TELEVISION
AND
SOCIAL BEHAVIOR

REPORTS AND PAPERS, VOLUME IV:
ELEVISION IN DAY-TO-DAY LIFE: PATTERNS OF USE

A TECHNICAL REPORT TO THE
SURGEON GENERAL'S SCIENTIFIC ADVISORY COMMITTEE
ON TELEVISION AND SOCIAL BEHAVIOR

Edited By
Eli A. Rubinstein, George A. Comstock, and John P. Murray
Editorial Coordination: Susan Lloyd-Jones

U.S. DEPARTMENT OF HEALTH, EDUCATION, AND WELFARE
Health Services and Mental Health Administration

National Institute of Mental Health
5600 Fishers Lane
Rockville, Maryland

Staff Members

Eli A. Rubinstein	Vice Chairman, Surgeon General's Scientific Advisory Committee
George A. Comstock	Senior Research Coordinator
John P. Murray	Research Coordinator
Michael Adler	Staff Assistant
Eileen Marchak	Research Assistant
Susan S. Lloyd-Jones	Editor
Joseph D. Reckley	Administrative Officer
Margaret D. Salladay	Secretary
Laura A. De Lisi	Secretary

Former Staff Members

Douglas A. Fuchs	Senior Research Coordinator (through 6/70)
John P. Robinson	Research Coordinator (through 9/70)
Harold Leigh	Administrative Officer (through 10/70)
Thomas Brubeck	Information Officer (through 5/71)
Deborah Cutler	Research Assistant (through 8/70)
Jan W. Lipkin	Secretary (through 4/70)

Advisory Committee Members

Ira H. Cisin	Charles A. Pinderhughes
Thomas E. Coffin	Ithiel de Sola Pool
Irving L. Janis	Alberta E. Siegel
Joseph T. Klapper	Anthony F. C. Wallace
Harold Mendelsohn	Andrew S. Watson
Eveline Omwake	Gerhart D. Wiebe

Preface

This document is one of five volumes of technical reports resulting from a broad scientific inquiry about television and its impact on the viewer. In the spring of 1969, by Congressional request, the DHEW initiated a special program under the general auspices of a Surgeon General's Scientific Advisory Committee on Television and Social Behavior. The major emphasis was to be on an examination of the relationship between televised violence and the attitudes and behavior of children. During the ensuing two years, more than fifty scientists participated directly in this program of research and produced over forty scientific reports.

The reports which are included in these five volumes are the independent work of the participating researchers. These results have all been made available to the Scientific Advisory Committee as evidence which the Committee could then evaluate and draw its own conclusions in the preparation of its own report. However, this work is of significance in its own right and is being published independently as source material for other researchers and for such interest as the general public may have in these technical reports.

In any broad scientific undertaking of this nature, where many individuals are involved, a careful balance between collaboration and independence of responsibility must be established. During the two and half years that this program of research was active, a constant effort was made to protect the scientific independence of the individual investigators and, at the same time: 1) to foster both cooperation and exchange among the researchers, 2) to develop as much of a total program structure as possible, and 3) to permit maximum communication and feedback among the researchers, the full-time staff responsible for planning and implementing the total research program, and the Scientific Advisory Committee responsible for the final assessment and evaluation of research.

This is not the place to describe in detail how that balance of collaboration and independence was established and maintained. I believe, however, that these five volumes of technical reports provide an accurate and meaningful indication of our success in achieving the goal. The reports themselves are the products of the respective authors. They have been edited only to insure some comparability of format and to delete any excessive redundancies in review of the literature or introductory material. In some instances, where a report seemed initially too long the author was requested to reduce the report without deleting any critical material. All editing done by staff was submitted for the author's approval. We believe the result has made each of these five volumes a more readable and integrated totality than would otherwise be expected from a collection of research reports produced under the time constraints of this program.

In each instance, the integration of the five volumes was further established by the inclusion of an overview paper which attempts to summarize and relate the papers in that volume. These overview papers are also the independent work of the respective authors.

It would be difficult to convey to the reader the extraordinary efforts required by all participants in this research program to bring the endeavor to its published conclusion within the time allotted. Despite that time pressure, these volumes demonstrate an unusually high level of both productivity and quality for an area of research which has had more than its share of complexity and controversy.

In addition to the work of all persons directly engaged in this program, a very large number of individuals at one time or another provided advice and guidance to the researchers, to the staff, and to the Scientific Advisory Committee. It would be impossible to provide a complete list of these additional consultants. The total count is in the hundreds. While their names are not visible in these products, their counsel was often a very significant factor in the course of an individual piece of research or in a decision on the direction of the research program. To all those individuals, this program owes a special debt of gratitude for the collective wisdom made available to us.

And finally, on behalf both of the members of the Scientific Advisory Committee and of the staff who served the program, I wish especially to express much appreciation to the participating researchers who did the work and wrote the reports that contributed the new knowledge contained in these volumes.

Eli A. Rubinstein
Vice-Chairman, Surgeon General's
Scientific Advisory Committee on
Television and Social Behavior

Contents

Page

Television in Daily Life: Patterns of Use (Overview)
Jack Lyle 1
A National Inventory of Television Viewing Behavior.
Leonard A. LoSciuto 33
Demographic Characteristics of Viewers of Television Violence and News Programs.
Harold Israel and John P. Robinson 87
Children's Use of Television and Other Media.
Jack Lyle and Heidi R. Hoffman 129
Explorations in Patterns of Television Viewing by Preschool-age Children.
Jack Lyle and Heidi R. Hoffman 257
Correlates Between Observed Behavior and Questionnaire Responses on Television Viewing.
Robert B. Bechtel, Clark Achelpohl, and Roger Akers 274
Television in Inner-city Homes: Viewing Behavior of Young Boys.
John P. Murray 345
Children's Television Behaviors as Perceived by Mother and Child.
Bradley S. Greenberg, Philip M. Ericson, and
Mantha Vlahos 395
Television's Impact on Everyday Life: Some Cross-national Evidence.
John P. Robinson 410
Effects of Television Advertising on Children and Adolescents.
Scott Ward 432

A Cognitive Developmental Study of Children's Reactions to Television Advertising.
Joan Blatt, Lyle Spencer, and Scott Ward 452

Children's Perceptions, Explanations, and Judgments of Television Advertising: A Further Exploration.
Scott Ward, Greg Reale, and David Levinson 468

Children's Attention to Television Advertising.
Scott Ward, David Levinson, and Daniel Wackman 491

v

vi

Television Advertising and Intrafamily Influence: Children's Purchase Influence Attempts and Parental Yielding.
Scott Ward and *Daniel Wackman* 516

Adolescent Attitudes Toward Television Advertising: Preliminary Findings.
Scott Ward and *Thomas S. Robertson* 526

Racial Differences in Responses to Advertising Among Adolescents.
Daniel B. Wackman, Greg Reale, and *Scott Ward* 543

Family and Media Influences on Adolescent Consumer Learning.
Scott Ward and *Daniel Wackman* 554

Toward Defining the Functions of Television.
John P. Robinson 568

Television in Daily Life: Patterns of Use Overview

In the span of only a quarter-century, television has achieved a place in American homes unmatched by any other appliance, convenience, or medium of communication. Not only is it ubiquitous—over 96 percent of our homes contain at least one set—but audience rating services indicate that the amount of daily use made of these sets is truly staggering. The average home set is said to be turned on more than six hours per day.[1] It is only natural that those concerned with the nation's mores and morals are deeply interested in and frequently worried about the impact of television.

The studies contained in this series of volumes reflect that interest and worry. They represent the broadest research effort in this area to date.

1

Included are studies of television's content and of those responsible for producing that content. There are laboratory and field experiments investigating what kinds of effects television content can have on what kinds of people.

Any attempt to gain insight into the effects of television on the viewing public must also include an assessment of the amount and patterns of viewing by the various segments of the general population. The two major references for this purpose are *Television in the Lives of Our Children* by Schramm, Lyle, and Parker (1961) and Steiner's (1963) *The People Look at Television*. The information and conclusions presented in these works are based on data a decade old.

This volume attempts to provide a new picture of how much and what kind of television people watch in the 1970s, to see what role television plays in the everyday lives of Americans.

Eight research projects are reported in this volume. They range from general studies of national samples to studies which focus either on specific subpopulations or on audiences for specific types of programs. The studies were done independently and the methodologies used varied considerably. Thus the studies were not designed to fit together to provide a complete picture, but common elements run through them and aspects of one individual study complement those of others.

The purpose of this chapter is to pull together the common threads running through these studies and make a meaningful pattern of the results, to provide the "new picture" mentioned above. To provide greater detail and definition to this picture, reference is made to pertinent findings in studies included in the companion volumes and to other studies published elsewhere.

An appendix attached to this chapter seeks to capitalize on the use of different methods by providing a discussion of some basic methodological problems connected with field surveys of this type.

CAPSULE REVIEW OF STUDIES

Before outlining the patterns of use of and attitudes toward television, let us quickly review the projects contained in this volume.

Bechtel, Achelpohl, and Akers (1971) looked at the problem of validity in reports of viewing time. A small sample—20 families—participated. They were asked to keep diaries of viewing. Concurrently they allowed equipment to be installed to videotape their actual behavior while their television set was operative. The recorded behavior was then analyzed and compared with the respondents' own reports. The analysis also provides information on relative levels of viewer attention to the television screen during the broadcast of different types of programs.

Using 27 six-year-old Negro boys who had been studied by a team from the Catholic University of America for four years, Murray (1971) gathered data detailing television behavior and attitudes. Of particular interest was the longitudinal data on social adjustment which he was able to relate to viewing.

LoScuito (1971) collected viewing and attitudinal information from a sample of 252 households drawn on a national basis. Attempts were made to interview all adult and adolescent members and to have them keep diaries of viewing behavior and reactions for a one-week period. In all, 512 interviews and 452 diaries were collected.

The Lyle and Hoffman (1971) study was a general replication of the Schramm, Lyle, and Parker (1961) study. Working in a suburban school district in the Los Angeles area, they gathered data by self-administered questionnaires from the sixth- and tenth-grade populations and obtained interviews with a 25 percent sample of the first graders. Data collected covered viewing behavior over a five-day period together with use of other media, program preferences, attitudes toward the media, and demographic and social adjustment data. Additional information was obtained in telephone interviews with a subsample of mothers of first graders. A separate paper provides information on preschool-age children.

Israel and Robinson (1971) used data from national samples of the W.R. Simmons and Associates research firm to analyze attention by different segments of the population over a three-year period to news programs and to programs rated high on violence.

Ward's (1971) series of related studies focused on the effects of television commericals on children. Part of his data was gathered from samples of youngsters in Maryland and in the Boston area using self-administered questionnaires. The cooperation of mothers of young children was obtained to secure observational data on children's attention and reactions to television content generally and to commercials specifically. The mothers themselves completed questionnaires on their own attitudes toward controlling youngsters' viewing and on their perceptions of the impact of commercials upon their children. He also used clinical interviews in group situations to obtain insights into children's reactions to commercials.

Robinson (1971) obtained time-use data, gathered in over one dozen studies in the United States, Europe, and South America, which included information on television availability and use. Using this data, he was able to analyze displacement of other activities by television.

In the final paper of the volume, Robinson (1971) uses data inputs from several studies (including those of Israel and Robinson and of Bechtel et al.) to seek to define certain aspects of television's meaning to the American public.

TELEVISION AVAILABILITY IN THE UNITED STATES

Hardly a person in the United States today does not have access to at least one television set in his or her own home. The U.S. Census estimates that 96 percent of all American homes have sets. The studies in this volume, dealing primarily with households in which there are children or adolescents, reported 98 to 99 percent saturation. Between 40 and 50 percent of the children surveyed watched on color sets.

Television watching is still primarily an experience shared by family members. The living room or another room serving as the family gathering place is the most frequently reported location for sets. By far the most viewing recorded was done in the company of other members of the family. This finding was common in all the studies of children, and there is little doubt that there is a strong relationship between various members of the family in amount of viewing and also in program selection. However, the nature of this relationship appears to be very complex.

Chaffee, McLeod, and Atkin (1970) report that three-quarters of adolescents they studied in several locations in two states said they sometimes watched television because their parents were watching. Two-thirds of them said they felt their parents sometimes watched because they (the youngsters) were watching. In another report on the same data, Chaffee and McLeod (1971) state that the strongest relationship appeared to be between youngsters and their mothers and that this relationship did weaken in the high school years. They went on to state that their interpretation of the data is that this does not represent a simply modeling situation in which the youngster learns patterns of viewing from his parents. Their analysis suggested that the teenagers may be influencing their parents rather than the other way around. They do not present data on young children, and it seems far more likely that there is modeling among this group, particularly in view of the dynamics of program selection which are reported later herein. It also seems likely that young children model their viewing habits on that of older siblings.

When parents are heavy viewers of television, it is likely that their children will become heavy viewers. Greenberg, Ericson and Vlahos (1971) found that the more children viewed in the company of their parents, the more violent programs they saw.

This relationship among the viewing patterns of different members of the household is understandable in a situation where family members are contending for control of a single set. However, the number of multiset homes is increasing. There are indications that the presence of an additional set or sets increases as the family grows, as the children age. Thus Lyle and Hoffman (1971) found that 71 percent of their first graders reported only one set in the house, but 61 percent of their tenth graders said there were two or more sets available. Although there was some variation from study to study, generally it appears that multiple sets are as common in working class and minority homes as in white collar homes but that white collar children are more likely to have access to a color set.

One would think that the addition of a second set to the home would reduce the relationship between parent and child viewing. Chaffee, McLeod, and Atkin (1970) report that viewing time for both mothers and their adolescent offspring was higher in multiset homes than in single set homes. Lyle and Hoffman (1971) suggest that with the addition of a second set in a home, one set becomes a "children's set"; they note that there were lower levels of conflict over program selection between children and parents than between children and their siblings in multiset homes. Further, most children reported more viewing in the company of siblings than in the company of parents.

However, in his family data, LoSciuto (1971) found that respondents in multiset homes estimated that 91 percent of their viewing was done on the main set. This suggests that the impact of additional sets on changing interfamily patterns may not be as great as might be expected.

LoSciuto also found that most families interviewed had access to stations carrying all three networks plus at least one additional channel. The handicap facing UHF (ultra high frequency) stations—which include many of the noncommerical "educational" stations—is illustrated by the fact that although 67 percent of LoSciuto's families lived within signal range of a UHF station, only 47 percent had sets equipped to receive UHF signals. However, both Murray (1971) and Lyle and Hoffman (1971) found that the majority of families in their major metropolitan area samples—all of whom had school-age children—had UHF receivers.

AMOUNT OF USE

The 1971 volume of *Broadcasting Yearbook* estimates that home sets are turned on an average of six hours and 18 minutes per day. Averages for individual viewing time, however, are far less. Basically, it is neither realistic nor practical to speak of "average viewing time." Such averages are necessarily artifactual. Reading through the studies which give viewing behavior for various demographic groups will impress one with the wide variation in amount of viewing and program selection within the population.

Contrasting Lyle and Hoffman's (1971) data with that of McIntyre and Teevan (1971) or that of Chaffee, McLeod, and Atkin (1970) emphasizes the different "average" figures which may be obtained from approximately the same age groups in different locales.

Despite different averages, all three studies reveal similar patterns of relative viewing time for different age groups. The National Audience

Demographics Report of the A.C. Nielsen Company can be used to extend the comparison. The point is that there are differences in the viewing patterns of different age groups. Further, the "child audience" itself shows variations, with viewing building to a peak around the period of puberty and early adolescence, then declining in the high school years.

There are well-documented patterns of difference in racial and socioeconomic groups. Perhaps the best most intensive series of studies on this problem are those of Greenberg and his associates (e.g., Greenberg and Dominick, 1969a, 1969b). For both adults and children, these investigators found that Negroes view more than whites, that blue collar families view more than white collar families. McIntyre and Teevan (1971) report similar patterns: Negroes watch more than whites, children from low socioeconomic status homes watch more than those from high socioeconomic status homes. Lyle and Hoffman's community had too small a black population to make such a comparison reliable, but the small group of Negro students were the heaviest viewers in both the first and the sixth grades. Among their large Mexican-American groups they found that girls watched more than Caucasian girls but that boys from these groups did not show consistent differences. It should also be noted that these authors did not find consistent white collar-blue collar differences over the five-day period for which they had viewing records.

Robinson (1971) quotes data from a Maryland study which showed that students who reported their grade average as "A" watched less television than their "B" and "C" peers at the seventh, ninth and eleventh-grade levels. Lyle and Hoffman, using Lorge-Thorndike scores, found results reminiscent of the 1959 data reported by Schramm, Lyle, and Parker: at the sixth-grade level bright students tended to be among the heaviest viewers, but at the tenth-grade level their viewing was more likely to be somewhat lower than that of their peers. However, their results were far less clearcut than those of 1959, and the authors suggested that there had been some leveling of comparative viewing among students of different ability at the secondary level.

Another type of difference was illustrated by the Lyle and Hoffman data: the variation in viewing time for the same individual from day to day. Along a similar vein, an inspection of the periodic Nielsen Television Index shows that there are fluctuations in the audience over the seasons of the year.

All these examples underline a major problem of dealing with "average daily viewing time": it obscures the very important individual and group variations in viewing.

Granting this, what can be said about amount of viewing?

LoSciuto's data suggest that most adult Americans do watch daily and that they watch for at least two hours. However, up to 20 percent of the population will not watch any television on a given day. Women tend to watch more than men, probably because many women work at home and have more opportunity to watch during the day.

The amount of viewing among children is much more complex. Children have become purposeful viewers—having regular viewing times and favorite programs—long before they start school. The amounts and times of viewing change almost from year to year as the child grows older. Sex differences in program preferences are being manifested by the time the children begin school.

Most children do watch television every day, and most likely they watch at least two hours; many watch considerably longer. In his group of kindergarten and first-grade Negro boys, Murray (1971) found that total weekly viewing time ranged from five to 42 hours. In a study involving nursery school children, Stein and Friedrich (1971) documented an average weekly viewing time of 34.56 hours for boys, 32.44 hours for girls. This represented well over one-third of the children's total waking hours during the week. It was noted above that the amount of viewing increases through the elementary years but then decreases in the high school years. For instance Chaffee, McLeod, and Atkin (1970) reported that their senior high school students watched on the average about one and one-quarter hours less than their junior high students. They also found that girls watched more than boys at both age groups, thus approximating the results LoSciuto reports among his adults. McIntyre and Teevan found similar sex differences. Lyle and Hoffman's data, however, showed much less marked and consistent differences in viewing times for boys and girls at first, sixth, and tenth-grade levels.

It appears that there is greater uniformity among very young children in amount of time spent viewing; only about ten percent will not view on a given weekday. Among Lyle and Hoffman's sixth graders, nonviewers had increased to about one-quarter. At all age levels, these authors found a sizable group—again about one-quarter—who were heavy viewers, watching more than five hours on schooldays. Much of this viewing, particularly among the elementary-age children, was done in the afternoon. At least two-thirds of these children said they watched in the afternoon. At least one-fifth said they watched before school. Daytime viewing was much lower among the high school students, but the drop in afternoon viewing was sharper among boys than among girls; for many girls the television "soap operas" appeared to have great appeal.

Most of the younger children drop out of the audiences and are off to bed by 9 p.m. Sixth graders continue to be present in large numbers much later. Lyle and Hoffman found that one-third of their sixth graders watched until after 10 p.m. This suggests that many older elementary students are in the audience through most of the prime time period. The teenage audience appears to hold strong until the end of prime time at 11 p.m.

LEVEL OF ATTENTION

A problem which has important implications for the question of viewing time is the level or degree of attention which viewers give to the set
when they are "watching." As mentioned earlier, different measures of
"viewing" can yield considerably different results. Both Bechtel et al.
and LoSciuto found that individuals considerably overestimated their
own viewing time.

Most viewing by most people is done in the company of others. For
children this is most frequently siblings and/or parents. Ward (1971)
reports that among his elementary-age subjects, viewing with other
members of their families increased with age. And LoSciuto reports that
among his adults, only about one-third of viewing was reported as being
done in a solitary situation.

Most respondents—adult and child—reported considerable levels of
conversation while viewing; this conversation ranged over topics other
than the program being watched. Students said they were likely to study
with the television set on at least part of the time.

All the studies agree that children's viewing of television is likely to be
far from passive. More than 80 percent of Lyle and Hoffman's first graders reported engaging in other activities—eating, playing, talking—while
watching television. In his observations of the youngsters while they
viewed, Murray documented considerable activity, both verbal and
physical. He states that attention declined as the program progressed.

Ward also had observation data focusing on children's attention before and during commercials. His observers reported that children
were watching 65 percent of the time at the onset of commercials. Generally, attention was higher among the younger children. His data document that there is a drop in attention during the commercials, particularly among the older children who are likely to engage in other behavior.
Twenty-five percent of the time the children observed made (mostly
favorable) comments about the commercials.

LoSciuto's annotated diaries showed considerable variation in attention during "viewing time," and Israel and Robinson concluded that at
least one-third of the time during the prime evening hours, viewers are
giving the set less than full attention.

However, the most dramatic evidence on this point comes from the
videotapes Bechtel and his associates collected of families watching television in their homes. They found that time spent actually watching a
program during "viewing" time, when averaged over program categories, ranged from 55 to 76 percent of the total. In an appendix to their
report, the authors provide a minute-by-minute record of the activities
performed by members of a family during a period of viewing. This
record dramatically details the scope and range of behavior which may
accompany viewing.

An experimental study by Foulkes, Belvedere, and Brubaker (1971) also provided evidence on this point. He found that eye contact with the television screen dropped spectacularly when adolescent boys were in a situation where the television program had to compete with alternative attractions such as books, games, and toys.

PROGRAM PREFERENCES AND SELECTION

Children begin viewing at a very early age; almost as soon as they begin viewing, they develop program preferences and habits. For instance, Murray reports that his five- and six-year olds had well-established patterns of viewing time and program preferences. The mothers of the nursery school children studied by Stein and her associates were able to indicate programs favored by their children. Most of Lyle and Hoffman's preschool children were able to specify favorite programs.

The several studies providing data on younger children—preschool to first-grade—reveal generally similar patterns. Cartoon programs (which, according to Gerbner [1971], are among the highest in violent content of all program types) consistently stood highest. Noncartoon "children's" programs usually rated below situation comedies as well as below cartoons. Stein and her colleagues report more viewing of "children's " programs than of either cartoons or adult programs, but it should be noted that her data was based on mothers' reports. Murray, on the other hand, found not a single children's program in the "top ten" among his small sample. Several cartoon and children's programs stood among the most viewed programs reported by Lyle and Hoffman's first graders and preschool children.

It appears that as children grow up, their program preferences become increasingly diversified. In part, this is reflected by the fact that the percentage of each age group watching the most popular programs for that age group declined consistently. Lyle and Hoffman found that the most popular first grade program, *Gilligan's Island*, drew 48 percent of the first graders. The sixth-grade favorites, *World of Disney* and *Bill Cosby*, drew 41 percent of that group. The tenth-grade favorite, *Bill Cosby*, drew only 36 percent of the teenagers.

There were frequent discrepancies at all age levels between the programs students named as their "favorites" and the top programs for each age group in terms of actual viewing. This probably was due, at least in part, to compromises necessitated by programming conflicts and different preferences among family members. (In the case of Lyle and Hoffman's data it may also have been influenced by the fact that the viewing records were obtained in the "postseason" period. In this period, when series were beginning to repeat, students may have watched a competing program which they had not seen in preference to an episode of a "favorite" series which they had already seen.) There was considerable evidence of intrafamily conflict over program selection—which the age differences mentioned above would predict. This conflict persisted in the face of the increased number of multiset homes.

To summarize the patterns of program preferences in highly simplified form: the first graders most frequently chose situation comedies (*Gilligan's Island*, *I Love Lucy*) and cartoon programs. The sixth graders had dropped the cartoon programs, but showed heavy preference for situation comedies and were increasing the attention given to adventure programs. Adventure programs dominated the preferences of the tenth graders. The other two leading categories for the teenagers were music/variety and dramatic, a loose category which included *Bill Cosby* and *Room 222*. In a 1968 report, Gans states that adolescents' viewing habits generally resemble those of adults, although they show a higher viewing of comedy programs.

Both Murray and Lyle and Hoffman suggest that brighter youngsters show more variation in their program preferences. There was also a suggestion that diversified preferences are related to higher socioeconomic status. In their study of nursery school students, Stein and her associates identified two patterns of viewing behavior based on favorite programs and viewing frequencies. Generally, the distinction between the two patterns hinged on the amount of viewing of noncartoon programs containing violence. They state that the children in the nonviolent group were typically from higher socioeconomic status homes and had higher IQs than their companions who fell in the violence-viewing-category. Their parents also were more likely to restrict their program selection.[2]

Much of the impetus for the studies contained in this series of volumes stemmed from concern about the impact of television violence on the population, particularly children. Therefore, it is appropriate that we take a careful look at the data on children's actual viewing of and preference for programs high in violent content.

This type of program increases in importance as children grow older. For instance, among Lyle and Hoffman's sixth graders, only one "violent program," *It Takes a Thief*, was among the ten most popular shows. Among the tenth graders there were four: *Mod Squad*, *It Takes a Thief*, *Then Came Bronson*, and *Adam-12*. That there can be exceptions to this age relationship is underlined by Murray's report. Among the top ten programs for his small sample of large-city Negro boys of preschool/first-grade age were *Mod Squad*, *Gunsmoke*, *The FBI*, and *Land of the Giants*. *Mod Squad* had the biggest audience among this group of any programs: 94 percent of the children watched it.

McLeod, Atkin, and Chaffee (1971) report that, among their samples of adolescents, overall viewing time *declined* with age but time spent viewing violent programs and movies *increased*. Chaffee and McLeod

(1971) report that viewing of violent programs by adolescents is positively related to total viewing time, a finding also reported by Lyle and Hoffman and by Greenberg, Ericson, and Vlahos (1971). Further, Chaffee and McLeod found violent viewing to be lower among bright children than among their age peers. Blue collar children watched more violent programs than their white collar peers. These authors also report data suggesting that violent programs are more frequently watched by children with a high propensity for violence than by their less violence-prone peers. McIntyre and Teevan (1971) showed rather weak tendencies of a similar nature: high viewing of violent programs was related to both violent behavior and approval of violence. Among their teenagers, 25 percent named a "high" violence program as a favorite, and 12 percent named a "moderate" violence program. Like other authors, McIntyre and Teevan found violence viewing to be lower among girls than among boys.

Perhaps the strongest evidence along this line is that reported by Robinson and Bachman (1971). They found positive relations between preference for violent television programs and actual (self-reported) participation in aggressive delinquent behavior among young men just out of high school.

Among adult audiences, Israel and Robinson report that about 12 percent of Simmons's national survey samples were heavy viewers of programs judged as the most violent series on television. The violent programs drew disproportionately large numbers of viewers from this group. Thus, although the "violence viewers" constituted only one-eighth of the total population, they provided one-third of the audience for violent programs. Israel and Robinson found this situation to be constant over a three-year period.

A perhaps disturbing companion finding in Israel and Robinson's data suggests that the level of violence viewing increased consistently over the three-year period. Israel and Robinson chose their cutting points defining "high violence viewing" so as to maintain a relatively constant percentage of the total sample over the three years. In 1967, their cutting point was six hours or more of viewing of "violent programs." In 1968 they had to raise the cutting point to 7.5 hours, and in 1969 to 8.5 hours.

Israel and Robinson's data on adults parallel those reported for adolescent audiences. Men watch more violence than women. Negroes watch more than Caucasians. The poor and the less educated watch more than those with white collar status and those who have gone on to college. He found a particularly high rate of violence viewing among male young adults who were high school dropouts—a group which he points out is higher than average in reports of actual violent behavior.

Violent programs seem to gain relatively high levels of attention from their audience. In the Simmons surveys, respondents were asked to indicate in their viewing diaries the level of attention given to programs viewed. In analyzing this data, Israel and Robinson found that programs of violence were given disproportionately high attention compared with other types of programs. Both the Bechtel et al. and the LoSciuto studies had measures of attention level for programs viewed. Both report that programs of violence (as a category) did receive relatively high attention, but in neither case did the violent category lead all other categories.

Through their videotapes of people actually viewing television in home environment, Bechtel and his colleagues were able to measure the amount of time spent actually attending the television program while it was on. Among the families participating in the study, movies (and for children, children's programs) had higher attention levels than the violent programs. LoSciuto's respondents were asked to record their levels of interest for programs viewed. His diaries showed the strongest interest in dramatic and family situation comedy shows.

Not all television violence is found in the fictional programs. As the Mass Media Task Force to the National Commission on the Causes and Prevention of Violence pointed out, some of the bloodiest, most violent fare found on television is seen within the context of news programs (Baker and Ball, 1971). The impact of this remains to be documented.

All the studies containing pertinent data agree that educational programs are hardly watched at all by the vast majority of the population, adult and child. The sole possible exception seems to be Sesame Street among younger children.

Viewing of television news was also generally quite low. On any weekday Israel and Robinson found, about 25 percent of the adult men and 22 percent of the adult women reported that they watched a national news program. In a footnote, the authors call attention to the fact that this figure is considerably lower than the Nielsen ratings for the network news programs in the same period, which showed a news audience of 39 percent in the Nielsen homes. LoSciuto asked his respondents how frequently they watched news and obtained a figure very close to the Nielsen ratings. Thirty-eight percent of his respondents said they watched network news almost every night, and half of them said they regularly watched a local newscast.

There is an interesting apparent conflict between these findings—discrepant though they may be—and the results reported from the series of national studies by Roper, showing that most people now cite television as their major source of nonlocal news. In the most favorable of the findings above, only half the adults were regular television users, whereas over 90 percent of the Simmons samples said they read a newspaper daily.

When they examined the day-to-day diaries of viewing, Israel and Robinson found that there was a very high overlap of the news audience from one day to the next. They concluded that only 20 percent of their adults could be categorized as regular news viewers and that these constituted the bulk of the audience for news programs on any given day. Indeed, among their large national samples, over half the adults managed to avoid watching a single national news program for the entire two-week period during which they kept diaries. However, they pointed out that the men who do watch the news gave outstandingly high attention to the program.

News viewing was also quite low among the respondents in the various studies involving youngsters. McIntyre and Teevan (1971) report that only some 20 percent of their teenagers were news watchers. Lyle and Hoffman's young viewers lived in a market where there were many channels, so that several entertainment options competed with any news program. These youngsters almost totally avoided news programs, particularly during the dinner hour. This was as true of tenth graders as of the younger students.

Several studies were able to make separate analyses of program preferences for Negro and white students. All reported that programs featuring Negro characters were particularly popular among Negro youngsters. It should be noted that many of these programs—particularly *Room 222*, *Bill Cosby*, and *Flip Wilson*—were among the most popular programs for white children, too. Indeed, Lyle and Hoffman reported that among their first graders *Bill Cosby* and Cory, the son of *Julia*, scored high in both recognition and affect among both white and Negro children, but the results were attenuated among the Negro children. They found similar patterns among preschool youngsters.

There were no network shows featuring Mexican-American characters, so it is impossible to know whether a similar situation would exist for Mexican-American students. However, in Lyle and Hoffman's study town, the youngsters had available two UHF stations broadcasting almost exclusively in Spanish, for the most part using programs produced in Mexico and South America. There was almost no viewing of either of these stations by the Mexican-American students, even though both featured "soap operas," a type of program particularly popular with a large number of the tenth-grade Mexican-American girls. Only one or two of these girls named one of these programs as a favorite.

WHY PEOPLE WATCH TELEVISION

Much of the daily life of both children and adults is performed to the accompaniment of the television set. Whether it is actually being watched or not, there is a high likelihood in most homes that from midafternoon on through the evening the television set will be turned on. In their 1961 report, Schramm et al. stated that children seemed to take television for granted (and the authors appeared somewhat surprised at just how blasé the youngsters were). The evidence in the various studies included here underlines the fact that this is even more the case today. It also shows that television casts a long shadow over the daily activities of most people—activities both within and outside the home.

For the most part, people appear to use television to enrich their lives and/or to fill time. "Filling time" might be equated by some with "wasting time," but the value attached to this function of television viewing depends largely upon a variety of social and personal factors. For many people, simply having television to help them pass or fill time is "enrichment," even though the more critical might look on disapprovingly. Foley (1968) found that many persons used television to help them forget pressures and problems. Such escape may be functionally beneficial for many people in some circumstances. The crucial question, of course, becomes the degree to which persons may become so dependent upon this relief that they begin to divorce themselves from the real world. More will be said about this later, but let us quickly note that Foley also reported that people use television as a vehicle to social interaction. It provided an opportunity for them to be with their family, a stimulus to conversation.

Among the adults in LoSciuto's sample, the overwhelming consensus was that television viewing was primarily done for relaxation and enjoyment. In studies done in the early days of television—indeed as late as Steiner's 1963 national study—many expressed embarrassment about the possibility that they might use television in this manner. Such embarrassment was particularly prevalent among the white collar professional group. This embarrassment appears to have faded. Only a minority of LoSciuto's sample (about 12 percent) stated that they watched for "constructive" purposes: to keep up with current events, to widen their knowledge, to improve themselves. By far the majority said that they watched for enjoyment and to occupy their time. Furthermore, most of them thought that their viewing was "worthwhile." Only a small number thought this type of viewing was "wasting time."

A similar approach—and lack of embarrassment—was found among Lyle and Hoffman's sixth and tenth graders. Greenberg and Dominick (1969a) report that among fourth and fifth graders, Negro youngsters and children from low income white families more frequently stated that they watched to learn than did children from higher status white families. The latter group were more likely to say they watched to be "excited." This stands in strong contrast to the 1959 findings of Schramm et al.

One of the interesting aspects of Lyle and Hoffman's data was that they found relatively small differences in reported viewing time over the five-day period by blue and white collar children. A decade ago there were very distinct socioeconomic differences.

These results suggest that there may have been a leveling in the differences of viewing patterns by different socioeconomic groups. However, the white collar youngsters in the Lyle and Hoffman study were far more critical and skeptical of television content than their blue collar classmates. Greenberg and Dominick also found that the lower status children were more likely to accept what they saw on television as realistic.

Among both adults and students, viewing was relatively opportunistic and unplanned. True, most of the studies reported considerable use of program schedules and guides, but it appears that while some programs might be preselected, unplanned viewing was likely to follow. The viewer often continued watching whatever came on next or flipped around the dial. Only 20 percent of the adults said that at least sometimes they found there just wasn't anything on that they wanted to watch. This percentage was smaller than the percentage saying they sometimes had to miss programs they'd really like to have watched. The majority of the youngsters said that at least sometimes they did turn the set off because they couldn't find anything on that they wanted to watch. However, a majority also said that they most frequently just turned the set on and flipped around hunting for a program to watch.

All-in-all, the answers on program selectivity (or the relative lack of it) and the generally low levels of involvement discussed earlier suggest that while television may be ubiquitous, it is frequently little noticed. Robinson goes further and develops the thesis that viewing time is actually a continuum of short periods of full attention to the set interspersed with periods of partial or non-attention. Thus the individual viewer "tunes in and out" during programs according to his evaluation of cues as to whether discrete episodes will or will not interest him. Robinson points out that if this is the case, it means that the viewer may see only the crime or the violence and not the retribution—or may see the retribution without seeing what provoked it.

Regardless of the actual levels of attention during viewing, television is deeply integrated into our lives. The data on both adults and children testified to the fact that television plays a part in our daily lives far beyond actual viewing. It not only serves to "fill time" while we view; it also provides topics of conversation both among members of the family and among friends, not only while we watch but in social interactions away from the set. And despite the low level of actual viewing, television news is used as frequently as newspaper items as a topic of conversation.

With regard to intrafamily dynamics, it should be noted that television plays another important role, as a focus of parent-child conflict and of sibling rivalry. The amount of parental control of television viewing (or attempt threat) was found to be small in study after study.

Lyle and Hoffman, for instance, found that the majority of mothers of their first graders said they made no effort to set hours or restrict the amount of viewing, although three-quarters did say they exercised some control over program selection. Similarly, Hess and Goldman (1962) reported that mothers felt the choice of programs more important than the amount of time their children spent viewing. They believed that they were best able to judge which programs were good for their children, and they expressed the feeling that there must be "something wrong" with children who were heavy viewers. Yet, while they stated that the "good mother" was not indulgent regarding television, in half the homes children actually viewed at will. In practice, it appeared that the mothers' main concern was to help their children avoid programs featuring physical violence. In a large sample survey of Ohio mothers, Niven (1960) found that children controlled the set in the afternoons but that in the evening decisions were made by the family as a unit.

Among the mothers and teenagers interviewed by Chaffee, McLeod, and Atkin (1970), only ten percent of the families represented had established viewing rules for the children. However, many of the parents did seem to worry that they should be doing something to shape their children's viewing. About one-third of the students in Lyle and Hoffman's study were aware that their parents either did try to restrict their viewing or had done so when they were younger. Greenberg and Dominick (1969a) found that children in poor homes reported less adult control over viewing than their more fortunate peers. However, only one-third of these fourth and fifth graders said they had control over program selection. Three out of five said they were told they couldn't watch some shows, and two-thirds said there was a definite cutoff hour beyond which they were forbidden to watch.

Over two-thirds of Lyle and Hoffman's students admitted that their parents at least occasionally complained about their viewing. Television was reported as a cause of parental complaint more frequently than any other medium, including radio and record playing. Most of the students also admitted that they at least occasionally quarreled over program selection. Such quarrels were much more frequent with their siblings than with their parents.

One-third of the mothers in LoSciuto's family groups mentioned that their children had been frightened by something seen on television. Lyle and Hoffman asked their young children whether or not they ever suffered such fright. Forty percent of the first-grade boys and 59 percent of the girls said they were at least sometimes frightened. About 70 percent of the preschool children gave this response. When asked what frightened them, the children most frequently cited monster cartoons and pictures. Care should be taken in interpreting this result. Children do enjoy being moderately frightened under at least some circumstances, and, significantly, some of the shows children mentioned as having frightened them were also named as their favorites.

The same authors found that about 40 percent of both boys and girls in the first grade could remember dreaming about things seen on television. Some of the mothers interviewed by Hess felt that television was a habit-forming source of nightmares. In a large-scale study of mothers in 1963-65, Roberts and Baird (1971) found that almost 30 percent of the parents felt that television and radio hindered their children's falling to sleep at night and were a cause of bad dreams. Only four percent of Lyle and Hoffman's preschool mothers could recall instances of television-related bad dreams.

Among his adult respondents, LoSciuto found a very low occurence of being upset by something seen on television. In the few cases where a respondent said he or she had been upset, the cause was almost always violent content seen on a newscast.

In a study of adults, Hazard (1967) reported that he found high levels of anxiety to be related to fantasy viewing, particularly among those of low socioeconomic status and those who had low levels of cultural participation. From his findings he inferred a causal relationship between anxiety and both low activity and high use of television for fantasy escape.

LEARNING FROM TELEVISION

So far we've seen that television news is regularly watched by only a rather small minority of the population, educational programs by a still smaller group (with the possible exception of *Sesame Street* among preschool children). Most people say they watch for entertainment and relaxation. Yet did the adults interviewed by LoSciuto not only said they felt their viewing was worthwhile; many also felt that they were learning from what they saw. Similarly, a large majority of Lyle and Hoffman's youngsters felt that they were learning from television at least some of the time. About one-quarter said that such learning occurred frequently.

LoSciuto attempted to test for acquisition of specific knowledge concerning news, public figures, and principles of meteorology among this adult sample; Robinson reports data from a similar attempt with teenagers. The results offer little support for the idea that amount of television news viewing was related to being able to identify news events and figures, but a positive relation was found with newspaper reading. The results were somewhat more encouraging when viewing of weather forecasts was related to meteorological knowledge, but still the relationship was hardly an impressive one.

When asked directly what they felt they were learning from television, LoSciuto's adults gave vague answers about what might be termed "social learning": learning about the world, how to handle social situations, how to cope with personal problems. He found that adults generally accepted television dramas as reflecting life realistically. The results were strongly reminiscent of those reported by Herzog in her 1942 study of housewives' use of radio soap operas.

Gans got similar responses in his 1968 study of New York adults and adolescents: one-third said they thought television helped them understand personal problems and make decisions. He found that television was perceived as more helpful by those who thought they had more problems than others. Foley (1968) reported that some of his parents used examples shown in television programs as models or support in interactions with their own children.

Gans (1968) states that his adolescents exceeded adults in believing that television gave illustrations relevant to their own lives. In the studies included in the present volume, a somewhat different picture emerges, perhaps reflecting differences in methodology. For the most part, the students in these studies expressed at least some skepticism about the verisimilitude of television drama. Generally there was corroboration of the Greenberg and Dominick (1969a) data which showed that minority and lower-class youngsters exhibited the highest acceptance of television as an accurate depiction of life, as a reliable means of "finding out what life is all about."

Both the preschool and first-grade children studied by Lyle and Hoffman were able to identify a large number and a wide range of television characters. Among the first graders there were considerably higher rates of correct identification of child characters than of adult characters—with the notable exceptions of Gilligan and Lucy, both of whom had phenomenal popularity among these young children. Further, among the first graders there appeared to be differences of affect: boys were more likely to have affect for male characters, girls for female characters; Negroes to have higher affect for Negro than for white characters. Unfortunately, these authors did not gather comparable data from their sixth and tenth graders. A study by Johnson, Friedman, and Gross (1971) showed that identification of characters was related to such factors as socioeconomic status, race, and whether or not there was a male adult in the household.

In their interviews with mothers of young children, Lyle and Hoffman found that the vast majority—nine out of ten—felt that their children were learning from television. Hess and Goldman (1962) also reported that mothers viewed television as an educational and enlightening experience for their children. Among the California mothers, this learning was seen primarily as beneficial; only about one-fifth mentioned negative learning. LoSciuto also reports that mothers in his sample said their children learned from television. At least some of them felt this learning was not all good, that television was making their children too curious about such things as sex and drugs.

As for the beneficial learning, Lyle and Hoffman were most frequently told that television was increasing vocabulary and helping to prepare young children for school as well as teaching them "about life." This recalls the 1959 finding of Schramm et al. (1961). Youngsters in their study town with television had Stanford-Binet oral vocabulary scores which, on the average, were one year higher than those of children in the study town without television. It might be further noted that the scores of the nontelevision town youngsters were in line with the normative scores of that period (which dated from the early 1930s). LaPlante (1969) found that preschool children did acquire a stock of sight vocabulary words from watching programs on commercial television, although he notes that the performance rates were not as high as had been predicted by some education writers. He reports that, relative to the whole group, boys and children from white collar homes had higher scores.

Murray, Ward, and Lyle and Hoffman all found that children learn and repeat behavior they see on television at home. Murray's observers reported that many youngsters copied behavior performed by characters on programs while watching. When asked if they ever "played" things they saw on television, the majority of Lyle and Hoffman's first graders said that they did use television as a model for play with friends. About one-third said they sometimes used such themes in play by themselves. Little play of this type was reported before age five.

Ward focused on the impact of commercials on children. The mothers he interviewed stated that their children were able to identify packages and brand names from commercials. He interprets his data as suggesting that television, particularly commercial content, has become a part of the child's informal training for adulthood. He found not only that commercials frequently served as a form of vicarious consumption by children, but also that they taught children about consumerism and product evaluation. These effects were positively related to interest in consumption, to positive attitudes on the part of parents to commercials, and to discussion of products and shopping between parent and child. The mothers felt that the impact of television was greater on younger children, and they gauged its influence by attempts of the children to influence product purchases. In analyzing the responses, Ward found that children's attempts to influence purchases increased with mother's viewing time and with a positive feeling on her part about television. Similarly, the heavy viewing mothers and mothers favorable toward television were more likely to perceive television as influencing their children, and they were more likely to yield to the child's attempt to influence purchases. Almost all the mothers of preschool children interviewed by Lyle and Hoffman said their children requested things seen in commercials.

In his interviews with children, Ward found that while kindergarten children didn't know the purpose of commercials, second graders had a clear understanding that commercials were trying to sell things. By the fourth grade, children were making clear distinctions between commercials and the products shown and had become critics of techniques used in the commercials.

SELECTED ATTITUDES

Several studies provide data on attitudes toward specific content of television: violence, sex, commercials, and news. Across all age groups commercials were the major focus of complaints and negative attitudes toward television. LoSciuto found that three-quarters of his respondents felt there were too many commercials, in contrast to less than half who said there was too much violence, and one-third who thought there was too much sex. The studies involving students showed similar or even stronger antipathies. For instance, the first-grade mothers interviewed by Lyle and Hoffman mentioned commercials most frequently in their volunteered complaints about television. Violence ran second. However, violence was first among complaints from preschool mothers. These authors report that the majority of their sixth and tenth graders felt commercials not only were annoying, but also were more frequently deceptive than truthful.

In his intensive study about commercials, Ward found that by the second grade, youngsters were reporting mistrust of commercials based on personal experience. By the sixth grade, he says, the children were exhibiting "global mistrust" of commercials. Three-quarters said most commercials were too long, and almost as many found them to be annoying and in bad taste. Among older students, commercials were criticized on a stylistic basis as well.

However, it should be noted that attitudes toward commercials were not totally negative. Ward says that his youngest respondents appreciated the entertainment aspect of some commercials. While fourth graders exhibited distrust, they did enjoy humor in commercials. The sixth graders also enjoyed the humor, but they exhibited contempt toward commercials as well.

Generally, the more time they spent with television, the more tolerant persons were of content, including commercials. There also appeared to be evidence of at least a moderate tendency for minority and lower income groups to have less antagonism toward commercials.

Only a small minority of both adults and children in the various studies felt that there was too much news on television. A majority of the students—about two-thirds in the Lyle and Hoffman study—felt that television news was generally reliable.

Lyle and Hoffman gathered data from their older students regarding attitudes toward social mores, "establishment," and authority. When these were cross-tabulated with various media use and attitude questions, little relationship was found. For instance, negative attitudes toward the news were not correlated with negative attitudes toward authority. Heavy viewing of violent programs did not correlate with any of these measures. Negative attitudes toward commercials did not relate to "antimaterialism." But there was a significant relation between negative attitudes toward commercials and a rejection of television news as unreliable.

TELEVISION'S ROLE IN THE SOCIAL LIFE OF CHILDREN

It has been frequently suggested by critics of television that excessive television viewing may interfere with a person's "normal" social life. This suggestion is based on the assumption that if one views great amounts of television, one must necessarily restrict other activities.

Definitive answers to this problem are not at hand and, indeed, would require agreement on what is "excessive" viewing and what is "normal" social interaction. The present data provide some insights on the general question of television's impact on social relations and suggest that "higher than average" viewing alone is not necessarily related to a lower level of other activities.

For one thing, as has been pointed out above, much television time is not actually viewing time. People often engage in one or more other activities at the same time they have the television set on. Further, most viewing is done in the company of the family, among whom there is frequent interaction while viewing. At least two studies have suggested that television actually facilitates interfamily interaction. Foley (1968) reports that some respondents said they viewed as an excuse to be with their family or friends or as a source for conversation. Ward states that regardless of the attitude toward them, commercials did stimulate family discussion.

Among their sixth and tenth graders, Lyle and Hoffman found that heavier than average television use did not necessarily correlate with a lower level of participation in extramural sports and organizations, hobbies and artistic activities, after-school chores or work. Heavy television viewing without accompanying high reading was related to lower levels of such activities, but so was low use of all media, including television. Actually, children who were heavy users of both television and print were among the most active in all areas. Unfortunately, in their 1959 data collection Schramm et al. (1961) did not obtain measures on these types of activities, so there is no basis for judging whether or not there has been a general decline in these activities as television has become more widespread.

In his examination of cross-national data on adult populations, Robinson found evidence that television not only reduced use of functionally equivalent media (such as radio and movies), but also seemed to reduce social interaction outside the home and to cause some trade off with chores. He also found that interaction with the family appeared to increase with the presence of television.

Lyle and Hoffman asked their students about loneliness, popularity, and their social interactions with peers. They found no significant relationships between responses to these questions and the amount of television viewing. There was a trend in the first grade for these children who spent the most time with television to report the lowest levels of loneliness. However, they also found that this group reported lower frequency of play with others after school. This suggested that children with social problems at this age turn to television to find companionship. From the low level of loneliness, one might argue that television was successful in filling a void.

Murray's results support this suggestion. He found that the very heavy viewers among his panel were the most likely to have problems of social adjustment: to be passive in interpersonal situations, bashful, more distractable. The longitudinal data on these children, it should be noted, showed that these children had exhibited these characteristics as early as age three. On this basis, Murray suggests that the heavy viewing may be a symptom, not a cause, of a retreat from social interaction. This recalls what Schramm et al. observed a decade earlier: that abnormally heavy use of television may occur "when the child retreats from unpleasant problems of reality to soothing fantasy and finds the difference so great and his responses so pleasantly reinforced by television, in contrast to what happens to them in reality, that he retreats ever more deeply."

Further logical support for this view comes from the fact that the studies both of Murray and of Lyle and Hoffman report that young children had a higher preference for play than for television watching during much of their free time, particularly during daylight hours when it is possible to play out of doors. Even in the evening hours, when play opportunities are more restricted, play rivaled television as the child's most preferred activity.

However, it should be noted that McLeod et al. (1971a, 1971b) reported a very low correlation between television viewing time and their measures of alienation. Among their adolescents, the newspaper was the mostly likely route to "escape."

The sixth and tenth graders in Lyle and Hoffman's study differed somewhat in their patterns of self-perceived reasons for using television. Both age groups primarily saw television as a source of entertainment or relaxation. The sixth-graders, particularly the boys, said they were likely to turn to television when lonely, but this was not true among the tenth graders. Most youngsters, with the exception of the sixth-grade boys, were more likely to seek out personal companionship when lonely or to listen to music than they were to turn to television. The use of television for relief from anger or hurt feelings was very low among both age groups, although it should be noted that more reliance upon television in this situation was reported by heavy viewers than by light viewers.

A fact which stands out in bold relief in this data is the great importance of music for the teenagers. "Listening to music" scored higher than "watching television" among the tenth graders for relaxation and entertainment as well as for relief from loneliness, anger and hurt feelings. Radio listening alone claimed more of the tenth graders' time than did television watching. When record listening time is added, the role of music in the everyday life space becomes even greater.

Even among the sixth graders, music was beginning to play an important part in the child's life.

In their 1959 data, Schramm et al. (1961) found heavy use of television to be related to conflict with parents. Lyle and Hoffman did not find this relationship in their study, although it should be noted that they used a different, more detailed measure of parent-child conflict. They did, however, find that conflict was positively related to high viewing of "most violent" programs.

SUMMARY

Overall, the studies suggest several changes over the decade in the public's use of and attitudes toward television. It seems that more time is spent in the company of the set, but it appears that the level of attention to program content fluctuates markedly.

One recalls that in the early days of television, when people were first acquiring sets, they watched for great periods of time, then gradually reduced their viewing time. Today it appears that the set is largely just left on and the viewer "drops in and out" of programs. This raises the possibility that while television has become ever more interwoven with our lives, its hold upon our attention has perhaps been reduced. Indeed, one might ask if the public's general affect for television has perhaps fallen despite apparent increases in "viewing time."

Certainly in one regard the public has become more critical of the medium. The present data showed a high level of antagonism toward commercials, not only with regard to their frequency but also as reflected in a strong tendency to reject them as deceitful, if not flatly untrue. This antagonism was stronger among teenagers than among adults.

Lyle and Hoffman suggest that there has been a leveling of television viewing among young people—that heavy vs light viewing per se does not work as a predictor of mental ability, social class, parental conflict, and social isolation in 1970 as it seemed to do in 1959. Differences in attitudes toward the medium and in manners of use, however, do seem to continue to discriminate. Further, they found that although reported television viewing time had apparently increased, there was little parallel reduction in the use of other media.

LoSciuto and Robinson interpret their data on adults as indicating that television was not displacing other activities valued by the individual, but more likely was being used to fill time which overwise would have been filled by generally "nonconstructive" activities. Murray suggests that the socially maladjusted youngsters who were heavy viewers would have been maladjusted without television. What is disturbing is the evidence, like that of Israel and Robinson and of Robinson and Bachman (1971) that social misfits or those perhaps more prone to violent behavior are most likely to view violent programs.

Although individuals may devote large amounts of time to television, primarily seeking relaxation, there is little in the data to suggest that this is turning them into escapists, social isolates, or deviants.

But we do know that there is learning from television. Such learning can be good; it can also be bad. Ward's data suggest that effects of learning from television can be strongly mediated by parental influence. Many of the studies mentioned above document that mothers feel they have evidence that their children, preschool-age as well as older, are learning from television. A sizable number feel that some of this learning is bad, and considerable uneasiness is reported among mothers concerning the impact of television upon their children. It is therefore disturbing to read in so many of the studies that, despite uneasiness and intentions of mothers to guide the viewing of their young children, much of the viewing of even very young children is unsupervised, unmonitored.

It is interesting, but not particularly comforting, to note that a recent report on the impact of television on Japanese children (Furu, 1971) comes to much the same conclusion. The author concludes with an appeal to parents and teachers to undertake to systematically create good viewing habits.

Greenberg, Ericson, and Vlahos report that viewing of violent programs increased according to the amount of viewing ten-year-olds did in the company of their parents. Lyle and Hoffman suggest that parental influence may account for the fact that actual viewing of violent programs was higher than their stated preference. One may well wonder who made the program selections which resulted in Mod Squad's being the most-viewed program among Murray's five- and six-year-old boys.

With these findings in mind, it is difficult to be sanguine about the possibility that parents will accept the responsibility for undertaking a sustained program of directing their children's exposure to television, even if they do recognize the potential impact of the medium—good and bad —on their children. Giving the ubiquity of the medium, perhaps this is not only an unrealistic, but an unfair, expectation.

One might have higher hopes for the schools, but it must be recognized that by the time the child reaches school, he has already accumulated considerable experience with television content, has acquired viewing habits, and probably has acquired knowledge and predispositions from what he has seen.

There is also a quandary for the broadcaster, given the competitive nature of our broadcasting system. There is no one "child audience." Interests change rapidly as the child grows older. *Sesame Street* may appeal to preschoolers, but it's "kid stuff" once they enter school. Conversely, the evidence is also clear that "adult programs" are likely to be seen by large numbers of youngsters, including some who are quite young. What is the broadcaster to do: program nothing but "family-rated" shows?

Television today is an integral part of our everyday life. It appears that it is not an unmixed blessing. To the extent that it can be dysfunctional to individuals and (by extension) to the social fabric, the manner in which it is intertwined in our daily lives makes it an exceedingly difficult problem to deal with. This does not mean it is an impossible problem. But the findings reported herein suggest that even those most directly concerned—the mothers of young children—do not have the will to come to grips with it.

Appendix

Accurate measurement of television viewing behavior is a vexing problem, one which has long been recognized. Schramm et al. (1961), for instance, discussed it in Appendix III of their book, making use of discrepancies noted in results using several different approaches on the same children. The varieties of methodologies used in the studies in this series present several problems, as well as opportunities to make observations on this problem.

Running through all the studies was a general finding that people tend to overestimate when asked to estimate their daily viewing time. At least, the figures obtained through this approach generally are higher than those which result from more specific measures such as aided recall or diaries.

The study of Bechtel and his associates is particularly valuable, in that it is one of the few studies which provides a check on the validity of self-reported viewing. In this instance the self-reports in diary form were checked against videotapes of actual viewing. The diaries provided much higher figures than the videotape observations for the same periods of "viewing."

The Bechtel et al. data is impressive both for its imaginative approach and for the documentation it provides concerning the scope and diversity of activities which may be concurrent with "television viewing." However, these authors developed their results from the standpoint that "viewing time" is only time actually spent looking at the television screen, or what is sometimes called "eye contact" time.

This raises some very real questions about the nature of television viewing which must be faced in any attempt to measure viewing time. Foremost is the question of whether or not "attention time" is restricted to "eye contact" time. The housewife who irons in front of the television set has only limited eye contact with the screen. Does she consider that she is "watching television?" The man of the house who attends to various chores while having the set tuned in to a football game may only turn his eyes to the set when the aural cues alert him that a play is about to begin. Is he "watching television?" What about the children playing in a room in which the television is pouring forth a stream of cartoons?

By Bechtel's criteria their viewing time would be limited to eye contact time; yet if they were asked, they possibly would reply that during the entire period they were "watching television." The comparative analysis of the videotapes and the diary records suggests this is probably the case.

Thus the Bechtel et al. study underlines the very real quandary of establishing the validity of such measures. Objective measures such as eye contact measures will produce one result, but viewer response may give another. It could be argued that the latter is perhaps the more valid measure in terms of reflecting the respondent's orientation to the television screen. He or she may not be actually watching, but an ear is cocked, so to speak, so that at critical moments they can focus their attention on the set.

Bechtel and his associates have, in effect, documented what informal observation has suggested: television viewing is a complex of behaviors which occur at different levels of attention. This situaton is very likely a major contributor to the overestimates of viewing time which result from abstract self-assessment.

The encouraging fact that emerges from these various studies, where it was possible to compare various self-reports and objective measures, is that regardless of the discrepancies in measures of time spent viewing, the measures are positively correlated. In other words, a person who is classified as a heavy viewer by one measure generally turns out to be a heavy viewer according to the other measures. Similarly, light viewers tend to be light viewers by whatever measure is used.

The import of this is that perhaps we would be wise to deemphasize reports of specific viewing time and deal more in categories of relative use. Certainly until we have solved the definitional problem of "viewing time," this is true. But the individual fluctuations from day to day documented by Lyle and Hoffman suggest that, even with a better definition, caution should be exercised in using measures which are based on behavior on a single day or even on an "average day."

LoSciuto's study underlines the difficulty of obtaining diary records and particularly measures of attention level and interest through self-administered diaries. He had a 28 percent initial loss of households whose members refused to cooperate even for interviews, and only 45 percent of the original sample provided both interviews and diaries. But significantly, he reports that 80 percent of the diaries that were obtained had few descriptive or meaningful responses to the open-end questions; only 5 percent had abundant meaningful or interesting answers.

The study by Greenberg, Ericson, and Vlahos is one of the most detailed documentations to date of the dangers of using mothers as informants concerning their children's viewing behavior. Working with ten-year-olds and their mothers, they found that the children reported twice as much viewing time as that estimated by their mothers. Similar gross discrepancies were found in the reports of viewing of violent programs given by the children and that estimated by their mothers. Mothers also tended to underestimate the reality of television for the child and of solitary viewing by the child.

In sum, the authors state, "Mother and child tended to disagree sharply on whatever television behavior was being analyzed, but there was no systematic relationship among the discrepancies across the measures."

This makes the Lyle and Hoffman work with first graders and pre-school-age children particularly interesting. While the children were not able to estimate amounts of time viewed, the majority of children as young as three were able to provide information on their general patterns of viewing and of the viewing environments in their homes. The investigators were able to obtain information on actual viewing time and program selection for the first graders by having interviewers go through the previous day's log with the children. This was time-consuming and required considerable patience, but it was possible. There remains the problem of how reliable and valid the children's reports were, for Lyle and Hoffman were able to make no checks.

One further, personal, observation is pertinent. The present author supervised the field work for several of the 1959 studies reported by Schramm et al. and supervised the work among the tenth graders in the 1970 study of Lyle and Hoffman. A very definite change of attitude was apparent among students of this age. A decade ago the dominant response of students was one of interest and cooperation. In 1970 the response was more likely to be one of acquiescence mixed with occasional complaint and outright hostility. Because the data was collected within the classroom, the students did participate and most appeared to be honest in their responses. But without the aura of classroom authority, it is doubtful if participation would have been as complete. Informal discussion with the classroom teachers on this situation brought forth comments by them that this was a reflection of general changes they had perceived in the attitudes of their students over recent years.

Perhaps the general import of all these observations is that in the future it will be advisable to concentrate more on depth personal interviews and observations rather than on large sample surveys. Further, it may well be more meaningful to put more focus on actual program selections and attention than on viewing time *per se*.

FOOTNOTES

1. *Broadcasting Yearbook, 1971.*
2. Some reservations may be entertained about this finding since, as noted above, the reports of both program favorites and viewing behavior were provided by the parents themselves. Greenberg, Ericson, and Vlahos provide data which raise serious questions about the value of such parental reports.

REFERENCES

Baker, R. K., and Ball, S. J. *Mass media and violence:* a report to the National Commission on the Causes and Prevention of Violence. Washington, D.C.: U.S. Government Printing Office, 1969.

Bechtel, R. B., Achelpohl, C., and Akers, R. Correlates between observed behavior and questionnaire responses on television viewing. In *Television and social behavior,* Vol. 4 (this volume).

Broadcasting yearbook, 1971. Washington, D.C.: Broadcasting Publications, Inc., 1971.

Chaffee, S. H., and McLeod, J. M. Adolescent television use in the family context. In *Television and social behavior,* Vol. 3 (this series). Washington, D.C.: U.S. Government Printing Office, 1971.

Chaffee, S.H., McLeod, J.M., and Atkin, C.K. Parent-adolescent similarities in television use. Paper presented at the meeting of the Association for Education in Journalism, Washington, D.C., August 1970.

Foley, J. M. A functional analysis of television viewing. Doctoral dissertation, University of Iowa, 1968.

Foulkes, D., Belevedere, E., and Brubaker, T. Televised violence and dream content. In *Television and social behavior,* Vol. 5 (this series). Washington, D.C.: U. S. Government Printing Office, 1971.

Furu, T. The function of television for children and adolescents. Tokyo: Sophia University Press, 1971.

Gans, H. J. *The uses of television and their educational implications.* New York: The Center for Urban Education, 1968.

Gerbner, G. Violence in television drama: trends and symbolic functions. In *Television and social behavior,* Vol. 1 (this series). Washington, D.C.: U.S. Government Printing Office, 1971.

Greenberg, B.S., and Dominick, J.R. Race and social class differences in teenagers' use of television. *Journal of Broadcasting,* 1969, **13,** 331-44. (a)

Greenberg, B.S., and Dominick, J.R. *Television behavior among disadvantaged children.* East Lansing, Mich.: Michigan State University Department of Communication, 1969. (b)

Greenberg, B.S., Ericson, P.M., and Vlahos, M. Children's television behaviors as perceived by mother and child. In *Television and social behavior,* Vol. 4 (this volume).

Hazard, W. R. Anxiety and preference for television fantasy. *Journalism Quarterly,* 1967, **44,** 461-69.

Herzog, H. Motivations and gratifications of daily serial listeners. Reprinted in Schramm, W. *Process and effects of mass communication.* Urbana, Ill.: University of Illinois Press, 1961.

Hess, R.D., and Goldman, H. Parents' views of the effects of television on their children. *Child Development,* 1962, **33,** 411-26.

Israel, H., and Robinson, J.P. Demographic characteristics of viewers of television violence and news programs. In *Television and social behavior*, Vol. 4 (this volume).

Johnson, R.L., Friedman, H.L., and Gross, H.S. Four masculine styles in television programming: a study of the viewing preferences of adolescent males. In *Television and social behavior*, Vol. 3 (this series). Washington, D.C.: U.S. Government Printing Office, 1971.

LaPlante, W. A. An investigation of the sight vocabulary of preschool children as measured by their ability to recognize words shown frequently on commercial television. Doctoral dissertation, Temple University, 1968.

LoSciuto, L.A. A national inventory of television viewing behavior. In *Television and social behavior*. Vol. 4 (this volume).

Lyle, J., and Hoffman, H. R. Children's use of television and other media. In *Television and social behavior*, Vol. 4 (this volume). 1971 a.

Lyle, J., and Hoffman, H. R. Explorations in patterns of television viewing by preschool-age children. In *Television and social behavior*, Vol. 4 (this volume). 1971 b.

McIntyre, J., and Teevan, J. Television and deviant behavior. In Television and social behavior, Vol. 3 (this series). Washington, D.C.: U.S. Government Printing Office, 1971.

McLeod, J. M., Atkin, C. K., and Chaffee, S. H. Adolescents, parents, and television use: adolescent self-report measures from Maryland and Wisconsin samples. In *Television and social behavior*, Vol. 3 (this series). Washington, D.C.: U.S. Government Printing Office, 1971. (a)

McLeod, J. M., Atkin, C. K., and Chaffee, S. H. Adolescents, parents, and television use: self-report and other-report measures from the Wisconsin sample. In *Television and social behavior*, Vol. 3 (this series). Washington, D.C.: U. S. Government Printing Office, 1971. (b)

Murray, J. P. Television in inner-city homes: viewing behavior of young boys. In *Television and social behavior*, Vol. 4 (this volume).

Niven, H. Who in the family selects the TV program? *Journalism Quarterly*, 1960, **37**(1), 110-11.

Roberts, J., and Baird, J. T. Parent ratings of behavior patterns of children in the United States. Vital and Health Statistics, National Center for Health Statistics, Series 11, No. 108, PHS No. 1000.

Robinson, J. P. Television's impact on everyday life: some cross-national evidence. In *Television and social behavior*, Vol. 4 (this volume). 1971 a.

Robinson, J. P. Toward defining the functions of television. In *Television and social behavior*, Vol. 4 (this volume). 1971 b.

Robinson, J.P., and Bachman, J. G. Television viewing habits and aggression. In *Television and social behavior*, Vol. 3 (this series). Washington, D. C.: U. S. Government Printing Office, 1971.

Schramm, W., Lyle, J., and Parker, E. B. *Television in the lives of our children*. Stanford, Calif.: Stanford University Press, 1961.

Stein, A., and Friedrich, L. Television content and young children's behavior. In *Television and social behavior*, Vol. 2 (this series). Washington, D.C.: U. S. Government Printing Office, 1971.

Steiner, G. *The people look at television*. New York: Alfred A. Knopf, 1963.

Ward, S. Effects of television advertising on children and adolescents. In *Television and social behavior*, Vol. 4 (this volume).

A National Inventory of Television Viewing Behavior

Leonard A. LoSciuto

Institute for Survey Research, Temple University

For close to a quarter century, television has been a central American institution with almost universally acknowledged implications for pervasive influence on attitudes and behavior. Television has even radically affected other sources of influence on American society. For example, the content of the other mass media has drastically shifted—movies to provide entertainment fare not available on television ("spectaculars," nudity), radio and magazines to arrange content which appeals to specialized audiences, newspapers to emphasize more pictures and shorter stories.

Such positive effects as increased vocabulary of primary school children have been attributed by some to television. On the other hand, it has been suggested by other social observers that television has detrimentally rearranged the basic manner in which man perceives his environment, has increased his appetite for trivial goods, and has even decreased his sensitivity to the pain and suffering of his fellow man.

All in all, the effects of television on American society remains a topic of considerable speculation, with little empirical evidence to substantiate the most interesting of these effects. For example, the effects of violence on television is a present topic of particularly heated debate. A number of laboratory experiments (Bandura, 1965; Berkowitz, 1965) have amassed evidence which strongly suggests that antisocial behavior can be stimulated by viewing aggressive content either on film or on television. However, there is ample precedent for taking a skeptical view of the applicability of these results to the effects of real-life viewing. Hovland (1959), reflecting on his classical laboratory studies on the effects of the mass media, noted the limited generalizability of his body of research findings about attitude change to ongoing attitude processes in the natural environment. He recognized that in the laboratory the experimenter has control over the messages the audience receives, while outside the laboratory audiences tend to select messages according to their already existing predispositions; that in the laboratory setting only short-run changes are usually observed, while in ongoing life the cumulative effects of media are crucial; and that individuals in experiments are not allowed to interact with their peers, while this is perhaps the most powerful barrier to attitude change in real life.

Of course, none of these factors is enough to invalidate the results of laboratory studies, since conditions in these studies were deliberately established to allow the maximum likelihood of effects to be shown, rather than attempting to replicate real-life situations. Nevertheless, it is unfortunate that better information is not available on the conditions of home viewing so that one could at least estimate how serious these differential viewing conditions are. In general, it is surprising to discover how little is known about the patterns of viewing behavior in the United States, even about as basic a statistic as how much time people watch television. For example, probably the most widely cited indicator of the pervasiveness of television in American culture is the amount of time that people spend in front of the set.

Yet a review of the various methods of collecting data on time use reveals that certain systematic differences derive from differing methodological approaches. Nielsen's "audimeters" produce the largest estimates of viewing, because these devices record the total time that the television set is on for the entire household and, of course, not all family members necessarily view the set while it is on. In fact, when Allen (1965) took pictures of the home television audience, he found that during 20 percent of the time the set was on, no one was within its viewing area. Schramm, Lyle, and Parker (1961) found systematic differences in viewing time according to the type of question that was employed in the interview; an unsupervised diary elicited almost 20 percent less reported viewing than aided recall methods. In preliminary research carried out by National Institute of Mental Health staff members, a question asked by the Roper (1969) organization (requiring respondents to estimate how much time they viewed on an average day) generated television viewing estimates for about 250 adolescents that averaged out to be 50 percent larger than if the adolescents were asked how much time they had viewed "yesterday." The difference is not explainable in terms of differential viewing by day of the week.

However, Robinson (1969) reported that in many instances differences of such magnitude were obtained by researchers using even the same basic methods and questions, so that methodological reasons alone do not account for the failure of researchers to agree on a single estimate of television viewing. Robinson's own research (which produced a relatively low estimate of television viewing time), utilizing a diary in which respondents reported all of their activities for one particular day, provided one likely source of discrepancy. This was viewing as a "secondary" activity—that is, viewing while reading, eating, talking, etc.— which comprised almost 30 percent of television viewing time.

Nevertheless, since the purpose of this research instrument was the description of all behavior, sufficient attention was not given to the subtleties involved in isolating the actual amount of viewing in such multiple-activity circumstances. Reasonable but arbitrary coding procedures were devised to deal with this problem so that quantitative analysis could proceed, but it is obvious that future studies should focus more attention on the problems attendant to the analysis of secondary activity viewing.

It seems worthwhile then to investigate not only amount of viewing time (which must be estimated by a number of different methods) but also conditions and contexts in which viewing takes place. It also seems worthwhile to investigate self-reported "effects" of the programs that are viewed with an eye toward answering questions such as: What aspects of the program provided most enjoyment and most interest? Did the viewer learn anything or claim to learn anything by viewing the program? If the program was of a dramatic nature, did he find it mainly realistic or unrealistic? Was there anything in the program that was objectionable or upsetting? Which was more interesting, the basic story line or the character development? Was any behavior seen that the viewer himself would consider appropriate in his own life? Even more fundamentally: Why do people watch television? Are no alternative activities available? How much do people watch even when the available content

is distasteful, as in the case of a dull political preemption on all networks? What activities draw them away from their sets and how often
do they feel that they would rather have watched television instead?
Only through testing is it possible to determine whether reliable information of this type can be elicited in the survey research setting.

In assessing effects, the factor of attention to the set may well turn out
to be a pivotal variable. In Allen's (1965) time series photographs (which
unfortunately have been destroyed), even when there was someone
within viewing range of the set, a substantial minority of viewers did not
have their eyes on the set at all. (Whether this means that they were not
"attending" to the set in any way is another question entirely, one only
partially covered in the present study.) Two other studies (Simmons,
1967; Steiner, 1966) indicate somewhat more attention to the set than
Allen's research, but even here only about two-thirds of the time was
the potential audience paying full attention to the set. Both studies
found less attention to the set for women, for younger persons, and for
the better educated.

There are undoubtedly a number of other variables that would provide
significant insights into the functions of everyday television viewing
beyond those already discussed. For example, under the heading "effects" one can think of results such as information gain, attitude
change, euphoria (as when one's favorite football team wins a big
game), discontent (as when an unpopular political figure appears on the
screen), and relief from loneliness.

It is obvious that survey interviews can shed light on only a few of
these issues (especially in a single study), but it seems worthwhile to
begin exploring methods of gauging these subtle social effects of television which have thus far been ignored in empirical research.

GENERAL OBJECTIVES AND SCOPE OF THE STUDY

The major purpose of the present survey was to collect benchmark
data relating to television viewing behavior in the United States. Such
data are necessary prerequisites to understanding the degree to which
the effects of television programs are seriously influenced by certain sit-
uational factors in the television viewing environment. Towards that
end, a national sample of 512 individuals selected by probability sampling methods were interviewed concerning their television viewing
behavior. Individuals provided unique data on their usual uses of television and other media and attitudes toward various facets of television
content. Data were collected to fill in gaps in the current state of knowledge about how people use television in everyday life.

There have been few attempts to describe the viewing habits of Americans beyond the behaviorally superficial nose-count data collected regularly by Nielsen and the rating services. It is true that Steiner (1963)

collected a considerable amount of descriptive data, and many parts of that study are currently being repeated. The present study, however, deals with aspects of television viewing not captured in this replication and was conducted with full knowledge of the Steiner replication effort (through the kind efforts of Robert Bower of the Bureau of Social Science Research who is responsible for this replication). The focus in the survey reported here is not on the meaning of television for each individual, but rather to a large extent on how people actually behave and react when the television set is on.

It should be pointed out at the outset that financial limitations and the highly exploratory nature of the data collection demand that the study be viewed strictly as a pilot project. In spite of this, it was deemed advisable to employ a national sample, rather than one from a more limited geographical area, in order to capture a fully representative range of responses to television. Moreover, the cost differential of the local *vs* the national survey was marginal for the increased representativeness gained.

There is little to dispute that the small basic sample size may force social researchers to consider the study deficient for the usual estimations attempted from national surveys. Since many social analysts still feel sample sizes as large as 1,500 are insufficient for estimations of national characteristics, we cannot hope to convince such persons that samples of one-third this size are almost as useful. And the effective sample size was further reduced by another feature of the study design —the decision to sample whole family units and all individuals 12 years of age or over in such households. This clustering effect reduced the effective sample size to about 250—the number of households participating in the study. Again, our purpose was to move into hitherto unexplored territory with new and interested questions, rather than to provide precise body counts.

Our study design was meant to focus on population characteristics on a gross level. We were interested, for example, in the gross proportion of the population that used printed television guides to choose television programs whether it was 30 or 60 or 90 percent. Since an effective sample size of 250 is sufficient to estimate proportions within a $\pm$ 7 percent range with 95 percent confidence, it was thought to be of sufficient size to provide answers to such broad inquiries. It was thought that the more provocative results obtained from this survey could subsequently be replicated using much larger samples. (It should be pointed out that even a simple random sample of 1,500 has a $\pm$ 3 percent tolerance range.) In any case, this project was conceived as a pilot inventory of television viewing, intent on exploring many complex aspects of the phenomenon, with little regard for generating precise inferences to population parameters.

Perhaps the major disadvantage of the small sample size is the lack of sufficiently stable bases from which to establish the correlations of television use variables with various background and psychological factors. Some attempt in this rather risky direction is made in a separate report by Dr. John Robinson, who consulted with ISR on various aspects of this project. The present report will concentrate instead on overall descriptions of the many facets of television viewing that were investigated. Time constraints have also played a role in this formatting, since we have had only two months after the data decks were properly cleaned and available for analysis to complete this report. Much of the data are, therefore, presently reported in undigested form. Far more thorough analyses of these data are planned for the future.

The measuring instruments employed in the study were designed from a multiple indicator perspective. That is, it is assumed that there is no single way of asking a question on a survey that perfectly and reliably satisfies all the aims of the researcher. The different formats at times make the estimation process in survey research a formidable task.

A prime example of this phenomenon is the seemingly simple matter of estimating how much time is spent watching television, toward which goal a good deal of effort was expended in the current study. We approached this question from three perspectives: (1) gross subjective estimates of how much time respondents thought they watched television on an average day; (2) recalling from a television guide all the programs and time spent watching television on the preceding day; and (3) the amount of viewing recorded in a log of viewing activity which respondents kept for a one-week period. It will be seen shortly that dramatically different estimates are generated by the three procedures.

A large number of viewing parameters were estimated by this "triangulation" from gross subjective reports, recall of viewing immediately preceding the interview, and daily recordings of one week's viewing activities. The major viewing parameters involved, in addition to time spent viewing, consisted of reasons for viewing, intensity of viewing, the degree to which television content brought pleasure or discomfort, and other self-reported effects of television content. In addition, nontriangulated information was collected on what people appear to learn from watching television, their use of other mass media, mother's reports on viewing of their children under 12 years of age, the number and type of sets available for viewing in the home, and, to a very limited extent in the present report, personality characteristics (e.g., aggression, alienation) that might relate to various facets of television viewing.

METHODOLOGY AND COMPARISONS WITH OTHER DATA

We recognized that data collection in this relatively new research area would ideally be accomplished over a long time period, with several pretestings employing rigorously designed experimental procedures to provide cross-checks of various methods of eliciting viewing data. Time constraints, however, allowed only two experimental pretests on nine households each to improve the questionnaire and study design. All conditions for the pretest except sample selection were designed to reflect the way the study was to be carried out in the field.

Data collection in general

The questionnaire, which may be found in Appendix A, was designed to (and did) take about an hour's interviewing time for the average respondent, including a small self-administered portion. A second data collection instrument was a television diary—a copy of which is in Appendix B. The diaries were to be filled out by each individual in a household over a one-week viewing period.

The present study was designed to be conducted in two waves. It was thought desirable to interview about half the sample during one one-week time period and the second half during another one-week period. The advantages of such a procedure are several—for example, if one separates the two periods by a sufficient length of time, one is able to amend the second wave questionnaire on the basis of experience with the first wave. One may also make other adjustments in the interview process, such as clarifying instructions to interviewers. Another advantage is the ability to use many of the same interviewers on the two waves and to keep the number of interviewers relatively small for control purposes. Still another reason for the two waves is the likelihood of cancelling out chance factors which might spuriously affect the results of one wave, but which probably would not affect the other.

The particular weeks chosen for diary keeping were those beginning Saturday, November 14 and Saturday, December 12, 1970. It was reasoned that these periods were far enough in advance of the Thanksgiving and Christmas holidays to reflect typical rather than holiday viewing patterns. It should also be noted that not all interviews were completed during these one-week periods. Interviewers were actually given two weeks beginning with November 11 and December 9 respectively (and, in rare cases, three weeks when necessary) in which to collect the interviews from all household members. However, the diaries were to be filled out by each family member during the specified one-week period, and virtually no deviation from this rule was permitted.

Interviewing procedures and problems

No unexpected national or local events of particular significance seem to have transpired during the study weeks to affect the television viewing pattern of the sample. As the second wave went on, however, it was necessary to conduct a number of interviews during the week right before Christmas, which may have affected viewing behavior to some extent.

A total of 118 interviewers worked on the study. Of these, 27 worked on wave 1 only, 25 were employed for wave 2 only, and 66 conducted interviews on both waves. All those collecting data were professional female interviewers, each of whom had been trained by ISR in general interviewing techniques and in the specifics of the study. Specific study training in this case was by mail. A very detailed manual of instructions was sent to each interviewer describing not only the questionnaires and diary, but the basic approach to be taken and steps to be followed in soliciting cooperation.

Interviewers were told to follow the screening form and questionnaire instructions exactly so that all potential respondents would be recruited in the same way. First the door answerer was to be told that the study was under the auspices of the Department of Health, Education, and Welfare and that it had to do with television viewing. Respondents were not told about the diaries until an interview had been taken with the male or female head of the house. Immediately after that initial interview, respondents were asked to cooperate and to promise the cooperation of other family members of 12 years of age or older in being interviewed and filling out diaries. One- or two-person households were offered $5.00 for cooperation, including diary keeping, while three-member or larger families were offered $10.00. It was felt that at least this much inducement was necessary for success of the study.

After gaining the cooperation of the male and female heads of house, interviewers had to call back to complete other interviews in the household, to check on the way diaries were being filled out, and finally to collect the diaries after the one-week viewing period.

A sample of each interviewer's work was checked for error and general quality before she was allowed to proceed with her assignment. Further, each household in which interviews were conducted was contacted by mail after the study and asked to fill out and return a validation form. A random sample of the nonreturns were then telephoned for purposes of validation. Neither mail nor telephone validations revealed significant problems with regard to honesty or accuracy of information collected by the interviewers. Copies of the validation forms may be found in Appendix C.

Since it is anticipated that studies like the present one (though more extensive in scope) will be carried out in the future, it is worthwhile to note the general and specific problems that were experienced in conducting this survey. Perhaps most worthy of note is that although completion rates were not particularly high, field administration personnel and interviewers reported relatively few fundamental problems and frustrations in staffing and in field work, since the topic was offensive or sensitive to very few interviewers or respondents. The field and related problems that did arise were largely the result of two study design features—multiple interviews per household and the task of diary completion.

With regard to multiple interviews, logistics problems in setting sample size and compromises with regard to clustering effects have already been discussed. The related problems of intraclass correlations and possible contamination through discussion of household members may be considered undesirable consequences of the decision to conduct multiple interviews within households. On the other hand, of course, such a design not only is economical, but also permits examination of family viewing patterns. It also obviates the necessity for statistical weighting according to household composition, since all eligibles within a household are selected for interviews.

One direct consequence of multiple interviews is that a screening refusal or a refusal of the head of household generally means that no interviews will be completed in that housing unit. This is mitigated by the advantages of added likelihood of participation of all household members in initially cooperative households.

Diary keeping for one week turned out to be a difficult requirement for many respondents and for many interviewers. Some of the problems outlined were unique, although most are common to virtually all studies employing diaries. The interviewers encountered a number of refusals at the diary request stage from people who had agreed to give interviews, despite the fact that incentive was offered for diary keeping. The necessity for this incentive is itself a problem and the actual amount is another. While providing a morale lift for the interviewer and some motivation for the respondent, it also creates a great deal of extra paper work regarding receipts, checks, etc. However, it is probable that diary keeping would be refused considerably more often without some inducement. (The diary and interview completion rates are given in the next section). Interviewers had to make a number of diary-related calls on each household—to secure initial cooperation, to see that they were being properly filled out, and to collect them at the end of the one-week period. (It might be added that the physical bulk of the diaries and interviews together made these calls somewhat awkward for the interviewer.)

However, even with all these calls, it was not always possible to arrange for each member to fill the diary out himself. In these cases female heads of house were allowed to do it for other individuals—meaning that recorded responses and reactions were not always the respondent's own. Further, as in many surveys, females tended to be somewhat more cooperative than males, so that often the point of view which is missing is that of the male head of the house.

The timing of the various parts of the survey was unavoidably inconsistent; individuals were interviewed at different points in time from when they started their diaries. Since individuals were interviewed on different days, the influence of days of the week had to be taken into account in assessing the questionnaire results.

Another set of difficulties resulted when interviewers, despite careful instruction to respondents and actual checking, were not always able to insure adequate diary completion. Many responses are cryptic and some missing completely. There is, of course, often more resistance to writing a response than to verbalizing one. In addition, respondents to a diary are able to avoid responses that send them on to other questions, so that replies to contingency questions may be somewhat restricted. Indeed, ratings of diary quality which were assigned by ISR's Coding Department showed the majority of diaries to have at least some inadequacies. Only two were regarded as completely unusable, however.

Interviewers sometimes found respondents who would not continue after a few days of diary keeping, so the one week time period may have been overlong and tedious. Perhaps in future studies it may be better to collect some information over the full week, with most questions concerning only the previous day or two.

Other field problems which materialized were for the most part potential obstacles in all national survey work—for example, winter weather, slowness of mail, and errors in questionnaire printing—so little can be gained by outlining them. However, it should be pointed out that such factors substantially affect both completion rate and the rates at which interviewers may be expected to drop out of the study.

Coding procedures and problems

The complexity of a particular coding assignment is determined by a number of factors: the size of the sample; the length of the questionnaire; the form in which the data is collected—whether it can be keypunched directly from the questionnaire and, if not, the extent to which it must be transformed by the coder; the extent to which the codes have been finalized at the time the coding operation begins; and the amount of copying and tallying of individual responses required of the coder.

In this study, the size of the sample was relatively small and the questionnaire was not of unusual length. However, in respect to the other factors mentioned, coding of this interview questionnaire was a relatively complicated assignment.

First, it was necessary to transfer data from the questionnaire to code sheets for keypunching. For only 70 of the 350 variables were precodes in the questionnaire used. In the remaining 280, some transformation of the data was required. These variables included those for open-end questions; others where the coder referred to a list of items, such as names of television programs, magazines, or colleges; and still another group where summary codes were used, requiring the coder to summarize data from several questions, often from different sections of the questionnaire.

Contributing to the complexity of the coding task was the need to refer frequently to television guides in order to code a program title and the day and time of watching. A further complication was the fact that codes for approximately a fourth of the variables could not be finalized until coding of the first wave was near completion. Tallies were kept of these responses, and when final codes were constructed, it was necessary to go back to the questionnaires and transfer sheets to complete the coding.

There was considerable variation in the amount of time required to code a diary, since this was dependent upon the quality of the diary keeping and the number of programs watched during the week. The major problem encountered was the failure of the person who kept the diary to record the exact name of the program watched or the time it began or ended. Again the television guide was used and the coder was able in most cases to secure from this source the omitted information. Extensive check coding and card cleaning operations were also required because of the nature of the data.

Although there were many problems in coding this study, one positive aspect was the high degree of involvement and interest the coders seemed to have in the project.

The sample

The nature of the study objectives seemed to necessitate only a relatively small sample, which would admittedly have the disadvantage of high sampling error so that precise projections to the population could not be made. A sample size of at least 200 families was initially agreed upon as necessary to meet the minimum requirements for the study. In fact, the actual final number of participating families in the study was 252. Sample size determinations were naturally accomplished through a set of considerations involving compromises. For example it was felt that if the sample size were relatively small it would be possible for interviewers to interact more often and more fully with household members.

At the same time, capability of making some inferences to the national population was desirable. These inferences cannot be based on precise data, since a simple random sample size of 250 estimates a population percentage of 50 percent with only seven percent accuracy. And although all family members 12 years of age and older within each household were to be interviewed, the actual consequent increase in sample size (to 512 interviews and 452 diaries) is compensated for to a large degree by the increase in clustering resulting from taking multiple interviews per household. Therefore the effective sample size is radically reduced.

The sample was selected in two stages. The first was the selection of 49 primary sampling units, and the second was the selection of two clusters of average size 3.6 housing units within each selected primary sampling unit. The primary sampling units were each comprised of 10,000 housing units (in 1960) which in most cases were located in the same county or in a contiguous set of counties. The primary sampling units were stratified by census division (as defined in the 1960 Census of the United States) and by location in a central city of a Standard Metropolitan Statistical Area (as defined in the 1960 Census), suburb of a central city, or nonmetropolitan area.

The two clusters of dwellings were selected randomly within each primary sampling unit included in the sample. Within each sample cluster the housing units were located on the same block or in a contiguous set of blocks, but the housing units were not adjacent to one another. In most cases they were separated by an interval of five to 15 housing units. The dwellings in each sample cluster were subdivided for inclusion in the first and second waves of interviewing. On the average, 4/7 of the dwellings in each cluster were included in the first wave and the remaining 3/7 in the second. A total of 354 housing units were selected, yielding 348 eligible households. As we have said, 252 of these households participated in the study. Each sample dwelling was selected with equal probability so the sample can be considered to be self-weighting.

Comparisons of ISR sample and U.S. Census data

Tables 1-7 present comparison of our sample with U.S. population data. In general it may be said, summing up all the tables, that sample characteristics do not differ greatly from those describing the population at large.

Table 1: Geographic region—U.S. population and sample data

	1970 census (100%)	ISR sample (100%)
New England	6%	11%
Middle Atlantic	18	9
East North Central	20	19
West North Central	8	12
South Atlantic	15	21
East South Central	6	5
West South Central	10	6
Mountain	4	4
Pacific	13	12

Table 2: City size—U.S. population and sample data

	1969 census (100%)	ISR sample (100%)
Center cities more than one million	15%	12%
Suburbs of above	20	19
Center cities less than one million	14	9
Suburbs of above	16	25
Nonmetropolitan	35	35

Preliminary examinations of the marginal distributions showed no significant differences between the demographic characteristics and the survey results for waves 1 and 2. Also no differences in completion rates and related data were found between the two waves. Therefore, this report concerns itself almost exclusively with the combined results of both waves. However, a full set of marginals for waves 1 and 2 are included as Appendix D to the report, should the reader wish to view the basic results separately for each wave. Also, responses to some key questions in the study are compared for the two waves in Table 15.

Table 3: Occupations—U.S. population and sample data

	1969 census (100%)	ISR sample (100%)
Professional	16%	14%
Managerial	17	16
Clerical	7	4
Sales	5	5
Craftsmen and firemen	21	21
Operators	19	18
Laborers (nonfarm)	5	3
Service	6	10
Farm labor	4	8

Table 4: Sex--U.S. population and sample data

	1970 census (100%)	ISR sample (100%)
Male	49%	45%
Female	51	55

Tables 1 and 2 reflect the results of the basic sample stratifications of geographic region and city size. Comparing these results with census data, it is evident that, geographically, the sample somewhat overrepresents the New England, South Atlantic, and West North Central states, while underrepresenting the Middle Atlantic and West South Central states. The implications of these imbalances are not at all clear, since consistent differences among these groups of regions are not particularly prominent in the survey data.

Table 5: Race—U.S. population and sample data

	1970 census (100%)	ISR sample (100%)
White	88%	85%
Black	11	13
Other	1	2

Table 6: Age (12 years and older)—U.S. population and sample data

	1969 census (100%)	ISR sample (100%)
12-19	20%	21%
20-29	18	22
30-39	15	12
40-49	15	16
50-59	13	11
60-69	10	10
70 and over	9	8

Somewhat fewer large center city residents are included in ISR's sample, and more residents of suburbs of smaller cities. But viewing data are not much different for these groups either.

Table 7: Education—U.S. population and sample data

	1969 census (100%)	ISR sample (100%)
None-7th grade	14%	14%
8th grade	14	12
9-11th grade	22	23
12th grade	32	29
13-15th grade	10	11
16th	5	6
16th +	3	5

Table 3 presents standard occupational breakdowns for employed male adults in the United States (U.S. Census) and for heads of house, male or female, in the ISR sample. Since no census data were available specifically for male and female heads of house, it was thought that the distribution of employed males might provide the best comparisons. In general the two distributions are matched fairly closely, especially considering the relatively small ISR sample size. Only some slight over-representation of farm personnel at the expense of clerical workers is evident, and these differences are quite small.

Completion rates and related data

Table 8 shows that a total of 354 households were selected for the study, only six of which were found to be ineligible. Of the 348 remaining housing units, 252 or 72 percent yielded at least one completed interview with a male or female head of house. In almost half (45 percent) of the eligible households, all eligible respondents were interviewed and kept diaries. In 11 percent of the households diary keeping was refused by all household members even though some interviews were taken.

Table 8: Final completion status for households

Total households visited	(354)	
Total eligible households	(348)	100%
Total eligible cooperating households	(252)	72%*
All eligibles completed interviews and kept diary	(158)	45%
Not all interviews or diaries completed	(57)	16%
Some interviews, but all refuse to keep diary	(37)	11%
Total eligible noncooperating households	(96)	28%
No eligible respondent home	(23)	7%
Refused household listing	(15)	4%
Refused interview and diary keeping	(43)	12%
Language barrier	(2)	1%
Other	(13)	4%

*These 252 households yielded 512 interviews and 452 completed diaries.

Twenty-eight percent of the eligible households did not agree to participate at all. Refusals of interviewing and diary keeping account for almost half of these nonparticipants. The refusal rate is relatively high compared to other studies done at ISR and would seem to be topic-related; that is, although individuals who do not watch television or watch it infrequently were asked to participate, many of them refused because they had no real interest in the study. Estimates of television viewing time are much lower for those who refused the interview than for those who responded. It should also be noted that refusals here are not due to the diary, since an interview was attempted before the request for diary completion was made. The reason most often given for refusal, as in most surveys, was lack of time. However, there is evidence that this reason is many times only a convenient excuse to avoid the interview, and interviewers are instructed to propose alternate times and dates. It is then that aversion or lack of interest in the topic is often brought out.

Other factors undoubtedly lowering the completion rate have already been mentioned. Winter weather made some houses almost inaccessible to call-backs after initial failure to find a respondent at home, and mail delays and losses prevented some interviewers from receiving their assignments until it was too late to make a sufficient number of calls on given households.

One approach to the problem of nonresponse is to compare the respondents with nonrespondents when possible to see if significant differences (usually demographic) exist between them. A problem here of course is that one most often does not have a full set of even demographic data on nonrespondents. This is true of the present study, and although some differences do appear (e.g., nonparticipating households tend more often to have heads who are unemployed and to have fewer people in the household), the bases are far too small to warrant confidence. We have already seen that the characteristics of individuals in cooperating households are similar to those described in U.S. Census data. Perhaps, then, it is worthwhile only to emphasize again that heavier viewers are more likely to participate than light viewers and nonviewers, so estimates of viewing time are likely to be on the high side (see Table 18). From a methodological or tactical point of view, it is also of interest to note that refusals are much more prevalent when the door answerer was a male than when it was a female adult or an adolescent of either sex. Where cooperation was gained, a female adult was much more likely to be the door answerer (Table 9). This may also be related to some extent to interest in the survey, since the substantive data show women to be heavier viewers than men. Procedurally, future studies might do well to avoid revealing the subject matter of the interview at least until the respondent has been somewhat warmed up to the task.

Table 9: Sex and age group of door answerer in cooperating households

	Number of households	
Total number of participating families	(251)*	100%
Male adult	(91)	36%
Female adult	(152)	60%
Male adolescent	(–)	0%
Female adolescent	(8)	3%

*Excludes one no-answer

Table 10 presents data reflecting on the sex and age composition of cooperating households. The distribution is such that female heads of house are present in almost all cases, with somewhat fewer male heads of house in evidence. The next most populous group was children 3-11, while male and female adolescents and children under three are about equally represented. This distribution corresponds reasonably well to U. S. census figures.

A total of 512 interviews were taken from the sample of 252 participating households, for an average of about two interviews per household (Table 11). As expected, fewer diaries were completed—the total number is 452, or about 1.8 per household. These figures are not surprising, since slightly over half of the households giving information on eligibles

Table 10: Sex and age group composition of cooperating households

	Number of HH with one or more of each group	
Male adult	(207)	82%
Female adult	(233)	92%
Male adolescent	(41)	16%
Female adolescent	(47)	19%
Children, 3-11 years old	(77)	31%
Children under 3	(44)	17%

Base for each percentage is 252—the number of participating households.

contained just two individuals 12 years of age or older (Tables 12 and 13). Thirty percent had three or more, and 16 percent had only one eligible. These tables also show that percentage of interview and diary completions does not vary systematically with number of eligibles per household.

Table 11: Number of completed interviews and diaries by sex and age group of respondent

	Completed interviews		Completed diaries	
Total	(512)	100%	(452)	100%
Male adult	(172)	33%	(157)	34%
Female adult	(235)	45%	(202)	44%
Male adolescent	(51)	10%	(47)	10%
Female adolescent	(54)	11%	(46)	10%

The age-sex distributions in Table 11 are very similar for the interviews and diaries, so evidently there was no general age- or sex-related resistance or inability to fill out the diary. However, the age breakdowns are not at all fine and it may be that the very old, for example, were at a disadvantage not revealed by these data. Indeed, interviewers reported a number of incidents in which the respondent was too old and infirm to participate. Most often poor eyesight was the direct cause.

The distributions in Table 11 also give evidence that adult females are more receptive to both interviews and diary keeping than are adult males, while male and female adolescents do not differ in their rate of cooperation.

Table 12: Number of completed interviews by number of eligible respondents per household

		Number of completed interviews							
Number of eligibles		0	1	2	3	4	5	6	7
1	53	13	40	–	–	–	–	–	–
2	154	22	35	97	–	–	–	–	–
3	41	3	3	7	28	–	–	–	–
4	30	1	5	3	11	10	–	1	–
5	6	–	–	–	2	–	4	–	–
6	6	3	–	–	–	–	–	3	–
7	4	–	1	–	2	–	–	–	1

The coding department was asked to rate on a four-point scale one day's diary recording for each respondent to get some idea of how well the task was carried out. The rating categories were: (1) no comments, or very brief, vague, nondescriptive ones; (2) few comments, mainly ones that are vague or nondescriptive; (3) few comments, all meaningful or numerous comments, some meaningful; and (4) numerous comments, most meaningful or interesting.

Table 13: Number of completed diaries by number of eligible respondents per household

		Number of completed diaries							
Number of eligibles		0	1	2	3	4	5	6	7
1	53	22	31	–	–	–	–	–	–
2	154	40	23	91	–	–	–	–	–
3	41	5	2	7	27	–	–	–	–
4	30	8	1	2	8	11	–	–	–
5	6	1	–	–	1	–	4	–	–
6	6	3	–	–	–	–	2	1	–
7	4	3	–	–	–	–	–	–	1

Table 14 shows the results of these evaluations for four sex-age groups. For the most part, diary content was rated as relatively poor by coders. Eighty percent of the diaries were found to have few descriptive and meaningful comments in response to open-end questions. Only five percent were found to contain numerous meaningful and interesting answers. Females tended to do better than males; in particular, the diaries of adult females were found to be superior to those of other household members. In future studies, it may be well to consider allowing only female heads of house to fill out these diaries for themselves and, perhaps, for other family members. In the present study, they were asked to fill out diaries for husbands and children only when these individuals would not fill them out themselves.

Table 14: Coder evaluation of quality of diary keeping—by sex and age group of diary keeper

		1	2	3	4
Adult male	(N=144)	45%	39%	13%	4%
Adult female	(191)	29%	45%	19%	6%
Adolescent male	(44)	57%	32%	7%	5%
Adolescent female	(38)	40%	45%	13%	3%

Comparison of critical questions—ISR sample and other surveys

It remains to compare the results of ISR's survey with data gathered in previous studies on a number of key items. ISR data is presented separately for Wave 1 and Wave 2 as well as for totals of the two.

Table 15 lists a number of items describing the physical availability and characteristics of television in the home, and some questions tapping attitudes toward television and other media. All of these items have been asked on previous studies, so that comparison of results is possible.

The similarities of results from Wave 1 to Wave 2 and from this study to previous studies are striking. In only three of the 12 cases are the differences between the ISR survey and previous studies greater than five percent—and one of these differences is contingent upon another at that. (That is, more people now feel television to be the most unbiased news medium, causing some other media—particularly newspapers—to be regarded less highly.) The only other change of more than five percent is an increase in the proportion of people who say they use a television guide.

Table 15: Television characteristics and attitudes—ISR sample and comparable data

	Spring 1970	ISR 1970		
		Wave 1	Wave 2	Total
		(N=310)	(N=202)	(N=512)
Within range of UHF channel	71%	67%	66%	67%
Have more than one set in home	41	43	39	42
Major set in living room	71	72	66	71
Major set is color	38	35	46	40
Major set can pick up UHF	46	46	50	47
Major set on cable	10	7	4	6
Spend too much time watching TV	20	16	15	16
Uses a TV guide to choose programs	73	79	77	79
Most unbiased news from TV	39	50	49	50
Most unbiased news from radio	23	23	24	23
Most unbiased news from magazines	11	8	10	8
Most unbiased news from newspapers	27	15	25	19

In Table 16, results are given for a three alternative present life satisfaction index. Here, too, the distributions of ISR and previous data are extremely similar, so the measurement seems at least reliable across time and survey variations.

Present estimates of viewing time do differ somewhat from previous surveys. For example, in a study conducted by the Roper organization for the Television Information Office in January 1971, respondents were asked how many hours they watched television on an average day. The median estimated was two hours and 50 minutes. ISR's data, on the other hand, show a median estimate of three hours and three minutes for respondents. However, if nonrespondents are taken into account, the ISR figure is reduced considerably.

Table 16: Life satisfaction index—ISR sample and comparable data

	Fall 1970 100%	ISR 1970		
		Wave 1	Wave 2	Total
Completely satisfying	22%	22%	31%	26%
Pretty satisfying	64%	64%	55%	60%
Not very satisfying	14%	14%	14%	14%

AVAILABILITY AND CHARACTERISTICS OF TELEVISION SETS IN THE HOME

Only 1.4 percent of our respondents did *not* have a television set in working order in their homes (including refusals, the nonownership rate rose closer to the 4 percent nonownership figure recently reported by the U.S. Census Bureau). The majority of the population, 57 percent, lived in one-set households, while 42 percent had more than one set in their households. Various characteristics of these sets are outlined in Table 17.

The major television set is almost universally located in the "group quarters" of the household environment, with 71 percent of first sets in the living room, nine percent in family or recreation rooms, and 11 percent in dens, libraries, or studies. Some three percent have their major set in the kitchen or living room and another four percent in an adult's bedroom. Second and especially third sets, in contrast, are found in adult or children's bedrooms, almost never in the living room. It is the first set that receives the vast bulk of use in the household, indicating second set use to be confined to merely occasional viewing. When asked to estimate the percentage of time they watch each set, 74 percent of the sample report watching all of their television on the first set in the household. In averaging these percentage estimates, we come up with 91 percent of viewing done on the first or only set, four percent on the second set, and one percent on the third set. (The fact that the totals do not add to 100 percent can be attributed to the difficulty many respondents have in thinking in percentage terms.)

Overall, 40 percent of respondents had color sets. This, of course, was usually the major set in the household, although 12 percent of second sets were in color.

The first set (not unexpectedly) was able to receive more channels (median 4.7 channels) than second or third sets (median 3.9 channels). These figures are only slightly under the median number of channels (6.0) that interviewers estimated were available for reception in that area. The discrepancy is largely due to the fact that most respondents reported being unable to pick up UHF stations. While interviewers

Table 17: Characteristics of TV sets in households

	First set	Second set	Third set
Location:			
Living room	71%	2%	–
Family or rec room	9	5	–
Den, library, study	11	4	–
Kitchen, dining room	3	3	–
Adult's bedroom	4	15	1
Child's bedroom	–	7	5
Other room	1	5	1
No answer, no set	2	59	93
	100%	100%	100%
Percent of time watching set (of those with such sets):			
(Average)	91%	4%	1%
Set is color:	40%	12%	0%
Median channels received:	4.7	3.9	3.9
Receive less than four channels:	23%	21%	26%
Can receive UHF:	47%	33%	24%
Antenna (of those with set):			
Roof antenna	52%	29%	14%
Rabbit ears	36%	56%	78%
Cable	6%	1%	0%
Other	7%	14%	8%
	100%	100%	100%

claimed that 67 percent of these homes were in the range of a UHF station, only 47 percent of respondents reported their main set could pick up UHF, the figures dropping to 33 percent and 24 percent, respectively, for second and third sets. Nevertheless, less than a quarter of all sets could pick up fewer than four stations, so that most respondents had an ample number of stations to choose from. In fact, some 15 percent reported having eight or more channels available (although interviewers estimated that 30 percent were in the range of eight or more channels, again probably mainly attributable to lack of UHF capabilities on many sets).

Despite what appears to be the universal presence of television antennas in all residential areas in America, only 52 percent of viewers have their main set attached to a roof antenna. The usage of antenna couplers must be infrequent since less than a quarter of multiple sets are attached to roof antennas, instead relying on "rabbit ears." In the fall of 1970, CATV was even more a rarity, with only six percent of respondents reporting a cable hookup. Another ten percent or so of sets have a miscellany of other antenna arrangements, such as connections to appliances, set-ups in attics, etc.

HOW MUCH TELEVISION PEOPLE WATCH

In order to establish a global estimate of how much time is spent watching television, the question regularly employed by the Roper Organization's television study was utilized: "On an average day, about how many hours do you personally spend watching television?"

Roper (1969) found that the median viewing time was 167 minutes, or two hours and 47 minutes. (An as-yet unpublished study indicates that in January 1971, this figure had risen by 3 minutes.) It should be noted that Roper's samples responded to omnibus surveys, so questions on television were not perceived by the respondents as the central focus of the studies. The present study, however, was obviously oriented toward television, and those participating were likely to be more interested in television than those who did not take part in the survey. The present sample, possibly because of this greater interest, reported a slightly higher median time of 183 minutes, or three hours and three minutes (Table 18). Only four percent of our respondents reported they watched no television on an average day, as compared to 15 percent who reported they watched six hours or more on an average day (more than double the national median figure). This results in the average amount of viewing being greater than the median figure by almost 20 minutes. The average viewing time for respondents is three hours and 20 minutes.[1]

Table 18: Viewing time in minutes for three
different measurement approaches

	Median	Mean
Average day's viewing	183	200*
Previous day's viewing	120	125
Average diary days' viewing	105	119

*ISR corrected mean = 174 minutes
Roper median = 170 minutes

The viewing figure is, however, considerably in excess of that inferred from respondents' recounting of the television programs viewed on the day preceding the interview. Totalling up the programs that respondents reported viewing on the previous day results in a median figure of 120 minutes (or two hours) and an average of 125 minutes. In contrast to their estimates for an average day, some 20 percent did not watch television on the preceding day and only four percent watched for six or more hours. (These figures are slightly inaccurate, since the days of the week for which television viewing information was collected were not equally distributed as they should have been. About 20 percent of these "yesterdays" were Mondays, Tuesdays, and Wednesdays; 15 percent were Sundays; ten percent were Thursdays and Fridays; and only five percent were Saturdays. Although the amount of watching time did not vary greatly here by day of week, Mondays and Sundays were somewhat heavier viewing days, while Fridays and Saturdays were light. Weighing days of the week equally results in a median figure of 110 minutes.)

Even these figures are larger than those reported in the week-long diary, undoubtedly reflecting to some extent the trouble involved in keeping these records. Of course, it is also possible (though unlikely) that the diary method may be reflecting most accurately the average amount of viewing, since respondents presumably fill out the diaries in closer proximity to the actual time of viewing. For all diary respondents (averaging over all days in the week and both waves), 23 percent reported that they did not watch television on an average day, slightly more than the 20 percent who said they did not watch television on the "previous day" question, and much greater than the four percent who reported they watched no television "on an average day." (It is interesting, incidentally, that many of these individuals apparently did not watch only because they had to work.) The median number of minutes watched was 105. This is 35 minutes lower than the median found from the question on the "previous day." The mean or average is 119 minutes—six minutes less than that found for the previous day's viewing in the questionnaire. The median is probably a better index of viewing time than the mean since the mean is considerably affected by a relatively small number of individuals who watch television throughout many of their waking hours.

It is somewhat surprising that the general amount of watching reported in the diaries varies little with a variety of demographic characteristics. For example, when the percentage of respondents who did not watch television "today" are compared across census geographic regions, the various areas do not differ significantly from each other. The range is also quite small across sizes of community, with somewhat more individuals (81 percent) in the most populated (over one million) metropolitan center city areas reporting viewing than the average (75 percent).

Nor do viewing patterns differ radically for male and female diary keepers of different ages. It is true, however, that somewhat more viewing is reported by women (79 percent) than by men (71 percent). No such difference exists between adolescent boys and girls.

Likewise, total number of programs and total number of minutes watched daily do not vary a great deal either by region or community size. Sex makes some difference; women tend to watch more programs and spend more time watching than do men. On the questionnaire, 21 percent of all women in the sample said they watched six or more hours on "the average day" compared to only 7 percent of men. Again, roughly the same viewing times are found for adolescent boys as for adolescent girls.

Surprisingly, the diaries also do not show great differences among days of the week with regard to whether television is watched or not. Fewest respondents said they watched television on Friday (66 percent), most on Tuesday (81 percent) and Sunday (80 percent).

Whatever the true amount of viewing may be, respondents felt little personal guilt about the time they do spend watching television. Only 16 percent felt that they spent too much time watching television. Those feeling guilty (somewhat more prevalent among the heavier viewers) invariably said that there were better things they could have been doing with their time. In the same vein, those who replied negatively gave as their reason the explanation that they were also quite busily engaged in other outside activities. Substantial numbers also defended their viewing time by saying that they watched only what they liked, that viewing provided them with some specific benefits, or that they really didn't feel that they watched that much compared to others.

These results differ from those of Steiner (1963), who found a great deal of ambivalence on the part of respondents who felt that television wastes much time that should be better spent. As he reported, to watch television is to be doing nothing, after all, except relaxing, which seems to be in conflict with the stress on activity and achievement among mobile Americans. This was more true of the better-educated. It may be that in the ten years or so since data were collected for the Steiner study, Americans have learned to be more accepting of television in its central role as entertainer and relaxing agent, perhaps partly because of greater familiarity with the medium. This would mean that television has been gradually rearranging thought patterns concerning leisure time so that to a limited extent it has come to determine what people do, rather than vice versa.

Also because of increased experience with television, secondary and even tertiary concurrent activities may be more prevalent now, so that television can be watched at the same time that more active pursuits—such as child care, housework, and hobbies—are followed. In any event, it might be speculated that as television continues to grow in familiarity, its use is likely to excite fewer feelings, either positive or negative, among the viewing public.

HOW PEOPLE WATCH TELEVISION

Time spent viewing, of course, is only a superficial indicator of how people use television. For one thing, as Robinson (1969) found, familiarity with having a set in the household becomes associated with an ability to accomplish other activities in conjunction with television viewing. Indeed, some 34 percent of the programs that respondents listed in their previous days' viewing were reported as viewed while the respondent was engaged in other activities. Work and housework were the most frequently mentioned activities concurrent with television viewing, with eating, talking, reading and child care following in that order. Other relatively frequent mentions were sewing or other needlework for women, personal care, hobbies, and schoolwork.

Five percent of all programs seen were viewed while respondents said they were engaged in two other concurrent activities. Talking was the most frequently mentioned tertiary activity.

The diary figures in the main substantiate these figures. They also show that the incidence of talking is higher when specific probes are utilized, since the diaries specifically offered "talking" as a response alternative. An average of 40 percent of the respondents reported talking during particular programs. In addition, 30 percent of the respondents said that they engaged in some other activity during the programs. As in the questionnaires, the most frequent of these activities was work or housework, followed by eating or drinking, reading, and child care in that order. Television also provided a topic of conversation afterwards for some 20 percent of diary respondents, who reported discussing a variety of dramatic shows, news, sports events, and other programs after seeing them.

Secondary activities detract from attention to the set while the person is presumably within viewing range, but they do not necessarily result in missing program content. For one thing, the diary data show that about half the respondents who were talking during programs were talking about the programs themselves. We also asked in the questionnaire about whether respondents actually did miss portions of each program and found that only 60 percent of the programs were watched from beginning to end. For 22 percent of the programs listed, respondents had seen less than half of the total program.

The diaries reflect on this issue in a slightly different way and indicate even less attention. Only ten percent of all programs watched were reported as viewed in their entirety by as many as 90 percent of the people who were watching them. Only an additional 23 percent of programs were reported viewed in their entirety by between 80 and 90 percent of their actual audience. So the audience for the average television show cannot be said to be very attentive. Only 33 percent of programs are actually watched all the way through by as many as 80 percent of the people who have turned on the programs.

All evidence certainly points to television viewing as a very disjointed series of experiences. Many viewers either find the programs so redundant or uninteresting that they can afford to miss large segments of the show without sacrificing enjoyment or are compelled by more urgent outside activities to see only bits and pieces. In either event, the dynamics of these viewing processes undoubtedly have strong implications for script writers or editors and what they hope to accomplish with the stories they put together for television. Interestingly, watching program from beginning to end drops to 52 percent of questionnaire respondents for the last viewed program, undoubtedly reflecting television's role as a sleep-inducing agent. However, our 60 percent figure (the percentage of programs watched from beginning to end as found from questionnaire data) may be high, since the manner in which we structured this series of questions meant that we oversampled prime-time viewing relative to earlier viewing (which is characterized by far more disjointed attention to the set).

This is corroborated by the findings from the diaries, which cancel out the biasing effects of selective viewing periods. When an average day's viewing is summed up for the diaries, we find that only one-third of the programs seen were actually viewed all the way through by 80 percent or more of the people who had tuned in. This figure was much higher for prime time shows in certain categories. Dramatic shows (other than adventure shows) and family situation comedies are characterized by high levels of audience attention. (These are shows such as *Marcus Welby, Medical Center, Bracken's World*, and soap operas).

If this popular type of program is compared to other types, a consistent pattern is seen in the way people watch these shows and in the amount of attention given them. First, more respondents said they planned to watch these dramatic shows and that they chose to watch them. Second, more people said they watched these shows all the way through than was true for any other program type. Further, few reported talking while the show was on, or carrying on potentially distracting activities. At the end of the program, most respondents in the dramatic show audience had good things to say about it. Compared with other shows, more respondents reported the program to have been really worth watching. It should be noted here that these dramatic programs are not chosen as favorites as often as are some other shows (e.g., comedy and variety shows), despite their advantages in attention value.

Some other shows with apparently limited audiences (like *Mayberry RFD*) receive full attention from those who do watch them. Interestingly, these programs with small but devoted audiences seem often to be reruns of shows which were very popular a few years ago (e.g., *Beverly Hillbillies, Green Acres*). In any case, it brings up the question of whether it is not as valuable (from a programmer's point of view) to have a restricted but attentive audience as it is to have one which is relatively large but easily distracted.

Programs receiving relatively little attention are variety-comedy or variety-music, education, and sports shows.

The social context of viewing also places important constraints on how viewing occurs. In their preceding days' viewing, respondents listed 32 percent of programs as watched alone, 43 percent in the company of one other person, and 25 percent in the company of more than one other person. The presence of other people in the room obviously affects what programs are selected for viewing, and, excluding programs viewed alone (presumably all in a sense chosen by the respondent himself), these were programs as likely to be chosen by other viewers as by the respondent himself. Of programs chosen when other viewers were present, the respondent claimed the choice was his for 38 percent of the programs viewed, someone else's for 33 percent of the programs viewed, and a joint decision for 29 percent of programs seen.

In the diaries, we see that on the average 68 percent of the respondents maintain that they had the major say in choosing a particular program. In fact, for only five percent of the programs was this proportion (of respondents reporting they had the major say in choosing the program) less than 50 percent on the average. However, 12 percent of the respondents reported that another adult had the major say in picking a given program, while 11 percent reported a consensus being reached between them and some other individuals in the room. It should be noted that these figures include data on many programs seen alone. When they are eliminated, the influence of other persons on program choice is indeed substantial.

All in all, these sets of questions indicate most television viewing to be a rather chaotic and discontinuous phenomenon, highly influenced by whoever happens to be in the room and how strongly they feel about the programs available for viewing. Program choice appears even more determined by whatever happens to appear on the screen than by the suggestions or demands of other people in the room.

WHY PEOPLE WATCH TELEVISION

In the early portions of the interview, respondents were asked directly about the main reasons they watched television. Over 60 percent listed more than two reasons for viewing. As can be seen in Table 19, entertainment and relaxation were the major reasons given by the majority of respondents. Another 18 percent gave "killing time" as their major reason for viewing. Yet a minority does put a more constructive perspective on their viewing, eight percent saying "to keep up with what was going on" and four percent saying that they were participating in a learning or self-improvement experience. Such reasons became even more prominent in second and third reasons for viewing. It would appear, therefore, that a substantial minority of viewers feel that their television viewing is not entirely a frivolous or escapist use of time.

When asked to choose which of three reasons best described their use of television, 62 percent chose "relaxing," confirming the Table 19 results that indicate most people do not look to their television sets for edification or self-improvement. As Steiner (1963) found, aside from the day's news or weather(which are watched with regularity), respondents rarely use the set as a deliberate source of information. Public affairs programs and specials, for example, received relatively little attention from our sample. However, more people (17 percent) claimed television to be "a useful way of spending time" than chose "a way of killing time" (11 percent), again indicating that a minority do take their viewing seriously.

Certain questions on both the weekly diary and the inquiry into the viewing of most recently seen programs also bear on why people watch television. Relatively few people describe particular programs they have seen as a waste of time. This is surprising in view of the reasons that people give for viewing the program in the first place. While a majority (61 percent) did claim to have planned to watch the program beforehand, some 28 percent watched just because it came on a channel they were

Tabel 19: Main reasons for watching television

	100%
For entertainment	32%
For relaxation	26%
To kill time	18%
To keep up with current events	8%
For learning or self-improvement	4%
For social reasons	4%
To see specific show	2%
Other	2%
No answer, no reason	4%

already watching, and another 11 percent watched because someone else in the household wanted to see the program. Such rationales do not argue well for television being a highly selective or well-planned activity.

The diary results at least partially confirm these conclusions. Here, a larger majority (69 percent) of the respondents on the average claimed to have planned to watch given programs that they actually watched. Only 20 percent reported watching programs just because they came on the channel then, and eight percent because someone else wanted to watch them. The diaries, then, result in somewhat higher estimates of planned television behavior, possibly because planning activity is remembered better in that situation, and possibly also because participation in the study encourages more attention to television viewing behavior. It might be speculated that diary keeping encourages individuals to be more selective in their viewing. This might result in more time spent planning what shows to watch and also perhaps in more attention paid to the programs that are watched. This is partly substantiated by the fact that the diaries show both fewer television shows watched and fewer minutes missed during the programs that are watched. It is still true, even in the diaries, however, that most programs are not watched in their entirety by all (or even 80 percent) of the respondents in their audiences.

These replies are not inconsistent with some interview question dealing with the use of printed television guides in the choice of programs. Almost 80 percent of our respondents said they used such guides—22 percent saying they used them for almost every program they chose, 21 percent for most programs, 18 percent for some programs, and 18 percent for only a few programs. The 20 percent who did not use these guides said either that they already knew when programs they wanted to watch would be on, or that the listings were too difficult or bothersome, or that they didn't watch television enough to justify use of a program guide.

Of the listings available, the following patterns of use were reported by those who used printed listings: 22 percent *TV Guide* magazine only; 33 percent weekly newspaper guide only; 19 percent daily newspaper guide only; five percent *TV Guide* + weekly paper; seven percent *TV*

Guide + daily paper; seven percent weekly paper + daily paper; six percent *TV Guide* + weekly paper + daily paper; two percent other guides or combinations.

When respondents who listed more than one guide were asked to nominate their most used source, and when their answers are merged with those using only one source, weekly newspaper guides came out to be major or only source for 42 percent of respondents and daily newspaper guides for 28 percent. Even though it has the largest circulation of any weekly magazine in America, *TV Guide* was listed by only 30 percent of those using guides as their major source. Moreover, as can be seen above, almost as many readers of the magazine supplement it with newspaper listings as use it by itself. Probably these multiple users are occasional buyers rather than weekly subscribers to the magazine.

Two sets of data were collected on why people did *not* watch television. The first was a report of a question first asked by Robinson (1969): "Were there times yesterday when you DID NOT watch TV because there were no programs worth watching on at that time?"

When asked about the preceding day's viewing in the interview, over 20 percent of the sample said yes, there was a time on the preceding day that they did something else because the choice of programs was so poor. The activities chosen instead were surprisingly as likely to be obligatory as to be free-time activities. The most frequently mentioned activities were housework and certain leisure activities (e.g., reading, playing). This potential but unused television time averaged 135 minutes per day for those who could not find suitable content. As Robinson (1969) found previously, however, relatively little (14 percent) of this boycotted television occurred during the prime time evening hours.

Although the incidence of reported boycotting was much lower in the diaries, very much the same impression emerges. Eight percent of the respondents reported times during the day when they wished to watch television but did not because nothing was on. Once again, relatively little of this time was during the evening prime time hours.

The second item on reasons for not viewing dealt with the reverse question—namely, times when respondents were unable to see something they wanted to see. The proportion of questionnaire respondents experiencing this feeling, 26 percent, is slightly larger than the proportion who had turned off their sets because of poor program choice (20 percent). Dramatic, comedy, and adventure programs on at prime time led the list of programs respondents regretted having missed. Relatively few sports events or specials were mentioned, which could mean either that they were of little salience to respondents or that most respondents made sure they did not miss these programs. No single set of activities kept viewers from programs they wanted to see. Shopping, leisure, working, visiting, entertaining, housework, organizational activity, and studying (in that order) were all listed relatively frequently.

Again, the diary entries tend to corroborate these findings to some extent, although not in all details. For example, 24 percent of respondents who answered the question reported that there had been programs on that day that they wanted to watch but didn't. This is a much greater proportion than those who rejected television during the day because there were no good programs to watch (eight percent). However the data do not clearly indicate any particular programs or program types as especially missed. To the extent that identification of "missed" program types is possible here, the leading contenders are soap operas for women and football for men. Prime time television is only a little more regretted than shows in other time slots.

For those reporting programs that they wanted to watch but didn't, the leading substitute activity during that time slot was shopping and personal care (such as sleeping or eating). This is followed closely by work of some kind, with entertainment and visiting next.

The lower estimates reflected in the diary data of television boycotting and of desired but unaccomplished viewing are quite possibly results of underreporting. After all, diary respondents knew that positive responses to these questions would lead them to still other questions and so may have tended to respond negatively.

In both questionnaires and diaries, respondents report some potential but unused television time to be more the result of presumably unavoidable missing of desirable programs than of poor programming. This is one indication, at least, that television programming may be registering more pluses than minuses with its audience.

HOW PEOPLE FEEL ABOUT WHAT THEY SEE

When we asked people to list their four favorite programs, we found comedy and variety shows leading the list, with crime-adventure, other adventure (including westerns), other dramatic (*Marcus Welby* and soap operas) shows close behind. Movies, singer-variety, sports, family-comedy, and situation-comedy programs each were mentioned generally about half as often as the preceding types of programs. Less than 20 percent of the respondents listed a news program, documentary, or other education programs as one of their four favorites, again reinforcing respondents' verbal statements that they use television predominantly for entertainment and relaxation.[2]

After listing their four favorite programs, respondents were asked to tell us what they liked about their *two* favorite *fictional* programs. The most common response to this open-ended question was that the particular program had good stories or plots. Specific reasons for liking centered mainly around specific characteristics of stories, such as typical plots or details of story line. Also frequently mentioned were effects on the viewer ("It makes me laugh," "You see what's happening"). General characteristics of the programs ("It's entertaining," "I like westerns") were next in order of popularity of response. Somewhat less frequent were responses centering on some action or character who appeared on the well-liked program. Still other reasons commonly given for liking a program involved respondents' perceptions that the program was realistic or portrayed things that could happen and were happening in real life.

Respondents were then asked whether it was the stories or the people on their favorite dramatic program that they enjoyed more. Although previous questions had resulted in many more story-related than people-related comments, the results here were for all practical purposes equally divided among stories, people, and both. When those who had replied "stories" or ("both") were asked what it was they liked about the stories, responses indicating realism or accuracy of real-life depictions were again the most frequent responses. Several respondents also noted the excitement or humor in these programs.

Those who said they liked their favorite show for the people (or both the stories and the people) were asked to name the people on the program. Most of these respondents were able to list several characters on that particular program. Few child actors and fewer adolescents were named, an interesting comment on the limited successful role models that television provides for preadults (since 20 percent of our sample were adolescents). Perhaps even more revealing is the fact that of the adult characters mentioned, males were listed three times more often than females, even though most of our respondents were female.

When asked what it was they liked about these characters, viewers gave several types of answers, not all of which yielded very specific information. The most frequent type of description given often indicated only that the person was evaluated highly ("He's good," "He's honest"). In addition to receiving positive character evaluations, story figures were often also credited with being "active" and doing "interesting things."

It is obvious that asking questions about positive experiences with television is likely to elicit only part of the story. Therefore respondents were later asked about television content that they *disliked*. Respondents were asked first if there was anything on television they would like to see changed. Then they were given four specific complaints and asked whether they agreed or disagreed with them. The results are portrayed side by side in Table 20.

It can be seen that the relative ordering of major complaints is quite consistent across the two types of questions. The most prevalent complaint voiced by viewers dealt with commercial interruptions; almost three of every four respondents agreed with this complaint when it was stated explicitly in the questionnaire. Although only five percent spontaneously complained about sex on television, 33 percent agreed there was too much of it on television when the question was asked directly. Few respondents to either question indicated there were too many news programs on television. While there were some complaints about news in the open-ended question, remarks were more likely to center around the content of the news than about frequency of news reports.

Table 20: Percentage of respondents giving various complaints about television

	Anything you would like to see changed?*	Agree as a complaint
Too many commercials	25%	73%
Too much violence	11	43
Too much sex	5	33
Too many news programs	2	13
Fewer particular types of programs (westerns, sports, etc.)	19	Not asked
More educational or cultural program	5	Not asked
More particular kinds of programs	6	Not asked
Poor scheduling of programs	5	Not asked
Greater variety of program	5	Not asked
Better children's programming	4	Not asked
Better or less biased news coverage	4	Not asked
Other complaints (e.g., too many blacks, irrelevant content)	11	Not asked

*Multiple answers are included, so figures add to more than 100%.

Another frequent verbal complaint centered on excessive violence (a large number of these remarks concerned its negative influence on children), and 43 percent agreed with this complaint. This is a subject which particularly concerns us here and which should be examined more closely. Do people choose violent programs over nonviolent or less violent programs? How much attention do these programs receive from their audience, and how well are they liked?

Partial answers to the questions are provided by the diaries, and these answers are somewhat surprising. If programs are divided on the basis of content analyses into three groups (ranging from those presenting least violence to those presenting most), it is apparent that the violent shows are proportionally no more popular than the nonviolent. Further, more attention and involvement seems to be characteristic of nonviolent than violent programs. More nonviolent programs are planned for and chosen by the respondents, and more are watched in their entirety. In addition, less talking and to some extent less other activities go on while the nonviolent programs are on the air.

Respondents' comments about violent as opposed to nonviolent shows are not particularly illuminating—many of the same reasons are given for watching each, centering around pleasing effects on the viewer such as "entertaining" and "relaxing." However, nonviolent programs are more likely to have something liked and nothing disliked about them than are violent programs, even though they are no more likely to be thought well worth watching.

In sum, it cannot be said from the evidence that violent television content is more positively evaluated or intensely viewed than nonviolent content. This, of course, says nothing of effects, about which no direct statement can be made from these data in their present state of analysis.

Several complaints were mentioned in response to the open-end question, although 28 percent of respondents had no suggestions at all. A very large number of suggestions for change centered on the removal or expansion of certain types of programs, be they westerns, sports, soap operas, or situation comedies. Fewer, but a still noteworthy proportion, seven percent, said there ought to be more educational and cultural content. Roughly five percent complained about poor scheduling of programs, the limited variety of programs available, or inadequate children's programming. All in all, it can be concluded that violent and sexual content on television is relatively high on, but not at the top of, the list of things that the public feels need to be changed. At the top of the list are programming changes which are unfortunately inconsistent from one respondent to another.

A somewhat different perspective on negatively evaluated television content emerged from a question probing recent things seen on television that had bothered or upset the respondent. While only two percent of the respondents said they had encountered such content, over half of these objectionable items appeared on news programs.[3] Other items included miscellaneous references to specific drama show content, advertising, action-adventure programs, and sports (usually when a respondent's favorite team lost).

The question was also asked in the context of programs that were seen on the previous day; here the complaint rate (nine percent) for a particular day was somewhat higher. Again, news programs eclipsed all other sources of distressing television content seen. When diary responses are tallied to the question asking for things that "bothered or upset you" that day on television, news content again is the most typical response, followed by advertising features or particular commercials. It should be noted, however, that the vast majority (88 percent) were not bothered or upset by anything on that day. If indeed television is used almost exclusively as an entertainment medium, one which provides pleasant though not particularly meaningful relaxation, it is not surprising that news programs' content, especially if it is violent, may have a jarring effect on the viewer, one which may be quite out of context psychologically.

However, these negative attitudes toward television pale by comparison with the positive assessments respondents gave the programs they had seen on the previous day. For each program seen, the respondent was asked: "Looking back, would you say that for you the program was a waste of time, really worth watching, or what?"

Despite the inviting way we presented the alternative, only 17 percent of the programs seen were described as a waste of time, compared to 75 percent which were described as "really worth watching." Another eight percent described their reactions as mixed, as did adults who turned on programs for their children's enjoyment. The diaries, which encompass a far greater sample of programs, show an even smaller average percentage who felt that a given program was a waste of time (six percent). In comparison, 38 percent felt the program just watched to be "really worth watching" while a majority (54 percent) thought the program was "O.K." Diary keepers may be somewhat more conservative in their comments regarding a program's worth as well as more selective in viewing. However, it is even more likely that the greater neutrality in the diaries is due to provision of the middle category as a response alternative. It was not present in the questionnaire.

Another rather enthusiastic endorsement of programming efforts is seen in the fact that 20 percent of questionnaire respondents volunteered the opinion that one of the programs they had seen the previous day was worth seeing again if it were repeated. Dramatic programs were most often mentioned in this connection, ranging from *Ironside* to the *Mary Tyler Moore Show*.

The diaries also included questions on specific things liked or disliked about programs. On the average, 21 percent of the diary respondents were unable to specify something they liked about the program they watched. But (as was true of the questionnaire) those who did respond to the open-end question, "What things did you like about the program?" often mentioned specific show characteristics like details of plot, story line, or general descriptive phrases (good acting, fast moving, etc.). Specific characteristics accounted for 20 percent of all responses, while general descriptions made up eight percent. In addition, five percent of respondents offered reactions to the general type of show, rather than to the show itself.

Another relevant general response category was that reflecting the effects of the show on the viewer (20 percent). Comments, for example, often were made such as, "It's always interesting" or "very relaxing" or "uplifting." Almost equal in mention (19 percent) were depictions of specific characters or actors in the well-liked programs. Characters (as opposed to story features), then, receive somewhat greater positive attention from viewers in the diary than in the questionnaires. However, the results of both methods generally agreed on ordering of liked features.

Disliked program features were also asked for in the diaries. Here the large majority (82 percent) said they disliked nothing. Those features mentioned were typically specific plot or story characteristics. One might conclude once again from these figures that programs that are watched tend to be evaluated highly by viewers.

Indeed, when other comments were solicited on an open-ended question about the days' viewing, positive opinions about particular shows and programming were far more numerous than adverse opinions. Most respondents (86 percent), however, offered no spontaneous comments in either direction.

Programs in general, then, are considered fairly good, although television is not particularly involving or exciting. Respondents seem for the most part content to watch the shows as they come on, although a minority offer a variety of changes they think would improve the medium.

WHAT PEOPLE LEARN FROM TELEVISION

Several questions designed to gain insight into what people learned from television were included in the survey. Since television is not the only source of media information, additional questions dealt with use of the other mass media: radio, newspapers, magazines, and movies. Three separate possible sources of learning were considered: news, weather programs, and dramatic programs.

News programs

Respondents were first told that we wanted them to tell us about network and local news broadcasts separately. They were asked to estimate how often they watched each type of newscast. The results are presented in Table 21, and show somewhat higher daily viewing of local (50 percent) than of network (38 percent) news.

Table 21: Estimated percentages watching various numbers of news programs during a week

	Network news programs	Local news programs
Almost every night	38%	50%
Two-three times per week	23%	24%
About once a week	12%	5%
Less often	7%	6%
Don't watch	19%	14%
No answer	1%*	1%
	100%	100%
Average night*	43%	54%

*Projected from above distribution

A series of three subsequent questions were asked in order to gauge respondents' concern about violence on network news. When asked for complaints about these news programs, only two percent mentioned excessive violence. (The most common complaints were biased news coverage, voiced by eight percent of respondents, and being on the air too much, mentioned by three percent.) When asked about things on the news that bothered or upset them, only three percent mentioned violence explicitly, although another eight percent mentioned events and fighting in Vietnam and three percent spoke of civil disorders. However, when asked specifically whether the network news gave too much, the right amount, or not enough attention to violence, 31 percent felt there was too much coverage of violence compared to 42 percent who said "the right amount" and six percent who said "not enough." (21 percent did not watch the news or gave no answer.) As expected, the three groups gave different rationales for their answers; some of those choosing the "too much attention" option felt that people often developed harmful ideas from viewing such content. Others felt simply that the amount of violence was exaggerated by the media. Those saying that violence coverage in the news was about right felt that the news should "tell it like it is" in order to make the public aware of what is happening, however unpleasant. The minority choosing the "not enough attention" alternative, however, claimed that even more violence was going on than the news showed.

Only the "bothered or upset" question was repeated for local news, but here almost half the answers concerned violence, including some violence that occurred to acquaintances of the respondent.

In order to focus more clearly on specific information that respondents may have gleaned from these newscasts, two sets of items were employed: recognition of seven stories that had appeared in these newscasts sometime over the previous six months, and identification of eight individuals who had been prominent in the news. These items are portrayed in Tables 22 and 23, along with the proportions of respondents who showed awareness of each of them.

It can be seen, by comparing results in Tables 22 and 23, that respondents' levels of self-acknowledged recognition of news items far surpassed their ability to correctly identify individuals in the news. Of course, if respondents had been asked instead to identify what each of the news stories was about, recognition levels in Table 22 would undoubtedly have dropped precipitously. Something, however, may be learned from the ordering of new stories in Table 22 in terms of what stories seemed to make greater or less impact on the American public. The My Lai massacre (the trial had not begun when most respondents were interviewed) easily led the list on this score, with only nine percent of our respondents not having heard this story. The deaths of Janis Joplin and Jimi Hendrix and the California courtroom shootout were next most heard, although almost 30 percent of respondents had not heard of these stories. Unawareness levels rose to 35 percent and more for Agnew's attacks on the news media, Nixon's statement about the Manson trial, and Robert Choate's testimony about breakfast cereals.[4] The least recognized item was the battle over Harold Carswell's nomination to the Supreme Court.

Table 22: Percentage hearing and being interested in
various new stories

	Heard	Heard and interested	Not heard
American soldiers accused of massacre of Vietnam civilians	91%	79%	9%
Rock singers die of drug overdose	73	48	27
Prisoners capture and shoot judge in courtroom	71	60	29
Agnew attacks the news media	65	38	35
Nixon makes statement about Manson trial	64	45	36
Nutrition expert criticizes breakfast cereals	62	43	38
Carswell nominated to Supreme Court	56	31	44

Granted that these news stories were at different levels of freshness in the mind of the public, it is worthwhile noting that the three most recognized new stories all had violence and/or death as a central element. Lower recognition levels were found for two items (Agnew's attacks and Carswell's nomination) which had been headline material for several weeks and for the breakfast cereal story, which should have had considerable personal relevance for most citizens. This is also reflected in the professed interest among respondents who had heard of each story. The average interest rate for the three stories with violence and death was 80 percent, compared to 63 percent for the other four.

The identification quiz obviously demanded more from most respondents than they could give. Nine out of ten could identify Spiro Agnew (included as a "warm-up" item), but when it came to Robert Finch, Ralph Nader, Martha Mitchell, and Bob Dylan only about three in ten were able to provide any reasonable identification (including partially correct answers such as "politics" or "government" for Finch or "entertainer" for Dylan). Maryland's then Senator Tydings, professional football's 1969 rookie-of-the-year Calvin Hill, and political activist-revolutionary Tom Hayden were even more remote from the minds of our respondents.

Table 23: Percentages identifying various people in the news

	Partially correct	Basically correct	TOTAL Partially or completely correct
Spiro Agnew	3%	86%	89%
Robert Finch	11	21	32
Ralph Nader	13	16	29
Martha Mitchell	8	18	27
Bob Dylan	3	23	26
Joseph Tydings	4	14	18
Calvin Hill	*	13	14
Tom Hayden	*	2	3

*Less than 0.5%

While it is rather presumptuous to expect the average citizen to have instant recognition of several of these individuals, the fact that the significant and continuing media exposure given individuals like Ralph Nader and Martha Mitchell had so little impact in registering their personalities with the public is worthy of attention.

For both the story recognition and news personalities "quizzes," however, the focus was far less on levels of awareness *per se* than on patterns of television and other media use that were associated with higher or lower levels of awareness. This analysis appears in the overview paper by Robinson (1971) and will not be carried further here. Particularly crucial in that analysis will be the degree to which awareness is related to use of the other news media—newspapers and radio (estimated as used daily by 65 percent and 71 percent respectively of our respondents), and magazines (two percent of our respondents reported regular readership of an analytic commentary magazine, 13 percent of a news magazine, and 17 percent of *Life* or *Look*). Despite these higher daily contact rates for newspaper and radio than for television news, however, almost twice as many of our respondents claim to get most of their news from television than either from newspapers or from the radio. Whether these respondents pick up proportionately more information is an empirical question that can be investigated with these data.

Weather programs

One type of television program whose impact has not been researched, but which occurs several times of the day on most television stations, is the weather forecast. Almost half of our respondents said they watched the forecasts at least once a night, and less than 20 percent said they failed to catch at least one forecast a week.

It is interesting to speculate about whether such programs have brought greater preparation for future behavior (e.g. leaving home early for projected poor weather, selecting clothing in line with what weather forecasts predict) than occurred before television. However, in the present analysis, attention was concentrated on direct information gain as one possible impact of seeing forecasts night after night over a long period. Since the weather map is the standard visual device used by television weathermen, we sought to inquire how well certain established principles of weather prediction viewers were able to pick up from such repeated exposures. Respondents were asked to estimate how much weather programs had helped them to understand weather maps. Of those replying, only 15 percent said a great deal, 26 percent said somewhat, 26 percent a little, and 33 percent not at all.

Questions on two principles of weather maps which are clearly implicit in the weather forecasters' use of these maps were then asked: the direction the weather usually comes from and the consequences of a low pressure system moving in. Except for South Florida, the prevailing direction for weather in this country is west, and 24 percent of our respondents correctly said so. Another 12 percent said west along with other directions, which could also be considered a correct answer. However, 45 percent chose other directions only, and another 19 percent did not attempt a guess. Only a little more than a third, then, appeared to comprehend the basic principle that weather flows from the west to east.

Far more respondents (32 percent) would not attempt an answer to the next question, dealing with the likely weather conditions following the arrival of a low pressure system. Of those who did, the vast majority correctly said that it meant the skies would be more cloudy. Overall, 53 percent gave this answer, compared to only seven percent who said skies would become clearer or stay the same and eight percent who said temperatures would go up (technically correct but not as correct as skies becoming cloudier)—combinations of these two answers being included in the 53 percent figure above. Whether respondents could apply this cloudier-low pressure association into interpreting a weather map is a moot point, since the semantic connection between "low" and "cloudy" could well have indicated the correct answer. This is not to denigrate our respondents' performance on this question, but it is inconsistent with their abilities displayed on the previous question about the direction of the weather.[5]

One final item on the weather concerned the perceived accuracy of weather forecasts on television, since one might suspect that a good deal of skepticism abounds about the profession, given the numerous occasions in which forecasts turn out incorrectly. Indeed, the public does underestimate the weatherman's performance, if one accepts the 80-85 percent figure widely publicized as the weatherman's level of accuracy. Only about a quarter of the population is willing to grant him that degree of accuracy, the average rating being 61 percent.

A number of interesting questions remain about the interplay of these variables, and analyses are planned which will verify the extent (if any) to which steadier viewers of weather programs feel the forecasts are more accurate, feel they have learned more about weather maps, and are able to answer the weather questions correctly. Also, we expect to find greater confidence in the weatherman among those with higher education, since these respondents should presumably place more reliance on the scientific underpinnings of weather forecasts.

Dramatic programs

Since the bulk of viewing time is spent on dramatic programs and these are programs that viewers overwhelmingly choose as favorites for viewing, we also inquired about whether or what respondents felt they were learning from such content. From the responses to the two questions, it is obvious that far more research needs to be done in this area.

Respondents were asked to judge whether they learned anything or didn't learn anything from viewing their two favorite dramatic programs.[6] For 56 percent of the dramatic programs mentioned, respondents said they did learn something from these programs; from 44 percent respondents said they learned nothing. Surprisingly, the things most often reported as learned are how to solve problems—one's own problems in the case of soap operas or crime problems in the case of detective shows—and how people behave or react in various situations.

It was also surprising to find, in the same vein, the amount of realism that respondents perceived in these programs. Twice as many respondents (60 percent) said their favorite program showed "life as it really is" than said it did not (30 percent); the remaining 10 percent claimed it was only partially realistic. When asked to explain their answer about programs being realistic, the majority pointed out that "things like this happen in real life," while others mentioned the realism of the acting or characters or the way they think, or even physical characteristics of the situation (scenery, props). Those who felt the programs were unrealistic explained that these were just stories, that only actors were used, or that the situations were romanticized or glorified. Some viewers exercised their critical faculties by pointing to specific incongruities within the story line. Such responses deserve more extended research attention than we were able to provide in this survey. For example, it would be of great psychological and sociological interest to know the degree of carryover to their own lives that respondents perceive as emanating from lessons and knowledge gained in these programs.

No testable information questions were included in the diaries. However, when respondents to the diaries were asked if they had learned anything seen on television that day, 82 percent replied that they had not. Of those who had, news or current events programs provided the common learning experiences. Of particular interest here is that sizable numbers of those reporting that they had "learned something" referred to practical knowledge and ways of problem solving. Once again, it would seem that at least some viewers see the shows they watch as directly relevant to their own lives. If many of these shows are drama or situation comedies, the fiction is evidently capable of yielding perceived insight into everyday real world transactions.

HOW CHILDREN USE TELEVISION

Our research plan called for a thorough inventory of all users of television in a household. While children between the ages of three and 12 are indeed heavy users, our previous experiences with interviewing these younger children suggested that we would be unlikely to collect reliable data from them. However, we did ask mothers of these youngsters a series of questions about their viewing habits. These questions concerned the child's favorite programs, which programs the mother thought were not good for the child to watch, and television content that the mother had observed as frightening or upsetting to the child. In all, mothers' reports were obtained for about 140 youngsters, with about equal numbers of children at each year of age.

Favorite programs listed by the mothers consisted largely of cartoons, children's programs (like *Captain Kangaroo*), and family comedies. Fewer mothers mentioned educational programs such as *Sesame Street* or *Misterogers Neighborhood*. The only action-adventure programs mentioned tended to be reruns rather than those currently on at prime time. In asking mothers for children's favorites, one might suspect that the list would represent some sample of programs that mothers felt were good for their children to watch. But the fact that many more mothers felt educational programs were good for their children than reported them as favorites indicates that mothers' judgments of childrens' favorites were not entirely dictated by social desirability. It may also indicate that some mothers experience difficulty getting their children to watch educational programs.

Only about half these reports included programs that mothers could name as not good for the child to watch, perhaps indicating some lack of concern about what their younger children were exposed to on television. Few of the programs named were on during prime time hours (with the exception of *Mod Squad*), and most seemed to be locally originated programs that had never been on the networks. Specific soap operas (particularly *Dark Shadows*) and reruns of action-adventure westerns were next most often mentioned. In general, many movies on television were seen as unfit for children, especially those featuring violence and sex. Unfortunately, specific names or even categories of these movies were usually not given by respondents. Cartoon shows with much violence or "idiocy" are also condemned by a minority of mothers.

Fewer mothers, about one-third, reported that television programs or parts of programs had frightened or upset their children. These included mainly monster pictures or other supernatural stories, parts of the program *Dark Shadows*, and depicted acts of violence or abuse toward children or animals.

Some mothers' comments indicate those programs to be bad which make children "more inquisitive" or plain "nosy" about sensitive issues like sex, drugs, and death.

OTHER QUESTIONS

Final analyses on the present data have by no means been carried out. It remains to outline analysis planned for questionnaire items less central to television behavior, and to give some indication of crucial questions which may be fruitful targets of future analysis and future research plans.

Personality variables and violence

In addition to the traditional background factors incorporated at the end of social surveys (age, education, occupation), respondents were asked to provide information on personality factors and other aspects of their social background. Since these are of practically no relevance *per se* in terms of television, these questions are merely listed in Table 24. The aggression and self-esteem items were taken mainly from standard personal agression scales; some were developed by NIMH's TV and Social Behavior staff. Both sets were found to have discriminant validity in previous studies. The alienation items come from Srole's well-known Anomie Scale.

Table 24: Personality items and percentages of respondents
giving various answers

Item	% Agree
Aggression	
Even if you don't like a person you should still try to help him.	92%
Whoever insults me or my family is asking for a fight.	38
I demand that people respect my rights.	69
If you don't watch yourself, people will take advantage of you.	71
Lately I have been kind of grouchy.	36
Alienation	
Nowadays a person has to live pretty much for today and let tomorrow take care of itself.	40
It's hardly fair to bring children into the world with the way things look for the future	35
These days a person doesn't know whom he can count on.	56
Self-esteem	
I am a useful person to have around.	85
I wish I could have more respect for myself.	40
You're waiting in a long line and someone tries to cut in ahead of you. Would you feel like:	
pushing him out of line	16
other physical aggression	13
A friend of yours tells other people a secret about you that embarrasses you. Do you feel like:	
threatening to beat him up	4
other physical aggression	0
Your ten year old brother or son is beaten up by an older boy. Would you feel like:	
beating up the older boy	6
other physical aggression	0

Correlational analysis involving the aggression items and violent television content will be undertaken with suitable multivariate controls added. The alienation and self-esteem items will be analyzed mainly against extent of television use, as will items measuring the respondent's professed satisfaction with life. The hypothesis to be explored here is whether those with high alienation, low self-esteem, and low life satisfaction are heavier and more avid television viewers than their counterparts at the reverse ends of these scales. With the three variables, it will be possible to find which (if any) contributes most to explaining heavy television use.

We also expect two other "social pressure" factors to explain a good deal of variance in amount of television use: the amount of time respondents feel they have excess time on their hands, and the number of evenings spent away from home. Less than 20 percent of our respondents said they had time on their hands with nothing to do more than once a week—which, on the surface, would indicate that this factor has little effect on how much time is spent watching television. Roughly the same proportion said they usuallly spent all of their evenings at home, with 49 percent saying they were out one or two nights per week, 19 percent three to four nights, and 12 percent five to seven nights per week. For most respondents, activities that took them away from home were leisure activities, particularly organizational activity, visiting, sports, and hobbies.

Some preliminary inspection of the questionnaires indicates that participants in at least one of these activities are quite likely to show a distinctive pattern of television use. People who report participating in church activities in the evening are particularly likely to be infrequent viewers of television, to feel that television is a waste of time, and to take more objection to sex and violence on the screen than other respondents.

Future research

Other questions raised by the more provocative of our findings can be resolved only partly by further analyses of current data. Future large-scale research is needed to examine a great number of topics:

Few people seem to regard television viewing as a waste of time, yet there is relatively little real attention given many programs. What are the factors that lead people to watch discontinuously, and how do these factors differ by program type?

What are the consequences of secondary and even tertiary activities engaged in concurrently with television viewing? How and to what extent does each affect watching?

What is the relationship between fictionalized television content and actual life situations? What is the perceived degree of carryover into real life of knowledge and information thought to be gained through television drama?

To what extent is increased (or retarded) physical and social interaction among family members seen as a result of television? What are the dynamics of these interactions and how do they affect other aspects of family life?

How are decisions made among family members to watch one program rather than another, assuming there is some conflict over the programs chosen?

What is the extent of commitment to or involvement with certain programs and program types? What is the degree of regret felt for having missed particularly favorite programs compared to other disappointments not related to television?

Finally, what is the change over time, if any, in the perceived legitimate functioning of television? Will it continue to be regarded almost entirely as an entertainer, or will more serious purposes prevail? How will attention values shift with time (assuming future programing levels and quality remain about the same)? Do parents continuously attempt to influence their children's program choices, and if so to what degree? If children are permitted to make their own choices, what are the factors that lead to selecting one program or program type rather than another?

It is our intention to devote attention to these and other questions by further perusal of the data collected in the project. It will be necessary however, to initiate other more intensive investigations if full answers are to be obtained about the use of television.

SUMMARY AND CONCLUSIONS

Availability and characteristics of television sets in the home

If nonrespondents as well as respondents are accounted for, virtually all of the households we contacted in attempting to gain cooperation were found to contain at least one television set, and about two-fifths of these households contained a color set. The major set in the household was usually to be found in the living room, although most rooms received at least a few mentions.

Broadcast coverage was fairly good among our sample members, with a median of about five channels received on the major set in the household. In addition, only one-quarter of the sample households received less than four channels, and about one-half were able to receive UHF channels.

Opportunities for viewing then were relatively unrestricted among our sample households, insuring at least a representative range of program and time choices about which to gather our data and make observations.

How much television people watch

Three methods of establishing viewing time estimates provide quite different results. The Roper question "On an average day—" produces by far the highest estimates, possibly because respondents are thinking of an average day on which they watch television and are excluding days when they do not. The diaries result in the lowest estimates of television viewing, possibly due to conscious underreporting on the part of respondents who resist writing responses more than they would verbalizing them and who wish to avoid further questions. A less likely possibility is that diary keepers become somewhat more selective in their viewing by virtue of a kind of panel effect. The requests to recount previous day's viewing provide an estimate between these two extremes which is possibly most accurate since it is free of the biases of both the other questions. This median estimate is less than two hours daily when proper weights are assigned for days of the week. This is considerably lower than usual estimates provided by commercial services.

Within method of questioning, amounts of television viewing time are relatively consistent across a variety of demographics such as region and community size. However, the watching is somewhat heavier among certain population groups (e.g., the less educated and women).

Even among those who watch a great deal of television, few feel that they watch too much, either because they are also engaged in other outside activities, because viewing benefits them, or because they feel others watch a great deal too. Evidently, while television is not necessarily seen to be of great value, neither is it regarded as a way of killing or wasting time, and guilt does not usually accrue from watching even a great amount. The ambivalence toward television watching found in at least one previous study (Steiner, 1963) is not much in evidence. Perhaps this indicates that with increasing familiarity over time, the amount of use of television becomes less a matter of either negative or positive concern to individual viewers, regardless of amount of time spent watching.

How people watch television

We have pointed out that television is often watched in conjunction with one or even two other activities such as paid work, housework, talking, eating, reading, and child care. The effect of these secondary activities on television viewing is not clear. However, it cannot be said that the average program audience is very attentive since so many respondents report missing segments of each program. Moreover, the diary data are even more extreme in showing that less than a third of the programs are seen in their entirety by as much as 80 percent of their audiences. Certain shows featuring drama or stories receive consistently more attention along a number of dimensions, especially if they have small (but presumably devoted) audiences. Large audience shows featuring "variety" probably receive least thorough attention. From a programming point of view, we have raised the question of whether a small attentive audience may not be at least as desirable as a large, easily distracted one.

There is more evidence that television viewing is not generally a thoroughly involving activity in itself, since items of either business or pleasure are quite likely to provide moments of distraction for the viewer. Further, people often watch television together. Some two-thirds of the programs were reported as watched with at least one other person. Since these individuals must somehow reach agreement (even if by fiat) on the programs to be viewed, the social environment and the particular aggregation of individual family members certainly influence the programs that are watched. Thus, even if one family member is thoroughly involved with a particular program, there are likely to be others who are not particularly interested in it or who are relatively inattentive. Since the incidence of talking and other at least semisocial activities is great, it appears that television may be used as a social facilitation device, to provide a context for gathering together. The programs themselves provide topics of conversation among family members during the show and among acquaintances afterwards.

Why people watch television

Most respondents say they watch television for entertainment and relaxation; this is evidently considered a legitimate motivation, distinct from killing or wasting time. In fact, a number of respondents find television often personally beneficial or uplifting at the same time that it is relaxing and entertaining. The fact that relatively few view television as a way of killing time or view specific programs as a waste of time is surprising considering the degree of inattention and noninvolvement with television which has already been implied. It is also surprising if one considers that a substantial minority report viewing programs just because they come on a channel they were already watching or because other people in the household wanted to watch them.

Less than half the viewers use television guides for all or even most programs, although the great majority of viewers use them occasionally to help them plan their watching. The diaries, it is true, give more indication that television watching is planned and rational, with a clear majority on the average saying they planned to watch a given program. This may be partially an artifact of the diary keeping situation, a sort of panel effect in which the respondent is made more attentive than he might otherwise be to general and specific programming. At any rate, the diaries too show that most programs are not watched all the way through by most respondents.

Whatever the degree of planning that goes into viewing, television programming is certainly not condemned by the majority. More individuals report regret over having missed particular programs than report avoiding television at times because nothing worthwhile is on. This is perhaps one indication that people are liking, more than disliking, currently available programs. It is also true, of course, that missing favorite programs like soap operas and football games may have more salience than the absence of worthy programs at a time when it might be pleasant to watch television. Evidently, boycotted television time amounting to more than two hours a day is used to fit in obligatory activities such as housework, as well as more leisurely pursuits, with relatively little of this boycotted time occurring during prime time hours.

Incidences of both missed programs and boycotting tend to be lower in the diaries, again probably due to underreporting.

The evidence accumulates, then, that television is used as a relatively noninvolving way of relaxing, being entertained, and perhaps socializing with family members. A number of viewers feel specifically benefited from television programming, although programs are surely not watched with complete attention, and lack of selectivity is such that less than half the viewers use television program guides for most programs.

Very little information gain or self-improvement from television was spontaneously mentioned by respondents. It appears once again that television is seen almost exclusively as an entertainer rather than a teacher. Although programs with information value (e.g., news and weather shows) are frequently watched, the instructional functions of television in themselves do not provide great motivation to view. Public affairs and information broadcasts and specials were rarely attended to by our sample.

How people feel about what they view

Favorite programs are most often comedy and variety shows with crime-adventure, other adventure, other dramatic, and soap operas close behind. The diaries, however, show that game shows and news account for much actual viewing, whether or not they are chosen as favorite programs. They also show that attention value of programs is not necessarily directly related to their audience size or expressed popularity.

Specific reasons for liking comedy or dramatic programs are most often couched in terms of specific characteristics of stories such as typical plots or story lines. Favorite characters or actors, when mentioned, are virtually all adults and mostly male even though one-fifth of our respondents were adolescents and more than half were female. This presents an interesting paradox with regard to role identification for a majority of the television audience.

In view of the frequent and heavy criticism leveled at television, it is somewhat surprising that rather positive attitudes toward specific and general programming are prevalent. Few programs are thought of as a waste of time, and one-fifth of the questionnaire respondents even expressed the wish to see particular programs again that they had just viewed the previous day. Moreover, spontaneous comments, though made by few, were much more likely to be positive than negative. Complaints about television—things that should be changed—most often involve number of commercials and expansion or removal of various types of programs. Unfortunately, this list of program types on both sides is too diverse and conflicting to be of much value to programmers. Violence and, to some extent, sex on television are matters of some concern to viewers but seem of lower priority than the basic programming issues.

In the same context, most viewers report having seen nothing recently on television that bothered or upset them. But of those who were bothered, the cause was most often the content of a news story, especially involving violence. When programs are grouped into three categories reflecting amount of violence in program content, we found that violent programs are not watched disproportionately to their numbers. It is also somewhat surprising to find consistently more attention being paid to nonviolent than to violent shows along a number of different dimensions. To some extent, there is also more satisfaction with them. This is perhaps one more indication that people watch television primarily for entertainment and relaxation and do not wish to confront violence or perhaps even discomfort on any extensive continuous basis. It may also be true that fictional violence on television has become so commonplace that its attention value is significantly less than it used to be. There is less evidence for this numbing effect with respect to violent news stories and information features, which seem to be better remembered than other items. This does not imply that they are enjoyed, however, or even seen as a primary function of television.

In any case, whatever the effects of violence on television may be, there does not seem to be any large scale involvement with, or commitment to, current programs featuring violence, compared with other more pacific programs.

What people learn from television

It is difficult to make definitive statements about how much people learn from television, especially without comparative information from different media and other sources of information. It is also not possible to build causative relationships, since the effects of these other sources as contributors to knowledge cannot be ruled out or controlled. In addition, even correlational analyses on our data involving viewing time and performance on information quizzes have not yet been carried out.

Within these constraints, some conclusions may be drawn. First, it may be said that while reported recognition of stories in the news appears fairly high, the level would undoubtedly be considerably reduced if respondents had been asked to recall details of the stories. Considering the indifference with which violent dramatic programs seem to be viewed, it is interesting that highest recognition was found for stories in which violence played a major role, and greater interest was also expressed in these stories.

When respondents were asked to identify eight national figures, few were able to properly describe any but Vice President Agnew. It is of note that national figures like Ralph Nader and Martha Mitchell, who have received extensive television (and other media) coverage, were so infrequently identified correctly. It seems to indicate once again that television is not used deliberately or particularly well as an educational medium with regard to matters of serious national concern. Yet television is seen as providing unbiased news and is reported the source of most news for a majority of respondents.

Weather programs were watched by almost half the respondents every night, although skepticism about the weatherman's forecast was perhaps greater than deserved among viewers. This too seems to indicate that great information gain is not expected from television programs. About one-third were able to correctly cite the west as the direction from which our weather emanates. Roughly the same proportion correctly identified the consequences of the arrival of a low pressure weather system. Since no baseline data is available, we do not know whether these figures reflect an information gain brought about by television news and weather programs or not. Future correlational analyses using suitable controls will give at least partial answers by establishing relationships (or lack of them) between viewing patterns and knowledge in these areas.

In another context, whatever may be the actual level of factual information gathered from intentionally instructive television programs, most individuals seem to feel that they learn something from watching their favorite dramatic programs. Surprisingly, practical knowledge and methods of problem-solving lead the list of knowledge reported acquired through these programs. Furthermore, these dramatic programs are most often seen as realistic and showing life as it really is. Many viewers then seem to be seeing the shows they value as directly relevant to their own lives.

Since favorite shows are usually fictional, a fascinating interface of fantasy and real world concerns is implied, and a fruitful area of future research would seem to be exploration of the degree of perceived carryover of learning from programs to situations in the respondent's life. In any event, many viewers evidently take the fictionalized content of dramatic programs more seriously and literally than most social thinkers and behavioral scientists have recognized.

How children use television

Mothers' reports on the viewing habits and preferences of their children 3-12 years of age indicate that cartoons, children's programs, and family comedies are the heavy favorites, with educational programs such as *Sesame Street* next in preference. As might be expected, educational programs were somewhat more favorably regarded by mothers than is reflected in children's actual viewing, perhaps indicating that mothers do not always succeed in influencing program choice.

Programs seen as bad for children to watch were named by only about half the mothers queried, so either television programming for children is regarded as adequate, or mothers are not overly concerned with younger children's viewing fare. Those specific program categories which are seen as bad are some soap operas (particularly *Dark Shadows*), certain action-adventure westerns, adult movies, monster or supernatural shows, and even certain cartoon shows with too much violence or foolishness.

Many of these programs are also the ones which are reported occasionally to bother or upset the children in question. It might be noted, however, that some programs seem to upset the parents without upsetting the children, such as the adult movies, action-adventure westerns, and cartoons mentioned above. There is some indication that programs on such sensitive issues as sex, drugs, and death lead to questions from children that parents are reluctant to deal with.

All in all, it cannot be said that mothers are particularly critical of current television programming for young children. Many more comments are directed toward favorite shows then toward those which are seen as harmful. This is not to say that parents are not concerned at all with what their children see—not a few mothers condemn programs which may, for example, "teach (them) bad things," or cause children to "learn the harm in life." However, there is little evidence here that the issue is particularly salient among our sample.

A brief overview

The average television viewer in our survey spends a good deal of time in front of the set, although not as much as some previous studies have indicated. Exactly how much time depends on how the estimate is established. If the middle one of three estimates is tentatively accepted, properly weighted and corrected for nonresponse, the median value is somewhat less than two hours per day per person.

Television is watched primarily for entertainment and relaxation and is rarely used deliberately as an educational device or source of information apart from regular news and weather programs. Yet it is not generally regarded as a way of killing time or as a waste of time. Little ambivalence is felt even with heavy use if the viewer manages to fit in other more active pursuits, if he feels watching television benefits him some way, or if he simply feels that others watch just as much as he does.

Watching television often is accompanied by other activities such as reading, child care, housework, and even hobbies. Since people most often watch television together, talking about the shows and other family social interactions are common during viewing.

Levels of current programming, while not remarkably stimulating or overpowering, are more positively than negatively evaluated by viewers. Favorite programs are regretted when missed, and more favorable than unfavorable comments are directed at specific shows and at general programming. Further, few report being bothered or upset by things they have seen on television. There are, to be sure, areas of dissatisfaction—the commercials, sex and violence, daytime television, and widely diverse specific programs that different people feel should be removed immediately. However, the general tone is positive, even with regard to children's programming, and there are few recommendations by viewers for major reform or change in the current system.

This is not to say that audiences are particularly enthusiastic. Surprisingly little attention is paid to many popular programs, with viewers watching whatever comes on the channel, carrying on a variety of other activities during the show, and watching, at best, discontinuously. It is true that when the viewer himself plans to watch a particular program and makes the choice himself, he pays somewhat more attention to the show, and certain programs, especially in the dramatic category, have more attention value than others.

However, for the most part, television viewing emerges as a relatively unplanned, discontinuous phenomenon characterized by at least 'surface noninvolvement on the part of the viewer. In this study at least, programs with violent content fare worse than nonviolent programs in attention value along the dimensions we have been considering.

Despite the apparent lack of involvement or expressed enthusiasm, however, we have also found that the fictional content of dramatic programs is often regarded as realistic, describing the way life really is. A number of respondents feel that they learn practical methods of problem-solving from these programs. An important area for future investigation will be pinpointing the perceived degree of transfer of lessons or information learned from these programs to the viewer's everyday life.

FOOTNOTES

1. For those nonrespondents who gave us the information, the average viewing time was about two hours. Although the number of nonrespondents who gave estimates of viewing time is too small (N=29) to provide reliable estimates, it is possible to calculate a weighted average of viewing time based on the assumption that the 29 individuals are representative of all 102 nonrespondents. When this is done, the average viewing time is two hours and 54 minutes.
2. The five most often mentioned favorites were those that scored highly in the Nielsen ratings: football games, *Marcus Welby, Flip Wilson, Mod Squad,* and *Medical Center.* The diary data, however, reveal that game shows, movies, and news account for much actual viewing time whether or not they are chosen as "favorite programs."
3. The question about being bothered or upset was repeated in the specific context of news programs; here the proportion reporting being bothered by something on the news rose to almost 30 percent, even though a substantial number of respondents admitted to being infrequent news viewers. Violent news (Vietnam, disruptions, etc.) was the major source of such bothersome content.
4. For those who had heard of this nutrition story, we included several questions about how Choate's testimony had been perceived. We anticipated mainly negative reaction because of the popularity of such food products, the subsequent rebuttal by some other scientists, and possible public weariness of muckraking. Of the 44 percent who ventured an opinion, however, almost four in five said Choate "knew what he was talking about," mainly citing the quality of his analysis of cereals and his expertise. Those who dissented referred far more often to the irrelevance of scientific evidence in the area than to the countertestimony presented after Choate's allegations.
5. Respondents were also asked how sure they were about the correctness of their answers to these two questions. It may be of some comfort to survey researchers to find that those who knew the correct answers were more sure of themselves than those who did not give the correct answers. (On the direction question, 83 percent of those who answered "west" were absolutely or pretty sure they were right, compared with 57 percent of those who gave other directions. On the low pressure question, 69 percent of those with correct answers were absolutely or pretty sure *vs* 47 percent of those with incorrect answers.) There is, of course, a reversal overall in that respondents were more confident on direction than on the low pressure question, even though the low pressure question had a higher proportion of correct answers. This adds some support to our concern about the clue implicit in the low pressure question.

6. These favorite dramatic programs consist of roughly equivalent numbers of crime-detective, western-adventure, general dramatic, soap opera, and situation comedy shows.

REFERENCES

Allen, C. Photographing the TV audience. *Journal of Advertising Research*, 1965, **5**, 2-8.

Bandura, A. Influence of models' reinforcement contingencies on the acquisition of imitative responses. *Journal of Personality and Social Psychology*, 1965, **1**, 589-95.

Berkowitz, L. Some aspects of observed aggression. *Journal of Personality and Social Psychology*, 1965, **2**, 359-69.

Bogart, L. *Strategy in advertising.* New York: Harcourt, Brace and World, 1967.

Hovland, C. Results from studies of attitude change. *The American Psychologist*, 1959, **14**, 8-17.

Nielson, A.C. *The television audience 1968.* New York: A.C. Nielson Company, 1968.

Robinson, J. On defining the functions of television. *Television and social behavior,* Vol. 4 (this volume). Washington, D.C.: U.S. Government Printing Office, 1971.

Robinson, J. Television and leisure time: yesterday, today, and (maybe) tomorrrow. *Public Opinion Quarterly*, 1969, **33**, 210-22.

Roper, B. *A ten-year view of public attitudes toward television and other mass media, 1959-1968.* New York: Television Information Office, 1969.

Schramm, W., Lyle, J., and Parker, E. *Television in the lives of our children.* Stanford: Stanford University Press, 1961.

Simmons, W.R., Associates. *Taking a new look at TV audiences.* New York, 1969.

Steiner, G. *The people look at television.* New York: Alfred A. Knopf, 1963.

Steiner, G. The people look at commerials: a study of audience behavior. *Journal of Business*, April 1966, 272-304.

Weiss, W. Effects of the mass media of communication. In Lindzey, G., and Aronsen, E. (Eds.) *Handbook of social psychology*, Vol. 5. Reading, Mass.: Addison-Wesley, 1968.

Demographic Characteristics of Viewers of Television Violence and News Programs

Harold Israel

W. R. Simmons and Associates

and

John P. Robinson

National Institute of Mental Health

Two separate analyses of the television viewing audience are contained in this report. The first is of viewers of television violence, the second of network television news viewers. The analysis of violence viewers uses data collected by W. R. Simmons and Associates during the 1967-68, 1968-69, and 1969-70 television seasons. The news analysis is confined to the 1969-70 season.

The Simmons organization has been engaged in collecting two-week diaries of television viewing and national probability samples of the public since 1964. The Simmons data are not collected for the purpose for

which they are used in this paper. They are collected to provide advertisers with estimates of the potential size and characteristics of the audience that can be reached by television programs rather than by national
magazines. Each year the Simmons organization collects data on the
readership of more than 50 national magazines. The Simmons national
sample stratified to ensure better representation of the higher income
segment of the population (which is likely to read more magazines) is
polled twice during the year.

During the second polling, a subset of the original respondents are
asked to fill out a two-week diary of the television programs they have
viewed (including supplementary data on the degree of attention paid to
each program). In the 1969-70 study, for example, 15,000 respondents
aged 18 and over were interviewed in the original sample. (Only one respondent per household was interviewed.) Of these, 10,000 were designated in the TV diary subsample. Respondents were offered a gift, such
as a transistor radio or a travel alarm clock, for their participation. Diaries were to be kept for various two-week periods between October 12
and November 15, 1969. Of those contacted:

6,834	filled out usable diary forms
349	filled out unusable diary forms
961	had moved from their previous residence and could not be located
192	were deceased or too ill to complete the diary
516	could not be found at home (despite repeated call backs), and
1,148	refused to participate
10,000	

The calculations which follow are based on the two-week diaries of
the 6,834 respondents, specially weighted to insure figures which can be
projected to the national population. Further details on data collection
procedures for the 1969-70 study are provided in the Appendix to this
report. Practically identical descriptions apply to the 1967-68 and 1968-
69 samples.

DEMOGRAPHIC CORRELATES OF VIEWERS OF VIOLENT TELEVISION PROGRAMS

Attempting to establish a link between mass media content and subsequent behavior of the audience is a complex undertaking. In the current
debate about the effects of television violence, the most persuasive evidence comes from laboratory studies which have used young children and
college students as subjects. Until recently, these segments of the population have not been responsible for much of the violent behavior that

plagues our society. Nor, in terms of sheer numbers, can they account for very substantial portions of the viewing audience for violent programs on television—the audience needed to keep these programs on the air.

A crucial factor in assessing the effects of television violence is the type of viewer who creates a demand for programs which emphasize and (in the eyes of many social observers) glorify the use of violence to resolve conflict. Are such viewers highly or poorly educated, old or young, from rural or urban environments? These questions are of limited scope and shed no direct light on the more central question: what are the effects of violent programs on audience members? However, identifying the audience for violence is a necessary first step in such an operation, one that has not been given much attention in previous literature and one that is needed to gain proper perspective on the functions of such television programs in society.

The basic computer tabulations on which the following report is based were calculated at the request of the Television and Social Behavior program staff. The Simmons organization supervised the translation of these research requests for computer processing.

The research in this report follows an analysis of the adult audience for violent television programming which was done for the 1967-68 TV season (Simmons, 1968). The original research is expanded in two basic directions: (a) attempting to replicate the findings of 1967-68 for audiences in 1968-69 and 1969-70; and (b) extending this demographic analysis to control for important background variables like amount of viewing, education, and race. As much as possible, procedures used in the original Simmons analysis were followed in order to preserve comparability of survey results.

Analysis procedures

The analysis procedures can be divided roughly into four steps: (a) identifying the most violent television programs; (b) calculating from each person's diary how many hours he had spent viewing such programs over the two-week period; (c) establishing a criterion amount of viewing that would classify a respondent as a "heavy viewer" of television violence; and (d) finding out which demographic groups had especially high or low proportions of heavy violence viewers in their ranks.

For the original report, Simmons (1968) asked three prominent television critics to rate prime time shows on a five-point scale from "not at all violent" to "extremely violent." The 13 programs that all three critics rated at the violent end of the scale are listed in the final column of Table 1.

Comparable critics' data were not available for the 1968-69 and 1969-70 seasons, so alternative sources of ratings had to be utilized. The best available source for the 1968-69 lay in ratings from graduate students collected by Smith (1969). Since the Smith ratings were also collected for the 1967-68 season, some adaptation of these ratings to the Simmons list had to be made. It was arbitrarily decided to select ten of the most violently rated of the programs of 1967-68 still on the air in the fall of 1968 and to add three new programs that seemed equivalent in terms of violence: *Mod Squad, Ironside,* and *Hawaii Five-O.* This group comprises the middle list in Table 1.[1]

Nine of the programs classified as most violent during the 1968-69 season are listed again in Table 1 for the 1969-70 season. (Only five programs carried over from 1967-68 to 1968-69.)

Table 1: Programs nominated as 13 most violent

1969-70	1968-69	1967-68
Mod Squad	Mod Squad	Big Valley
Mannix	Mannix	Mannix
Mission Impossible	Mission Impossible	Man from Uncle
Hawaii Five-O	Hawaii Five-O	Cimmaron Strip
Virginian	Virginian	Custer
The F.B.I.	The F.B.I.	Garrison's Gorillas
Gunsmoke	Gunsmoke	Guns of Will Sonnett
High Chapparal	High Chapparal	High Chapparal
Ironside	Ironside	Hondo
Bonanza	Felony Squad	Bonanza
It Taks a Thief	Avengers	Judd for the Defense
Land of the Giants	N.Y.P.D.	N.Y.P.D.
Lancer	Wild Wild West	Wild Wild West

The nominations for the 1969-70 season list were based on a composite of ratings obtained from Greenberg and Gordon's national sample of television critics and from a Detroit telephone sample of adults. (The Greenberg and Gordon ratings and procedures are described in a separate report submitted to the NIMH Television and Social Behavior program.)

For their 1967-68 analysis (hereafter referred to as the 1968 sample), Simmons defined heavy viewers of violent television as those who had watched more than six hours of violent (as defined by the list of 13) programs during the two-week diary period. Some 11 percent of the male adult population and eight percent of female adult population met this criterion. For the 1969 and 1970 samples, the viewing criteria had to be moved up to include approximately the same number of heavy viewers, since we are interested in contrasting populations that are comparable on social grounds rather than on obsolete levels of television viewing. The following corresponding figures were obtained:

	1968-69	1969-70
Hours viewed	7.5 or more	8.5 or more
Percent of males	11.1	12.4
Percent of females	10.8	10.7

The increased criteria indicate that programs selected as violent in Table 1 reached larger audiences over the years, even though the total amount of reported television viewing was in a period of decline. During all three seasons, these heavy viewers constituted one-third of the audience for all the programs labeled as violent in Table 1, despite the fact that they constituted only one-tenth of the total sample.

The analysis tables which follow chart the concentrations of these heavy viewers within various demographic subgroups of American society. These tables utilize an index which simply describes the relative prevalence of heavy viewers within a population subgroup. If the proportion of heavy viewers of violence within the subgroup is exactly the same as for the total sample, then the index registers 100. If the proportion is twice as high, the index registers 200; if it is only half as high, 50.

A concrete example may help. In the 1970 data, the following breakdown by education was obtained for men:

Attended or graduated from college	28.0 percent
Graduated from high school	30.5
Did not graduate from high school	41.5
	100.0 percent

The distribution of heavy viewers and the resulting index for each group are:

		Index
College	16.9	60
High school grad	21.7	71
Non-high school grad	61.4	148
	100.0	

The index of 60 for male respondents who had either attended or graduated from college indicated that the proportion of heavy viewers of television violence in this subset of the population (16.9 percent) represents only 60 percent of the total proportion of such persons in the sample (28.0 percent). The index of 148 for men who did not graduate from high school, on the other hand, indicated that this group contains almost one-and-one-half times as many heavy viewers of violence as would be expected from this group as a whole. Put another way, the following percentages of each group are heavy consumers of violent television fare:

College	7.5 percent
High school grad	8.9 percent
Non-high school grad	18.5 percent

Compared to the overall figure of heavy viewers of violence among men of 12.4 percent, the 18.5 percent figure for men who have not graduated from school is almost half again as great.

Results

Tables 2-7 contain the values of this index for various demographic groupings across the three years. Table 2 examines variations in the index for men by age, income, education, race, number of children, and ownership of color sets; parallel data for women are laid out in Table 3. Degree of violent viewing by age and race within educational categories is shown for men in Table 4 and for women in Table 5. Table 6 explores a three-way breakdown (Region x Urbanity x Income) separately for

Table 2: Indices* of degrees of viewing of violent television programs for various demographic groupings: men only

	All male viewers			Males who are heavy viewers of TV		
	1970	1969	1968	1970	1969	1968
Age: 18-24	62	90	90	92	104	106
25-34	72	78	99	66	97	100
35-49	68	54	114	78	58	109
50-64	144	148	80	129	130	78
65+	173	162	117	123	116	111
Income: $15,000+	54	61	55	70	74	88
10 -14,999	82	79	73	97	85	83
8 - 9,999	111	109	90	110	107	95
5 - 7,999	150	148	118	123	127	105
Under $5,000	150	148	118	123	127	105
Education:						
Attended college	60	60	38	81	62	38
High school grad	71	87	114	72	87	114
Did not graduate high school	148	134	128	127	126	128
Race: White	97	96	91	99	99	98
Nonwhite	127	132	163	110	114	141
No children	122	119	NA	111	110	95
One-Two children	85	89	NA	82	88	NA
Under 6	108	87	–	81	90	–
6-12	106	64	–	116	69	–
13-17	45	72	–	54	81	–
Three or more children	71	77	NA	99	96	NA
Under 6	50	–	–	63	–	–
6-12	74	–	–	104	–	–
13-17	83	–	–	109	–	–
Color set	100	78	129	100	65	107
Black and white set	100	107	95	100	111	98

*See text for description of the index.

men and for women. This arrangement of breakdowns thus proceeds from univariate to more complex multivariate analyses.

Tables 2 and 3 generally verify the initial Simmons analysis, which isolated race, income, education, and age as major correlates of violent TV viewing. In more recent years, age, income, and education have increased in explanatory power, while race—the leading correlate in the initial study—has produced noticeably less differentiation. Two interesting variables in 1968—region (not shown in Tables 2 and 3) and ownership of color television sets—failed to appear as correlates for the 1969 and 1970 data. For women, in a reversal of a 1968 finding, presence of children in the household was associated with slightly *less* viewing of violence in 1969 and 1970. However, no consistent tendency for either number or age of children to affect viewing appears in the two tables. While education, income, and age again appear as correlates of violent viewing in Table 3, race remains the leading correlate of violent viewing for women.

Table 3: Indices of degrees of viewing of violent programs for
various demographic groupings: Women

	All women			Women who are heavy viewers		
	1970	1969	1968	1970	1969	1968
Age: 18-24	66	84	73	78	80	78
25-34	77	87	86	63	90	91
35-49	91	81	105	100	104	101
50-64	139	125	132	130	118	122
65+	122	132	89	111	100	94
Income: $15,000+	81	69	37	119	98	57
10-14,999	66	69	73	83	69	73
8- 9,999	76	84	71	76	78	74
5- 7,999	113	115	126	90	116	118
Under $5,000	137	128	123	121	112	116
Education:						
Attended college	53	69	46	67	79	72
High school grad	73	105	108	70	112	96
Did not graduate high school	146	110	117	131	96	110
Race: White	92	96	94	96	95	96
Nonwhite	160	137	149	124	131	130
No childtren	110	118	95	107	109	94
One-two children	88	96	NA	92	99	NA
Under 6	77	113	–	77	102	–｡
6-12	80	64	–	86	70	–
13-17	101	75	–	112	87	–
Three or more children	95	66	NA	95	79	NA
Under 6	91	–	–	82	–	–
6-12	98	–	–	98	–	–
13-17	102	–	–	114	–	–
Color set	99	124	109	94	125	91
Black and white set	103	93	99	104	94	103

The right sides of Tables 2 and 3 show corresponding indices for the heaviest viewing segments of the population. (Using this strategy, we have a basic control on the influence of total amount of set usage on viewing of violence.) These heavy TV users almost by definition watch more violence, simply because they watch more television.[2] In point of fact they watch twice as much violent programming as the average member of the general audiences. This would not pose a methodological problem if the average amount of viewing were constant across the population subgroups. However, heavy viewing is concentrated in the lower-education, lower-income, black, and aged portions of the United States population (Bogart, 1958; Robinson, 1969)—the same portions already noted as heavy viewers of violence. The control on amount of viewing is therefore essential before proper estimates of the effects of the demographic variables can be made.

Indeed, when such control is applied, the differentials of the top four variables in Tables 2 and 3 drop considerably.[3] In fact, viewing in the oldest age category (65 and over) drops below that in the second oldest age group (50-64). Nevertheless, education and income continue to be the leading correlates for men, and race the leading correlate for women.

Tables 4 and 5 attempt to get a better perspective on the interactions among three of these important correlates: education, age, and race. Internal instability is evident in the two sets of tables; that is, violent viewing does not increase consistently as age increases (or education decreases) within various age (or education) categories. Of the two, variations by education are more consistent than variations by age. But (at least in the 1970 data) there is, in Coombs's (1965) term a "disjunctive" cast to the interaction of the two variables: one must *either* be over 50 *or* not have finished high school to be a heavy viewer of violence. Particularly intriguing in both the 1969 and the 1970 data in Table 4 is the high viewing of violence among young male high school dropouts, a group particularly prone to aggressive activity (Campbell and Schuman, 1969; Baker and Ball, 1969).

Considerable instability also appears in the relation between viewing violence and education for blacks in Tables 4 and 5. Among black men, high school graduates watched the most violence in 1970; in 1969, those who had not finished high school watched most. Among black women, almost the opposite patterns occurred. Of course, the small sample sizes preclude anything but idle speculation about the meaning of these data.

Further instability is found within the four-way breakdown of the white population in Table 6. However, the relation between heavy viewing of violence and lower income holds up across regional, urban, and sex boundaries. A relation between violence viewing and location was also found. That higher violent viewing would be characteristic of nonmetropolitan locations, especially in the South, was not expected. These

Table 4: Degree of viewing of violent programs by age and education and by race and education: Men

| | | All males | | | | Males who are heavy television viewers | | |
| | | | Education | | | | | Education | |
	TOTAL	Did not graduate high school	High school grad	Attended college	TOTAL	Did not graduate high school	High school grad	Attended college
1970								
AGE 18-24	62	145*	66	22	92	157**	93***	50**
25-34	72	81	76	64	66	55*	64	75
35-49	68	137	28	36	78	134	33	50
50+	158	164	140	133	126	130	115	119
RACE White	97	153	63	60	99	131	63	81
Nonwhite	127	127	167*	72*	110	106*	138**	75**
		148	71	60		127	72	81
1969								
AGE 18-24	90	235*	82	18	104	193**	119**	0**
25-35	78	88	69	79	97	138	64	105
35-49	54	78	39	40	58	83	35	45
50+	155	160	165	115	130	131	133	81
RACE White	96	123	91	63	98	120	88	67
Nonwhite	132	187	62*	8*	114	157*	81**	6**
		134	87	60		126	87	62

*Sample size not large enough for high stability.
**Sample size too small for reliability.

Table 5: Degree of viewing of violent programs by age and education and by race and education: Women

	All females				Females who are heavy television viewers			
		Education				Education		
	TOTAL	Did not graduate high school	High school grad	Attended college	TOTAL	Did not graduate high school	High school grad	Attended college
1970								
AGE 18-24	66	124	48	45	78	104*	67	54**
25-34	77	148	67	24	63	111	53	17
35-49	91	144	68	35	100	149	54	63*
50+	132	151	106	98	120	133	100	110
RACE White	92	133	74	49	96	125	74	59
Nonwhite	160	205	54	100	124	158	43*	142**
		146	73	53		131	70	66
1969								
AGE 18-24	84	76	101	57	80	69*	91	54**
25-34	87	115	99	43	90	100	106	54
35-49	81	86	81	71	109	113	96	119
50+	128	129	143	94	110	97	149	95
RACE White	96	113	97	64	95	95	105	70
Nonwhite	137	111	208	140*	131	102	208*	190**
		110	105	69		96	112	79

*Sample size not large enough for high stability.
**Sample size too small for reliability.

Table 6: Degree of viewing of violent programs by income and location (whites only)

A. Men

WHITES		1970				1969			
		Non-South		South		Non-South		South	
		Metro	Non-metro	Metro	Non-metro	Metro	Non-metro	Metro	Non-metro
INCOME	$8000+	74	80	36	168	81	69	62	125
	Under $8000	146	133	26	135	107	103	50	161
		97	106	32	151	90	89	55	156

B. Women

WHITES		1970				1969			
		Non-South		South		Non-South		South	
		Metro	Non-metro	Metro	Non-metro	Metro	Non-metro	Metro	Non-metro
INCOME	$8000+	73	64	62	87	61	110	90	69
	Under $8000	112	103	98	156	112	115	129	134
		89	85	79	131	82	113	110	116

Table 7: Top 13 evening programs in degree of attentiveness of audience
(Numbers are percentages who say they are paying "full attention" when the program is on)

MEN

	1970		1969		1968
83	Mannix*	88	Judd for the Defense	89	Sunday News/Reasoner
83	Bonanza*	86	Mission Impossible*	89	High Chaparral*
83	Hawaii Five-O*	86	Name of the Game	88	Bonanza*
82	Harry Reasoner (Sunday News)	85	Star Trek	88	Big Valley*
82	Ironside*	85	Outcasts	86	Mission Impossible
82	Virginian*	84	It Takes a Thief	86	I Spy
82	Walter Cronkite	84	Gunsmoke*	85	Hondo*
81	Gunsmoke*	84	Guns of Will Sonnett	85	Cimarron Strip*
81	The FBI	84	Ironside*	85	FBI
81	High Chapparal*	83	Hogan's Heroes	84	Felony Squad
80	Name of the Game	83	Hawaii Five-O*	84	Sunday Night Movie
80	Mission Impossible*	83	Journey to the Unknown	83	Guns of Will Sonnett*
80	Dragnet	83	Virginian*	83	Gunsmoke

WOMEN

	1970		1969		1968
84	Marcus Welby, M.D.	84	Peyton Place	88	Peyton Place I
84	Medical Center	84	Kraft Music Hall	88	Peyton Place II
80	Bold Ones	82	Family Affair	87	Sunday Night Movie
80	Newlywed Game	82	Lawrence Welk	85	ABC Scope
79	Ironside*	82	My Three Sons	84	Big Valley*
79	Lawrence Welk	82	Julia	84	Bonanza*
79	Mannix*	81	Ironside*	84	Judd for the Defense*
79	Jimmy Durante - Lennon Sisters	80	Judd for the Defense	83	Saturday Night Movie
78	Hawaii Five-O*	80	Walt Disney	82	Ironside
78	Virginian*	79	Bonanza	82	Thursday Night Movie
78	Then Came Bronson	79	Big Valley	82	Run for Your Life
78	Let's Make a Deal	79	Mission Impossible*	81	Mission Impossible
78	Bonanza*	79	Star Trek	81	Wednesday Night Movie

are locations in which the type of violence seen on television is least likely to occur. The finding holds when controlled for income and sex in Table 6. In contrast, figures for the black population (parallel to Table 6) show no stable trends whatsoever.

One of the unique features of the Simmons diary data on television viewing is that respondents are asked to indicate for each program whether they paid full attention for most of the viewing period, paid only some attention, or were mainly out of the room. This becomes an important facet of viewing behavior; respondents report paying less than full attention to the set for almost one-third of their viewing time during prime time hours.[4] It may be useful, therefore, to inquire about what kinds of programs are most likely to capture complete viewer attention.

Table 7 contains, in rank order, the 13 programs from the 1968, 1969, and 1970 seasons that were most likely to have full viewer attention. In the 1970 season, nine of the 13 programs for male viewers were also among the most violent programs on television. In 1969, the number drops to five of 13—but this still represents 38 percent of the most violent programs. Only eight of the remaining 72 less violent or nonviolent programs (11 percent) rated as high on the attentiveness factor (and all eight of these programs contain some degree of violence). In 1968, the figure is six of 13, and again most of the remaining seven top attention programs contain some violence.

Table 7 indicates that violence has much less appeal to women than to men. In 1970, five (38 percent) of the most attentively viewed programs were among the most violent; in 1968 and 1969, only two and three were among the most violent. Over all three seasons, however, violent programs do appear to generate disproportionately higher attention to the set among women than do other programs.[5]

Nevertheless, male viewing patterns provide the most striking figures in Table 7. These figures take on even greater significance when one examines male degree of attentiveness to what is stereotypically considered the programming that generates greatest involvement—professional football. The attentiveness rating for NFL pro football in 1970 was 71; for AFL football it was 65.[6]

Summary and comment

In all three seasons studied, the male audience for the most violent television programs has been drawn disproportionately from the lower-status segments, in terms of income and education, of American society. Heavy viewers of violence also tend to be past age 50 and to be black, although these factors do not operate consistently within each status grouping. Particularly high viewing of violence characterizes those males 18-24 who were high school dropouts. These findings hold, (although less significantly), when viewing of violence is controlled for total amount of television viewing, which is also highest among persons of lower social status, among the elderly, and among blacks.

The same factors tend to characterize heavy viewers of television violence among women, but their relative predominance differs from among men. Race seems to be the major determinant of violence viewing among women; education, income, and age play less important roles.

Among both men and women factors which in previous analyses had been correlates of violence viewing—ownership of a color set, region of the country, and number and age of children—failed to replicate over the years or when controlled for total amount of viewing. One new variable, size of community, appeared promising in the 1970 data, but further checks over future seasons are needed.

Despite the consistency with which these results appear (across seasons when these programs faced highly variable competing programs), it would be premature to conclude that the factors analyzed are immutable concomitants of violence viewing. The data are restricted to, and reflect public response to, current evening television dramatic fare. The recent favorable response among better-educated Americans to movies like *Bonnie and Clyde, The Wild Bunch, Butch Cassidy and the Sundance Kid*, and the James Bond series leaves little doubt that violence can be dressed up to have greater appeal to those of higher social status.[7] The introduction of more television series like *The Avengers* and *Mission: Impossible* (both of which in fact drew disproportionately from the college-exposed segment of the public) would result in a reversal of the findings of this report. The gradual disappearance of television westerns (only five were on in the 1969-70 season) may hasten such a trend.

Nevertheless, the greater exposure to television violence among those portions of our society in which violence is already more likely to be an accepted way of life offers little hope that television is helping to orient our society in a less violent direction. In no way can any causal inferences about television be read into these data.[8] But they certainly do not diminish the likelihood that more detailed investigation would reveal television, in a very subtle and continuous fashion, playing an important social role as reinforcer of the norm of justified violence.

The findings on attentiveness, on the other hand, remind us that there are many criteria by which to assess the function of such programming to a society and that its positive social consequences need to be considered as well. While available research offers little evidence that the greater attentiveness to violent programming can be translated into a catharsis effect on personal aggression, the greater appeal of violence over the fare on the television screen may betoken a considerable lessening of feelings of apathy and boredom in the viewing public. A recent Gallup poll found that three times more lower-status than higher-status respondents described their lives as dull and unexciting. Perhaps television violence is partially filling this void in the lives of a significant number of our citizens. Certainly this function needs to be considered in the growing debate on the effects of television violence on American society.

VIEWERS OF NATIONAL NEWS PROGRAMS

Surprisingly little is known about the audiences of national news programs on television. Survey data have shown that television news viewers tend to be better informed about news events than nonviewers (Robinson, 1967; Wade and Schramm, 1969). Numerous social observers have also conjectured that national news programs have created a greater national consciousness at the expense of public concern about local political matters. Almost all recent surveys have shown vast majorities of the public claiming television to be their main source of news (Roper, 1969), not only generally but also during special periods such as elections (Robinson, 1967; Converse, 1966; Hero, 1959).

Nevertheless, a number of important pieces of information are lacking in our understanding of the function of television news programs in American society. Most notably, no researcher has yet examined the ways public perceptions of our sociopolitical environment change in response to important news events as they are reported in the various mass media. It is undoubtedly true that recent public concern about pollution and student unrest are largely the result of mass media coverage of these topics. But *how* have public attitudes changed? What groups have changed their views more than others? What types of people have become engaged in political or social behavior as a result of media coverage? These and other fundamental questions, while quite complex to research, are the kinds to which more research needs to be directed.

Unfortunately, the research in this report bears only indirectly on these fascinating issues. It is concerned with more mundane questions: What proportion of the population is reached by a national news broadcast over a two-week period? What are some demographic correlates of persons who watch these programs frequently? Are heavy viewers of television news more likely than nonviewers or light viewers to use other sources of news like magazines and newspapers? How much attention do viewers pay to their sets when news programs rather than other kinds are on the air? Answers to such questions do widen our understanding of how television news functions in the process of keeping our citizenry informed on the crucial issues of the day.

The data reported here were collected by the W. R. Simmons organization from television viewing diaries of a national probability sample of persons 18 years and older. The sampling procedures have been described in detail in Part I. The diaries were kept by 6,834 viewers for various two-week periods between October 12 and November 15, 1969.

These data offer unique advantages over those collected in previous studies of news viewers. The sample is over three times larger then those few previous studies of news viewing that had a nationwide probability base. Considerable experience and care in collecting valid data on highly specific aspects of mass media usage are built into the Simmons data gathering operation. Simmons collects usage data on three media simultaneously from respondents. The fact that the data are collected by a commercial concern, minimizes the likelihood that respondents overreport their news-seeking behavior because it might be expected of them (as is to be feared when the subject of the survey is news and the respondent knows it).

Amount of news viewing

On an average weekday, 25 percent of adult men and 22 percent of adult women reported watching the national news programs of either Reynolds-Smith (ABC), Walter Cronkite (CBS), or Huntley-Brinkley (NBC). However, the pattern of viewing such programs over a two-week time period is far from the random one which would result if the vast majority of viewers saw at least one of these news programs over a two-week period—despite this relatively low proportion of daily viewers. In fact, as can be seen in Table 8, the majority of the population (52 percent of men and 54 percent of women) did not report seeing even one national news program during the two-week period.

Table 8: Percentages of the sample viewing news programs over a two-week period

Saw	Men	(by chance)	Women	(by chance)
No program	52%	(6%)	54%	(8%)
One program	9	(18)	11	(23)
Two	7	(28)	6	(27)
Three	3	(25)	4	(24)
Four	5	(15)	4	(12)
Five	4	(6)	4	(5)
Six	4	(2)	3	(1)
Seven	3	(*)	3	(*)
Eight	3	(*)	3	(*)
Nine	4	(*)	3	(*)
Ten or more	6	(*)	5	(*)
	100%	(100%)	100%	(100%)

*Less than 0.5 percent

Table 8 shows the proportion of men and women who saw up to ten news programs over the two week period.[9] In parentheses we have also given the corresponding proportions as if news behavior were a random phenomenon—that is, viewers who watch the news on one evening are no more likely than nonviewers to watch the next evening. It can be seen that under random conditions, only six percent of men would have seen

no news show over a two-week period. The actual percentage who saw
no programs is almost nine times as high. The 20 percent of male viewers, at the other end of the scale, who saw more than five shows is similarly about nine times higher than that expected by chance. Hence there
is tremendous overlap in news audience from one evening to the next,
and only about 20 percent of the viewing audience could be categorized
as regular viewers of national news programs.

It is this 20 percent of viewers—those who are more likely than not to
watch a news program on a given evening—on which we now focus attention. We shall be concerned with two characteristics of this group on
which the Simmons data offer us perspective: (a) How do their members
compare with the rest of the society in age, education, and race? (b)
How do their magazine and newspaper reading habits differ from those
of less regular viewers or nonviewers of news?

Some demographic correlates

Our first concern is with the way news viewing varies with age and
education among white people. The proportion of blacks in the Simmons
sample is too small to subdivide in this manner; the news viewing of
blacks, which, as we shall see, varies somewhat from the patterns for
whites, will be covered separately.

Table 2 contains figures indicating the prevalence of regular news
viewers in various age and education categories of the sample. The index used is described in detail in Part I of this report. (Briefly, the index
is constructed to read 100 when the proportion of regular news viewers

Table 9: Index of regular news viewers in various age and education categories
(corresponding figures for heavy television viewers in parentheses)

	High school (not complete)		High school grad		Some college		College grad	
White men by age:								
18-24	32*	(64**)	25	(41**)	42	(47**)	32*	(100**)
25-39	46	(52*)	46	(57)	35	(16**)	58	(71*)
35-49	90	(92)	59	(53)	44	(78*)	75	(116*)
50+	188	(143)	197	(148)	80	(63*)	162	(115)
	143	(124)	80	(81)	49	(55)	85	(103)
White women by age:								
18-24	53	(77*)	16	(18*)	61	(94**)	100*	(71**)
25-34	40	(38)	48	(56)	7	(7*)	18	(40**)
35-49	87	(90)	94	(99)	70	(56*)	81	(154**)
50+	139	(116)	183	(156)	168	(158*)	244	(242*)
	108	(98)	92	(97)	77	(82)	133	(177)
Black men:	87	(105*)	80	(91**)	61*	(63**)	282**	(166**)
Black women:	96	(112)	81	(67*)	52*	(42**)	370**	(174**)

*Sample size too small for high reliability.
**Sample size too small for reliability.

in a category is exactly equal to the proportion of viewers in the rest of the sample, to read in varying degrees over 100 when there are disproportionate numbers of regular news viewers, and to read in varying degrees less than 100 when there are fewer regular news viewers than average.) Table 9 indicates a fairly consistent increase in news viewing as age increases but shows a curvilinear viewing pattern as educaton increases. Among women, viewing dips in the 25-34 age category, the years when family responsibilities apparently reach a peak leaving little time for keeping up with the news.

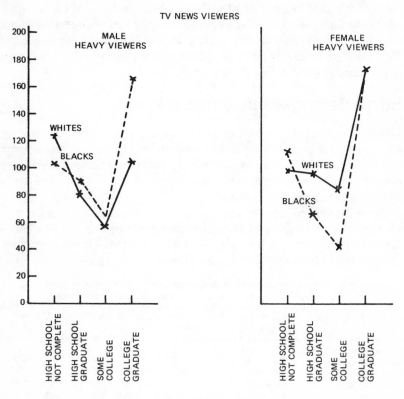

Figure 1: Indices of viewing of national news by educational level, age, and sex

The curvilinear pattern of news viewing with education is such that heaviest viewing is found among those with the lowest and the highest degrees of educational attainment. Among men, college graduates are less likely to be heavy news viewers than those who have not finished high school; among women, college graduates watch more than the least educated group.

While the data are not shown in Table 8, the same conclusions emerge from a parallel analysis of the nonviewers of television news, the majority of the sample that did not watch any news programs over the two-week period. Likewise, controls for amount of television viewing (see the figures in parentheses in Table 9, which refer to indices of viewing among the 40 percent of the population who watch the most television) confirm these trends, although the news viewing of college graduates appears more pronounced than that of those who have not finished high school. The curvilinear nature of these viewing data can be seen graphically in Figure 1.

Among blacks this control for amount of viewing results in the opposite effect of educational differentials on news viewing. This is due to the fact that, contrary to the pattern for whites, television viewing tends to be greater among the more educated blacks. Thus, when controls for amount of viewing are imposed, the strikingly high indices (282 for men, 370 for women) for black college graduates become considerably attenuated. However, in both raw and controlled sets of figures, the same basic curvilinear nature of viewing patterns is found.

Use of printed news media

The Simmons data offer an opportunity to explore the use that regular television news viewers make of the printed media. In this section, we shall inquire into their use of daily newspapers and of various news-oriented magazines.

Newspaper readers are identified by a "yesterday recall" method. They are asked the names of any newspapers read in the past week. Only those who read the newspaper "yesterday" or on an average weekday are counted as newspaper readers; 90 percent of both men and women qualified as newspaper readers in 1970. As can be seen in Table 10, newspaper readership was not very strongly related to television news viewing among men or women.[10]

Readership of magazines is assessed by what Simmons calls the "through-the-book" technique, in which copies of ten articles appearing in a recent issue of the magazine are presented to the respondent; he is asked to rate them according to his interest in them. After rating the ten articles, the respondent is asked whether he has seen this issue of the magazine before. Respondents must affirm past exposure to the issue to qualify as readers. Respondents who kept television diaries not only gave this information in the fall survey but also had completed the procedure some months earlier.

For the present survey, magazines were grouped into four categories that had been previously found predictive of awareness of items in the news (Robinson, 1967). The four categories are: analytic commentary (for example, *Atlantic*), news (*Time*), general interest (*Look*), and business (*Fortune*). To qualify in the "two or more" category in Table 10, the respondent had to read two different magazines in that category in either interview. For example, a person who read *Time* in both the spring and the fall interviews falls into the "one" category in Table 3; but the person who read *Newsweek* in the spring and *Time* in the fall qualifies for the "two or more" category.[11]

Table 10: Indices of regular television news viewing by readership of various magazines and newspapers

Reader of:	All men			College expposed men		
	None	One	Two or more	None	One	Two or more
Daily newspaper	106	99	X	61	102	X
Analytic mag[1]	99	107	89	89	144	79
News mag[2]	100	104	91	94	90	117
General interest mag[3]	98	94	104	82	91	106
Business mag[4]	102	100	77	102	80	115
Reader of:	All women			College exposed women		
Daily newspaper	82	102	X	69	102	X
Analytic mag	98	100	200	103	56	140
News mag	92	124	124	76	132	106
General interest mag	94	91	108	52	84	116
Business mag	98	124	172	91	106	258

[1] Includes *Atlantic, Harpers, New Yorker, Saturday Review or Esquire*
[2] Includes *Time, Newsweek, U.S. News and World Report*
[3] Includes *Look, Life, Readers Digest, Parade, Family Weekly*
[4] Includes *Barrons, Business Management, Business Week, Duns Review, Forbes, Fortune, Nation's Business, Wall Street Journal*

The data in Table 10 provide only limited support for the notion of a "news-seeking syndrome," in which individuals who are news-seekers will try to keep up with the news in as many media as possible. There is in fact no relation between news viewing and readership of magazines among the total male sample. There is some tendency in this direction among college-educated men, although news viewing does not increase monotonically with number of magazines read (especially analytic commentary magazines), as we would expect to be the case if there were a strong bond linking the two forms of media behavior.[12]

Among women, however, the news-seeking syndrome holds more often than not. Readers of each type of magazine are more likely to be regular news viewers than are nonreaders; those who read two or more such magazines are as likely or more likely to be regular news viewers than are those who read only one magazine. This monotonicity does not hold for analytic and news magazine readers among women who had been to college. Nevertheless, a link between television and printed media news behavior is generally supported among the female portion of the sample.

Among blacks, no strong or consistent relation could be found between television news behavior and magazine readership or newspaper readership.[13]

Attentiveness to news programs

Table 7 showed that many news programs scored high in capturing viewer attention. Of the three news programs considered in the present analysis, Walter Cronkite received the highest attention score (82 percent of the audience was paying full attention), with Huntley-Brinkley and Reynolds-Smith (both at 78 percent) commanding only slightly less attention. All three ratings were considerably above the average attention score for evening television programs.

On the other hand, among women the attention ratings dropped to well below average (64 percent for Walter Cronkite and Huntley-Brinkley and 57 percent for Reynolds-Smith). To some extent, this can be attributed to the fact that these programs are on the air during the dinner hours. When one looks at attention to other news programs, women's ratings are about on a par with those of men. For the program *60 Minutes,* full attention is claimed by 80 percent of the men and 76 percent of the women, for Harry Reasoner 82 percent and 76 percent for Roger Mudd 78 percent and 71 percent, for *Meet the Press* 71 percent and 71 percent, for *Face the Nation* 63 percent and 66 percent, respectively.

Summary and comments

We have attempted to utilize some unique aspects of media data to gain a better understanding of news viewing behavior among adults in the United States. We have found that:

1) The 20 percent of the population who view national evening news regularly (at least six times over a two-week period) is far larger in number than one would expect if news viewing from one evening to the next were a random phenomenon. It seems justified, therefore, to separate the viewing public into regular and nonregular news viewers.

2) Both male and female regular news viewers are drawn disproportionately from older people in our society, regardless of their educational level or amount of overall television viewing.

3) Regular news viewing shows a curvilinear relation with educational level for both men and women, with those of least and most educational achievement most likely to be regular news viewers.

4) The proportion of regular news viewers among black college graduates is strikingly high.

5) The supposition that regular viewers supplement their information through their more extensive contact with printed media was supported by women but not by men. Regular male news viewers were not consistently more likely than nonviewers to be readers of news-oriented magazines.

6) While attention to evening news is notably higher among men that women, this does not appear to hold true for news-related programs at

other times of the day. Male attention to all television news shows tends to be much higher than that given to average entertainment programs.

The findings bear on rather disparate aspects of television news behavior and seem incapable of integration into a single summary theme. The data point out definite differences in news viewing between men and women, between blacks and whites, between the better and the less educated, and between older and younger people. With regard to age, we are reminded of data indicating a decided increase in attention to and awareness of news and politics among parents once their children begin to leave home (Robinson, 1967).

Perhaps the most striking statistic in the report, however, is the 52 percent of the population who did not report watching a single evening news show over the two-week diary period.[14] This figure is difficult to comprehend alongside the 59 percent of the population who reported that they received most of their news from television in a recent Roper (1969) survey. On the average day, the Simmons data suggest that 90 percent of the population read a newspaper while less than 25 percent watch national television news.

It is obvious that more detailed knowledge is needed about the ways mass media operate in the context of specific news events, so that dependence on people's recall or general attitudes or perceptions is not necessary. Are people who have seen television news coverage of some event or story more or less likely to seek and/or read more details in the printed media? What segments of the tremendous amount of news to which a person is exposed in an average day does he remember the next day or the next week? What type of news is most likely to be brought up and discussed in interpersonal conversation? It would seem most fruitful to examine these questions in the context of microscopic daily behavior (as we have done here) rather than to make oversimplified projections based on personal intuition or superficial polls.

FOOTNOTES

1. There are some discrepancies between the Smith and Simmons ratings. Smith's raters would probably have included *Felony Squad, Mission Impossible, Gunsmoke, Avengers,* and *Rat Patrol* on the 1967-68 list, and dropped *Cimarron Strip, Guns of Will Sonnett, Bonanza, Big Valley,* and *Judd for the Defense.* Nevertheless, both sets of raters basically agreed that the other eight programs belonged on the list, and it seems unlikely that either set of judges would deny that any of the above programs contained considerable amounts of violence.

2. The following amounts of weekly hours of television viewing qualify the respondent as a heavy viewer:

	Men	Women
1969	21.5+	27.0+
1970	19.8+	26.0+

These criteria include the top 40 percent of the viewing public.
3. The differentiation appears to increase, however, if one looks only at the remaining 60 percent of the population—the "nonheavy viewers." In the 1970 data, the following indices obtain for education for this 60 percent: attended college—44, graduated from high school—69, and did not graduate from high school—161. For, race, the following indices obtained: white—92, nonwhite—164.
4. These demographic factors have been found to be generally associated with greater attentiveness: lower education, lower income, greater age, male sex, smaller family size, and no children in the household. Attention to the set is highest during the prime time hours and drops to well below half during weekday daytime hours. These data are from the Simmons Newsletter, Vol. 1 No. 1 (November 1967), entitled "Taking a New Look at TV Audience." Subsequent validational research has shown attentiveness to be strongly related to respondents' abilities to recall commercial messages broadcast during the program.
5. A number of daytime serials not considered in Table 7 also rate high in inattentiveness among women. In the 1970 data, for example, *Another World, As the World Turns,* and *Days of Our Lives* all commanded the full attention of more than 75 percent of women viewers. Attentiveness scores for games shows like *Hollywood Squares* (50 percent), reruns like *The Lucy Show* (47 percent), *The Today Show* (38 percent), and *Captain Kangaroo* (12 percent) pale by comparison.
6. College football actually has a slightly more attentive (although much smaller) audience with 76 percent of viewers claiming full attention. In 1969, college and pro football rated about equally in attentiveness. (These figures must be considered in the light of the time of year in which they were collected. Professional games in October and November are more likely to be lopsided contests, to have less overall significance, and to have to compete with more favorable weather than those later in the year. It would be interesting to have comparable figures for playoff games.)
7. A significant amount of movie violence appears on television (particularly in movies made especially for television); this movie violence (too complicated to analyze in the present data) is more likely to attract the better-educated than the less-educated audience.
8. Questions dealing with respondents' attitudes toward and experience of violence might be included in future surveys of television viewing behavior in order to examine the way viewing of television

violence relates to personal orientations toward violence. Some questions of this type were considered for the 1970 Simmons survey, but constraints imposed by time and finances combined to make this infeasible.

However, a number of behavioral items already included in the Simmons survey which could be interpreted as violence-related were correlated with the amount of violence viewed by men in the sample. The following items were actually negatively related to violence viewing: purchase of a gun or rifle during the previous year (index of violence viewing 34 for these respondents); purchase of a target gun or rifle during the previous year (index of violence viewing 34 for these respondents); purchase of a target gun during the previous year (index 35); purchase of factory-loaded ammunition (index 61). Nor did heavy viewing relate to the reading of various "masculine" magazines; readers of adventure magazines like *True* indexed at 71, of automobile magazines like *Hot Rod* at 66, and of hunting magazines like Field and Stream at 109. Multivariate controls need to be imposed on these data before they can be properly interpreted, but there is little reason to expect such controls to result in a reversal of the direction of these results.

9. Some 1.8 percent of men and .7 percent of women watched more than ten news programs over the two-week period. These news-hungry viewers obviously lived in areas in which the three news programs are not on the air at the same time.

10. One intriguing differential pattern of newspaper readership appears when amount of education is controlled. Among both men and women who have attended college, nonreaders are more likely to be nonviewers. Among those with less education, nonreaders are less likely to be nonviewers. However, intriguing these data are, the trends are neither strong enough nor appropriate enough (the newspaper reading day is not coincident with the TV day) to warrant more than this brief comment.

11. By these criteria, the overall percentage of whites reading at least one of the analytic commentary magazines was 12 percent; the percentage reading one of the news magazines was 35 percent; of the general interest magazines, 79 percent; and of the business magazines, 21 percent. Men were considerably more likely to be readers of magazines in all categories except general interest. Respondents who had been to college were even more likely to be readers than those who had not been to college for many magazines the reading rates among college-attenders was twice as high.

12. The education control in Table 3 was unfortunately written into the computer analysis at the same time as the education-by-age breakdowns were written in. If the researchers had been aware of the notable differences between the newsviewing of college graduates

and that of those who had not finished college (Table 2), we would have restricted the control in Table 3 to college graduates in order to utilize a group with more homogenous news viewing behavior.

13. Blacks were less likely to be readers of these magazines than whites. However, college-exposed blacks were more likely to be magazine readers than were college-exposed whites.

14. It should be pointed out that the figures from the A.C. Nielson rating firm indicate considerably higher news viewing. On an average day in October-November 1969, Nielson figures show about 39 percent of the population tuned in to national television news (as opposed to the 23 percent daily figure found in the Simmons diaries). While the Nielson data do corroborate some curvilinear relational tendency between news viewing and education, it is far less severe than that suggested in Table 9. The Nielson data indicate 44 percent news viewing by high school dropouts, 35 percent by high school graduates, 36 percent by persons with some college, and 37 percent by college graduates. Whatever methodological differences account for such differences between the two surveys cannot be explained here, but it is worthwhile to note that the Simmons data might not replicate if different sources of data were used.

Since the Nielson data are collected across many years and during all seasons of the year, it is useful to note that October-November is relatively heavy news viewing period, 20-30 percent higher than May-September and roughly ten percent lower than December-February. Nielson news-viewing figures for the fall of 1969 were at about the same level as those for the same period in 1966—indicating a relatively stable audience size over the years.

REFERENCES

Baker, R., and Ball S. *Violence and the media.* Washington, D.C.: United States Government Printing Office, 1969.

Bogart, L. *The age of television.* New York, Ungar, 1958.

Campbell, A., and Schuman, H. *Racial attitudes in fifteen American cities.* Ann Arbor, Mich.: Institute for Social Research, 1968.

Converse, P. Information flow and the stability of partisan attitudes. In A. Campbell et al. *Elections and the Political Order,* New York: Wiley, 1966.

Coombs, C. *A theory of data.* New York: Wiley, 1965.

Gallup, G. Do you find life exciting or dull? Princeton, N. J.: American Institute of Public Opinion, October 9, 1969.

Hero, A. *Mass media and world affairs.* Boston: World Peace Foundation, 1959.

Robinson, J. *Public information about world affairs.* Ann Arbor, Mich.: Institute for Social Research, 1967.

Robinson, J. Television and leisure time. *Public Opinion Quarterly,* 169, **33,** 210-22.

Roper, B. A ten-year view of public attitudes toward television and other mass media 1959-1968. New York: Television Information Office, 1969.

Simmons, W. R. Violence on television. *Media/Scope,* 1969, 12, 36-78.

Smith, J. Television violence and driving behavior. *Educational Broadcasting Review,* 1969, **3,** 23-28.

Wade, S., and Schramm, W. The mass media as sources of public affairs, science, and health knowledge. *Public Opinion Quarterly,* 1969, **33,** 197-209.

Appendix: Research design and methodology

The sample for the 1970 Study of Selective Markets and the Media Reaching Them was selected on a national probability basis. The television diary respondents consist of a subsample of the total sample. Therefore, an understanding of the selection procedures used for the total sample is necessary for a thorough understanding of the study. These procedures, as well as those used to select the diary subsample, are described in the first section of this Appendix.

SAMPLE DESIGN AND SELECTION PROCEDURES

The sample for the study of selective markets and of media reaching them was designed, drawn, and administered in such a way as to meet every requirement for obtaining reliable and unbiased findings, and is projectable within calculable tolerance limits to the population under study. It was designed and selected to assure that every individual in the defined population would have a known probability of inclusion. Equally important, the sampling procedures provided a high degree of administrative control in the field, so as to be certain that the selections made would be virtually identical to those demanded by the strict probability model on which the original design was based. The design utilized in this study involved a five-stage national area probability sample which was disproportionately allocated to high income areas.

Selection of census tracts and minor civil divisions within each primary sampling unit

Within each of the selected PSUs all census Tracts and all Minor Civil Divisions in untracted areas were stratified in terms of family income data from the 1960 Census, in such a way as to assure that each Census Tract and Minor Civil Division would fall into one and only one of four strata, which are defined as follows:

Stratum (a) Census Tracts and Minor Civil Divisions in which more than 25 per cent of the families reported incomes of $15,-000 or over at the time of the 1960 Census.

Stratum (b) Census Tracts and Minor Civil Divisions not included in Stratum "A", in which 10 percent to 25 per cent of the families reported incomes of $15,000 or over at the time of the 1960 Census, or in which more of the families are in the $8,000 or over categories than in either the $5,000 - $8,000 category, or under $5,000.

Stratum (c)   Census Tracts and Minor Civil Divisions not included in
               Strata "A" and "B" in which more families reported in-
               comes of $5,000 to $8,000 than reported incomes under
               $5,000.

Stratum (d)   Census tracts and Minor Civil Divisions not included in
               Strata "A", "B", or "C", i.e., in which more of the fam-
               ilies reported incomes of less than $5,000 at the time of
               the 1960 Census than was true of the other categories.

Specific Census tracts and Minor Civil Divisions were then selected
from within each stratum by a random process with probability proportionate to 1960 population, and with each stratum being sampled independently and at a different rate. The procedure followed thus assured
allocation of a disproportionately large number of interviews to the higher income strata, while at the same time providing a precisely known
probability of selection for each of the Census Tracts and Minor Civil
Divisions in the sample.

Selection of primary sampling units

Standard Metropolitan Statistical Areas (SMSA)—as defined by the
U.S. Census Bureau in October 1963—and nonmetropolitan counties
throughout the United States (coterminous 48 states) were first stratified
by a complex stratification plan which took into consideration geographic region, geographic location within region, population at the time of
the 1960 Census, per capita income, the rate of population change and
the ratio of white to nonwhite population. Thirty-eight SMSAs were selected with certainty. (That is, the selected SMSA and the stratum were
one and the same.) Fifty additional SMSAs were selected from the remaining metropolitan Statistical Area strata with probability proportionate to size. Seventy nonmetropolitan counties were also randomly selected from the nonmetropolitan strata. Selections were made with
probability proportionate to size based on 1960 Census counts. The total
number of Primary Sampling Units was 158; they contained a total of
304 counties.

Selection of interviewing areas (clusters)

Within each Census Tract covered by Block Statistics Reports, a
block or a predefined group of contiguous blocks were selected by a
random procedure with a probability proportionate to the 1960 household count. Within Census Tracts not so covered, or within Minor Civil
Divisions, a Census Enumeration District was selected by a random
procedure with probability proportionate to 1960 population. In some
instances, a predefined segment of the selected Enumeration District

was then selected randomly and with equal probability. Interviews were completed in a total of 937 such clusters.

Selection of households within the cluster

All housing units within the boundaries of each interviewing area were prelisted in advance of any interviewing in accordance with detailed listing instructions which required the interviewer to account for all structures within cluster boundaries and to indicate whether or not each structure contained any living quarters. In rural areas, interviewers were required to make a large-scale sketch map of the cluster, including any streets, roads, or country lanes which did not appear on the Census maps. The exact location of each dwelling place was indicated in such a way that it could be unambiguously identified even in the absence of street addresses and other aids to identification which are frequently lacking in open country areas.

Specific housing units (designated in terms of page-and-line numbers on the applicable prelisting forms) were selected in the New York office by trained sampling personnel using a random procedure.

At the time of interviewing, allowance was made for the inclusion of new housing units in the sample which were found to exist in the cluster but not included on the prelisting. The procedure followed, by which a sample of these new housing units was included, is known as the "half-open interval" procedure. The application of this procedure is simple and straight-forward. It only required that each new housing unit discovered immediately after a designated sample household and coming immediately before the next housing unit on the list, be taken by the interviewer as a sample case. Interviewers were instructed to be on the lookout for such housing units not previously listed, including cases where an apartment or a single family home was renovated to make additional housing units.

Selection of individual respondents

Within each designated household, only one adult, 18 years of age or older, was designated to be interviewed. In this way, the sample of individuals comes from a much larger number of households than the case where all adults residing in the household are interviewed. The total number of households in which interviews were conducted is 15,322.

Rather than use a procedure wherein the respondent would be selected from a list of all adults living in the household, each household was designated for interview with either a man or a woman. Thus, there was a separate sample of households for the adult male of adult female populations. In this way, a proper balance of male and female interviews could be assured. Further, the number of adults to be listed in each household was approximately one-half of the required listing if the selection was made from all adults of both sexes. Many families contain only one adult male and one adult female. Thus, with this procedure, it became almost automatic for the interviewer to select the person to be interviewed. Generally, the sex predesignation served to shorten the list from which each respondent was finally selected. When more than one adult of the designated sex resided in the household, a prescribed and random procedure for determining the selected respondent was provided to the interviewer. This procedure called for a list of eligible respondents to be made. The interviewers were instructed to list the male and female head first, then all others in order by age starting with the oldest. The interviewer was then referred to a table which was printed on the back of the questionnaire, out of the sight of the interviewer as she listed down the men and women on the front of the questionnaire. This table was worked out be selecting in advance on the basis of a systematic random procedure one number out of two, one out of three, etc., in such a way that every adult of the specified sex was given an equal participation in the selection of the respondent was confined to a reference to the pre-designated table which identified the respondent by line number. Once the identity of the designated respondent by line number was established, the designation was irrevocable and no substitutions were permitted for any reason whatsoever.

The net effect of these procedures was that two separately projectable samples existed; one of the male population, 18 years of age or older and another of the female population, 18 years of age or older. The distribution of the male sample was disproportionately allocated to a greater extent to the upper income A stratum.

Designation of television diary subsample

Since the respondents were initially interviewed on a year-round basis with the magazine and marketing questionnaires, it was expected that some of them would be deceased or residing somewhere else when the television data would be collected. Consequently, this expected loss needed to be considered in deciding upon the total subsample to be assigned to obtain approximately 7,000 completed two-week diaries. In total, return visits were made to 10,000 respondents to request their participation in the television portion of the survey. The selections were systematically made with random starting points in each cluster. As in the past, the respondents were encouraged to participate by the offer of a premium. Each respondent had a choice of four gifts from which to select.

RECOVERY OF SAMPLE RESPONDENTS

Among the 10,000 respondents who were the designated in the television diary subsample, it was found 961 had moved from their previous residence and 192 were either deceased or so seriously infirm so as to preclude them from further participation in the survey. It should be pointed out that the 961 respondents classified as no longer residing at previous residence does not include those who made changes of residence within the cluster area or who moved to nearby residence. Such respondents were pursued and in many cases their cooperation was obtained.

A total of 7,183 (81.2 percent) of the remaining 8,847 respondents agreed to maintain the two-week television diaries; 15.6 percent refused and 7.1 per cent could not be found at home despite repeated callbacks. Since the full two-weeks of data was required in order for a respondent to be tabulated in the television reach and frequency report, those respondents from whom diaries for both weeks could not be obtained were excluded. In total, therefore, 6,834 respondents (77.3 percent of the eligible respondents) with completed first and second week diaries were used in the tabulations. The total includes 2,884 men and 3,950 women.

The attainment of this high cooperation rate is attributable in great part to the skill and experience of the interviewers. Probably their two previous visits to the respondents served to develop a rapport which was helpful in achieving the diary cooperation. Throughout the course of their work the interviewers were repeatedly reminded of the need to maintain this rapport. The gifts previously given to the respondents for their cooperation with the market questionnaire must have also served to develop the necessary cooperative frame of mind. As a further inducement, however, more expensive additional gifts were offered to the respondents for their cooperation in keeping the diaries. These handsome gifts included a transistor radio, a flash equipped camer kit, a high intensity lamp and a traveling alarm clock.

The recovery was achieved despite the added disproportionate allocation to the twenty Simmons Marketing Areas and to the normally "hard-to-interview" upper income areas. A great many interviews were obtained only by virtue of the fact that interviewers made personal visits on as many different evenings as they felt were necessary in order to contact respondents not easily found at home.

In addition to the considerable effort made to place diaries with "hard-to-find" respondents, every attempt was made to overcome refusals. Interviewers were instructed on how to deal with problems of this nature. "Hard-core" refusal cases were turned over to special interviewers who had been particularly successful in overcoming refusals. Finally, personal letters explaining the nature and purpose of the study, telegrams, and even long distance calls were employed as a last resort.

WEIGHTING AND PROJECTING THE SAMPLE

Since the probability of selection was precisely known for each of the five stages of the selection process, the weights could be based on the reciprocal of these probabilities. The final weight applied to each completed interview, therefore, was determined by the sample selection procedures previously described plus an additional factor based on recovery in each interviewing area. Each separate population group measured, i.e., adult males and adult females, was weighted independently since they in fact constituted separate samples and differences in distribution and recovery of these samples may have had differential effect on the estimates.

As a first step in the weighting process, estimates of the number of households in the population were projected, taking into consideration the probability of selecting the cluster and the growth shown by the prelisting made for the cluster. The probability of selecting the cluster was obtained by multiplying the probabilities of the first three stages of selection, i.e., (p1)   X   (p2)   X   (p3)

where:

p1 = the probability that the Primary Sampling Unit in which the individual lives was selected from among all the Primary Sampling Units in the stratum.

p2 = the probability that the Census Tract or Minor Civil Division in which the individual lives was selected from among all the Census Tracts and Minor Civil Divisions in the Primary Sampling Unit.

p3 = the probability that the cluster (city block or Census Enumeration District) in which the individual lives was selected from among all the city blocks or Census Enumeration Districts in the Census Tract or Minor Civil Division.

The inverse of this probability was then multiplied by the aggregate number of housing units in the cluster, including the growth (or loss) as indicated by the prelisting.

Recovery equalization factors were then applied to the sampling rates for each within each cluster. When the number of interviews obtained in any one cluster was too small, similar or adjacent clusters in the same stratum were combined. In this way, the non-recovered households were accounted for separately for each sex, for each income stratum and for each Primary Sampling Unit. New households found at the time of the interviewing through the application of the "half-open interval" procedure were also given the composite weight for that cluster and sex.

Each recovered interview was also assigned a weight equal to the reciprocal of the probability with which the respondent was selected from among the eligible individuals in the household. For example, a female respondent living in a household with one other woman came into the sample with a probability of 1/2 and would have been given an additional weight of 2; a female respondent living in a household with two other women came into the sample with a probability of 1/3 and would have been given an additional weight of 3; etc.

Further, in order to equalize the contribution of each month's sample in the total projected sample, the interviews from each month were weighted to approximately equal totals. This served to count each magazine issue studied on an equal basis in making the audience estimates.

Weighting of the diary subsample

This stage in weighting proceeded by first multiplying the original weight each sample case had in the total sample by the inverse of the net effective subsampling rate. Essentially this gave the sample cases in the subsample a total weight equivalent to that of the total population under study. This total weight was then cross-tabulated into some thirty to forty demographic cells (not all of which were independent of one another). The distribution of these demographic criteria was then compared to the distribution as shown by the total sample. This served to pinpoint the population subgroups which were affected by differential recovery in the field. A series of ratio adjustments were then applied which brought the demographic distributions into line with those shown by the total sample.

AUDIENCE DETERMINATION AND DEFINITIONS

The audience of any program includes each person who recorded in his diary that he viewed any part of the average half-hour of the program. This year, audiences for all programs are reported in terms of the *average* half-hour—that is, the number of people viewing *any part of* each half hour of a program are summed and divided by the total number of half hours. Since each person kept a diary for a two-week period, the average half-hour audience for an hour program, shown once a week, would include the sum of all the people viewing each of the four half hours (over the two-week period) divided by four.

Audience estimates for weekday, daytime shows were obtained the same way. However, since these shows are generally shown every weekday, the audience for each of the ten weekdays (over a two-week period) was summed and divided by 10, producing an estimate for the average half-hour (or, in this case, average day).

Included in all audience estimates are estimates for delayed telecasts shown in particular localities at times other than their regularly scheduled times.

Handling preemptions

The diary period was actually spread over four weeks and each person kept a diary for a consecutive two weeks within this period. However, some shows were preempted during one or more of these weeks. Therefore, respondents maintaining diaries during any of the weeks that these shows were preempted would not have had an opportunity to be in the audience of the program for the week in question. In order to compensate for this, the following procedure was adopted:

Audience estimates (both the average audience and the two week net-unduplicated audiences) for each preempted show were tabulated from diaries in which respondents had an opportunity to view the show during one or both of the two weeks in which they kept the diaries. These audience estimates were then ratio adjusted up to the total population by the value of N/N_1 where N = the total population, and N_1 = the measured populaton with an opportunity to view the show. In ratio adjusting these estimates, the demographic proportions of the measured population were kept essentially intact. That is, this estimating procedure was used in a number of mutually exclusive demographic cells totally to the entire population studied.

To avoid the application of ratio factors in tabulating viewing was randomly ascribed to the preempted population. This was done separately within each of the demographic cells whereby the ratio adjusted estimates for that cell where achieved by the random assignment of viewing to individual diary keepers who were affected by the preemption, i.e., those who kept diaries during the period in which the preemption occurred.

There were three prime time programs which were affected twice by preemptions during the diary period. This precluded the possibility of producing reach and frequency estimates, and reduced the reliability of the average audience estimates. Consequently, estimates for these three programs, *Adam 12*, *Doris Day*, and *Kraft Music Hall* are excluded from the Television Audience Report and the Television Audience Reach and Frequency Report.

Audiences by day part and half-hour segments

The following day parts are shown:

a.   7:30 p.m. to 11:00 p.m.   Sunday through Saturday (prime time)
b.   11:00 p.m. to 1:00 a.m.   Sunday through Saturday (late fringe)

c.   5:00 p.m. to   7:30 p.m.   Monday through Friday (early fringe)

d.   8:00 a.m. to 10:00 a.m.   Monday through Friday

e.   1:00 p.m. to   5:00 p.m.   Monday through Friday

f.   8:00 a.m. to   1:00 p.m.   Saturday and Sunday

g.   1:00 p.m. to   5:00 p.m.   Saturday and Sunday

h.   5:00 p.m. to   7:30 p.m.   Saturday and Sunday

The time periods are presented in terms of network time (New York Time) rather than local time. Thus, in the Central Time zone and in the Mountain Time zone, where telecasts are shown one hour and two hours earlier, respectively, than in New York, the time of viewing was recoded to correspond to New York time. Telecasts in the Pacific Time zone follow the same time schedule as in New York.

For each day part, audience figures are shown for weekly and daily net reach as well as for the average half-hour. Weekly net reach includes all men (or women) who have viewed any television during a particular time period in an average week. Since all data is based on two full weeks of viewing information, the net audience for each week is summed and divided by two.

Daily net reach includes those adults reached during a particular day part in an average day. It is obtained by summing the audience estimates for each of 14 days (or ten days for weekday day parts or four days for weekend day parts) and dividing by 14 (or ten or four, respectively).

Average half-hour audiences are obtained by summing the audiences for each half-hour in a particular day part and then dividing by the total number of half-hours. In the case of prime time (7:30 p.m.-11:00 p.m.), this would be 98 half-hours. Thus, the average half-hour audience for any day part is proportionately weighted by the heavy viewers in that time segment.

Half-hour time periods are always based on an average day. Thus, the audience for each period is obtained by summing the audiences for each of the 14 days (or ten days for weekday time periods) and dividing by the total number of days.

Quintiles of frequency of viewing

The criterion used to classify respondents into viewing quintiles was based on the number of hours they viewed in the designated day part across an average week. That is, the number of hours each respondent viewed over a two-week period was summed and divided by two. The criteria used for each quintile are:

Range of number of hours viewed in an average week for each quintile

	Bottom 20%	Next 20%	Next 20%	Next 20%	Top 20%
MEN					
Total viewing	0- 7.00	7.25-13.50	13.75-19.50	19.75-28.25	28.50 and over
Prime time	0- 2.75	00- 6.00	6.25- 9.75	10.00-14.25	14.50 and over
WOMEN					
Total viewing	0-10.00	10.25-17.50	17.75-25.75	26.00-36.50	36.75 and over
Prime time	0- 4.00	4.25- 8.00	8.25-11.75	12.00-16.00	16.25 and over
Weekday daytime	0	0.25- 2.00	2.25- 5.50	5.75-11.75	12.00 and over

County size and geographic region

Two of the demographics used in the Comprehensive Report are county size and geographic region. They are defined as follows:

County size
County size A - All counties belonging to the 25 largest metropolitan areas.
County size B - Counties over 120,000 population that are not in Class A (25 largest Metro areas) plus counties that are part of the metropolitan area of cities in such B counties.
County size C - Counties not included under A or B having over 32,000 population plus counties that are part of the metropolitan area of cities in such C counties.
County size D - All remaining counties.

Geographic regions were determined in accordance with standard Bureau of the Census definitions. The four regions in this report represent state groupings as shown below:

Northeast .... Maine, Vermont, New Hampshire, Massachusetts, Connecticut, Rhode Island, New York, Pennsylvania, New Jersey.

South .... Delaware, Maryland, Washington, D. C., Virginia, West Virginia, North Carolina, South Carolina, Georgia, Florida, Kentucky, Tennessee, Mississippi, Alabama, Louisiana, Arkansas, Oklahoma, Texas.

Central .... Ohio, Indiana, Illinois, Wisconsin, Michigan, Minnesota, Iowa, Missouri, Kansas, Nebraska, South Dakota, North Dakota.

West .... Montana, Idaho, Wyoming, Colorado, New Mexico, Arizona, Utah, Nevada, Washington, Oregon, California.

ATTENTIVENESS OF VIEWING

This report includes the results of a new measurement that was shown for the first time in the 1967 Standard Television Report, "Attentiveness of Viewing". For each 15-minute period that a respondent reported viewing a program, he was asked to record whether he was:
1. Out of the television room for most of the period;

2. In the television room, paying some attention, for most of the period;

3. In the television room, paying full attention for most of the period.

Attention levels were tabulated in half-hour intervals. A respondent who reported differences in attention levels between two quarter hours of a half-hour program segment was tabulated as "Paying some attention" for the whole half-hour segment. This means of tabulation tends to understate somewhat the extremes of this scale and correspondingly overstate the "Paying some attention" portion of the scale.

Attention levels are reported for the average half-hour of each program. In addition, attention levels are shown by day part, by selected demographic characteristics within each day part and by half-hour time segments.

Day part audiences are based on average half-hour tabulations. That is, the audiences for each half-hour within a day part are summed, and this number is then divided by the total number of half-hours. Demographic characteristics within each day part are determined in a similar manner.

Attention levels for each half-hour segment represent an average day. To get this, the audiences for a specific half-hour segment are summed across a two-week period and divided by the total number of days (14 for evening programs, 10 for weekday daytime programs, etc.)

LISTING OF SHOWS WITHIN EACH PROGRAM TYPE

The classification of the programs included under each type, and the number of half-hour segments for each program, are as follows:

Prime time evening shows

Action/adventure: 11 half-hour segments, 5 programs
  It Takes A Thief (2)
  Land of the Giants (2)
  Mission Impossible (2)
  Name of the Game (3)
  Then Came Bronson (2)
Comedy/variety: 10 half-hour segments, 5 programs
  Carol Burnett (2)
  Jackie Gleason (2)
  Red Skelton (2)
  Rowan & Martin (2)
  Love American Style (2)
Family adventure: 6 half-hour segments, 4 programs
  Daniel Boone (2)
  Lassie (1)

    Walt Disney (Wonderful World of Color) (2)
    Wild Kingdom (1)
General drama: 12 half-hour segments, 6 programs
    Bold Ones (The) (2)
    Bracken's World (2)
    Marcus Welby MD (2)
    Medical Center (UMC) (2)
    New People (2)
    Survivors (The) (2)
General variety: 23 1/2 half-hour segments, 12 programs
    Andy Williams (2)
    Dean Martin (2)
    Ed Sullivan (2)
    Glen Campbell Hour (2)
    Hollywood Palace (2)
    Jimmy Durante-Lennon Sisters (2)
    Jim Nabor's Hour (2)
    Kraft Music Hall (2)
    Lawrence Welk (2)
    Leslie Uggams (2)
    Music Scene (1 1/2)
    This is Tom Jones (2)
Movies: 31 half-hour segments, 8 programs
    Sunday Night Movie (4)
    Monday Night Movie (4)
    Tuesday Night Movie (4)
    Wednesday Night Movie (4)
    Thursday Night Movie (4)
    Friday Night Movie (4)
    Saturday Night Movie (4)
    Movie of the Week (3)
Mystery/police drama: 12 half-hour segments, 7 programs
    Adam 12 (1)
    Dragnet (1)
    FBI (2)
    Hawaii Five-O (2)
    Ironsides (2)
    Mannix (2)
    Mod Squad (2)
Situation comedy: 27 half-hour segments, 27 programs
    Beverly Hillbillies (1)
    Bewitched (1)
    Bill Cosby Show (1)
    Brady Bunch (1)
    Courtship of Eddie's Father (1)

Debbie Reynolds (1)
Doris Day (1)
Family Affair (1)
Flying Nun (1)
Get Smart (1)
Ghost & Mrs. Muir (1)
Governor & J. J. (1)
Good Guys (1)
Green Acres (1)
Here Come the Brides (1)
Here's Lucy (1)
Hogan's Heroes (1)
I Dream of Jeanie (1)
Julia (1)
Mayberry RFD (1)
Mr. Deeds Goes To Town (1)
My World and Welcome To It (1)
Room 222 (1)
My Three Sons (1)
Petticoat Junction (1)
That Girl (1)
To Rome With Love (1)
Western: 11 half-hour segments, 5 programs
Bonanza (2)
Gunsmoke (2)
High Chaparral (2)
Lancer (2)
Virginian (3)
Quiz/audience participation: 3 half-hour segments, 3 programs
Let's Make a Deal (1)
Newlywed Game (1)
Dating Game (1)
Quiz/audience participation: 13 half-hour segments, 13 programs
Anniversary Game (1)
Concentration (1)
Dating Game (1)
Dream House (1)
Hollywood Squares (1)
It Takes Two (1)
It's Your Bet (1)
Jeopardy (1)
Let's Make a Deal (1)
Name Droppers (1)
Newlywed Game (1)

Sale of the Century (1)
You're Putting Me On (1)
Serials: 15 half-hour segments, 15 programs
Another World (1)
As the World Turns (1)
Bright Promise (1)
Dark Shadows (1)
Days of Our Lives (1)
Doctors (1)
Edge of Night (1)
General Hospital (1)
Guiding Light (1)
Love is a Many Splendored Thing (1)
Love of Life (1)
One Life to Live (1)
Search for Tomorrow (1)
Secret Storm (1)
Where the Heart Is (1)
Situation comedy: 7 half-hour segments, 7 programs
Andy of Mayberry (1)
Bewitched (1)
Beverly Hillbillies (1)
Gomer Pyle USMC (1)
Letters to Laugh In (1)
Lucy (1)
That Girl (1)

RELIABILITY OF RESULTS

Estimates for television program audiences are based on the sample of respondents who maintained television diaries for the two-week period.

The tolerance limits applicable to the audience figures depend upon the variation among sampling units within each stratum, the number of sampling units selected, and the method of their selection of each stage at which sampling operations were performed. Each variable estimated will be affected somewhat differently as a result of this variation, and therefore each reported figure will have its own tolerance.

The following table shows average estimates of two-sigma tolerances, as applicable to adult audiences of different sizes. These estimated tolerances were computed based on the relative variation within audience estimates.

Estimated two-sigma tolerance** (in thousands)

Level of estimate (000)	Programs of a half hour duration or individual half hours*	Average half hour estimates for progragrams of one hour duration	Average half hour estimates for programs of more than one hour duration
20,000	1450	1350	1250
15,000	1275	1200	1100
12,500	1100	1050	920
10,000	900	860	810
9,000	870	825	790
8,000	830	800	760
7,000	800	750	720
6,000	780	725	700
5,000	720	675	625
4,000	650	625	590
3,000	575	525	475
2,500	550	475	450
1,000	350	325	300

*Tolerances for Daytime (Daily) TV audiences are approximately 1/2 of those for evening shows.

**This means that if every individual in the population under study had been interviewed using the same questionnaire, there are 19 chances out of 20 that the results obtained would not differ from the reported figure by more than the number shown.

Children's Use of Television and Other Media

Jack Lyle
and
Heidi R. Hoffman

University of California at Los Angeles

This report begins with a section briefly summarizing the major findings of the study, devoid of technical details and with a minimum of tables. We hope this will make it easier for the general reader to get an overview of our results. Those who wish more details will find them in the sections which follow and in the Technical Appendix.

TELEVISION IN THE DAILY LIVES OF CHILDREN

How much time do children spend watching television? What programs do children watch?

How does television viewing—in terms of both the time spent watching and the programs selected—relate to such factors as age, sex, ability, socioeconomic and racial characteristics, and factors of social adjustment?

How does the relationship of children to television compare with that which existed a decade earlier?

These were the major questions addressed by the study reported here. Put another way, this study sought to document some baselines concerning the actual day-to-day use children make of television.

This type of data is not available from the usual television rating services. And while there have been various studies over the years looking either at some aspects of children's viewing or of specific subgroups of students (See Atkin, Murray and Nayman, 1971), the last comprehensive effort in this field was *Television in the Lives of Our Children* (Schramm, Lyle, and Parker), a book published in 1961 and based on data collected in 1959. The decade which has passed since that work was published has been one of considerable change, particularly with regard to "youth culture" and with regard to the impact of television upon society and upon children in particular. Thus, there was some urgency for a new look at children's actual use of television and other media.

To obtain this "new look" we turned to a small town on the fringes of the greater Los Angeles complex. We obtained individual interviews and one-day viewing records from a 25 percent sample of first graders—274 youngsters in the 12 public and three church elementary schools. Followup telephone interviews were conducted with 114 mothers of first graders. Data, including viewing records for a five-day period (Sunday through Thursday), were gathered from the community's population of sixth and tenth graders, using self-administered questionnaires. Because of absences, the number of sixth and tenth graders varied from day to day, but generally we were dealing with over 800 sixth graders and about 500 tenth graders each day.

Details about the town, its schools, and the methodology used are provided in the Technical Appendix.

In brief, the town is a working-class community with a mixed economy based on heavy industry and agriculture. Of the 21,000 residents, 16 percent are Mexican-American, and six percent black. Residents can receive the seven Los Angeles VHF television stations plus six UHF stations, including two noncommercial educational stations and two which program almost exclusively in the Spanish language.

The study was conducted in early May 1970.[1]

Basic findings on amount of use

There is hardly a child in this country who does not have access to a television set. The 1970 Census estimated that 96 percent of all American homes contain a television set. Among our students, the figure was

98 percent. There was also a high likelihood that the home contained more than one set, particularly if there were older children in the household. While only 29 percent of the first graders said there was more than one set at home, 61 percent of the tenth graders said their family had two or more sets. And over half the children had access to a color set.

How much time did children spend watching television? This is a complex question. There may be great variation in viewing time for the same individual from day to day. Further, it is specious to think of *the* "child audience." Patterns of viewing time and program selection change almost from year to year so that there are very different audiences at different ages of childhood and adolescence. Sex differences, particularly in program preferences, are apparent by the time the child enters the first grade.

Most children do watch at least some television every day. Most watch for at least two hours; many may watch considerably longer. In the study town, over one-quarter of the sixth graders and only a slightly smaller proportion of the tenth graders watched at least five and one-half hours on a given school day (Table 6).[2] About equal proportions spent no time before the set. Well over one-third of the first graders watched for four hours or more, but the proportion of non-viewers was less than ten percent. For older children, viewing time increased on Sundays.

Television watching, together with sleep and school, is one of the major activities of the vast majority of children. Over a week-long period, the first graders spent the equivalent of just less than one full day watching television; sixth and tenth graders exceeded that level (see Table 1).

Several things appear to happen to viewing patterns as the child grows older. The amount of time spent viewing builds to a peak somewhere around the period at which the child approaches adolescence. Then it begins a decline. Sixth and tenth graders spent more time watching over the weekend than the first graders did; first and sixth graders spent more time watching in the afternoons than did the tenth graders.

For the younger children the later afternoon was a peak viewing period (Table 8). Almost two-thirds of the first graders and over half the sixth graders were at their sets just before dinner. Tenth grade viewing, on the other hand, did not peak until prime time began at 7 p.m., although one-third of this older group also did some afternoon viewing.

Many of the younger children—one-third of the first graders, one-fifth of those in grade six—watched in the morning before going to school.

Most of the first graders had dropped out of the audience (and were in bed) by 9 p.m. The sixth grade audience began to decline at 9:30 p.m., but as many as 25 percent might still be watching as late as 11 p.m. The teenage audience held strong until 11 p.m., then dropped to well under 20 percent.

Table 1: Projected weekly total viewing time*

	First grade		Sixth grade		Tenth grade	
	Boys	Girls	Boys	Girls	Boys	Girls
Weekdays only	17:43	17:00	17:12	18:21	16:07	17:80
Week total	22:03	23:57	30:17	31:17	27:23	28:28

*These figures were arrived at by estimated Friday viewing as equal to the average of viewing time on other week days and by assuming that viewing on Saturday was equal to Sunday viewing. Both assumptions, particularly the latter, are open to challenge.

The number of black students was too small to provide reliable comparisons, but among the small sample available they tended to spend more time viewing than their age peers. There was also a marked difference in the average viewing time of Mexican-American and "Anglo" girls at both the sixth and tenth grade levels, but the difference between the boys was not consistent (Table 72B).

Among the sixth graders the brightest students were among the heaviest users of all media, including television. In the tenth grade, the brighter students viewed somewhat less television than their classmates (Table 68.)

Program preferences

Students were asked to name their four favorite programs (Tables 12 and 13). From their recall diaries of previous day viewing, we were able to measure the audience of individual programs Sunday through Thursday for each age group (Table 11).

Among the first graders, the most popular programs were situation comedies and cartoon shows. The sixth graders had dropped the cartoons and were giving increased attention to family situation comedies and to adventure programs. Adventure programs dominated the preferences of tenth graders, who had replaced family situation comedies with dramatic and music/variety shows as favorites.

Scrutiny of the lists suggests that children of the several age groups were attracted to shows featuring characters near to them in age. This was further supported by first-grade responses to questions on character identification and preference. Black children were also strongly attracted to shows featuring black characters.

The students in this town had two educational stations available. Both were UHF stations, but the vast majority of students indicated that their home sets were equipped for UHF reception. For all practical purposes, however, there was no viewing of either of these stations by students at any grade level. There also was very little viewing of the two Spanish-language stations by the Mexican-American students.

Further, there was almost no viewing of news programs, even among the tenth graders. This was particulary true during the 5-7:30 p.m. period when the major daily news presentations are scheduled. It should be noted that the largest audiences of young students were gathered in this time period. But they were watching *Gilligan's Island, Flintstones, My Favorite Martian*, and *I Love Lucy* reruns, not the news.

One of the intriguing findings of the study was the immense popularity of these programs and their characters among the elementary school age children. They seemed content to watch these programs over and over and still over once again.

Viewing of violent programs

And what about viewing of violence? In another study of this series (Greenberg and Gordon), a list of the 20 most violent television series was established using ratings by a sample of the public and of television critics. Of the 20 "most violent" programs, 14 were regularly scheduled in ten time slots during the five-day period for which viewing records were available. Thus the youngsters could have watched as many as ten of these programs during the five days.

An analysis was made of the records for the sixth- and tenth-grade students for whom there was a complete set of viewing records for the five-day period.[3] The average number of these programs watched over the five days was two. Almost one-quarter of each age group saw none of these shows; one-fifth of each age group watched four or more. No one saw more than eight (Table 107).

The differences in the audience won by these programs are interesting (Table 108). Two of the shows clearly dominated their time slots: *Bonanza* and *Mod Squad. Mod Squad's* dominance was particularly pronounced among the tenth graders. *Mission Impossible* and *The Bold Ones* competed against each other. Between them, they had over 80 percent of the youngsters watching in those time periods. In another competition situation, *Then Came Bronson* had almost twice as many tenth grade viewers as *Hawaii Five-O*, but *Bronson* was less popular among the sixth graders. More significantly, *Room 222*, which was also shown in this time slot, led among the sixth graders and was well ahead of *Hawaii Five-0* (but not *Bronson*) among the tenth graders. *Ironsides* was eclipsed by *Bewitched* among both grade groups.

The point to be drawn is that many of these "most violent" programs were on the air when there were many young people in the audience—as many as 64 percent of the sixth graders—and that they frequently did command the greatest share of these young audiences.

Higher than average viewing of violent programs did relate to certain aspects of the child's social and family life at the sixth and tenth grade levels. The heavy viewers of violence reported significantly higher levels of conflict with their parents over grades and spending. Among the sixth-grade heavy violence viewers, there was also greater conflict over clothes and hair styles.

At the tenth grade level, the heavy violence viewers reported a higher incidence of parental complaint about their television viewing; they were more likely to watch television when they were lonely; they were more likely to accept the people they saw on television as being like people they meet in real life.

Program selection

At all age levels, it appeared that students were most likely to just turn the set on and flip channels to see if there was a program on that interested them, although most of them said that they at least sometimes used a television log prior to viewing (Tables 9 and 10).[4]

However, most of the students—even at the first-grade level—said that if they didn't find anything on that interested them, they turned the set off. The majority of both sixth and tenth graders said that this occurred at least "sometimes," and almost one-third said it was "usually" the case.

Most viewing was done in the company of siblings, parents, or both (Table 43). There was a high incidence of reported conflict with both siblings and parents over program selection (Table 48 and 49). While compromise solutions increased with age, generally the younger party to the conflict deferred to an older person. For the sixth and tenth graders, this most frequently meant bowing to parental desires, particularly those of the father.

Similarly, of all the mass media, television was the most frequent source of parental complaint; well over one-third of the older students said their parents did complain at least "now and then." The complaints were fairly evenly divided among "watching too much," "watching too late," and program selection (Table 45).

Although the majority of the first grade mothers interviewed stated that they did try to guide program selection for their young children, few indicated that they attempted to restrict the amount of viewing. About one-third of the students themselves said that their parents tried to control their viewing, either "now" or "when they were younger" (Tables 46 and 47).

Television's impact on other activities

Not only does the child spend a large share of his waking hours with television, but he also uses it in connection with other activities. Just as viewing time begins to decline in adolescence, so there is evidence that the importance of television to the youngsters begins to slide in this period.

About half the first graders said that they use things they've seen on television as a model for social play "sometimes" or "often." Solitary play based on television content was reported by 30 percent (Table 52).

Television did intrude on the dreams of these children. Four out of ten of the first graders said that they remembered dreaming about things they'd seen on television (Table 60).

Children admitted to having been frightened by television — 40 percent of the first-grade boys, 60 percent of the girls (Table 60). It is difficult to say exactly what this means. Many of the shows children mentioned as having frightened them were also their favorites. We must keep in mind that children do seem to enjoy being frightened to some degree.

Things seen on television provided students at all ages with a major topic of conversation. Television appeared to be more frequently discussed with friends than with parents, among sixth graders than among tenth graders (Tables 50 and 51).

Sixth and tenth graders were asked how likely they thought they would be to engage in a variety of activities under five different circumstances: when lonely, when angry, when their feelings had been hurt, when they just wanted to relax, and when they wanted to be entertained.[5] Television scored highest relative to other activities for entertainment, relaxation, and relief from loneliness. It was a much less likely choice when angry or suffering from hurt feelings (Table 64).

Again, there was strong evidence that television's personal importance declined with age. Except for entertainment, the percentages feeling that they'd be likely to turn to television were lower in each situation among tenth than among sixth graders. Among the older students, music surged to the front, even in the entertainment category (Table 65).

Schramm and his colleagues commented on the fact that brighter students among their sixth graders somehow managed to combine large amounts of television viewing with higher than average use of other media. Among the 1970 children, this held true for the tenth graders as well. The brighter tenth-grade students were likely to be high in television viewing as well as in reading and in sports, hobbies, and social activities. There was a relationship between high television viewing and decreased social activity among high viewers who did not also read.

This raises the speculation that perhaps this generation of 1970, the second television generation, has grown up under conditions which have taught youngsters so inclined to accommodate large amounts of television without sacrificing other activities. It is true that there was some evidence of a slight decline in the use of some other media compared to the 1959 levels—particularly reading. But the 1959 levels were already low, particularly among tenth graders.

The most disturbing results uncovered in this area were that the heavy viewers among first graders did report a lower incidence of after-school play with other children—even though play remained their preferred activity. Yet those sixth and tenth graders who were habitual heavy viewers of television on schoolday afternoons showed little evidence to suggest that the television viewing was related to social isolation of the students. The level of participation in various social, recreational, hobby, and work activities was not significantly related to the amount of time spent watching television—either total viewing time or afternoon viewing time.

Attitudes toward television

The majority of the sixth and tenth graders—more than three-quarters —felt that they were learning from television at least some of the time. And nine out of ten of the first grade mothers said that they felt their children were learning from television. For the most part they felt this learning was beneficial, although one-fifth of them did mention negative aspects. The mothers felt the television increasing the vocabularies of the young children, helping prepare them for school, and teaching them "about life."

Most students, even at the first-grade level, expressed considerable skepticism about the realism of what they saw on television. It is difficult to attach a value judgment to this finding; one might argue that much, if not most, television content is designed to entertain rather than to present a realistic portrayal of the world. It is interesting to note that first graders were more likely to accept child characters on television as being like themselves and their friends than they were to accept television adults as being like the grownups they knew.

As to television news—which most students did not watch, 60 percent felt that if they saw something on television news, they could be sure it was true at least most of the time.

Eight percent of the mothers felt that there were bad aspects of television. About one-quarter of these mothers volunteered complaints about violence in television programs. More mothers—over one-third—complained about commercials.

Nine out of ten of the students at both sixth and tenth grade levels felt that there were too many commercials, and the majority gave commercials a low vote on credibility. The students showed very low levels of concern about the amount of sex and violence on television.

Television viewing is not passive

The responses of students at all three age groups document that much of the time recorded as "television viewing time" is actually divided among the television set and other activities. Fewer than 20 percent of the first graders said that they never did other things while watching television. About half the older students said that they sometimes study while the television set is on. Students generally reported a high frequency of discussion with parents and siblings while they watch television. The largest part of this discussion did touch on program content, but it also ranged over other topics (Table 16 and 18).

Comparison with 1959

Compared with the children in the seven United States cities and towns used in the 1959 study, the children in this 1970 study town at all three age levels were watching more television (Table 2). Using the data from "Clifton," the 1959 study community most similar to the present one, both first and sixth graders were watching about an hour more per schoolday. Sunday viewing was up more than 15 minutes for first graders and more than two and one-half hours for sixth graders. (The Clifton data included only elementary school students, but the present tenth graders had higher schoolday and Sunday viewing than the 1959 tenth graders in San Francisco and all five Rocky Mountain towns studied.)

Table 2: Comparison of viewing times, 1959 and 1970

| | Median estimated viewing time for weekdays* — 1959 | | | | 1970 | |
| | San Francisco | | Rocky Mt. towns | | Present study | |
	Boys	Girls	Boys	Girls	Boys	Girls
First grade	2:00	2:00	Not available		Not available	
Sixth grade	2:30	2:30	3:05 to 3:24		3:19	3:42
Tenth grade	2:45	2:48	2:12 to 3:00		3:03	3:13

	Median Recorded Viewing Time**	
	1959	1970
	"Clifton"	Present study
		Boys	Girls
Weekdays			
First grade	2:18	3:32	3:26
Sixth grade	2:30	3:26	3:40
Tenth grade	Not available	3:13	3:26
Sunday			
First grade	2:24	2:15	3:19
Sixth grade	3:54	6:37	6:28
Tenth grade	Not available	5:38	5:40

*These figures are based on responses to a question asking students to estimate how much time they spent watching television on an average school day.

**These figures are based on recall diaries of previous day viewing. Only elementary school students were included in the "Clifton" study.

The first graders in the present study, on the average, were in bed by 8:30 p.m. compared to 8 p.m. in 1959. Sixth grade bedtime also was later, 9:45 p.m. compared to 9:30 p.m. for the "Clifton" children.

Viewing before school on weekdays was about the same among first graders in 1959 and 1970, somewhat increased among sixth graders. There was a strong suggestion that television had increased its claim on the afternoon hours of children during this decade.

In 1959, the bright students in the sixth grade were among the heaviest users of all media, including television. In the tenth grade, the brighter students showed less viewing of television than their age peers and heavier use of books.

The situation remained much the same in 1970 among the sixth graders. Among the tenth graders, however, there was a change. While the high book users were predominantly brighter students, the fact remained that more of the brightest students were heavy users of television than were heavy users of books.

In both sixth and tenth grade there was a trend reminiscent of the differences found in 1959 between children of blue-collar and white-collar families: blue-collar children tended to watch more television than white-collar children.

While the difference in viewing time and patterns of media use did not appear as marked in 1970 as they were in the 1959 studies, there still were marked differences between these various groups in many of their attitudes toward television. White-collar and brighter students generally showed a more critical attitude toward television, specifically regarding commercials and the acceptance of television situations and characters as being lifelike. They also tended to be more selective in their viewing and to have a higher expectation of television (as reflected by their rejection of the statements that television should just be "fun" and that there is too much news on television).

In 1959, heavy use of television among white-collar children was found to be related to high conflict with parents. The 1970 situation was far less clearcut, perhaps due to the generally higher levels of viewing among all the groups. There was a trend for high viewing time to be related to high conflict. As already noted, significant relationships were found between heavy viewing of violent programs and conflict with parents.

Comparison of program selection in 1959 and 1970 shows considerable change. But it must be remembered that the program mix on the networks in 1959 was quite different from that in 1970. Students' program choices undoubtedly were influenced by the mix of programs available to them. For instance, the single most striking difference was the decline of westerns among the 1970 students compared to the 1959 students. But the number of westerns in 1970 was considerably smaller than that in 1959, and it should be noted that both *Bonanza* and *Gunsmoke* did fare reasonably well among older students. Another striking difference was the lower popularity of the *World of Disney* among the 1970 first graders. But again, this may reflect a change of emphasis in the content of this series, which now seems to feature more dramatic stories at the expense of the animated adventures which were more common in 1959.

Summary

For all practical purposes, every child in this town had access to at least one television set. Most youngsters, from first to tenth grade, spent at least two hours with the television set on school days. While young children watched in greatest numbers during the late afternoon, the largest child audiences went to programs which were made for adult or family audiences, not to "child programs." Beyond the first grade there appeared to be little parental monitoring or control of viewing, although the fact that much viewing was done in the evening meant it was done in the company of parents.

While the amount of time spent with television appeared to have increased over the past decade, heavy viewing of television *per se* did not appear to be related to reduced levels of other activities nor to use of other media. Indeed, children who were high users of both television and books were equally or more likely than their classmates to be among the most active in sports, recreation, and social activities. But the importance of television to youngsters did decline quite markedly during the adolescent years as they developed new social relationships and increasingly turned to music.

Neither the amount of television watched nor selection of violent programs was related to antiestablishment attitudes.

The authors of the 1959 studies remarked on how quickly children seemed to have adopted television viewing as normal behavior, to take its availability for granted. The younger generation of 1970 appeared to take television even more for granted. It is there; they expect it to be there, and they most likely will make extensive use of it during any given day. However, they also appeared to be somewhat blasé. Most learned at an early age to discount much of the content; most became antipathetic toward and resentful of commercials. But most also felt that they are learning from television.

Many of the most popular shows among youngsters are programs of adventure featuring excessive violence. But there is hope in the fact that low-key programs dealing with people their own age in situations they understand also can pull large audiences.

BASIC PATTERNS OF TELEVISION USE

The basic pattern of the life cycle was consistent through the school week for each age group. The rising and bedtimes for each are shown in Table 3. On Sundays the sixth and tenth graders went to bed approximately half an hour later than they did on weeknights.

The rising time reflected the exceptionally early high school day. Many of the children are bussed to school, a factor pushing their rising time earlier.

The school hours for each grade were:

First Grade	8:45 a.m. to 2:00 p.m.
Sixth Grade	8:45 a.m. to 3:00 p.m.
Tenth Grade	7:55 a.m. to 2:30 p.m.

Table 3: Basic dimensions of students' day

Average:	First grade	Sixth grade	Tenth grade
Rising time	7:20	6:40	6:10
Bed time	8:30	9:45	10:10
Number of waking hours	12:50	15:00	16:00
Hours in school (includes lunch time)	5:15	6:15	6:35

Television availability

Television saturation was almost total; only 2 percent of the students stated that there was not a working television set in their home. Among the older students most homes had multiple sets. The number of multiple sets and the presence of color was higher among the older students, but even at the first-grade level over half the homes had color (Table 4).

In most instances (78 percent) the set was located in the living room. The family room was the next most frequent location (11 percent). Only some 6 percent of the children reported having a set in their bedrooms.[6]

Table 4: TV sets in home

Number of sets:	First grade	Sixth grade	Tenth grade
1	71%	48%	39%
2	24	38	38
3 or more	3	13	20
No set	2	2	3
Homes with color set	52%	50%	61%

Daily television viewing time

The average amount of time spent watching television for each of the five study days is shown in Table 5. Table 6 provides a breakdown by categories of viewing time on Sunday and Wednesday.

Among the three age groups studied, viewing peaked with the sixth grades. However, on weekdays the variation between the three grades generally was not great—a quarter to a half-hour in most instances. The most dramatic difference was on Sunday, when both older groups showed far more viewing than the first graders and when the sixth graders spent almost an hour more than the tenth graders.

Table 7 gives the distribution of daytime viewing on Sunday and Wednesday for the sixth and tenth grades. Relating this table to Table 6 suggests that the higher total viewing among sixth graders as compared to tenth graders was primarily attributable to increased daytime viewing by this age group. It will also be noted that daytime viewing was also higher among sixth graders on the weekday.

Table 5: Average daily TV viewing time

	First grade		Sixth grade		Tenth grade	
	Boys	Girls	Boys	Girls	Boys	Girls
Sunday	2:15	3:19	6:37	6:28	5:38	5:40
Monday	3:30	3:03	3:42	3:58	3:27	3:31
Tuesday	3:05	3:10	3:39	3:47	3:16	3:21
Wednesday	4:14	3:13	3:09	3:10	2:57	3:13
Thursday	3:12	4:17	3:56	3:46	3:14	3:38

Table 6: Categories of viewing time

	First grade			Sixth grade		Tenth grade	
	Boys	Girls		Boys	Girls	Boys	Girls
Sunday							
Up to 1:00	30%	31%	Up to 3:00	30%	30%	37%	38%
1:30 to 3:00	48	22	3:30 to 5:00	19	22	22	22
3:30 to 5:00	18	19	5:30 to 8:00	20	23	19	18
5:30 or more	4	28	8:30 or more	31	25	22	22
Wednesday							
No viewing	0%	11%	No viewing	30%	29%	25%	24%
0:30 to 2:00	13	30	0:30 to 3:00	24	24	37	30
2:30 to 3:30	43	30	3:30 to 5:00	21	20	16	19
4:00 or more	43	29	5:30 or more	25	27	22	26

Table 7: Categories of daytime viewing

	Sixth grade		Tenth grade	
	Boys	Girls	Boys	Girls
Sunday				
No viewing	23%	26%	38%	37%
0:30 to 2:00	20	27	25	23
2:30 to 4:30	23	21	15	20
5:00 or more	34	26	22	20
Average	3:33	3:00	2:20	2:07
Wednesday				
No viewing	29%	29%	46%	36%
0:30 to 1:00	24	18	19	14
1:30 to 2:30	24	29	20	34
3:00 or more	23	24	15	16
Average	1:29	1:35	1:00	1:16

With few exceptions, viewing times were similar for boys and girls. Among the sixth and tenth grades, what differences did appear generally showed more viewing by girls than boys. The differences among first graders were larger, but were not consistent.

Profile of viewing during the day. Tables 8A and 8B detail the percentages of each age group who were watching television at various times during Sunday and each weekday covered by the study.

It is evident that there was a considerable amount of Sunday daytime viewing, but that evening viewing on Sunday did not quite match the

Table 8A: Profile of Sunday viewing

% viewing at:	First grade	Sixth grade	Tenth grade	% viewing at	First grade	Sixth grade	Tenth grade
7:00 a.m.	16%	19%	7%	3:30 p.m.	2%	21%	21%
7:30	24	14	5	4:00	5	24	23
8:00	38	35	13	4:30	16	33	26
8:30	40	34	16	5:00	20	41	38
9:00	24	32	15	5:30	22	34	31
9:30	25	33	17	6:00	24	36	38
10:00	25	34	18	6:30	14	35	38
10:30	29	37	24	7:00	31	41	36
11:00	38	37	28	7:30	44	57	48
11:30	22	29	21	8:00	38	56	49
12 NOON	18	30	23	8:30	25	60	54
12:30 p.m.	22	34	27	9:00	16	52	57
1:00	16	35	33	9:30	11	42	43
1:30	18	29	28	10:00	-	28	38
2:00	16	30	29	10:30	-	23	32
2:30	16	33	30	11:00	-	9	12
3:00	9	28	24	11:30	-	8	10

Table 8B: Profile of weekday viewing

	First grade				Sixth grade				Tenth grade			
	M	Tu	W	Th	M	Tu	W	Th	M	Tu	W	Th
7:00 a.m.	35%	24%	20%	29%	17%	15%	17%	16%	3%	7%	3%	6%
7:30	18	17	26	29	22	22	21	23	3	4	3	5
3:00 p.m.	43	47	36	41	34	32	34	33	37	33	35	36
3:30	43	42	52	46	41	39	40	33	36	32	37	32
4:00	47	44	48	46	44	43	40	40	36	31	33	34
4:30	39	44	44	49	37	56	43	44	32	33	45	37
5:00	49	61	62	49	36	40	40	39	30	31	42	34
5:30	55	63	56	56	48	51	52	48	39	36	50	40
6:00	65	66	78	57	49	51	54	53	49	43	54	47
6:30	65	66	78	56	43	45	51	48	44	41	53	45
7:00	55	44	58	59	46	46	52	52	43	38	51	41
7:30	43	41	56	57	54	63	63	61	46	54	59	50
8:00	45	35	46	57	60	54	56	63	56	50	58	53
8:30	39	36	34	41	63	61	57	64	57	55	60	58
9:00	8	8	8	30	52	48	46	49	59	50	57	55
9:30	2	34	10	12	40	30	44	38	51	39	53	52
10:00	-	14	2	5	32	22	32	24	46	34	53	41
10:30	-	2	-	5	25	19	24	21	35	30	48	36
11:00	-	-	-	2	10	9	8	9	18	15	14	15
11:30	-	-	-	-	9	8	8	8	13	10	10	6

levels reached during the week. The younger children generally were more likely to watch television in the morning than were the tenth graders. The pattern of daytime viewing on Sunday was for the first graders to start earlier than either other group. By 8 a.m., over one-third of both the first and sixth graders were viewing. Sixth grade viewing continued at a fairly even rate throughout the day on Sunday, while the first graders trailed off and by midafternoon only a handful were still watching. Through the week there was little morning viewing by the tenth graders. However, one-third of these students were in the audience each weekday afternoon.

First grade viewing each evening peaked by 8 p.m., while the sixth grade audience held strong until 9 p.m. and the tenth graders until 11 p.m. It is interesting to note that while the student audience at 11:30 was generally small, the proportion of sixth graders watching was approximately equal to that of tenth graders among this hard core of late viewers.

The overall pattern appeared relatively stable throughout the week for each age group, suggesting that viewing might be largely habitual regardless of content. Therefore, let us now look at responses to items dealing with program selection.

Selection of programs. First graders were asked, "When you decide to watch TV, how do you decide what program to watch?" Almost half indicated some premeditation, about one-fourth indicated indiscriminate or opportunistic selection, and about one in ten said the selection was made by someone else—primarily a parent (Table 9).

Table 9: First grader program selection

When you decide to watch TV, how do you decide what to watch?	
Turn on to show I like	33%
Check the TV guide	16
Just turn the set on	11
Switch around the dial	17
Parent selects program	9
Sibling selects program	3
Other	11

When you're watching TV do you ever find that there's nothing on you want to watch? If so, what do you do?	Boys	Girls
Never find this the case	25%	12%
Keep on watching	15	18
Turn the set off	60	70
		p=.02

Other evidence suggesting discriminatory viewing by first graders was provided by their responses to the question "When you're watching television do you ever find that there's nothing on you want to watch?" If so, what do you do?" Roughly eight out of ten (82 percent) said that they did sometimes find this the case; of those, 80 percent said that in such cases they turned the set off. Boys were significantly less discriminating in this regard than girls.

The matter of program selection was treated somewhat differently among the older students. They were asked a series of three questions detailed in Table 10. Just turning the set on was more typical than checking the log for both sixth and tenth graders, but at both age levels most students said that they were likely to turn the set off if they couldn't find a program they wanted to watch.

Table 11 details the actual audience (in terms of the percentage of students at each grade level) for the most popular programs during the test week. The most obvious aspect of this set of data is the difference in general pattern of viewing by age groups. The early bedtime of the first graders meant that they had little chance to view many of the prime time programs. Indeed, the afternoon programs generally had larger audiences among the first graders than the evening programs, and two of the evening programs with the largest audience among this age group were repeats in the period prior to 7:30 p.m.

Table 10: Program selection by sixth and tenth graders

How often do you:

Turn the set on and change channels until you find something you like?

	Sixth grade		Tenth grade	
	Boys	Girls	Boys	Girls
Never	10%	9%	9%	9%
Not very often	15	18	20	21
Sometimes	29	29	28	32
Usually	45	43	43	39

Look at the TV log and decide whether to turn the set on or not?

	Sixth grade		Tenth grade	
Never	18%	13%	17%	9%
Not very often	19	19	24	17
Sometimes	32	30	53	47
Usually	31	38	33	45
				p=.02

Turn the set on and find there's nothing you want to watch and so turn the set off?

	Sixth grade		Tenth grade	
Never	10%	7%	10%	7%
Not very often	21	20	23	24
Sometimes	36	41	42	39
Usually	33	32	26	30

Daytime viewing was also important among the sixth graders. Four of the daytime series had a sixth grade audience as large or larger than all but ten prime time programs. It should be noted that among both first and sixth graders, the percentages viewing and the share of audience for the afternoon programs was relatively constant from day to day. With the exception of *Hobo Kelly* and *Abbott and Costello,* these programs were repeats of old networks series.

As was indicated in Table 7, daytime viewing was lower among the tenth graders. Further, whereas the day time viewing among the younger students was concentrated on a few series of repeats and cartoons, the older students were more diversified in their program selection. In particular, the serial dramas were beginning to split the audience with the repeats.

Looking at the prime time viewing, the general patterns for sixth and tenth graders were similar. The main difference was that audience levels were generally lower among the tenth graders than among the sixth graders. This similarity was perhaps due more to forced sharing of sets than to preference.

The program logs for all three age groups showed negligible viewing of educational programs—even *Sesame Street,* despite the fairly high acquaintance levels reported. Further, both sixth and tenth graders avoided news programs. For instance, Walter Cronkite's largest audience of tenth graders during the week contained 12 viewers.

Favorite programs and characters

All participating students were asked to name their four favorite television programs. Table 12 lists the 20 most frequently named shows for each grade level, showing the percentage of students naming specific shows as one of their four favorites.[7] Table 13 shows the percent of mentions grouped by program category. It should be remembered that

Table 11: Most popular programs for the five test days

First Grade		Sixth Grade		Tenth Grade	
Prime Time:					
45%	My Favorite Martian*	41%	World of Disney	36%	Bill Cosby
37	I Love Lucy*	41	Bill Cosby	35	Mod Squad
37	World of Disney	35	Bewitched	33	Bonanza
27	Laugh-In	34	Laugh-In	29	World of Disney
21	Bill Cosby	32	Mod Squad	28	Laugh-In
20	Bewitched	29	Bonanza	27	Bewitched
18	Family Affair*	29	I Love Lucy*	22	Dragnet
18	Daniel Boone	26	That Girl	21	That Girl
		26	My Favorite Martian*	19	It Takes a Thief
		24	Julia	19	Red Skelton
		22	Beverly Hillbillies	19	Tom Jones
		22	Red Skelton	18	Mayberry RFD
		21	Mayberry RFD	18	Medical Center
		20	Doris Day	17	Beverly Hillbillies
		19	Here's Lucy	17	Daniel Boone
		18	Hee Haw	17	Then Came Bronson
		18	Courtship of	17	Mission Impossible
			Eddie's Father	15	Ironside
		18	Ironside	15	Governor and JJ
		17	Tom Jones	14	Courtship of
		17	Family Affair*		Eddie's Father
		17	Governor and JJ	14	Bold Ones
		17	Gunsmoke	14	Here's Lucy
Sunday daytime:					
38%	Wonderama	33%	Wonderama		
29	Flintstones*	21	Flintstones*		
22	Batman*	21	Abbott & Costello		
Weekday daytime:					
48%	Gilligan's Island*	29%	Gilligan's Island*		
45	Flintstones*	28	Munsters*		
37	Munsters*	26	Flintstones*		
31	Hobo Kelly	24	Abbott & Costello		
29	Batman*				

*Repeat series.

the number of programs in categories was not equal; however, some indication of general types of program preferences is provided. Both maturational and sex differences are pronounced.

Maturational differences. There was a marked difference in the preference patterns for each age group, the sixth graders being very much a transitional group between the children's program preferences of first graders and the more adult-like preferences of the tenth graders. Like

Table 12: Twenty favorite shows for each age group

(Number in parentheses is actual number naming show)

	First grade		Sixth grade		Tenth grade	
1	Gilligan's Island	(121)	Gilligan's Island	(215)	Laugh-In	(167)
2	Flintstones	(78)	Mod Squad	(145)	Mod Squad	(134)
3	Lucy	(66)	Laugh-In	(145)	Takes a Thief	(117)
4	My Favorite Martian	(55)	Brady Bunch	(118)	Star Trek	(69)
5	Batman	(54)	Flintstones	(115)	Eddie's Father	(74)
6	Brady Bunch	(45)	Eddie's Father	(117)	Room 222	(55)
7	Hobo Kelly	(33)	I Love Lucy	(106)	Bill Cosby	(55)
8	Bewitched	(32)	Here Come Brides	(87)	Then Came Bronson	(53)
9	Bozo	(25)	My Favorite Martian	(86)	Love American Style	(45)
10	Eddie's Father	(25)	Takes a Thief	(86)	Adam-12	(44)
10	Munsters	(25)	Star Trek	(86)	Here Come Brides	(38)
12	Adam-12	(22)	Room 222	(86)	Disney	(35)
13	Star Trek	(21)	Adam 12	(79)	Dark Shadows	(31)
14	Beat the Clock	(19)	Gunsmoke	(72)	Highway Patrol	(29)
15	Disney	(14)	Bill Cosby	(69)	Gunsmoke	(23)
16	Bill Cosby	(14)	Disney	(69)	Gilligan's Island	(21)
17	Julia	(14)	Here's Lucy	(65)	I Love Lucy	(19)
18	Ghost & Mrs. Muir	(14)	Dark Shadows	(65)	Munsters	(18)
19	Popeye	(12)	Nanny	(58)	Doris Day	(18)
20	Gumby	(10)	Doris Day	(57)	Gomer Pyle	(14)
					My Favorite Martian	(14)
	(N=274)		(N=940)		(N=579)	

Table 13: Favorite program choices grouped by type

	First grade	Sixth grade	Tenth grade
Hip adventure	10%	14%	20%
Situation comedy	22	17	9
Family situation comedy	25	23	9
Cop/detective	3	5	6
Cartoon/kiddie	24	5	1
Music/variety/talk	3	5	13
Serial dramas	-	3	9
Dramatic	2	6	13
News	-	1	1
Education/culture	4	3	2
Western	3	8	7
Game	2	4	2
Sports	-	2	2
Movies	2	4	6

the first graders, the sixth grade students had *Gilligan's Island* as their overwhelming favorite, and the cartoon family of the *Flintstones* remained in the top five. Among the tenth graders *Gilligan* dropped to sixteenth place and the *Flintstones* disappeared from the top 20. But while retaining these types of juvenile preferences, the sixth grade had begun to take an interest in *Laugh-In*, the "hip adventure" and high school locale shows *Bill Cosby* and *Room 222* which also scored highly with the tenth graders.

Generally, there was an increase with age in the preference for hip adventure, *Laugh-In*, and dramatic shows and, at a somewhat lower rate of increase, for cop shows, westerns, and movies. Complimenting this was a decrease with age in preference for both family and general situation comedies and of course, kiddie-cartoon programs (which, with the exception of the *Flintstones*, all disappeared as favorites by the sixth grade).

Some shows — a diverse group — showed stability across the ages: *The Courtship of Eddie's Father, Adam-12,* and the *Disney* program.

The appeal of characters of their own age group was clearly shown in the results. The most popular family situation comedies among the younger children were those featuring children their age, although this is clearly not a sufficient stimulus to popularity, since some shows featuring young children were seldom mentioned. The one family situation comedy popular with tenth graders was not one of the teenage family programs (like *My Three Sons*), but *The Courtship of Eddie's Father* (which, it might be noted, features a rather "hippie" uncle-figure and a widower father who is both appealing and moderately "mod"). On the other hand, the shows using high school locales — *Room 222* and *Bill Cosby*—and the teenage "hip adventure" *Mod Squad* were already popular with sixth graders. The popularity of the high schools shows pulled up sharply, though, between the sixth and the tenth grade.

Living in an area with a large number of channels, these students had a considerably broader spectrum of choice than their peers in many communities. Much of this choice consisted of repeated reruns of former network series. Many of these shows rated high with the students, particularly the younger classes. Four of the five top shows of the first graders were rerun series, four of the sixth graders' top ten, seven of the tenth graders top 20.

Sex Differences. The present data underline, as did the 1959 data, that differences in the program preferences of boys and girls appear as early as the first grade. Table 14 shows the top programs for first grade boys and girls. Six of the programs showed similar ranking — *Gilligan, Flintstones, Lucy, My Favorite Martian, The Brady Bunch,* and *Hobo Kelly,* although only *Gilligan, My Favorite Martian,* and *Hobo Kelly* were close in the actual numbers of boys and girls naming them. Boys generally seemed to show an earlier preference than girls for action programs

—which, incidentally, usually feature strong male characters. The girls in the first grade were already fond of the family situation comedies in which women either predominate or are coequal with the male lead: *Lucy, Brady Bunch, Bewitched* (and one might add the *Flintstones*). *The Courtship of Eddie's Father,* however, scored higher with girls than boys.

Table 14: First grade favorite programs, boys and girls compared

	Boys	Girls
1	Gilligan's Island	Gilligan's Island
2	Batman	Flintstones
3	Flintstones	Lucy
4	My Favorite Martian	Brady Bunch
5	Lucy	My Favorite Martian
6	Brady Bunch	Bewitched
7	Adam-12	Hobo Kelly
8	Star Trek	Courtship of Eddie's Father
9	Hobo Kelly	Batman
10	Bozo/	Munsters
	Disney	

In an attempt to assess the depth of the personal involvement of first graders with (or at least knowledge of) television characters, the children were asked if they "knew" 17 different characters or groups of characters. If they did know them, they were asked how well they liked or disliked them. Five of the identifications were children characters. The adult characters were selected to represent a range of programs, from situation comedy to western and police-type programs. The results are summarized in Table 15.

Officer Mally of *Adam-12* was better known among girls, his popularity was higher among boys. Misterogers not only was known by more boys than girls, but the boys also liked him better than did girls.

A word is in order regarding both *Misterogers* and *Sesame Street.* Both shows are available to these children only on UHF. Despite this handicap (and the fact that these shows both are generally aimed at preschool children), the characters of *Sesame Street* were better known than those of several commercial programs, including such long time favorites as Hoss of *Bonanza* and Matt Dillon of *Gunsmoke.* Misterogers, however, was the least recognized of the names among both boys and girls, although it should be noted that his showing was not markedly worse than some other characters, particularly among the boys.

Some implications. Age, sex and ethnic group differences were important factors in students' preferences among programs, and the latter two types of differences were manifested by the first grade. (Ethnic group differences will be discussed in a later section.)

One of the most important aspects of program popularity appeared to be the presence of characters in the program with which the children

Table 15: Acquaintance with TV characters—first grade

	Boys		Girls	
	Didn't know	Of those who knew: liked very much	Didn't know	Of those who knew: liked very much
Julia's Cory	33%	47%	28%	41%
Kids on Lassie	14	48	22	33
Brady Bunch kids	16	61	15	59
Eddie	20	56	23	46
Mrs. Muir's kids	27	38	21	33
Marshall Dillon	47%	33%	61%	25%
Gilligan	7	63	4	60
Misterogers	60	38	72	23
Samantha (Bewitched)	12	36	20	52
Hoss (Bonanza)	56	32	66	30
Chief Ironside	58	28	61	26
Sesame Street adults	56	32	61	36
Malloy (Adam-12)	55	53	44	41
Bill Cosby	24	56	31	40
Lucy	8	41	4	53
Maxwell Smart	27	42	44	38
Pat Paulsen	47	33	55	29

could identify. Characters their own age had great appeal, and black characters had an added advantage for the black students. Unfortunately there were no Chicano characters in any of the series. Although there were two Spanish-language stations available on UHF channels, these did little programming specifically for children and they were seldom mentioned by children. A few of the older girls did name "soap operas" — produced in Mexico City — shown on these channels.

Violence did not appear to be an attraction in and of itself, particularly among the tenth graders. Hip adventures did predominate in the choices of this age group, but the two most popular of these shows — Mod Squad and It Takes a Thief —featured youth-oriented characters and styles which may have been more important than the violence as the base of attraction. The most popular character of other top hip adventure, Star Trek, was a nonearthling whose superior intellect was a frequent foil to violence, particularly that of the earthling captain.

The one cop show which did achieve consistent popularity while featuring violence, Adam-12, was one of the most low-key shows in its category.

Perhaps more disturbing is the second-rank position of cartoon/kiddie programs among the first graders. According to the analysis of Gerbner (1971) and his colleagues, the cartoon programs are among the highest in levels of violent content.

Two characters — both adults — were particularly salient among these children: Gilligan and Lucy. The popularity of his show was confirmed by Gilligan's position as the overwhelmingly most popular person among the group.

Looking at the five child character groups, the general level of acquaintance was high. The vast majority of the students knew all the characters. In terms of popularity, the children of *The Brady Bunch* were dominant, followed by Eddie of *The Courtship of Eddie's Father*. In all cases a higher level of liking was reported by boys than girls, the differences being fairly marked with the sole exception of *The Brady Bunch*. The fact that most of the child characters presented for identification were boys may have been a factor in this result.

Except for Gilligan and Lucy, adult characters fared considerably poorer. Samantha of *Bewitched* fared well among both boys and girls (and it might be noted that this show has a child character which sometimes appears).

Sex differences were apparent both in the acquaintance reported and in the levels of liking. But among the boys and girls situation comedies did better than other types of programs. The two female characters — Lucy and Samantha — did much better among girls than among boys.

Other activities while watching

Television viewing was generally not a passive behavior for first graders. When asked if they ever did other things at the same time, 81 percent replied that they did. Most of these indicated that they were likely to do a combination of activities (see Table 16).

Table 16: Activities while watching—first grade

Do you ever do other things at the same time you're watching TV?	
No	19%
Of those responding yes:	
Eat	16%
Talk	10
Play	9
Draw	7
Study	2
Read	2
Other single act	1
Combination	53

Older children were asked directly how often they studied with the television set on. As can be seen in Table 17, almost half the students did so at least sometimes, and such behavior was more frequent among girls, particularly at the tenth grade level.

Table 17: Study with the TV set on

	Sixth grade		Tenth grade	
	Boys	Girls	Boys	Girls
Never	30%	25%	35%	21%
Not very often	28	27	26	26
Sometimes	23	31	27	33
Usually	19	18	12	21

$p < .001$

The older students were also asked if they and their family talked while watching television. Of those who reported that they did watch with other members of the family, over eight out of ten said that they did at least occasionally talk, and two out of ten said there was quite a bit of talk (see Table 18).

Table 18: Discussion while watching TV

	Sixth grade		Tenth grade	
	Boys	Girls	Boys	Girls
Do you and your family talk to each other while watching TV? (Figures based only on students saying they do watch with family)				
Not very often	22%	23%	24%	20%
Sometimes	56	59	57	62
Quite a bit	23	18	19	18
If you do talk, is it mostly about:				
The TV show	29%	24%	16%	16%
Other things	27	22	32	20
Half and half	44	54	52	64

$p < .01$ $p < .01$

While television viewing was a time for family chatting, it should be noted that the chatting for the most part was not exclusively about the show being watched but ranged over other topics as well.

OTHER USES OF LEISURE TIME

Television is only one of the options available to children as a means of using their leisure time. In this section are detailed the norms of other types of leisure activities, beginning with use of other media.

Use of other media

Movies. The sole remaining walk-in movie theater in the community operated only on weekends, although there were theaters in surrounding areas operating on a full-time basis. This may have influenced the level of movie attendance.

Fully half the first graders could not remember the last time they had gone to a movie; 12 percent said that they had been within the last week.

Moviegoing was also infrequent among the older students, as shown in Table 19.

Table 19: Movie attendance

	Sixth grade	Tenth grade
Number of movies seen in the last month:		
None	52%	57%
1	20	19
2	13	13
3 or more	15	11
Saw a movie on a weekday during the last week:	3%	9%
Saw a movie over the past weekend:	11%	11%

Radio. Radio, like television, is a ubiquitous medium in American homes. Not only was it present in practically all of the homes, but personal ownership of receivers was high among the students (Table 20). Even at the first grade level, 25 percent of the students reported having their own radio sets.

Table 20: Ownership of radio receivers

Personally own:	Sixth grade	Tenth grade
A portable	28%	20%
Clock radio	12	19
Hi-fi receiver	4	6
Regular table model	16	13
Other types	1	1
More than one	21	27
None	18	14

Among the older students, the figures were quite impressive. Roughly one-quarter reported owning more than one set.

Because of the difficulty younger students have in estimating time periods, first graders were only asked if they had listened to the radio, not for how long. Almost half — 46 percent — said that they had listened the preceding day, and 26 percent had listened within the last week. There was no difference between boys and girls.

Older children were asked to estimate their radio listening time on school days. Two things stand out in the results (Table 21): radio listening increased markedly in the teenage years, and girls spent more time listening than did boys.

Table 21: Radio listening

	Sixth grade		Tenth grade	
Time spent listening:	Boys	Girls	Boys	Girls
Didn't listen	23%	14%	9%	3%
Less than 1 hour	33	28	18	13
1 hour	16	15	11	8
2 hours	10	16	19	19
3 hours	6	11	18	17
4 hours	3	8	6	11
5 hours or more	10	9	19	28
	p=.001		p=.02	

Records. Personal ownership of record players of one type or another was also high. Over half the sixth graders and two-thirds of the tenth graders reported having their own equipment. While there was no difference between boys and girls on whether or not they owned a machine, boys were more likely than girls to have gone into tapes and cassettes (Table 22).

Table 22: Ownership of record players

	Sixth grade		Tenth grade	
Own:	Boys	Girls	Boys	Girls
Record players	29%	44%	36%	46%
Cassette player	7	3	10	3
Tape recorder	5	2	6	2
Record player and tape or cassette player	15	9	16	13
None	44	42	30	35
	p=.001		p=.01	

The younger children were asked if they had records of their own or that they shared with siblings. Only 33 percent said that they had no records; 44 percent said they had records of their own, and 23 percent said they had records shared with siblings.

Half the first graders said they had played records at least within the last week, and 22 percent said they had done so "yesterday". It is interesting to note that while the difference was not statistically significant at this age, the girls were showing a trend to more record playing than boys. This difference became very marked among the sixth graders, as seen in Table 23, and then faded among the teenagers where the overall level of record playing is higher.

Table 23: Record playing

	First grade	
	Boys	Girls
When was the last time you played records?		
Yesterday	18%	26%
Within last week	26	31
Longer ago	27	19
Never	28	23

	Sixth grade		Tenth grade	
	Boys	Girls	Boys	Girls
How much time do you spend listening to records or tapes on school days as a rule?				
None	30%	28%	23%	17%
Less than 1 hour	36	26	25	28
1 hour	14	20	16	22
2 hours	9	13	15	14
3 hours	4	7	8	11
4 hours	2	3	3	3
5 hours or more	6	3	8	5

p=.01

Comic books. First graders were asked whether or not they liked to read comic books, and 82 percent responded "yes." Only 0.7 percent said their parents did not allow them to read comic books. Boys had a higher frequency of comic book reading than girls, a situation which fades in the older years as the general level of reading declines sharply (see Table 24).

As to the types of comic books preferred, 51 percent of the first graders chose "funny books" and 29 percent chose adventure characters. No other category was mentioned by more than two percent. The choices of the older students are shown in Table 25. There were strong sex differences among both the sixth and tenth graders. There was a generally high interest in adult humor comics, such as *Peanuts*, even at the sixth grade level, along with a high interest in teenage characters by sixth grade girls. More sixth than tenth graders chose teenage comics, like *Archie*. This is true even if the figures are adjusted using only those with a favorite as the base. This suggests the possibility that sixth graders may use these as modeling guides.

Magazine reading. Magazine reading was almost as high among the first graders as among older students (Table 26). When asked if they read

Table 24: Comic book reading

| | First grade | |
How often do you read comic books?	Boys	Girls
Every day	17%	4%
Within last week	43	47
Can't remember	40	49

p=.01

Number of comic books read in last month:	Sixth grade	Tenth grade
None	35%	64%
1	9	6
2	8	8
3	7	7
4	8	4
5-8	13	6
9 or more	19	4

Table 25: Types of comic books preferred

| | Sixth grade | | Tenth grade | |
Favorite type of comic book:	Boys	Girls	Boys	Girls
No favorite	21%	25%	41%	36%
Mystery/detective	8	6	4	1
Western	4	1	1	1
Romance	3	9	2	10
War	8	0	5	4
Horror/science fiction	15	3	4	2
Teenage	10	26	7	19
Animal characters	12	12	8	3
Adult humor	20	15	28	26
More than one type	2	3	1	1

or looked at magazines at home, 16 percent said "often," 46 percent "sometimes," and 38 percent "never." Twenty-four percent said that they got magazines of their own.

Table 26: Magazine reading

Number of magazines read in last month:	Sixth Grade	Tenth Grade
None	29%	32%
1	17	15
2	14	15
3	10	14
4	7	10
5-8	12	9
9 or more	10	5

There was little difference in the age groups overall, nor were there marked sex differences in the amount of magazine reading. However, there were different patterns of selection for boys and girls, as seen in Table 27. The patterns remain consistent across age, although the level generally increases.

Table 27: Types of magazines read

	Sixth grade		Tenth grade	
	Boys	Girls	Boys	Girls
Young people's (like *Seventeen*)	10%	25%	12%	40%
Look or *Life*	24	29	42	38
News magazines	7	7	13	6
Men's (*Playboy, Esquire*)	20	5	41	7
Women's (*McCalls*, etc.)	4	26	6	33
Fashion	3	18	4	23
Homemaking	4	22	6	24
Sports	29	7	39	5
Reader's Digest	15	22	27	30
Quality (*Atlantic, Geographic*)	7	6	10	6
Religious	3	5	5	7
Humor (*Mad*)	28	21	37	16
Romance	6	14	7	26
Detective/mystery	9	9	6	7
Negro	4	2	5	3

Books. As a lead-in to asking first graders about their book reading, they were asked if their parents ever read to them. Slightly more than one-third (36 percent) said "no," 55 percent said "sometimes," and 9 percent said "daily." Most reading was done by the mother, (62 percent) compared to 15 percent by the father and 22 percent combination.

When asked if they ever read or looked at books by themselves, 9 percent said "no" and 63 percent said that they did read books, while 28 percent said they only looked at them. Twenty percent said they either looked at or read books daily. As to the kinds of books, 9 percent said they read picture books, 24 percent "funny" or "pretend" books, 29 percent regular books, and 38 percent a combination.

For the older students a distinction was made between hardcover and paperback reading. The number of each type of book reported read in the last month (exclusive of school reading) is shown in Table 28.

The older students were also asked to check categories of books that they did read (Table 29). As with magazines, the sex differences follow expected patterns at both age groups. The most popular types among girls were mysteries, love stories, popular novels, and science fiction. For boys the leaders were mysteries, science fiction, science, (for the sixth graders) westerns, and (for the tenth graders) popular novels.

Newspaper. Most of the students do have a daily newspaper available to them in their home (Table 30). The figures are relatively constant for

Table 28: Book reading

Number read in last month:	Paperbacks		Hardcover	
	6th grade	10th grade	6th grade	10th grade
None	30%	49%	25%	66%
1	17	22	17	16
2	14	15	13	9
3	10	7	9	4
4	8	3	10	2
5	6	2	6	1
6 or more	14	2	20	1

Table 29: Types of books read

	Sixth grade		Tenth grade	
	Boys	Girls	Boys	Girls
Mysteries/detectives	26%	41%	25%	34%
Westerns	11	7	7	7
Popular novels	8	16	15	24
Love stories	7	22	9	45
Biography	9	13	15	7
Science	11	5	8	1
Classics	6	11	5	8
Science fiction	17	11	22	15
Other	16	14	19	9

Table 30: Newspaper availability

Does your family get a paper delivered to your home?	Sixth grade	Tenth grade
No	21%	27%
The local paper only	36	31
Local paper and another	17	13
San Bernardino *Sun*	19	22
Los Angeles *Times*	3	2
Other	4	4

the sixth and tenth graders and appear to reflect the general known pattern of circulation.

Most of the first graders had begun at least casual exposure to the newspaper. When asked if they ever looked at the paper, 7 percent said they did so daily, 45 percent said they did so sometimes during the week, 9 percent said they looked at the Sunday paper and 39 percent said "no." For the most part — 64 percent —they were only looking at the funnies; 8 percent said they looked at the funnies and the pictures, 6 percent the funnies and headlines.

There was a continuing increase of regular newspaper reading with age (Table 31), but even among the tenth graders less than half were

Table 31: Newspaper reading

Read newspaper:	Sixth grade	Tenth grade
Daily	31%	47%
Several times a week	30	25
Sunday only	14	4
Seldom or never	25	24

reading the paper on a daily basis; one-fourth said they seldom or never read the paper. There were no sex differences in the frequency of reading.

Table 32 shows the percentage of those who did read the paper who reported reading various sections or content of the paper. It is obvious that the tenth graders were not only reading the paper more frequently than the sixth graders, but also reading more of the paper. Among the sixth graders, readership was limited primarily to the funnies, the front page, and, for the boys, sports. By the tenth grade the front page was almost equal to comics. Local news and, for girls, women's news, advice columns, school news, and the entertainment section were becoming important. The higher interest in advice columns among girls than boys might be expected. More interesting, perhaps, is the higher interest expressed by girls in local news and school news along with the entertainment section.

Table 32: Content of newspaper read

	Sixth grade		Tenth grade	
	Boys	Girls	Boys	Girls
Comics	44%	51%	52%	52%
Front page	25	30	48	45
Local news	11	17	28	34
School news	12	19	18	34
Editorial and political columns	7	8	12	10
Advice columns	9	16	13	32
Sports	32	12	45	2
Women's section	4	16	3	39
Entertainment section	17	19	18	34
Crossword puzzle	10	16	6	6

Because of the phenomenon of "underground" press which has become an object of increasing frequency and interest in recent years, the sixth and tenth graders were asked if they knew what an underground paper was and whether or not they had read one. There was considerable ignorance of these papers even at the tenth grade level, and very few students reported having read one (Table 33). Undoubtedly the figures would be higher among teenagers in central Los Angeles (and perhaps most central cities), where these papers are widely displayed and sold.[8]

Table 33: Exposure to "underground" newspapers

	Sixth grade	Tenth grade
Don't know what an "underground" paper is	57%	41%
Know, but never read one	37	50
Have read one	6	9

Personal purchase of media

It is generally accepted that the nation's youth — particularly teenagers — today constitute a major market segment. We decided to ascertain to what extent these students were active participants in the market for commercial mass media: to what extent they spend money for purchase of media.

Moviegoing does require money and so might be considered as a "media purchase." We reported earlier that 12 percent of the first graders had seen a movie in the last week; 48 percent of the sixth graders and 43 percent of the tenth graders had seen at least one movie during the past month. Thus, despite the rather limited local access to movies, almost half of the two older groups were active in the "movie market."

The older students were asked directly about personal purchase of recordings, magazines, and books.

Purchase of recordings of various types within the last month is detailed in Table 34. The majority of students in both grades had not bought any recordings. As might be expected, there was a slightly higher rate of purchase among the tenth graders. One other difference is noteworthy: while sixth graders were most likely to purchase singles, the tenth graders were equally likely to buy singles and LPs.

Although purchase of tapes and cassettes was reported by only about 10 percent of the tenth graders and by still fewer sixth graders, when these figures are compared to the purchase rate of disc recordings they appear to have claimed between one-fifth and one-fourth of the market.

It is appropriate to recall that 44 percent of the first graders said they had records of their own—in other words, records bought specifically for them.

Personal purchase of or subscription to magazines (Table 35) was reported by four out of ten of the students, and there was a slight decrease

Table 34: Purchase of recordings

% of total recordings purchased:	Sixth grade	Tenth grade
Singles	49%	38%
LPs	30	39
Reel-to-reel tape	14	14
Cassettes	7	9

in such consumption between the sixth and tenth grades. (It will be recalled that 24 percent of the first graders said they got magazines of their own.)

Table 35: Purchase of magazines

Number of magazines bought in last month:	Sixth grade	Tenth grade
None	60%	62%
1	16	17
2	7	8
3	4	6
4 or more	13	7

Book purchases (Table 36) reflected the general low readership of books and also declined between the sixth and tenth grades. Paperbacks have established themselves as the dominant book market for these students.

Table 36: Purchase of books

	Sixth grade		Tenth grade	
Number of books bought in last month:	Paperback	Hardcover	Paperback	Hardcover
None	61%	74%	80%	91%
1	11	10	9	5
2	8	5	5	2
3	7	3	3	1
4 or more	13	8	3	1

Other types of leisure activities

First graders. As an attempt to obtain a picture of how television viewing fits with other leisure activities of the first graders, these children were asked a series of questions concerning out-of-school activities. They were asked what they best liked to do after school and between supper and bedtime. Then they were asked what they were most likely to do on the weekends. The results are shown in Table 37.

While television obviously dominated the evening hours, play activity was the most frequent activity during the daylight periods. It is worth noting that even in the evening less than half the children preferred television, and play activity still was a strong contender. However, almost one-third of the children mentioned television for Saturday morning, a peak period of cartoon programming.

The sample of first grade mothers was asked what they thought their children would do with the time spent watching television if television were not available. The major categories of response are summarized in Table 38.

Play obviously dominates the responses. There is a fairly strong indication in the responses that the mothers think the replacement activity would be likely to be one performed alone rather than a social one.

Sixth and tenth graders. The older students were asked a series of questions about nonclassroom and nonmedia activities. First they were asked how many school and how many nonschool organizations they belonged to. The majority of the students belonged to no organizations (Table 39).

Another series of questions asked for the frequency of participation in various activities. These are shown in Table 40, together with an index consisting of the summer scores of all six items. The amount of such participation shows a sharp decline between the sixth and tenth grades. Boys have a higher level of activity in the sixth grade group, but this difference fades among the tenth graders. The higher index scores are primarily a result of the particularly high involvement of boys in sports activities. Girls did report higher levels in church and music activities.

The students were also asked the frequency of their work activities, both chores at home and work at a paying job. The vast majority of the students indicated that they do chores at home at least several times a

Table 37: First graders' preferred leisure activities

	School Days		Saturday			Sunday		
	After-noon	PM	AM	After-noon	PM	AM	After-noon	PM
Watch TV	20%	44%	31%	22%	42%	17%	14%	49%
Play	58	34	39	51	34	23	53	27
TV/play	6	7	3	4	4	2	3	4
Chores			11	6	4	4	4	3
Shopping			2	2	1		2	1
Read/study	5	5						
Snack	3							
Visit friends			1	3	2	2	7	2
Church						48	6	2

Table 38: Mothers' responses to: Suppose there wasn't any TV—what do you think your child would do with the time now spent watching TV?

	Boys	Girls
Play—general	20%	11%
Play activities, alone	22	29
Play activities, with others	18	13
Play and read	12	11
Play and activities	6	4
Read	12	8

Table 39: Organizational membership

	Sixth grade		Tenth grade	
	Boys	Girls	Boys	Girls
School organizations, including teams:				
None	59%	73%	62%	52%
1	25	18	23	29
2 or more	16	9	15	19
Nonschool organizations				
None	62%	57%	76%	72%
1	27	30	20	18
2 or more	11	13	4	10

week, and the frequency was markedly higher among girls than boys. Boys, on the other hand, were more likely to have paying jobs (Table 41).

The tenth graders were asked how frequently they dated. Boys and girls reported identical frequencies: 17 percent said several times a week and 23 percent said they dated about once a week.

Finally, the students were asked how frequently they talked with friends on the telephone. As can be seen in Table 42, there is a sharp increase in this type of activity between the sixth and tenth grades. In both grades the girls are far more active in use of telephone than boys.

MEDIA AS AGENTS OF SOCIAL INTERACTIONS

Most media can be used in a social situation, either as a common activity, as the stimulus for conversation, or as the model for social behavior. While most reading is an exception, for young children parental reading does provide a social interaction and, as previously reported, two-thirds of the first graders said that their parents read to them at least occasionally.

Watching television was most frequently done in a social context, as can be seen by the data in Table 43. However, it should be noted that solitary viewing did appear to be considerably higher among sixth graders than first graders, and a further increase was shown among tenth graders.

At all three age levels siblings were the most frequent companions while viewing. The first graders reported very little viewing with friends, and among the older students friends are much less frequent television companions than either siblings or parents.

Of all media activity, moviegoing was overwhelmingly the most "social." Practically all movie going at all three age levels was done with

Table 40: Recreational activities

	Sixth grade		Tenth grade	
	Boys	Girls	Boys	Girls
Individual sports:				
Never	26%	34%	33%	36%
Monthly	20	24	21	26
2–3 times a week	20	21	24	25
Almost daily	34	21	22	13
Scouts or club meetings:				
Never	70%	72%	89%	90%
Church activities:				
Never	37%	29%	56%	54%
Monthly	19	24	19	20
Weekly or more often	44	47	25	26
Play music or dance:				
Never	53%	37%	59%	39%
Monthly	11	7	12	13
2–3 times a week	18	21	10	21
Almost daily	18	35	19	27
Work on hobby activities:				
Never	23%	33%	39%	46%
Monthly	28	20	19	19
Weekly or more often	49	47	42	35
After school activities or sports:				
Never	27%	44%	62%	58%
Monthly	15	13	11	20
2–3 times a week	23	15	6	16
Almost daily	35	28	21	1
Summary index of activities:				
Low	27%	35%	55%	59%
Moderate	44	38	35	31
High	29	27	10	10

p=.05

companions (Table 44). Only the identity of the companions changed with age. First graders went mostly with the family group. By the sixth grade, the peer group had become slightly more important than the family. Among the tenth graders, the peer group was clearly dominant, and dating had become an important subdivision.

Listening to records was also largely a social activity. Only 31 percent of both sixth and tenth graders said that they usually listened to records alone. (At the sixth-grade level, boys were more likely than girls to be solitary listeners.) The amount of social listening was higher among sixth graders than tenth graders. Among the younger group, 39 percent

Table 41: Work activities

	Sixth grade		Tenth grade	
	Boys	Girls	Boys	Girls
Work at a paying job:				
Almost never	47%	64%	48%	62%
Monthly	19	12	10	15
2–3 times a week	20	12	21	16
Almost daily	14	12	21	7
	p=.001		p=.001	
Do work at home:				
Almost never	10%	9%	12%	11%
Monthly	16	9	15	7
2–3 times a week	30	21	37	19
Almost daily	43	61	36	63
	p=.001		p=.001	

Table 42: Frequency of telephone conversations with friends

	Sixth grade		Tenth grade	
	Boys	Girls	Boys	Girls
Daily	11%	31%	24%	44%
Several times a week	22	26	25	23
Weekly	13	8	10	7
Now and then	28	18	24	20
Almost never	26	17	17	7
	p=.001		p=.001	

said they usually listened to records with friends and 30 percent said it was about half and half, with friends and alone. Of the tenth graders, 27 percent said they usually listened with friends, and 42 percent said half and half.

Media as source of conflict with parents

Since media — and particularly television — claim a very large share of the child's time and interest, it is perhaps only natural that they may be a point of irritation between parent and child. A series of questions was included to ascertain the frequency with which the older students perceived their parents complaining about their media activity. The results are summarized in Table 45.

As might be expected from its dominance in the child's media use, television was the medium causing most parental complaints. The music media — radio and recordings — which ranked next to television in use

Table 43: Social viewing of television

First graders

When you watch TV, most of the time are you alone
or is someone else watching with you?

Watch with siblings	37%
Watch with parents	8
Watch with siblings and parents	27
Watch with friends	3
Half alone, half with someone	14
Mostly alone	11

Sixth and tenth graders

How often do you watch television:

	With parents		With siblings		With friends		By yourself	
	6th	10th*	6th	10th	6th	10th**	6th	10th
Never	3%	6%	6%	10%	8%	13%	9%	6%
Not very often	10	16	12	15	36	40	22	18
Sometimes	37	42	19	27	36	34	42	43
Usually	50	36	63	48	20	13	27	33

*Sex difference p $<$ .05, girls higher
**Sex difference p $<$ .001, girls higher

Table 44: Social aspect of moviegoing

When you go to the movies, it is usually with:

	First grade	Sixth grade	Tenth grade
Family	77%	36%	12%
Siblings	9	16	8
Friends	4	34	43
Date	-	7	32
Combination	8	5	4
Alone	1	2	1

time also ranked next as focus of parental complaint. Movies and books
were the least frequent causes of complaints. Parental objections about
television and movie declined somewhat between the sixth and tenth
grades, while there was a slight increase in the frequency of complaints
about the music media.

The nature of the parental complaints show an interesting pattern. For
both television and movies, the content selection was cited as the most
frequent cause of complaints (although this dominance is far less in the
case of television than movies). For both recordings and radio, paprental complaints focused on the volume at which music was played. There
was a higher frequency of parent complaints about the music media

Table 45: Parental complaints about media use

	Television		Movies	
	6th grade	10th grade	6th grade	10th grade
Parents complain:				
Never	27%	38%	56%	67%
Not very often	29	26	25	17
Now and then	34	32	13	12
Pretty often	10	4	6	4
Complain about:				
Watch too much	27%	22%	Go too often 14%	7%
Watch too late	27	27	When you go 12	6
Selection	29	35	Selection 42	54
			Companion 6	6

	Record playing		Radio	
Complain:				
Never	50%	46%*	50%	44%**
Not very often	29	30	27	28
Now and then	17	19	14	22
Pretty often	4	5	9	6
About:				
Play too loud	63%	69%	60%	62%
Too much	6	4	5	7
Selection	18	13	24	20
Spend too much	5	5	-	-

	Books	
Never complain	66%	70%***
Should read more	25	24
Should read less	5	4

*Sex difference, p $<$ .01, girls more complaints
**Sex difference, p $<$ .01, girls more complaints
***Sex difference, p $<$ .01, girls more complaints

among girls than among boys at the tenth grade level, perhaps reflecting the fact that girls did spend more time with both these media than boys (although, it should be noted, that this was also true at the sixth grade level where there was no difference regarding complaints).

The major complaint parents made regarding books was that the child read too few books, particularly in the case of the tenth-grade boys.

Parental control of television

Another point for consideration is whether or not parents attempt to control the child's exposure to television.

Student perception of whether or not their parents attempt to impose (or have attempted to do so in the past) a limit on television viewing is shown in Table 46. It is interesting to note that the two categories combined give the same total for both sixth and tenth graders, indicating that something over one-third of these students felt they either presently were or had been previously under a limit.

Table 46: Do parents limit TV viewing?

	First grade	Sixth grade	Tenth grade
Yes	19%	22%	9%
Not now, but did when child was younger		14	27

This was considerably higher than the 19 percent of first graders who recognized that their parents set a limit. Since there was the possibility that these younger children might not recognize subtle forms of parental control, this area was explored in the interviews with the subsample of first grader mothers. The results of this series of questions are shown in Table 47.

Table 47: Parental restrictions on TV viewing
First grade mother responses

	Girls			Boys		
Do you or your husband ever:	Never	Occasionally	Often	Never	Occasionally	Often
Set special hours when the child can and cannot watch TV	52%	35%	13%	65%	23%	12%
Restrict the total amount of time he/she can watch TV	63	26	11	73	14	13
Decide which programs he/she can watch	26	48	26	37	42	21
Encourage him/her to watch TV just to keep him/her quiet or occupied	65	27	8	69	23	8
Encourage him/her to watch just to keep him/her at home	82	16	2	90	8	2
Punish him/her by not letting him/her watch TV	55	39	7	69	25	4
Reward him/her by letting him/her watch more TV, later TV, or special programs	50	45	3	56	40	2

Among these mothers the most frequent form of control was supervising the actual selection of programs their first grade child watched. The proportion actually setting special hours or "often" restricting the amount of viewing time was pretty much in line with the number of children recognizing control. Very little use of television viewing to keep the child occupied or indoors was reported. It is interesting to note that there is a consistent trend through all these questions for mothers of girls to report more control than the mothers of boys.

Television deprivation as punishment

The importance of television in the lives of most students creates the opportunity for parents to use deprivation of television viewing privilege as a form of punishment. A considerably higher proportion of the first graders — 31 percent — answered that they were sometimes punished in this manner. As can be seen by the last two items in Table 47, the mothers themselves reported a higher incidence of using expanded viewing as a reward than of restricted viewing a punishment.

Among the sixth graders 35 percent reported that their parents used this form of punishment at the present time, and another 13 percent said that they had been so punished when they were younger. Only 15 percent of the tenth graders said they were now punished in this fashion, but another 19 percent said they had been when younger.

Conflict with siblings was generally higher than conflict with parents (Table 48) and peaked among the sixth graders (who, of course, were most likely to be in the middle of a sibling hierarchy residing together). First graders were also asked the age of siblings with whom they most frequently disagreed. Older siblings were cited by 61 percent compared to 33 percent for younger siblings and 6 percent who said they argued equally with older and younger siblings.

The "pecking order" differences shown by responses to the conflict resolution question (Table 49) are interesting. First graders predomi-

Table 48: Frequency of family conflict over television

	Conflict with parents			Conflict with siblings		
	First grade	Sixth grade	Tenth grade	First grade	Sixth grade	Tenth grade
Never	60%	36%	34%	42%	13%	18%
Not very often	13	36	35	11	27	31
Now and then	24	15	17	24	19	16
Pretty often	5	13	13	22	41	35
None—we have our own set	-	15	19	-	4	9

nantly perceived themselves and older siblings — with whom they have the most conflict — as winning in almost equal numbers. Among sixth graders older siblings had greater dominance than self, but by the tenth grade self was once more dominant over older siblings. Perhaps the most important difference is the change which occurs between first and sixth grade for mutual agreement or compromise to become the most frequent form of resolution—a situation which persevered into the tenth grade. The strong position of father at all three age groups is also noteworthy.

Table 49: Resolution of conflict over television

Who wins:	First grade	Sixth grade	Tenth grade
Father	17%	25%	22%
Mother	7	16	12
Older sibling	28	12	6
Younger sibling	5	4	3
I do	29	8	15
Compromise	14	29	31

A final point concerns responses by older students that there was no occasion for conflict because they had their own set. Almost one-fifth of the tenth graders and 15 percent of the sixth graders said this was the case regarding their parents; the percentages for a similar response regarding siblings were much lower. This suggests that when a family becomes a multiset household, the custom is to reserve one set for adults and one for the children.

Media as topics of conversation

In addition to serving as an activity which can be socially shared, media and their content can also be socially used as topics of conversation. The older students were asked how frequently they discussed the media both with their parents and with their friends. The results are summarized in Table 50.

All the media were used with considerable frequency as topics of conversation with both parents and peers, but there were some differences in the patterns. Television programs and movies predominated as the subject of discussion with friends. With parents, discussion was considerably more evenly distributed among the media.

Discussion of television programs, movies, and magazines was higher with friends than with parents, whereas television news, newspaper items, and books were more likely to be discussed with parents than with friends. (This pattern was not perfect for the newspaper.)

There was considerably greater difference between the sexes in the tenth grade in discussion with parents than with friends. In most instances girls showed a higher level of discussion with parents than did the boys.

To put the matter of conversation into a broader context, Table 51A and 51B show the percentage of students saying they "sometimes" or "often" discussed television and a range of other topics, such as personal problems and public issues. The second half of the table shows the ranking of each of the topics for boys and girls in each grade. School

Table 50: Frequency of discussions concerning media

| | With friends | | | | With parents | | | |
| | Sixth grade | | Tenth grade | | Sixth grade | | Tenth grade | |
	Boys	Girls	Boys	Girls	Boys	Girls	Boys	Girls
Television:								
Never	7%	6%	10%	7%	18%	14%	22%	13%
Not very often	18	18	26	30	30	30	41	32
Sometimes	49	54	50	52	36	42	31	44
Often	25	22	14	11	16	15	6	11
								p ⟨.001
Movies:								
Never	6%	7%	8%	3%	17%	15%	25%	14%
Not very often	22	23	22	16	31	28	37	23
Sometimes	42	46	48	53	34	41	33	47
Often	30	24	23	28	17	16	6	11
				p=.02				p ⟨.001
Books:								
Never	21%	13%	36%	28%	28%	21%	44%	30%
Not very often	39	40	44	45	33	28	37	37
Sometimes	28	32	18	20	28	39	15	25
Often	12	15	3	7	12	12	4	8
		p ⟨.02				p ⟨.01		p ⟨.01
Magazines:								
Never	25%	22%	24%	14%	27%	25%	31%	17%
Not very often	27	31	36	33	31	35	36	36
Sometimes	31	32	32	40	29	27	24	39
Often	17	15	18	13	14	13	9	8
				p=.01				p ⟨.001
Newspaper items:								
Never	25%	25%	21%	14%	25%	24%	27%	16%
Not very often	32	35	35	31	24	32	27	30
Sometimes	32	29	36	44	34	30	35	40
Often	11	10	8	11	10	15	10	14
								p=.01
Television news items:								
Never	21%	28%	24%	21%	21%	24%	23%	16%
Not very often	36	31	33	36	27	32	30	30
Sometimes	28	29	36	33	35	29	36	38
Often	15	12	7	10	17	15	11	16
		p=.05						

Table 51A: Television compared to other conversation topics

% discussing "sometimes" or "often"	With friends				With parents			
	Sixth grade		Tenth grade		Sixth grade		Tenth grade	
	Boys	Girls	Boys	Girls	Boys	Girls	Boys	Girls
Television	74%	76%	64%	63%	52%	57%	37%	58%
School events	79	83	87	92	74	83	66	79
Friends	61	63	58	72	58	69	49	66
Personal problems	38	38	28	53	57	57	33	48
Family problems	(not asked)				59	60	50	66
School problems	56	56	71	75	60	60	49	66
Problems of Young people	39	38	36	62	45	44	36	56
Clothes/fads	42	65	40	74	47	65	51	64
Plans for future	57	58	55	69	55	56	55	64
Student protest	33	33	30	45	54	46	28	38
Pollution	52	52	54	50	53	54	46	40
Politics	28	29	21	22	35	36	33	27
Vietnam	58	39	56	58	56	42	50	55

events dominated conversation across age, sex, and conversational partners. Television's relative importance appeared to decline somewhat with age, and it also figured as a more important topic with friends than with parents.

Television as a model for play

Another type of social use which can be made of the media is as a stimulus or suggestion for play activity. The first graders were asked whether or not they ever played about things they had seen on television. As can be seen in Table 52, they reported using television much more frequently as a model for social play than for solitary play activity. When asked what types of programs were copied in play activity, 24 percent cited adventure shows (such as *Batman*), 21 percent cited several types, 14 percent situation comedies, 12 percent cartoons, 7 percent cowboys.

Table 51B: Rank order of conversation topics

	With friends				With parents			
	Sixth grade		Tenth grade		Sixth grade		Tenth grade	
	Boys	Girls	Boys	Girls	Boys	Girls	Boys	Girls
	School events	School events	School events	School events	School events	School events	School events	School events
	Television	Television	School problems	School problems	School problems	Friends	Future	Friends
	Friends	Clothes	Television	Clothes	Family problems	Clothes	Clothes	Family problems
	Vietnam	Friends	Friends	Friends	Friends	Family problems	Family problems	School problems
	Future	Future	Vietnam	Future	Personal problems	School problems	Vietnam	Clothes
	School problems	School problems	Future	Television	Vietnam	Television	Friends	Future
	Pollution	Pollution	Pollution	Youth problems	Future	Personal problems / Future	School problems / Pollution	Television
	Clothes	Vietnam	Clothes	Vietnam	Student protest	Pollution	Television	Youth problems
	Youth problems	Personal problems	Youth problems	Personal problems	Pollution	Student protest	Youth problems	Vietnam
	Personal problems	Youth problems	Student protest	Pollution	Television	Youth problems	Personal problems	Personal problems
	Student protest	Student protest	Personal problems	Student protest	Clothes	Vietnam	Politics	Pollution
	Politics	Politics	Politics	Politics	Youth problems	Politics	Student protest	Student protest
					Politics			Politics

Television's ranking as a leisure time option

In the course of the first-grade interviews, children were asked a series of questions as to what they most like to do when they are not in school. The results were presented in Table 37.

While there is no denying the impact of television, it is significant that, with one exception—Saturday morning—it was not the most popular choice for daylight hours. Play — which some have called "children's work" — was dominant as the afternoon choice and remained a strong second even into the evening hours when television does clearly dominate. Church and Sunday School were very important Sunday morning activities. Forty-six percent of these children said they had gone to church the preceding Sunday, and another 30 percent said they sometimes go.

The Saturday morning figures are interesting because of the heavy emphasis on cartoon and kiddie programming by television stations during that period.

Table 52: First grade use of TV as model for play

Do you remember if you ever play either by yourself or with friends about things you've seen on TV?	By self	With friends
Often	5%	7%
Sometimes	25	42
Not very often	16	14
Never	54	37
	(N=274)	

ATTITUDES TOWARD TELEVISION

Reflecting the sense of wonder which most adults felt toward the "miracle of television" in its early years, Schramm, Lyle, and Parker remarked upon the fact that the children they studied in 1959 calmly accepted television as one of the ordinary accommodations of their lives. In 1970 television was, if anything, even more commonplace for all youngsters.

In this working class town, only 2 percent of the students said they did not have a working television set in their homes. Color was available in over half the homes, and a large minority of the homes contained two or more sets. With this universal availability of the medium, it is not surprising that the students had developed a fairly high level of critical sophistication toward the medium.

Even at the first grade level, students had begun to develop a differentiation between life as portrayed on television and what they themselves experienced. This is reflected in the data presented in Table 53. It is interesting to note that these children were more likely to distinguish between television and real life with regard to grown ups than with regard to children.

Slightly different questions about the "realism" of television were put to the sixth and tenth graders. Responses to these are also shown in Table 53. The sixth graders appeared to be considerably advanced over the first graders in rejecting television as an accurate reflection of life, and there was a further increase reflected among the tenth graders.

Schramm, Lyle, and Parker commented on a tendency for children to reject the concept of television as "educational" and to hold to the opinion that it was to be "fun" or "entertaining." Another possible reflection of a growing sophistication concerning the medium were answers to questions about whether or not television should be just for fun and whether or not the students felt that they learned from watching television.

As can be seen in Table 54, when directly asked if television should be for fun rather than education, more students disagreed than agreed. This is not meant to imply that the students actually wanted a heavier emphasis on educational content in television. It will be recalled that their actual program selection reflected almost no viewing of educational or public affairs and news programs. But most students did feel that they do learn something from television at least part of the time, as shown in the second part of Table 54.

Table 53: Acceptance of TV as realistic

	First graders	
	Are grown ups on TV like grown ups you know?	Do you think kids on TV are like you and your friends?
Just like	6%	5%
Pretty much	39	48
Not very much	32	25
Not at all	23	22

	Sixth and tenth graders			
	The programs on TV tell about life the way it really is.		The people you see on TV are just like people you meet in real life.	
	Sixth grade	Tenth grade	Sixth grade	Tenth grade
Always	1%	1%	19%	8%
Most of the time	8	8	18	17
Some of the time	48	43	24	33
Now and then	37	41	20	24
Never	6	7	18	19

Table 54:

	Sixth grade	Tenth grade
Television programs should be for fun, not education.		
Strongly	8%	13%
Agree	12	20
Not sure	26	26
Disagree	34	31
Strongly disagree	20	9
You learn a lot from watching TV.		
Strongly agree	5%	4%
Agree	20	25
Some of the time	37	48
Most of the time	29	20
Always	9	4

Television news. The small amount of viewing of television news is reflected in the further finding that 45 percent of the sixth graders and 40 percent of the tenth graders felt that there were *too many* news programs presented on television, despite the fact that in this area the multiplicity of channels meant that there was always a nonnews alternative available on one or more channels.

Despite their apparent avoidance of television news programs, students generally rated television news high, as shown in Table 55. Most students were inclined to agree that the average person could get all the news he needs from television. The other half of the table, showing perceived need for the newspaper, complements this. It should be noted that the tenth graders, who were considerably higher in their newspaper readership, indicated a higher need for the newspapers and were somewhat polarized regarding television news.

Table 55:

	The average person can get all the news he needs each day from TV.		To be well informed a person must read the newspaper.	
	Sixth grade	Tenth grade	Sixth grade	Tenth grade
Strongly agree	10%	10%	10%	11%
Agree	32	40	25	36
Not sure	33	20	23	18
Disagree	20	28	33	29
Strongly disagree	6	2	10	7

Television news did have high credibility among the students who also gave it a high rating regarding fairness to minority groups (Table 56).

Table 56:

	If you see something on TV news you can be sure it is true.		TV is not fair to some groups like Blacks and Chicanos.	
	Sixth grade	Tenth grade	Sixth grade	Tenth grade
Never	8%	10%	22%	39%
Now and then	14	14	26	23
Some of the time	17	16	26	21
Most of the time	34	45	15	10
Always	27	16	11	7

Commercials. The greatest criticism of and discontent toward television was reflected in the questions concerning commercials. Nine out of ten of the students thought there were too many commercials (88 percent in the sixth grade, 92 percent in the tenth grade). Furthermore, commercials were rated as annoying and in poor taste (Table 57). At the six-grade level, girls showed a higher tolerance than boys, but still 43 percent said commercials were annoying "most of the time" or "always."

Perhaps the most devastating results were the replies to the question concerning truthfulness of commercials. The majority of the students at both grade levels responded that commercials never tell the truth or, at best, only "some of the time" (Table 57).

Table 57:

	Commercials are in poor taste and annoying.		Television commercials tell the truth.	
	Sixth grade	Tenth grade	Sixth grade	Tenth grade
Never	10%	5%	23%	23%
Now and then	20	25	35	47
Some of the time	23	19	31	26
Most of the time	24	26	10	4
Always	24	25	2	0

To provide a basis of comparison for television commercials, students were asked to rate the truthfulness of newspaper advertisements. Although considerable skecpticism was also registered toward these, their acceptance was higher than that of the television commercials (Table 58). Again, there was a considerable decrease in acceptance between sixth and tenth grades.

Offensive content. Although many adults may be in a furor over violence and sex on television, little discontent was evidenced by the sixth and tenth graders, as is seen in Table 59. With regard to both, there was a decline in the objections with age, and this decline was particularly marked regarding sex.

Table 58

		Newspaper advertisements tell the truth.
	Sixth grade	Tenth grade
Never	6%	7%
Now and then	23	35
Some of the time	32	36
Most of the time	26	20
Always	12	2

Table 59

	Television has too much:	
	Sex	Violence
Sixth grade	33%	24%
Tenth grade	20%	7%

First graders were asked whether or not they were ever frightened by what they saw on television and whether or not they remembered ever dreaming about things they'd seen on television. About half of the children said they were sometimes frightened and over one-third remembered dreaming about television (Table 60). Boys were less likely than girls to say they were frightened, but there was no difference in the report of dreaming.

Of those who did say they were frightened, the cause was overwhelmingly—88 percent—programs of the "chiller/monster" category. Shooting and detective type violence was cited by eight percent of the children. "Chiller/monster" shows were also the predominant stimulus of dreams—68 percent—followed by incidents in situation comedy shows. Cartoons and shootings were remembered as dream incidents by seven percent.

Table 60

	Do you ever get scared by things you see on TV?		Do you ever dream about something you saw on TV?	
First grade	Boys	Girls	Boys	Girls
Often	7%	9%	7%	10%
Sometimes	33	50	32	27
Not very often	12	10	10	10
Never	48	31	51	54

$P < .02$

Attitudes of first-grade mothers. The sample of mothers of first grad-ers were asked three questions to provide indications of their qualitative assessment of television's role in their child's life. First they were asked if there was anything about television or specific programs which they felt was good or useful for the child. Second they were asked about things they felt were bad or annoying, and finally, what kinds of things they felt the child learned from television.

The vast majority of mothers did choose to specify some good aspect of television for their young children. Aspects of learning were the most frequently mentioned (Table 61). In response to the question asking about learning specifically, almost nine out of ten mothers felt that their child was learning from television. The types of learning reported are detailed in Table 62, in which (it will be noted) the mothers of boys named more types of learning—including negative things—than mothers of girls.

Most mothers also specified things they felt were bad about television for their young children. The area of most frequent complaint was commercials, followed by violence and horror content (Table 63).

Table 61: Good points of television mentioned by first grade mothers

| | Mothers of: | |
	Boys	Girls
School-oriented learning	10%	16%
General learning	15	18
News and special events	25	10
Sesame Street	12	18
Capt. Kangaroo, Romper Room, etc.	21	10
Entertainment value	15	18
Animal shows	21	21
Cartoons	14	14
Keeps child occupied	17	6

(Multiple responses were permitted.)

Table 62: Learning reported by mothers

| | Mothers of: | |
	Boys	Girls
No learning	6%	3%
Not sure	6	10
Increased vocabulary	39	30
School-oriented learning	31	29
Nature-oriented learning	31	29
Learning about "life"	48	25
General learning	27	14
Negative things learned	27	14

(Multiple responses were permitted.)

Table 63: Bad points of television mentioned by first grade mothers

| | Mothers of: | |
	Boys	Girls
Cigarette/alcohol commercials	12%	11%
Commercials generally	23	31
Violence and horror content	27	19
Sex in programs	12	11
"Too adult"	14	11
Cartoon content objectionable	14	13
"Nothing bad"	14	19

(Multiple responses were permitted.)

Utility of television. An aspect of media attitudes is the perceived usefulness of a medium or activity for different types of personal needs. Taking a lead from Steiner's (1963) work, we included a series of questions for this purpose in the sixth and tenth grade instruments. The students were asked to mark a degree of likeliness to engage in seven different behaviors under five different situations:

When you just want to relax
When you just want to be entertained
When you feel lonely
When someone has hurt your feelings
When someone has made you angry.

The behaviors were:

Watch TV
Go to a movie
Read a book or magazine
Listen to music
Play a game or sport
Talk to somebody
Go off by yourself

Through these questions we hoped to get some indication of the relative utility of different media and personal interactions in situations reflecting different levels of tensions.   The overall results are summarized in Tables 64A and 64B. These show considerable change between the two age groups and very marked sex differences. However, the number of sex differences declines among the teenage group.

Table 65 regroups the data to facilitate the comparison between media, summarizing only the proportion reporting themselves "likely" or "very likely" to use a particular behavior.

As was expected, television is perceived by all age and sex groups primarily as a source of entertainment. It is interesting to note that all groups also rated it higher as a means of reducing loneliness than as a means of relaxation. The importance of television as a "companion" was more marked among the sixth than among the tenth graders. Among

Table 64A: Comparative use of media and activities for personal reasons

How likely would you be to use each of these in the following situations:	Boys				Sixth grade — Girls				
	Not very likely	Maybe	Likely	Very likely	Not very likely	Maybe	Likely	Very likely	
When you just want to relax									
Watch TV	16%	26%	21%	37%	12%	33%	23%	32%	p< .01
Listen to music	33	20	21	26	22	28	21	29	
Go to a movie	54	20	12	14	60	18	11	11	p< .001
Read book/magazine	47	22	17	14	32	31	21	16	
Go off by yourself	38	25	16	21	39	27	15	19	p< .001
Play a game or sport	30	25	19	26	47	22	16	15	p< .01
Talk to somebody	33	28	10	10	22	30	26	22	
When someone has hurt your feelings									
Watch TV	49	25	12	14	53	24	16	7	p< .01
Listen to music	43	25	16	17	34	30	16	20	
Go to a movie	66	14	11	9	67	17	9	7	
Read book/magazine	53	22	14	11	42	25	21	13	p< .01
Go off by yourself	22	14	19	45	20	16	17	47	
Play a game or sport	48	20	13	18	63	19	9	8	p< .001
Talk to somebody	43	23	24	19	36	23	13	28	p< .05
When you want to be entertained									
Watch TV	18	14	19	50	15	18	17	50	p< .001
Listen to music	25	24	19	31	13	23	28	36	
Go to a movie	31	19	17	33	37	18	18	27	
Read book/magazine	50	23	12	15	38	27	16	18	p< .02
Go off by yourself	59	15	13	13	63	17	11	9	
Play a game or sport	24	19	16	51	21	23	21	36	
Talk to somebody	33	25	21	21	45	25	12	18	p< .02

Table 64A: (Continued)

How likely would you be to use each of these in the following situations:	Sixth grade								
	Boys				Girls				
	Not very likely	Maybe	Likely	Very likely	Not very likely	Maybe	Likely	Very likely	
When someone has made you angry									
Watch TV	45%	25%	12%	18%	46%	22%	15%	17%	$p < .01$
Listen to music	44	26	14	16	32	30	15	24	$p < .05$
Go to a movie	57	17	13	15	59	23	8	10	$p < .02$
Read book/magazine	53	21	11	15	41	25	17	17	$p < .02$
Go off by yourself	29	16	19	36	20	17	17	45	$p < .001$
Play a game or sport	42	23	13	23	53	24	14	9	
Talk to somebody	43	20	19	18	38	22	15	25	
When you feel lonely									
Watch TV	21	15	17	47	19	17	21	44	
Listen to music	26	23	17	34	13	24	27	37	$p < .001$
Go to a movie	43	21	14	22	51	17	18	14	$p < .02$
Read book/magazine	42	26	16	16	32	30	16	21	$p < .05$
Go off by yourself	47	18	12	23	21	16	24	29	
Play a game or sport	21	16	24	29	33	21	20	26	$p < .001$
Talk to somebody	27	17	19	37	13	17	16	54	$p < .001$

Table 64B: Comparative use of media and activities for personal reasons

How likely would you be to use each of these in the following situations:	Tenth grade								
	Boys				Girls				
	Not very likely	Maybe	Likely	Very likely	Not very likely	Maybe	Likely	Very likely	
When you just want to relax									
Watch TV	20%	33%	26%	22%	15%	36%	23%	26%	
Listen to music	7	18	25	50	4	13	27	56	
Go to a movie	58	23	10	9	56	24	10	9	
Read book/magazine	59	23	9	9	43	29	14	14	$p < .02$
Go off by yourself	36	32	17	16	23	21	19	28	$p < .001$
Play a game or sport	44	22	16	18	60	26	8	7	$p < .001$
Talk to somebody	23	30	28	19	21	28	31	19	$p < .001$
When someone has hurt your feelings									
Watch TV	63	21	8	8	68	13	11	9	
Listen to music	19	23	16	42	13	23	20	45	
Go to a movie	72	15	8	6	75	15	4	6	
Read book/magazine	69	18	5	8	58	23	10	9	
Go off by yourself	21	19	19	41	8	9	16	67	$p < .001$
Play a game or sport	56	24	10	11	80	11	5	4	$p < .001$
Talk to somebody	35	25	19	21	23	20	21	36	$p < .01$
When you want to be entertained									
Watch TV	12	19	26	43	10	17	33	40	
Listen to music	9	15	29	47	3	15	25	59	$p < .01$
Go to a movie	28	20	21	31	21	18	21	40	
Read book/magazine	54	24	11	11	45	25	17	12	
Go off by yourself	71	21	5	4	67	17	10	6	
Play a game or sport	26	16	19	39	30	20	22	27	
Talk to somebody	23	28	27	22	11	21	33	34	$p < .001$

Table 64B: (Continued)

How likely would you be to use each of these in the following situations:	Boys				Girls (Tenth grade)				
	Not very likely	Maybe	Likely	Very likely	Not very likely	Maybe	Likely	Very likely	
When someone has made you angry									
Watch TV	51%	25%	13%	11%	51%	22%	13%	14%	
Listen to music	22	22	19	37	13	22	23	42	
Go to a movie	69	16	8	7	66	18	10	7	
Read book/magazine	66	20	9	6	57	20	10	13	p < .05
Go off by yourself	23	19	17	42	14	11	20	55	p < .01
Play a game or sport	55	19	12	14	70	14	7	9	p < .02
Talk to somebody	41	20	22	17	25	15	27	33	p < .001
When you feel lonely									
Watch TV	21	26	20	33	20	23	23	34	
Listen to music	7	16	26	52	7	15	19	59	
Go to a movie	54	21	12	14	55	20	11	14	
Read book/magazine	56	23	12	9	49	20	17	14	
Go off by yourself	52	18	12	18	50	15	12	23	
Play a game or sport	36	18	20	26	48	16	18	18	
Talk to somebody	17	13	18	52	8	11	17	64	p < .02

the younger boys, television even ranked above personal interaction—talking to somebody. Among the sixth grade girls, television stood a close second to talking to somebody.

While television was still an important relief from loneliness for the tenth graders, it had fallen behind music. One of the most significant points in the data, perhaps, is the testimony of the overwhelming importance of music in the life of the teenagers. Listening to music outscored television even for entertainment and had an overwhelming lead for relaxation and for relief from loneliness. Music was becoming important for these purposes for the sixth graders—particularly the girls, but among the tenth graders it reigned supreme. The sole exception was that talking to somebody rated slightly higher among the older girls.

The other point deserving particular emphasis is television's relatively low standing as a relief from hurt feelings or anger. The sixth graders indicated that they would most likely resort to seeking solitude or go talk to somebody. While solitude still led among the tenth graders, music was now as likely a relief as seeking out someone for conversation.

MEDIA BEHAVIOR RELATED TO ABILITY, FATHER'S OCCUPATION, AND ETHNIC GROUP

Ability

"Ability" for the first graders was based on ratings by the individual student's classroom teacher. The teachers were asked to rate each student interviewed as in the upper, middle, or lower third of the class. (There was no formal "tracking" by ability in the class assignment of students.) The results showed a slight bias toward the upper part of the continuum, and it will be noted from the summary below that this bias was primarily in ratings of girls:

	Girls	Boys	Total
Upper third	58	41	99
Middle third	44	49	93
Lower third	33	44	77

(Actual numbers)

The weekday viewing time reported by these students is presented in Table 66.

Table 67 is a general summary of media behavior and attitudes for the children of the different ability levels. (Areas or questions where there was no noteworthy difference are ommitted.)

Table 65: Comparative use of media and activities

"Likely" or "Very likely" to:	Watch TV	Listen to music	Go to movie	Read	Go off by self	Play, sports	Talk to somebody
Sixth grade boys							
For relaxation	58%	47%	36%	31%	37%	45%	38%
For entertainment	69	50	50	27	26	67	42
When lonely	64	51	36	32	35	53	56
When feelings are hurt	26	33	20	25	64	31	43
When angry	30	30	26	26	54	36	37
Sixth grade girls							
For relaxation	55	50	22	37	34	31	48
For entertainment	67	64	45	34	20	57	30
When lonely	65	63	32	37	53	46	70
When feelings are hurt	23	36	16	34	64	17	41
When angry	32	39	18	34	62	23	40
Tenth grade boys							
For relaxation	48	75	19	18	33	34	47
For entertainment	69	76	52	22	9	58	49
When lonely	53	78	26	21	30	46	70
When feelings are hurt	16	58	14	13	60	21	40
When angry	24	56	15	15	59	26	39
Tenth grade girls							
For relaxation	49	83	19	28	47	15	50
For entertainment	73	84	61	29	16	49	67
When lonely	57	78	25	31	35	36	81
When feelings are hurt	20	65	10	19	83	9	57
When angry	27	65	17	23	75	16	60

Table 66: First grade television viewing by ability groups

TV viewing	Girls			Boys		
Hours:	Low	Mod	High	Low	Mod	High
0 – 1:00	4%	7%	12%	4%	10%	9%
1:30 – 3:00	4	12	9	15	12	6
3:30 – 4:30	5	7	8	6	4	8
5:00 – more	10	7	13	7	10	7

(Weekdays only)

It will be noted that the low ability children perceived that they watch more television than their classmates. This was particularly marked among the boys.

The personal impact of television did appear to be different among the groups, and this difference was consistent among boys and girls. The higher-rated children were somewhat *more likely* to use television as a play motif. There was a slight tendency for them to remember dreaming about television *less frequently*. More significant, both from the standpoint of intrinsic interest and statistical difference, was the fact that the children rated highest on ability were *more likely* to report that they were frightened by things on television. This was most marked among the girls.

There were also differences in the patterns of family interactions related to television. Disagreement with both parents and siblings over the selection of programs was *inversely* related to ability. The relationship to the withdrawing of television privileges as punishment showed *reverse* relationship to ability for boys and for girls. The *more able* girls and the *least able* boys had the *lowest* percentage reporting such punishment.

Another instance where sex was an intervening variable was the question on whether or not the child ever found that there was nothing on that she or he wanted to watch, and, if so, what action was taken? Among the boys there was no difference in the ability groups in responses. A large majority of all three groups said they did encounter such situations and that their reaction was to turn the set off. This response was typical of the high ability girls, but the lower ability girls had sizable groups who said they never found this the case.

With regard to other media, the picture was considerably mixed. There was not a consistent higher use of print by the higher ability children. They were more likely to report reading books for themselves— particularly the more able boys, but it was the low ability girls who reported the highest use of magazines and the middle ability group of both sexes who were most favorable to comic books. As for the newspaper, the low ability girls did fall lower than any other group in use.

Table 67: Ability differences — first grade

	Girls			Boys		
	High	Mod	Low	High	Mod	Low
TV time compared to friends						
Watch more than friends	36%	36%	45%	29%	47%	46%
Same as friends	19	20	18	22	12	16
Less than friends	38	30	33	17	18	14
Don't know	7	14	3	12	8	9
Ever frightened by things on TV						
Never or not very often	31	41	58	51	63	68
Ever dream about things seen on TV?						
Never or not very often	67	63	58	63	59	59
Ever play with friends about things seen on TV?						
Often or sometimes	48	43	39	59	53	51
Ever disagree with parents on TV programs?						
Never	47	64	61	54	61	73
Ever disagree with siblings on TV programs?						
Never	39	30	55	44	38	57
Ever punished by withdrawal of TV privileges?						
Yes	24	36	36	34	35	23
If watching TV and there's nothing on you want to see, what do you do?						
Never find this the case	18	27	36	10	12	14
Keep on watching anyway	14	16	15	22	16	18
Turn the set off	68	57	49	68	71	68
Listened to radio yesterday	41	43	54	44	47	50
Played records yesterday	19	25	39	15	16	23
Read books for self	74	64	61	66	59	48
Never read magazines	36	27	46	42	43	36
Like to read comic books	79	86	79	80	92	73
Have read comic books within last week at least	54	48	52	56	67	57
Look at newspaper during week	53	57	42	49	51	54

With radio and record playing, there was a consistent trend for use to be higher among the lower ability groups, particularly among the girls.

Sixth and tenth graders. Students in the sixth and tenth grades had been given the Lorge-Thorndike inventory the preceding fall, and results were made available to the investigators. The overall score was used. The distribution was generally skewed to the low side. For the analysis which is discussed in the following section, students were divided into three groups. The "low" group contains those with scores under 85, "moderate" those with scores of 85-99, and "high" those with scores of 100 or higher. The basic numbers in each group are presented below:

	Sixth grade		Tenth grade	
	Boys	Girls	Boys	Girls
Low	221	160	116	87
Moderate	119	122	93	80
High	116	133	106	72

There was little difference (Table 68) in the amount of television viewing among ability groups in the sixth grade, but in the tenth grade there was some evidence of the expected tendency for brighter students to watch less television.

The point of most interest regarding the relation of intelligence scores to use of other media had to do with the use of print media. These results are presented in Table 69.

Daily reading of the newspaper is the activity which showed the highest relation to intelligence. The low group of both sexes reported the lowest frequency of newspaper reading, and there was very little increase from the sixth to the tenth grades.

Among the middle and high score boys, there was no increase from sixth to tenth grade. Indeed, the boys in the middle ability bracket reflected a decrease in this period. Girls, however, showed a strong increase, and the high ability girls at the tenth grade level had the highest reading of the newpaper of any group.

With regard to comic book reading, the high ability students were actually among the highest users in the sixth grade group, but by the tenth grade level they showed a heavier decrease of use than the other groups.

The ability differences in magazine reading were found primarily among the girls. Lower ability girls at both grade levels had a higher proportion reading no magazines.

As to books, the trend for low ability students to be the most likely to read no books—either paperback or hard cover—was surprisingly low. However, when one looks at the last section of the table, very different attitudes toward books are found in the groups. The low ability students

Table 68: Television viewing by ability groups

	Sixth grade						Tenth grade					
	Boys			Girls			Boys			Girls		
	Low	Mod	High	Low	Mod	High	Low	Mod	High	Low	Mod	High
Sunday viewing												
0–3:00	32%	25%	31%	30%	36%	25%	44%	34%	33%	39%	40%	33%
3:30–5:00	16	20	24	20	23	25	16	26	26	18	21	28
5:30–8:00	22	17	19	25	21	23	8	23	28	15	18	21
8:30+	29	38	25	25	20	27	32	17	13	28	21	18
Wednesday viewing												
0	38	26	22	47	30	21	24	20	30	25	27	25
0:30–3:00	19	24	31	5	24	32	38	38	36	22	31	32
3:30–5:00	19	25	22	18	20	23	12	16	20	20	18	19
5:30+	24	25	25	30	26	24	26	26	14	33	24	24

Table 69: Use of print media related to ability

| | Sixth grade | | | | | | Tenth grade | | | | | |
| | Boys | | | Girls | | | Boys | | | Girls | | |
	Low	Mod	High	Low	Mod	High	Low	Mod	High	Low	Mod	High
Read newspaper Daily	22%	69%	53%	20%	33%	57%	28%	54%	52%	35%	50%	78%
Comic books Read none	33	29	28	42	36	37	54	63	68	67	64	76
Magazines Read none	36	26	30	35	23	24	22	21	24	32	32	15
Paperbacks Read none	35	24	31	38	31	24	55	53	50	45	41	42
Hard cover books Read none	35	19	31	23	19	21	76	71	65	59	67	54
Percent responding "not very likely" to read books:												
To relax	57	51	44	47	27	15	64	63	47	52	43	20
To be entertained	56	56	41	47	35	21	62	51	49	63	46	15
When lonely	46	38	37	40	32	25	61	60	46	53	51	30

were the least likely to consider books as a possible source of relaxation, entertainment, and solace for loneliness.

The situation regarding the relationship of intelligence or ability is seriously clouded by the fact that exceedingly strong relationships were found between socioeconomic status and the test scores of the sixth and tenth grades and the ability ratings provided by the first grade teachers. There was a further relationship between ethnicity and the scores or ratings. These relationships are shown in Table 70.

Because of this situation, heavier emphasis has been placed on the comparison of media behaviors and attitudes as reflected by groups based on these variables rather than on intelligence.

SES and ethnic background

Both socioeconomic status and the ethnic background of individuals have been found frequently to relate to the use of television and other media. As pointed out in the introduction, the present study location was a predominantly blue collar community. However, in the upper grades the numbers were sufficiently large to make possible comparisons between students from blue collar and white collar families, which are here equated with socioeconomic status.

Father's occupation was categorized using the North-Hatt scale. Those categories 50 and above were put into the "white collar" group, those below into the "blue collar" group.

The number of Mexican-American students (based upon identification of Spanish surname) was sufficient to allow comparison to Caucasian students at all three grade levels. However, the number of Negro students (identified by classroom teacher) was smaller than anticipated and in most instances was insufficient for reliable comparison.

As usual there was a high-order relationship between socioeconomic status and ethnic background. All the Mexican-American (Chicano) students fell into the blue collar group.

Television availability and use. Neither socioeconomic status nor ethnic background appeared to be related to the number of television sets within the household. Both were important factors related to the presence of a color set in the home, as can be seen in Table 71. There is a general tendency in all three grades for Caucasian students to have a greater accessibility to color sets than either the Mexican-American or Negro students. The SES data is less clearcut. In the tenth grade the expected positive relationship between white collar status and possession of color was present, but in the sixth grade the only difference was between ethnic groups.

At both the sixth- and tenth-grade levels, Mexican-American girls were heavier viewers than their "Anglo" peers (Table 72A and B). This difference ranged from a half-hour to an hour and a half more than the

Table 70: Ability and grade equivalence
related to SES and ethnic background

	First grade		
	Teacher's rating of ability		
	Lower third	Middle third	Upper third
Boys			
Caucasian	27%	42%	31%
Mexican—American	46	19	35
Negro	43	43	14
Girls			
Caucasian	20	31	49
Mexican—American	27	42	31
Negro	60	1	30

	Percent identified as underachievers
Caucasian	24%
Mexican—American	15
Negro	29

	Sixth and tenth grades					
	IQ			Grade equivalence		
	Under 85	85—99	Over 100	Low	Modal	High
Sixth grade boys						
Caucasian, white collar	6%	37%	57%	12%	70%	18%
Caucasian, blue collar	28	47	25	44	43	12
Mexican—American	42	42	16	56	40	4
Sixth grade girls						
Caucasian, white collar	13	15	72	13	58	29
Caucasian, blue collar	20	47	33	35	53	12
Mexican—American	35	43	22	48	44	8
Sixth grade Negroes	53	36	11	75	21	3
Tenth grade boys						
Caucasian, white collar	7	31	62	27	73	
Caucasian, blue collar	18	50	32	25	75	
Mexican—American	32	59	9	50	50	
Tenth grade girls						
Caucasian, white collar	3	53	44	7	93	
Caucasian, blue collar	22	52	26	28	72	
Mexican—American	33	52	15	33	66	

Table 71: Color TV in the home

	White Collar	Caucasian	Mexican-American	Negro	
First grade		57%	41%	29%	p=.02

	White Collar		Blue Collar		
		Caucasian	Mex.–Am.	Negro	
Sixth grade	59%	63%	51%	48%	n.s.
Tenth grade	77%	62%	44%	—	p=.001

Chicanos. For the boys, on the other hand, there was no difference at the sixth-grade level, and among the tenth graders the results were inconsistent. The Chicanos watched more on Sunday, less on the weekdays. This pattern of results meant that there was more difference between Mexican-American boys and girls than between Caucasian boys and girls.

Program selection. In response to the question concerning how they select television programs, the first graders of various ethnic groups showed no marked differences (Tables 73A-73C). However, when asked if they ever found that there was nothing on they wanted to watch, significant differences appeared. The Negro children were far more likely

Table 72A: Viewing averages for white collar and blue collar groups

	Sunday	Monday	Tuesday	Wednesday	Thursday
Sixth grade boys					
Blue collar	7:24	3:46	3:25	3:29	3:56
White collar	6:54	3:20	3:27	3:56	3:65
Sixth grade girls					
Blue collar	7:49	3:35	3:48	3:56	3:44
White collar	6:39	3:14	3:39	4:01	3:35
Tenth grade boys					
Blue collar	6:19	3:28	3:19	3:22	3:30
White collar	6:22	3:22	3:07	3:16	2:59
Tenth grade girls					
Blue collar	6:28	3:43	3:23	3:46	3:50
White collar	5:20	2:52	3:13	3:24	2:49

Table 72B: Viewing averages for Mexican—American
and Caucasian students

	Sixth grade				Tenth grade			
	Boys		Girls		Boys		Girls	
	Mex-		Mex-		Mex-		Mex-	
	Am.	Cau.	Am.	Cau.	Am.	Cau.	Am.	Cau.
Sunday	6:29	6:34	6:37	6:07	6:14	5:31	6:46	5:47
Weekday	3:00	2:52	3:22	2:49	2:38	3:07	4:30	3:04

than the others to say that they never found this to be the case, and, further, if they did, they were more likely than the others to keep on watching anyway. The Mexican-American children also were more likely than Caucasians to say this was never the case.

The pattern of program selection for older children is more complex since three questions were asked.

Caucasian children in the sixth grade were more likely than either minority group to consult the program log, and a similar trend was apparent among the tenth graders.

When asked how often they just turned the set on and flipped the dial, it was the blue collar sixth graders (including both minority groups) who indicated that they were most likely to do this. A similar trend was evident among tenth-grade boys.

However, when asked if they turned the set off when they found nothing on they wanted to watch, the pattern was that white collar children at both grade levels were less likely to turn the set off. This, of course, could be a result of the higher probability that they had checked the program log before turning the set on.

Favorite programs. Among the first graders the only major difference in the categories of programs named as favorites was that the small number of Negroes overwhelmingly chose situation comedies. While this category was also the most popular among Caucasian and Chicano students, its dominance was far less marked (Table 74). A considerable number of both Caucasian and Mexican-American children named cartoon shows.

Both ethnic and socioeconomic difference, however, began to emerge in the preferences among sixth and, especially, tenth graders. The older children were asked to name their four favorite programs. In Table 74, the percentages of programs of various types have been summed over the four possible choices.

Sixth-grade preferences were concentrated in four program types: hip adventure, situation comedies, family situation comedies, and music-

Table 73A: Selection of programs

	First grade		
	Caucasian	Mexican—American	Negro
When you decide to watch TV, how to you decide what program to watch?			
Just turn the set on	11%	11%	6%
Switch the dial	16	21	18
Turn on for specific show	33	34	35
Parent selects	9	8	18
Sibling selects	4	—	—
Look at TV guide	17	13	6
Other	9	13	18

	Sixth and tenth grades	
	Not very often or never	Sometimes or usually
How often do you turn the set on and change channels until you find something you like?		
Sixth grade boys		
Caucasian, white collar	36%	64%
Caucasian, blue collar	21	79
Mexican—American	27	73
Sixth grade girls		
Caucasian, white collar	37	63
Caucasian, blue collar	25	75
Mexican—American	33	67
Sixth grade Negroes	12	88

		Sometimes	Usually
Tenth grade boys			
Caucasian, white collar	36%	31%	33%
Caucasian, blue collar	27	28	45
Mexican—American	26	18	56
Tenth grade girls			
Caucasian, white collar	27	37	36
Caucasian, blue collar	31	30	39
Mexican—American	28	34	38

variety. The differences were more marked for boys than girls. Among the boys, the Caucasians gave first preference to situation comedies while the Chicanos chose family situation comedies. Hip adventure programs scored higher among blue collar group boys generally, and Chicanos were higher for program types, but the blue collar girls showed the same rank order of program types, but the blue collar girls tended to be more diversified, as reflected by a more even spread of choices.

The differences were more marked among the tenth graders. White collar boys preferred a far more varied selection of programs than their blue collar peers. While hip adventure shows dominated the choices of all three groups of boys, the blue collar Caucasians showed a stronger preference than their peers for situation comedies and for cop/detective shows.

The most mixed pattern of all was shown by the tenth-grade girls. Mexican-American girls this age showed partiality for the hip adventures and, secondly, situation comedies. Among blue collar Caucasians

Table 73B

	Sixth and tenth grades		
How often do you look at the TV log and decide whether to turn the set on or not?	Never or not very often	Sometimes	Usually
Sixth grade boys			
Caucasian, white collar	41%	20%	39%
Caucasian, blue collar	35	31	34
Mexican—American	40	43	17
Sixth grade girls			
Caucasian, white collar	24	22	54
Caucasian, blue collar	34	25	41
Mexican—American	40	32	28
Sixth grade Negroes	16	48	36
Tenth grade boys			
Caucasian, white collar	39	24	37
Caucasian, blue collar	38	27	35
Mexican—American	47	32	21
Tenth grade girls			
Caucasian, white collar	18	32	50
Caucasian, blue collar	33	27	40
Mexican—American	28	31	41

Sixth grade overall, p=.02

Table 73C

When you're watching TV do you ever find that there's nothing on you want to watch? If so, what do you do?	First grade		
	Never find this true	Keep on watching	Turn the set off
Caucasian	14%	17%	69%
Mexican—American	26	13	60
Negro	41	29	29

p=.02

How often do you turn the set on and find there's nothing on you want to watch and so turn the set off?	Sixth and tenth grades		
	Never or not very often	Sometimes	Usually
Sixth grade goys			
Caucasian, white collar	36%	36%	28%
Caucasian, blue collar	27	35	38
Mexican—American	35	34	31
Sixth grade girls			
Caucasian, white collar	32	41	27
Caucasian, blue collar	26	36	38
Mexican—American	32	40	28
Sixth grade Negroes	32	52	16
Tenth grade boys			
Caucasian, white collar	38	48	14
Caucasian, blue collar	33	40	27
Mexican—American	27	38	35
Tenth grade girls			
Caucasian, white collar	29	50	21
Caucasian, blue collar	31	41	28
Mexican—American	24	31	45

the order was reversed. White collar girls were most equally partial to family situation comedies and dramatic shows.

From these differences, there does not appear to be any consistent pattern of either SES or ethnic differences for the sex and age groups. Perhaps the most that can be said is that the results underscore the fact that the television audience is indeed a diverse one and that the concept of "most popular program" on a population basis is highly artifactual.

Table 74: Favorite program index

	First grade		
	Caucasian	Mexican—American	Negro
Situation comedy	47%	53%	82%
Cartoons	21	28	6
Dramatic	10	8	12
Cowboy	4	4	0
Variety	6	2	0

	Sixth and tenth grades						
	Hip Adventure	Comedy	Family	Westerns	Cops	Music	Drama
Sixth grade boys							
Caucasian, white collar	50%	97%	81%	X	X	43%	X
Caucasian, blue collar	70	92	65	X	X	35	X
Mexican—American	65	68	106	X	X	61	X
Sixth grade girls							
Caucasian, white collar	38	113	133	X	X	35	X
Caucasian, blue collar	42	90	108	X	X	32	X
Mexican—American	39	98	143	X	X	27	X
Sixth grade Negroes	69	68	82	X	X	26	X
Tenth grade boys							
Caucasian, white collar	88	38	35	41	35	65	62
Caucasian, blue collar	108	69	21	36	58	52	19
Mexican—American	135	37	42	26	30	53	21
Tenth grade girls							
Caucasian, white collar	46	49	70	15	10	48	68
Caucasian, blue collar	70	84	57	15	12	59	14
Mexican—American	94	74	58	25	19	43	12

At the sixth-grade level, situation comedies and family situation comedies did clearly dominate, and among tenth-grade boys the hip adventures reigned supreme.

There were some differences in the knowledge of and affect toward television characters by the first-grade ethnic groups. As might be expected, the most pronounced differences were that the two black characters—Cory (Julia's son) and Bill Cosby—scored even higher with Negro students than they did with the other groups. The only other major differences were that Gilligan and the Brady Bunch—both among the most popular overall—were less popular among the two minority groups than among the Caucasian students.

Attitudes toward television

The realism of television. Among the first graders, Caucasian children are less likely than minority group children to accept the children they see on television as realistic (in the sense of being like people they know) (Table 75). There is no difference between the Caucasian and Mexican-

Table 75: The realism of television

Do you think the children you see on TV are pretty much like you and your friends?	First grade	
	Not at all, Not very much	Pretty much, Just like us
Caucasian	51%	49%
Mexican—American	40	60
Negro	25	75
	p=.05	

What about the grownups and the way they act on TV — do they act like the grownups you know?		
Caucasian	56%	44%
Mexican—American	58	42
Negro	38	62

The programs on TV tell about life the way it really is.	Sixth and tenth grades		
	Never now & then	Some of the time	Most of time, always
Sixth grade boys			
Caucasian, white collar	52%	44%	4%
Caucasian, blue collar	44	45	11
Mexican—American	39	38	23
Sixth grade girls			
Caucasian, white collar	48	48	4
Caucasian, blue collar	43	52	5
Mexican—American	32	58	10
Sixth grade Negroes	37	52	11
Tenth grade boys			
Caucasian, white collar	47	45	8
Caucasian, blue collar	52	44	4
Mexican-American	40	47	13
Tenth grade girls			
Caucasian, white collar	57	37	6
Caucasian, blue collar	40	50	10
Mexican—American	50	38	12
Sixth grade overall p=.01			

Table 75 (Continued)

The people you see on TV are just like people you meet in real life.	Sixth and tenth grades		
	Never now & then	Some of the time	Most of time, always
Sixth grade boys			
Caucasian, white collar	51%	22%	27%
Caucasian, blue collar	42	20	38
Mexican—American	30	23	47
Sixth grade girls			
Caucasian, white collar	35	30	35
Caucasian, blue collar	32	29	39
Mexican—American	39	20	41
Sixth grade Negroes	37	26	37
Tenth grade boys			
Caucasian, white collar	51	24	24
Caucasian, blue collar	41	34	25
Mexican—American	33	33	33
Tenth grade girls			
Caucasian, white collar	32	44	24
Caucasian, blue collar	44	30	26
Mexican—American	54	29	17

Sixth grade overall $p=.05$

American children in the acceptance/rejection of television adults as realistic but the small group of Negroes were considerably more likely to accept the adults than the others.

Caucasians, particularly white collar children, in the sixth grade were significantly less credulous in accepting television as telling about life realistically than their peers. But among the tenth graders there was no significant nor consistent pattern.

In evaluating television characters, in the sixth grade there was a significant difference only among the boys. Again Caucasian and particularly the white collar boys were less accepting of the television characters than the Mexican-American boys. In the tenth grade there was no consistent pattern, and the differences, while in some cases appearing large, did not prove statistically significant.

Acceptance/rejection of commercials. The minority group students generally showed a greater tolerance and credulity regarding commercials than the Caucasian students, but there was no consistent SES difference. The only major exception was that among the tenth-grade girls, Mexican-Americans showed the least credulity of commercials (Table 76).

Table 76: Acceptance/rejection of commercials

TV commercials tell the truth.	Sixth and Tenth grades		
	Never now & then	Some of the time	Most of time, always
Sixth grade boys			
Caucasian, white collar	67%	24%	9%
Caucasian, blue collar	63	27	10
Mexican—American	48	35	17
Sixth grade girls			
Caucasian, white collar	74	18	8
Cuacasian, blue collar	51	34	15
Mexican—American	54	35	11
Sixth grade Negroes	50	46	4
	p=.01		
Tenth grade boys			
Caucasian, white collar	66	32	2
Caucasian, blue collar	76	19	5
Mexican—American	60	30	10
Tenth grade girls			
Caucasian, white collar	70	30	
Caucasian, blue collar	67	30	3
Mexican—American	75	17	8

Commercials are in poor taste and very annoying.			
Sixth grade boys			
Caucasian, white collar	20%	18%	62%
Caucasian, blue collar	28	23	59
Mexican—American	31	22	47
Sixth grade girls			
Caucasian, white collar	27	22	51
Caucasian, blue collar	32	27	41
Mexican—American	38	23	39
Sixth grade Negroes	44	19	37
Tenth grade boys			
Caucasian, white collar	22	19	59
Caucasian, blue collar	26	16	58
Mexican—American	50	17	33
Tenth grade girls			
Caucasian, white collar	35	9	56
Caucasian, blue collar	33	15	52
Mexican—American	33	42	25

Tenth grade ethnic difference p= .01

Television news. In response to the query about the sufficiency of television news for the needs of the average person, there was no real difference among the SES and ethnic groups at the tenth-grade level (Table 77). Among the sixth graders, Caucasian students, and particularly the white collar ones, were more polarized in their opinions than the Mexican-American students. Thus more white collar Caucasians both agreed and disagreed with the statement than members of the other groups. This, of course, may be related to the correlations also found between SES and intelligence scores and grade equivalence performance among these students.

As to the reliability of television news, there is an interesting reversal from the sixth to the tenth grades. Among the sixth graders, the Caucasian (and particularly the white collar) students have the highest acceptance of television news as reliable, but among the tenth graders they show the lowest acceptance.

Racial fairness of television. When asked whether or not television is ever unfair to ethnic groups like Negroes and Chicanos, the minority students in the sixth grade tended to give the medium a stronger acquittal than did Caucasian students. However, the maturation and growing militancy that has been generally seen among teenagers was reflected in the present data. Among the tenth graders, the Mexican-American students were significantly more critical of the medium on this count than their Caucasian peers (Table 78).

Television as fun. Since it is generally assumed that immediate gratification is more important to blue collar persons than to white collar persons, and since education is generally assumed to be deferred gratification, the older students were asked whether or not they thought television should be for fun, not for education.

Among the tenth graders, the white collar students were significantly less likely to accept this statement. A similar general pattern was shown by the sixth graders, although among the girls at that level the difference was between ethnic, not SES, groups (Table 79).

Uses of other media

Moviegoing. Although as noted earlier, moviegoing generally is not frequent among the students of this town, there is evidence of an SES difference at all three grade levels (Table 80). Generally white collar students are more likely to have gone to a movie than blue collar students, regardless of ethnic group. Two major exceptions stand out. Sixth-grade Negroes reported the highest level of movie going of any group, and among the sixth-grade girls the difference was between Caucasian and Mexican-Americans rather than between white collar and blue collar.

Table 77: Television news

The average person can get all the news he needs each day from TV.	Agree	Not sure	Disagree
Sixth grade boys			
Caucasian, white collar	53%	13%	33%
Caucasian, blue collar	49	23	27
Mexican—American	39	41	20
Sixth grade girls			
Caucasian, white collar	44	20	36
Caucasian, blue collar	33	41	26
Mexican—American	26	58	16
Sixth grade Negroes	30	37	33
Tenth grade boys			
Caucasian, white collar	53	13	34
Caucasian, blue collar	50	21	29
Mexican—American	48	24	28
Tenth grade girls			
Caucasian, white collar	49	17	34
Caucasian, blue collar	43	20	37
Mexican—American	46	25	29

Sixth grade overall p=0.001

If you see something on TV news you can be sure it is true.	Never, now & then	Some of the time	Most of time, always
Sixth grade boys			
Caucasian, white collar	18%	9%	73%
Caucasian, blue collar	20	16	64
Mexican—American	29	23	48
Sixth grade girls			
Caucasian, white collar	14	6	80
Caucasian, blue collar	21	17	62
Mexican—American	18	25	57
Sixth grade Negroes	33	21	46
Tenth grade boys			
Caucasian, white collar	29	8	63
Caucasian, blue collar	23	12	65
Mexican—American	11	18	71
Tenth grade girls			
Caucasian, white collar	43	11	46
Caucasian, blue collar	20	18	62
Mexican—American	33	29	38

Sixth grade overall p=.01
Tenth grade overall p=.05

Table 78: Racial fairness of television

TV is not fair to some groups, like Negroes and Chicanos.	Never, now & then	Some of the time	Most of time, always
Sixth-grade boys			
Caucasian, white collar	44%	36%	20%
Caucasian, blue collar	46	25	29
Mexican—American	54	14	32
Sixth grade girls			
Caucasian, white collar	50	33	17
Caucasian, blue collar	46	27	27
Mexican—American	56	29	15
Sixth grade Negroes	54	29	17
Tenth grade boys			
Caucasian, white collar	74	13	13
Caucasian, blue collar	69	14	17
Mexican—American	48	26	26
Tenth grade girls			
Caucasian, white collar	65	24	12
Caucasian, blue collar	64	18	18
Mexican—American	41	36	23

Tenth grade ethnic comparison p=.01

Table 79: Television as fun

TV should be for fun, not for education.	Agree	Not sure	Disagree
Sixth grade boys			
Caucasian, white collar	13%	27%	60%
Caucasian, blue collar	21	28	51
Mexican—American	23	26	51
Sixth grade girls			
Caucasian, white collar	16	21	63
Caucasian, blue collar	17	22	61
Mexican—American	29	21	50
Sixth grade Negroes	22	33	55
Tenth grade boys			
Caucasian, white collar	21	32	47
Caucasian, blue collar	36	21	43
Mexican—American	28	29	45
Tenth grade girls			
Caucasian, white collar	26	31	43
Caucasian, blue collar	36	23	41
Mexican—American	38	29	33

Tenth grade overall p=.05

Table 80: Movie going

	First grade		
	Caucasian	Mexican—American	Negro
Can't remember last time went to movies.	46%	60%	53%

	Sixth and tenth grades			
Have been to no movies in the last motnh.	Caucasian		Mexican—American	Negro Boys & Girls
	White Collar	Blue Collar		
Sixth grade boys	43%	54%	52%	35%
Sixth grade girls	53	52	59	
Tenth grade boys	54	64	60	
Tenth grade girls	45	54	50	

Sixth grade overall p=.001
Tenth grade overall p=.02

Radio listening. Although the ethnic group difference among first graders was statistically significant, this was primarily based on the divergence of the small sample of Negro students who had a higher overall percentage of radio listeners than the other two groups (Table 81).

Among the older students, there was a consistent trend, statistically significant at the sixth-grade level, for Mexican-Americans to be heavier users of radio than Caucasians, regardless of SES.

Record listening. Record listening was generally higher in the first grade among the Caucasian students than among minority students (Table 82). Among the sixth graders there is a trend for record listening to be higher among white collar family students than among the blue collar students, regardless of ethnic group. This situation changes in the tenth grade where the Mexican-American students showed a higher overall use of records than their Caucasian classmates.

Comic books. In the past comic book reading has been found to be negatively related to high SES status. Among these students the situation was somewhat mixed (Table 83). At the tenth-grade level the white collar students did have the lowest level of readership, and among the blue collar students the Mexican-American students showed a higher readership than their Caucasian peers. A similar situation held among the sixth-grade girls, but for the boys there was not real difference among the groups. In the first grade only the small sample of Negroes showed a distinct pattern, a pattern of low readership.

Table 81: Radio listening

Listened to radio:	First grade		
	Caucasian	Mexican—American	Negro
Yesterday	47%	45%	41%
Within last week	24	23	41
Longer ago	29	32	18

Overall p=.05

Radio listening time yesterday:	Sixth and tenth grades		
	Less than 1 hour	1—3 hours	4 hours or more
Sixth grade boys			
Caucasian, white collar	57%	23%	19%
Caucasian, blue collar	59	30	11
Mexican—American	45	43	12
Sixth grade girls			
Caucasian, white collar	48	41	11
Caucasian, blue collar	50	45	15
Mexican—American	37	32	31
Sixth grade Negroes	65	35	0
Tenth grade boys			
Caucasian, white collar	29	48	23
Caucasian, blue collar	24	50	26
Mexican—American	17	63	20
Tenth grade girls			
Caucasian, white collar	19	37	45
Caucasian, blue collar	16	56	37
Mexican—American	4	45	50

Sixth grade overall p=.05

Newspaper reading. Newspaper reading has generally shown the opposite relation to SES as comic books: a positive relationship with SES. This relationship consistently appears across grades and sexes (Table 84). It should be noted that the small sample of Negroes in the first grade showed a parallel pattern to Caucasian students. At the sixth-grade level the difference in daily reading of the newspaper appears to be primarily an SES difference, but at the tenth-grade level there was also a further decline among Mexican-American students compared to their blue collar Caucasian peers.

Magazine reading. The pattern for magazine reading is very inconsistent, with the boys and girls within each grade level showing very different patterns (Table 85). Only the tenth-grade boys produced a non-chance pattern which showed higher reading to have a positive relationship to higher SES among Caucasians and Mexican-Americans to be primarily moderate readers of magazines.

Book reading. There was no difference among the ethnic groups of the first grade in reported parental reading, nor in general personal attention to books, although Negro children were less likely than the others to actually read books themselves (Table 86).

Again, among the older children boys and girls showed different patterns. The boys generally exhibited a tendency for white collar students

Table 82: Record listening

Listened to records:	First grade		
	Caucasian	Mexican—American	Negro
Yesterday	29%	20%	23%
Within last week	53	29	23
Longer ago/never	18	51	54

p=.05

Record listening time yesterday:	Sixth and tenth grades		
	Less than 1 hour	1—3 hours	4 hours or more
Sixth grade boys			
Caucasian, white collar	34%	57%	9%
Caucasian, blue collar	28	60	12
Mexican—American	25	60	15
Sixth grade girls			
Caucasian, white collar	21	72	7
Caucasian, blue collar	29	57	14
Mexican—American	30	55	15
Sixth grade Negroes	13	69	18
Tenth grade boys			
Caucasian, white collar	23	61	16
Caucasian, blue collar	22	55	23
Mexican—American	9	71	20
Tenth grade girls			
Caucasian, white collar	13	61	26
Caucasian, blue collar	21	65	14
Mexican—American	8	58	34

Table 83: Comic book reading

How often read comic books:	First grade		
	Caucasian	Mexican—American	Negro
Every day	12%	8%	6%
Within last week	47	45	23
Can't remember	41	47	71

Comic books read in last month:	Sixth and tenth grades			
	None	1—4	5—8	9 or more
Sixth grade boys				
Caucasian, white collar	34%	21%	17%	28%
Caucasian, blue collar	35	31	16	18
Mexican—American	32	28	16	24
Sixth grade girls				
Caucasian, white collar	41	36	10	13
Caucasian, blue collar	38	30	14	18
Mexican—American	26	31	18	26
Sixth grade Negroes	22	48	13	17

	None	1—4	5 or more	
Tenth grade boys				
Caucasian, white collar	67	24	9	
Caucasian, blue collar	63	24	13	
Mexican—American	53	29	17	
Tenth grade girls				
Caucasian, white collar	73	17	10	
Caucasian, blue collar	67	25	8	
Mexican—American	56	37	7	

Tenth grade, boys and girls combined, readers vs nonreaders p=.001

to be the heavier users. However, at the sixth-grade level, the boys actually showed more of an ethnic difference than an SES difference. Caucasian boys generally reported higher use of both paperbacks and hard cover books than their Mexican-American peers. A similar ethnic pattern was shown by girls in their paperback use, but not in use of hard cover books.

The tenth-grade boys did show the classic SES pattern with the white collar students clearly heavier users of both types of books. Among the girls, the Mexican-American students were actually heavier users than Caucasians regardless of SES.

Use of Spanish-language media

The Mexican-American students at the two grade levels showed different patterns in the use of Spanish-language media, and it would be perhaps futile to try to make meaning out of them. However, there are two points which seem worth noting. One is the reversal of use of Spanish-language newspapers between the sixth and tenth grades among the sex groups. In this connection, it should be recalled that there is a complementary reversal (though not nearly so marked) in the use of general newspapers: boys showing a slight increase between the sixth and tenth grades, girls showing a slight decrease.

Table 84: Newspaper reading

Do you ever look at the newspaper?	First grade		
	Caucasian	Mexican–American	Negro
No	36%	49%	35%
Sundays only	10	6	8
Do look at least sometimes	54	45	57

How often do you read the newspaper?	Sixth and tenth grades		
	Seldom/never	Several times a a week	Daily
Sixth grade boys			
Caucasian, white collar	4%	35%	51%
Caucasian, blue collar	28	41	31
Mexican–American	23	46	31
Sixth grade girls			
Caucasian, white collar	24	31	45
Caucasian, blue collar	22	48	30
Mexican–American	18	49	33
Sixth grade Negroes	33	33	33
Tenth grade boys			
Caucasian, white collar	18	31	51
Caucasian, blue collar	28	26	46
Mexican–American	18	41	41
Tenth grade girls			
Caucasian, white collar	15	23	62
Caucasian, blue collar	20	31	49
Mexican–American	26	33	41

Sixth grade sexes combined,
readers vs other p=.01

Table 85: Magazine Reading

How often do you look at or read magazines at home:	First grade		
	Caucasian	Mexican—American	Negro
Often	38%	42%	47%
Sometimes	48	43	29
Never	14	15	27

How many magazines would you say you usually read each month?	Sixth and tenth grades		
	None	1—3	4 or more
Sixth grade boys			
Caucasian, white collar	21%	48%	31%
Caucasian, blue collar	31	42	27
Mexican—American	26	39	35
Sixth grade girls			
Caucasian, white collar	28	42	30
Caucasian, blue collar	26	43	31
Mexican—American	34	46	20
Sixth grade Negroes	39	52	9
Tenth grade boys			
Caucasian, white collar	33	33	33
Caucasian, blue collar	37	39	24
Mexican—American	26	65	9
Tenth grade girls			
Caucasian, white collar	25	50	25
Caucasian, blue collar	27	50	23
Mexican—American	22	56	23

Tenth grade boys $p=.001$

The other point is the vast jump in attendance of Spanish-language movies by the older girls, while such attendance declines among the boys.

Perhaps the most significant overall point to be drawn from these figures is the fact that with only two exceptions—both of these among the tenth-grade girls—less than half of either age group showed any use. The girls did show a consistent increase of use of Spanish media between the two grades, while the boys actually declined in their reported use of Spanish-language newspapers and movies (Table 87).

Other factors related to leisure time

Loneliness. Since a frequent thesis is that television (and mass media generally) are used as social substitutes, it is worth noting the self-reports of loneliness by the various groups.

Table 86: Book reading

Does either mother or father ever read to you?	First grade		
	Cacuasian	Mexican—American	Negro
No, never	34%	37%	35%

Do you ever read or look at books at home by yourself?			
No	8	13	12
Look, don't read	26	30	35
Read for self	66	67	53

Number read in last month	Sixth and tenth grades					
	Paperback			Hard cover		
	None	1	2 or more	None	1	2 or more
Sixth grade boys						
Caucasian, white collar	21%	27%	52%	28%	15%	57%
Caucasian, blue collar	32	16	52	28	14	58
Mexican—American	35	17	48	26	24	50
Sixth grade girls						
Caucasian, white collar	31	17	52	27	17	56
Caucasian, blue collar	28	19	53	22	14	64
Mexican—American	42	12	46	29	14	57
Sixth grade Negroes	26	9	65	9	22	69
Tenth grade boys						
Caucasian, white collar	46	20	34	61	14	25
Caucasian, blue collar	53	24	23	71	15	14
Mexican—American	53	29	18	76	15	11
Tenth grade girls						
Caucasian, white collar	42	28	30	62	18	20
Caucasian, blue collar	42	24	34	62	18	20
Mexican—American	41	11	48	56	22	12

Sixth grade girls paperback reading p=.05

There were no differences among the ethnic groups in the first grade (Table 88). However, among the sixth graders Mexican-American boys showed a significantly higher amount of loneliness than their classmates, and in the tenth grade this situation held for both Mexican-American boys and girls.

Organizational memberships. Organizational membership—both in school groups and teams and in nonschool groups—showed a distinct

Table 87: Use of Spanish language media by Mexican—American students

Do you read or go to Spanish language:	Sixth grade		Tenth grade	
	Boys	Girls	Boys	Girls
Books	24%	30%	38%	44%
Magazines	35	24	41	52
Newspapers	42	27	29	43
Movies	42	45	30	70

Table 88: Loneliness

	First grade		
Do you ever feel lonely?	Caucasian	Mexican—American	Negro
Never	43%	38%	41%
Not very often/now and then	45	47	47
Often/most of the time	12	15	12

	Sixth and tenth grades		
How often do you feel lonely?	Never, now & then	Once a week	Most of time, pretty often
Sixth grade boys			
Caucasian, white collar	76%	10%	14%
Caucasian, blue collar	68	13	19
Mexican—American	51	14	35
Sixth grade girls			
Caucasian, white collar	64	19	17
Caucasian, blue collar	65	11	24
Mexican—American	68	7	25
Sixth grade Negroes	77	5	18
Tenth grade boys			
Caucasian, white collar	71	16	13
Caucasian, blue collar	76	11	13
Mexican—American	63	8	29
Tenth grade girls			
Caucasian, white collar	65	15	20
Caucasian, blue collar	58	10	32
Mexican—American	57	4	39

Sixth grade boys p=.01
Tenth grade overall p=.001

SES difference at the sixth-grade level (Table 89). White collar students reported the highest levels of membership. However, the pattern falls apart for the tenth graders. Among Caucasian students, the SES pattern still generally prevails, but for school organizations the Mexican-American students equal or surpass the white collar students in memberships.

Table 89: Organization memberships

	Membership in school organizations	Membership in non-school organizations
Sixth grade boys		
Caucasian, white collar	62%	54%
Caucasian, blue collar	40	40
Mexican—American	34	37
Sixth grade girls		
Caucasian, white collar	43	53
Caucasian, blue collar	24	47
Mexican—American	28	34
Sixth grade Negroes	35	13
Tenth grade boys		
Caucasian, white collar	51	27
Caucasian, blue collar	34	26
Mexican—American	50	18
Tenth grade girls		
Caucasian, white collar	52	50
Caucasian, blue collar	44	25
Mexican—American	79	14

Sixth grade school organizations overall $p=.01$
Sixth grade non-school organizations overall $p=.001$
Tenth grade school organizations overall $p=.01$
Tenth grade non-school organizations overall $p=.001$

Chores and jobs. White collar students in the sixth grade appear to have more of their time claimed by work activities than their peers (Table 90). This is primarily due to the higher numbers of white collar students who report doing daily chores at home. The blue collar students are more likely to occasionally "hire out" for pay, but the amount of daily working for pay is very low at this age and there is no dfference among the SES or ethnic groups in the amount of *daily* work for pay, which generally is quite low.

Chores obviously have become less important for the tenth-grade boys, who are more likely to be working at paying jobs. But here there is a significant trend for white collar boys to be more likely to work for pay than blue collar, and within the blue collar group for Caucasians to do more pay work than Mexican-Americans. Although chores continued to be more important for girls, working for pay shows the same SES and ethnic pattern for girls as for boys. In both cases these results may reflect differential opportunities. Certainly it seems likely that white collar teenagers are far more likely to have baby-sitting opportunities than their blue collar peers. And for the boys, the white collar teenagers are far more likely to have fathers or family contacts who are responsible for hiring decisions than the blue collar youths.

Use of media and activities for personal reasons. Out of the complex set of data contained in Table 91 perhaps the most significant point is the comparatively high use of television by white collar boys in the sixth grade for relief of anger. Their peers are more likely to go off by themselves, talk to somebody, or seek catharsis through sports.

The high percentage of tenth-grade Mexican-American girls who would be likely to play a game or sports reflects a finding reported earlier. These girls showed a very high frequency of after-school activities.

The relatively higher use of music listening for entertainment and relaxation by sixth-grade Chicano boys recalls their higher preference for music/variety programs on television.

While many of the comparisons are statistically significant, the patterns of differences were seldom consistent across sex and age groups.

Table 90: Chores and jobs

	Do chores at home daily	Work at paying job at least occasionally
Sixth grade boys		
Caucasian, white collar	57%	43%
Caucasian, blue collar	44	53
Mexican—American	39	58
Sixth grade girls		
Caucasian, white collar	67	22
Caucasian, blue collar	63	37
Mexican—American	60	38
Sixth grade Negroes	42	54
Tenth grade boys		
Caucasian, white collar	32	61
Caucasian, blue collar	40	51
Mexican—American	33	41
Tenth grade girls		
Caucasian, white collar	73	43
Caucasian, blue collar	61	38
Mexican—American	73	33

Sixth grade chores overall p=.001
Sixth grade job overall p=.02
Tenth grade chores overall p=.001
Tenth grade chores overall p=.01

Table 91: Use of media and activites for personal reasons — socio-economic status and ethnicity

| | Sixth grade | | | | | | | |
| | Boys | | | Girls | | | Negro | |
Likely or very likely to use:	Mex.–Am.	Cau. BC	Cau. WC	Mex.–Am.	Cau. BC	Cau. WC	Both sexes	
When you just want to relax								
Watch TV	56%	44%	53%	52%	55%	63%	59%	
Listen to music	58	49	34	58	45	51	47	$p < .05$
Go to a movie	32	26	20	29	20	18	53	$p < .01$
Read book/magazine	31	28	39	40	34	50	47	
Go off by yourself	36	37	34	31	36	29	31	
Play a game or sport	48	44	45	45	27	27	53	$p < .001$
Talk to someone	43	35	29	45	53	41	33	$p < .05$
When someone has hurt your feelings								
Watch TV	22	26	28	14	26	20	35	
Listen to music	35	33	31	35	38	36	17	
Go to movie	30	20	17	17	16	8	47	$p < .001$
Read book/magazine	27	24	33	40	32	41	19	
Go off by yourself	57	67	71	54	66	66	74	
Play a game or sport	37	33	36	30	15	9	35	$p < .01$
Talk to someone	41	31	40	40	42	34	26	
When you want to be entertained								
Watch TV	64	70	76	66	68	75	73	$p < .02$
Listen to music	63	48	51	53	64	66	54	
Go to a movie	56	51	49	41	46	54	50	
Read book/magazine	35	24	29	35	34	49	27	
Go off by yourself	38	24	17	26	18	8	35	
Play a game or sport	55	62	47	52	56	60	65	
Talk to someone	56	38	29	52	51	43	47	

Continued

Table 91: Continued

	Sixth grade							
	Boys			Girls			Negro	
Likely or very likely to use:	Mex.–Am.	Cau. BC	Cau. WC	Mex.–Am.	Cau. BC	Cau. WC	Both sexes	
When someone has made you angry								
Watch TV	30	28	46	21	34	29	43	
Listen to music	40	27	32	33	40	26	11	
Go to a movie	40	26	18	25	16	9	55	
Read book/magazine	40	23	41	19	45	43	28	
Go off by yourself	51	59	46	50	66	63	75	
Play a game or sport	53	32	31	39	21	20	39	
Talk to someone	38	38	32	34	41	38	41	$p < .01$
When you are lonely								
Watch TV	66	66	72	50	65	70	45	
Listen to music	60	48	57	52	66	59	50	$p < .05$
Go to a movie	47	31	29	32	32	29	53	$p < .001$
Read book/magazine	29	29	43	31	40	44	40	$p < .001$
Go off by yourself	46	35	23	33	40	33	29	
Play a game or sport	73	59	61	46	46	41	61	
Talk to someone	55	58	49	65	74	73	60	$p < .01$

Table 91: Continued

Likely or very likely to use:	Boys			Girls			
	Mex.–Am.	Cau. BC	Cau. WC	Mex.–Am.	Cau. BC	Cau. WC	
When you just want to relax							
Watch TV	52%	47%	50%	39%	55%	44%	
Listen to music	93	74	61	94	79	87	
Go to a movie	24	14	23	18	25	9	
Read book/magazine	38	15	20	36	29	33	
Go off by yourself	36	31	40	50	52	75	
Play a game or sport	33	34	35	5	16	8	
Talk to someone	55	44	45	41	57	38	$p < .05$
When someone has hurt your feelings							
Watch TV	12	19	13	19	24	13	
Listen to music	62	58	60	67	65	71	
Go to a movie	23	10	10	10	11	4	
Read book/magazine	24	10	11	32	21	17	
Go off by yourself	89	55	62	83	79	88	$p < .05$
Play a game or sport	11	20	29	4	11	4	$p < .05$
Talk to someone	48	50	37	59	58	59	
When you want to be entertained							
Watch TV	69	69	58	74	78	80	
Listen to music	77	79	71	86	82	91	
Go to a movie	58	50	57	52	60	79	
Read book/magazine	24	32	21	29	36	30	
Go off by yourself	26	4	3	29	14	13	$p < .05$
Play a game or sport	60	60	50	76	44	44	$p < .01$
Talk to someone	65	57	53	72	70	65	

Tenth grade

Continued

Table 91: Continued

	Boys			Tenth grade Girls		
Likely or very likely to use:	Mex.–Am.	Cau. BC	Cau. WC	Mex.–Am.	Cau. BC	Cau. WC
When someone has made you angry						
Watch TV	15	24	27	19	32	29
Listen to music	59	55	62	71	63	75
Go to a movie	23	11	14	16	21	4
Read book/magazine	19	13	17	25	21	29
Go off by yourself	70	54	71	65	76	83
Play a game or sport	29	26	28	19	17	17
Talk to someone	42	37	38	50	58	71
When you feel lonely						
Watch TV	60	51	52	57	61	48
Listen to music	92	77	82	80	76	79
Go to a movie	46	22	21	16	33	21
Read book/magazine	25	17	21	35	32	34
Go off by yourself	50	24	31	30	33	35
Play a game or sport	48	46	43	52	32	36
Talk to someone	84	77	76	83	83	77

$p < .05$

HIGH AND LOW USERS OF TELEVISION AND PRINT CONTRASTED

The preceding section analyzed differences in media use among socioeconomic, ability, and ethnic groups. In the present section we will focus on categories of users to see how they may differ.

In doing this we have followed the basic methodology used by Schramm, Lyle, and Parker in their 1961 report. Four basic groups were established in each grade by dividing students into high and low users of television and books. "High" and "low" were defined independently for each age group relative to the norms of that age group. These criteria were as follows:

	Weekday Television times	Books read
First grade		
Low users	0-3:00	Do *not* read for self
High print	0-3:00	Do read for self
High television	3:30 or more	Do *not* read for self
High users	3:30 or more	Do read for self
Sixth grade		
Low users	0-2:30	0-1 books per month
High print	0-2:30	2 or more books
High television	3:00 or more	0-1 books
High users	3:00 or more	2 or more books
Tenth grade		
Low users	0-2:30	No books
High print	0-2:30	1 or more books
High television	3:00 or more	No books
High users	3:00 or more	1 or more books

Division of students in each grade according to these criteria produced the following distributions:

	First grade	Sixth grade	Tenth grade
Low users	55 (20%)	111 (17%)	136 (27%)
High print	91 (33%)	136 (20%)	75 (15%)
High television	47 (17%)	150 (23%)	203 (40%)
High users	81 (30%)	262 (40%)	97 (19%)

Demographic relations

Schramm, Lyle, and Parker demonstrated a relationship between similar divisions and such variables as socioeconomic status and intelligence. As might be suspected from the analysis in the preceding section, these relations were far less clearcut in the present data.

Intelligence. Table 92 details the findings for intelligence among the sixth and tenth graders, using intelligence first as the dependent variable and then as the independent variable. At both age levels the High Print and High User groups had a higher average intelligence than the High Television group, this being more marked the sixth than among the tenth graders. Turning the table around, one sees that at both levels there was a trend—not very strong—for brighter students to be disproportionately (compared to the marginals) high in High Print and High Use. The low intelligence group was disproportionately higher in the High Television category, particularly at the sixth-grade level. However, it must be noted that at the tenth-grade level more high-intelligence students went into the High Television group than into any other group. Among the high-intelligence sixth graders, the largest number went into the High User group, a finding which paralleled that of the 1961 study.

In sum, the High Print group (and at the sixth grade level the High User group) did tend to be more intelligent than the other groups; however, it cannot be said that children of high intelligence are markedly lower users of television than their peers.

Socioeconomic status. Many earlier studies, including that of Schramm, Lyle, and Parker, have reported higher viewing among blue

Table 92: Media use categories related to intelligence

Intelligence:	Sixth grade				Tenth grade			
	Low user	High print	High TV	High user	Low user	High print	High TV	High user
Low	30%	22%	35%	22%	31%	12%	23%	24%
Middle	33	48	39	46	39	47	52	37
High	37	30	26	32	30	42	26	39
	Intelligence				Intelligence			
	Low	Mid.	High		Low	Mid.	High	
Low users	18%	13%	19%		35%	23%	25%	
High print	17	23	20		7	14	18	
High television	32	22	20		40	48	34	
High users	33	42	41		18	15	23	

p=.01

collar children compared to white collar children. Table 93 shows the socioeconomic comparison for the present data. There is little more than a suggestion of the relationship reported in earlier studies. True, at both grade levels the High Print group has the highest percentage of white collar family students, and among white collar students there is a smaller proportion in the High Television group than among blue collar students, but these differences are not beyond the .05 chance level.

Table 93: Media use categories related to socio-economic status

| | Sixth grade | | | | Tenth grade | | | |
	Low user	High print	High TV	High user	Low user	High print	High TV	High user
Blue collar	83%	80%	86%	85%	80%	71%	83%	79%
White collar	17	20	14	15	20	29	17	21

	Blue collar	White collar	Blue collar	White collar
Low user	16%	19%	28%	28%
High print	20	26	13	21
High TV	25	21	41	32
High user	39	34	18	19

Ethnic groups. The distribution of ethnic groups into the four media use categories presents a rather complex picture, one complicated by age differences (Table 94). The most clearcut point is that Negro students in both first and sixth grades were far heavier viewers of television than their peers, but that at the sixth grade level they were concentrated in the High User group.

Chicano students at the first-grade level were disproportionately low in the High Print category, disproportionately high in the Low User category. In the sixth grade they were disproportionately low in the High User category and slightly high in both the High Print and the High Television groups. In the tenth grade they were disproportionately high in the High User group and, particularly, in the High TV group.

Table 94: Media use categories related to ethnic groups

| | First grade | | | Sixth grade | | | Tenth grade | |
	Cau- casian	Mex.— Am.	Negro	Cau- casian	Mex.— Am.	Negro	Cau- casian	Mex.— Am.
Low user	19%	28%	9%	17%	19%	14%	28%	18%
High print	37	28	12	20	25	9	16	8
High TV	15	15	47	24	27	18	38	48
High user	29	28	41	39	29	59	18	25

Parental relations

Students in the sixth and tenth grades were asked a series of questions to ascertain frequency of disagreement or conflict with their parents over grades, friends, their clothes, their hair, and money. An index of conflict with parents was formed by summing responses to these five items. Table 95 shows the relation of media use categories to conflict index scores.

Table 95: Media use categories related to conflict index scores

	Sixth grade				Tenth grade			
Conflict:	Low user	High print	High TV	High user	Low user	High print	High TV	High user
Low	17%	12%	6%	9%	12%	4%	8%	4%
Moderate low	36	29	29	28	36	39	31	40
Moderate high	42	43	47	44	40	48	47	45
High	15	16	18	19	13	9	14	11

	Conflict				Conflict			
	Low	Mod. low	Mod. high	High	Low	Mod. low	Mod. high	High
Low user	14%	20%	16%	15%	42%	28%	24%	28%
High print	28	19	19	18	8	16	16	10
High TV	17	25	27	26	39	34	40	45
High user	42	36	38	41	11	23	20	17

No real relationship appears between these two variables.

Two other indices of relations with parents were formed. One summed scores on the items detailing the frequency with which students discussed current issues with their parents, and the other the summed items dealing with the discussion of personal or family problems. The relationship of these index scores is shown in Table 96.

Among the sixth graders there were significant differences. High television users were less likely than others to discuss issues with their parents and, together with the Low Users, less likely to discuss their personal problems with their parents. Tenth graders showed no difference in discussion of problems, and only the Low Users showed a markedly lower discussion of issues with their parents.

Regarding parents' efforts to control the child's television viewing, somewhat different patterns emerged among the sixth and tenth graders, as shown in Table 97.

There was no difference among the sixth graders in parenttal limitation on television viewing nor on the amount of parental complaints

Table 96: Media use categories related to parental discussion indices

	Sixth grade				Tenth grade			
	Low user	High print	High TV	High user	Low user	High print	High TV	High user
Discussion of issues								
Low	31%	29%	44%	30%	41%	28%	33%	24%
Moderate	35	41	32	36	36	47	45	50
High	34	30	24	34	23	25	21	26
Discussion of problems								
Low	29	21	26	19	33	29	28	27
Moderate	51	52	54	48	44	49	48	49
High	20	27	20	33	23	22	24	24

p=.01

Table 97: Media use categories related to parental control of viewing

	Sixth grade				Tenth grade			
	Low user	High print	High TV	High user	Low user	High print	High TV	High user
Parents have limited TV viewing	37%	38%	37%	38%	34%	30%	34%	46%
Parents have used TV deprivation as punishment	51	53	50	42	32	41	34	50
Parents do complain about TV	48	48	49	45	27	37	40	56
Of those complaining, subject of the complaint is:								
Watch too much	21	33	32	24	12	23	24	46
Watch too late	34	20	23	30	29	31	24	18
Program selection	28	28	26	29	38	31	37	21

about viewing. However, the High Users reported the least amount of parental use of television deprivation as punishment. Of the complaints cited, parents of the High Print and High Television groups most often complained of too much viewing, while those of the Low Users and High Users were more likely to complain about watching too late or about the programs selected.

A considerably different pattern emerged among the tenth graders where the High Users were the most frequent subjects of parental limitation, punishment, and complaints concerning television. Further, the amount of time spent viewing was the overwhelming subject of parental complaints in this group, while among the other groups parents complained mostly about watching too late or about program selection.

Students who were heavy viewers were far more likely to have parents who were heavy viewers than students who were light viewers, as is shown in Table 98.

Table 98: Media use categories related to parents' TV time

	Sixth grade				Tenth grade			
	Low user	High print	High TV	High user	Low user	High print	High TV	High user
Mother's TV time								
0 – 1 hour	39%	30%	13%	16%	24%	26%	21%	19%
1½ – 3 hours	27	33	36	30	41	46	34	31
3½ – hours or more	24	37	51	54	16	17	39	39
p=.001	p=.05							
Father's TV time								
0 – 1 hour	56	45	29	32	55	49	31	21
1½ – 3 hours	28	38	32	29	35	34	44	24
3½ hours or more	16	17	39	39	10	17	24	34
p=.001	p=.01							

Social adjustment and peer relations

An obvious question regarding the child's use of television is whether or not it interferes with the child's social relations and his integration into the peer group. A series of questions aimed at this problem were included in the data collection.[9] For the most part, the results lend no more than modest support to the thesis that heavy television viewing interferes with the child having a normal social life. Table 99 details the relationship between media use categories and the students' self-reported levels of loneliness. The only sizable difference is among the first graders, where the High Users showed the *lowest* level of loneliness.

Similarly, self-rated popularity of the sixth and tenth graders showed no difference related to media use category. The High Print students in the tenth grade did show a significantly higher perception of teacher interest than all three other groups, and a similar trend was apparent among the sixth graders.

Table 99: Media use categories related to reported loneliness

	First grade			Sixth grade			Tenth grade		
	Low	Mod.	High	Low	Mod.	High	Low	Mod.	High
Low users	47%	36%	17%	65%	14%	21%	74%	9%	19%
High print	57	27	16	60	13	27	63	14	23
High TV	53	36	11	61	15	24	67	12	21
High users	67	26	7	68	12	20	63	8	29

Among the first graders it is noteworthy that both the Low User and High Print groups reported a higher level of daily play with other children compared to the High Television and High User groups. This perhaps was the single strongest indicator that television viewing may be dysfunctional to social activity.

The series of items in the sixth and tenth grade questionnaire dealing with leisure time activities were summed to form an "activity" index.[10] In neither grade was there a significant relationship between media use categories and activity index scores. One item in the index—frequency of participation in after-school activities or sports—showed a significant relationship among tenth graders. The High Television group showed a far lower level of such activity than the other three groups.

A separate check was made to see if high activity index scores might be inversely related to daytime viewing. There was no difference among the groups. Daily home chores did show a trend in this direction among the tenth graders.

Discussion with friends of various topics, ranging from current issues to friends and events at school to personal problems was also compared for the four media use groups.[11] Although there were general age differences in the levels of discussion of various topics, a general pattern held for both sixth and tenth grades (Table 100A and B). High Print and High User groups had generally higher levels of discussion than the other two groups. Significantly, although television was one of the leading topics of discussion for all groups, it was somewhat less important among the Low Users and the High Print groups. Another highly suggestive difference, far more pronounced at the tenth grade level than at the sixth, was that the High Print group had a higher level of discussion of the future than all three other groups.

Indices of discussion of issues and personal problems with peers similar to those for discussion with parents were constructed by summing over items. When the scores on these indices were related to the media use categories, there were no differences among the sixth graders. At the tenth-grade level the High Print group was significantly higher (at the .05 level) in discussion of issues than the other groups. There was a similar, but not statistically significant, trend for discussion of personal problems among the tenth graders.

Table 100A: Media use categories related to frequent discussion of topics with friends — sixth grade*

	Low users	High print	High TV	High users
80%'s	School (80%)	School (80%)	School (84%)	School (82%)
70%'s	— (—)	TV (73%)	TV (77%) Movies (70%)	TV (78%) Movies (70%)
60%'s	TV (68%) Movies (67%) Friends (63%)	Movies (69%)		Friends (66%)
50%'s	Dissatisfaction at school (53%) Future (51%) Clothes (50%)	Friends (53%) Future (55%) Pollution (53%) Dissatisfaction at school (52%) Books (51%) Vietnam (50%)	Friends (58%) Clothes (56%) Future (52%) Dissatisfaction at school (50%) Pollution (50%)	Clothes (58%) Dissatisfaction at school (57%) Future (56%) Pollution (52%)
40%'s	Pollution (48%) Books (46%) Vietnam (45%) Magazines (45%) TV news (40%) Newspaper (40%)	Newspaper (49%) Magazines (48%) Clothes (45%) TV news (40%)	Magazines (44%) Books (41%)	Vietnam (49%) Magazines (48%) Books (45%) TV news (43%) Newspaper (41%) Problems of youth (41%)
30%'s	Problems of youth (39%) Personal problems (38%) Student protest (31%)	Problems of youth (38%) Personal problems (35%) Student protest (32%) Politics (31%)	TV News (39%) Newspapers (38%) Problems of youth (38%) Vietnam (38%) Personal problems (36%) Student protest (34%)	Personal problems (38%) Student protest (31%) Politics (30%)
20%'s	Politics (28%)		Politics (21%)	

*Percentage of students indicating "frequent" discussion given in parentheses.

Table 100B: Media use categories related to frequent discussion of topics with friends — tenth grade*

	Low users	High print	High TV	High users
90's	School (92%)	School (92%)	School (91%)	— (—)
80's	—	Movies (82%)	—	School (83%)
70's	Movies (70%)	Dissatisfaction at school (73%) Future (71%)	Movies (77%)	Movies (77%)
60's	Dissatisfaction at school (68%) Friends (64%)	Friends (66%) TV (62%)	TV (69%) Friends (69%) Dissatisfaction at school (66%) Clothes (65%)	TV (69%) Dissatisfaction at school (67%) Friends (61%)
50's	Future (56%) TV (54%)	Problems of youth (59%) Clothes (58%) Newspaper (55%) Pollution (53%) Vietnam (53%) Magazines (52%)	Future (53%) Vietnam (53%)	Future (56%) Newspaper (57%) Vietnam (54%) Clothes (54%) Magazines (52%)
40's	Vietnam (48%) Pollution (47%) Magazines (46%) Clothes (44%) Problems of youth (42%) TV News (40%)	TV news (45%)	Newspaper (48%) Problems of youth (48%) TV news (42%) Magazines (41%) Pollution (40%)	Problems of youth (49%) Pollution (48%) TV news (48%) Books (40%)
30's	Personal problems (36%)	Personal problems (37%) Student protest (36%) Books (34%)	Student protest (37%) Personal problems (36%)	Personal problems (37%) Student protest (36%)
20's	Student protest (29%)	Politics (24%)	Books (20%) Politics (20%)	Politics (28%)
10's	Books (19%) Politics (14%)			

Viewing behavior

There was no consistent evidence that the Low User or High Print groups were more selective in their television viewing. Among the sixth graders there were some suggestions that the High Print group might be more discriminating and the television group less so than the other groups, but among the tenth graders differences were small and inconsistent.

The High Television and High User groups were more likely to study with the television set on at both age levels, and the High User group at both age levels was most likely to watch in the company of parents and siblings. Among the first graders, both the High Television and particularly the High User groups were higher than the other groups in their viewing in the company of siblings. Disagreement with siblings over program selection was highest among the first-grade High Television group and among the tenth-grade High User group. There was no difference among the sixth-grade groups.

Talking while watching showed little difference among the groups, nor did other activities (other than studying), although the High Print groups had a slightly higher level of such activities.

Use of other media

Very little was found in the way of relations between the media use categories and use of other media among the first graders, as is seen in Table 101. The High Television group was low in record playing and movie attendance; High Print students were high on comic book reading; Low Use group students were highest in readership of magazines, lowest in daily looking at the newspaper.

Similarly at the sixth and tenth-grade levels there were no consistent patterns of either positive correlation or displacement (Table 102).

Table 101: Media use categories related to use of other media

	First grade			
	Low users	High print	High TV	High users
Listened to radio yesterday	44%	50%	49%	42%
Listened to records yesterday	20	29	13	22
Saw movie last week	11	19	2	10
Parents read to them	62	68	60	64
Read magazines	24	14	13	15
Read comic books daily	6	19	4	9
Don't look at newspaper	54	32	34	37

Table 102: Media use categories related to use of other media

	Sixth grade					Tenth grade			
	Low user	High print	High TV	High user		Low user	High print	High TV	High user
Radio time yesterday									
None	26%	21%	16%	16%		8%	5%	4%	7%
5 hours or more	7	6	9	12		21	18	28	21
Phonograph playing									
None	36	36	28	21		18	26	24	16
5 hours or more	3	2	4	6		6	5	9	4
No movies in last month	62	48	58	46		55	52	60	53
Read newspaper									
No	30	19	29	22		23	20	27	17
Daily	27	38	28	32		49	51	46	52
Comic books read									
None	45	35	44	25		72	53	66	57
9 or more	12	22	13	24		4	8	2	6
Magazines read									
None	37	24	38	24		33	25	40	18
9 or more	3	12	6	15		6	7	3	4

Program preferences

The different media use groups did show variations in the categories of shows they named as their favorites. Again, however, the pattern of differences was not consistent over age (Table 103). Among the first graders, the Low User group was somewhat lower in preference for situation comedies, the High Print group somewhat lower in preference for cartoon shows.

At the sixth-grade level the family situation comedies were considerably more important among the High Television and High User groups. Among the tenth graders, hip adventures stood considerably higher with the High Print and High User groups. Family Situation comedies were more important for the High Print group, which was low on music programs compared to the other groups. Dramatic shows scored higher with the High User and High Television groups.

Attitudes toward television

Examining the responses of the members of the media use groups to the various questions concerning attitudes toward the media, several differences did stand out.

Table 103: Media use categories related to program preferences

	Hip Adventure	Situation Comedy	Family Situation Comedy	Music	Drama	Cartoon
First grade						
Low user		42%			9%	26%
High print		53			13	16
High TV		53			8	26
High user		52			21	7
Sixth grade*						
Low user	66%	86	82%	38%		
High print	54	84	87	35		
High TV	49	95	100	37		
High user	53	89	104	34		
Tenth grade*						
Low user	90	55	37	57	32	
High print	110	66	62	45	25	
High TV	90	68	38	52	44	
High user	109	45	32	55	43	

*Each individual allowed to name four favorite programs, hence percentages may total more than 100.

At the first grade level the High User and High Television group were significantly more accepting of television children as being like themselves than were the Low User and High Print groups (Table 104). This difference did not hold concerning acceptance of television adults, although it should be noted that the High User group did show the highest level of acceptance. This group also showed the highest amount of use of television for play modeling, in both solitary and social play. The High Television group was the most likely to dream about things seen on television, but it was the Low User group which showed the highest level of being frightened by television content.

Among the sixth graders there were no nonchance differences between the media use groups in their responses to the various attitudinal questions concerning television (Table 105). Several differences, however, might be noted. The High User group was the most accepting of television characters as being lifelike. The High Print group registered the strongest disagreement with the statement that television should be fun rather than educational.

Three differences among the tenth graders were statistically significant. The High User and High Television groups were less likely to view television news as inadequate. The High Print group showed the strongest disagreement with the statement that television should just be fun

Table 104: Media use categories related to TV influence

	First grade				
	Low users	High print	High TV	High users	
Kids on TV like self	44%	41%	64%	68%	p=.01
Adults on TV lifelike	42	41	40	53	
Frightened by TV content	56	47	45	49	
Dream about TV content	34	38	49	32	
Use TV for solitary play	22	22	21	31	
Use TV for social play	47	45	45	52	

Table 105: Media use categories related to attitudes of sixth and tenth graders

	Sixth grade				Tenth grade			
	Low user	High print	High TV	High user	Low user	High print	High TV	High user
People on TV not like real life	50%	42%	38%	34%	42%	57%	36%	24%
TV not like real life	47	44	39	44	49	63	48	35
						p=.01		
Too much news on TV	32	43	54	49	42	29	41	39
TV news not truthful	22	18	25	22	22	36	24	21
TV news not sufficient	22	29	25	25	41	40	27	27
						p=.01		
TV unfair to minorities	23	27	23	26	20	24	16	15
Commercials annoying	50	49	48	46	64	55	50	46
Commercials untruthful	65	56	60	58	75	66	68	72
TV should not be just for fun	49	61	52	57	40	58	32	47
						p=.05		
One doesn't learn from TV	26	30	23	26	28	32	25	32

and also the highest rejection of programs as being realistic. Similarly, although the difference did not reach statistical significance, this group showed the highest rejection of television characters as being lifelike and the highest rejection of television news as being trustworthy, although they were also the least likely to think there was too much news on television. It might also be noted that both the High Use and High Television group were more tolerant of commercials.

Comparative use of media and activities

Table 106 shows the relative levels of choice of different media and activities by the four media use groups for entertainment, relaxation, and solace from loneliness, anger, or hurt feelings. The general pattern

Table 106: Media use categories related to comparative use of media and activities

% likely to use:	Sixth grade					Tenth grade				
	Low user	High print	High TV	High user	p	Low user	High print	High TV	High user	p
For entertainment										
Watch television	62%	59%	71%	70%	.05	63%	64%	75%	74%	
Listen music	47	52	59	60	.05	80	82	76	86	
Go to movie	39	48	50	47		59	46	57	71	
Read book	27	31	24	36	.05	26	38	20	51	.001
Go off by self	20	24	23	24		13	8	11	10	
Play game/sport	56	56	57	58		58	36	52	66	
Talk to someone	35	44	44	52		56	59	57	57	
For relaxation										
Watch television	44	41	65	60	.001	36	29	56	68	.001
Listen to music	47	49	48	50		77	83	78	77	
Go to movie	21	21	26	24		19	30	17	18	
Read book	25	41	29	35	.05	21	39	18	46	.001
Go off by self	38	34	40	30		45	40	40	59	
Play game/sport	44	46	33	37		27	22	24	24	
Talk to someone	41	40	40	46		52	50	47	46	
When lonely										
Watch television	50	55	68	70	.05	45	57	61	61	
Listen to music	50	58	56	59		73	81	76	83	
Go to movie	30	29	32	38		22	31	31	29	
Read book	34	33	31	43		25	38	20	41	
Go off by self	44	35	38	37		37	37	29	41	
Play game/sport	55	56	49	58		40	37	43	44	
Talk to someone	66	59	60	66		71	73	78	69	
When angry										
Watch television	30	18	31	38	.05	16	25	30	42	.05
Listen to music	27	32	31	38		61	59	59	66	
Go to movie	23	20	24	19		13	11	14	24	
Read book	24	34	25	35		13	25	17	36	.001
Go off by self	51	49	61	65		69	46	65	59	
Play game/sport	35	35	27	31		28	7	18	32	
Talk to someone	30	26	42	42	.05	45	54	46	53	
When feelings hurt										
Watch television	17	21	26	27		12	11	22	29	
Listen to music	32	35	39	38		63	54	59	60	
Go to movie	14	19	17	19		12	7	10	18	
Read book	30	33	23	38		16	33	12	18	
Go off by self	59	57	69	67		75	42	70	74	
Play game/sport	26	31	26	27		20	7	10	20	
Talk to someone	30	33	40	35		50	36	49	40	

holds for both grade levels. In effect, the pattern is for television to be more important for all purposes to the High Television and High User groups, for print to be more important to the High Print and High User groups. This, of course, suggests that those who are heavier users of each medium do obtain greater and more general satisfaction from them which should, in turn, reinforce their use.

But perhaps just as important is the fact that even among the heavy users of television at both grade levels—whether High Television or High User—television is a secondary medium for relieving both anger and hurt feelings. It is, however, a significant solace for loneliness for these students.

SPECIAL PATTERNS OF VIEWING AND ATTITUDES

Viewing of violent programs

Using ratings by a sample of the general public and of television critics, Greenberg and Gordon (1971) established a list of the 20 most violent series shown during the 1969-70 television series.

Fourteen of these shows were scheduled during the five days for which sixth and tenth graders provided recall diaries of their television viewing. In four instances, two of the programs competed in the same time period. This meant that the students could have watched as many as ten complete programs.

Table 107 shows the share of audience for each grade gained by these programs together with the ratings for other major station programs in the same time period. It should be emphasized that the percentages for each program are based on the number of people watching in that time period, not on the population of sixth and tenth graders. The percentage of each grade population who were watching is given at the top of each time period.

Some of these programs scored rather spectacularly. *Mod Squad*, for instance, attracted two-thirds of the tenth graders who were watching and well over half of the sixth graders. *Bonanza* was watched by 57 percent of the audience from both grades. *Mission Impossible* also scored well among both age groups, but it should be noted that the audience at that time period was relatively small.

By contrast, in two different periods of peak viewing, *The Virginian* and *Ironside* did relatively poorly. *Hee Haw* outpulled *The Virginian* and *Bewitched* was far ahead of *Ironside*.

Age differences were pronounced in several cases. *It Takes a Thief* and *Then Came Bronson* did much better among the tenth graders than among the sixth graders. *Paris 7000* scored strongly with the sixth graders but not with the tenth graders. However, this situation may have been happenstance. In the survey week the *Grammy Awards* were

Table 107: Share of audience gained by "most violent programs" ("most violent programs" shown in capital letters)

	Grade 6	Grade 10
SUNDAY		
9 p.m.		
% of sample viewing	52%	57%
Glen Campbell	14%	12%
BONANZA	57	57
Roller Game	12	10
Movie	12	16
Movie	1	3
Movie	3	2
News	1	1
7 p.m.		
% of sample viewing	41%	36%
Lassie	20%	15%
Wild Kingdom	23	19
LAND OF THE GIANTS	33	31
Showcase Five		2
Rat Patrol*	8	16
Movie	3	5
Star Trek	13	18
10 p.m.		
% of sample viewing	28%	38%
MISSION IMPOSSIBLE	45%	46%
BOLD ONES	34	37
News	2	2
Movie	14	13
Let Me Talk To:	1	1
News	3	
Labor Report	1	

	Grade 6	Grade 10
MONDAY		
7:30 p.m.		
% of sample viewing	54%	46%
GUNSMOKE	25%	20%
My World and Welcome To It	25	18
IT TAKES A THIEF	28	41
Steve Allen	2	6
Movie	3	2
Truth/Consequences	13	10
Perry Mason	4	3
TUESDAY		
7 p.m.		
% of sample viewing	63%	54%
LANCER	14%	10%
Once Before I Die	10	6
MOD SQUAD	54	67
Steve Allen		4
Movie	8	11
Truth/Consequences	11	3
Perry Mason	2	
WEDNESDAY		
7:30 p.m.		
% of sample viewing	63%	69%
Hee Haw	32%	27%
VIRGINIAN	17	25
Steve Allen	2	6
Movie	23	17
Kentuckian*	12	16

	Grade 6	Grade 10
WEDNESDAY (continued)		
Truth/Consequences	11%	9%
Perry Mason	4	2
10 p.m.		
% of sample viewing	32%	53%
HAWAII FIVE-O	28%	23%
THEN CAME BRONSON	24	40
Room 222	37	27
I Spy*	6	6
News	1	2
News		
Twelve O'clock High	4	1
THURSDAY		
7:30 p.m.		
% of sample viewing	61%	50%
Family Affair	30%	26%
DANIEL BOONE	38	34
Steve Allen	2	5
Animal World	9	9
Movie	8	15
Truth/Consequences	10	8
Perry Mason	3	4
8:30 p.m.		
% of sample viewing	64%	58%
Jim Nabors	10	8
IRONSIDE	18	26
Boxing	4	3

Continued

*These programs, which generally contain considerable violence, were shown as re-runs. The "most violent ratings" were based only on network prime time shows for that season.

Table 107: Continued

	Grade	
	6	10
THURSDAY (continued)		
8:30 p.m.		
% of sample viewing	64%	58%
Bewitched	56%	47%
Movie	7	11
David Frost	1	2
Big Valley	4	2
10 p.m.		
% of sample viewing	24%	41%
Movie	11%	20%
Grammy Awards	18	36
Boxing	6	3
PARIS 7000	45	14
I Spy	16	24
News	2	1
Major Adams	2	2

*These programs, which generally contain considerable violence, were shown as re-runs. The "most violent ratings" were based only on network prime time shows for that season.

broadcast as a special in the same time period as *Paris 7000* and walked away with the largest share of the tenth-grade audience. The special appeal of music for tenth graders, documented in earlier sections, may have meant that this program drew regular viewers away from *Paris 7000*. It should be noted that a rerun series (and a violent one), *I Spy*, drew a considerably larger segment of the tenth-grade audience.[12]

It is worth noting that in addition to *Hee Haw* and *Bewitched*, several other programs without violence competed successfully against the violent programs. The gentle *My World and Welcome to It* did very well among the sixth graders. *Room 222* and *Family Affair* did well among both grade groups. All three featured young people.

The most popular programs for the five-day period and the percentage of all the students in each group watching the programs were given in Table 11. Table 108 shows the "most violent" programs among the leaders for each age group.

Table 108: "Most violent programs" among most popular programs for each age group (% are proportion of all students in group watching program.)

First grade (of eight programs)	Sixth grade (of 22 programs)	Tenth grade (of 22 programs)
18% Daniel Boone	32% Mod Squad 29% Bonanza 18% Ironside	35% Mod Squad 35% Bonanza 22% Dragnet 19% It Takes a Thief 17% Daniel Boone 17% Then Came Bronson 17% Mission Impossible 15% Ironside 14% Bold Ones

Turning to the programs which students listed as their "favorites" (Table 74), the "most violent" programs appearing are given in Table 109.

It is obvious that preference for violent programs, both in terms of actual viewing and as favorites, increases with age.

Table 109: "Most violent programs" among favorite programs for each age group

First grade	Sixth grade	Tenth grade
	Mod Squad It Takes a Thief Gunsmoke	Mod Squad It Takes a Thief Then Came Bronson Gunsmoke (Highway Patrol)*

* A re-run series containing considerable violence.

Turning to the students for whom there were complete five-day viewing diaries, a count was made of how many of the "most violent" programs each student watched. Table 110 shows the distribution. (It
should be remembered that the maximum number of shows any student
could see was ten.) There was no difference between the boys and girls,
so the results are combined in the table.

Table 110: Number of "most violent programs" viewed

	Sixth grade	Tenth grade
None	23.1%	23.8%
1	23.1	24.2
2	20.2	16.1
3	15.1	15.7
4	10.1	10.9
5	3.9	4.4
6	3.1	2.0
7	1.0	1.6
8	0.2	1.2
	(N=484)	(N=248)
Mean number	2.0	2.0

The distributions for the two age groups were almost identical. At first
glance this might seem to contradict what has just been said concerning
popularity of such programs among the age groups. However, the larger
number of violent programs in the top 22 programs of the tenth graders
was largely due to the fact that the tenth graders viewed somewhat less
overall than did the sixth graders, and their viewing was more broadly
spread over programs. In other words, the top 22 tenth grade programs
included programs with smaller audiences than was the case with the top
22 of the sixth graders.

A series of cross tabulations were made to see if the viewing of violent
programs was related to various attitudinal and personal characteristic
measures included in the survey. Students who watched four or more of
the "most violent" programs were classified as "heavy violence viewers." As might be expected, heavy violence viewing was positively
related to total viewing time. It was felt this factor should be controlled
to see if those students who were light viewers of television but heavy
viewers of violent programs were unique. Inspection of the frequency
tables, however, showed that wherever differences were found, they
were functions of violence viewing independent of total viewing time.

While there was no difference between boys and girls in the number of
violent programs seen, there were different patterns of relationships.
The most interesting relationship found was the positive relationship
between heavy viewing of violent programs and the index of conflict

with parents. This relationship was significant among boys at both sixth- and tenth-grade levels. For the girls there were trends in the same direction, but they did not pass the .05 nonchance level. Examination of the individual items making up the index showed that violence viewing was most strongly related to conflict over hair and money spending, with conflict over clothes and grades following. Conflict with parents over friends was not related to violence viewing. The only item which showed a significant relationship among the girls was conflict over hair, which among the sixth-grade girls was positively related to violence viewing.

Generally there were no significant relationships between violence viewing and attitudes toward "establishment" and authority. Among the sixth graders, boys who were high violence viewers were significantly more likely than their peers to think that older people do not understand young people. There was a similar trend among the sixth-grade girls. In the tenth grade, the relationship was significant among the girls but not among the boys.

Violence viewing tended to be related to lower intelligence among boys of both grade groups, but the differences were not beyond the .05 chance level.

Among the tenth graders there were trends, not beyond the .05 chance level, for violence viewing to be more prevalent among blue collar than among white collar youths.

Those tenth-grade boys who were heavy violence viewers did show a significantly higher acceptance of television characters as being like people they know.

Habitual afternoon viewing

It might be expected that youngsters who habitually watch a large amount of television in the afternoon on school days might have problems of social adjustment. To see if this might be the case, a "habitual afternoon viewer" variable was established. Using only those students for whom there were complete sets of viewing diaries for the four schoolday afternoons (Monday through Thursday), those students who watched at least one and one-half hours each afternoon were labeled the "habitual afternoon viewers." The dividing point was arbitrary. Most students did watch at least some television most afternoons. The criterion of an hour and one-half or more meant that these children spent close to half of their total nonschool afternoon hours with television and also yielded a large enough group to make meaningful comparisons possible.

Table 111 shows the distribution of "habitual afternoon viewers" for both grades. As expected from the general viewing patterns previously reported, the proportion of students falling into this group showed a decline among the boys of the tenth grade as contrasted to the sixth grade, but there was no similar decline among the girls.

Table 111: "Habitual daytime viewers"

"Habitual daytime viewers" watch at least 1½ hours of television every schoolday afternoon.

	Sixth grade		Tenth grade	
	Boys	Girls	Boys	Girls
Habitual daytime viewers	29%	28%	16%	27%
Others	17	72	84	73
	(N=288)	(N=238)	(N=153)	(N=123)

Contrary to expectations, there were no significant relationships between habitual daytime viewing and any of the social adjustment variables such as reported loneliness, self-rated popularity, or perceived teacher interest. The habitual daytime viewers in the tenth grade showed only a slightly lower score on the social/recreational activity index than their peers. The difference was not statistically significant. Sixth-grade girls and tenth graders—both boys and girls—in this group also showed a slight, but not significant, trend to have higher scores on the parental conflict index.

There was a consistent trend over the age groups for the habitual daytime viewing to be related to low intelligence. This relationship was highly significant ($p = .001$) among the tenth grade girls. There was a similarly consistent trend in responses to the question concerning the students' educational goals. They also reported significantly lower grade averages. They were also significantly more likely to watch alone (the tenth grade boys showed a similar trend) and to study with the television set on.

Attitudinal relationships

A final area of investigation concerned possible relationships between students' attitudes toward the media and their attitudes toward "establishment" values and authority.

Attitudes toward commercials, acceptance of television news as reliable, and acceptance of the newspaper as fair toward young people were all run against the questions concerning obedience to the law, authority of principals, older people's understanding of youth, optimism for the future, and "materialism."

Only one significant relationship was found. Among the tenth graders a negative attitude toward the truthfulness of commercials was related to "antimaterialism" (as measured by response to the question "Most people think too much about things like cars, money, clothes, etc.").

Among both sixth and tenth graders, a belief that commercials were untruthful was significantly related to skepticism about the reliability of television news.

FOOTNOTES

1. We would like to give special recognition to several people whose assistance was of particular importance to the project. Ziporah Suesskind helped with the preliminary literature review and pretesting. Three members of the UCLA Survey Research Center staff, Debbie Hensler, Winnie Hom and David Landes, helped us through many a problem and crisis. Richard A. Stone came into the project in its later phases and took over the computer work. Hazel Richmond of the Journalism Department staff proved herself a typist of supreme skill and patience. Finally, Dr. Douglas A. Fuchs provided ideas and guidance which were of great value to the study, and Dr. Frederick Gottlieb of UCLA's Neuropsychiatric Institute provided insights for the work with the younger children.

2. Throughout this section, reference is made to tables on which statements are based. These tables will be found later in the paper.

3. Since we had only one-day viewing records for first graders, we could not make a similar analysis of that age group.

4. The fact that the survey was done at the end of the season when program schedules were well-established may have meant that there was little need to use the log.

5. The other activities were: going to a movie, listening to music, reading, talking to someone, going off to oneself, and playing a game.

6. Throughout the following sections, significance levels are given only for comparisons yielding a chi-square value sufficient for the .05 level or less.

7. The question of rank order is cloudy here as students were not asked to assign rank order to their selections. The ranking in the table, therefore, is based upon the total number of mentions for a program, regardless of whether it was the first, second, third, or fourth show named. An analysis was made, weighing the order of mention, which showed that the rank order remained pretty much the same. In a few cases where the total percentages were close, the order was reversed.

8. So far as local school officials were aware, no "underground" paper had been issued by local students. Such papers have sporadically appeared in many (if not most) of the high schools in more urbanized sections of the Los Angeles complex.

9. See Technical Appendix for details on these items.

10. See Technical Appendix.

11. See Technical Appendix.

12. Several violent programs from previous seasons were appearing as reruns on the nonnetwork stations.

REFERENCES

Atkin, C., Murray, J., and Nayman, O. *Television and social behavior: an annotated bibliography*. National Institute of Mental Health, 1971.

Gerbner, G. Violence in television drama: trends and symbolic functions. *Television and Social Behavior*, Volume 1. Washington, D.C.: United States Government Printing Office, 1971.

Greenberg, B., and Gordon, T. Perceptions of violence in TV programs: critics and the public. *Television and Social Behavior*, Volume I.

Schramm, W., Lyle, J., and Parker, E. *Television in the lives of our children*. Stanford: Stanford University Press, 1961.

Steiner, G. *The people look at television*. New York: Knopf, 1963.

Technical Appendix

The criteria for selecting the study location were predominately pragmatic.

To avoid the expense and problems of constructing a sample of students in a large system, it was decided to seek a unified district of a size making it feasible to work with population groups at the sixth and tenth grade levels. In California there are Elementary School Districts, High School Districts and Unified School Districts. The unified districts offer instruction from kindergarten through grade 12. In some cases (as in the district used in this study), the unified district was created by the merger of earlier elementary and high school districts.

Since comparison of ethnic groups was intended, it was necessary to seek a system with a mixed population.

For ease of field supervision, it was desired that the test city be located within commuting distance of the UCLA campus.

Because of the sensitivity currently encountered in many communities among parents and school officials concerning "psychological testing" of children, it was necessary to find a system with a progressive administrative staff willing to participate and competent to cope with possible parental resistance.

The school district

The school district itself extends beyond the limits of the town and contains a school-age population of approximately 13,000 for kindergarten through twelfth grade. At the time of this study it operated 12 elementary schools, three junior high schools (grades 7-9), and one senior high school (grades 10-12), plus a special school for the handicapped.

In addition to the public schools, there are two Roman Catholic and one Protestant elementary day schools drawing enrollment from the local area. Through the good offices of the public school officials, arrangements were made to include children from these schools in the study, thus insuring coverage of all the school population with the exception of those in the special school.

Although minority students tend to be concentrated in certain elementary schools because of residential patterns, in all cases they are integrated into a predominately Caucasian student body.

Disciplinary and racial problems within the district appear to be fairly typical. There have been some outbreaks of racial antagonism, but no

major violence. A dress code council exists in the high school and the
rules on hair and clothing appear relatively moderate, but some student
grumbling persists. While some use of narcotics is recognized, it is not
seen as a problem that is out of hand. At least some teachers, however,
feel parents are closing their eyes to the drug situation.

Methodology

Data were collected from students in the first, sixth, and tenth grades
and from mothers of first graders. These age groups were used to con-
form to the major pattern of data collection in the 1959 study. The methodology differed for the first graders and the older children.

Sixth and tenth grades. In these two groups, self-administered instruments were distributed by the classroom teachers to all students in attendance on each day of the test week. Monday through Thursday the
questionnaire consisted of a program log for the preceding day plus an
additional page of questions. Students were asked to mark the programs
they had watched and to answer the questions. This took 5-10 minutes of
class time.

On Friday a longer instrument was distributed. In addition to the program log for Thursday, it included the bulk of questions for other variables identified for analysis. This instrument was constructed so that
most tenth graders would be able to complete it in a regular 50-minute
class period.

The questionnaires were distributed and collected each day. In the
high school, English classes were used, because English was a required
subject for all tenth graders. The elementary schools were organized in
all-day classes, most of them at separate grade levels. Individual sixth-
grade classes were used, with the teacher distributing the instrument at a
convenient time within the day's activities. On Friday many teachers had
their students work on the questionnaire in two sessions to offset fa-
tigue. In the several nongraded classes, teachers gave the instrument
only to those students of sixth-grade age.

Students put their names on the instruments so that their responses
over the five days could be collated. Teachers were asked to identify
black students on class rosters, and this information was transferred to
appropriate individual records. Spanish surnames were used as an indicator of Mexican-American students.

Intelligence test scores and grade equivalence performance scores on
the Lorge-Thorndike battery were provided from the records of the current year's testings for the majority of the sixth- and tenth-grade students. Data was missing for some students who had been absent or who
had moved into the district after the testing. No test scores were available for parochial school students.

The daily data collection provided a record of viewing for Sunday and four weekdays, Monday through Thursday. Assuming that absences were random, this provided a representative profile of viewing for the age groups for each of these five days. The extension of data collection over a five-day period during which there were normal absences means that there was not a complete data file for all students. It was not feasible to have "make-up" administration. Thus any cross-tabulations of data gathered on different days are based on a reduced sample.

The instruments for the older children were pretested through the cooperation of another school district within the Los Angeles complex.

First graders. The 1959 experience suggested that parents were not necessarily reliable sources of information about children's media behavior. Therefore a decision was made to gather information directly from the first graders by personal interview rather than by parent questionnaires as in 1959. Pretesting on a small sample of first-grade children proved the feasibility of the technique.

A staff of women experienced in working with young children was recruited from the University of California Riverside campus. Included were both Negro and Mexican-American girls, all of the latter being able to interview children in Spanish if they felt it reduced anxiety. The staff was deployed so that all black students were interviewed by a black interviewer and all Chicanos by a Chicana. It should be noted that these interviewers also dealt with Caucasian students. This did not appear to present any problems of rapport for this age group. (The presence of some minority group teachers in the schools probably was a factor in this situation.) The staff received special training and was supervised by the junior author, who had worked in child care centers and who did the pretesting.

A 25 percent sample was stipulated, since the yield of approximately 300 would be sufficient to the cross-tabulations planned. Classroom teachers were asked to designate every fourth student on their roster for interviewing. (As it turned out, oversampling should have been made for black students. Prior estimates concerning the number of these students were incorrect and the straight sampling produced only 17 black first graders.)

Interviewing continued over a two-week period. Each interviewer reported to the principal of her assigned school. The principals and their staffs provided the liaison between interviewers and classroom teachers and provided a convenient place for the interviewing. Children were sent individually to the interviewer, who put great emphasis on reducing tension and allaying fears the child might feel at being "sent out of the room."

Since children of this age are not able to give reliable information about parents' occupations and education, followup interviews were planned with their mothers. Home phone numbers were obtained wherever possible for this purpose. These interviews also provided the opportunity to obtain information on mothers' attitudes about various aspects of television's relationship to their children.

Several unanticipated administrative problems caused the delay of this stage of the study until the following fall term. This was unfortunate, because it contributed to a heavy reduction in the number of mothers reached.

Where phone numbers were available, attempts were made to interview the mothers through this medium. For those without known phones, interviewers went to the listed address. Call-backs were made in all cases, but many of the mothers remained unreached. Further, many addresses and phone numbers were no longer accurate, due in part to an apparent increase in family mobility because of the rise in local unemployment.

Date of study. Data collection for the sixth and tenth graders proceeded during the first week of May 1970. First-grade interviews continued through the following week. As noted above, the followup interviews with mothers of first graders were completed after the opening of the school term in the fall of 1970.

The timing of the primary data collection was not ideal. It was late in the school year, when absences—particularly at the high school level—tend to run higher than normal. Further, it was after the end of the regular television season, and summer "reruns" had begun on the regular schedules—a factor which could have influenced the amount of viewing time and program selection.

Another problem was the Cambodian/Kent State upheaval which began during the data collection. While this did not have any apparent impact in the schools of the test town, the situation did produce anxiety among the field staff. Further, the presence of AFROTC facilities in the same building as the Journalism Department on the UCLA campus stimulated some physical damage. It was decided to evacuate all study materials from the building and the staff worked for the remainder of the term at the home of the senior project director.

However, there was little choice. The study was not funded until the end of February, making it impossible to get into the field at an earlier date. To have delayed data collection until the opening of the following term would have left insufficient time for data processing.

After editing, data was punched onto computer tape, and analysis proceeded using the facilities of the UCLA Campus Computing Network and the programming staff of the UCLA Survey Research Center. Most of the analysis made use of SPSS (Statistical Programs for Social Sciences).

The sample

Information was gathered from a total of 274 first graders, 137 boys and 137 girls. This was from a total population of 1,047. Due to absences (which were running higher than normal because of the closeness of the end of term and the warm weather), the totals for the sixth and tenth grades varied from day to day. The actual daily figures are detailed in Table A.1.

Table A.1: Daily sample figures for sixth and tenth grades

| | Sixth grade | | | Tenth grade | | |
	Boys	Girls	Total	Boys	Girls	Total
Monday	455	422	877	268	223	491
Tuesday	446	412	858	260	223	483
Wednesday	419	374	793	262	207	469
Thursday	431	385	816	300	248	548
Friday	451	407	858	285	220	505

The ethnic breakdown is given in Table A.2, along with the socioeconomic status distribution for the sixth and tenth grades. (SES was based on father's occupation. The derivation is detailed elsewhere in the report.)

Table A.2: Ethnic and socioeconomic status data

	First grade	Sixth grade	Tenth grade
Ethnic			
Caucasian	72%	82%	86%
Mexican—American	19	15	12
Negro	6	3	2
Asian/Indian	3	*	*
Socioeconomic			
Blue collar	*	65%	68%
White collar		13	17
Unemployed/retired		10	6
Undetermined		12	9

*Data not available.

The vast majority of the children lived with two parents: 84 percent of first and tenth graders and 86 percent of sixth graders. One in ten of the first graders reported that their parents were divorced; the rate almost doubled for the sixth and tenth graders.

Family size was slightly larger among the sixth graders and the number of only children was quite small in all three grades (Table A.3).

The incidence of working mothers was much higher for the high school students than for either elementary groups. (Table A.4.)

The level of education was predominately high school or less for both mother and father (Table A.5). It should be noted that the number of sixth

Table A.3: Family size

	First grade*	Sixth grade	Tenth grade
Only child	4%	6%	4%
Number of persons in household:			
Three	4%	7%	12%
Four	24	17	23
Five	25	24	22
Six	22	21	19
Seven	13	16	9
Eight	6	6	8
Nine or more	5	7	4

*Based on subsample of 114 mother interview.

Table A.4: Percent of students with working mothers

Mother works:	First grade	Sixth grade	Tenth grade
Full time	22%	25%	43%
Part time	*	32	27

*First graders were not asked to distinguish frequency.

graders who could not answer this query was quite high, reflecting a generally low level of awareness (also shown by the vagueness of answers concerning father's occupation).

As would be expected due to natural age orders, older students were more likely to have a sibling who had attended or was presently enrolled

Table A.5: Parents' educational level

	Father			Mother		
	First grade	Sixth grade	Tenth grade	First grade	Sixth grade	Tenth grade
	*			*		
Less than high school	41%	21%	41%	44	20%	40%
High school	25	22	27	35	28	36
Technical training	7	2	2	8	2	3
Some college	17	7	9	11	7	8
Finished college	4	10	8	2	11	6
Graduate work	2	3	1	0	1	0
Don't know	4	35	11	0	30	8

*Based on subsample of 114 mother interviews.

in college. Thirty-five percent of the tenth graders had collegiate siblings, 27 percent of the sixth graders.

Reflecting the nature of the community, the single unit dwelling was the overwhelming mode. Only 11 percent of the first graders, 14 percent of the sixth graders and 6 percent of the tenth graders lived in other types of domiciles, primarily apartments. The number of students having a room of their own increased with age, from 24 percent for the first graders to 37 percent for the sixth and 52 percent for the tenth graders.

Table A.6: Mobility indicators

	Sixth grade	Tenth grade
How long have you lived here?		
A year or less	8%	3%
2 — 4 years	21	15
5 — 9 years	23	18
10 years or more	34	38
Where else have you lived?		
Near this town	34%	28%
Los Angeles area	16	15
Other Southern California	8	15
Nothern California	5	4
Other states	25	32
Combination of places	9	6

Most of the students—about two-thirds—had lived in other towns, and between one-quarter and one-third of these had lived in other states.

As an indicator of family interaction, frequency of family meals was asked. Daily family eating is detailed in Table A.7, which shows that the evening meal is the only one commonly eaten as a family gathering; even this one shows a marked decline among the tenth graders.

Table A.7: Meals eaten daily with family

	First grade	Sixth grade	Tenth grade
Breakfast	39%	47%	25%
Lunch	7	22	8
Dinner	81	84	71

Attitudinal questions

A series of questions aimed at tapping the attitudes of sixth and tenth graders in several areas was included. These included a variety of moral issues, attitudes toward the "establishment" and middle-class mores, and optimism/pessimism.

The marginals for these questions are presented in Table A.8. Generally there was little difference between boys and girls at each age group; what differences did exist were primarily differences of degree, not of direction. One exception was that the tenth-grade boys were less likely than girls to think it unsafe to be out alone on the streets of their home city at night (item 24).

There was considerable disagreement with the concept of a dress code (item 1) and with unquestioned acceptance of the authority of principals (item 2). Questioning the authority of principals increased markedly in the tenth grade. There was a strong belief that older people do not understand young people's feelings and problems (item 3), and among the tenth graders there was considerable sentiment that young people should be free from their parents (item 4).

However, both age groups were strongly supportive of the idea that people should obey all laws (items 5 and 6).

Most students felt that one should seek new and unusual experiences (item 7), yet they strongly agreed that cigarettes, whiskey, and marijuana are harmful (items 8, 9, and 10). However, for all three the degree of condemnation was lower among tenth graders than among sixth graders. This decline was most marked with regard to marijuana.

There was general agreement that people think too much about material things (item 11).

The idea that one should let emotions rather than reason guide actions was strongly rejected (items 12 and 13).

There was strong acceptance of the concept of delayed rewards, at least inasmuch as saying that hard work, planning, and study are necessary to succeed (items 14, 15).

Strong endorsement was given to the concept that anyone—minority groups and women—can get good jobs (items 16 and 17), but there was also a strong feeling that there will always be poor among us (item 18).

Generally, strong optimism was not expressed about general improvement in society during the coming 20 years (item 19 and 20). Both pollution and overpopulation were rated as serious threats to the future of our society (items 21 and 22), and the overwhelming majority of students agreed that most American cities were dangerous places because of crime (item 23). They tended to see their own hometown as less threatening (item 24). Only a minority of the tenth graders accepted the proposition that it was unsafe to be out alone on their hometown streets.

Conflict with parents

Five questions were included in the sixth- and tenth-grade questionnaires concerning the frequency of disagreement with parents over grades, friends, clothes, hair, and spending. The distribution of responses is shown in Table A.9. As noted earlier, scores on these five items were summed to constitute a Parental Conflict Index.

Table A.8: Attitudinal question

| | Sixth grade | | Tenth grade | |
	Boys	Girls	Boys	Girls
1. Some kind of school dress code is necessary.				
Strongly disagree	17.8%	10.2%	22.6%	16.3%
Disagree	22.4	23.0	21.4	23.8
Don't know	23.6	22.1	7.4	5.9
Agree	25.9	32.6	37.0	41.6
Strongly agree	10.2	12.2	11.5	12.4
2. Principals generally know best and students shouldn't question their decisions.				
Strongly disagree	16.7	15.8	29.2	21.9
Disagree	21.7	22.9	33.3	41.3
Don't know	22.6	26.4	21.8	17.9
Agree	24.9	24.0	10.7	13.9
Strongly agree	14.1	10.9	4.9	5.0
3. Most older people don't understand young people's feelings and problems.				
Strongly disagree	9.1	8.4	3.7	4.0
Disagree	9.1	15.1	7.8	14.5
Don't know	19.6	19.1	14.3	12.0
Agree	33.6	30.4	35.9	37.5
Strongly agree	28.7	27.0	38.4	32.0
4. Young people should be allowed freedom from their parents.				
Strongly disagree	19.6	20.9	10.7	10.4
Disagree	24.0	27.3	29.1	27.7
Don't know	24.3	29.9	22.1	22.3
Agree	16.1	9.0	24.2	23.8
Strongly agree	16.1	12.8	13.9	15.8
5. You should obey only those laws you think just and reasonable.				
Strongly disagree	29.5	32.8	22.4	26.2
Disagree	22.2	24.1	49.4	44.1
Don't know	16.4	20.3	11.0	9.9
Agree	19.9	14.8	10.2	14.4
Strongly agree	12.1	8.1	6.9	5.4
6. It's a person's duty to obey all laws since they are for our own good.				
Strongly disagree	2.6	2.0	2.4	1.5
Disagree	4.7	3.5	6.5	5.4
Don't know	11.2	10.5	13.8	11.3
Agree	37.9	43.4	48.0	53.7
Strongly agree	43.5	49.5	29.3	28.1

Continued

Table A.8: Continued

| | Sixth grade | | Tenth grade | |
	Boys	Girls	Boys	Girls
7. To grow and develop as an individual person you should seek every new and unusual experience you can get.				
Strongly disagree	6.7%	8.5%	4.9%	5.4%
Disagree	11.7	15.8	20.1	21.7
Don't know	34.5	37.4	26.2	24.6
Agree	28.9	27.2	31.6	34.0
Strongly agree	18.1	11.1	17.2	14.3
8. People who smoke cigarettes are harming themselves.				
Strongly disagree	5.6	5.5	2.0	4.4
Disagree	5.6	2.9	6.1	4.9
Don't know	4.5	6.7	9.4	12.8
Agree	15.7	22.1	36.7	34.0
Strongly agree	68.5	62.8	45.7	43.8
9. People who drink whiskey or liquor are harming themselves.				
Strongly disagree	8.7	6.7	7.8	6.1
Disagree	9.3	10.7	20.0	14.6
Don't know	10.5	17.1	17.1	20.7
Agree	27.7	26.7	34.7	31.3
Strongly agree	43.7	38.8	20.4	27.3
10. People who smoke marijuana are hurting themselves.				
Strongly disagree	6.8	4.7	9.5	9.4
Disagree	3.8	3.2	14.0	10.9
Don't know	5.9	5.3	21.8	16.8
Agree	16.6	14.1	21.4	22.3
Strongly agree	66.9	72.7	33.3	40.6
11. Most people think too much about things like cars, money, clothes, etc.				
Strongly disagree	10.4	5.8	9.3	3.0
Disagree	15.9	12.7	17.9	17.0
Don't know	25.8	35.2	14.6	18.0
Agree	33.9	36.0	34.5	46.5
Strongly agree	13.9	10.4	14.6	15.5

Continued

Table A.8: Continued

| | Sixth grade | | Tenth grade | |
	Boys	Girls	Boys	Girls
12. People should let their emotions direct their actions.				
Strongly disagree	20.8%	17.4%	25.5%	17.4%
Disagree	23.7	23.5	38.7	43.8
Don't know	35.4	42.9	23.5	19.9
Agree	14.6	12.1	7.8	16.4
Strongly agree	5.6	4.1	4.5	2.5
13. One should keep a cool head and think before acting.				
Strongly disagree	1.2	1.2	1.2	0.5
Disagree	2.1	2.0	0.4	1.0
Don't know	9.4	9.9	6.5	4.5
Agree	45.5	42.9	49.8	47.3
Strongly agree	41.9	44.0	42.0	46.8
14. The good things in life usually require hard work and planning.				
Strongly disagree	3.2	3.2	2.4	1.5
Disagree	5.6	6.4	7.8	8.4
Don't know	13.7	17.7	8.2	6.9
Agree	41.2	47.0	44.1	50.0
Strongly agree	36.3	25.8	37.6	33.2
15. Everybody should study and work to get ahead as far as they can — it pays off in the end.				
Strongly disagree	2.6	1.4	1.6	0.5
Disagree	2.1	2.0	5.7	3.9
Don't know	10.9	13.3	10.2	5.9
Agree	34.9	37.7	45.5	50.7
Strongly agree	49.6	45.5	36.9	38.9
16. Girls and women can have good jobs if they want to.				
Strongly disagree	2.9	1.7	1.6	1.5
Disagree	4.6	4.0	2.0	4.9
Don't know	13.3	11.8	11.1	7.4
Agree	48.4	46.2	61.5	47.8
Strongly agree	30.7	36.1	23.8	38.4
17. Anyone — no matter color or background — who is willing to work hard can get ahead in the U.S.				
Strongly disagree	4.7	3.2	5.3	4.5
Disagree	9.1	8.1	12.7	8.4
Don't know	16.4	22.8	12.2	8.4
Agree	31.1	32.4	33.5	35.6
Strongly agree	38.7	33.5	36.3	43.1

Continued

Table A.8: Continued

| | Sixth grade | | Tenth grade | |
	Boys	Girls	Boys	Girls
18. There will always be some people who are poor.				
Strongly disagree	5.0%	2.0%	2.5%	2.0%
Disagree	5.0	4.4	2.9	4.9
Don't know	10.7	15.4	6.6	7.4
Agree	52.7	48.5	65.2	60.6
Strongly agree	26.6	29.7	23.0	25.1
19. There will be lots of changes in the next 20 years because my generation is going to change things for the better.				
Strongly disagree	7.6	6.1	6.9	1.5
Disagree	10.0	13.3	10.6	12.0
Don't know	38.2	48.4	45.3	53.0
Agree	26.5	22.6	24.1	23.5
Strongly agree	17.6	9.6	13.1	10.0
20. The world will probably be in an even worse mess in 20 years than it is now.				
Strongly disagree	7.6	6.5	5.8	6.9
Disagree	7.6	11.2	13.2	13.3
Don't know	38.2	46.8	35.0	42.9
Agree	19.8	18.8	18.1	23.6
Strongly agree	26.8	16.8	28.0	13.3
21. Pollution is a serious threat to our future.				
Strongly disagree	3.5	2.3	1.6	2.0
Disagree	5.2	4.6	0.8	2.9
Don't know	15.9	24.9	4.9	8.8
Agree	21.4	25.4	27.8	27.5
Strongly agree	53.9	42.8	64.9	58.8
22. Overpopulation is a serious threat to our future.				
Strongly disagree	5.2	3.8	3.3	2.0
Disagree	7.6	9.0	2.4	6.9
Don't know	23.3	39.4	13.0	16.3
Agree	29.1	26.4	38.6	44.3
Strongly agree	34.9	21.4	42.7	30.5

Continued

Table A.8: Continued

| | Sixth grade | | Tenth grade | |
	Boys	Girls	Boys	Girls
23. Crime makes most of our cities unsafe.				
Strongly disagree	5.6%	5.8%	2.5%	3.0%
Disagree	6.7	3.8	7.0	9.5
Don't know	9.4	10.7	14.3	10.9
Agree	32.7	39.3	49.6	42.8
Strongly agree	45.6	40.5	26.6	33.8
24. It is not safe to be out alone at night in (this town).				
Strongly disagree	12.9	10.2	25.8	10.4
Disagree	18.8	17.2	40.6	33.8
Don't know	21.2	20.3	13.9	22.4
Agree	25.3	27.9	14.3	18.9
Strongly agree	21.8	24.4	5.3	14.4

The two leading subjects of conflict were hair and grades. For the tenth grade girls, clothes replaced hair. The frequency of disputes over spending declined somewhat from the sixth to the tenth grade.

Table A.9: Questions concerning conflict with parents

| | Sixth grade | | Tenth grade | |
	Boys	Girls	Boys	Girls
Frequency of conflict with parents:				
About grades				
Never	28.6%	28.2%	20.5%	25.2%
Not very often	24.8	24.1	22.6	28.7
Sometimes	27.8	28.2	32.2	29.2
Often	18.8	19.5	24.7	16.8
About friends				
Never	32.9	32.7	30.1	28.0
Not very often	30.6	30.9	30.1	33.5
Sometimes	26.1	25.5	28.0	28.5
Often	10.4	10.9	11.7	10.0
About clothes				
Never	29.6	28.6	35.0	25.1
Not very often	30.3	30.4	33.8	31.7
Sometimes	24.2	25.7	19.4	29.1
Often	15.9	15.4	11.8	14.1

Continued

Table A.9: Continued

| | Sixth grade | | Tenth grade | |
	Boys	Girls	Boys	Girls
About hair				
Never	25.1	26.2	20.6	41.5
Not very often	22.7	22.5	23.9	25.5
Sometimes	25.9	26.0	29.8	20.5
Often	26.2	25.3	25.6	12.5
About spending				
Never	32.5	31.7	31.9	44.2
Not very often	24.6	24.5	32.4	21.6
Sometimes	20.5	21.9	21.4	20.1
Often	22.4	22.0	14.3	14.1

Explorations in Patterns of Television Viewing by Preschool-age Children

Jack Lyle and Heidi R. Hoffman

University of California at Los Angeles

It is generally accepted that the preschool years are among the most important in a child's development. With television present in almost every American home, this medium undoubtedly is a factor contributing to the developmental experiences of young children. Yet very little is known about the norms of viewing behavior among this age group. Most of what has been reported is based on interviews with mothers about the behavior of their young children.

This study was an attempt to gather information directly from pre-school-age children themselves. It focused on use of television and other media together; some questions also probed children's cognitive reactions to television.

In effect, it was an exploratory study. The sample is not a random one; rather, selection was purposeful to guarantee inclusion of a variety of types of children. The children were recruited through the cooperation of day care centers and nursery schools. These ranged from centers operated with public funds to private and church programs. Followup interviews were obtained with mothers of approximately half the children. (See Appendix A for a fuller discussion of methodology.)

THE SAMPLE

Basic demographic characteristics of the 158 children interviewed are detailed in Table 1. There was a roughly even division between boys and girls and between students in half-day and full-day programs. Four-year-olds constituted about half the sample; the remainder was divided about equally between three- and five-year-olds. Over half the children were Caucasian, but sufficient numbers of blacks and Mexican-Americans were included to make comparisons possible. The Mexican-Americans tended to be older than the other groups. The age profiles for boys and girls were relatively even.

Table 1: Characteristics of the sample

	N=158
Girls	48.7%
Boys	51.3
Age 3	24.7%
Age 4	52.5
Age 5	22.2
Age 6	.6
Caucasian	55.7%
Negro	23.4
Mexican—American	17.7
Other	3.1
Poverty level	41.7%
Middle-class	58.3
Full-day students	48.7%
Part-day students	51.3

Four of every ten children came from poor or welfare families. These were primarily the minority children, and review of the cross tabulations suggested that the two were basically redundant. Therefore, in the analysis which follows, the emphasis has been on ethnic rather than on socioeconomic comparisons.

RESULTS

Before beginning a discussion of the responses provided by these children and their mothers, let us caution the reader against extrapolation of the data. Certainly it cannot be said that the sample is a representative one. However, we do feel that the results are suggestive of the patterns of media use and development. Differences between some of the groups within the sample are particularly intriguing.

Despite the fact that there were many quite poor children in the sample, only two youngsters reported that there was no television in their home. Color was present in 52 percent of the homes and actually was more prevalent in the poor homes than in the middle-class homes. Two-thirds of the Negro children said they had color, compared with 55 percent of the Caucasian and 36 percent of the Mexican-American youngsters.

The living room was the most common location of the television set, with 65 percent of the children citing that location and 22 percent citing the family room. But 45 percent of the children reported that their parents had a set in their bedrooms and 12 percent said they had a set in their own bedrooms. The percentages add to more than 100 percent, reflecting the presence of multiple sets in many homes.

Television is immensely popular: 98 percent of the children said they do like to watch television.

Since children of this age generally have not developed the ability to tell time, it was impractical to ask them for reports on viewing time. Instead, they were asked if they were allowed to watch at various periods of the day. The results are shown in Table 2. The afternoon figures as the predominant viewing time; nine out of ten say they are allowed to watch then. But over 80 percent said they also can watch in the evening after supper and in the mornings. Six out of ten say they are allowed to watch while eating.

Table 2: Periods of television viewing

	Are you allowed to watch television:				
	In the afternoon	After supper	While eating supper	In the morning	Saturday morning
All children	91.1%	82.8%	62.0%	82.3%	84.8%
Full-time students	93.7%	80.5%	61.0%	76.6%	88.3%
Part-time students	88.8	85.0	63.0	87.7	81.5
Mother works	90.6%	90.6%	56.3%	71.9%	84.4%
Mother doesn't work	90.5	78.6	52.4	95.2	83.3

There was a marked difference between ethnic groups in these responses. For instance, 78 percent of the Negro youngsters said they could watch while eating, compared to 64 percent of the Mexican-American and only 53 percent of the Caucasian children.

Children whose mothers work were more likely than their peers to watch after supper, but the other children were more likely to say they could watch in the morning. This latter difference reflected the fact that they were more likely to be part-time students and hence at home where television was available in the morning period.

To provide a rough index of total viewing time, responses to these five items were summed. This provided possible scores of 0-5. Table 3 presents the distribution of index scores. Over three-quarters of the youngsters responded that they were allowed to watch in at least four of the five time periods. Mexican-American children had the highest scores, followed by blacks; Caucasians had the lowest scores. However, the basic difference between the groups was whether they said they could watch in four or five of the time periods. Similar patterns of differences were found between full-time and part-time students and between those whose mothers worked and those whose mothers did not.

Table 3: Number of time periods child can view

	0 − 3	4	5
All children	23.5%	32.5%	43.9%
Girls	29.0%	25.0%	46.1%
Boys	18.0	39.5	42.0
Caucasian	24.1%	37.9%	37.9%
Negro	24.3	27.0	48.6
Mexican—American	21.1	21.4	57.1
Full-time student	25.9%	37.7%	36.4%
Part-time student	21.2	27.5	51.3
Mother works	24.9%	43.8%	31.3%
Mother doesn't work	23.8	35.7	40.5

Solitary watching was definitely a rarity; only 11 percent of all the children said they did so. The major difference here was that such viewing was higher among the younger children: 17 percent of the three-year-olds said they viewed alone, compared with 11 percent of the four-year-olds and six percent of the five-year-olds.

An age difference was also apparent in responses to the question of who selects programs for viewing. The pattern of responses is shown in Table 4. The majority of five-year-olds say they make their own selections, compared with only about one-third of the three- and four-year-olds. Selection by mother falls sharply after age three. Children whose mothers work are more likely to say they make their own program selection or that they acquiese to older siblings, while the influence of non-working mothers is stronger.

Table 4: Who selects programs

	I do	Mother	Older sibling
All children	39.2%	16.3%	15.0%
Girls	33.3%	19.4%	18.1%
Boys	44.4	13.6	15.0
Mother works	43.8%	12.5%	21.9%
Mother doesn't work	38.1	26.2	7.2
Age 3	33.3%	27.8%	13.9%
Age 4	35.4	13.4	18.3
Age 5	52.9	11.8	8.8

*Other responses account for missing percentages.

Children were asked to name their favorite program, and the responses were categorized according to program type. The results are shown in Table 5. Cartoon shows of various types accounted for almost two-thirds of the choices.

The cartoon show *The Flintstones* led in popularity with over one-quarter of the children naming it. *Sesame Street,* named by 16 percent, was the only other individual program achieving a sizable frequency.

It is interesting to note that *Sesame Street* was the most popular among the youngest children, the three-year-olds. It also was much more frequently named by Caucasian youngsters than by minority youngsters.

The Flintstones' popularity increased with age and it also scored much higher among girls than among boys, among minority groups than among Caucasians.

The violent action character cartoons were mentioned by 11 percent, pulling higher response among boys than among girls, among older children than among the three-year-olds.

Almost one-fifth, 19 percent, of the youngest group did not comprehend the concept of a favorite program.

Children were shown a series of photographs of persons featured in various television series and asked if they could name them. The characters were selected to provide a cross-section of both cartoon and regular programs, of both adult and child characters.

The responses are detailed in Table 6.

Table 5: Favorite program categories

	All children	Girls	Boys	Age 3	Age 4	Age 5	Caucasian	Negro	Mex.-American
Flintstones	26.1%	39.3%	19.0%	10.8%	28.9%	36.4%	17.2%	34.3%	40.7%
Mickey Mouse type cartoon	5.2	6.7	3.8	2.7	3.6	12.1	4.6	2.9	7.4
General cartoon	11.8	9.3	13.9	8.1	15.7	6.1	10.3	14.3	7.4
Violent cartoon	11.1	5.3	16.5	2.7	14.5	12.1	12.6	5.7	14.8
Bozo, etc.	3.3	4.0	2.5	8.1	2.4	—	3.4	5.7	—
Sesame Street	16.3	17.3	15.2	29.7	13.3	12.0	25.3	8.6	—
Misterogers	2.0	—	3.8	2.7	2.4	—	3.4	—	—
Situation comedy	4.6	5.3	3.8	—	3.6	12.1	5.7	2.9	3.7
Family situation comedy	3.9	4.0	3.8	5.4	2.4	6.1	4.6	5.7	—
No favorite	4.6	4.0	5.1	5.4	4.8	3.0	3.4	2.9	11.1
Don't understand	7.2	8.0	6.3	18.9	3.6	3.0	4.6	11.4	11.1

(Miscellaneous program choices account for the missing residual percentages.)

Given the popularity of *The Flintstones*, it should be no surprise that Fred Flintstone was the most frequently identified character. His wife, Wilma, scored considerably below Fred but still was one of the three most frequently identified characters. The second best-known character was Big Bird from *Sesame Street*.

Although the other *Sesame Street* characters presented to the children obtained good recognition levels, they were far less well-known than Big Bird. It is impossible to say whether this is due to the character's inherent attraction of the or to the fact that Big Bird has been more widely featured than his colleagues in guest appearances on major network programs.

There were marked differences in the level of recognition of *Sesame Street* characters among ethnic groups. In all instances Caucasian children had the highest levels of recognition and, with the exception of Big Bird, black children the lowest. There also was a consistently higher recognition level of these characters among boys than girls. The fact that the human character and the two handpuppet characters were all males may have contaminated this difference.

A similar sex difference was apparent for Fred Rogers. However, far more marked was the ethnic difference. Only six percent of the Negro children recognized him, compared with 27 percent of the Mexican-American and 53 percent of the Caucasian youngsters.

Generally there was relatively low recognition of child characters from family situation comedies. This was particularly true among the younger children. Several characters—Buffy of *Family Affair*, Eddie, and *Julia's* Cory—showed a sharp increased recognition among the five-year-olds.

But several adult characters from situation comedy programs scored much higher than any child character. Lucy, Gilligan and his foil Skipper, together with Samantha of *Bewitched* were particularly well known. It should be noted that these are characters in programs which are broadcast as repeats during daytime hours. The other adult characters—and, indeed, all the child characters—are on programs shown only in the evening. The fact that adult characters like Malloy, Julia, and Tom Corbett were most widely recognized by five-year-olds may be a reflection of this situation, since they are apt to be allowed to view later into the evening.

There was no age difference in recognition of Gilligan, a daytime-only character. Lucy's recognition did increase markedly with age, but she was seen both in daytime repeats as well as in her current evening series.

Perhaps most interesting of all the differences is the recognition of black characters. Bill Cosby was identified by only one-quarter of the total sample, but over half the Negro children named him. Similar differences are seen for Julia and for her son, Cory. By contrast, however, Gordon, a black adult from *Sesame Street*, was identified by over 60 per-

Table 6: Levels of identification for characters
(Percent able to identify characters from pictures)

	All child-ren	Girls	Boys	Age 3	Age 4	Age 5	Cauca-sian	Negro	Mex.–Amer-ican
Fred Flintstone	92.3%	89.3%	95.1%	87.2%	92.6%	97.1%	89.8%	100.0%	92.6%
Wilma Flintstone	71.6	71.6	71.6	61.2	72.5	82.9	64.4	77.8	85.2
Scooby Do	48.4	45.2	51.3	25.6	52.6	65.7	40.2	55.6	65.4
Lucy	64.1	68.0	60.5	53.8	66.7	71.4	59.1	83.3	59.3
Malloy (Adam-12)	17.6	18.1	17.1	8.1	16.9	27.3	5.9	32.4	41.7
Bill Cosby	24.7	21.9	27.2	17.9	26.3	29.4	17.2	52.8	11.5
Samantha (Bewitched)	49.7	54.1	45.6	28.2	54.4	62.9	38.6	63.9	70.8
Gilligan	57.5	54.8	60.0	48.7	54.4	71.4	53.4	63.9	70.8
Skipper (Gilligan)	54.6	50.7	58.2	46.2	52.6	65.7	52.9	55.6	66.7
Tom Corbett (Eddie's Father)	24.0	18.9	28.8	23.1	20.3	34.3	18.4	40.0	25.9
Julia	11.8	13.3	10.3	5.4	8.8	25.7	3.4	31.4	15.4
Danny Partridge	21.3	20.3	22.2	17.9	23.5	20.6	11.4	38.9	34.6
Buffy (Family Affair)	25.2	27.0	23.5	23.1	21.0	38.2	15.9	44.4	26.9

Continued

Table 6: Continued

	All child- ren	Girls	Boys	Age 3	Age 4	Age 5	Cauca- sian	Negro	Mex.– Amer.- ican
Marcia Brady	13.0%	15.1%	11.1%	20.5%	7.4%	18.2%	8.0%	30.6%	7.7%
Eddie (Eddie's Father)	23.4	17.6	28.8	20.5	20.3	34.3	18.4	40.0	22.2
Cory (Julia)	11.3	12.0	10.5	8.1	8.9	20.6	1.2	35.3	15.4
Sesame Street: Big Bird	77.6	73.3	81.5	74.4	76.5	82.9	85.2	75.0	51.9
Ernie	50.4	41.3	56.8	48.7	54.3	40.0	62.5	22.2	44.4
Bert	50.3	43.2	56.8	58.7	55.0	42.9	64.4	22.2	44.4
Gordon	46.1	37.0	54.3	41.0	49.4	45.7	60.9	19.4	38.5
Fred Rogers (Misterogers)	36.8	31.1	42.0	33.3	36.3	42.9	53.4	5.6	26.9

cent of the Caucasian youngsters, but only 19 percent of the black children knew him. He even did better among Mexican-American children, 38 percent of whom knew him.

Since the children who were in the centers and nursery schools all day generally had less time for television viewing than their peers who were there only part of the day, it was thought that they might have lower levels of recognition. However, there were no consistent patterns of differences when these two groups were compared—not even for daytime programs.

It is interesting to compare the recognition of characters by these preschool youngsters with the first graders studied by Lyle and Hoffman (1971). The pattern of best-known characters is quite similar, particularly among the five-year-olds: Lucy, Gilligan, Samantha and, above all, Fred Flintstone. Two differences do stand out: the higher recognition of *Sesame Street* characters and of Fred Rogers by these young children, and their lower level of recognition of child characters. The first graders tended to have higher recognition of child characters than of adult ones; this was not true of these preschool-age youngsters.

The children were asked whether or not they "played things they saw on television" in their activities with friends. Over half—55 percent—of the children said that they did not. However, there was a marked tendency for such play to increase with age. Whereas 64 percent of the three-year-olds said they *didn't* engage in such play, 61.5 percent of the five-year-olds said that they *did*. The types of things used as models for play were too varied to present any meaningful pattern.

Another question put to the children was, "What kinds of scary things are there on television?" Two-thirds of the children named "scary" things, and the responses overwhelmingly dealt with "monsters." Only 26.7 percent said that there weren't any scary things; another 8.7 percent did not understand the question. As noted in the report on first graders, care must be taken in equating this with an unpleasant experience. Many children responded with obvious relish at the thought of these "scary monsters" of television.

Several questions were included to try to ascertain whether or not the child had any concept of people on television as "real." The children were asked, "How do kids get to be on your TV?" Sixteen percent did not understand the question, and another 40 percent stated that they did not know. Only 22 percent showed signs of real comprehension about the nature of television. A parallel question asked, "Where do the people and kids and things on your TV go when your TV is turned off?" On this item 24 percent couldn't understand the question and another 29 percent didn't know; only 20 percent showed understanding. The major increase in comprehension came between ages three and four, but even among the older children the vast majority still did not grasp the nature of television pictures.

The youngsters were also asked whether or not they thought the children they saw on television were like themselves and their friends. Fifty-five percent replied "yes." Minority children were somewhat more likely to think this way than were Caucasian children; 71 percent of the Mexican-American youngsters replied yes, compared with 59 percent of the Negroes and 51 percent of the Caucasians.

Followup interviews were obtained from 76 mothers of children interviewed. Because of difficulties encountered in contacting minority group mothers, these tended to be mostly Caucasian mothers. Of those interviewed, 58 percent were employed and 42 percent did not work.

Since the educational stations in the Los Angeles area are UHF channels, it was necessary to ascertain the availability of reliable UHF reception in the homes. Only 13 percent of the mothers said they did not have UHF receivers. Twenty-two percent said they had receivers but could not get good reception. Sixty-four percent indicated they had adquate UHF reception in their home.

The mothers were asked to estimate the amount of time their children spent watching television in different periods of the day. The results are detailed in Table 7. Generally, viewing appeared to be heaviest on weekday afternoons and Saturday mornings. With the exception of weekday mornings, there was no marked difference in the responses of working and nonworking mothers. However, 61 percent of the nonworking mothers said their children were not allowed to watch on weekday mornings, compared with only 21 percent of the working mothers.

Table 7: Children's viewing time, reported by mother

	Weekday morning	Weekday afternoon	Weekday evening	Saturday morning	Sunday morning
None	37.9%	20.3%	10.5%	8.0%	16.4%
1 hour or less	34.9	9.5	36.9	25.3	38.4
1.5 - 2 hours	24.2	47.3	21.1	30.7	28.7
2.5 hours or more	3.0	36.5	19.7	34.7	16.4

Most of the children were up by 7 a.m., and most were put to bed by 8 p.m. Nonworking mothers said their children got up earlier, although they were not put to bed any earlier than those of working mothers. However, 94 percent of the nonworking mothers said their children went to sleep immediately, compared with 80 percent of the working mothers. On the other hand, only 34 percent of the children of nonworking mothers were said to take naps, compared with 51 percent of those of working mothers.

There was little difference between the responses of working and nonworking mothers to questions about use of television deprivation as a punishment of extended viewing as a reward. Less than one-quarter of the mothers said they used these techniques. There was a difference in their reports of selecting programs for their children: 70 percent of the working mothers said they did select programs, but only 41 percent of the nonworking mothers said they did so.

Almost three-quarters, 74 percent, of the mothers said their young children sang commercial jingles learned from television, 62 percent saying that this had begun the time the child was age two, another 31 percent saying by age three.

The impact of advertising was further emphasized by the fact that 87 percent of the mothers said their preschool-age children asked for food items they saw on television; 91 percent said their children asked for toys they saw on television. Only 22 percent of the mothers said they usually denied the request outright, but working mothers were twice as likely as nonworking mothers to do so. The most typical action was to sidetrack the child's request.

Most of the mothers felt that their children were learning both good and bad things from television. Nine out of ten felt that beneficial learning did occur, 17 percent citing learning "about life." Twenty-eight percent felt there was "school-readiness" learning, and another 22 percent mentioned learning from *Sesame Street* and *Misterogers*. A variety of other responses accounted for the remainder.

As to bad learning, only nine percent were certain that no bad learning occurred; another 28 percent were not sure. The only type of bad learning specified with any marked frequency had to do with violence. Twenty-four percent of these mothers felt that their young children were learning violent or aggressive behavior from the things they viewed on television.

Slightly more than half the mothers, 53 percent, thought their children were sometimes frightened by television. Monsters were specified by 2.1 percent of the mothers as the cause; this was the only specific type of stimulus mentioned by a sizable number. As we have pointed out, the children themselves also most frequently said they were frightened by television monsters.

Only 12 percent said their children's sleep was interrupted by bad dreams; another 66 percent said this occurred only infrequently, and 22 percent said it didn't happen at all. Only four percent of the mothers could recall dreams they could trace to television.

USE OF OTHER MEDIA

The children were asked about the availability of radios and phonographs in their homes. These were equally present: 84 percent of the children said they had a radio, and 86 percent said they had a phono-graph or record player. Nineteen percent said they had records of their own. Interestingly, the children seemed to have more access to record players than to radios. When asked if they were allowed to play them when they wanted to, 64 percent said they had free access to the record player; only 51 percent said they had access to the radio. As might be expected, there was a general age progression on these responses: the five-year-olds reported more accessiblility to both radio and phonograph than did the younger children.

◄Books appeared to be generally available to the children; 87 percent said they had books of their own. When asked what were their favorites, the three most frequent categories named were classic story books (29 percent), books like the *Sesame Street* series (27 percent), and the Dr. Seuss books (13 percent).

When asked if their mother ever read to them, only 15 percent said "no"; 48 percent said she did so at bedtime. The remainder named dif-ferent times but indicated that she did read for them. There was clear evidence of decreased reading by mothers as children grow. Only three percent of the three-year-olds said their mothers did not read to them, compared with 27 percent of the four-year-olds and 41 percent of the five-year-olds.

Particularly marked were differences in parental reading among the ethnic subgroups. Whereas 87 percent of the Caucasian youngsters said their mothers read to them, only 61 percent of the Negro and 52 percent of the Mexican-American children reported reading.

As can be seen from Table 8, these children did spend considerable time in play activities, particularly with siblings and friends.

Table 8: Children's play time, reported by mother

Play with:	Alone	Siblings	Friends	Mother	Father
1 hours or less	57.3%	29.3%	9.6%	77.6%	69.3%
2 hours	22.7	17.3	11.0	10.5	13.3
3 hours or more	20.0	53.3	79.4	11.8	17.4

SUMMARY

The responses of these three-, four-, and five-year-olds drawn from disparate backgrounds provide strong testimony to the fact that mass media—and particularly television—do play an important part in their lives, do claim large shares of the children's time. Even the youngest children indicated that they do watch television regularly on a daily ba-sis. Viewing was particularly heavy during afternoons and on Saturday mornings, but the majority also indicated that they watched on weekday mornings and in the evenings.

Even the youngest children generally had favorite programs and showed high ability to identify at least some television characters; almost nine out of ten of the three-year-olds could identify Fred Flintstone; seven out of ten could identify Big Bird from *Sesame Street;* over half of them knew Lucy.

Almost nine out of ten of the mothers said their children had learned commercial jingles from television, and that the children were stimulated by commercials to ask for food and toy items featured in television commercials.

Sex and ethnic differences were already apparent in the program choices of these preschool-age youngsters.

Generally, then, the responses of these children and their mothers strongly support the thesis that much of the framework of a child's patterns of television use and reactions to the television stimulus has already begun taking shape before the child begins his formal education in the first grade.

REFERENCES

Lyle, J., and Hoffman, H. Children's use of television and other media. In *Television and social behavior*, Vol. 4 (this volume). Washington, D.C.: U.S. Government Printing Office, 1971.

Appendix A:

A note on methodology

As noted at the outset, this study was an exploratory one. Not only did it attempt to gather data on a segment of the population about whose media use knowledge is sketchy, but it attempted to gather this data by direct interview with the young children themselves rather than by using reports from mothers. Interviewing with very young children is still a relatively rare and undeveloped area of field survey research.

For the present study, the techniques employed were developed primarily as adaptations of those used in the interviews with the first graders in the major portion of this study (Lyle and Hoffman, 1971). The junior author was primarily responsible for developing the techniques and in doing so was able to draw upon considerable personal experience in working with young children in day care centers and nursery schools. In addition, helpful ideas and suggestions came from the authors of several other studies in this series who drew upon their experiences with young children, particularly Aimee Leifer, Donald Roberts, and Aletha Stein and her associates. Conversations with Dr. Fred Gottleib of UCLA's Neuropsychiatric Institute and Dr. Alberta Siegal of Stanford's Psychiatry Department provided other valuable inputs.

In the early stages of development, it was anticipated that it might be necessary to rely heavily on projective devices. However, pretesting soon showed that even three-year-olds were knowledgeable about television and, for the most part, could respond directly to verbal questioning. As a result, the technique used in the field relied upon direct questioning together with a series of photographs of television characters which the children were asked to identify.

Great care was taken in recruiting interviewers who could relate to children of this age group and could make them feel at ease while still keeping their attention directed. The interviewers were young adults who had experience working with young children. Negro children were interviewed by Caucasians after consultation with the Negro teachers or directors of the centers and nurseries. Mexican-American children were interviewed in Spanish where it appeared that this was necessary to put them at ease.

Most interviewing was done within the nursery school or day care center environment. This procedure allowed the interviewer to appear on the scene before beginning to interview and to be accepted as part of the group before dealing with a child individually.

All interviews were conducted on an individual basis; the interviewer provided reinforcement and reassurance as needed to keep the child's attention and confidence. The interview consisted of 24 questions, after which the child was allowed to rest or stretch before being presented with the 21 photographs for identification.

The photographs were purposely kept until last to serve as something of a reward, since identifying them was found to be a generally pleasurable game-type activity for the children.

An interesting informal observation was that although the word "test" was never used by the interviewers, a number of the children themselves applied this term in inquiring when their turn would come. Even in the preschool ages, these youngsters had already become "test conscious."

Some difficulty was encountered both with the question about favorite programs and with the picture identifications. The responses were something of a puzzle. With regard to favorite programs, this was primarily due to the apparent tendency for some children to fail to distinguish among programs and between programs and commercials. In some instances, the children had definite answers which were not immediately meaningful to the interviewers. A wide knowledge of programs and characters was of prime necessity for the interviewers so that they could understand the response. Similarly, in response to the picture identification, children sometimes answered, not with the actual "name" of the character, but with a mimicking of the character's behavior or pet phrases.

The most serious difficulty encountered was the difficulty some children had in verbalization. At all three age levels considerable diversity of verbal skills was encountered. For instance, some children showed physical evidence—facial expression, body motion—that they recognized characters, but they couldn't respond with a verbal identification. Generally the difficulties in verbalization were more likely to be related to minority group membership and disadvantaged background than to age.

Correlates Between Observed Behavior and Questionnaire Responses on Television Viewing

Robert B. Bechtel, Clark Achelpohl, and Roger Akers

Greater Kansas City Mental Health Foundation
Epidemiological Field Station

Studies of television viewing and its effects have relied heavily on the use of self-report questionnaires to determine the extent of television viewing. When much evidence depends on questionnaires, it becomes imperative to validate the accuracy of this method. Should the questionnaire technique prove inaccurate in sufficient degree, a great many studies would be modified or rendered invalid.

The best method of validating a questionnaire is correlating responses on the questionnaire with a direct measure of the behavior in question. Since the behavior in question is the daily viewing habits of the subject, the best measure must be taken *in situ*, not in the laboratory.

A technique for measuring daily behavior in the home has been developed and used extensively by Barker and Wright (1955). This method collects written behavior specimen records which require detailed and exhausting observation of subjects. To perform such an operation in a home filled with children and adults watching television would require a team of observers who would be prohibitively obtrusive on the very behavior to be measured.

A compromise would be photographing the behavior and analyzing the film. Such a technique was demonstrated by Allen (1968) although he used time sequence photography rather than continuous surveillance.

The purpose of the present study was to explore the use of photographing the television audience as a technique for validating questionnaires about television viewing behavior.[1] The technique is expensive and does not permit the use of a large sample. Therefore the conclusions are intended only to demonstrate what directions must be taken in further research and to show how different from or how similar to the actual behavior questionnaire reports can be.

The question asked by Steiner (1963) needs to be answered empirically: "What does viewing mean in behavioral terms—how much real attention is ordinarily devoted to programs? When and for whom is viewing a primary or exclusive pursuit like reading, and when is it only of secondary or 'background' significance?"

METHODS

Subjects for the study were selected by resampling a previous survey population (52 subjects) representative of households in the first 99 census tracts of Kansas City, Missouri. All subjects were administered a preliminary questionnaire about television and asked if they would permit television cameras in their homes for a six-day period. When an insufficient number (eight) were found who would allow the surveillance technique in their homes, the remainder of families in the subject group (12) were made up of volunteers. Differences between those surveyed who agreed and those who did not were tested on 23 variables as a partial control. Differences between survey subjects and volunteers were also tested on the same variables.

Families whose viewing behavior was recorded answered three additional questionnaires about their viewing habits. The present study's results consist largely of the amount of agreement between these questionnaires and the observed viewing. Other data were obtained from descriptions of the types of behavior that accompany and/or interfere with television viewing.

Questionnaires

Four questionnaires on television were used in the study. The first (see Appendix A-1) asked general questions about the number of televi-

sion sets in the house, how many channels could be received, preferences for programs, and attitudes toward programs and television in
general. This questionnaire was administered to all 52 subjects selected
from the previous Mental Health Survey population.

As part of this questionnaire, the subject was asked if he would permit
the filming of his or her family while they watched television. Payment
of $75.00 for six days was offered. If the subject agreed, an appoint-
ment was made for a representative to call, and the subject signed an
agreement (see Appendix A-2). If the subject refused, the reason for
refusal was recorded on the questionnaire.

The second questionnaire was a diary of viewing that was filled out by
subjects who agreed to the surveillance (see Appendix A-3). The diary
was in the form of a chart with the entire day marked off into 15-minute
intervals. If the subject did not watch during more than half of a period,
he was requested not to mark that period; the later comparison with
observed viewing was not counted as a disagreement unless it showed
the subject watching for the full period when he claimed otherwise.

In most cases the lady of the house filled out the diary form for herself
and other members of the family present. The diary was administered on
the fourth day after the television camera was placed in the home—
usually a Saturday.

The third questionnaire (see Appendix A-4) asked the subject to specify the programs watched the previous day and to fill out one sheet for
each program. The subject was also asked to estimate amount of time
missed watching each program and to list the reasons why the time was
missed. The fourth questionnaire (see Appendix A-5) was administered
following the sixth day and merely asked for an estimate of viewing for
the five days during which the family was filmed. The subject was also
asked whether the presence of the camera interfered with normal viewing in any way and asked to estimate the effect of this interference.

The diary and previous day questionnaires have been used in previous
studies (Robinson, 1969) in similar form.

Subjects

The Greater Kansas City Mental Health Foundation's Epidemiological Field Station conducted a mental health survey of the first 99 census
tracts in Kansas City Missouri in 1969-70. From a sample of 4,000, 3,685
persons were successfully interviewed. Since the mental health survey
provided a population about which considerable information was available, we decided to resample this population in order to save interview
time. Since we anticipated that our request to install television cameras
in these homes would be refused at a rather high rate, we thought it
important to be able to measure whether refusals differed from acceptances on a wide range of variables.

Seventy-nine names were drawn at random from the survey population. Only 53 were located. Six had no addresses, 18 had moved away, and two were never found at home after ten callbacks. One person called on did not have a television set, and one other refused to talk at all. Fifty-one interviews were completed. Of these, only 13 agreed to having the television camera placed in their homes, making the refusal rate 75 percent. Since more single persons than families agreed to the surveillance, only eight subjects were finally used from the original survey population. The remainder of the families (12) were volunteers, usually known to the researchers or employees of the Greater Kansas City Mental Health Foundation.

Variables describing the subjects will be listed as part of the results. It must be stressed that the main effort was not to obtain a truly representative population but to gain knowledge about how to successfully measure the television viewing behavior of families.

Procedure

Eight of the subjects were already part of the mental health survey and did not need to fill out that survey form. The volunteers, however, filled out the mental health survey so they could be compared with the survey subjects. This was done before the television apparatus was installed.

Installation of equipment began on a Tuesday. The family was given Wednesday to get used to the presence of the camera. They thought the camera was in operation, but the researchers did not record until Thursday. There was no way to tell whether the camera was operating or not. The camera did not click or hum or in any way reveal whether it was functioning.

The equipment operator monitored the film recording from a rented truck parked in the driveway behind or beside the house. The largest bulk of the apparatus was mounted in the rear of the truck. The operator sat facing the screens and console, keeping a constant check on operation and changing tapes after about every hour of viewing. As he changed each tape, he spoke into the sound track and identified the family and the time. As each tape was taken off, the can was carefully labeled with the family name, date, and time.

The cameras operated automatically with the television set in the home. Whenever the family switched on the set, the tape would begin recording in the truck, provided the operator had his own equipment running.

After the tapes were recorded, they were collected and brought to the Field Station office for coding. Coders played the tapes and recorded viewing behavior for each two-and-one-half-minute interval. A six-point scale was used (see Table 1) for behavior, and a letter code identified type of program (see Table 2). After the tapes were coded, most were recycled for use again. Several thought to be typical of certain types of families and behavior were kept for later descriptive analysis.

Equipment

At first, we decided to use one-inch recording tape because we thought it would provide a clearer picture for finer discrimination in coding. However, we quickly discovered that one-inch equipment was not adaptable to changing temperatures and to the vicissitudes of continuous operation. Only the half-inch equipment was viable under field conditions. The one-inch tape picture was not noticeably clearer than the half-inch tape picture, even when the equipment was operating properly.

The equipment in the truck consisted of: 1) a Sony 3600 videotape recorder, 2) a microphone mixer that permitted pickup from three microphones in the house and one microphone in the truck so that all voices would be recorded simultaneously with the visual image, and 3) three nine-inch (screen) television monitors mounted with a control console in the truck. One monitor was used for each of the two cameras in the house, and one was used for the combined image with sound. A special effects generator was used to combine the two camera images for a corner insert.

In the house, two cameras and three microphones were placed in the television viewing room. The cameras were two Sony CVC 2100 models with wide angle lenses. Camera # 1 was mounted over the set to obtain the widest possible view of the room. Camera # 2 was aimed directly at the set so that it could pick up the programs being watched. The picture from camera #2 was inserted in the lower left corner of the picture from camera #1, providing a simultaneous view of the program and the viewers. The three microphones and two cameras were connected by cables to the equipment in the truck outside.

About seven minutes of viewing time were lost each time the tape was changed. In addition, the recording heads of the video tape recorder (VTR) had to be replaced at various times in an unpredictable fashion. Exactly why the heads stopped functioning was never clear, even to the manufacturer and supplier. Various other mechanical troubles developed in serial fashion: the special effects generator broke down, one of the monitors broke down, one of the cables failed. Each of the equipment failures cost considerably in lost recording time.

Lighting proved to be another obstacle. While the level in most rooms proved adequate for the sensitive camera, in a few instances the room was too dark for good observation.

The buildup of iron oxide from running tapes caused continuous recording problems. Even a microscopic deposit of oxide would prevent the tape from recording a clear picture. The heads had to be frequently cleaned, and the operator had to play back the first few minutes of each tape to make sure the tape was recording properly.

Coding

Videotapes were coded according to the degree subjects were engaged in watching and according to the type of program being watched.

A six-category classification of television viewing was developed, as in Table 1.

Table 1: Categories of involvement in television viewing

Code	Behavior
Attending screen	
1	Participating, actively responding to the TV set or to others regarding content from the set
2	Passively watching (doing nothing else)
3	Simultaneous activity (eating, knitting, etc.) while looking at the screen
Not attending screen	
4	Positioned to watch TV but reading, talking or attending to something other than television
5	In the viewing area of the TV but positioned away from the set in a way that would require turning to see it
6	Not in the room and unable to see the set or degree of impact of TV content

The six categories are not meant to imply subjective involvement. Letter codes were applied to the type of program, as in Table 2.

Table 2: Coding for type of program

A — Movie
B — Family comedy and variety
C — Commercial
D — Suspense
E — Melodrama
F — Game show
G — Talk show
H — Religious
J — News, weather, informative programs
K — Sports
L — Children's show and cartoons

The coder checked the viewing of all subjects on the screen every two and one-half minutes. This time interval was found necessary in order to collect enough information on commercials. Larger units would miss commercial time.

The coding sheet (Appendix B) was used for each tape. Since tapes lasted for about one hour, the sheet was calibrated accordingly. On the left side of the sheet, the amount of tape used was listed by number of feet. This enabled coders who used and reused tapes to pick up the same places in the tape for coding checks. (Each VTR unit had a counter that registers amount of tape used.)

The operator spoke into the tape the time that recording began. Thus the coder had an exact time for beginning and a second calibration in amount of feet used on the tape. Beginning and ending times are marked on each coding sheet.

Analysis of data

Computation of agreement with behavior and answers on question-naires. Subjects were instructed in the diary questionnaire to record as accurately as possible the time spent watching their programs. Since a significant amount of recording time was lost because of equipment failures, only the times for which the subject made his report and which were correspondingly recorded on television tapes were used for analysis. Agreement was calculated between reported time and time coded as watching or nonwatching according to Guetzkow's (1950) accepted formula. In the questionnaire asking for the previous day's viewing, the same formulas were used for calculating agreement, taking into consideration only those times for which tapes and reported viewing were parallel.

To define viewing time as watching, those two-and-one-half-minute units coded with a 1, 2, or 3 (see Table 1) were used to indicate times when the subject was considered actually watching the program. Categories 4 and 5 indicated the subject was in the room but not watching, and category 6 indicated that the subject was not present in the room.

Agreement was considered 100 percent when the subject reported viewing the program for a specific amount of time and was coded in the 1, 2, and 3 categories for the same amount of time. If subject actually viewed *less* than the amount he reported, the report was considered a case of *overreporting*. If subject was coded as viewing *more* than the reported amount, the report was considered *underreporting*. Underreporting seldom occurred; virtually all self-reports are overreported.

Because some data on tape was lost due to equipment failures, actual viewing time for the five-day estimate needed to be extrapolated from available data. In only one case did this extrapolation amount to more than 25 percent of data actually recorded.

Reliability of coding. Two coders were used throughout the project on 613 tapes. Reliability checks were made at the beginning, middle, and end of the project. Reliability was measured for agreement on watching (categories 1, 2, 3) *vs* not watching (4, 5, 6) and for agreement on the individual categories alone (agreement on 1, 2, or 3, 4, 5, or 6 separately).

Table 3: Reliabilities among coders

	Beginning	Middle	End
Watching-Nonwatching	96.0	92.2	94.3
Categories	96.0	87.3	82.0

RESULTS

Accepters and refusers

A comparison was made between the families who agreed to allow the cameras to be placed in their homes and those who refused. Twenty-three variables from the mental health survey were tested.

Table 4: Continuous variables tested for differences between acceptance and refusal families

Variable	N*	Mean for refusals	S.D.	N*	Accept-ances	S.D.	Tests	p
1. Number of people in house	40	3.67	2.05	13	3.31	2.37	†= .5289	n.s.
2. Number of children	40	1.30	1.54	13	1.76	1.96	†= .7583	n.s.
3. Age	34	48.06	17.21	13	47.15	14.48	†= .1646	n.s.
4. No. of rooms in house	40	5.45	1.48	12	5.42	1.32	†= .0688	n.s.
5. No. of times moved/2 yrs.	40	.45	1.04	13	.69	.99	†= .7202	n.s.
6. Job changes/2 yrs.	38	.34	.66	13	.31	.72	†= .1557	n.s.
7. No. marriages	40	1.03	.65	12	1.42	.95	†=1.5944	n.s.
8. Family income	37	6999.43	2493.28	10	7099.40	2256.44	†= .1122	n.s.
9. Last grade in school	40	10.17	4.30	12	11.33	2.24	†= .8799	n.s.
10. Tiffany Scale FE	39	46.00	27.87	13	45.31	32.12	†= .0671	n.s.
FI	39	55.00	30.44	13	41.46	32.41	†=3.1942	.01
DI	39	70.89	28.49	13	76.69	22.77	†= .7210	n.s.
OE	39	56.72	27.25	13	59.15	23.88	†= .2974	n.s.
11. Lubin Scale	40	5.83	3.30	13	6.85	3.32	†= .9490	n.s.
12. Katz Scale	40	36.50	4.72	13	38.08	4.39	†=1.0445	n.s.

*Ns for each test differ because not all subjects answered the questions or were appropriate for the category.

The 23 variables reported in Tables 4 and 5 constitute the bulk of demographic and psychological variables measured on the mental health survey. The Tiffany Scale (Tiffany, 1967) is a measure of the degree the subject feels he controls forces inside or outside himself. The only significant difference found was on the F1 Scale indicating refusal subjects seem to feel more control over internal forces within themselves than do acceptance subjects.

Other tests—the Lubin (1965), the Katz and Lyerly (1963), and the Who-Am-I (Garretson, 1962) showed no differences between acceptance and refusal families. Apparently, although the refusal rate was high (75 percent), there was not much difference between families that refused and those that accepted, at least on these measures.

Table 5: Nominal variables tested for differences between
acceptances and refusal families

Variable		Refusals	Acceptances	x^2	p
13. Race		28 white, 12 black	9 white, 4 black	.0870	n.s.
14. Who-Am-I	A	A 2, Others 33	A 0, Others 13	.0045	n.s.
	B	B10, Others 35	B 5, Others 8	˒ .6694	n.s.
	C	C16, Others 19	C 5, Others 8	1.0446	n.s.
	D	D 7, Others 28	D 3, Others 10	.0277	n.s.
15. Own/rent		Own 29, Rent 11	Own 6, rent 7	1.9753	n.s.
16. Type of residence		House 35, Apt. 5	House 9, Apt. 4	1.2076	n.s.
17. Religion		Prot. 31, Others 9	Prot. 7, Others 6	1.6651	n.s.
		Cath. 7, Others 33	Cath. 4, Others 9	.3984	n.s.
18. Where did you live most of your life		Rural 9, City 31	Rural 1, City 12		
19. Drinking problems		Yes 2, No 38	Yes 2, No 11	.3930	n.s.
20. Anything good happened in past month?		Yes 19, No 21	Yes 6, No 7	.0550	n.s.
21. Anything bad happened in past month?		Yes 15, No 25	Yes 3, No 10	.3805	n.s.
22. How happy are you?		Very 15, Fairly 25	Very 4, Fairly 9	.1100	n.s.
23. What scares you?		Nothing 10, Something 24	Nothing 1, Something 10	2.2385	n.s.

Accepters, refusers, and volunteers

A preliminary questionnaire was administered to all persons included
in the study—volunteers, survey subjects who accepted surveillance,
and those who refused to allow the television camera in the home. The
first item asked the number of television sets in the home. Volunteers
(N=12) had a mean of 1.58 sets, survey subject accepters (N=8) had
2.12 sets, and refusers (N=38) had 1.55 sets. None of these differences
was significant (F=1.64). The second item asked the number of color
sets. Volunteers had .41, accepters .50, and refusers .36. Again, the differences were not significant (F=.15). Volunteers, accepters, and refusers also did not differ in their ability to pick up UHF stations ($X^2= 5.43$).

When the subjects were asked to estimate the amount of time they
spent watching on an average day, however, differences were significant.

Table 6: Estimate of hours spent watching television on an average day

Volunteers (N=12)	Survey subjects (N=8)	Refusals (N=38)
6.20	3.31	3.09

H = 10.10   p < .01

The volunteers had significantly higher estimates than either accepters
or refusers. Since there were problems with homogeneity in the data

(F max = 4.31, p < .05), Kruskal Wallis one-way analysis of variance was used.

Significant differences were also found in estimates of time spent watching television yesterday.

Table 7: Estimate of hours spent watching television yesterday

Volunteers (N=12)	Survey subjects (N=8)	Refusals (N=38)
5.29	2.56	2.85

H = 14.66   p < .01

In general, then, preliminary estimates of viewing time by volunteers were significantly higher than those of either survey accepters or refusers.

Asked whether their favorite program 1) shows life as it really is, 2) does not show life as it really is, 3) both, or 4) don't know, subjects revealed no significant differences between volunteers, accepters, and refusers ($X^2 = 3.0829$, df = 6).

Asked the reason they liked the programs (because of 1) the stories, 2) people in the stories, 3) both, and 4) don't know), subjects showed no significant differences ($X^2 = 3.9447$, df = 4).

Subjects were asked to agree or disagree with four opinions about television programming in general: 1) too much sex, 2) too many commercials, 3) too much violence, 4) too many news programs. There were again, no significant differences ($X^2 = 3.7271, 2.2923$, and $.4840$ respectively, df = 2). Generally, then, only on estimates of viewing time did volunteers differ from accepters and refusers.

Accepters and volunteer subjects

Since only eight of the 13 acceptance families were used and the remaining 12 families were volunteers, it is imperative to show differences between "surveys" and volunteers.

Tables 8 and 9 show that some rather important differences exist between the volunteers and the accepters. The volunteers are about 16 years younger, moved five more times than the accepter families in the last two years, had many more job changes, are less depressed, and have a lower F1 score on the Tiffany (indicating that survey subjects feel they have a great deal more control over internal forces than volunteer subjects).

Thus, significant differences between survey and volunteer families prevent combining the two groups for generalizations about the population as a whole. Nevertheless, since the accepter population of eight families is so small, the two groups were combined for the purpose of

Table 8: Continuous variables tested for differences between survey and volunteer families

| | N=8 | | N=12 | | | |
Variable	Mean for survey	S.C.	Mean for volunteers	S.D.	Test	p
1. No. of people in house	3.63	2.11	4.67	1.49	t=1.1347	n.s.
2. No. of children	1.63	2.12	1.83	1.14	t= .2390	n.s.
3. Age	48.75	12.57	32.83	8.05	t=2.9838	< .01
4. No. rooms in house	6.00	.87	6.17	.80	t= .4100	n.s.
5. No. times moved/2 yrs.	.63	.99	5.42	1.32	t=8.7629	< .001
6. Job changes/ 2 yrs.	1.13	2.32	5.42	1.55	t=4.3253	< .01
7. Times married	1.63	1.11	1.17	.37	t=1.0547	n.s.
8. Family income	7,000.00	2,397.90	6,750.00	2,919.00	t= .1978	n.s.
9. Last year in school	11.25	1.56	12.17	1.06	t=1.3639	n.s.
10. Tiffany Scale						
FE	58.00	27.65	52.50	29.47	t= .4009	n.s.
FI	66.75	22.31	39.17	28.71	t=2.2825	< .05
DI	73.13	15.19	70.83	26.29	t= .2341	n.s.
OE	63.00	26.40	50.83	21.12	t= .9292	n.s.
11. Lubin Scale	6.75	3.27	3.33	2.66	t=2.3204	< .05
12. Katz Scale	38.13	4.14	36.17	10.50	t= .5545	n.s.

Table 9: Nominal variables tested for differences between survey and volunteer families

Variable	Survey N=8	Volunteers N=12	x^2	p
13. Race	(white 6, black 2)	(white 11, black 1)	.1470	n.s.
14. Who-Am-I A	none	none		
B	B 3, Others 5	B 5, Others 7	.0780	n.s.
C	C 3, Others 5	C 6, Others 6	.0082	n.s.
D	D 2, Others 6	D 1, Others 11	.1470	n.s.
15. Own/rent	own 5, rent 3	own 9, rent 3	.0092	n.s.
16. Type of residence	house 8, apt. 0	house 10, apt. 2	.2082	n.s.
17. Religion	Prot. 2, others 6	Prot. 8, others 4	1.8750	n.s.
	Cath. 5, others 3	Cath. 3, others 9	1.4670	n.s.
18. Where did you live live most of your life?	rural 1, city 7	rural 1, city 11	.2082	n.s.
19. Drinking problems	some 2, no 6	some 1, no 11	.1470	n.s.
20. Anything good happened in past month?	yes 7, no 1	yes 9, no 3	.0130	n.s.
21. Anything bad happened in past month?	yes 0, no 8	yes 6, no 6	3.5812	n.s.
22. How happy are you?	very 2, fairly 6	very 7, fairly 5	1.0185	n.s.
23. What scares you?	some 8, nothing 0	some 11, nothing 0	.0437	n.s.

reporting selected results. However, differences between the two groups in television viewing behavior are reported for most variables.

Diary questionnaire and observed viewing

Since the diary was the questionnaire most contiguous with the recorded viewing behavior, we expected that these results would correspond closest with behavior.

Table 10: Agreement of diary with observed behavior on a watch-nonwatch basis* for survey families

Family	% of Agreement
1	54
2	81
3	55
4	78
5	68
6	70
7	56
8	83

*See Table 1: 1-2-3 is watching. 4-5-6 is nonwatching

Cases of underreporting were infrequent (5.5 percent of total time), while overreporting was the general case (24.8 percent). This means that for roughly every four hours' watching reported, only three hours were actually spent watching.

Table 11: Agreement of diary with observed behavior on a watch-nonwatch basis for volunteer families

Family	% of Agreement
1	92
2	72
3	65
4	78
5	55
6	57
7	78
8	82
9	85
10	71
11	69
12	79

Average agreement among volunteers was 75.6 percent. The difference between volunteers and accepter families was not significant (Z= −.79).

Previous day reports and observations

Since the previous day questionnaire was one step removed from the diary in time, we expected that it would be less in agreement with observed behavior.

Table 12: Agreement of viewing time on previous day report with observed behavior for survey families*

Family	% of agreement
1	61
2	56
3	51
4	67
5	44
6	58
7	72

*One family reported no viewing during the previous day.

Table 13: Agreement of viewing time on previous day report with observed behavior for volunteers

Family*	% of agreement
1	77
2	29
3	0
4	55
5	71
6	22
7	49
8	61

*Three families reported no viewing on the previous day and one family's data was lost due to equipment failure.

Average percentage of agreement among volunteers is only 45.5 percent. This means that for over half the time they reported viewing, the subjects were not watching television. The difference between the average agreements of accepters and volunteers is not statistically significant ($Z = -.76$).

Five-day questionnaire estimates and observed behavior

Respondents were asked to estimate the number of hours viewed per day during the five-day period, both for themselves and for each member of the family. These estimates were compared with the actual times recorded by the VTR each day. In most cases, the recorded tapes did not exactly cover the times the set was on during the day because of the tape changing and equipment breakdowns. Total watching time was estimated by extrapolating from the watching-nonwatching data already recorded to the known time missed. In one case, this meant extrapolating nearly 50 percent of the total watching time. Most families, however, had less than 25 percent estimated time. The total percentage of estimated time for all families was 23.7 percent (135 hours of 570 hours observed). This amounts to about 6.7 hours for each family over the average five-day period. Time lost on tape changes amounted to 56.6 hours, or 3.8 hours per family over the average five-day period.

The total number of hours that each person watched was arrived at by taking the ratio of watch nonwatch time from the VTR tapes and applying this to the known missed time. For example, Mrs. M watched two hours (ten percent of the time) on 20 hours of VTR tapes. This one/ten ratio was applied to the known time missed by the VTR, which was five hours. One-tenth of five hours is 30 minutes, so total watching time for 25 hours was two hours and 30 minutes. This total was then averaged for the five-day period, resulting in average watching time of 30 minutes per day out of five hours each day the set is on.

On the five-day questionnaire, subjects reported viewing times in three ways: 1) how much time they generally watched television per day; 2) how much time they themselves watched television per day during the five-day period; and 3) how much time each member of the family watched per day during the five-day period. These questions are similar to the questions asked in a recent nationwide questionnaire (see Appendix A-1) and are repeats of estimates on the preliminary questionnaire. Question 1 was asked *before* the observation period, and questions 2 and 3 were asked one day *after* the observation period ended.

The three different estimates of average viewing time show remarkable agreement (F = .02 p > .05). Estimates 1 and 2 correlate .5109 (p < .05), but estimates 1 and 3 correlate only .0745 and 2 and 3 only −.0886. Nearly all overreport viewing, both for self and for others. One would expect an individual to estimate his own previous day's viewing time more accurately than he would estimate either others' viewing time or his viewing time in general. However, the estimate of viewing time for self turns out to be *less* accurate than the other two estimates. Surprisingly, estimates of viewing time in general turn out to be most accurate (Table 14).

Comparing the diary with previous day estimate and with the general estimate shows a decreasing continuum of accuracy, as would be expected. The further removed in time the respondent is from the immediate situation, the less accurate should be his estimates of behavior in that situation. The respondent begins this continuum, however, with a fairly high degree of inaccuracy (about 25 percent error).

Table 14: Comparison of observed viewing time
with estimates of viewing time in general

		% of agreement	Absolute difference in hours**
Survey subjects	1	100	0
	2	91.3*	−.5
	3	86.7	.4
	4	60.0	.8
	5	37.5	2.5
	6	34.5	3.6
	7	32.2	6.1
	8	20.0	.4
Weighted mean by hours		55.1	1.7
Volunteer subjects	1	90.6	.3
	2	85.5*	−.5
	3	57.8	1.9
	4	38.3	3.7
	5	36.0	3.2
	6	30.7	10.4
	7	30.0	8.4
	8	28.0	3.6
	9	22.5	3.2
	10	20.0	2.4
	11	2.8	3.4
	12	No data available	No data available
Weighted means by hours		38.3	3.6
Total combined weighted means		43.6	2.8

*The only two cases of *under*reporting; all other cases are *over*reporting
**Difference between volunteers and survey subjects is not significant (t = 1.58 > .05).

One possible explanation of the overreporting is that the subjects may have referred to the amount of time the set was on rather than the amount of time they watched. The evidence is mixed. For volunteers, the estimate of average viewing time was closer to the time the set was on than to the actual viewing time, but the reverse was true for accepted subjects. Yet the estimates of viewing made by all subjects showed a clear awareness that other activities interfered with watching; these were listed, showing that the estimates did not refer to the time the set was on. This was true for both volunteers and accepter subjects.

Influence of the camera

In the final questtionaire (see Appendix A-5), subjects were asked whether they thought the presence of the camera influenced them in any way. Ten replied they thought it did, and ten replied they thought it did not. Those who thought it did influence them gave the following reasons:

Table 15: Comparison of observed viewing time with estimates of individual average time watching during observation

		% of agreement	Absolute difference in hours**
Survey subjects	1	100	0
	2	92.1*	−.2
	3	60.0	.8
	4	57.8	1.9
	5	52.0	4.8
	6	37.5	2.5
	7	30.5	6.6
	8	10.0	.9
Weighted mean by hours		48.5	2.2
Volunteer subjects	1	83.3	.8
	2	72.5	1.1
	3	60.0	1.2
	4	52.0	2.4
	5	39.0	7.2
	6	38.3	3.7
	7	31.3	2.4
	8	28.0	3.6
	9	22.5	3.1
	10	17.6	2.8
	11	12.5	3.5
	12	2.5	3.9
Weighted mean by hours		35.6	3.8
Total combined weighted means		39.8	3.2

*The only case of underreporting; all other cases are overreporting.
**Difference between volunteers and survey subjects is not significant (t= .83, p > .05).

"We dressed better, used better language and watched more.'
"For the first day or so."
"Felt a little guilty about not watching."
"Husband wouldn't sit in the room in pajamas."
"Tried to be more careful."
"We were on our best behavior."
"My 14-year-old was constantly trying to watch himself."
"We turned it on more."
"Let's act like we have company."
"We didn't play."

When asked if answering questions on the questionnaires made them more aware of watching television, eight of the 20 respondents said it had.

Table 16: Comparison of observed viewing time with estimates of
average viewing time of entire family (including self)

		% of agreement	Absolute difference in hours per person, per day**
Survey	1	64.7	1.2
subjects	2	64.2	.7
	3	52.0	4.8
	4	50.0	1.0
	5	50.0	1.9
	6	40.0	.4
	7	36.0	3.7
	8	30.5	4.7
Weighted mean by hours		44.4	2.0
Volunteer	1	92.9	.3
subjects	2	67.9	1.3
	3	51.1	2.8
	4	48.7	2.5
	5	41.2	1.8
	6	40.9	2.3
	7	36.9	2.6
	8	31.9	2.5
	9	31.8	1.9
	10	26.5	9.7
	11	24.6	3.1
	12	11.9	4.6
Weighted mean by hours		31.5	2.9
Total combined weighted means		41.1	2.6

**Difference between volunteers and survey subjects is not significant ($t = .64$, $p > .05$).

Table 17: Comparison of general viewing estimates with
time set was on and time actually watched

	Volunteers (N=12)	Survey (N=8)
Time set on per day	7.90	7.20
Estimate of average viewing	6.20	3.31
Difference (hrs.)	1.70	3.89
Difference from hours actual viewing and estimate	3.20	2.20

Cluster analysis and classification of viewing types

In order to arrive at an empirical classification of viewing behavior types, the scores on the six categories of watching were clustered according to the BC TRY system (Tryon and Bailey, 1970), and each of 93 subjects from the 20 families was classified by 0-type analysis (Tryon and

Bailey, 1970, ch. 8). Rates, rather than raw data, were used for each category. 0-type analysis is a classification procedure that uses composite scores on the derived clusters to group the subjects into types. For example, the six categories produced two empirical clusters. Each subject was then given a composite score on each of the clusters and grouped into types according to whether his or her composite scores fell above or below the mean on each of the clusters. A finer classification divides subjects into thirds above, at, or below the mean; a still finer classification divides into fourths, and a final one divides into fifths.

The correlation matrix of the six categories showed fairly high correlations between category 6 and category 2 ($-.870$) and between category 6 and category 4 ($-.772$).

Table 18: Correlations among watching category scores

	1	2	3	4	5	6
1	—	−.134	.022	.057	−.049	−.002
2		—	.105	.444	−.133	−.870
3			—	.298	.005	−.258
4				—	.368	−.772
5					—	−.164
6						—

These high correlations indicate that those who stayed out of the room (6) were not passive watchers (2) and were not nonwatchers while facing the television screen (4). In simpler terms: most people's in-room behavior on categories 4 and 2 correlates negatively with being out of the room.

The clusters are best defined as : 1) *in the room*, and 2) *not watching*. The pivotal variable (6) in the first cluster is negative, meaning literally a negative absence rather than a positive presence of watching behavior. The pivotal variable for the second cluster is variable 5—positioned not facing the set and not watching.

Table 19: Clusters of watching categories

Cluster 1: in room	Cluster 2: not watching
6 (out of room)—pivotal variable, reflected	5 (positioned away from set)—pivotal variable
4 (not watching but facing set)	4 (not watching but facing set)
2 (passive watching)	

Categories 1 (active watching) and 3 (interrupted watching) were dropped because they had communality measures below .200. This means that they were not associated significantly with any of the other categories. Both clusters exhaust .9785 cumulative proportion of the raw correlation matrix. Reliability coefficient for cluster one is .8656 and for cluster two .7004.

Of course, the clusters overlap on category 5. The meaning of cluster two as a *not watching* cluster is clear, but there is some confusion in cluster one because it shows association with two seemingly contradictory elements, passive watching (2) and not watching but facing set (4). The purpose of this analysis was to classify viewing behavior empirically, not to impose arbitrary categories. What the data say then is that both watching in the passive sense (2) and not watching (4) tend to go together somewhat (corr. .444); at the same time, not watching (4) and positioning away from the set *also* go together somewhat but a little less strongly (corr. .368). In other words, the behaviors observed are not exclusive, except those in category 6. Intercorrelation between the two cluster domains is .6919, which means they are closely related.

The classification of the 93 subjects into behavioral types was done by 0-type analysis. The first classification, separating high from low scorers on each of the clusters (one cut) resulted in four 0-types. The overall homogeneity of these 0-types after condensation was .9432 for Type 1, .8886 for Type 2, .9258 for Type 3, and .8401 for Type 4. The second classification (two cuts) resulted in five types after condensation with overall homogeneities of .9393, .9376, .8679, .9124, and .9507. A third classification (three cuts) resulted in six types after condensation with homogeneities .9453, .8886, .9285, .9106, .7844, and .9507. A fourth classification of scores into five parts (four cuts) resulted in nine 0-types after condensation of overall homogeneities .9785, .9593, .9585, .9354, .7844, .9777, .9330, .9724, and .9507. Despite the fact that increasing 0-types usually increases homogeneities, after five types there is a decrease of homogeneity in one of the types for three, four, and five cuts, so that five types seem to optimize the homogeneity within each type— the lowest homogeneity there being .8679.

Using five types, then, the following classification table can be set up for all 93 subjects (two subjects were excluded because their scores did not fit homogeneously within any of the types, leaving an N of 91).

Table 20: Television viewing behavior types
Mean = 50,   S.D. = 10
Typology mean scores

Type 1-28 members, low on in-room cluster, low on not-watching
                39.36   42.84
Type 2-31 members, near mean on in-room cluster, near mean on not-watching
                48.19   47.34
Type 3- 8 members, above mean on in-room cluster, high on not-watching
                56.16   64.13
Type 4-18 members, above mean on in-room cluster, at mean on not-watching
                58.82   50.07
Type 5- 6 members, high on in-room cluster, high on not-watching
                73.28   64.61

The types of watchers can be further described as follows:
Type 1, the least present group, were the ones who spent the least

amount of time in the room and also least amount of time in the non-watching categories.

Type 2, the average group, were just slightly and equally below the means of both cluster scores.

Type 3, the nonwatchers, were those who spent more than an average amount of time in the room and who used most of it in nonwatching activity.

Type 4, the watchers. These people spent a lot of time in the room, were high in watching and only at the mean on nonwatching.

Type 5, the watch-nonwatchers. These people were highest on the in-room cluster and also highest on nonwatching. They both watched and didn't watch television while they were in the room.

A further breakdown of the types according to age, sex, and income reveals the following:

Type 1 had 28 members, 16 males, 12 females; mean age was 18.95, and $6,937.50 was mean income for the families. Only seven of the 28 were adults.

Type 2 had 31 members, 16 males and 15 females; mean age was 22.52, and $7,500 was mean income of families. Twelve were adults.

Type 3 had eight members, four males and four females; mean age was 26.44, and $6,937.50 was mean income of families. Five were adults.

Type 4 had 18 members, nine males and nine females; mean age was 30.11, and $4,638.89 was mean income of families. Nine were adults.

Type 5 had six members, one male and five females; mean age was 40.33, and $7,000 was mean income of families. All were adults.

The clearest trend is a rising mean age through all five types. The most inactive watchers (Type 1) had a mean age of 18.95, increasing to 22.52 for Type 2, 26.44 for Type 3, 30.11 for Type 4, and 40.33 for Type 5. Although the numbers of subjects are too small for generalization, this may suggest that television watching styles are correlated with age. Corresponding to that possible relationship, numbers of children decrease in the types from a large majority in Type 1, to no children in Type 5.

Income does not have the obvious linear quality that age does, but higher mean income does appear to be associated with inactivity (Type 1), while the lowest mean income is associated with watching (Type 4).

Sex is evenly divided among all types except Type 5, which is predominantly female. The watch-nonwatch style of watching may be related to a kind of housewife syndrome, but it must be noted that other housewives (17 of them) are scattered among the other types.

Table 21 lists three ways of measuring amounts of watching time in relation to the types of programs.[2] Part A lists the percent of total watching time devoted to each type of program. In other words, taking into account all the time periods in which subjects were scored 1, 2, or 3, 20.8 percent of that time occurred while subjects were watching a family type program. Part B shows the percent breakdown of total 4 and 5 scores by type of programs. Commercials, for example, account for 22.6 percent of all the time subjects were observed not watching. The relationship of watching to nonwatching is further illustrated by the fact that family programs account for 19.2 percent of nonwatching time as well as the largest amount of watching time. Commercials, in similar fashion, also account for the third largest amount of watching time (15 percent).

Table 21: Program categories ranked by percent of total watching time, total not-watching time, and percent of time watched while program was on

N = 20 families (93 persons)					
A Percentage of total watching time		B Percentage of total not-watching time		C Percentage of time watched while program was on	
Program type	%	Program type	%	Program type	%
Family	20.8	Commercial	22.6	Movies	76.0
Movies	18.5	Family	19.2	Children's	71.4
Commercial	15.0	Sports events	11.1	Suspense	68.1
Children's	11.8	Movies	10.7	Religious	66.7
Suspense	10.6	News	9.7	Family	66.4
Sports events	8.6	Suspense	9.1	Game show	65.9
News	5.6	Children's	8.7	Talk show	63.7
Melodrama	3.1	Melodrama	3.9	Melodrama	59.3
Talk show	2.5	Talk show	2.6	Sports events	58.7
Game show	2.4	Game show	2.3	News	55.2
Religious	.2	Religious	.2	Commercial	54.8

Although the relationships are not exact, a comparison of columns A and B shows that programs that tend to be watched, also tend to be not watched. This suggests that the watch-nonwatch pattern is generally not a function of type of program.

Column C in Table 21 shows the amount of time a type of program was watched while it was actually on the set, and it reflects the fact that for much of the time the sets were on, no one was watching. It appears that movies are watched 76 percent of the time they are on, while commercials, at the bottom of the list, are only watched 54.8 percent of the time they are on.

Column C is not a reciprocal or parallel to either column A or B, because A and B are calculated from scores in the 1-2-3 and 4-5 categories, while the time a particular program was on must take into account category 6 (indicating time people were out of the room).

Suspense programs are rated most violent by critics and public in the Greenberg-Gordon (1971) study.[3] Column A shows that suspense programs only account for 10.6 percent of total watching time and 9.1 percent of nonwatching time, but receive a fair amount of attention while they are on, being watched 68.1 percent of the time.

Table 22: Proportions of watching to not-watching for types of programs among volunteers and survey families

Type of program:		A	B	C	D	E	F	G	H	J	K	L	Total
		M	F	C	S	M	G	T	R	N	S	C	
		O	A	O	U	E	A	A	E	E	P	H	
		V	M	M	S	L	M	L	L	W	O	I	
		I	I	M	P	O	E	K	I	S	R	L	
		E	L	E	E	D	S		G		T	D	
		S	Y	R	N	R			I		S	R	
				C	S	A			O			E	
				I	E	M			U			N	
				A		A			S			'	
				L								S	
Volun- teers	% Watch	79.3	66.8	56.8	66.8	63.1	64.4	62.4	25.0	56.1	58.1	68.3	65.5
(N=12)	% Not- watch	20.7	33.2	43.2	33.1	36.9	35.6	37.6	75.0	43.9	41.9	31.7	34.5
Sur- vey	% Watch	65.2	65.6	49.7	73.5	34.4	73.5	74.1	71.4	52.5	59.3	78.3	62.6
(N=8)	% Not- watch	34.8	34.4	50.3	26.5	65.6	26.5	25.9	28.6	47.5	40.7	21.7	37.4

Volunteers and accepter subjects differed in the relative amounts of watching and nonwatching time devoted to each type of program. Table 22 shows that the two largest differences are for religious and melodrama programs. Volunteers watch much less than they "not-watch" (25 percent to 75 percent religious programs; accepters reverse this ratio (71 percent to 29 percent). Generally the same pattern exists for melodrama. Both volunteers and accepters have high watch/not-watch ratios for children's programs (68/22 percent and 68/32 percent respectively), but accepter subjects watched 10 percent more than volunteers. The same pattern is true for game shows, but differences between the two groups are smaller.

A breakdown of families by income shows no reversals of watch-not-watch ratios between those who make less than $9,000 and those who make more than $9,000 (Table 23). The under $9,000 group does watch children's programs a great deal more intensely (86 percent) than the over $9,000 group (67 percent).

The 93 subjects broke naturally into three distributions of age groups: 1-10, 11-19, and 20-75. Age was definitely a strong factor in determining watch and not-watch patterns for types of programs as well as the overall pattern for all programs. The 11-19 age group watched slightly more attentively than the 20-75 age group, and both these groups were considerably more attentive than the 1-10 age group.

As might be expected, the highest watch/not-watch ratio (86.5/13.5 percent) was for children's programs in the 1-10 age group. Correspond-

Table 23: Watching, nonwatching, and income

Type of program:	A	B	C	D	E	F	G	H	J	K	L	Total
	M O V I E S	F A M I L Y	C O M M E R C I A L	S U S P E N S E	M E L O D R A M A	G A M E S	T A L K	R E L I G I O U S	N E W S	S P O R T S	C H I L D R E N	

		A	B	C	D	E	F	G	H	J	K	L	Total
Under $9,000	% Watch	73.9	70.3	59.7	67.1	54.7	64.5	56.7	0	55.7	69.1	85.7	66.9
(N=9)	% Non-watch	26.1	29.7	40.3	32.9	45.3	35.5	43.3	0	44.3	30.9	14.3	33.1
Over $9,000	% Watch	80.8	65.3	54.3	71.6	68.9	68.9	67.3	66.7	55.0	58.6	67.0	65.0
(N=11)	% Non-watch	19.2	34.7	45.7	28.4	31.1	31.2	32.7	33.3	45.0	41.4	33.0	35.0

ingly, the highest not-watch/watch ratios (91.7/8.3 percent) are for sports and melodrama in the 1-10 age group.

The 11-19 age group is far more attentive to the violent suspense programs than are the 20-75 or the 1-10 age groups.

Table 24: Watching and not-watching for each type of program by age

		M O V I E S	F A M I L Y	C O M M E R C I A L	S U S P E N S E	M E L O D R A M A	G A M E S	T A L K	R E L I G I O U S	N E W S	S P O R T S	C H I L D R E N	Total
Age: 1-10	% Watch	38.6	53.6	41.5	54.3	8.3	—	50.0	57.1	12.3	8.3	86.5	52.2
(N=26)	% Not-watch	61.4	46.2	58.5	45.7	91.7	—	50.0	42.9	87.7	91.7	13.5	47.8
Age: 11-19	% Watch	73.2	74.6	55.8	84.1	—	—	—	50.0	55.8	43.0	83.5	68.8
(N=23)	% Not-watch	26.8	25.4	44.1	15.9	—	—	—	50.0	44.2	57.0	16.5	31.1
Age: 20-75	% Watch	77.9	67.6	51.8	76.8	67.2	73.5	70.2	76.9	60.6	64.8	54.8	65.3
(N=40)	% Not-watch	22.0	32.4	48.2	23.1	32.8	26.5	29.8	23.1	39.4	35.2	45.2	34.7

As age increases, the amount of relative time watching does, but there is some indication it may decrease again with older age. Perhaps attention to television follows the u-shaped curve of general attention span and age.

It is worth noting that the subjects in the 11-19 age group did not watch melodrama, games, or talk shows.

Behavior specimen of television viewing

Appendix D contains the complete record of a family watching television for one hour. Simultaneous records appear side by side on the pages for each member of the family so that interactions between their behavior can be seen. By no means can this record be considered a statistical mean of all the families observed. However, it can show just how varied is the behavior that accompanies television viewing. The record includes behavior that fits all of the categories of Table 1, including active participation in viewing. Children's general inattention during commercials can be seen. Probably the most consistently frequent type of behavior accompanying viewing, next to talking, is eating. Adults and children come and go during the period of observation. No conclusions can be drawn from this one record, but it serves to illustrate the watching-nonwatching pattern. The description provides the essential flavor of the 613 tapes scored for this study.

The behavior observed while viewing television included a surprising variety of items. This list only partially covers that variety:

Looking out window	Reciting
Picking nose	Wrestling
Scratching (someone else	Fighting
and self)	Crying
Doing homework	Throwing objects (toys, books,
Smoking	paper airplanes)
Rocking	Scolding children
Reading	Mimicking the TV
Dancing	Answering back to TV
Lying (on floor, couch, table)	Eating
Untying knots	Drinking
Sorting wash	Sleeping
Preparing meals	Playing Cards
Setting table	Picking up objects (toys, etc.)
Ironing.	Conversing
Dressing	Playing board games (Monopoly,
Undressing	Scrabble)
Posing	Answering phone
Doing exercises	Crawling
Singing	Fantasy play

Pacing   Teasing
Asking questions about TV program   Combing hair

Relatively well defined themes occur across the life styles of each family. These include the obvious meals, visits, phone calls, holidays, work, and school. There also seem to be wide varieties in children's play and bed times.

Styles of viewing also appear. Each family has "regular" programs family members always try to watch (as opposed to "fill ins" and "specials" or news events).

Present limitations of the study did not permit quantifying these themes across all the families, but it must be noted that viewing seems to be a part of these themes and is, perhaps, no more than one element of a family lifestyle. No doubt an aim of future research is determining the relationship among viewing time, viewing styles, and the larger framework of a family's life style.

SUMMARY AND DISCUSSION

When observed viewing time is compared with self-report of television viewing a clear trend of overreporting emerges. This tendency ranges from about 25 percent overreporting in a diary to a 40-50 percent overreport in estimates of viewing time for the previous day and general estimates of an average day's viewing.

Volunteers' general estimates of viewing time per day were close to those reported by a Nielsen survey—approximately six hours per day (Doan, 1971), while the estimates of randomly selected subjects were nearer those of another national survey—approximately three hours per day (Robinson, 1971). While the numbers are too small to be definitive, the possibility that Nielsen ratings might correspond with a volunteer rather than a random population needs further investigation.

In general, the subjects' consistent overreporting indicates a lack of awareness of the complexity of behavior during the time the television set is on. This finding is supported by the single other study which photographed the television audience (Allen, 1968).

Globally, the data point to an inseparable mixture of watching and nonwatching as a general style of television viewing behavior. Classifying 91 subjects into five types of viewing behavior shows a complex relationship between viewing behavior and age. The viewing types show a linear progression from youngest in the first type to oldest in the fifth type, but behavior, since it is based on several dimensions, does not function linearly with age. There is no evidence that viewing styles followed a family pattern or a sex-related pattern (except Type 5, which was made up almost entirely of women).

Family-type programs accounted for most of the total watching time, but movies received the greatest degree of attention while the set was on. The 11-19 age group was the most attentive, and the 1-10 age group the least attentive, to all programs. Commercials accounted for the largest block of nonwatching behavior. Generally, however, types of programs that were watched a great deal were also "not-watched" relatively the same amount compared to other types. This indicates that watching and not-watching are part of a general behavior pattern not related to program type.

The most violent type of programs—suspense—only accounted for 10.6 percent of watching behavior, but subjects in the 11-19 age group watched them very intently when they were on (84 percent of the time).

Volunteers were significantly different from subjects selected at random in their viewing patterns for certain types of programs. Volunteers pay much less attention to religious and melodrama programs when they are on than do subjects selected at random.

The findings point to the fact that television viewing is a complex and various form of behavior intricately interwoven with many other kinds of behavior. It will not be a simple matter to sort out how the way programs viewed finally impinge on the sense receptors, nor to interpret how the interfering behaviors filter out the television stimulus. Clearly, watching television is not a behavior in its own right but is a mixture with many threads of which the viewer seems only partially aware. Any interpretation of the way violence is or is not communicated from the television stimulus must take this complex "filter" of the stimulus into account. Television viewing does not occur in a vacuum; it is always to some degree background to a complex behavior pattern in the home.

FOOTNOTES

1. This research is one of a group of studies done under the sponsorship of the Surgeon General's Scientific Advisory Committee on Television and Social Behavior to provide evidence on the relationships between televised violence and the behavior of children and youth. Work was done under contract No. PH 43-67-1324 with the National Institute of Mental Health, Center for Epidemiological Studies. Special thanks are due to Roberta Haynes, Mario Fort, Charles Herrick, Cathy McCarthy, Jean Hicks and Jeanie Meyer for their work on this project. Bob Hayles and Patricia Banks recorded the specimen record of TV viewing behavior in Appendix D.
2. See Appendix C for a partial listing of programs for each type.
3. Includes *Mod Squad, Mannix, Mission Impossible, Hawaii Five-0, It Takes a Thief, The FBI, Gunsmoke, High Chapparal, Dragnet, Ironside, The Virginian, Name of the Game, Land of Giants,* and *The Bold Ones* as the most violent—and generally in that order.

REFERENCES

Allen, C.L. Photographing the TV audience *Journal of Advertising Research*, March 1968, 2-8.

Barker, R.G., and Wright, H. *Midwest and its children.* Evanston, Ill.: Row, Peterson, 1955.

Doan, R.K. The Doan report. *TV Guide* (Kansas City ed.), May 8, 1971.

Garretson, W. The consensual definition of social objects. *The Sociological Quarterly*, 1962, **3**, 107-13.

Greenberg, B., and Gordon, T. Perceptions of violence in TV programs: critics and the public. In *Television and social behavior*, Vol. 1 (this series). Washington, D.C.: U.S. Government Printing Office, 1971.

Guetzkow, H. Unitizing and categorizing problems in coding qualitative data. *Journal of Clinical Psychology*, 1950, **6**, 47-58.

Katz, M., and Lyerly, S. Methods of measuring adjustment and social behavior in the community: rationale, description, discriminative validity and scale development. *Psychological Reports*, 1963, **13**, 503-35.

Lubin, B., Adjective check lists for measurement of depression. *Archives of General Psychiatry*, 1965, **12**, 57-62.

Robinson, J.P. Television and leisure time: yesterday, today, and (maybe) tomorrow. *Public Opinion Quarterly*, 1969, **33**, 210-22.

Robinson, J.P. Television's impact on everyday life: some crossnational evidence. In *Television and social behavior*, Vol. 4 (this volume). Washington, D.C.: U.S. Government Printing Office, 1971.

Steiner, G. *The people look at television.* New York: Alfred A. Knopf, 1963.

Tiffany, D. Mental health, a function of experienced control. *Journal of Clinical Psychology*, 1967, **23**, 311-15.

Tryon, R., and Bailey, D. *Cluster analysis.* New York: McGraw Hill, 1970.

Appendix A-1: First questionnaire

My name is Ada Sylvie and I am conducting a poll for the Surgeon General's Scientific Advisory Committee on Television and Social Behavior. This survey is paid for by the Federal Government and your cooperation would be greatly appreciated.

May I come in and ask you a few questions. The poll should only take 15 or 20 minutes at the most.

1. a. How many TV sets (that work) do you have in your home?
   b. How many of these are color sets?
   c. Are any of these sets able to pick up the UHF stations (channels 19, 50)?
                         Yes_____   No_____
2. a. On an average day, about how many hours do you personally spend watching TV?_____ hours
   b. How many hours did you watch yesterday?   hours
3. What are your four favorite programs on television, the ones you try to watch every time they are on the air?
   a._____   c._____

   b._____   d._____

4. (FOR FIRST FICTIONAL PROGRAM MENTIONED IN Q. 3):
   a. Would you say that_____(PROGRAM)_____
   ____1. Shows life like it really is
   ____3. Does not show life like it really is
   ____2. Both
   ____8. Don't know
   b. Would you say you like these programs more for
   ____1. The stories
   ____3. The people in the stories
   ____2. Both
   ____8. Don't know
5. Would you agree or disagree with these complaints about TV?
   a. Too much sex   _____ Agree ____Disagree
   b. Too many commercials   _____ Agree ____Disagree
   c. Too much violence   _____ Agree ____Disagree
   d. Too many news programs _____ Agree ____Disagree

Thank you for answering the questions in the poll.

A part of the research being done on the effects of television concerns itself with the time people spend watching television and the ways they behave while watching it. Would you be willing to allow us to film (your family) (you) watching television?

Of course, we would pay you for the inconvenience. Payment is $75.00 for six days viewing.

1. Record refusal and reason.
2. Record acceptance and set up date for representative to call.

Appendix A-2: Subject agreement

I,_____am willing to permit two cameras and three microphones to be installed in my home for research on television viewing behavior. It is my understanding that viewing will take place for six (6) days and that I will be recompensed by payment of $75.00.

It is also my understanding that this information will be used only for purposes of scientific research sponsored by The Surgeon General's Scientific Advisory Committee on Television and Social Behavior and that the data are to remain anonymous.

_____
signed

Appendix A-3: Diary

TIME QUARTER HOURS	SET USE		STATION TUNED IN		NAME OF PROGRAM WATCHED		MAN OF HOUSE	LADY OF HOUSE	CHILDREN	OTHERS
	ON	OFF	CALL LETTERS	CHAN. NO.	AGE	SEX				
4:00–4:14										
4:15–4:29										
4:30–4:44										
4:45–4:59										
5:00–5:14										
5:15–5:29										
5:30–5:44										
5:45–5:59										
6:00–6:14										
6:15–6:29										
6:30–6:44										
6:45–6:59										
7:00–7:14										
7:15–7:29										
7:30–7:44										
7:45–7:59										
8:00–8:14										
8:15–8:29										
8:30–8:44										
8:45–8:59										
9:00–9:14										
9:15–9:29										

Appendix A-4: Previous day questionnaire

Now I'd like to go over with you the programs you watched on television yesterday, that is, _____ (NOTE THE SPECIFIC DAY, e.g., Saturday). Here is a television schedule to help you recall the programs on yesterday. Let's begin by asking what the first program you watched was after you got up yesterday._____

a) Program (or description with channel, if R cannot recall program)____

_____

b) And you watched that program between____ $\frac{AM}{PM}$ and ____ $\frac{AM}{PM}$

c) As best you can remember, what was the program about? (TRY TO GET R TO NOTE AT LEAST TWO DESCRIPTIVE SENTENCES ABOUT PROGRAM.) _____

_____

d) How did you happen to watch this show? Had you planned to watch it beforehand, did it just come on the channel you were already watching, or what?

Planned to watch   Came on channel

Other (explain)_____

e) Were you doing anything else while watching this program, or did the program have your complete attention from start to finish?

1. Complete attention   5. Doing something else

                                    f) What were you doing? _____

                                    g) How long were you doing it? __

h) Looking back, would you say that the program was a waste of time, really worth watching or what?

1. Waste of time   5. Worth watching

Other (explain) _____

i) Was anyone watching the program with you?

Yes   No

j) Who was that? _____

k) Did they have any say in choosing this program rather than other ones on at the same time?

Yes   No

l) Who had the main say as to watching?_____ (program watched)

m) Did you talk with anyone while the program was on?

Yes   No

n) What did you talk about?_____

Appendix A-5: Five-day questionnaire

I would like to ask about how much you watched T.V. during the past five days.

1. First, do you think having the camera present influenced you and your family in any way?

   Yes ☐   No ☐

   a. In what way?_____

   _____

2. Do you think our asking you questions has made you more aware of watching T.V.?

   Yes ☐   No ☐

3. How much T.V. did you watch during the last 5 days?

   a. Hours per day for you

   b. Hours per day for spouse

   c. Hours per day for children

      1.

      2.

      3.

      4.

      5.

4. Was the last five days in any way different from an ordinary week? Did anything unusual happen that might influence T.V. watching?

Appendix B: Coding sheet

T.V. OBSERVER: CODE SHEET

FAMILY NAME: _____   TAPE DATE: _____

SHEET NUMBER: # _____   TAPE TIME: _____ TO _____

CODE DATE: _____   REEL NUMBER # _____

NAME													
AGE													
SEX													
1. 40	C H												
2. 78	A N												
3. 115	N E												
4. 151	L												
5. 185													
6. 218													
7. 250													
8. 281													
9. 311													
10. 340													
11. 368													
12. 396													
13. 423													
14. 449													
15. 475													
16. 500													
17. 525													
18. 549													
19. 573													
20. 596													
21. 619													
22. 641													
23. 663													
24. 684													
25. 705													
26. 725													
27. 745													
28. 765													
29. 784													
30. 803													
31. 822													

Appendix C: Partial listing of program types

Category	Examples
A. Movie	*ABC Movie, NBC Movie, Wednesday Night Movie, Channel 5 Movie, Channel 9 Movie*
B. Family variety and comedy	*Glen Campbell Goodtime Hour, I Love Lucy, Don Knotts Show, All in the Family, Johnny Cash, Odd Couple, Bob Hope's Christmas Show, Love American Style, Fanfare, Hee Haw*
C. Commercial	*Commercials for products and paid political announcements.*
D. Suspense	*The FBI, Felony Squad, Perry Mason, Big Valley, Gunsmoke, Dragnet, The Avengers, Mannix, Alfred Hitchcock, Run for Your Life*
E. Melodrama	*Peyton Place, Where the Heart Is, General Hospital, Secret Storm, Edge of Night, Divorce Court, Love of Life, A World Apart*
F. Game show	*Truth or Consequences, Concentration, Movie Game, The Who, What, Where Game, Let's Make a Deal, Sale of the Century, You Don't Say*
G. Talk show	*Tonight Show, Dick Cavett, Merv Griffin, David Frost Show*
H. Religious	*Story of Jesus, Faith for Today, Oral Roberts, Unity Society, Herald of Truth, Rabbi Margolies, Revival Fires, Faith for Our Times*
J. News, weather, information programs	*Issues and Answers, Perspective, CBS News, NBC News, 10:00 News, Weather and Sports, Meet The Press, World Press, The Advocates, CBS News Special, Your Congressman, 60 Minutes*
K. Sports events	*Basketball—1970 Stanley Cup Highlights, Gold, Sportsman's Friend, NFL Football, Roller Derby*
L. Children's show and cartoons	*Tom & Jerry, Penelope Pitstop, Smokey the Bear, Captain Kangaroo, Sesame Street, Superman, Flintstones, Romper Room, Gomer Pyle*

Appendix D: Behavior specimen record of one family's television viewing for one hour

SKETCH OF BARKER FAMILY TV AREA
(View from above)

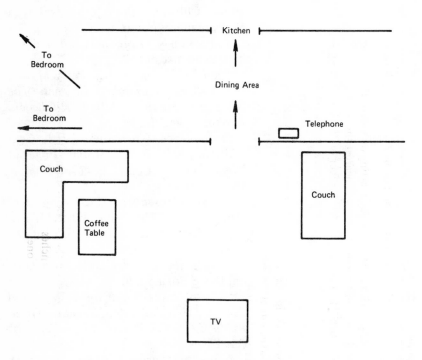

The following material came from:
Barker: Monday, 2/16/70, Tape #18
Time: approximately one hour

(TV is presenting the *I Love Lucy* show.)

Time		Tommie	Jamie	Mother	Father
0'	0"	Tommie sits with legs tucked under him on the right couch. He holds a drumstick-like object in his hand. He watches the set in a relaxed but attentive manner. He watches for 20 seconds without movement. Then, while still looking at the set, he gives the stick a flicking movement.	He is sitting on end of the couch nearest the set. He has his feet on the floor and his back resting on the couch; one hand is near his mouth. He is watching TV closely. He has his feet crossed. He wiggles his feet.	Out	Out
0'	30"	He continues to watch in a very still position.	He wiggles his feet. He continues to watch the set closely.	Out	Out
1'		Tommie's fixation on the set continues. He scrunches back in his seat giving one flick to his stick.	He is sitting still watching TV.	Out	Out

Time	Tommie	Jamie	Mother	Father
1' 30"	He is still like a statue, staring at the set.	He bounces feet to the rhythm of the song.	Out	Out
		("I've got the world on a string" is being sung on TV.)		
		He is bouncing his head to the beat a few times and then sits still with no movements.		
		(The song continues.)		
2'	Tommie is watching closely. He flicks stick.	Jamie sniffs a rose. He wiggles feet a little.	Out	Out
2' 30"	He is still watching closely. Without moving his eyes, he pushes his legs out from under himself. Now he is sitting feet down on the seat of the couch.	He is sitting still.	Out	Out
		(The music still continues.)		
3'	He is watching carefully and taking it all in. He brings his hand and arm across his face as if rubbing an itchy area.	He is still sitting in the original position.	Out	Out

Time		Tommie	Jamie	Mother	Father
3'	30"	Tommie draws his knees up and shifts his body slightly. He is still watching TV.	Jamie turns to look at his dad as he closes the dining room, for a few minutes. Then he returns to the original posture of watching TV.	Out	Out
4'		Tommie watches the set. Then he notices his dad crossing the dining area. He says something but does not receive an answer. Then he turns and comments briefly to Jamie (not heard). He looks back at the set.	Jamie pats his feet to the beat of the song for a few seconds. (The song on the set continues.)	Out	Out
4'	30"	He is still looking at the set. (The song ends.)	He stops beat.	Out	Out

Time	Tommie	Jamie	Mother	Father
		He uncrosses his feet, sits up, and scoots back on couch, places hand on his chin with elbow on knee. He watches TV attentively.		
		(Lucy of *The Lucy Show* is making a comment.)		
5′	Tommie watches closely. He pulls himself further back on the couch so that his feet are off the floor. He watches the set all the while.	He flutters his feet for 10 seconds and then stops. He removes his hand from his chin and leans back a little more.	Out	Out
		He glances into the dining area.		
		He quickly looks back at the TV.		
5′ 30″	Tommie sits quietly and comfortably. He watches.	He leans forward a little with his head and body and straightens up and places fingers in his mouth.	Out	Out
		He begins to whistle loudly for a few seconds.		

Time	Tommie	Jamie	Mother	Father
6'	He continues to watch TV. (He does not seem to notice his father passing through the dining room.)	He whistles off and on. He bounces his feet on the edge of the couch. (A commercial is on.) (Jamie does not notice his father passing through the dining area.)	Out	Out
6' 30"	Tommie gets off the couch still facing the set as he is about to leave. (You might say he is taking one last look.)	He continues to bounce his feet and whistle. He stops viewing the set to look at Tommie. He then beats the drumsticks and whistles. His head is now turning away from the TV.	Out	Out
7'	He walks out of the area.	Jamie looks back at TV. He continues to beat his leg with the drumstick. He gets up and goes over to the TV and adjusts the set, then returns to the couch. He slouches down on the couch. He then looks into the dining area.	Out	Out

Time	Tommie	Jamie	Mother	Father
7' 30"	Out	He looked back at TV. He's still in a slouched position. Jamie looks down at his hands that are playing with the drumstick. His feet are on the floor. He touches one foot to the other. He glances away from and then back to the TV set.	Out	Out
8'	Out	Jamie takes his right shoe off. He then bounces his foot on the shoe. He continues to watch TV while doing this.	Out	Out
8' 30"	Out	Jamie is playing around with his feet. He bounces them and touches them to each other. Jamie then puts his legs entirely onto the couch. He beats his drumstick. He looks at TV.	Out	Out

Time	Tommie	Jamie	Mother	Father
9'	Out	Jamie looks into the dining area and sits up. His legs are folded. He is laying on his side; the drumstick is held under his foot with his hands attached to each end.	Out	Out
9' 30"	Out	He continues to watch TV. Jamie beats his foot with the drumstick.	Out	We can hear him speaking.
10'	Out	Jamie scratches foot with his drumstick. (*Mayberry RFD* is on TV.)	Out	We can now neither see or hear the father.
10' 30"	Out	Jamie continues to play with his mouth holding it with his left hand.	Out	Out
11'	Out	He puts the stick in and out of his mouth holding it with his left hand.	Out	Out

Time	Tommie	Jamie	Mother	Father
11' 30"	Out	Jamie whistles.	Out	Out
		He then lies on his stomach facing TV. He beats something with his drumstick. Jamie continues to watch TV.		
12'	Out	Jamie looks down. He then beats on something.	Out	Out
		Jamie looks back at set.		
		He stops his beating.		
12' 30"	Out	Jamie watches the TV set.	Out	Out
		He puts his fingers near his mouth, he sniffs.		
13'	Out	Jamie still has his hand in front of mouth and nose.	Out	Out
13' 30"	Out	He lies down flatter on the couch. He keeps his eyes on the TV.	Out	Out
		He glares to the right for a second. Then he places his head on the arm of the couch.		

Time	Tommie	Jamie	Mother	Father
14'	Out	Jamie kicks his legs a little.	Out	Out
		He then beats the arm of the couch with his drumstick.		
14' 30"	Out	Jamie scoots forward and sits halfway up. He looks down and fiddles with the drumstick, beats on the couch and runs stick along the couch.	Out	Out
		He now resumes TV viewing.		
15'	Out	He beats an unknown object held in one hand with the drum stick.	Out	He leans forward now and can be seen sitting near the doorway.
15' 30"	Out	He is still watching TV and beating with the drumstick.	Out	Mr. Barker raises, lowers, and lowers his arm. He rests his elbows on the table and rests his head in his hands.
		He glances into dining area and back at the TV.		
16'	Out	He is still watching TV.	Out	Mr. Barker rubs his head with his hand.
				He tells Tommie "No" to an unheard question.

Time	Tommie	Jamie	Mother	Father
16′ 30″	Tommie returns with two cupcakes.	He accepts the cupcake from Tommie.	Out	He turns his head forward and gets up out of the chair.
	He gives one to Jamie.	He leans back and his head cannot be seen.		He goes out of sight.
	He climbs onto the couch and sits in a kneeling position.			
17′	Tommie squirms. He looks at cupcake, then back at TV.	Jamie sits up a ways with his head still out of sight.	Out	He is asked something by one of the boys.
				He gives a command.
	He wipes his nose with his elbow and turns head briefly.			
17′ 30″	He pounds one hand with the other while making sounds to the same rhythm. He nods his head a few times.	He leans his head forward and beats the cupcake wrapper with his drumstick. (He is not watching TV.)	Out	He gets some food out and then walks out of sight again.
	He speaks to Jamie (content unknown).			
18′	Tommie watches TV intently; he sits very still.	He is viewing TV.	Out	Out
		Jamie glances down and back at TV.		

Time		Tommie	Jamie	Mother	Father
18'	30"	He now moves to a kneeling position.	He beats his hand with the drumstick.	Out	Out
		He is still watching TV.	He is still watching TV.		
19'		He looks down at his cupcake and takes a bite.	He looks down and beats the cupcake with his drumstick.	Out	Out
		He watches TV.	He takes a bite from his cupcake.		
		He chews, too.			
		He leans forward to see around Jamie.			
19'	30"	He looks at the cupcake and takes another bite.	He drops a piece of cupcake, picks it up and eats it; he eats more of the cupcake.	Out	Out
		He looks into the dining area. (Someone moves in there.)			
20'		He sits very still with his legs straight out.	Now he is totally involved with eating the cupcake.	Out	Out
		He is still watching TV.	He is not viewing TV. He beats occasionally on his leg with rhythm.		
			(Marlboro commercial on TV.)		

Time		Tommie	Jamie	Mother	Father
20'	30"	He does not notice his father entering the room.	He glances at his dad as he enters the room.	She walks through the living room. She looks at the TV while moving.	Mr. B. enters the area and goes around TV.
			He resumes watching TV and beating the stick.		
			He sits up on the edge of the couch and faces across the room at his father.		
21'		He reclines and watches TV.	He eats the cupcake.	She walks out of the living room and out of view. (She had apparently come into the room to look for, or to get something)	He leaves the area.
			Jamie sits back and rocks over to one side.		
21'	30"	Tommie watches TV very intently with no reactions.	He watches TV. He eats some more cupcake at the same time.	Out	He returns and adjusts the pillows on the couch and sits with legs spread apart and feet on the floor.
22'		He watches TV while sitting very still.	He eats some more cupcake. He is still watching TV.	Out	He lifts his feet onto the couch and glances at them.
					He fingers his glasses.
					He cleans his ears.

Time		Tommie	Jamie	Mother	Father
22'	30"	Tommie continues watching.	He watches.	Out	He glances at the boys. He looks back at the set. He places his hands across his stomach.
23'		He watches.	He continues to watch TV. He also continues to eat on the cupcake.	Out	He scratches his chest. He digs in his ear and looks at the object (unknown) used for digging.
23'	30"	Tommie continues watching.	He watches.	Out	He looks at TV. Mr. B. grunts and yawns. He picks up a newspaper and holds it in front of him.
24'		He watches. Tommie sits very still without moving or reacting.	He watches.	Out	He is reading the newspaper and doing nothing else.
24'	30"	He watches.	He watches.	Out	He continues to read the newspaper. He moves his fingers a little.

Time	Tommie	Jamie	Mother	Father
25'	Tommie continues to watch. He leaves the area.	He beats his hand with the drumstick. He finishes the cupcake.	Out	The father now leans slightly over to one side, while still reading the paper.
25' 30"	Out	He beats the cupcake wrapper with the stick while holding the stick in one hand and the wrapper in the other.	Out	He continues to read.
26'	Out	Jamie is sitting with one leg down and the other bent at the knee with his arm resting on it. He puts the end of the stick into his mouth.	Out	He is still reading the paper. He places his fingers by his mouth. He has not looked up the whole 30 seconds.
26' 30"	Tommie returns. He sits on edge of the couch and watches TV intently.	He takes the stick away from his mouth. He glances at Tommie.	Out	The father looks up from the paper once. He is still fingering with the paper.
27'	He turns to his dad. He then watches TV quietly and intently.	He jumps up quickly and runs into the dining area.	Out	He moves the hand that is holding the paper. The paper almost completely conceals his face.

Time		Tommie	Jamie	Mother	Father
27'	30"	He still sits on edge of couch, and watches TV intently.	Out	Out	Mr. B. looks down. He moves the paper slightly. He puts his right hand up to his glasses and pushes them back on his face. Then he places right hand on top of and behind his head.
					He is still holding and reading his paper.
28'		He is watching TV with close attention.	Out	Out	He holds the same position.
					He turns his head to ask a question of Mrs. Barker.
					He moves the paper slightly.
					He looks back at paper.
28'	30"	Tommie rests his hand on his leg. He wipes his nose with his arm.	Jamie returns and sits on the couch. He sits all the way back with his feet extended straight out, and his hands between his thighs.	Mrs. Barker enters living room. She is carrying an article of clothing on a hanger. She glances at TV.	He looks up as mother passes through. (TV says at the same time "Hey look over there"). He watches set for 10 seconds. He then turns back to paper. Mother goes through. He looks up at set. (There is marching music on TV.)
		He then looks at his brother and dad.	He watches TV.		

Time	Tommie	Jamie	Mother	Father
29'	He says something to Jamie and something to Dad. He then leaves the room after looking at Dad and then at Jamie.	He watches TV intently. He answers his dad and looks at him for a few seconds.	She enters the living room and glances slightly at the television. She is carrying an article of clothing on a hanger into another room.	He takes his hand off his head and looks toward the boys. He asks something about what is on the television. He then moves his legs slightly.
29' 30"	Tommy returns and sits down on the couch. He places one leg out and one leg tucked underneath him. He wiggles his foot a little.	He flutters his feet as a swimmer does while kicking and then stops.	She returns to the living room where she stands in the doorway and does not pay attention to the television. She seems to be clearing something from the table.	He holds the paper up. I cannot tell if he is looking at it or the television.
30'	He wiggles his feet. He is still watching television intently.	He is still watching television intently with no movement.	She walks out of the room and returns by the living room and glances at the TV on the way by.	He maintains his same position but moves his feet up and down slightly.
30' 30"	From this time through 33 minutes, Tommie watches TV sitting very still with no reaction or movement.	He flutters his feet a little, still watching TV intently.	She is still out of the room.	He holds his same position while sitting on the couch reading the newspaper. He places his hand on back and on top of his head. He crosses his legs. He is reading the newspaper, definitely. He is holding it up with his left hand.

Time	Tommie	Jamie	Mother	Father
31'		He glances at Tommie. He folds one leg up and puts his hand in front of his mouth. Perhaps he puts a finger or two inside his mouth.	Mrs. Barker now leaves the room and does not return until 38 minutes.	He is still lying on the couch reading the newspaper. He maintains this behavior to 33 minutes 30 seconds.
31' 30"		He holds his left foot with his right hand. He then pats his left foot alternately with his right and left hands several times.	Out	
32'		He stops patting after 15 seconds.	Out	
32' 30"		Both his hands are fingering his feet.	Out	
33'	He still has no reaction to the TV or anyone in the room.	He stops, he glances down. He sniffs his nose, he fingers his foot with his hands and grabs one of his feet and pulls it up with both hands. He is still watching TV intently.	Out	

(A commercial advertising Benson & Hedges is now on.)

Time		Tommie	Jamie	Mother	Father
33′	30″	He glances into the dining area and then looks back at the television.	He puts his foot down and puts his hand near his mouth.	Out	He now raises his head slightly but I still cannot tell if he is watching TV and/or reading the newspaper.
			He now puts his legs down over the edge of the couch.		
34′		He glances at Jamie then back at the TV.	He now sits back on the couch with his hand near his mouth.	Out	He is in the same position on the couch with his legs crossed.
					He is reading the newspaper.
					He still has one hand on his head.
34′	30″	He is sitting still watching TV intently.	He is still watching TV with his hand at his mouth. He rubs one foot against the other one.	Out	He scratches his left leg with his right foot. His other body position remains the same.
35′		He glances at his dad reading the newspaper.	He is still watching TV with his hand near his mouth.	Out	

Time	Tommie	Jamie	Mother	Father
35' 30"	Tommie goes toward the dining room and when he is called by Dad he returns to the living room. He goes over to Dad by the couch to see what he wants.	Jamie claps his hands four times and looks at Tommie for a few seconds. He then folds his legs under him onto the couch.	Out	He moves his head slightly. He lowers his arm along with the paper. He then turns to see what the boys are doing and calls to Tommie.
	(The television show *Mayberry R.F.D.* is now going on.)			
	He now turns to watch the TV while standing in front of his dad. He does not react to Jamie's clapping.			
36'	He asks his dad for an aspirin. He then leaves the room and searches for his mom. Apparently, she will give him the aspirin.	He is sitting very still with his hand near his mouth watching TV. He makes no movements.	Out	
36' 30"	Tommie has not returned yet.	(At this point, *The Doris Day Show* begins.)	Out	He begins to pick at his nose while still reading the newspaper. He moves his left hand as if scanning up the side of the paper.

Time	Tommie	Jamie	Mother	Father
37'	Out	Jamie is still watching TV sitting very still with no movement or reaction.	Out	He folds a section of the paper and then scoots down further on the couch. He places one hand behind his head. He now has his legs sprawled apart on the couch.
37' 30"	Out	He now gets up slowly and walks slowly out of the room.	Out	He turns his head slightly still reading the newspaper. He then takes his arm from his head and scratches his shoulder, and then resumes his previous position.
38'	Tommie has returned. He enters the room and climbs onto the couch. He sits in a kneeling position. He now wipes his face with his hands. He glances at Dad for a few seconds.	Out	She walks into the living room and questions Mr. Barker about what is on TV. She then stands in the living room facing toward the television.	He now moves his legs around a little, scratches his head with his hand. He then glances for a second at the set. While he is glancing at the set, he is turning a page of the newspaper.

Time		Tommie	Jamie	Mother	Father
38′	30″	He rubs his nose with his fist and yawns. He then turns to speak with someone who is out of the room and cannot be seen.	Jamie is still out of the room.	She is still standing in front of the couch watching TV standing very still. After a few seconds she turns around to face toward the dining room. She places the article she was holding onto the dining room table.	He now turns his head for a second toward Tommie. He then turns back and watches television.
39′		Tommie looks around quickly and pays close attention to a light being cut on, probably by Jamie in the dining room.	Jamie is still out of the room.	Mrs. Barker does not respond to Mr. Barker or statement in Spanish. She now apparently goes to the bathroom. Mrs. Barker calls to one of the boys as she goes to the bathroom.	He turns back to the paper and then turns back to the TV to listen to an announcement about family planning. He then says something to Mrs. Barker in Spanish.
39′	30″	Tommie now watches TV intently in the same position.	Jamie returns to the room, carrying a little puppy in his arms.	Mrs. Barker is still out, apparently in the bathroom.	He returns to his reclining position on the couch still reading the newspaper.

Time		Tommie	Jamie	Mother	Father
40'		He has no reaction to the behavior going on in the room or the TV.	Jamie now sits on the couch, with the puppy in his arms.	Out	He now tells one of the boys to bring him the dog.
			He looks at his dad and upon request from Dad he takes the puppy over to Dad.		He talks to the boy about the dog and about what the boy has done.
			He hands the puppy to him and tells Dad what he has just done. Evidently, he has just cleaned the dog's pen.		He accepts the dog from Jamie and places the dog on his shoulder and begins to pet it.
40'	30'	Tommie looks at Dad as Dad is talking. He does not know to whom his dad is talking.	Jamie, after giving the dog to his dad, now leaves the room.	Out	He continues to play with the dog, petting it and stroking it.
		He gets up, goes over to Dad, and asks him what he is talking about.			
		He now climbs onto Dad and begins to play with the dog.			

Time	Tommie	Jamie	Mother	Father
41'	He is now kneeling on top of his dad. He turns to watch Jamie enter the room. He is still watching Dad pet the dog.	Jamie returns to the room and sits on the edge of the couch facing Dad.	Out	He moves his hand in an encouraging motion to the dog. He tries to get the dog to crawl on him. He is very attentively watching the dog.
41' 30"	Tommie watches his dad. He then crawls down, stands for a few seconds watching the TV.	Jamie sits back and begins watching TV. He is sitting up very straight. He wiggles his feet for a few seconds.	Out	He now picks up the paper. The dog is crawling on him. He lowered the paper as Jamie entered the room and then laughed as he looked at the dog.
				He now places his hand behind his head and continues reading the paper.
	(They are watching a Jif peanut butter commercial on TV.)			
42'	Tommie goes back and sits on the edge of the couch. He begins watching TV very intently.	Jamie glances at Dad for a few seconds.	Out	He then stops and strokes the dog once or twice.
	He places a finger in his mouth. He is sitting on the couch across from Dad.	He bounces his feet on the edge of his couch and then wiggles his feet.		He strokes the dog again and then looks down over at Tom.
				He places one hand behind his head and continues to read the paper.

Time	Tommie	Jamie	Mother	Father
42' 30"	Tommie watches his dad pet the dog, then he turns to watch Jamie. He rubs his eyes, and then looks back at the TV. He glances at Dad, then to the dining area, and then back at TV.		Out	He now raises up slightly to see what the dog is doing. The dog is under his chin. He keeps looking back and forth between the paper and the dog trying to keep up with what the dog is doing and occasionally reads a few lines on the paper. He now smiles and turns to glance at the TV.
43'	Tommie now gets up, looks at the TV for a second, and walks out of the room.	Jamie moves both hands down between his thighs. He flutters his feet up and down on the edge of the couch. He then glances at Dad and then looks back at the TV.	Out	He is still holding the paper with his left hand and he pats the dog with his right hand. He smiles briefly and then he turns to see what the boys are watching. He then turns back to look at the dog.
43' 30"	Out	Jamie sniffs his nose three times then places his hand near his mouth. He does all this while still watching TV.	Out	He is still stroking the dog with his left hand. He is holding the newspaper with his right hand. He now smiles, turns his head toward the boys for a second, then turns back and watches the dog.

Time	Tommie	Jamie	Mother	Father
44'	Out	Jamie is still watching TV intently. He bounces both feet on the edge of the couch.	Out	He continues to play with the dog, petting it and stroking it.
44' 30"	Out	Jamie is still bouncing his feet on the edge of the couch. At this instant the dog yelps loudly. Jamie turns suddenly toward the couch and comments that he was scared by the dog's loud yelping. He then resumes TV viewing.	Out	He places his hand down along his side for a moment. He looks to see if the boy is watching him, then he looks back at the dog. He smiles as the dog yelps.
45'	Out	He bounces his feet on the edge of the couch for about 10 seconds, then he watches TV intently.	Out	He smiles again and continues to stroke the dog while still holding the newspaper with the other hand.
45' 30"	Out	He now beats his legs a little with both hands very rapidly. He then bends his head down a little while doing this. He stops and looks over at Dad and the dog for a while. He begins to bounce his feet on the edge of the couch again. He then looks back at	Out	He makes a jerky movement toward the dog and then he smiles a little broader. He continues to pet the dog.

Time		Tommie	Jamie	Mother	Father
			the TV and relaxes. He also ceases all motion.		
46′		Tommie now returns. He walks over to the couch with Jamie and looks at the dog.	Jamie yawns. He does not notice Tommie entering the room. He continues to watch TV intently.	Mrs. Barker now comes out of the bath, comes toward the living room and glances at TV.	He continues to play with the dog, fingering him in the face and he continues to smile.
		He pets the dog.	He places his hand near his mouth. He sniffs his nose a couple of times. He glances at Dad and the dog and glances back at the TV.	As she goes by, she calls to Jamie and tells him to call Gus Jr., to tell him to come home.	He is also still holding the newspaper but not reading it. He now turns sideways a little so that his back is against the couch more so and he is resting more of his weight against the side.
46′	30″	Tommie now goes over to the other side of the room. He sits in a kneeling position.	After being asked to call Gus Jr., he says, "What's the number?" At this point, he leaves the room.		He quickly places his hand in front of the dog and quickly draws it away, teasing him. He continues to do this for several seconds.
		He places the drumstick in his mouth again and begins to watch TV intently.			
47′		Tommie takes the stick out of his mouth and is still watching TV intently.	Out	Out	He removes his hand from back of the dog and places it on top of his head and begins to read. Paper is perfectly still.

Time		Tommie	Jamie	Mother	Father
47′	30″	Tommie is still sitting on the couch very still in a kneeling position watching TV.	Out	Out	He is now reading the newspaper. He moves his hand up a little on the back of his head and moves it back and forth a little.
48′		A bell rings. Tommie turns his head for a second. He looks at the TV and then back at Dad and the dog. He switches back and forth several times between the TV, his dad and the dog.	Out	Out	At the sound of the bell, he looks up and looks up at the top edge of the paper.
48′	30″	Tommie now scratches his head several times while still watching TV.	Out	Out	He now turns his head toward the TV and makes a comment and then turns back to the paper. He does not answer to a comment made by Mrs. Barker in the other room.
49′		Tommie listens while Dad tells him something. He then goes over to Dad, picks up the dog and carries the dog out of the room.	Jamie returns to the room. He sits on the edge of the couch, facing his dad.	Out	Dad lies still for about 15 seconds, then he turns to Tom and tells him something.

Time	Tommie	Jamie	Mother	Father
49' 30"	Out	Jamie gets up, walks over to the couch where Dad is, looks over his shoulder at the newspaper for a few seconds. He then picks up a magazine off of the coffee table and leaves the room.	Out	He continues to read the newspaper lying on the couch.
50'	Out	Out	Out	He continues to read the newspaper. He appears to be reading the comic section for there is an occasional smile.
50' 30"	Out	Out	Out	He continues to read the newspaper and continues to laugh and smile on occasion.
51'	Out	Out	Out	He fingers the edge of the newspaper and continues to read.
51' 30"	Out	Out	Out	He continues to read the newspaper quietly now.
52'	Out	Out	Out	At this point, Mr. Barker is smiling broadly.

Time	Tommie	Jamie	Mother	Father
52' 30"	Out	Jamie has now entered the room. He walks to the end of the couch.	Out	After about 15 seconds, he stops and watches Jamie enter the room.
				He continues to smile.
		Jamie begins to look over Dad's shoulder. He now reaches to pet the dog.		
		He begins to poke at the dog, teasing it.		
53'	Out		Out	He begins to laugh now. He is still holding the paper with one hand.
				He now scoots up higher onto the seat.
				He glances over at the TV, and then back toward the dog.
53' 30"	Out	Jamie continues to tease and poke at the dog. The dog yelps. Then Jamie turns toward the TV, looks at it, glances at the dog and back at the TV.	Out	Mr. Barker looks up now and begins to watch Jamie play with the dog.
				He tells him, "That's enough now."

Time	Tommie	Jamie	Mother	Father
54'	At this point, Tommie returns with plate of food and sets it on the coffee table. He sits on edge of table.	Jamie places his hand in the dog's mouth, then looks at TV, and begins to lean on the wall and the couch.	Out	Mr. Barker holds the paper and moves it slightly.
				He looks at dog and smiles. He giggles a little. He glances at the TV, then rolls to the side.
	He gets up, walks around corner of table. He takes a bite of food.			He begins to watch again.
	He walks over to the TV, then sits down on couch opposite his Dad.			
54' 30"	He pounds on the table and the couch with the drumstick.	He is looking at dog (or paper?) for 15 seconds.	Out	He watches TV. He plays with dog while watching.
		He then looks back at TV.		He then looks back at the paper.
55'	He walks over to the table and gets the plate.	Jamie glances back and forth a few times from the TV to the dog.	Out	He looks at the paper, then at the dog.
	He takes it over to the couch and sets it down.			He glances at TV.

(The door bell rings.)

Time		Tommie	Jamie	Mother	Father
		He goes back over to the table to get the drumstick which he left on the first trip.	He runs out of the room.		
55'	30"	He returns to the couch. He sits down and watches TV.	Out	Out	He picks up the dog. He rolls over himself. He then places the dog on the floor. He is still holding the paper. He then looks up and says something in Spanish.
56'		He watches for a few seconds. He then leaves the room after Jamie does.	Out	Out	He looks back down at the dog. He motions with his head to have someone take the dog. He then begins to read the paper again. He lays back with his head resting on the back of the couch. One of his hands is up to his mouth, the other is holding the paper.

Time		Tommie	Jamie	Mother	Father
56'	30"	He returns to the couch immediately and climbs on. He takes some food off the plate and eats it.	Out	Out	(The telephone rings) He turns his head slightly, takes the phone and lowers the paper. He places the phone to his ear.
57'		He plays with the drum-stick (fingers it, and strokes it.)	Out	Out	He is listening on the phone.
57'	30"	He eats some more off the the plate. He eats slowly and con-tinues to watch TV.	Out	Out	He talks very slowly and is asking questions. He moves his legs slightly.
58'		He continues to eat. He also watches TV.	Out	Out	He keeps his position and talks. One cannot tell if he is look-ing at the paper in front of him or the TV set.
58'	30"	He watches TV. He continues to eat.	Out	Out	He has not moved.

Time		Tommie	Jamie	Mother	Father
59'		He watches TV. He continues to eat.	He walks into the room, straight toward the TV. He stands in front of it for a few seconds.	Out	He shifts his leg slightly and continues to talk.
59'	30"	He watches TV. He continues to eat.	He sits on couch, and places his hand near his mouth. He is sitting in a slouched position.	Out	He is talking quite forcefully, but does not move.
60'		He watches TV. He continues to eat.	He gets up and leaves the room.	Out	As he talks, he moves his leg slightly back and forth.
60'	30"	He watches TV. He continues to eat.	Out	Out	He is still talking. He has not moved, still has the paper in his hand. (We cannot tell if he is looking at the paper or the TV.)
61'		He watches TV. He continues to eat.	Out	Out	He maintains his position.
61'	30"	He watches TV.	Out	Out	He is in the same position, and continues to talk on the phone.

Time	Tommie	Jamie	Mother	Father
	All the while, he bounces his feet on the edge of the couch.			
62'	Tommie now plays with the drumstick. He beats his leg and then fingers the end of the drumstick.	Out	Out	Mr. Barker continues talking on the phone.
62' 30"	(End of TV tape observation.)	(End of TV tape observation.)	(End of TV tape observation.)	He moves the paper back, lays it down, puts his hand on top of his head and scratches his scalp.

He continues to talk.

(End of TV tape observation.) |

Television in Inner-city Homes: Viewing Behavior of Young Boys

John P. Murray

National Institute of Mental Health

The extent of television use and its potential impact on the child viewer has stimulated considerable research. (For recent reviews, see Atkin, Murray, and Nayman, 1971; Weiss, 1969.) The major lines of such research have been centered either on the effects of televiewing or on the patterns of use associated with this media form.

With regard to the effects of televiewing, Bandura and Walters (1963) have suggested that children can learn novel behaviors from the observation of a televised model. More specifically, several studies (e.g., Bandura and Huston, 1961; Bandura, Ross, and Ross, 1963; Berkowitz, Corwin, and Heironimus, 1963) have indicated that the observation of televised violence may instigate or facilitate the child's display of aggressive behavior. However, elaboration of the social learning principles underlying these formulations (Bandura, 1969) has generally restricted such studies to a laboratory setting and hence prevented clear demonstration of the applicability of such principles in accounting for spontaneous behavior occurring in naturalistic televiewing settings.

On the other hand, the task of mapping children's television use patterns has provided information on behaviors that are clearly related to the child's daily life. For example, Schramm, Lyle, and Parker (1961) surveyed the role television plays in the lives of children and indicated that the child viewer is a heavy user of this medium. Indeed, their data indicate a consistent increase in the amount of televiewing from about two hours per day in the first grade to a peak of three or four hours per day during the preteens, with a subsequent decrease during the teenage years. In general, the description of the function and role of television provided by Schramm, Lyle, and Parker (1961) is echoed by the findings of Himmelweit, Oppenheim, and Vince (1958) in their study of British school children. Other studies (e.g., Greenberg and Dervin, 1970) have described some aspects of mass media use patterns of selected subgroups of the population such as the "urban poor". One study in particular (Greenberg and Dominick, 1970) described the function television performs for disadvantaged children. Taken together, these studies provide a fairly comprehensive picture of children's televiewing in terms of media use and program preference patterns.

Research on the relationship between patterns of viewing and the impact of viewing on the child's social behavior has generally attempted to differentiate the program preference patterns of various "criterion groups" such as aggressive and nonaggressive boys (Eron, 1963; Lovibond, 1967). A recent study along these lines (Halloran, Brown, and Chaney, 1970) suggests that the delinquent boy differs from his nondelinquent counterpart not only in the type of program content he most prefers (i.e., exciting programs) but also in the likelihood that he will use television to rationalize his delinquent acts. Moreover, the results suggest that the observation of aggressive or destructive behavior may lead the child to conclude that such behavior is not severely prohibited by society; by inference, such viewing may facilitate delinquent behavior.

Although each of these previously described studies has been concerned with the broad issue of the role of television in childhood, most of the research focuses on the way television deals with children rather than asking how the child deals with television. The latter issue is the focal point of the present study. More specifically, this study is concerned not only with "what" children watch but also with "how" they watch television. It attempts to map the behavior setting and describe the spontaneous reactions of the child while viewing standard commercial television programming in his own home, and to relate these factors to other aspects of the child's total televiewing experience like program preferences, extent and duration of viewing, and cognitive/socialization variables.[1]

METHOD

Twenty-seven five- and six-year-old black males were selected from a sample of urban poor families in Washington, D.C. These boys had been participants for about four years in a longitudinal study of the impact of early childhood education.

The initial subject selection in the longitudinal study depended upon some degree of parental cooperation; therefore, the sample cannot be considered truly random. The details of the sampling procedures are outlined in reports on the Infant Education Research Project (Furfey, 1971).

Sample characteristics

Family unit. Thirteen (48 percent) of the 27 children lived in family units containing both mothers and fathers. An additional 13 children lived with just their mothers, and the remaining child lived with his grandmother. In general the parents represented a broad age range; 66 percent of the mothers and 49 percent of the fathers were between the ages of 26 and 40. The mothers tended to be somewhat younger than their husbands; 26 percent of the mothers and 11 percent of the fathers were below age 25. Five families indicated that both parents worked; overall 15(56 percent) of the mothers are employed on a part-time or full-time basis. The typical family unit consisted of one or two parents, the subject child, and several older siblings. Of the 27 families, 14(52 percent) had four or more children in addition to the subject child, while only two (seven percent) were one-child families. In 16 (59 percent) instances, the family consisted of one to three children who were *older* than the subject child. The subject child was a six year old male who was typically described by his tutor as an active, outgoing youngster who usually played well with both siblings and neighborhood playmates.

Home setting. Most of the families lived in either a residential (14/52 percent) or a primarily residential and mixed commercial (six/22 percent) neighborhood. The type of housing was either an apartment (59 percent) or a row house (30 percent); only three (11 percent) families lived in a detached single dwelling unit. The families were relatively mobile; 23(85 percent) had moved between two and five times in the previous four years. The physical condition of the housing was generally described by the tutors as fair to adequate. The typical home had five to six rooms (12/44 percent) with an indoor bathroom (25/93 percent) and adequate plumbing; 22 families indicated they had hot and cold running water. There were regular meal times in 19(70 percent) homes. Supervision or discipline was described as either variable or lax in 11(40 percent) of the homes, while three families supervised the children rather closely.

Available media. Each of the 27 families had at least one television set; six (22 percent) families had two or more, while only two families owned color television sets. In 16(59 percent) families, the main television set was in the living room; in seven homes, it was in the bedroom. Nineteen of the 28 families indicated that they owned at least one radio; it too was usually located in either the living room or the bedroom. In addition, 17 families possessed phonographs; they were likely to be located in the living room.

Procedure

In the present study, each child was observed and interviewed on several occasions during a one-year period from March 1970 to April 1971. The "interviewers" were the "tutors" in the longitudinal study; they had established considerable rapport with both the child and his family. The forms of data obtained from each child can be described as assessing either developmental variables (i.e., measures of cognitive or socialization processes) or televiewing variables (program preferences, behavior while viewing, media use patterns).

Developmental variables. Longitudinal trends of each child's intellectual and social development were obtained from both prior and concurrent measures. In the long-range study, intellectual development was assessed at ages three, four, five, and six (Stanford-Binet Intelligence Scale). The child's interpersonal behavior was assessed, in both home and classroom settings, at age six by asking the "interviewer-tutors" and teachers to complete a behavior rating scale (see Appendix B). This scale had been employed in the longitudinal study at age three; developmental comparisons could therefore assist in describing the child's characteristic behavior patterns.

Televiewing variables. Each child was interviewed on several occasions about his conception of television. The interviews covered such factors as the child's knowledge of and preference for various types of television programming. Additional questions focused on his daily activities, life style, and future goals. In some instances the tutor presented structured questions to the children; in other instances the child and tutor engaged in free dialogue.

During the week of February 15-21, 1971 each family maintained a "diary" of the subject child's television viewing. The diary (see Appendix C) provided data on such factors as programs viewed, duration and intensity of viewing, and reason for program selection. The diaries were distributed to each home approximately three days prior to the onset of the recording period. The "tutors" instructed the subject child's mother or teenage siblings in the recording procedures. The family was paid a small fee (seven dollars) for their cooperation in this phase of the study.

An additional source of information on the televiewing patterns of these children was provided by direct observation of each child's behavior while viewing several television programs. The observation form (see Appendix D) provided for the collection of both quantitative and qualitative data on each child's behavior while he viewed standard commercial television programming. Each child was observed on two occasions for periods of 45 minutes, while he viewed television in his home. The observer for the first observation period was the child's tutor, a familiar black female. The observer for the second observation session was a black male who was unknown to both the child and his family. In each instance, a standard observational schedule was employed, and the directions to the child never varied.

RESULTS

Patterns of Use

Television and daily activities. A major portion of the child's day was occupied with school-related activities, since each child was enrolled in either preschool or first grade. The time between the close of school and bedtime (which for most children was before 10 p.m.) was devoted to activities like playing or watching television. Most of the children indicated that they spent some time between school and supper (3 to 6 p.m.) either playing or watching television; 13(48 percent of the children devoted this time period primarily to play. In the evening (6 p.m. to bedtime), the children were more likely to watch television than to play outdoors. In this period, 17(63 percent) either played or watched television, as contrasted with ten(37 percent) who played or watched television in the afternoon time period. During both of these time periods the children indicated that they had free access to the television set and engaged in extensive viewing (between two and four hours of television programming each day), but they were most likely to watch in the after-school and evening time periods. However, on holidays and weekends, morning (9 a.m. to noon) is the heavy viewing period for nine(33 percent) of the children.

Most children have definite program preferences, and about 19(70 percent) of the children were able to name at least four favorite programs. With regard to control of television viewing, 19(70 percent) of the children indicated that they were not supervised and that the choice of television fare was primarily determined in 13(48 percent) homes by either the child or his siblings. Indeed, the characteristic television setting in 19(70 percent) families is one in which the child and his brothers and sisters are the primary users and controllers of television in the late afternoon and early evening hours.

Viewing times. A diary of the television programs viewed by each child during the week of February 15-21 provided data on the patterns of television usage for 24 of the 27 children. Table 1 displays the "television time budgets" of these child viewers according to four time periods: morning (sign-on to noon), midday (noon to 3 p.m.), after school (3 to 6 p.m.), and evening (6 p.m. to bedtime). The heavy viewing periods during the weekdays are concentrated in the after-school and evening hours, with the evening somewhat more popular. However, on Saturday and Sunday, the prime viewing period shifts to the morning hours with a correlative large decrease in after-school and evening viewing. This pattern most readily suggests that the children are selective about their television viewing. They at least choose specific viewing times and, by implication, specific classes of programs.

Table 1: Mean number of television programs viewed according to time and day of week during the week of February 15-21[a]

Time period	Monday[b]	Tuesday	Wednesday	Thursday	Friday	Saturday	Sunday	Total all week
Morning[c]	1.46	0.21	0.42	0.17	0.17	2.29	1.54	6.26
Midday	0.08	0.00	0.00	0.00	0.00	0.54	0.46	1.08
After-school	1.38	2.17	2.12	1.75	1.58	0.50	0.50	10.00
Evening	1.33	1.88	1.38	2.08	2.42	0.88	1.33	11.30
Total all day	4.25	4.26	3.92	4.00	4.17	4.21	3.83	

[a]N=24.

[b]Monday was a legal holiday (Washington's Birthday); hence heavy morning viewing was more typical of Saturday and Sunday.

[c]Morning (sign-on to noon); midday (noon to 3); Afterschool (3 to 6); Evening (6 to sign-off).

On Sunday, for example, the boys tuned in the children's programs in the morning but shunned the rest of the television day until Sunday evening—which turns out to be *Sunday Night at the Movies.* This inference about the child's selective viewing is further supported by Monday's viewing pattern. Monday of the survey week was functionally equivalent to the weekend because it was a legal holiday, and the boys had access to a full day's programming. We again see the pattern of viewing early morning children's programs, but the pattern also includes normal after-school and evening viewing. The children actively sought out their normal favorite after-school programs and, in effect, used the morning as an opportunity to view additional children's programming.

Television diet. Table 2 describes the television content viewed by the children for each day of the one-week recording period. All programs recorded in the diary were classified according to seven basic content

areas: situation comedy, cartoons, child adventure, action drama, quiz
and variety, general drama, and educational programming. Several of
these categories, like situation comedy (*Eddie's Father* and *Here's
Lucy*), cartoon (*Superman, Eightman, Batman, Speed Racer*), quiz
and variety (*Truth or Consequences* and *Ed Sullivan*), and educational
programs (*Sesame Street, Misterogers Neighborhood,* etc.) are relatively distinct categories. The "child adventure" category, on the other
hand, can be described as a melange of nonanimated, (noncartoon) adventure programs which seem to be designed specifically for children,
such as *Ultraman, The Little Rascals,* and *Lassie.* The "action drama"
category contains more adult fare such as *Mod Squad, Wild Wild West,
Mission Impossible, The FBI,* and similar prime time programs. The
"general drama" category, defined by social-dramatic content, was
composed of such shows as *Dark Shadows, Marcus Welby, M.D.,* and
the so-called "soap operas." The remaining category included movies,
sports and news or generic-unknown programs (*Cinderella,
Spaceman*).

Table 2: Mean number of television programs viewed according to content
(program category) and day of week for the week of February 15-21[a]

Program category	Monday	Tuesday	Wednesday	Thursday	Friday	Saturday	Sunday	Total all week
Situation comedy	1.62	1.42	1.08	1.33	2.08	0.88	0.29	8.70
Cartoon	0.88	0.88	1.04	0.50	0.71	1.88	0.33	6.22
Child adventure	0.38	0.62	0.58	0.33	0.46	0.38	0.50	3.25
Action drama	0.54	0.79	0.62	0.88	0.54	0.54	0.96	4.83
Quiz or variety	0.29	0.08	0.12	0.46	0.00	0.17	0.33	1.45
General drama	0.04	0.08	0.12	0.21	0.12	0.00	0.00	0.57
Educational	0.46	0.08	0.21	0.08	0.08	0.08	0.21	1.20
Other	0.04	0.38	0.12	0.08	0.21	0.29	1.17	2.29
Total all day	4.25	4.33	3.89	3.87	4.20	4.22	3.79	

[a]N = 24.

   It is apparent that the frequency with which a specific type of program
was viewed varied according to the day of the week. This finding can
most probably be accounted for by differences in the availability of various kinds of programming throughout the week; there are more situation comedy programs on weekdays (at a viewing time available to the
school-age child) than on weekends, for example. The data in Table 2
indicate that, in terms of the total week's viewing, situation comedy is
the front runner, followed by cartoons and action drama. However, on

weekends cartoons supplant situation comedy as the most frequently viewed programs primarily because of the Saturday morning "cartoon festival."

Table 2 also points up the very low incidence of viewing of educational programs (*Captain Kangaroo*, *Misterogers Neighborhood*, and *Sesame Street*). However, this may be due to the fact that many educational programs are available only on UHF in the Washington area. Most older television sets are not equipped for UHF reception and, when equipped, the reception is frequently poor. On the other hand, it should be noted that *Captain Kangaroo*, on standard (VHF) commercial channels, was also seldom viewed.

General drama programs, sports, and news broadcasts also had a low viewing index. The sharp increase in the "other" category for Sunday reflects the fact that many children viewed movies during the day; for the week recorded, the children viewed Shirley Temple and Blondie and Dagwood films in the morning, and *Whatever Happened to Baby Jane* and *The Blue Max* in the evening. However, the overall most frequently viewed programs for the total week were situation comedies and cartoons.

Extent and duration of viewing. In general, the children in this study spent approximately 21 hours viewing about 30 programs during the week. Their viewing, in terms of *number* of programs, was lighter on weekends than on weekdays. However, in terms of duration of viewing, the actual amount of viewing appeared to be heavier on weekends. Table 3 describes the average numbers of hours devoted to television for each day, derived from the one-week "diary" records. Weekday view-

Table 3: Mean number of daily television hours viewed (duration)
for the week of February 15-21[a]

Duration (hours and minutes) of daily viewing							
Monday	Tuesday	Wednesday	Thursday	Friday	Saturday	Sunday	Total all week
2:39	3:00	2:38	2:41	2:38	2:50	5:04	21:29

[a]N = 24.

ing averaged around two and one-half hours. The record for Saturday viewing indicated only a small increment, but Sunday viewing was distinctly atypical, with approximately five hours devoted to television. One plausible explanation of this finding is the fact that the Sunday programming contains a considerable number of movies; fourteen (58 percent) of the children viewed at least one movie during the day. This factor simultaneously inflated the duration and decreased the frequency of viewing for Sunday.

One finding not evident in Table 3 is that viewing, in terms of both daily and weekly averages and both duration and extent of viewing, varies greatly from child to child. Among the 24 boys, some could be considered "addicted" to television. Five boys (21 percent) watched 48 or more programs throughout the week; nine children (38 percent) watched 25-30 programs on weekdays. On the other hand, some children watched as few as five programs on weekdays and as a few as one program on the weekend. Some children watched as little as 30 minutes per day, while one child watched 12 and one-half hours on the recorded Sunday. The weekly viewing totals ranged from five to 42 hours.

Program preferences. When children were asked to name their favorite television programs, the viewing patterns they described differed only slightly from the diary records of their actual viewing. Table 4 describes the proportion of "favorite programs" occurring in eight content categories.

Table 4: Children's favorite television content

Program category	Percent — Favored Content	
	Time 1[a] index	Time 2[b] 1st choice
Situation comedy	19%	26%
Cartoon	50	44
Child adventure	14	4
Action drama	5	12
Quiz and variety	1	7
General drama	1	—
Educational	1	—
Other	9	7

[a]$N = 25$
[b]$N = 27$

On two separate occasions, the children were asked to name their four favorite television programs. All four programs mentioned by each of 25 boys in the first interview (Time 1) were combined in a summary preference index. The results of the second interview (Time 2) are presented in terms of the favorite program *first* mentioned by each child. The summary index of Time 1 is strongly related to the preference pattern displayed by the child's first-choice favorite programs of Time 2 ($r_s = .76$) and provides an index of good temporal stability of the child's preference structure.

In general, the programs most favored by the children were cartoons; the next favored were situation comedies. These two categories alone accounted for about 70 percent of all preferred programs. Programs in the "child adventure" and "action drama" categories accounted for another 20 percent of favored programs. This preference pattern is clearly related to *actual* viewing patterns as described by the viewing diary.

These children both prefer and watch a considerable amount of television besides that available during the "children's hours". Table 5 presents the ten prime time television programs most frequently viewed by these subjects. The list was obtained by presenting 16 children with a menu of all locally available prime time programming (81 programs) and asking each child to indicate the programs he frequently (very often or always) viewed. The product of this cafeteria selection was a television diet consisting mainly of situation comedies and action drama.

Table 5: Most frequently viewed prime time television programming[a]

Program name	Program content category	Percent of children viewing
Mod Squad	Action drama	94%
Here's Lucy	Situation comedy	81
Julia	Situation comedy	75
Gunsmoke	Action drama	69
Beverly Hillbillies	Situation comedy	69
Lassie	Child adventure	62
FBI	Action drama	62
Mayberry RFD	Situation comedy	62
Bewitched	Situation comedy	62
Land of the Giants	Action drama	62

[a]$N = 16$
Note: The data are based on number of children indicating that they "frequently" (i.e., very often or always) watch these programs. The child selected each program from a list of all currently available, network prime time programming (81 programs).

Do brighter children like to watch the same types of programs other children prefer? The data in Table 6 suggest that the brighter children (median-split, Stanford-Binet) are more likely to prefer programs *other* than cartoons or situation comedies. While the average child's favorite program is almost always a cartoon or situation comedy, the brighter child manifests a more varied preference structure (Fisher Exact Probability Test, p. $<.05$).

Table 6: Program preference patterns of bright and average children

		First-choice favorite program	
		Cartoons/situation comedy	Other programs
Intelligence	Bright	8	7
	Average	11	1

N=27

Heavy and casual viewers. The diary records for 24 boys indicate that the amount of time spent viewing television is highly variable. The figures on typical weekly viewing range from five to approximately 42

hours. Five children watched more than 33 hours per week, and five viewed less than 13 hours. Thus, the children could be clearly separated into groups of intensive and casual viewers on the basis of a median split on total weekly viewing time (addicted: $\tilde{X}$=1821.82, S.D.=531.9/casual: $\tilde{X}$=810.0, S.D. = 229.7). Table 7 presents a description of the program preference patterns of light and heavy television users. Both the intensive and the causal childviewers overwhelmingly preferred cartoons and situation comedies to other types of programming.

Table 7: Program preference patterns of heavy and casual viewers[a]

	First-choice favorite programs	
	Cartoon/comedy	Other
Television use		
Heavy	9	2
Casual	9	4

[a]N=24

The data in Table 8 suggest that a child's intellectual ability was not related to his "amount" of viewing. Thus, both bright and average children were equally represented in the heavy user category.

Table 8: Extent of televiewing among bright and average boys[a]

		Televiewing	
		Heavy	Casual
Intelligence	Bright	6	7
	Average	5	6

[a]N = 25

A more elaborate picture of the intensive child viewer emerges when comparisons are made between the children's television use patterns and their social behavior ratings. Table 9 displays the mean behavior ratings of heavy and casual viewers on three behavior dimensions: extraversion-introversion, hostility-considerateness, distractibility-task-orientation. The "current" ratings (age six) were provided by the "tutor-interviewers" who had been involved with the children for the previous four years. Ratings obtained for each child at age three are provided for longitudinal comparison.

From the current (age six) behavior ratings, the heavy television user can be generally described as a physically active but interpersonally passive child. He is *more* likely to forget instructions and drift from one activity to another with only passing interst, *less* likely to initiate interpersonal contact (like talking to visitors); he prefers to engage in solitary

Table 9: Mean social behavior ratings of heavy and casual televiewers

	Age 3[a]		Age 6[b]	
	Heavy	Casual	Heavy	Casual
Extraversion Introversion	32.27	35.30	32.80	37.18
Task orientation Distractibility	31.18	31.30	33.30	35.82
Considerateness Hostility	36.54	36.60	37.10	36.27

[a]$N = 21$
[b]$N = 21$
Note: Scores can range from 5 to 50. In these bi-dimensional scales, higher scores refer to the first dimension and lower scores refer to the second dimension (e.g., 40.03 = extroversion; 10.60 = introversion).

play. On the other hand, the casual viewer can be described as *less* distractible, *less* likely to be bashful about playing with others, and *more* likely to initiate interpersonal contact.

This suggested relationship between television use and the social behavior patterns of these six-year-old boys invites speculation about the causal influence of heavy television viewing on facilitating passivity. However, Table 9 also presents data on the social behavior patterns of these children when they were three-year-olds; the data show that the heavy viewers at age six manifested similar behavior at age three. Thus, it may be suggested that the child who is interpersonally passive becomes a heavy television user; passivity may lead to heavy viewing, rather than the reverse. However, it should be noted that, despite the trend of these findings, the conclusions remain tentative due to the restricted sample size. When the current (age six) social behavior ratings were dichotomized and recast in Table 10, Fisher Exact Probability tests failed to yield a reliable differentiation between the heavy and the casual viewer.

Table 10: Patterns of children's televiewing and social behavior[a]

	Social behavior ratings					
	Extraversion/Introversion		Task oriented/Distractible		Considerateness/Hostility	
	High	Low	High	Low	High	Low
Televiewing behavior						
Heavy	4	6	4	6	5	5
Casual	8	3	7	4	7	4

[a]$N = 21$

Televiewing behavior

Behavior setting. Each child was observed on two separate occasions (daytime and evening) while he viewed standard commercial television programming in his own home. The daytime observers were the two "tutor-interviewers," black females familiar to both the child and his family. The evening observer was a black male who was not previously known by either the child or his family. The observation period lasted 45 minutes and was divided into a five-minute "orientation" and eight alternating five-minute "structured" (eye contact) and "free response" recording periods (See Appendix D).

The 25 *daytime* observations took place in either the morning (13/52 percent) or the afternoon (12/48 percent) on any day except Sunday; most observations (16/64 percent) occurred on Friday and Saturday. The observations were conducted in the room in which the child regularly viewed television—usually (15/60 percent) the living room. This naturalistic setting necessitated the free inclusion of additional adults and children in the viewing environment. The total number of participants (including the observer and child) ranged from three to seven, fifteen (60 percent) of the settings included five or more participants. In 21(84 percent) of the observations only one adult, at most, was in the room, However, in 18(72 percent) observations, one to seven additional children were present, "one additional child" being the most likely (six/24 percent) of the possible combinations.

The 22 *evening* observations took place in the afternoon (50 percent) or evening (50 percent) on weekdays (Monday-Friday); Monday or Tuesday were most likely observation days (12/54 percent). The observations were usually conducted in the living room (16/73 percent), typically with three to five people in the room (12/54 percent) including the child and observer. The bulk of the additional viewers were usually children; in nine (41 percent) cases between two and four other children were present. However, in 13 (59 percent) instances, the observer was the only adult in the setting.

Correlates of viewing. Observation records indicate that the behavior exhibited by these children while viewing television ranged from passive staring to simultaneous imitation of behavior displayed on the screen. Table 11 presents the mean frequency of occurrence of four broad classes of behavior (staring, commentary, imitation, and reproduction) and a weighted index of reactivity based on these four scores (staring, 1 point; commentary, 2 points; imitation, 3 points; reproduction, 5 points) for the 20-minute "free response" observation period. The most likely event was passive staring more active forms of participation, such as imitation, occurred rather infrquently.

The behavioral content of each of these four categories is functionally discrete. *Staring* consists of merely passive gazing at the television set. *Commentary* is verbalizations about the program such as "I saw this yesterday" or "I like Lucy." *Imitation* consists of nonverbal imitation of televised behavior; or answering questions, talking back to the television character, and singing along with or repeating songs or dialogue.

Table 11: Children's reactivity while viewing television

Mean number of televiewing reactions

	Staring	Commentary	Imitation	Reproduction	Reactivity index
Daytime[a]	8.28	2.40	.64	.20	.16.04
Evening[b]	8.04	.54	.04	.00	9.05

[a]$N = 25$
[b]$N = 22$

Note: The reactivity index is based on a weighted score for each of the four categories of viewing reactions: staring (one point); commentary (two points); imitation (three points); and reproduction (five points).

The fourth category, *reproduction*, occurred very infrequently but was sufficiently unique to warrant separate description. Reproduction was typefied by the response of a child watching *Spiderman*, a cartoon serial: "No more monsters coming, no more Pete (a character in the film)." "I'm Spiderman!" (Stretching out hands, arms, and fingers and singing along with the music). In addition to these four categories, other behavior manifested during viewing included eating, interacting with other people, and solitary play.

Table 12 presents the relationship among the various viewing behaviors manifested by these six-year-old boys during the daytime observations. As anticipated, the amount of passive "staring" at the television set was clearly *inversely* related to all other behavior—with the obvious exception of "attention" (calculated in terms of frequency of eye contact with the screen during the 20-minute structured response recording period). The commentary and imitative behavior of these children were positively related to all other reactions—with the exception of "solitary play," which was antithetical to the more active responses. All these active responses were, by definition, positively related to the reactivity index. However, both reactivity and attention were inversely related to the competing influence of interpersonal contact and solitary play.

Table 12: Intercorrelation of children's viewing behavior (daytime)[a]

	1	2	3	4	5	6	7	8
Televiewing behavior								
1. Staring		-.60**	-.23	-.35	-.27	-.34	-.46**	+.28
2. Commentary			+.04	+.43**	+.77**	-.12	+.22	+.12
3. Imitation				+.23	+.42*	-.21	+.01	+.02
4. Reproduction					+.70**	-.14	-.14	-.07
5. Reactivity index						-.41*	-.09	+.28
6. Solitary play							+.08	-.68**
7. Interpersonal contact								-.16
8. Attention								—

[a]$N = 25$
*$p.05$
**$p.01$

Viewer involvement. In general, children's overall activity in front of the television set, measured in terms either of frequency of "eye contact" with the screen or of total reactivity (reactivity index) tended to decline over the 40-minute observation period. Table 13 presents the mean number of eye contacts (possible range 0-20) for each of the four "structured" five-minute observation periods and the mean reactivity index for the four "free response" observation periods for both daytime and evening observations. The table shows that the children were responding at a reliably lower rate during the last ten minutes of the home observation than during the first ten minutes (Wilcoxon Signed Ranks Test: T = 33.5, p < .01 contact, and T = 32.0, p < .01 reactivity—daytime; t = 16.0, p < .01 eye contact and T = 16.0, p < .01 eye contact and T = 32.0, p = .02 reactivity—evening). However, despite this overall decrease in response, the children continued to look at and respond to the television set throughout the observation period.

Table 13: Televiewing activity rates during daytime and evening observation periods

	Duration (in five-minute periods) of observation							
	5	10	15	20	25	30	35	40
				Daytime[a]				
Structured (eye contact)		15.36		15.08		13.60		8.56
Free response (reactivity index)	5.00		3.76		4.48		2.80	
				Evening[b]				
Structured (eye contact)		14.23		14.86		11.27		5.95
Free response (reactivity index)	2.73		2.14		2.64		1.54	

[a]N = 25
[b]N = 22

The attentiveness of the child viewer was assessed both by rating overall interest or attention and by recording the child's eye contact (every 15 seconds) during alternating five-minute periods throughout the 40-minute observation. A strong relationship between the tutor's global ratings of the child's overall attentiveness to the screen and the behavioral record of "eye contact" (r_{bis} = .73) provided internal consistency for both measures.

Attention (eye contact) to the television set was generally unrelated to either cognitive or socialization variables, including such factors as "task orientation." Moreover, Table 14 describes the relationship between the child's attentiveness (observer rating) and his behavior while viewing. While the patterns in Table 14 suggest that increased attentiveness is related to greater reactivity, Fisher Exact Probability tests on

Table 14: Televiewing reactions of attentive and nonattentive children[a]

		Televiewing reactions								
		Staring		Commentary		Imitation		Reactivity index		
		Low	High	Low	High	None	Some	Low	High	
Attentiveness	High	6	11	High 7	10	High 10	7	High 6	11	
	Low	5	3	Low 5	3	Low 7	1	Low 6	2	

[a]N = 25

Note: "Attentiveness" is based on the observer's rating of the overall attention to the television set, manifested during the 40-minute observation period.

each contingency table failed to reliably differentiate the televiewing activity of attentive from that of nonattentive children.

Daytime and evening televiewing. Interobserver reliability was difficult to assess in this study, since three observers in a home to record a child's behavior would be extremely disruptive of the behavior to be observed. However, two indicies were devised to test the "goodness-of-fit" between the observer's record and the actual behavior observed. The first of these indicies required each of three observers (two daytime, one evening) to view four five-minute videotapes of a child viewing television in his own home and record the child's behavior. The completed observation records were coded; the reactivity index for each of the four five-minute periods were ranked for each observer. A Kendall Coefficient of Concordance (Siegel, 1956) computed on these rankings indicated only fair agreement ($W = .56$, $p > .05$) between the three observers. On the other hand, the second index provided a measure of the validity of the observational record as a description of the behavior setting. This "narrative" measure, presented in Appendix F, compares the three observer's comments with a transcript of the videotaped behavior specimen. Although quantitative analyses are not possible, inspection suggests that the observers were able to accurately describe the child's television viewing behavior. Indeed, the conjoint observational record produced by the three observers directly paralleled the transcript of the videotape.[2]

Further analyses, however, revealed some clear differences between the daytime and evening observation periods. Table 11 indicates that the overall reactivity of the child (reactivity index) was clearly depressed during the evening observations ($t = 3.88$, d.f. $= 21$, p. $< .001$). While there was no reliable difference in the amount of passive "staring," it is evident that imitation and commentary are virtually nonexistent in the evening observation period. There are three possible explanations for this discrepency between daytime and evening observations: differential behavior settings for the child (watching television with parents/siblings); unfamiliar observer; or differential stimulus materials (viewing different kinds of programs in the evening).

Most of the significant aspects of the behavior setting, such as the number of children and adults in the room, remained unchanged in the evening observations. On the other hand, one factor which may have altered the evening behavior setting was the presence of an unfamiliar male observer. Despite the fact that the observer was carefully "introduced" to the family, this strangeness factor may have contributed to generalized inhibition of overt reactions to the television program. However, a plausible alternative explanation of the reactivity differences between day and evening viewing rests on demonstrable differences in the stimulus material. Table 15 describes the proportion of children viewing various types of programs during the two observation periods. Inspection of these data indicates that the differences are indeed like "night and day"; cartoons and child adventure shows accounted for 57 percent of all programs viewed during the daytime observation periods but for only 15 percent of the programs viewed in the evening.

Table 15: Programs viewed during daytime and evening home observations

	Observation periods	
	Daytime[a]	Evening[b]
Program content	Percent viewed	
Situation comedy	20%	45%
Cartoon	34	08
Child adventure	23	07
Action drama	00	20
Quiz variety	03	08
General drama	02	00
Educational	16	00
Other	01	05
No answer	01	07

[a]$N = 25$
[b]$N = 32$

In the evening the programs most frequently viewed (65 percent) were in the situation comedy and action drama categories. Since it has been demonstrated that cartoons are overwhelmingly the favorite progams of these children, it is plausible that they would manifest greater reactivity while viewing cartoons (daytime observations) then while watching the less favored situation comedies and action dramas. It is also conceivable that programs specifically designed for children, like cartoons, are more likely to elicit spontaneous imitation and commentary than the more adult fare (action drama and situation comedy) broadcast during prime time.

Patterns of use and viewing

Heavy televiewing. Do children who view extensive amounts of television react to programs in a unique manner? The data in Table 16, although speculative, suggest a possible pattern. In general, the addicted viewer is *less* responsive to television, *less* attentive, and *more* likely to engage in solitary play while viewing. This pattern of viewing behavior is quite similar to the previous description of the heavy viewer's social behavior: the heavy television user is *less* likely to initiate interpersonal contact, *more* likely to prefer playing alone, and *more* distractible. Although attenuation of both sample size and range of observed behaviors prevents a clear differentiation between heavy and casual viewers, these parallel patterns of *social* and *viewing* behavior provide some support for the construct of television-addiction.

Table 16: Televiewing behavior of heavy and casual viewers[a]

	Televiewing behavior		
Television use	Reactivity index	Solitary play	Eye contact
Heavy	14.50	3.08	52.25
Casual	18.40	2.30	54.80

[a]N = 25

Program preference and televiewing. In general, the subjects' reactivity and attentiveness to the television set were highly variable. It was previously demonstrated that children's viewing activity during the home observations tended to decline throughout the duration of the 40 minutes of observation. It was also demonstrated that the child's activity during the evening observation period was much more restricted and passive than his behavior during the daytime observations. One potential explanation of this daytime/evening contrast was the difference in the television content viewed during the evening; more adult programs were viewed at night than during the daytime. Table 17 describes the attentiveness and reactivity of the child viewers while they watched either children's or adult programming during the daytime observation

Table 17: Attention and reactivity to varying program content during daytime observations of televiewing behavior[a]

	Observation period						
	0-10 minutes		11-20 minutes		21-30 minutes		31-40 minutes	
Program content	Eye contact	Reactivity index	Eye contact	Reactivity index	Eye contact	Reactivity index	Eye contact	Reactivity index
Children's programming	16.31	5.46	15.31	4.38	14.46	3.62	6.67	2.11
Adult programming	14.11	4.00	14.89	2.78	13.22	6.00	10.08	3.54

[a]N = 25

period. The general trend (despite the fluctuation during the last ten minutes of observation) is one of greater attention and higher reactivity while viewing children's programming. The trend reversal during the final ten minutes of the observation period may be related to the fact that the observation period usually began with the start of a program; the programs generally terminated after 30 minutes, possibly producing a minor disruption of the flow of viewing activity.

DISCUSSION

The results of this study provide a description of the role television plays in the daily lives of several young children, in terms of both the child's "use" of television (program preferences, extent of viewing) and his "reactivity" to the medium (viewing behavior). However, the findings should be considered primarily descriptive of the children in this study; generalizations to other ages and other groups should reference the particular characteristics of this sample. Despite this limitation, however, some intriguing and stable viewing patterns did emerge.

In general, the viewing behavior displayed by these children suggests highly differentiated patterns of television use. By the time these boys were six years old, they had developed similar tastes in the programs they preferred and viewed most often, but the extent and duration of their actual viewing varied greatly.

These boys overwhelmingly chose cartoons as their favorite form of television entertainment and regularly avoided all "educational" programming; this indifference was manifested both in the nominations of favorite programs and in diary records of one week's viewing. On the few occasions when educational programs were mentioned as most preferred, they were usually nominated by the brighter children. Indeed, there was a reliable difference between the preferences of bright and those of average children; the brighter children manifested a more diversified preference pattern.

It should also be noted that the boys frequently viewed and, by implication, endorsed programs besides those specifically designed for children. The second most preferred program category was situation comedy; when each child was asked to indicate the *evening* (prime time) programs he most frequently viewed, both situation comedies and action dramas were the front runners. The finding that young children are extensively exposed to adult programming stands in contrast to the results of Schramm, Lyle, and Parker (1961), who found that preschoolers rarely viewed other than children's programming. Moreover, their findings suggested a developmental progression (during the preschool to teenage years) in the child's "taste" in television programming from cartoons and child-adventure, to westerns and situation comedies, and finally to pop music and public affairs. In the present study, inspection of the diary records of a total week's viewing indicated that although children's programming (cartoon and child adventure) was heavily viewed, more adult fare like situation comedy and action drama accounted for almost 48 percent of all programs viewed by these six-year-old boys. However, it is conceivable that the differential amount of adult programming viewed by the young children in the present study, as contrasted with that reported by Schramm, Lyle, and Parker (1961), may be merely reflective of variations in the types of programs available a decade later. In this regard, some measure of the fluidity of television programming is provided by Shelby's (1964) history of the continuous modification in children's programming, from "live" broadcasts in the 1948-52, to the Disneyland era in the mid-1950s, and finally to the cartoon festivals of Saturday morning in the 1960s.

The magnitude of television's involvement in the daily life of the child can be calculated in terms of the extent and duration of his viewing. On the average, these young boys spent half of an adult's workweek (21 hours) watching approximately 30 programs. They were most likely to watch in the morning on weekends and in the afternoon and early evening during the week. The pattern of viewing on a weekday that coincided with a school holiday (Washington's Birthday) closely corresponded to the weekend viewing pattern. Thus, the child seems to structure his viewing in terms of both content preferences *and* available time. When given the opportunity to select from an entire day's programming, the child will focus both on early morning children's programming and on his next-favored, adult evening programs. There were however, clear individual differences in the total amount of time devoted to television. Indeed, the *heavy viewers* of television viewed extensively enough to be considered "addicted"—as much as 42 hours per week. This differential utilization of television did not appear to be related either to the child's intellectual ability or to his program preference patterns.

The conclusions of the Himmelweit, Oppenheim, and Vince (1958) study, which suggest that the "addicted" child viewer may be distinguished from his less involved counterpart by his interpersonal behavior, received some support in the present study of six year old boys. Ratings of each child's social behavior on three broad dimensions (extraversion-introversion, task orientation-distractibility; considerateness-hostility) tended to describe the heavy viewer as more interpersonally passive or shy, preferring solitary play to peer interaction. The casual viewer was described as more likely to initiate interpersonal contact and as more task-oriented. In addition, the finding that similarly differentiated social behavior patterns were manifested by the addicted and casual viewers when they were three-year-olds led to the speculation that heavy television use *per se* does not produce the interpersonal passivity; rather, such children turn to television as a means of maintaining a more solitary environment. It is conceivable that an "electronic peer" is a more accessible playmate for a passive child.

The patterns of behavior exhibited by these young boys while viewing television in their own homes varied from passive staring to more active participation in the process of viewing. The frequency of these reactions to televised programming was not uniform across all behavior categories. Passive staring was the most likely reaction, but commentary and imitation were also evident (in that order). Observers were able to record numerous instances of spontaneous imitation of televised behavior. The child who claimed to be Spiderman, the children who sang along with commercials, and the child who copied the behavior of *Romper Room's* "Miss Nancy" and sang along with *Sesame Street* (see Appendix A) were manifesting, in a naturalistic setting, behavior more typically observed in experimental investigations of social learning phenomena (Bandura and Walters, 1963). The frequency or "reality" of this spontaneous imitation, despite the presence of an observer in the home setting, suggests that the actual occurrence of this behavior in the course of daily interaction with the television set is probably much greater than the number of instances recorded in the present study.

The fact that the child's reactivity to the television set was affected both by the type of program content viewed and/or by "observer effects" demonstrates that the child's performance of behavior acquired while watching television is highly susceptible to environmental influences. General reactivity to television appears to vary in relation to the amount of "attention" the child pays to the television program, and this attention seems to be related to previously developed patterns of social behavior. It seems reasonable to conclude that what the child brings to the television set will determine, in some measure, the potential impact of television on him.

The television "addict" seems to be somewhat different from the casual viewer. Moreover, the child's previously acquired program preferences exert an influence on his attentiveness and reaction to particular programming. Consequently, the results of the present study suggest that prediction of the potential impact of television requires a relatively precise specification of the characteristics of the child as well as a description of the content of the program viewed. However, it must be remembered that observers who watched children viewing television in their own homes were able to record numerous instances of spontaneous imitation of televised behavior. Thus, these children demonstrate, in a naturalistic setting, imitative behavior which usually has been observed only in an experimental setting.

FOOTNOTES

1. The author is indebted to Paul Hanly Furfey, director, Bureau of
   Social Research, Catholic University of America, for providing research facilities and a working paper (see Appendix A) on observer
   impressions of television's impact on the children of the present
   study. Moreover, the author is especially grateful for the assistance of
   Lucile Banks, Lilly Davidson, and Robert Davidson who were the
   observers and interviewers. The author is further indebted to Earl S.
   Schaefer and May Aaronson, Center for Studies of Child and Family
   Mental Health, National Institute of Mental Health for permission to
   use materials developed in a prior study of the impact of infant education. Finally, the author is very grateful for the assistance of Eileen
   Marchak whose research skills greatly facilitated this study.

   The research on which this report is based was supported, in part,
   by Contract No. HSM-42-70-50 between the Catholic University of
   America and the National Institute of Mental Health, Health Services and Mental Health Administration, U.S. Department of Health,
   Education, and Welfare.
2. The videotaped behavior specimen of television viewing was provided by Robert B. Bechtel, Epidemiological Field Station, Greater
   Kansas City Mental Health Foundation.

REFERENCES

Atkin, C.K., Murray, J.P., and Nayman, O.B. *Television and social behavior: an annotated bibliography of research focusing on television's impact on children.* Public Health Service Publication No. 2099. Washington: National Institute of Mental Health, 1971.

Bandura, A. Social learning theory of identificatory processes. In Goslin, D.A. (Ed.) *Handbook of socialization theory and research.* Chicago: Rand McNally, 1969.

Bandura, A., and Huston, A.C. Identification as a process of incidental learning. *Journal of Abnormal and Social Psychology,* 1961, **63** (2), 311-18.

Bandura, A., and Walters, R. H. *Social Learning and Personality Development.* New York: Holt, Rinehart & Winston, 1963.

Bandura, A., Ross, D., and Ross, S.A. Imitation of film-mediated aggressive models. *Journal of Abnormal and Social Psychology,* 1963, **66**(1), 3-11.

Berkowitz, L., Corwin, R. and Heironimus, M. Film violence and subsequent aggressive tendencies. *Public Opinion Quarterly,* 1963, **27,** 217-29.

Eron, L. Relationship of TV viewing habits and aggressive behavior in children. *Journal of Abnormal and Social Psychology,* 1963, **67**(2), 193-96

Furfey, P.H. The subculture of the ghetto. *Studies from the Bureau of Social Research,* No. 5. Washington, D.C.: Catholic University of America Press, 1971.

Greenberg, B.S. and Dervin, B. *Use of the mass media by the urban poor.* New York: Praeger, 1970.

Greenberg, B.S. and Dominick, J.R. Television behavior among disadvantaged children. In Greenberg, B.S. and Dervin, B. (Eds.) *Use of the mass media by the urban poor.* New York: Praeger, 1970.

Halloran, J.D., Brown, R.L., and Chaney, D.C. Television and delinquency. *Television Research Committee Working Paper No. 3.* Leicester: Leicester University Press, 1970.

Himmelweit, H., Oppenheim, A.N., and Vince, P. *Television and the child: an empirical study of the effect of television on the young.* London: Oxford University Press, 1958.

Lovibond, S.H. The effect of media stressing crime and violence upon children's attitudes. *Social Problems,* 1967, 15, 91-100.

Schramm, W., Lyle, J., and Parker, E. *Television in the lives of our children.* Stanford: Stanford University Press, 1961.

Shelby, M. Children's programming trends on network television. *Journal of Broadcasting,* 1964, **8,** 247-54.

Siegel, S. *Nonparametric statistics for the behavioral sciences.* New York: McGraw-Hill, 1956.

Weiss, W. Effects of mass media of communication. In Lindzey, G., and Aronson, E. (Eds.) *The handbook of social psychology.* Reading, Mass.: Addison-Wesley, 1969, pp. 77-195.

Appendix A: First Graders Watching Television

Paul Hanly Furfey
Catholic University of America

Staff members of the Infant Education Research Project visited the homes of 25 six-year-old children and observed for approximately one hour while these boys watched television. The observers described their general impressions of the child's television viewing by drawing both on their observation period and on their general knowledge of these children and their families. The 25 reports varied in length from about half a typed page to a full page. The present memo is based on these reports.

It must be admitted at the outset that this anecdotal information does not permit clear generalizations about the part that television played in the lives of the subject children. However, it was interesting to note that in a number of cases television was chosen for a lack of something more interesting to do. One child said he watched television "when there is nothing better to do." Another chose it for lack of "something better or more exciting." Four boys explicitly stated that they preferred outdoor play but fell back on television when the weather was bad. The homes where these boys live are often crowded, dark, and unpleasant. Therefore, when outdoor play is impossible, television looms large. There are probably far fewer alternatives than in middle-class homes. Of one boy the observer said, "In inclement weather, this is his main entertainment."

Many published studies give quantitative data on the total amount of time children spend watching television or the amount of time they watch specific programs, but they do not distinguish qualitatively among different kinds of watching. One point brought out clearly by the present series of observations is that a child may react to television in many different ways. There are many varieties of "watching."

Staff members observed that in several cases a child's reaction to television was "passive." Of one boy it was said that "his television observation was quite passive." One child was allowed to choose his program; but even though the program was his own choice, he sat passively. Then the staff member allowed him to choose another program, but his reaction "was basically the same." Another boy was reported by his mother to "love" television; yet he impressed the visiting staff member as "a passive television viewer." Of one child, the staff member remarked that throughout the staff's contact with him he had been "observed as a passive, introverted, nonverbal child." She was therefore not surprised that he should also be "a passive viewer" of television.

On the other hand, more than half the subject children gave some proof of a genuinely active interest in the programs they watched. It was reported of one child that "each time the commercial came on he sang along and appeared to know the entire commercial. He also hummed or sang along with the music that accompanied the cartoons he watched." Another "appeared to enjoy particularly the programs in which he could actively participate. As he watched *Sesame Street*, he said his alphabet, counted and sang along with the TV."

Six of the subject children knew by name the characters appearing on certain programs and could discuss them and what they did. For example, it was reported of one boy that "he is familiar with some characters who appear in the programs and can describe verbally various aspects of the programs, particularly those he is most fond of. . . .He tries to imitate some of the people he watches."

One subject child gets up early regularly every morning to watch a favorite program before he goes to school. In a couple of instances, observers remarked that a child would be so interested in a program that he could not be distracted by noisy siblings and would dislike being interrupted to answer questions. One child sat so close to the television screen that the observer was afraid this might injure his eyes; probably this, too, should be interpreted as an evidence of interest.

To one little boy, television seemed to have a good deal of psychological importance: "Being an only child, he relies on the television for companionship. He spends a good deal of time watching television. . . .It appears that without television he might be a very lonely child."

The following excerpt from a report shows another way in which television may capture a child's interest: "This child appears to have a close relationship with his father. They often, from the child's report, watch television together. On occasion, Mrs. W. says, the child really gets a big kick out of choosing the winner on *The Dating Game* along with his father."

The examples which have just been cited are cases in which subject children prove that they have a more than passive interest in television. The most striking examples, however, are those in which the child appears to confuse the "make-believe" on the television screen with reality. Several instances of this sort of thing occurred during the observations now being discussed.

The first was reported as follows: "In the course of the program there was a scene about a garage. An argument took place over the ownership of the garage. The subject child seemed somewhat disturbed by the argument. It was my impression that he really took the argument seriously from the worried expression on his face. Then he looked at me as if to read my reaction to the argument. Then he smiled." In this case, by taking the argument too seriously, the subject child seemed to show that he was confusing a story with real life.

A second case was thus reported: "While watching *The Flintstones,* the subject child turned to me and said, 'If Superman and Mighty Mouse were to fight, who would win?' This to me indicated that the child did not recognize the difference between the cartoons and the human characters." It seems rather striking that a child should consider the bizarre cartoon characters to be real.

Another instance seems a little special. One subject child was reported by his grandmother to like to imitate the characters he watches on television. The report continues. "Sometimes he pretends that he is able to fly and then falls and hursts himself." Somehow television was able to induce in this child the false belief that he could fly. In the face of common sense, he tried to do so and thus hurt himself. One would like to know a good deal more about this incident.

The fourth case is the most striking of all. The report is as follows: "His baby sitter reported that on one occasion some time ago, he was watching *Li'l Rascals* on television and decided to run away. By the time the police apprehended him, he was at Union Station ready to board a train. When asked where he was going, he replied, 'to California, to see the Li'l Rascals.'"

In children, like our six-year-old subjects, the dividing line between the real and the imaginary is far less sharp than with adults. Of course this is a general truth and is not confined to the world of television. However, children often watch television a great deal, and some of them, like some of our subject children, are fascinated by it. Television presents the imaginary, but it presents it with a peculiar and persuasive vividness. Thus television adds a powerful source of confusion of the real and the unreal in the minds of the young.

The data from our present series of observations are rather tantalizing. They show that television can blur the distinction between reality and imagination in the minds of the young, but they do not show under what conditions this happens nor what the long-term effects may be.

When one child got from television the false notion that he could fly, no great harm resulted. He soon learned that he could not; and he did not harm himself seriously in the process. What may be infinitely more serious is television's effect on the child's ultimate *Weltanschauung.* When growing up, a child must learn to adapt himself to reality. He must learn how to meet life's problems, and one does not solve life's problems by magic, as on television. Of course fairy tales also distort reality, but television is much more vivid than a fairy tale and its effect may be much greater.

At the present state of our knowledge, we can say little about these issues beyond the fact that television can distort reality in the minds of our subject children. But whether this distortion is a harmless and trifling matter or whether it can be serious, we simply do not know. Even to speculate about answers would be bad science.

Appendix B: Home Behavior Inventory

Earl S. Schaefer and May Aaronson

Child's Name_____ Class___ Teacher_____

Date_____

INSTRUCTIONS

Please describe as accurately as possible how your child behaves by circling one
of the five responses to each question. Give a response to every item and Base
YOUR RESPONSE UPON YOUR PERSONAL OBSERVATION AND EXPER-
IENCE.

	Almost always	Fre-quently	Half the time	Some-times	Almost never
1. Goes up to other and makes friends; doesn't wait until they come to him.	5	4	3	2	1
2. Sticks to something he starts until its finished.	5	4	3	2	1
3. Prefers to be by himself; wants to be let alone.	5	4	3	2	1
4. Gets in a temper if he can't have his way.	5	4	3	2	1
5. Likes to run around rather than to settle down to quiet play.	5	4	3	2	1
6. Is kind and sympathetic to someone who is upset or in trouble.	5	4	3	2	1
7. Likes to be with people rather than by himself.	5	4	3	2	1
8. Quietly sticks to what he's doing when others are mak-ing noise or doing things nearby.	5	4	3	2	1
9. Plays by himself rather than with others.	5	4	3	2	1
10. Gets angry when he has to wait his turn or share with others.	5	4	3	2	1

	Almost always	Fre-quently	Half the time	Some-times	Almost never
11. Forgets a job or errand he started, as his mind wanders to other things.	5	4	3	2	1
12. Tries to make life easier for others; doesn't want to hurt them.	5	4	3	2	1
13. Looks for someone to talk with or play with.	5	4	3	2	1
14. Spends a long time with things that interest him.	5	4	3	2	1
15. Pulls away, hides, leaves the room when visitors come.	5	4	3	2	1
16. Pushes, hits, kicks others.	5	4	3	2	1
17. His attention wanders from what you're telling him.	5	4	3	2	1
18. Is willing to share candy, food or belongings with others.	5	4	3	2	1
19. Likes to talk to visitors.	5	4	3	2	1
20. Keeps trying even if something is hard to do.	5	4	3	2	1
21. Watches others, but doesn't join in with them.	5	4	3	2	1
22. Picks fights.	5	4	3	2	1
23. Goes from one thing to another; quickly loses interest in things.	5	4	3	2	1
24. Tries to help when he's asked.	5	4	3	2	1
25. Tries to get attention by smiling and talking to people.	5	4	3	2	1
26. Tries to do something the best he can, even if it takes a long time.	5	4	3	2	1
27. Is too shy or bashful to play with others.	5	4	3	2	1
28. Sulks, gets resentful, and won't do things he should.	5	4	3	2	1

29. Gives up on what he's trying to   5   4   3   2   1
    do if it takes more than a
    short time.
30. Tries to please others.   5   4   3   2   1

Appendix C: Televiewing diary record (sample page)

SAMPLE PAGE   MONDAY

1. NAME OF PROGRAM	ON CHANNEL	TIME OF PROGRAM
Monday Night at the Movies (Beach Blanket Bingo)	4	9-11:15 A.M. P.M.

2.   Did you watch the entire program?

☐ Yes

☒ No, I missed part of the program ⟶ a. Between what times did you miss part of the program?

         9 ___ and *9:45 PM*

         10 ___ and *10:30*

3.   Reason for watching *(Check one):*

☐ I planned to watch this program

☒ It just came on the channel

☐ Other *(Please explain)* _____

4.   Who had the main say in choosing this program?

☐ Me

☐ Someone else *(Who?)* *nobody, it just came on the channel*

5.   Did you talk at all while you were watching the program?

☐ No, I didn't say anything. *(GO TO QUESTION 6)*

☒ Yes ⟶ a. Did you talk about ☐ the TV program

                       ☒ something else

         b. How long were you talking? *20* Minutes

6.   Did you do anything else during the program *(e.g., reading, child care, etc.)*?

☐ No, *(GO TO QUESTION 7)*

☒ Yes ⟶ a. What were you doing? *fell asleep; played checkers with youngest daughter*

         b. How long were you doing this? *15* Minutes

7.   How did you feel about the program?   *(Check one):*

☒ Waste of time

☐ OK

☐ Really worth watching

8.   What things did you like about the program?

_____

                                  ☒ NOTHING

9.   What things did you dislike about the program? *stupid plot; acting was terrible*

                                  ☐ NOTHING

SAMPLE PAGE   MONDAY

1. NAME OF PROGRAM | ON CHANNEL | TIME OF PROGRAM

Bonanza | 7 | _9-10_ A.M. / P.M.

2. Did you watch the entire program?

☐ Yes

☒ No, I missed part of the program ──────→ a. Between what times did you miss part of the program?

___9___ and ___9:05___
___9:45___ and ___9:50___

3. Reason for watching *(Check one):*

☐ I planned to watch this program

☐ It just came on the channel

☒ Other *(Please explain)* ___my husband wanted to watch___

4. Who had the main say in choosing this program?

☐ Me

☒ Someone else *(Who?)* ___husband___

5. Did you talk at all while you were watching the program?

☐ No, I didn't say anything. *(GO TO QUESTION 6)*

☒ Yes ──────→ a. Did you talk about ☒ the TV program
                                      ☒ something else

b. How long were you talking? ___20___ Minutes

6. Did you do anything else during the program *(e.g., reading, child care, etc.)?*

☐ No, *(GO TO QUESTION 7)*

☒ Yes ──────→ a. What were you doing? ___taking care of children;___
___reading magazine___

b. How long were you doing this? ___10___ Minutes

7. How did you feel about the program? *(Check one):*

☐ Waste of time

☒ OK

☐ Really worth watching

8. What things did you like about the program? ___the way Pa Cartwright___
___kidded Hoss; beautiful scenery___   ☐ NOTHING

9. What things did you dislike about the program? ___Story was very slow___
___and boring___   ☐ NOTHING

Appendix D: Observation schedule—home televiewing

OBSERVATION SCHEDULE

Name of child: _____

Date: _____ Day of week: _____

Time: _____

GENERAL DIRECTIONS: Make sure the television is on. Explain to the child that the reason you are there is to watch TV with him.

ORIENTATION PERIOD: Observe for five minutes and describe the setting. Description should include number of people in room and their activities, room in which TV is located, and general impressions of the setting.

_____

_____

_____

_____

_____

_____

_____

_____

_____

_____

_____

_____

_____

_____

_____

NEXT FIVE MINUTES: Description of child and his activity (e.g. sits with legs crossed, sucks thumb, punches brother, etc.) for each minute.

Minutes   Name of program: _____   Time: _____

1   _____

_____

2   _____

_____

3   _____

_____

4   _____

_____

5   _____

_____

_____

=======================================

NEXT FIVE MINUTES: Eye Contact—Record what child is looking at using fifteen second intervals.

Minutes	0	15	30	45	60
6					
7					
8					
9					
10					

NEXT FIVE MINUTES: Description of child and his activity (e.g., sits with legs crossed, sucks thumb, punches brother, etc.) for each minute.

Name of program: _____ Time: _____

11 _____

_____

=======================================

12 _____

_____

=======================================

13 _____

_____

=======================================

Minutes

14 _____

_____

_____

15 _____

_____

_____

NEXT FIVE MINUTES: Eye Contact—Record what child is looking at using fifteen second intervals.

	0	15	30	45	60
16					
17					
18					
19					
20					

NEXT FIVE MINUTES: Description of child and his activity (e.g., sits with legs crossed, sucks thumb, punches brother, etc.) for each minute.

Name of program: _____ Time: _____

21 _____

_____

_____

22 _____

_____

Minutes

23

24

25

NEXT FIVE MINUTES:Eye Contact—Record what child is looking at using fifteen second intervals.

	0	15	30	45	60
26					
27					
28					
29					
30					

NEXT FIVE MINUTES: Description of child and his activity (e.g.,
sits with legs crossed, sucks thumbs, punches brother, etc.) for each
minute.

Name of program: _____ Time: _____

NEXT FIVE MINUTES: Description of child and his activity (e.g.,
sits with legs crossed, sucks thumb, punches brother, etc.) for each
minute.

31 _____

32 _____

33 _____

34 _____

35 _____

NEXT FIVE MINUTES: Eye Contact—Record what child is looking at using fifteen second intervals.

	0	15	30	45	60
36					
37					
38					
39					
40					

Summary of Observation Period

1) Child watched:

        _____ very attentively

        _____ somewhat attentively

        _____ not very attentively

2) Who chose programs? (Check as many as apply.)

        _____ child

        _____ sibling

        _____ parent or other adult

        _____ observer

        _____ friend

        _____ other

3) Setting during programs:

        _____ noisy

        _____ quiet

        _____ both noisy and quiet at times

4) Interactions of child during programs: (Check as many as apply.)

        _____ parents or other adults made demands on child or interrupted his viewing

        _____ siblings interacted with child

        _____ friends interacted with child

        _____ child played with toys or other materials (i.e., books, pets, etc.) other (describe)

        _____

        _____

5) Emotional responses during programs: (Check as many as apply.)

        _____ no emotional response

        _____ laughter

        _____ surprise

        _____ sadness

        _____ fear

        _____ bewilderment

        _____ boredom

        _____ other (describe)_____

Postviewing Questions

1) What programs did you watch today?

_____

_____

_____

_____

2) What do you remember about what happened on TV today?

_____

_____

_____

_____

_____

3) What did you like best about the shows you saw today?

_____

_____

_____

_____

_____

Appendix E:
Media use and
daily activities questionnaires*

Home Setting

Family Name:_____

Address: _____

Type of Housing (e.g., apt., row/detached)*

_____

_____

*General description

Neighborhood Characteristics

_____

_____

_____

_____

Description of Household

Color:

No. of Rooms   No. of TV sets   Yes____ No ___
Indoor Bathroom   Yes   No   Location   1. _____
Adequate Plumbing   Yes   No   of   2. _____
No. of Bedrooms   TV's   3. _____

No. of Radios _____
Location   1. _____
   of   2._____
Radios   3._____
Phonograph: Yes   No
             ____   ____

Location_____

Furniture: Old   New

---

*Note: These questionnaires area composite of structured and semi-
          structured interviews with each child and his teachers, tutors,
          and parents.

Background Information

Parents:	Birthdate	Age	Hours Usually At Work	At Home
Mother	_____	( )	_____	_____
Father	_____	( )	_____	_____
Other Male	_____	( )	_____	_____

Children and Other Adults: (in order)

1. _____   _____

2. _____   _____

3. _____   _____

4. _____   _____

5. _____   _____

6. _____   _____

7. _____   _____

8. _____   _____

Discipline in Family: _____

_____

No. and Location of Previous Residences (in order)

1. _____

2. _____

3. _____

4. _____

Is family on welfare?   Amount of additional support _____

Yes _____ No_____   Source of support _____

Child's Daily Activities

Child's Name _____ Age _____

School _____

Please indicate how he spends a typical day. _____

I. School: What do you know about his behavior in school? _____

_____

_____

What kind of student is he? _____

II. After School:

3:00 — 6:00 p.m. _____

_____

_____

6:00 p.m. — bedtime _____

_____

_____

_____

When is bedtime? _____

Are meals served regularly? _____

General comments

Television Viewing

About how much time per day does the child spend watching TV?_____

When is he most likely to watch? (Please give specific times)

Does he watch most often with: brothers and sisters

whole family

alone (Please circle
answer

other

What are his favorite shows?.

Does he receive parental supervision of the TV fare he watches?

Is he free to choose what he will watch or do others make the selection?

In the following space please indicate anything you have learned about the child's television viewing behaviors or attitudes, how TV has affected him, what specific facts or behaviors he has learned from watching TV, etc.

Program Preference Schedule

Childrens' Television Interview

What are your favorite—TV programs?

_____

_____

_____

_____

What do you like about   (Program 1) _____ ?

What do you like about   (Program 2) _____ ?

What do you like about   (Program 3) _____ ?

What do you like about   (Program 4) _____ ?

Here is a list of weekly programs that are on network television during the evening.

Circle each program that you have seen all the way through ten times or more since January 1, 1970. (Each program has been on about 15 weeks.)

MONDAY

Gunsmoke	My World/Welcome	It Takes a Thief
Here's Lucy	Laugh-In	ABC Monday Movie
Mayberry RFD	Monday Movies	
Carol Burnett		

TUESDAY

Lancer	I dream of Jeannie	Mod Squad
Red Skelton	Debbie Reynolds	Movie of the Week
Governor and J.J.	Julia	Marcus Welby, MD.
Sixty Minutes	Tuesday Movies	

WEDNESDAY

Hee Haw	The Virginian	Nanny and the Professor
Beverly Hillbillies	Kraft Music Hall	Courtship of Eddie's Father
Medical Center	Then Came Bronson	Room 222
Hawaii Five-O		Johnny Cash
		Engelbert Humperdinck

THURSDAY

Family Affair	Daniel Boone	Pat Paulsen 1/2 Comedy Hour
Jim Nabors	Ironside	That Girl
Thursday Movie	Dragnat	Bewitched
	Dean Martin	Tom Jones
		Paris 7000

FRIDAY

Get Smart	High Chaparral	Flying Nun
Tim Conway	Name of the Game	Brady Bunch
Hogan's Heroes	Bracken's World	Ghost and Mrs. Muir
Friday Movie		Here Comes the Brides
		Love, American Style

SATURDAY

Jackie Gleason	*Andy Williams*	*Let's Make a Deal*
My Three Sons	*Adam-12*	*Newlywed Game*
Green Acres	*Saturday Movie*	*Lawrence Welk*
Petticoat Junction		*Hollywood Palace*
Mannix		*Cesar's World*

SUNDAY

Lassie	*Marlin Perkins*	*Land of the Giants*
To Rome with	*Walt Disney*	*The FBI*
Love	*Bill Cosby*	
Ed Sullivan	*Bonanza*	
Glen Campbell		

Appendix F: Observer record and behavior specimen transcript

Table F-1: Observer Record and Behavior Specimen Transcript

Observer Record	Transcript
Minute 1	
1. Leaning on sofa looking at T.V. feet crossed — still laying back on sofa.	He is sitting on end of the couch nearest the set. He has his feet on the floor and his back resting on the couch; one hand is near his mouth. He is watching TV closely. He has his feet crossed. He wiggles his feet. He continues to watch the set closely.
2. Leaning back on couch while watching has legs crossed, hand to face	
3. Two children are sitting on couch; older child is partially seen; presumed to be viewing — both children are silent	
Minute 2	
1. Patting feet to music still looking — looking at TV	He is sitting still watching TV. He bounces feet to the rhythm of the song. He is bouncing his head to the beat a few times and then sits still with no movements.
2. Same position but moving feet to music	
3. Younger child shifts to another position older child remains in same position. Music is the dominant theme at this moment	
Minute 3	
1. Looking intently same position	Jamie sniffs a rose. He wiggles feet a little. He is sitting still.
2. Same position — still moving feet to music	
3. Exchange of words occur between the two children . . . on time to watch.	
Minute 4	
1. Looking intently feet crossed. Moving feet. Raising feet up and down.	He is still sitting in the original position. Jamie turns to look at his dad as he closes the dining room, for a few minutes. Then he returns to the original posture of watching TV.
2. Child still has legs crossed but moved hand from fact momentarily — moving it to music.	
3. Children watching, both are silent — older child moves both feet.	
Minute 5	
1. Still leaning back on sofa looking at TV. Moving feet.	Jamie pats his feet to the beat of the song for a few seconds. He stops beat. He uncrosses his feet, sits up, and scoots back on couch, places hand on his chin with elbow on knee. He watches TV attentively.
2. Song ended — Child moves back on the couch to get more comfortable feet moving in up and down motion.	
3. Older child can be seen sitting up; full profile is in view.	

Table F-1: Observer Record and Behavior Specimen Transcript (Continued)

Observer Record	Transcript

Minute 6

1. Sitting back on sofa looking intently. Gets up adjusts screen sits down, continues looking.
2. Child has toy in hand and whistle gets up to get something and sits again on sofa.
3. Child is striking object leg — approaches television changes channels — returns to sofa and leans back.

Jamie looks back at TV. He continues to beat his leg with the drumstick. He gets up and goes over to the TV and adjusts the set, then returns to the couch. He slouches down on the couch. He then looks into the dining area. He looked back at TV. He's still in a slouched

Minute 6 (Continued)

position. Jamie looks down at his hands that are playing with the drumstick. His feet are on the floor. He touches one foot to the other. He glances away from and then back to the TV set.

Minute 7

1. Same sitting position — looking intently. Sits up then leans back.
2. Sitting on couch moving right foot up and down (shoe off).
3. Child raises up look toward other room says something to another person. Child is not watching — continues to play with object.

Jamie takes his right shoe off. He then bounces his foot on the shoe. He continues to watch TV while doing this. Jamie is playing around with his feet. He bounces them and touches them to each other. Jamie then puts his legs entirely onto the couch. He beats his drumstick. He looks at TV.

Minute 8

1. Changes position — moves arm. Playing with stick watching TV.
2. Child looking toward kitchen — has legs crossed, toy in hand.
3. Child is presumed to be watching.

Jamie looks into the dining area and sits up. His legs are folded. He is laying on his side the drumstick is held under his foot with his hands attached to each end. He continues to watch TV. Jamie beats his foot with the drumstick.

Minute 9

1. Raises leg. Sitting back on sofa looking at TV.
2. Same position but probing foot with toy that he has (both feet on couch).
3. Child turns to prone position watches somewhat attentively. Child is watching.

Jamie scratches foot with his drumstick. Jamie continues to play with his mouth holding it with his left hand.

Minute 10

1. Props leg up continues to lay back on sofa. Lays on stomach hitting stick on something. Watching TV.
2. Right leg raised has toy in hand, blowing whistle (not too interested).
3. Child plays with object — continues to watch.

He puts the stick in and out of his mouth holding it with his left hand.

Children's Television Behaviors as Perceived by Mother and Child

Bradley S. Greenberg, Philip M. Ericson, and Mantha Vlahos

Department of Communication
Michigan State University

This study examined the relationship among a child's interaction with his parents, his exposure to violent and nonviolent television content, and his attitudes toward the medium. It studied these phenomena from the twin vantage points of the child's description of his own behavior, and a description of that child's behavior by his mother.

A basic methodological concern was to obtain an estimate of the extent of agreement between the two principal sources of information. Some studies rely primarily on data obtained from the child, others on parent data. Schramm, Lyle, and Parker (1961) obtained time exposure estimates from both parties, found them discrepant, and subsequently relied on a combination of parental estimates, aided recall, and whole family interviews. They examined none of their other media variables for possible additional disagreements. Himmelweit, Oppenheim, and Vince (1958) based their classic British study primarily on the responses obtained from children on questionnaires, diaries, and program-recall lists. Parental estimates of the children's behavior provided only minimal data. The present study examined extent of agreement across a wide range of television behaviors.[1]

The basic theoretic notion was that extensive family interaction between the parent and the child should result in fewer discrepancies between the estimates made by both about the child's television behaviors. It was posited that if a child and his mother and father interact verbally across a wide range of issues, the increased parental awareness of the child's attitudes, interests, etc., should manifest itself in greater awareness of the child's television habits. In our measure of interaction, we focused on the child's talking with parents about school matters, about family decision-making situations, and "just sitting around and talking."

Here, interaction was considered in terms of its frequency and not in terms of specific content, nor in terms of the role of the child in such interaction. In a series of studies at the University of Wisconsin, McLeod, Chaffee, and Wachman (1967, 1970) have focused on the kind of family communication which occurs, and have related this to media use and family influence on socialization. In families, for example, where the child is exposed to controversial material and is relatively free of social restraints, he is more politically active and more often uses the media for information.

For the present study, it was posited that in families where there was extensive interaction between mother and child, the mother and child would have clearer perceptions and/or data on the child's behavior. Thus, if both were asked what the child's favorite programs were, or how realistic television was perceived to be by the child, etc., the answers would be more harmonious than those of a parent and child who, by their own reports, interact little. In fact, the latter ought not even agree on the extent to which they interact.

Relating such interaction, regardless of the content of the discussions, to the child's aggressiveness is a more tenuous matter. Basically, we proposed that if a child were exposed to a considerable diet of television violence and had attitudes which were supportive of the use of violence in problem-solving situations, then such attitudes would be somewhat ameliorated through extended family interaction. That is, the direction of family interaction would be biased against the learning or reinforcement of proviolence attitudes.

Finally, this study examined the clustering of television-related behaviors as estimated by both the child and his mother. We anticipated that the watching of more violent programs would be positively related to total television exposure, perceived reality of television, and self-watching and would be negatively related to such variables as perceived amount of violence on television and the existence of household rules about television. Rather than a concise conceptual framework for these latter expectations, the study findings were to provide pilot data for subsequent, more precise hypothesis testing.

In summary, this initial study sought (1) to determine the extent of agreement between a mother and one of her children as to the child's television habits and (2) to analyze the role of frequency of family interaction in their coorientation toward television and toward the use of violence.

METHODS

During the fall of 1970, approximately 100 children from fourth and fifth grade classes in a single elementary school in western Michigan were interviewed. Questionnaires were distributed during normal classtime, explained by the investigator, and completed by the children. The school was purposively selected as a middle-class school, and all fourth and fifth grade children present on the testing day were interviewed, except one class.

The parents of all the children interviewed had been notified in advance of the study and were asked if they would consent to interviews. This resulted in completed interviews with 85 mothers of the children tested. It is this paired grouping of 85 children with their mothers whose responses were analyzed. The mothers were interviewed in their homes on the same day as the children were queried. Of the 85 children, 44 were girls and 41 were boys. Four-fifths of the children were white, and the remainder were black.

Variables

A mother's estimates of her child's viewing habits and television behavior patterns were obtained in order to compare them to the child's own estimates. The specific variables and their operationalizations were:

Television exposure. We assessed regularity of exposure to violent and nonviolent shows and the amount of time spent watching television on an average weekday and on Saturday morning. Respondents identified programs they (their child) watched every week from a list of ten shows previously judged as having violent content (e.g., *Mannix, Hawaii Five-O, F.B.I.*) and from a list of ten shows previously judged as having nonviolent content (e.g., *Family Affair, Hee Haw, My Three Sons*). These programs were identified in a study by Greenberg and

Gordon (1971). The 20 programs were interspersed in a common listing. Both parent and child estimated how much time, in hours, the child spent watching television on an average weekday and on Saturday morning.

Context of viewing. This consisted of five items which asked how often the child watched television with his (a) mother, (b)·father, (c) friends, (d) brothers or sisters, and how often (e) by himself. Respondents indicated, for each question, whether it was always, often, sometimes, not very much, or never.

Program selection. These variables sought to determine where the child got information about what shows were on television and which ones he should watch, and who had the most control over what he watched. The first variable was indexed by asking the parent (and the child) the open-ended question, "When your child (you) wants to watch television, how does he (do you) find out what shows are on?" Major responses were: TV guide, turn channel, newspaper, memory, and mother. For the second measure, respondents indicated whether parents and teachers suggested that the child watch certain shows. The third was based on the question, "Who has the most to say over what your child (you) watches (watch)—child, parent, brother or sister, or someone else?" In the analysis, this became a dichotomy between self and other.

Perceived reality of television. Five items formed this index and measured respondents' judgments about how realistic television content is compared with real-life situations and people. Parents and children were asked about such statements as "Families I see on TV are just like my family" or "The shows I see on TV tell about life the way it really is." Response categories were agree, disagree, and not sure.

Rules about television watching. Four items concerned parental regulation of the child's viewing habits. One item asked if there were any rules about how late the child could watch television. Another asked if there were some shows the child was not allowed to watch. Two items dealt with the loss of viewing privileges as punishment and extended viewing privileges as reward for something special the child did. All items had yes/no response categories.

Amount of violence on television. Three items were used to determine how much violence respondents perceived on television in general and on shows they liked to watch. For this measure the parent did not estimate the child's response, but gave her own perceptions.

Family interaction. Three items assessed how much and in what aspects the child verbally interacted with his parents. They asked how often the child talked about things going on in school, participated in family decisions, and just talked about things. Each item had the foils of very often, sometimes, not very often, and not at all.

Violence justification. Four items asked respondents to agree or disagree with statements such as "It's okay for a teacher to hit one of her students'' or ''It's all right if a man slaps his wife.'' The four items were assumed to create a violence justification index.

Hypothetical situations involving the child's behavior. Respondents were asked to estimate how the child would behave in situations in which (a) another child took something from him, (b) another child started ordering him around, (c) another child his age pushed him down, and (d) he wanted something with which another child his age was playing. Open-ended responses were coded as either ''verbal'' (indicating that the child would speak to the other child), as ''violent'' (indicating that the child would react with some physical force toward the other child), or as neither.

RESULTS

Five issues were examined in the data analysis: (1) What is the relationship between the measure of the child's verbal interaction with his (her) parents and the degree of discrepancy between parent and child in estimating the child's television behaviors? (2) To what extent is some particular television viewing behavior of a child, as reported by a parent, correlated with the behavioral report of the child? (3) What is the magnitude and nature of the differences between the base levels of the behaviors reported by the two sources? (4) Is there some general pattern of discrepancies; do reported differences in one behavior relate systematically to reported differences in other behaviors? (5) What television habits are related, according to the child, and then according to the mother?

Family interaction and parent-child discrepancies

For each of the measures obtained from both the mother and her child, a difference score was calculated. This score was correlated against the family interaction index obtained for both the parent and the child. The general expectation was that the higher the level of family interaction, the smaller would be the discrepancy between the mother and child in estimating the child's behavior. There was no support for this proposition; across 30 correlations (15 for the child and 15 for the parent), none achieved statistical significance. Approximately half had positive correlations, and half had negative ones. Therefore, the extent to which parents and their child talked about decisions, problems, or anything did not result in a common perception of the child's television habits. Indeed, they did not have very similar perceptions of the extent to which they interacted; the interaction indices correlated only .239 (p < .05). The remainder of these analyses then deal with the nature and magnitude of the differences in perceptions between the mother and her child.

Mother-child correlations in reports of child's television behaviors

Table 1 correlates each of the television behaviors, as described by the mother with the self-description of her fourth- or fifth-grade youngster.

The general pattern was one of statistical significance; there was sufficient linearity in the relationships to indicate nonindependence. However, the size of the correlations in most instances was small.

Table 1: Correlations between mother and child in estimating child's TV behaviors (n=85)

Variable	r^1
1. Exposure	
a. Violent shows watched weekly	.219
b. Nonviolent shows watched weekly	.522
c. TV hours/day	.069
d. TV hours/Saturday	.221
2. Context of viewing	
a. Frequency with mother or father	.404
b. Frequency with friends	.382
c. Frequency by himself	.274
3. Program selection	
a. Does mother suggest shows?	.315
b. Who has most to say about what is watched?	.219
4. Perceived reality of TV	.318
5. Rules about TV watching	.190
6. Family interaction index	.239

[1] Pearson product-moment correlations. An r of .213 is significant at the .05 level; an r of .278 is significant at the .01 level.

In terms of the exposure measures used, the mother and child agreed best on the nonviolent television diet of the child (r = .522). Indeed, that correlation was significantly larger (p < .05) than that for any other of the exposure measures. Agreement between parent and child on the violent shows watched was minimally significant. There was no correlation in terms of how much time the child watched television on an average weekday. Estimates of viewing time on Saturday were marginally correlated.

As to viewing partners, the mother and child agreed best on the frequency with which one or the other parent was present during television time. Agreement on frequency of vewing with friends was correlated to the same extent. Reliability on self-viewing by the child was substantially smaller than either of these other two viewing contexts.

A positive correlation was obtained between the two data sources as to the extent the child perceived television to be true-to-life *vis a vis* the series of reality items.

There existed a moderate correlation for program suggestions by the mother, but less so for whether the child or others had the most to say about program selection. There was insignificant agreement between the mother and child about the rules associated with watching television.

As noted, a moderate correlation was found on the family interaction index. There was some—but not very much agreement—about the role of the child in talking about various issues and problems with the parents.

There was no correlation between the parent's and child's statements about the child's perception of the justification of the uses of violence. For hypothetical problem situations, however, mother and child estimates on the frequency of verbal responses correlated .216, and their estimates that the child would make a physically violent response correlated .240.

In summary, there was relatively strong agreement on only three aspects of the child's TV habits—the nonviolent shows he watched and his frequency of watching with either his parents or his friends.

Mother-child baseline differences in reports of child's television habits

Table 2 presents the means for each of the measures. In this way, it is possible to examine the baselines obtained for each measure and the magnitude of the differences between the reporting groups.

On the exposure indices, the child reported watching four of ten possible violent shows weekly; the mother said the child watched 1.5 such shows. The child reported watching television for six hours on an average day; the mother reported 2.5 hours for the child. The Saturday time estimates were equally discrepant.

There was far more agreement on the frequency of watching nonviolent shows, with about one show's difference in the two estimates. Apparently the mother either was more knowledgeable about the child's watching of nonviolent programs than about his violent program diet or was prone to report it more accurately.

As might be expected, the mother was best able to estimate how often her child watched television with her or with the other children in the same family. There was no significant difference between the child's and the mother's estimates. However, the mother reported significantly less viewing for the child with the father, with friends, and by himself. The grossest discrepancy was with self-viewing. Half the children said that they often or always watched television alone; less than one-sixth of the mothers had that perception of the child's viewing habits.

In program selection procedures, the children were asked, "Do your parents ever suggest you watch certain shows?" Three-fifths of the youngsters responded affirmatively, compared with more than four-fifths of their mothers to a parallel question. In reverse fashion, half the

Table 2: Mother-child discrepancies in child's TV behaviors (n = 85)

Variable	Mother's description of child	Child's self-estimate	(p)[1]
1. Exposure			
a. Violent shows watched weekly	1.54	3.93	< .001
b. Nonviolent shows watched weekly	4.32	5.73	< .001
c. TV hours/day	2.55	5.88	< .001
d. TVhours/Saturday	2.56	5.06	< .001
2. Context of viewing[2]			
a. With mother	36%	41%	n.s.
b. With father	22%	48%	< .01
c. With friends	12%	23%	< .10
d. With siblings	78%	76%	n.s.
e. By himself	14%	51%	< .001
3. Program selection			
a. Uses TV Guide	31%	52%	< .001
b. Mother suggests shows	82%	60%	< .001
c. Teacher suggest shows	47%	41%	n.s.
d. Child has most to say about what he watches	29%	46%	< .05
4. Perceived reality of TV			
a. Index of five items	8.06	9.51	< .01
5. Family Interaction[3]			
a. Talk about school	81%	53%	< .001
b. Participate in family decisions	35%	22%	< .001
c. Just talk	53%	28%	< .001
6. Rules about TV watching			
a-d. No difference on four items			

[1] The probability estimate comes from a Chi-Square analysis of the frequency data for the two groups of respondents for each variable.
[2] Cell entry is percent who said "often" or "always."
[3] Cell entry is percent who said "very often."

children claimed to have the most to say about what was watched, but less than one-third of their mothers agreed. Nearly half of each group said that teachers made program watching suggestions.

How realistic is television for the child? More than the mother thinks it is, and far more than the mother's personal perceptions, which were also obtained. The reality index scores ranged from 5-15 across five items, with three response categories each. The mean for the mothers' personal attitudes was 7.10, a clear statement of disbelief in the reality of television. Her estimate for her child was 8.06, whereas the child's own response, a mean of 9.51, was very near the midpoint on the reality scale. For the child, there was neither belief nor disbelief, but uncertainty.

As to child-parent interaction—talking about school, family decisions, or just talking—the child perceived about three-fifths as much a role for himself as his mother indicated he had. The mother said "Oh, yes," the child participated heavily, while the child denied majority participation.

The mother and her child did not differ in terms of questions about television rules in the household. All of the parents and 90 percent of the youngsters said there were rules about how late television could be watched; two-thirds of each group said there were some forbidden shows; one-third said there was punishment in the form of not being allowed to watch television; one-third of the children and one-fifth of the parents said more television watching was used as a reward for good behavior. Although these distributions are very similar, they do not indicate extensive agreement between a mother and her own child. The low correlation (.190) between the two on this index attests to this.

Some nontabled findings are of interest. In terms of perceived violence, where the parent was giving personal responses, not projective ones, the mothers said there was significantly more violence ($p < .05$) on television overall than did their children. In reverse fashion, the children said there was significantly more violence ($p < .01$), on the programs they liked to watch than did their mothers.

On the measures of when violence is justified, there were counterbalancing differences between mother and child. The child was more likely than the mother to say that it was okay for a man to slap his wife ($p < .001$) and for a mother to hit her child ($p < .001$). The mothers said it was okay for a teacher to hit one of her students ($p < .05$) and for two boys to fight ($p < .01$), more so than did the children.

Relationships among the mother-child discrepancies

For each variable, the difference between the mother and the child was computed. These differences were intercorrelated to determine whether there were any general pattern of discrepancies. The general expectation was that such discrepancies would be nonindependent. A mother and a child who disagreed on one aspect of the child's television behavior should likely be in disagreement on other aspects. This was not the case. Across a 16 x 16 correlation matrix, with 120 possible comparisons, only 12 yielded significant correlations, and eight of those were negative. Although it is of some interest to note that discrepancy in estimating number of nonviolent shows watched was positively correlated ($p < .01$) with discrepancy in estimating number of violent shows watched and with total amount of television exposure time ($p < .05$), the more general finding here was one of inconsistency. Mother and child tended to disagree sharply on whatever television behavior was being analyzed, but there was no systematic relationship among the discrepancies across the measures.

Relationships among behaviors

Here we shall attempt to summarize our analysis of the intercorrelations among these variables separately for the mother and her child. This will be done primarily in a descriptive fashion, indicating what sets of variables appear to cluster.[2]

In terms of the original concern of this project for the anticipated (but unsupported) role of family interaction, one finding is critical. It might well be the capstone for interpreting the perceptions of the mother which are correlated, and the relationships among the child's reported behaviors. For the child, family interaction was positively correlated (.226) with watching television with his parents; in turn, such watching was significantly related to watching more total television, more of the violent shows, etc. For the parent, extensive interaction with the child was negatively related (-.251) to reported watching of television with the child and with the child's total television exposure. So the child has said if we talk a lot, we watch a lot together; the mother perceived the situation to be just the opposite.

Child's reported behaviors. The range of correlations reported here is from .226 to .365.

As the child's weekday television time increased, his exposure to violent shows increased, as did his exposure to Saturday television and the frequency of his watching with his parents. With more watching time, he perceived more reality in to what he viewed.

With Saturday viewing, there was more self-watching and less parental suggestions about what to watch.

Another subset of correlations indicates that if the child perceived strong family interaction, he was less likely to give violent responses to hypothetical aggression situations. He perceived less violence on television, was more likely to choose a response of verbal aggression, and was less likely to perceive violence as a justified means of problem solving.

Mother's reports of children's behaviors. Here, one can cluster the major behaviors of the child, as perceived by the mother, around the concept of total television time—either weekday or Saturday. Positively and significantly related to total exposure were the frequency of watching violent and nonviolent shows, watching with parents, the perceived existence of rules about watching, and the reality of the television content.

If the child reported he watched a large number of nonviolent shows, the mother said she watched a large number of such shows (r = .656) and reported that the child perceived a lesser amount of violence on television. If the child watched a large number of violent programs, so did the parent in her own viewing (r = .312), and the child purportedly perceived more general television violence. This watching of more violent shows was in the context of more watching with a parent, according to the mother.

When the mother watched a substantial number of violent programs, she stated that the child would more often find the use of violence justified and would make more violent responses to specified problem situations.

Across these separate sets of correlations, there was an intriguing consistency to contrast with the significant disagreement about the role of family interaction: it was in terms of the context of watching violent shows. From both vantage points, there was more viewing of programs considered violent among children who did a significant amount of television watching with one or both of their parents present. When such time was spent watching television, a good share (of necessity) went to more violent programs. Much of this tended to be family viewing time, rather than self-viewing.

DISCUSSION

A discussion of these findings might focus on these three issues:

(1) Why is there so much disagreement between mother and ten-year-old about what the child's television behaviors and attitudes are? Who is right?

(2) Given the watching that is done with parents (both with greater total television exposure and particularly with exposure to the more violent shows), what occurs in that context?

(3) What is family interaction all about if, for the child, it is concurrent with more television watching with his parents and, for the parent, it is concurrent with less television watching?

These questions are not answerable directly from this project but testify to subsequent research needs.

That the mother and child strongly disagree is apparent. Given this noncurrence between the two, one would predict an even more dismal situation if data were collected from the father. Does the child overstate television watching because within his reference group it is prestigious to do so? Does the mother underestimate the child's preoccupation because she devalues that activity? One requires an independent assessment of the child's behavior to isolate one or both of these plausible explanations.

Certainly prior research data based on parental reports of the child's behaviors and attitudes must remain highly suspect. Biases which may be present in such reports are unlikely to be self-cancelling. One might expect mothers to be better reporters for children younger than those examined here, and worse reporters as the children approach and attain puberty.

If the child does engage in as much watching by himself as he indicates—and there is little reason to associate status with that kind of viewing—this may be a major source of certain discrepancies. The mother may not know how much or what kind of television is consumed in the context of the child's self-watching. Attitudes toward television, toward program content, and toward the use of violence may be misperceived if they are never discussed.

This leads directly to the issue of what goes on while children view television with their parents. The parallel question of what goes on while they view with peers, siblings—or anyone for that matter—is also relevant. Is there any discussion of program, of characterization, of plot? If so, what is the content of the discussion? Is it unidirectional? Which direction(s)? Is there any analysis of the role of aggression or violence during those programs which feature such activities? Is there an examination of the general reality levels of television dramatizations?

One might propose to develop an educational effort for young people in terms of how to use the medium of television, and a second effort for parents. The books on raising children give little space (most give none at all) to the issue of the media. Yet television occupies a large portion of one's life space; it is absorbed without formal training in its use and offers few criteria for selecting among its offerings. Of course, the research necessary for indicating principles of television viewing remains largely undone.

One begins to surmise that the family get-together for watching television is largely unaccompanied by any significant interaction directed toward the medium. Television viewing may be the master of the situation, not the servant.

This suggests some reasons why the family interaction measure constructed in this study "washed out" so completely. It failed to explain discrepancies between parent and child in perceptions of the child's behaviors. It was not a correlate in its own right of what the child does with the television medium. It did not relate to concepts dealing with the use of violence. The measure, it will be recalled, determined the frequency of interaction between parent and child in terms of talking about school, family decisions, or "sitting around and just talking about things." It did not deal at all with the content of such discussions, nor with the role of the child in such discussions (e.g., passive receiver, active source).

The empirical evidence indicates that such interaction, for the child, is intimately associated with watching television with one's parents. The mother claims that such interaction is not only *not* associated with that context, but occurs in a television-free setting. We may begin to suspect that, for the child, sitting around and just talking is a television-related phenomenon. In that case, family discussion may be considered a secondary activity and in practice may be just that. The parent may perhaps envision a situation in which such discussion is the focal point of the togetherness, not ancillary.

All these musings require more precise data than are available at this point. These questions may be paramount: Do children interact with their parents over the content of television programs? How? Does communication about violent content on television affect the child's perceptions of and attitudes toward violence?

Perhaps the closing speculation of largest import would be that the American family has not seemingly specified a role for television in the process of family growth and development. It is just there. Always there. No one has decided what to do about it, or with it. There are limits on how much it is to be used, but they probably are observed as much in their nonobservance. Television's merits, deficits, and utility have not been assessed and implemented in the American home, yet it remains a central feature of family activity.

FOOTNOTES

1. The research upon which this report is based was performed pursuant to Contract No. HSM 42-70-32 with the National Institute of Mental Health, Health Services and Mental Health Administration, U.S. Department of Health, Education and Welfare. Miss Christine Liebrock was a project assistant.
2. The full correlation matrix from which these findings were extracted is available from the authors.

REFERENCES

Chaffee, S.H., McLeod, J.M., and Wackman, D.B. Family communication patterns and adolescent political participation. In Dennis, J. (Ed.) *Explorations of political socialization: a reader of contemporary research.* New York: Wiley, 1970.

Greenberg, B.S., and Gordon, T.F. Perceptions of violence in television programs: critics and the public. *Television and social behavior:* a report to the Surgeon General's Scientific Advisory Committee, Vol. 1. Washington, D.C.: U.S. Government Printing Office, 1971.

Himmelweit, H.T., Oppenheim, A.N., and Vince, P. *Television and the child.* London: Oxford University Press, 1958.

McLeod, J.M., Chaffee, S.H., and Wackman, D.B. Family communication: an updated report. Paper presented at a meeting of the Communication Theory and Methodology division of the Association for Education in Journalism, Boulder, Colo., 1967.

Schramm, W., Lyle, J., and Parker, E.B. *Television in the lives of our children.* Stanford: Stanford University Press, 1961.

Television's Impact on Everyday Life: Some Cross-national Evidence

John P. Robinson

National Institute of Mental Health

Only now, 20 years after the introduction of television to American society, are the magnitude and dimensions of its impact being recognized. Not surprisingly, speculation about the effects of television remains more provocative than the few well-documented empirical findings that have been published.

Sociologists in the "mass society" tradition have alleged that television has brought about increased cultural homogeneity in dress, customs, and language. Such students of communication as Marshall McLuhan note that television changes the way in which man perceives and reacts to his environment, and social critics believe that this pervasive form of mass media debases taste and increases public tolerance for violence.

Satisfactory empirical research bearing on such interesting issues is almost nonexistent, because social measurement tools for assessing such variables are still in an embryonic stage. In areas where measurement is more straightforward, certain facts about television's effects have been uncovered with assuring regularity across a variety of study locations and populations. An example is television's effect on the timetable of people's lives. The arrival of the television set obviously displaced leisure activities which are "functional equivalents" (Weiss, 1970; Bogart, 1957; Himmelweit, Oppenheim, and Vince, 1958)—most notably radio listening and movie attendance, and to a lesser extent the reading of newspapers, magazines, and books. One particularly well-documented set of quantitative data comes from Coffin (1955), who examined the daily media behavior of a panel of 2,500 persons in Fort Wayne, Indiana, over a six-month period during which the city acquired its first television station. The time devoted to media by the respondents who had purchased a set was calculated as follows:

	Before Television was available	Time spent after purchase of a set	Difference
Magazines	17 Min/day	10 Min/day	−7
Newspapers	39	32	−7
Radio	122	52	−70
Television	12	173	+161
	190 Min/day	267 Min/day	+ 77

Coffin's documentation also showed that the media behavior of persons who did not purchase a television set over the six-month period was virtually identical with the behavior of all the nonowners before television was available, thus strongly ruling out the possibility that media behavior changes were due to general historical shifts in population time allocation.

The data also show that while television has made deep inroads on functionally equivalent media behavior, it must have affected nonmedia behavior as well. According to the Coffin data, television owners spent 77 minutes watching television that was formerly spent on other nonmedia activities.[1] This represents a 41 percent increase in time devoted to the mass media. The next crucial question thus becomes which nonmedia activities set owners gave up.

Belson's (1969) study of the impact of television in Britain in the early 1950s did attempt to isolate the ways in which nine other leisure activities were affected by the acquisition of television. He located considerable decreases in theater and ballet attendance and in visits to places of historical interest (each of which could be seen in a broad context as a mass medium), lesser decreases in card playing and phonograph record playing, and little or no change in gardening and attending organizational meetings. Two activities actually showed considerable gains in participation—visits to art galleries and attendance at sporting events (especially horse racing and horse jumping), and Belson noted that substantial amounts of television time had been devoted to popularized coverage of these activities. In a subsequent study which looked at different leisure activities, Belson (1960) found that families with television sets engaged in considerably more entertaining in their homes that did nonowners, though owners were far less involved in social activities outside the home.

The ten-year study of Videotown (New Brunswick, N.J.) between 1948 and 1958 is the most extensive longitudinal study of the impact of television in the United States (Cunningham and Walsh, 1958). In 1951, the year when television ownership in the town jumped from 20 to 50 percent, the amount of visiting and entertaining in the community dropped decidedly (from 25 to 13 percent on a typical day). After remaining at this lower level for five years, these social activities began to increase moderately, although the study was terminated before any definitive trends could be isolated. Other gregarious activities—attending meetings, going out to dinner, attending sports events—were engaged in rather infrequently on a daily basis, with no significant up or down trend emerging over the ten-year period.

While these data shed light on how nonmedia aspects of leisure time are affected by television, they offer only limited glimpses of the full round of daily activities affected by an innovation like television.

A number of activities might be affected: Do people sleep less when they frequently stay up to watch late programs?Does late viewing cause workers to be late reporting to work? Do homemakers take shortcuts in caring for children and household chores in order to compensate for television viewing?

A major weakness of the available literature has been its failure to employ an adequate sampling framework of daily life with which to assess television's full impact. The major purpose of this paper is to show that time budget methodology contains within itself an ideal sampling procedure for this task. However, there are certain requirements that time budget studies must fulfill in order to prove equal to the task; very few time budget studies in the past have met these requirements.

The major asset of the time variable is that it is a universal "container" of all phenomena. Any behavior that occurs in a day can be indexed and catalogued by the amount of time it takes. In order to actually exploit this feature of the time variable, however, researchers must examine (or sample at random from) the full 24-hour day. If observations during early morning or daytime work hours are excluded, as they are by some investigators, the probability of subtle shifts in daily behavior could be significant. For example, it might be a mistake to conclude that evening viewing makes inroads into the amount of sleep which people obtain; data collected during morning hours might reveal that late-hour viewers compensate by getting up later in the morning. It would seem wise, therefore, to utilize the full 1,440 minutes of the day as the proper sampling framework.

Once this sampling framework is accepted, the crucial problem is devising a suitable coding framework into which activities can be classified. The more detailed the code, the more specific the changes that can be detected. If, for example, one locates a decrease in "work time," it would be instructive to know that this decrease was due to decreased participation in second jobs or to fewer coffee breaks rather than to less actual time on the job. The coding scheme, of course, also should be broad enough to capture the full range of activities performed during the 24-hour day.

While numerous problems remain, sampling and coding are probably the most important. Among the others that remain unresolved are: (1) ensuring that various days of the week are weighted equally, so that time estimates are not biased by day of the week differences; (2) ensuring that various seasons of the year are represented proportionately; and (3) ensuring that various segments of the population are not excluded or underrepresented. Attaining reasonable response rates and encouraging respondents to record daily activities in appropriate detail across the entire day typify steps which must be taken to ensure accurate representation.

It is unlikely that time budget studies that will ideally resolve each of the above problems can be carried out in the near future, but the research reported here offers hope that quantitative data can be collected that satisfactorily represent patterns of daily behavior and hence are fully capable of shedding light on how these patterns are affected by the presence of television. The data on which this report is based come from the Multination Time Budget Research Project (Szalai, 1966.)[2]

TIME BUDGETS

Time budgets of human behavior have only sporadically caught the attention of social researchers; for this reason knowledge about optimal procedures of collecting such data has accumulated slowly. The best-known studies of time use in America were conducted in the 1930s under the direction of two leading sociologists of that period, George Lundberg (Lundberg, Kanarovski, and McInerny, 1934) and Pitrim Sorokin (Sorokin and Berger, 1939). In retrospect, helpful as they were in charting new territory, these pioneer efforts seem sadly unsophisticated in their methods of sampling individuals and days of the week and in their coding procedures. Nevertheless, both sets of investigators did take advantage of the full 24-hour day, so some extremely blurred glimpses of daily life in this interesting pretelevision period are implicit in these data.

In a recent paper, Robinson and Converse (1970) compared time budget data collected from a national probability sample of 1,243 urban adults in 1965-66 with those collected by Lundberg et al. and by Sorokin-Berger. In the national study (which was supplemented with a probability sample of the single community of Jackson, Michigan), 73 percent of the respondents approached (from households in which least one person under 65 was employed, in order to increase standardization) recorded an entire day's activities; respondents were randomly assigned to fill out diaries on either a weekday or a weekend day, and approximately equal numbers of diaries were obtained for each day of the week. These activities were then coded into one of 96 coding categories. (These categories were subsequently collapsed to the 37 activities noted in Table 3.) Further details on procedures and coding categories can be found in Robinson (1969) and Robinson (1970).

When these time budget data were compared with those collected in the 1930s, Robinson and Converse found respondents in 1965-66 reporting significantly less time sleeping, eating, reading, frequenting places of entertainment (especially movies), listening to the radio, playing sports and games, talking, pleasure driving, dancing, and going to church services. Most of these activities have already been isolated in previous studies of the effects of television, but some new changes appear, especially in nondiscretionary activities like sleeping and eating. Needless to say, these results can be treated only as the crudest reflection of television's impact, since a number of 1960s activities besides television viewing showed increases over the 1930s: working, traveling, shopping, and caring for children. It is unlikely that these changes in daily life are the results directly of television; rather, they are due to other social influences that changed during the time period in which television was introduced.

In the present paper we concentrate on the differential activity patterns of television owners and nonowners in the 1965-66 study. Such a contrast is necessarily confounded by other factors, most notably the fact that nonowners differ from owners in ways other than the mere presence of a set in the household. Almost from television's inception in the United States, set owners have been drawn quite disproportionately from households with children and with higher incomes.[3] Moreover, the ownership rate for respondents at the time of this survey was over 98 percent, leaving very few respondents in the important nonowner category.

These United States survey sites, however, represented only two of the fifteen (mainly European) locations in which parallel time budget data were concurrently collected. Ownership rates in the other 13 sites varied between 26 and 85 percent, offering a much wider spectrum of societies from which to compare the behavior of owners and nonowners. Fourteen of the sites (the data from the Soviet Union, with an ownership rate near 50 percent, were not available for computation in this paper) are described in Table 1. The table gives, for each site, sample sizes, ownership rates, and time spent watching television. The 14 sites, drawn from 11 different countries, are mainly cities (and their environs) with populations between 50,000 and 150,000 and with more than 30 percent of their work force engaged in industry. In this way, a certain degree of standardization of respondents across countries was attained. Household sampling methods, field procedures, and coding methods were identical to those described for the United States survey. The research in each survey site was carried out by indigenous survey organizations and personnel; a UNESCO center in Vienna acted as a central coordinating agency. The project was directed by a Hungarian sociologist, Alexander Szalai, who has described the background procedures in more detail in the December 1966 issue of the *American Behavioral Scientist* (Szalai et al., 1966).

The data were collected for the purpose of better understanding the effects of industrialization on everyday life; hence they are not ideal for the study of television. Had television been the central focus, the study would have been more successful had it employed the panel design utilized in the Coffin study (in which the *same* respondents reported behavior before and after the acquisition of television). Nevertheless, encouraged by Coffin's findings that identical figures and conclusions would have been obtained with a single "after" survey, we assume that it will be profitable to examine the figures from our "after only" survey. Moreover, the present study has the further leverage of being able to isolate patterns that hold across a variety of societies in different stages of television diffusion.

Table 1 reveals a constancy of time spent viewing television across the survey sites. With the exception of those in Kazanlik, Bulgaria, percentages of owners viewing television (as a primary activity) on a particular day vary only between 61 percent and 77 percent; the amount of time spent viewing varies only between 70 and 107 minutes. This basic trend toward cross-national inelasticity in viewing times was noted at the aggregative level in an earlier paper (Robinson, 1969). In that study the viewing figures for the Soviet Union were also found to be on a par with countries where similar ownership patterns were found and where further evidence for inelasticity was reviewed (from different studies of the United States viewing public, which employed quite different research methodologies).

Subtracting the total viewing of owners from that of nonowners, the investigators arrived at a cross-national average of almost 80 minutes

Table 1: Ownership rates and time viewing for TV owners and nonowners across the survey sites

	SAMPLE SIZE	TV OWNERS				NONOWNERS		
		Percent ownership	Percent viewing at home	Average time viewing (in minutes per day)		Percent viewing at home	Average time viewing (in minutes per day)	
				At home	Away from home		At home	Away from home
United States cities	1243	97%	70%	93	1	11%	19	0
Jackson, United States	778	98%	71%	100	2	7%	7	0
West Germany, national	1501	67%	68%	86	1	10%	11	2
Osnabruck, West Germany	979	77%	72%	92	1	4%	6	8
Belgium, national	2077	72%	77%	107	2	6%	7	6
French cities	2805	64%	76%	82	2	1%	2	5
Olomouc, Czechoslovakia	2194	73%	61%	81	1	13%	15	5
Torun, Poland	2759	59%	76%	101	2	6%	7	12
Hoyerswerda, East Germany	1650	85%	73%	91	1	8%	9	2
Gyor, Hungary	1994	45%	65%	83	1	2%	2	7
Kazanlik, Bulgaria	2096	26%	50%	46	1	2%	2	2
Maribor, Yugoslavia	1995	49%	72%	79	*	4%	4	1
Kragujevac, Yugoslavia	2125	35%	67%	85	*	5%	6	4
Lima-Callao, Peru	782	49%	71%	86	2	3%	6	3
	24,978	63.3%	72%	86.5%	1.1 min.	5.8%	7.3 min.	4.0 min.

*Less than 1 minute per day average.

per day of increased viewing at home.[4] Unsurprisingly, viewing away from home decreases substantially, from four minutes to one minute per day. The relatively small magnitude of this "guest" viewing indicates that persons who do not have sets view very little and that the full impact of television is only felt when people have personal access to a set in their own households.

The similarity of viewing patterns across these countries becomes especially striking when one notes the contrasting patterns of viewing by social status. In the Western European and American survey sites, respondents with less education and in blue collar occupations reported substantially more viewing than did their white collar counterparts; in Eastern Europe either the opposite trend or no trend at all was found by educational level (Robinson and Converse, 1966). Such trends are also reflected in ownership rates in Table 2 for individuals in various occupational and family status cateogires.[5] It can be seen that while individuals in blue collar households generally show lower ownership than those in white collar homes, the effect is especially pronounced in Eastern European countries. Table 2 also shows that, overall, employed married men with children have four percent higher television ownership than do other employed men. These subdivisions of the sample will be used when we attempt to find out whether differences in time allocations of owners and nonowners hold up across various subdivisions of the sample.

TIME ALLOCATIONS OF TELEVISION OWNERS AND NONOWNERS

Table 3 shows the cross-national average time expenditures of owners and nonowners on 37 activities comprising the entire day's behavior. Where differences can be directly attributed to the more detailed code of 96 activities, these differences will be mentioned in the following discussion). It can be seen, first, that the 79-minute average increase in television viewing at home appears to have its greatest impact on other media activities, as previous research has already suggested. Especially large decreases are noted for radio listening (down eight minutes), book reading (down six minutes), and movie viewing (down three minutes). Magazine and newspaper reading seem least affected. Overall, television owners still spent almost an hour more than nonowners in contact with the mass media.

The Table 3 data suggest that this extra hour is drawn about equally from both free time and nonfree time activities (if the reader accepts the investigators' definition of free time).[7] The main free time activities engaged in less by television set owners are social gatherings outside one's own home (12 minutes less), conversation (five minutes less), hobbies (five minutes less), and travel associated with all leisure activities (four

Table 2: Percentages of various demographic groupings owning television sets across survey sites (see text for definitions)

	TOTAL SAMPLE	EMPLOYED MEN		EMPLOYED WOMEN		HOUSEWIVES		EMPLOYED MARRIED MEN WITH CHILDREN
		White collar	Blue collar	White collar	Blue collar	White collar	Blue collar	
United States cities	97%	97%	99%	95%	88%	98%	100%	99.5%
Jackson, United States	98	98	100	92	100	98	96*	100
West Germany, national	67	70	68*	61	76	70	67	72
Osnabruck, West Germany	77	80	80	62	82	82	71	87
Belgium, national	72	67	73	61	80	78	73	76
French cities	64	70	63	54	50	73	70	74
Olomouc, Czechoslovakia	73	73	80	76	79	74	71	84
Torun, Poland	59	74	50	65	45	62	47	72
Hoyerswerda, East Germany	85	83	87	82	82	82	90	89
Gyor, Hungary	45	69	39	65	38	68*	25	54
Kazanlik, Bulgaria	26	38	16	29	23	43**	7*	30
Maribor, Yugoslavia	49	85	31	79	29	74	25	58
Kragujevac, Yugoslavia	35	67	12	67	12	69	16	33
Lima-Callao, Peru	49	83	21	86*	28	84	43	51
	64%	75%	58%	70%	58%	75%	57%	70%

*Sample size less than 30
**Sample size less than 10

Table 3: Differences in the cross-national average of time spent on all activities for TV owners and nonowners

(in minutes per day; data are weighted to ensure equality of days of the week and respondents per household)

	TV Owners	Nonowners	Difference	Percent Difference
1. Main job	254.2	253.2	+ 1.0	—
2. Second job	3.7	4.1	− .4	− .10
3. At work other	10.6	10.8	− .2	− .02
4. Travel to job	28.1	28.4	− .3	− .01
TOTAL WORK			+ 0.1	
5. Cooking	55.0	56.7	− 1.7	− .03
6. Home chores	57.9	58.1	− 0.2	—
7. Laundry	27.9	32.9	− 5.0	− .02
8. Marketing	18.1	18.1	0	
TOTAL HOUSEWORK			− 6.9	
9. Animal, garden	11.5	17.6	− 6.1	− .35
10. Shopping	7.7	6.4	+ 1.3	+ .20
11. Other house	19.1	20.8	− 1.7	− .08
HOUSEHOLD CARE			− 6.7	
12. Child care	17.9	16.8	+ 1.1	+ .07
13. Other child	11.5	10.1	+ 1.4	+ .14
TOTAL CHILD CARE			+ 2.5	
14. Personal care	55.0	59.5	− 4.5	− .09
15. Eating	84.7	84.6	+ 0.1	—
16. Sleep	479.3	491.8	−12.5	− .04
PERSONAL NEEDS			−17.4	
17. Personal travel	18.4	19.0	− 0.6	− .03
18. Leisure travel	16.4	20.5	− 4.1	− .20
NON-WORK TRAVEL			− 4.7	
19. Study	15.7	18.1	− 2.4	− .13
20. Religion	3.5	6.2	− 2.7	− .44
21. Organizations	5.3	3.6	+ 1.7	+ .47
STUDY & PARTICIPATION			− 3.4	
22. Radio	5.2	13.2	− 8.0	− .61
23. TV (home)	86.5	7.3	+79.2	+10.85
24. TV (away)	1.1	4.0	− 2.9	− .73
25. Read paper	15.2	15.3	− 0.1	− .01
26. Read magazine	3.9	5.4	− 1.5	− .28
27. Read books	8.3	14.1	− 5.8	− .41
28. Movies	3.1	6.5	− 3.4	− .52
TOTAL MASS MEDIA			+57.5	
29. Social (home)	14.6	11.7	+ 2.9	+ .25
30. Social (away)	22.4	33.9	−11.5	− .34
31. Conversation	14.5	19.5	− 5.0	− .26
32. Active sports	2.4	2.6	− 0.2	− .08
33. Outdoors	15.8	17.5	− 1.7	− .10
34. Entertainment	3.9	3.9	0	—
35. Cultural events	1.0	1.1	− 0.1	− .09
36. Resting	23.8	24.8	− 1.0	− .04
37. Other leisure	16.7	21.9	− 5.2	− .24
TOTAL LEISURE			−23.3	
TOTAL MINUTES PER DAY	1440.0	1440.0		

minutes less). Entertaining in one's own home increases, perhaps (as Belson [1960] found) as a result of having "television guests."

The major "nonfree" time activity engaged in less often by television set owners is sleep (13 minutes less), indicating perhaps that television set owners do "trade off" their sleep in order to watch television. Less substantial decreases are noted for garden and/or pet care (Six minutes less), washing and caring for clothes (five minutes less), and personal care (five minutes less). Perhaps the most surprising finding is the greater amount of child care for television set owners. Although the difference is small, it holds up when presence of children is controlled.

The final column in Table 3 alerts us not to overemphasize the absolute differences in time allocations. These figures indicate the relative percentage differences in time expenditures—the degree to which television set owners spent more or less time on various activities. In this perspective other media activities appear to suffer much greater losses from television: television away from home down 73 percent, radio down 61 percent, and movies down 52 percent. No nonmedia activity shows a difference greater than 50 percent. Sleep, the activity which showed the greatest absolute amount of difference (13 minutes), takes only four percent less time among owners than among nonowners.

Since we have been examining only gross aggregate figures, at least two sorts of statistical controls need to be placed on the Table 3 data before they can be reliably interpreted. First, we need to show that such differences are not the result of aberrant figures for one or two countries but reflect differences that hold across a reasonable number of survey sites. This aspect of the data is examined in Table 4. Second, we should establish that these differences hold for various demographic groupings within each sample. This control is exercised in Table 5.

The distribution of survey sites according to how well differences between owners and nonowners hold up is shown in Table 4. The entries in the extreme left column represent the number of sites in which owners spent six or more minutes *more* time than nonowners on the activity, while those in the corresponding right column represent the number of sites in which owners spent six or more minutes *less* time than nonowners. Differences of one minute or less are coded in the middle ("only slight change") category, with all other differences coded in the two adjoining categories. These distributions are presented for the 20 activities in Table 3 in which owners and nonowners differed by more than 1.5 minutes in their time allocations. It can be seen, for example, that owners reported six or more minutes less sleep than nonowners in 12 of the 14 sites.

Of the 20 activities, 11 show regular and consistent differences across the survey sites. Two activities that drew noticeably lower participation among television owners—gardening and laundry—in Table 3 appear to have resulted from abnormally large differences in two or three sites.

Table 4: Number of survey sites showing various differences in time spent on 20 activities apparently affected by TV ownership.

	6 or more minutes more by TV owners	2–5 minutes more by TV owners	1 minute more or less by TV owners (+1 to −1)	2–5 minutes less by TV owners	6 or more minutes less by TV owners	TOTAL CHANGE (in minutes)
Trend holds regularly across survey sites						
16. Sleep	2	0	0	0	12	−13
30. Social, away	0	1	1	4	8	−12
22. Radio	0	1	0	0	12	− 8
27. Read book	0	1	3	3	7	− 6
37. Other leisure	1	0	3	3	7	− 5
31. Conversation	0	0	2	6	6	− 5
18. Leisure travel	0	1	3	7	3	− 4
28. Movies	0	1	3	7	3	− 3
24. TV, away	0	1	5	5	3	− 3
20. Religion	0	0	11	1	2	− 3
11. Other house	1	1	3	6	3	− 2
Trend holds irregularly across survey sites						
9. Garden	1	2	6	2	3	− 6
7. Laundry	2	0	4	5	3	− 5
14. Personal care	1	1	6	2	4	− 5
19. Study	4	2	2	3	3	− 2
26. Read magazine	0	1	10	1	2	− 2
33. Outdoors	1	3	3	5	2	− 2
5. Cooking	1	4	2	3	4	− 2
21. Organization	2	6	3	3	0	+ 2
29. Social, at home	3	4	3	3	1	+ 3

The large cross-national differences in gardening, for example, appear to have resulted from the very great differences recorded in Maribor (Yugoslavia) and Gyor (Hungary); owners in the United States and West German sites actually recorded more garden and pet care than did nonowners.[8] Similarly, the large difference in laundry activities appears to have been unduly influenced by an abnormal discrepancy among rents in Peru; differences in magazine reading resulted from differences in West Germany. The two activities which showed *larger* time expenditures for owners in Table 3—organizational activity and social engagements at home—did not hold up when this consistency test was applied.

Seven of these nine activities at the botton of Table 3 also fare badly when tested by the Table 5 control, which reflects the popularity with which differences hold across demographic groupings within the survey sites. The calculations for the Table 5 entries were arrived at by the same method as the Table 3 figures, but in Table 5 only the relevant population subdivisions (identified earlier in Table 2) within each survey site were examined. Where less than ten respondents fell into a category, the country was excluded from the calculations. The lower amounts of magazine reading and outdoor activities (mainly promenades) for television set owners hold up more regularly in Table 5 than in Table 4, although the reverse holds true for religious activities, travel associated with all leisure activities, and personal care. Again, differences for the two activities in which television set owners engaged *more* extensively than nonowners did not hold regularly across demographic groups.[9]

The nine activities which survive both tests most regularly are sleeping, radio listening, social gatherings away from home, book reading, other leisure activities (mainly correspondence and knitting), conversation, movies, television viewed away from home, and other household care (mainly heat and water supply). Of these, two are nonfree time activities, four are media activities, and the remaining three are nonmedia leisure activities. In the perspective of previous research studies, the apparent implication of these data in isolating tradeoffs of television for sleep[10] and other household care[11] provide insights that are not possible without time budget data. That figures for these two activities emerge as significant, while nonleisure activities related to housework, paid work, child care, personal needs, and travel show little if any apparent effect, deserves reflection, though our data are too tentative to view as reflecting universal "effects" of television.

OTHER ASPECTS OF TIME USAGE

Further aspects of time usage were examined in this study: secondary activities accompanying the primary activities described in the previous section, the location of each activity, and the personal contacts with

Table 5: Difference in time spent by TV owners (vs. non-owners) in 20 activities apparently most affected by TV as a function of demographic groupings (in minutes per day)

	TOTAL SAMPLE	Employed men		Employed women		Housewives		Employed men with children
		White collar	Blue collar	White collar	Blue collar	White collar	Blue collar	
Trend holds regularly across demographic groupings								
16. Sleep	−13	−21	− 9	− 6	−19	−13	−36	−13
30. Social, away	−12	−11	−11	−12	− 7	− 5	− 5	− 4
22. Radio	− 8	−16	−11	− 9	− 6	− 8	− 8	− 8
27. Read book	− 6	− 5	− 4	− 9	− 3	− 8	− 5	− 3
37. Other leisure	− 5	− 4	− 3	− 5	0	− 7	− 9	− 1
31. Conversation	− 5	− 3	+ 1	− 2	− 5	−10	− 7	− 5
28. Movies	− 3	− 6	− 2	− 3	− 1	0	− 1	− 2
24. Television, away	− 3	− 2	− 4	− 3	− 1	− 6	− 3	− 4
11. Other house	− 2	+ 3	− 6	− 5	− 1	− 1	0	− 6
26. Read magazine	− 2	− 2	− 3	− 3	− 1	− 5	− 1	− 1
33. Outdoors	− 2	− 6	− 3	− 9	+ 2	− 2	−10	− 1

Continued

Table 5: Continued

	TOTAL SAMPLE	Employed men		Employed women		Housewives		Employed men with children
		White collar	Blue collar	White collar	Blue collar	White collar	Blue collar	
Trend holds irregularly across demographic groupings								
9. Garden	− 6	− 7	−10	+ 2	− 4	+ 7	−15	−10
7. Laundry	− 5	0	+ 2	0	+ 1	+ 4	− 5	0
14. Personal care	− 5	− 4	+ 1	− 4	− 2	+ 3	+ 1	− 2
18. Leisure travel	− 4	− 6	+ 3	− 8	− 1	− 3	+ 2	− 2
20. Religion	− 3	− 1	0	− 1	0	+ 1	0	− 1
5. Cooking	− 2	− 3	− 3	+ 6	− 3	− 7	+ 4	0
19. Study	− 2	0	− 3	− 1	0	− 3	+22	+ 6
21. Organization	+ 2	0	− 1	+ 2	0	+ 1	0	0
29. Social, at home	+ 3	0	+ 1	− 4	− 4	+ 5	+ 3	0

whom the activity was performed. Table 6 shows differences between television set owners and nonowners on these aspects of time usage. Cross-national averages are reported both for the total sample and for one subsegment of the sample—employed married men with children—which might be most likely to show different patterns of reactions to television within the entire sample.[12]

The ten prevalent secondary activities are examined first in Table 6. The most overwhelming result (not surprisingly) is the lesser amount of radio listening as a secondary activity for television set owners. The decrease in secondary radio listening is almost matched by owners' greater expenditure of time on secondary television viewing. Television viewing away from home (which is slightly more prevalent as a secondary activity than as a primary activity) is also lower for owners. The only other secondary activity showing any shift is conversation, but here the figures are contradictory: owners report more conversation (although the trend holds true only in eight of 14 sites), while television-owning males with children report less conversation.

The largest difference in the ways owners and nonowners spend their time is found inside their own places of residence, a finding that holds across all sites except Olomouc, Czechoslovakia. As the middle portion of Table 6 shows, it also holds for employed married men with children—those who have more requirements keeping them at home. This difference is offset mainly by the smaller amount of time that owners spend in the immediate environs of their home (perhaps gardening or maintaining heat and water supply), in other persons' homes (a corollary of the Table 1 finding of less visiting by owners), in streets (related to decreased time in leisure travel), in indoor leisure (less time in movie theatres), and in restaurants and cafes. Other differences are either trivial or do not hold consistently for the two groups in Table 6 or across most survey sites.

Television set owners spend less time alone than nonowners in all sites (except Lima-Callao, Peru), although employed men with children report similar amounts of time alone whether they are owners or nonowners, perhaps indicating that nonowners are likely to spend more time alone to begin with.[13] Both owners and nonowners among married men with children report similar amounts of time spent with their families, though these amounts of time are generally higher among owners. Owners and nonowners reported substantial differences in amount of time spent with friends, relatives, and neighbors, though again married men with children reported similar amounts of time whether they were owners or nonowners. The greater amounts of contact that television set owners reported having with other adult members of their households, work colleagues, and formal acquaintances (like clients) did not hold across a sufficient number of sites to warrant generalization.

Table 6: Differences in total time in selected secondary activities, at various locations, and with various types of people for TV owners and non-owners (in minutes per day; data are weighted to ensure equality of days of the week and number of eligible respondents per household)

	Total sample	Employed married men with children
SECONDARY ACTIVITIES		
MASS MEDIA		
Radio	−22	−21
TV, home	+ 19	+ 13
TV, away	− 5	− 3
Read paper	0	0
Read magazine	0	+ 2
Read book	− 1	0
NON-MEDIA		
Child care	0	0
Social, at home	0	− 1
Social, away	0	+ 1
Conversation	+ 3	− 8
LOCATION		
At home, inside	+32	+42
At home, outside	−13	−18
Others' homes	−10	− 5
Work	− 1	− 7
Streets	− 4	−11
Stores, business	− 2	+ 6
Indoor leisure	− 3	− 3
Outdoor leisure	+ 1	− 1
Restaurant	− 2	− 2
Other	0	− 3
COMPANY		
All alone	−36	− 7
Alone in a crowd	− 5	− 5
With spouse	+ 12	+ 8
With children	+ 10	+ 10
Spouse and children together	+30	+ 4
Other household adults	+ 4	0
Friends, relatives	−14	− 3
Neighbors	− 9	− 5
Work colleagues	+ 7	+ 4
Organization members	0	0
Formal contacts	+ 3	− 1
Other	− 3	− 9

SUMMARY AND CONCLUSIONS

We have compared the daily expenditures of time of persons with television sets in their households with those of persons who do not have sets across fourteen diverse locations in Eastern and Western Europe and North and South America. These time budget data were not collected with this comparison as the research aim, and they fall short on several research design desiderata. Little background information on the habits and experiences of respondents with television sets was collected; the survey locations were at widely different stages of television diffusion; the data were collected at only one period rather than on a longitudinal basis (so that the investigators could not ensure that individuals with and without television did not differ in their activity patterns before the survey).

Nevertheless, these data afford an excellent opportunity to observe the ways television appears to have quantitatively affected daily behavior in the Western world. Time budget data are uniquely capable of measuring the impact of an innovation like television in the perspective of the full cycle of daily activities. Thus, while the data in this paper reinforce a large body of studies that have rightly emphasized the effects of television on usage of the other mass media (particularly radio, movies, and book reading), they indicate that expenditures of time on certain nonmedia activities have also been affected. Particularly noteworthy are the lesser amounts of time that television set owners spend in the nonleisure activities of sleep and miscellaneous household care.

The differences in time spent on other leisure activities are also interesting. Some social observers may be alarmed at the reduced amounts of time that television owners spend in conversation, in correspondence, or in visits to the homes of friends, relatives, and neighbors, but they should also note that these may be balanced by increased amounts of time in contact with the owners' immediate families, including children. Whether such shifts result in greater benefit or harm to the social fabric of society remains a moot point.

Despite the convergences that appear in these data, it is necessary to reiterate that these "one-shot" surveys undoubtedly fail to illuminate some of the dynamics of change that occurs over time. The Belson (1967) and Videotown (Cunningham and Walsh, 1958) longitudinal studies both indicate that television has its greatest effect on daily life during the first few years of set ownership. Belson found that set owners' "initiative" dropped significantly with the acquisition of television but rose to pretelevision levels within two years. The Videotown study showed that within a few years set owners began to resume many of their pretelevision activities, though without decreasing the time spent watching television.

A further finding from the Videotown study concerns the effects of television on moviegoing. Movie attendance in Videotown dropped drastically with the introduction of television. However, in the year that television diffusion made its initial spurt, the drop in movie attendance was noted for *both* owners and nonowners. Even persons without television sets were thus feeling some fundamental change in daily life that television might have brought in its wake.

More data are needed on the everyday activities of television owners when they do not watch television. Such figures are now available only for employed men, and more stringent controls need to be imposed on these data before they can be interpreted with suitable confidence. Nevertheless, these figures indicate that only a few of the activities we have characterized as "casualties" of television are the activities that appear to recapture viewers away from their sets. Of the two activities that most substantially differentiate owners who watch from owners who do not, only one was isolated in our analysis—social visiting. The other, organizational activity, was engaged in slightly more by owners than by nonowners.

The same mixed pattern holds for other activities that nonviewing owners appeared to choose in place of viewing. Movie attendance, a prime casualty from the earlier analysis, is markedly higher for nonviewing owners than for viewing owners, but so is attendance at theatres, nightclubs, and museums. Most interestingly, however, there are only insignificant differences between nonviewers and viewers for three of the most prominent casualties identified above—sleeping, radio listening, and book reading. These may be permanent casualties of television.

Finally, it is of considerable interest to compare television with other innovations of the twentieth century. Comparing the amount of travel by owners of automobiles with that of nonowners, we were especially surprised that cross-nationally automobile owners on the average spent only six percent more time in transit than nonowners. While automobile owners were undoubtedly able to cover far more territory in the time they spent traveling, the overall shift is pale indeed compared with the 58 percent increase in media usage apparently occasioned by the influence of television. Cross-national data also indicates that time spent on housework is not grossly affected by the acquisition of home appliances like washing machines and dryers. Rather, it appears that time saved on these basic chores as a result of laborsaving devices is quickly channeled into other activities designed to improve the appearance of the home. Thus, at least in the temporal sense, television appears to have had a greater influence on the structure of daily life than any other innovation in this century.

FOOTNOTES

1. Coffin's data exlude the media activities of movie attendance and book reading, but these could constitute at best only a small part of the 77-minute difference.

2. The author wishes to thank Professor Szalai for granting access to the data prior to the publication of a two-volume series detailing procedures and results of this pioneering research venture. The author also thanks Professor Philip Stone of the Department of Social Relations at Harvard University for preparing the complex computer program that generated the calculations for this paper. In no way can either of them be held responsible for any liberties the author has taken in interpreting these data.

3. The relation with education has been more complex, tending toward curvilinearlity, with the least- and best-educated segments of the population reporting least ownership.

4. An embarrassing proportion of individuals (six percent over all sites) reported that they did not own a television set and yet reported viewing television at home on the day they kept their diary of activities. Whether this is due to respondents' unwillingness to divulge ownership (perhaps because of nonpayment of state fees on set usage; or to coding error is not possible to determine from the present data. The possibility of such a discrepancy would have been given greater attention had the study been more directly focused on television. It should be primary concern of future time budget studies.

5. The definitions used in Table 2 represent the two extremes, not the middle, of the status distribution. The designation "white collar" refers to men who were either employed in managerial or responsible jobs *or* exposed to some college. "Blue collar" men, on the other hand, had to both work in a blue collar occupation *and* have finished no more than primary education. For both employed women and housewives, these definitions applied to the head of the household—the husband, if he was employed, or the employed woman herself if she was not married. These groupings are less than elegant conceptually but were used in order to include roughly equivalent numbers of respondents in each country without imposing separate definitions for each country.

6. These activities refer to the "primary" activity in which the respondent was engaged. A considerable amount of secondary activity (done to the accompaniment of primary activities, like eating while reading, caring for children while watching television) is considered separately in Table 6.

7. The present definition of free time includes activities numbered 18-37 in Table 3. In essence it includes all daily activities besides paid work, housework, child care, shopping, sleep, and personal care. In some instances, of course, this division results in less than satisfactory assignment: coffee breaks and playing with children are coded as obligatory activities, while attending meetings and knitting are considered free time activities.

8. This activity should be more accurately differentiated in future time budget studies. The "gardening" of Eastern European respondents, which provides them with extra staple foods, is an entirely different social function from the flower gardening and pet care of the United States and West Germany.

9. Some interesting social patterns in Table 5 deserve consideration: differences in home social gatherings hold for housewives but not for employed women; differences in gardening hold more strongly for respondents in blue collar households than those in white collar households.

10. Our overall difference of 13 minutes for sleep corresponds exactly with the 13-minute later bedtimes reported by American television children in Schramm, Lyle, and Parker (1961) and is very close to the changes in children's bedtimes reported in Himmelweit, Oppenheim, and Vince (1958) and Maccoby (1951). But figures from these studies refer to times at which children go to bed and do not indicate whether these children sleep later in the mornings as compensation. Although these bedtime data do not distinguish between owners and nonowners, research from Japan (Nakanishi, 1966) and from the United States (Robinson and Converse, 1970) show both later retiring and later rising times for adults in the last 15 years.

11. It is possible that nontelevision households, despite the controls we have already applied, are more primitive in respect to ownership of other conveniences like running water and central heating. This factor, if true, might better explain this difference than the presence of television.

12. Elaborations on Table 6 differences along the lines of Tables 4 and 5 are not presented because such differentiation produces practically no changes in the Table 6 results.

13. Unlike the figures for location or primary activities, those for personal contact are not mutually exclusive and do not add up to 1440 minutes for all demographic groups.

REFERENCES

Belson, W. The effects of television upon family life. *Discovery*, 1960, **21**, 1-5.

Belson, W. *The impact of television*. Hamden, Conn.: Archon Books, 1967.

Bogart, L. *The age of television*. New York: Ungar, 1958.

Coffin, T. Television's impact on society. *American Psychologist*, 1955, **10**, 630-41.

Cunningham and Walsh. *Videotown: 1948-1958*. New York: Cunningham and Walsh, 1959.

Himmelweit, H. Oppenheim, A., and Vince, P. *Television and the child*. London: Oxford, 1958.

Lundberg, G.; Komarovski, M., and McInerny, M. *Leisure: a suburban study*. New York: Columbia University Press, 1934.

Maccoby, E. Television: its impact on school children. *Public Opinion Quarterly*, 1951, **15**, 421-44.

Nakanishi, N. *A report on the how do people spend their time survey in 1965*. Tokyo: NHK Public Opinion Research Institute, 1966.

Robinson, J. Television and leisure time: yesterday, today, and (maybe) tomorrow. *Public Opinion Quarterly*, 1969, **33**, 210-22.

Robinson, J. Daily participation in sport across twelve countries. In G. Luschen (ed.), *The cross-cultural analysis of sport and games*. Champaign, Ill.: Stipes Publishing, 1970.

Robinson, J. and Converse, P. The impact of television on mass media usage: a cross-national comparison. Paper read at the Sixth World Congress of Sociology in Evian, France, September, 1966.

Robinson, J. and Converse, P. Social change reflected in the use of time. In A. Campbell and P. Converse (eds.), *Indicators of Social Change*. New York: Russell Sage, 1970.

Schramm, W.; Lyle, J., and Parker, E. *Television in the lives of our children*. Stanford University Press, 1961.

Sorokin, P., and Berger, C. *Time-budgets of human behavior*. Cambridge, Mass.: Harvard University Press, 1939.

Szalai, A., *et al.* The multinational comparative time budget research project. *American Behavioral Scientist*, December, 1966 (whole issue).

Weiss, W. Effects of the mass media of communication. In G. Lindsay and E. Aronson, *Handbook of Social Psychology, Vol. 5*. Reading, Mass.: Addison-Wesley, 1970.

Effects of Television Advertising on Children and Adolescents

Scott Ward

Harvard University
Graduate School of Business Administration
and
Marketing Science Institute

Questions about the effects of television advertising on children have frequently been raised by television's critics. Surprisingly, little published research exists in this area. Investigators have examined the effects of television programming on children, but they have not been concerned with television advertising; conversely, much research has examined effects of television advertising, but the focus has been on adults rather than on children. It would be naive to use these sources to derive hypotheses for research studies of effects of commercials on children. The content, structure, and repetitive presentation of commercial messages are different from programming, so the effects on viewers should be different. Moreover, hypotheses about effects of television advertising on children cannot simply be derived from research with adults.

For these reasons, the overall purpose of the present program of research was to provide exploratory baseline data on the effects of television advertising on children and teenagers. The objective was to conduct studies in several areas which might suggest a range of effects of television advertising on children and teenagers from five to 18 years old. This research program sought to stimulate future hypothesis-testing research rather than to explicitly undertake such research. Seven separate studies were undertaken for this project. Four concern effects of television advertising on preteenage children; three concern effects on adolescents and are based on a survey in a Maryland school district. Four additional papers, summarizing various aspects of the data, reporting preliminary data, or dealing with related aspects of the research, are listed in Appendix A. The purpose of this overview paper is to summarize the areas of research, the methodologies employed, and the major findings.

AREAS OF RESEARCH

Figure 1 presents a descriptive model of the various areas of research in this project.

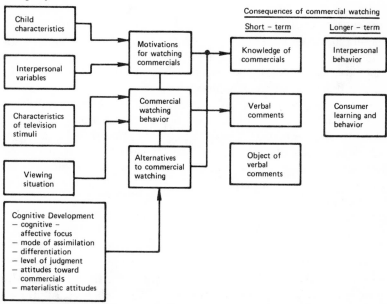

Figure 1: Major variables in studies of effects of television advertising on youth

Three areas of research were of primary concern in the studies of young children (ages 5-12): commercial watching behavior, effects on cognitive development, and effects on interpersonal behavior.

Commercial watching is a necessary condition for learning from commercials; among young children, such learning presumably affects more complex learning during adolescence and early adulthood, when cognitive orientations and skills relevant to behavior as consumers are acquired.

Our study of "commercial watching" focuses on the degree of children's attention to commercials and on the incidence of alternative or coterminous activities during commercial exposure. We also examine some determinants of watching behavior and short-term consequences of commercial watching. Our concern is with child characteristics, characteristics of television stimuli, and the viewing situation as determinants of commercial watching. We examine verbal comments about the objects advertised in commercials or about the commercials themselves as one kind of short-term consequence of commercial watching.

The second area of research with younger children is the relationship between responses to television advertising and stages of cognitive growth. Four aspects of cognitive development interest us: a) *cognitive-affective focus,* referring to the kind or quality of physical, emotional, or intellectual stimuli which are most likely to affect children; b) *mode of assimilation,* referring to the ways in which children recall and use the information they receive from television advertisements; c) *differentiation,* referring to the degree to which children can discriminate fantasy from fact, products advertised from the advertisements themselves, and elements of commercials, and d) *level of judgment,* referring to the stage of cognitive or ego development at which a child judges commercials, or is susceptible to commercial appeals.

The third area of concern is the effects of television advertising on interpersonal behavior—specifically, the extent to which children attempt to influence parental purchasing. One study reports data from mothers of young children—their perceptions of the frequency with which television commercials influence their children to want advertised products, and the extent to which they yield to children's purchase influence attempts.

Among adolescents, television advertising is one influence on the process of "consumer learning"—the process of developing attitudes, skills, and norms relevant to consumption behavior. We are concerned with the relative impact of television advertising on four aspects of "consumption behavior": attitudes toward advertising, materialistic attitudes, knowledge of commercials, and buying behavior. Additonally, we are interested in the motivations of adolescents to watch commercials and in the relationship of television advertising to intrafamily communication about consumption matters. Finally, data from adolescent samples are analyzed by race, to determine whether television advertising differentially affects black and white adolescents.

To summarize, while much mass communication research is concerned with the role of mass media in persuasion, the focus of this project is on learning—what children and adolescents learn from television advertising. Moreover, the project attempts to relate television advertising to different kinds of learning which are relevant to different age groups. Among young children, we examine actual commercial watching behavior as well as relatively simple aspects of learning from commercials. Among adolescents, television advertising is considered one input to more complex processes of acquiring skills and attitudes relevant to consumption behavior.

METHODOLOGY

Three surveys and one clinical investigation were conducted during the course of this research project. The initial survey was conducted in April 1970 among 1,094 junior and senior high school students in the Prince Georges County, Maryland, school district. During the following autumn, a subsequent supplementary survey was conducted in school districts with high proportions of black students. The purpose of this initial survey was to gather basic information about adolescent attitudes toward advertising and toward commercials, the nature and extent of intrafamily communication about consumption matters, the effects of commercials on buying behavior, materialistic attitudes, and so forth.

A second survey was conducted in spring 1971 in the Boston area. For this study 134 mothers of 5-12 year old children were asked to observe one of their children watching television—and commercials—for six to ten hours during the child's normal viewing times over a ten-day period.

A third survey involved mail questionnaires completed by each of these 134 mothers. The objective of this study was to relate mothers' perceptions of the influence of commercials on their children to such interpersonal behavior as the child's purchase influence attempts and parental yielding to these requests.

Finally, exploratory research was conducted with four groups of five children each, drawn from kindergarten, second, fourth, and sixth grades in a Boston area school. While sample size in this clinical examination was quite limited, the objective was to suggest some effects of commercials on young viewers, and to relate these effects to stages of cognitive development.

Table 1 summarizes the five major study areas, the objectives for each area, and the methodology employed.

It should be emphasized that this research relies upon cross-sectional rather than longitudinal data. Thus our research concerns age-related

Table 1: Summary of studies, objectives, methodology in "effects of television advertising on youth" project

Study	Objectives	Methodology
A Cognitive Developmental Study of Children's Reactions to Television Advertising (Blatt, Spencer, and Ward)	To gather exploratory data concerning effects of commercials on young children and to relate effects to stages of cognitive development	Four groups of five children each were exposed to a videotape recording of Saturday morning programming and commercials. The following day group interviews were conducted. Age groups were 5—12, with children drawn from kindergarten, second, fourth, and sixth grades.
Children's Attention to Television Advertising (Ward, Levinson, and Wackman)	To examine determinants and short-term consequences of commercial watching; to examine degree of children's attention to commercials, and the incidence of alternative or coterminus activities during commercial exposure	134 mothers of 5—12 year old children were recruited from service clubs sampled from various socio-economic areas of the Boston metropolitan area. The mothers were trained in the use of code sheets for unobtrusively observing one of their children watching television. Observation periods were scheduled according to a sample of each child's estimated normal viewing behavior. Mothers observed for a minimum of six and a maximum of ten hours and were paid $10 each for their participation. Data from 65 mothers were coded in 3 age groups: 5—7 (n=2a), 8—10 (n=18) and 11—12 (n=18). Data are based on a sample of one-fifth of the 6,465 commercials watched by 65 children during the 10-day period.
Television Advertising and Intra-Family Influences: Children's Purchase Influence Attempts and Parental Yielding (Ward and Wackman)	To examine effects of commercials on children's attempts to influence mother's purchases; mother's responses to influence attempts; perceived frequency of commercial influence on children[4]	The 134 mothers participating in the watching behavior study received a self-administered questionnaire. Analyses are based on 109 returned instruments (81% of the mothers)

Continued

Table 1: Continued

Study	Objectives	Methodology
Adolescent Attitudes Toward Television Advertising (Ward and Robertson)	To examine the nature of attitudes toward television advertising among adolescents from different racial and socio-economic backgrounds; to examine predictors of attitudes, and to relate attitudes to other variables, e.g., intra-family communication, television use, aspirations, etc.	Self-administered questionnaires were completed by 1,094 adolescents (8th—12th grades) in randomly-selected classrooms in the Prince Georges County, Maryland, school district. A subsequent survey gathered data from adolescents in predominantly Black schools
Family and Media Influences on Adolescent Consumer Learning (Ward and Wackman)	To analyze the influence of demographic variables, motivations for watching commercials, quantity of media use, and intra-family communication, on four aspects of acquiring consumer skills and values: recall of advertising content, attitudes toward commercials, materialistic attitudes, and buying behavior	Subsequent analysis of Prince Georges County survey data, and supplementary data from primarily black districts.

differences but not age-related change. Taken as a whole, the data suggest different effects of commercials on children in different age groups, but they are not meant to suggest an explicit developmental process. The division of studies into those concerning young children (ages 5-12) and those concerning adolescents (ages 13-18) is arbitrary.

FINDINGS: RESEARCH AMONG PRETEËNAGE CHILDREN

Children's commercial watching behavior

The study by Ward, Levinson, and Wackman examined two aspects of commercial watching behavior: degree of attention and types of behavior at commercial onset, and degree of attention and types of behavior during commercial exposure. Four determinants of watching behavior were examined: (1) personal characteristics (age and sex); (2) characteristics of the viewing situation (time and day of viewing, who child views with); (3) characteristics of the viewing situation (duration of commercial, position of commercial, object of commercial—product category); (4) prior watching behavior (degree of attention to program just before commercial appears).

Analysis of marginal data indicates that children pay full attention to prior programming about 65 percent of the viewing time, although somewhat higher incidence of full attention is found among younger children (under ten years old). Children make some verbal response at commercial outset about 25 percent of the time. When such a response is made, it is most likely to be favorable ("here's a good commercial," "now watch this," etc.).

Across all product categories, times of viewing, number of companions, and so on, all children exhibit a drop in attention during commercial exposure from attention to prior programming. The drop in full attention is least for the youngest children (5-7 years old) and greatest for the oldest children (11-12 years old). Talking with others during commercial exposure—either a result of or an alternative to commercial watching—occurs during about 25 percent of the commercial exposures for 11-12-year-olds, somewhat less for younger children.

Comments about the commercial and/or the product are made after about 20 percent of commercial exposures. When comments are made, they are most likely to be made by younger children (under ten), and they are more likely to be about the product advertised than about the commercial. The incidence of comments about the commercial itself increases with age: when young children make comments after a commercial, they are most likely to be about the product advertised; among older children, about half the comments are about the product, and about half are about the commercial.

No significant sex differences were observed, although girls in the oldest age group talked during 28 percent of the commercial exposures, while boys in the same age group talked during 20 percent.

The data are divided into two groups (that for 5-8-year olds and that for 9-12-year-olds) for analysis of time of viewing as a determinant of commercial watching behavior. Older children watch less Saturday morning television; when they do, they pay less attention to prior programming and less attention during commercial exposure than do young children. They are also more likely to make negative comments at commercial onset than at other viewing times, and are more likely to make such comments than the younger children.

Another aspect of the viewing situation is the other people who may be watching television with the child. Viewing with siblings and with father ("family viewing") increased with age (the mother was always present, *de facto,* observing the child's behavior), but paying full attention to commercials during family viewing decreased with age; talking with others increased with age, suggesting that older children use the opportunity of commercial breaks for interpersonal communication with family members more than younger children do.

Characteristics of television stimuli are another class of determinants of commercial watching. One such characteristic is the length of the commercial. Regardless of commercial length, older children paid less attention to commercials than did younger children. Least "full" attention was paid to ten-second commercials. With the exception of the youngest age group, most attention was paid to 60-second commercials.

Another characteristic which may affect differential commercial watching is the position of a commercial within a "block" of commercials. While children in all age groups had similar (and high) prior attention to programming, attention level decreased more rapidly during a sequence of commercials for the oldest children.

Attention was greatest to commercials at the beginning of programs for all three age groups. Full attention among older children decreased as the program progressed, while younger children showed little differences in full attention regardless of the commercial's position in program context.

The product category of the advertising may also determine watching behavior. Advertisements for food products were *a priori* designated "relevant" to children. Advertisements for cleaning products, cosmetics, and patent medicines were considered less relevant. The drop in full attention to commercials for relevant products is roughly equivalent for the three age groups. However, for commercials in the "less relevant" product group, young children's attention actually increased slightly from prior attention to programming. As age increased, attention to the less relevant commercials decreased. It may be that children are so familiar with food products—through advertising exposure, direct consumption, and intrafamily influence attempts—that advertising for food products is actually less relevant than advertising for products associated with adult roles.

A final determinant of commercial watching behavior is the watching behavior of children just prior to commercial exposure. Among children paying full prior attention to programming, attention falls off during commercial exposure for all age groups. However, the drop in full attention is smallest for the 5-7-year-olds; the greatest drop occurs among the 11-12-year-olds. Older children were more likely to engage in other behaviors—getting up, talking, etc.—than younger children. Among children paying no attention or partial attention to prior programming, increases to full attention were observed during only 12 percent of commercial exposures, with slight age differences.

Reactions to television advertising and stages of cognitive development

In the exploratory study by Blatt, Spencer, and Ward, eight categories of responses to commercials were identified and related to stages of cognitive development: (1) *Reality*. Children in all age groups could identify the term "commercials," but kindergartern children exhibited confusion and judged the relationship between commercials and reality based on coincidental reasoning or affect. (2) *Purpose*. While kindergarten students exhibited no understanding of the purpose of commercials, second graders exhibited clear understanding that commercials are intended to sell goods, and fourth and sixth graders commented on techniques employed in constructing commercials. (3) *Discrimination between product and advertisement*. The youngest children do not discriminate between commercials and products advertised. Second graders exhibited some confusion, but fourth and sixth graders made a clear differentiation between commercials and actual products.

(4) *Classes of products recalled*. The youngest children spontaneously recalled food product advertisements, while second graders recalled advertising for products with which they could identify and which they could exhibit some competence in using (car games, dolls). Fourth graders frequently mentioned household cleaning products, but sixth graders exhibited no consistent pattern of recall according to product groups. They seem more likely to recall advertisements on the basis of message characteristics. (5) *Complexity of recall*. Recall of commercials became more multidimensional and complex with age. (6) *Significant others*. Older children tended to see parents and celebrities as significant others. Sixth graders tended to project themselves as significant others ("I'd probably try the product out first").

(7) *Perceived validity and credibility of advertisements.* Kindergarten students exhibited confusion, but second graders indicated concrete distrust of commercials, often based on experience with advertised products. Fourth graders exhibited mistrust for specific commercials and "tricky" elements of commercials; sixth graders exhibited global mistrust—except, if probed, of public service announcements. (8) *Affective response to commercials.* The youngest children showed some positive responses to the entertainment value of commercials; second graders had slightly negative associations, but these were not strongly felt; fourth graders exhibited distrust, but appeared to enjoy humor (especially slapstick and sadistic humor); sixth graders enjoyed humor but were generally contemptuous.

The data suggest that kindergarten children's memory of commercials, their reasoning about them, and their responses to them are concerned with concrete products—especially food products which relate to immediate impulsive needs. Second graders are primarily concerned with competence in sex roles, and their responses to classes of commercials reflect this orientation. Fourth grade children appear to be concerned with social relationships and the reactions of others to approved roles. Sixth grade children tend to evaluate advertisements on rational, "conscientious" bases.

Television advertising and intrafamily behavior

The study by Ward and Wackman is based on mail questionnaires returned from 109 of the 134 mothers recruited for the study of watching behavior. We were interested in relationships between frequency of children's purchase influence attempts for various products, mother's yielding to these attempts, and mother's perceivd influence of commercials in stimulating desires of children for specific products. Data were analyzed by the three age groups employed in the watching behavior study (5-7, 8-10, 11-12); however, observation data from that study have not been related to these data from mothers.

The data indicate that mothers feel commercials influence younger children more than older children, and they appear to gauge this influence by the frequency of purchase influence attempts for particular products. Although influence attempts may decrease with age, parental yielding to requests increases with age, probably reflecting the perceived increased competence of older children to make purchase decisions.

Aspects of parent-child conflict are related to influence attempts and yielding. The data suggest that influence attempts may be part of more general parent-child conflict problems; furthermore, mothers who restrict viewing are likely not to yield to purchase influence attempts. Finally, mothers' time spent watching television is positively related to influence attempts, yielding, and perceived influence, while recall of commercials is related to influence attempts and perceived influence. Mothers with positive attitudes toward advertising are more likely than mothers with negative attitudes to yield to influence attempts.

FINDINGS: RESEARCH AMONG ADOLESCENTS

Previous research indicates that patterns of media use change during adolescent years, from childhood years. Time spent with television generally decreases, and use of other media increases. Our general hypothesis was that adolescents would also respond to television advertising differently than would younger children. As we have seen, younger children may respond impulsively to commercials, and cynical attitudes toward commercials may develop by the time a child reaches second grade. Attention to commercials also appears to decrease with age.

While the development of cynical and negative attitudes toward television advertising should probably continue during adolescence, we should also expect commercials to become more relevant to teenagers, who are becoming increasingly active consumers of goods and services. Therefore, television advertising may be one input to more general processes of "consumer learning"—acquiring skills and values relating to consumption behavior. In the case of preteenage children, television commercials were related to intrafamily purchase influence attempts. Such second-order consequences probably also occur during adolescence, but we should also expect different consequences of advertising exposure among teenagers, since adolescents engage in consumption behavior directly. They have more available money than younger children, and they increasingly assume consumer roles.

The general model for our research with adolescents is described in Figure 2.

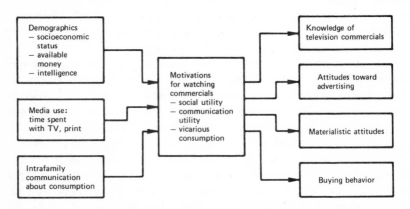

Figure 2: Major variables in studies of effects of television advertising on adolescents

Adolescent attitudes toward television advertising

One aspect of consumer learning is the development of attitudes toward advertising; the relationship of these attitudes with other aspects of learning and with behavior is important. In this case, "attitudes" refers both to specific affective attitudes toward television commercials and to more general attitudes toward the institution of television advertising.

In studies by Ward and Robertson and by Wackman, Reale, and Ward, adolescents were asked open-ended questions about the television advertising they felt was representative of the "best" and the "worst" on television, and their reasons for these attitudes. While there were slight differences between junior high and senior high school adolescents, the most liked categories of commercials were those for drug and patent medicines, automobile advertising, and soft drink advertising. The most liked category among black adolescents was advertising for food and gum products; otherwise, their rankings were parallel to those for white adolescents.

The adolescents were most favorable to those commercials seen as "funny" and/or "straightforward." There was some tendency for younger adolescents to cite humor as their primary reasons for liking and for older adolescents to cite commercials seen as "straightforward." Both black and white adolescents ranked their reasons for liking commercials similarly.

Cigarette advertising was listed as the most disliked category of commercials. Of those adolescents answering the question, over 20 percent cited this product category as "worst" advertising. While the data indicate that white adolescents were more critical of cigarette advertising than blacks, this result may reflect the fact that data from black adolescents were gathered during fall 1971, shortly before cigarette advertising was banned from television. The second category of disliked advertising was that for deodorants and cosmetics.

More than one-third of the adolescents criticized commercials because they were "stupid. . .insult intelligence." The second most salient reason was that commercials were seen as "false" or "hypocritical." Interestingly, junior high and senior high school adolescents are alike in their ranking of reasons for disliking commercials, but senior high adolescents also cite stylistic reasons (e.g. "bad acting") more than junior high adolescents do. Black students are somewhat more likely than white students to cite stylistic characteristics as a reason for disliking commercials.

One puzzling aspect of these attitudinal data is that about one-third of the adolescents did not respond to the questions on liked and disliked commercials. This nonresponse rate was greater than for other open-ended items in the questionnaire, and the rate was higher among black adolescents than among white adolescents. This may suggest that television commercials are simply not very salient for adolescents.

For purposes of analysis, a scale of attitudes toward the institution of television advertising was developed, based on four-point questionnaire items. About three-quarters of the sample agreed with the statement, "Most commercials are too long," and almost 70 percent agreed that "most commercials are in bad taste and are very annoying." Only about one-third of the adolescents agreed that "TV commercials tell the truth."

The higher an adolescent's social class, the more negative were his attitudes toward television advertising. However, social class was not a particularly important predictor of other aspects of consumer learning, nor was it important in analyses comparing black and white adolescents.

Among white adolescents, watching greater amounts of television was associated with positive attitudes toward television advertising, at least among middle and upper social classes.

Adolescents from families in which consumption matters are discussed relatively frequently—in which parents and teenagers seek and give advice about consumption of goods and services, are more likely to have positive attitudes toward advertising than are adolescents from families in which consumption matters are discussed less frequently. However, students who perceive that their parents want them to achieve higher socioeconomic status than the family's present status—adolescents who perceive that their parents have high expectations for them— are no more likely to have positive attitudes toward television advertising than adolescents who do not have this perception. Similarly, there are no differences in attitudes between adolescents who hold high occupation expectations for themselves and those who hold less ambitious occupational goals. It might be expected that television advertising, which often portrays success in interpersonal and occupational roles, might be more appealing to adolescents from environments in which striving for success in such roles is important. This does not seem to be the case, however, at least in terms of perceived parental expectations and the adolescent's own expectations.

A mild relationship was found, however, between attitudes toward advertising and "materialism." "Materialism" was defined as an orientation emphasizing material possessions and money for personal happiness and social progress. Adolescents scoring high in materialism had more positive attitudes than less materialistic adolescents.

Consumer learning

During adolescence, most young people begin buying goods and services for themselves. Television advertising often portrays buying behavior, and attractive life styles are presented as the consequence of buying certain products or services. Thus, we should expect adolescents to use television advertising as one input to learning values and skills as consumers.

Four aspects of such consumer learning were analyzed in the present studies: *recall of commercial content* is the measure of knowledge of advertised products; *attitudes toward commercials* and *"materialistic" attitudes* are measures of more complex cognitive development; self-reported influence of commercials on specific product purchases is the measure of behavior.

We expected that various demographic indices would be related to these criterion variables. Our interest was in demographic characteristics, of adolescents which, in effect, "locate" the adolescent in the social environment, such as socioeconomic status, intelligence, and available money. Within demographically defined groups, however, we expected that adolescent consumer learning would vary depending on the relative presence or absence of intrafamily communication about consumption matters and on the adolescent's media use. Our concern was with two dimensions of media use: amount of print and television use, and motivations or reasons adolescents watch television commercials. The specific "reasons for watching commercials" in the study by Ward and Wackman were derived from student-written essays on the subject. Content analysis of these essays revealed three major dimensions of reasons adolescents watch commercials. The major dimension was "social utility"—watching commercials in order to gain information about the "social significance" of products or brands and association of advertised objects with social roles and life styles.

A second major reason for watching commercials was "communication utility"—watching in order to provide a basis for later interpersonal communication. Finally, the teenagers indicated that they watch for "vicarious consumption" reasons—as a means of vicarious participation in desired life styles or as a means of vicarious association with attractive others.

These three clusters of motivations for watching commercials were measured by a series of questionnaire items. While most adolescents indicated that they did not usually watch commercials for these reasons, our interest was in the relative incidence of watching for these reasons among black and white adolescents and in the relative influence of these reasons on the four aspects of consumer learning.

Black adolescents indicated that they watched for social utility, communication utility, and vicarious consumption reasons more than white adolescents. Black adolescents also watched television and listened to the radio more than whites; white adolescents spent more time with print media.

No differences were observed between the white and black adolescents in recall of commercials and in attitudes toward advertising. However, blacks were more materialistic than white adolescents, and they indicated that television advertising influenced their purchases more than white adolescents.

Further analyses of consumer learning processes were conducted for white adolescents only, because we had insufficient data from black adolescents. We were interested in differences in consumer learning processes between younger and older adolescents. The data indicated no differences between the two groups on the dependent variables, but some differences between younger and older adolescents on the communication variables. Thus, younger and older adolescents appear to be at the same level of consumer learning, but processes of learning differ for the two groups.

The four aspects of consumer learning appear generally to be independent of each other, and relationships between them do not appear to change over time; intercorrelations among the dependent variables are essentially zero, for both younger and older adolescents.

A step-up regression analysis was used to analyze the relationships between the independent variables and the four measures of consumer learning. The results may be summarized as follows:

(1) *Recall.* Recall of commercial themes and slogans represents a fundamental aspect of consumer learning. For younger and older adolescents, intelligence was the best predictor of recall. The fact that media exposure is a less certain correlate is not surprising, considering the redundancy of commercial messages. Even minimal exposure to media insures commercial exposure; but storing and retrieving their content seems mainly a function of intelligence—at least, as measured by tests of "intelligence."

(2) *Attitudes toward commercials.* Markedly different processes seem to be involved in learning general attitudes toward commercials among younger and older adolescents. Social utility reasons for watching commercials and time spent viewing account for much of the variance for younger viewers. By contrast, vicarious consumption reasons and intrafamily communication about consumption matters are important variables for older adolescents.

(3) *Materialism.* Another measure of more complex kinds of consumer learning is "materialism"—an orientation which views material goods and money as important for personal happiness and social progress. For both younger and older adolescents, social utility and vicarious consumption reasons for watching commercials account for much of the variance. However, for younger adolescents, a third factor was available money; for older adolescents, a third factor was intelligence, which was negatively related to materialism.

(4) *Effects of commercials on buying behavior.* Our measure of effects of television advertising on buying behavior is a self-report item which

asks whether the adolescent feels he has been directly influenced by television advertising in buying a specific product.

The data indicate that three variables are important predictors of this kind of learning for both younger and older adolescents: communication in the family about consumption, social utility reasons for viewing television commercials, and amount of exposure to magazines. In addition, for younger adolescents, a fourth variable is important—communicatory utility reasons for viewing commercials, which is negatively related to effects of advertisements on buying.

To summarize the research on consumer learning: the data suggest that television advertising is not a sufficient condition for buying—especially among older adolescents. Intrafamily communication about consumption intervenes between communication exposure and purchase. For younger adolescents, reasons for watching commercials are also important intervening variables between exposure and behavior. Specifically, the data suggest that:

(1) Different aspects of consumer learning are not well integrated among either younger or older adolescents;

(2) Different clusters of variables have effects on the different kinds of consumer learning examined in this study;

(3) For any particular kind of consumer learning, essentially the same cluster of variables affects that kind of learning for both younger and older adolescents. Therefore, even though younger adolescents are exposed to more commercial content, talk with parents more about consumer goods, and watch commercials more for social utility and communicatory utility reasons, the predictive power of these variables is essentially the same in both groups of adolescents.

Three major processes seem to be involved in the different kinds of consumer learning:

The learning of advertising slogans seems to be mainly a function of the *intelligence* of the adolescent.

The learning of more cognitive orientations, such as attitudes toward television advertising and a materialistic orientation, seems to be mainly a function of the adolescent's *reasons for viewing* commercials. Thus, these cognitive orientations develop as a function of the adolescent's television behavior but not simply of exposure time. Rather, the orientations develop as a function of the uses the adolescent makes of commercial content, several of which are basically social uses.

A third process which seems to be involved in the formation of purchasing patterns is clearly an overt social process. In this process, *communication with parents* about advertising, consumer goods, and consumption processes seems to be an important variable intervening between exposure to advertising and the purchase of consumer goods.

SUMMARY

Since the overall objective of this program of research was to bring exploratory data to bear on a broad range of television advertising's effects, no attempt is made to integrate the various findings presented in each of the discrete studies which comprise this research project. We hope that these studies will help make such conceptual integration possible, so that we may have more complete, explicit, and integrated knowledge of televisision advertising's effects on children and adolescents.

Five areas of this research seem particularly important, both in terms of policy implications and in terms of promise for future research possibilities:

1. *Young children's reactions to television advertising reflect stages in cognitive development.* While our data in this area are quite tentative due to several methodological limitations, it appears that responses to television advertising become increasingly differentiated and complex with age. Children progress from confused perceptions of commercials —not discriminating between program and commercials, nor between advertisements and products—to the beginnings of cynicism about advertising and perceptions of the intent of advertising by second and fourth grade. By sixth grade, we find that children have relatively well-developed attitudes toward commercials; they respond to them in terms of the message and evaluate advertised objects in terms of their relevance to them.

2. *"Selectivity" in viewing commercials increases with age, but processes of commercial watching are highly complex.* It does not appear that young children automatically "tune in" to commercials, as one popular criticism of television advertising suggests. Generally, paying of full attention to commercials decreases with age, although the viewing situation, characteristics of television stimuli, attention to prior programming, and personal characteristics all affect children's attention to commercials.

Just as previous research suggests that adults selectively attend to programming and commercials, the same patterns are observed with pre-teenage children. Generally, all children seem to pay more attention to programming than adults, but the drop in attention during commercials is not as great as for adults. The drop in attention is greatest for older children, least for youngest children.

Perhaps the central importance of the research concerning commercial watching behavior is that the data may be related to consequences of watching in other aspects of children's lives—i.e., to learning from commercials, intrafamily influence, and attitudinal development.

3. *Mother's perceive that television advertising influences their children, and they estimate commercials' effects by the frequency with*

which their children attempt to influence purchases. While most of our research concerns relatively direct effects of television advertising on children's behavior and cognitive development, the study of intrafamily influence is concerned with second-order consequences of television advertising—namely, do television advertisements stimulate desires of children for advertised goods, and do young children then engage in behavior directed at acquiring these goods? Direct measurement of such effects is impossible, but we asked mothers to estimate the frequency with which commercials influenced their children to want specific advertised products. The mothers had no straightforward, independent measure of commercial's effects, so their estimates of advertising's influence were based on purchase influence attempts. The mothers appeared to reason that, the more their children asked for products which were advertised on television, the more advertising was influencing their children. (Interestingly, however, even the placing of relatively stringent restrictions on viewing did not seem to inhibit purchase influence attempts, suggesting that television advertising was not the sole cause of such interpersonal influence attempts.)

4. *Adolescents hold negative attitudes toward television advertising, and there are only slight differences between black and white adolescents in attitudes.* Generally, adolescents are quite cynical about television advertising, feeling that commercials are not straightforward and are often hypocritical. Cigarette advertising—still on the air at the time of the research—was especially disliked, while advertising for drug and patent medicines was particularly liked. (Most adolescents who cited drug and patent medicine advertising as most liked advertising seem to like it because it was seen as funny. Thus, the data may reflect the widespread popularity of one product in this category which was advertised in quite humorous ways.)

It is interesting to note that most adolescents like advertising for stylistic, entertainment reasons—not because commercials are seen as helpful or informative. On the other hand, the bases of their negative attitudes are along dimensions of trust, truthfulness, straightforwardness.

5. *Adolescents acquire consumer attitudes and skills from television advertising. Such consumer learning occurs as a function of the quality of television advertising use, more than the quantity of media use.* Understanding the broad effects of television advertising among adolescents requires an understanding of the context of advertising communication for adolescents. This context reflects the adolescent's growing interest in adult roles and activities and the relevance of television advertising to associated consumer roles and activities. Our interest was in knowledge of advertising, general cognitive orientations (attitudes toward advertising and materialistic attitudes), and buying behavior as aspects of consumer attitudes and skills.

It appears that the most important predictors of the development of these aspects of consumer behavior are the motivations of adolescents for watching television commercials. Our data suggest that, beyond verbal attitudes toward television advertising (which are generally negative and cynical), adolescents do learn from television advertising, and this learning is related to developing skills and attitudes relevant to consumer roles.

FUTURE RESEARCH

Future research will require further conceptual development and refinement as well as further empirical work. The conceptual framework shown in Figure 1 has guided the present research, but some of the concepts in this framework are too abstract and general for guiding empirical research "consumer behavior," "alternatives to commercial watching," etc. Thus, a first step in future research will be the development of lower-level, more specific concepts to describe buying behavior, reactions to advertisements, etc. Conceptual development in the areas of socialization and personality-cognition development should be especially useful—as indeed they already have been in guiding this research. For example, Brim's conceptualization of role development has been useful in conceptualizing "consumer role learning," and Piaget's and Erikson's conceptualizations of stages of cognitive development and personality development have been useful in guiding our clinical research on stages of development in children's reactions to television commercials. Besides concept development, further research will need to specify theoretical linkages between concepts, building upon and supplementing the relationships already found in the present research.

At the same time, empirical research to develop adequate measures of these concepts must be carried out. For example, standardized measures of the dimensions of reactions to ads should be developed and administered to larger samples of children, so that baseline estimates of stages of development in reactions to ads can be made. Measures which will tap the several dimensions of buying behavior should be developed; in fact, a start has been made with two questionnaires which have been administered in Ann Arbor, Michigan, and in the Boston area.

Furthermore, research is needed to fill in gaps in the present research. Some of this research will simply involve analysis of data already collected—for example, analysis of the relation between children's watching behavior and purchase influence attempts. By collecting more data from the children in the watching behavior study, we can analyze the relation between attitudes toward advertising, purchase behavior, and watching behavior to determine long-term consequences of differences in children's commercial watching behavior.

Research is also needed to clarify some of the conflicts in the present data. Our research on adolescents indicates that by the seventh grade, adolescent attitudes toward advertising are quite negative, and that these attitudes do not change markedly through junior and senior high schools. The watching behavior study indicated that negative reactions to commercials occur frequently among 11- and 12-year-olds, but not among younger children. On the other hand, the clinical study indicated that most fourth graders (8-10-year-olds) were quite negative toward advertising, and that some second graders (6-8-year-olds) were rather negative toward commercials because of their experiences with products advertised. Research is needed to determine when these negative attitudes begin to develop and what variables in the child's media behavior, interpersonal behavior, cognitive development, etc., are related to this development.

Finally, subsequent research must fulfill two methodological requirements: (a) In order to investigate earlier development in watching behavior and reactions to advertising, sampling must include children younger than those studied in the present research, those under five years old. (b) Cross-sectional research is useful for identifying important variables and for determining age group differences on these variables, but longitudinal research is necessary to investigate developmental phases and trends.

A Cognitive Development Study of Children's Reactions to Television Advertising

Joan Blatt, Lyle Spencer, and Scott Ward

The purpose of the present investigation was to observe and attempt to identify cognitive developmental trends in children's perceptions, explanations, and judgments of the content and purpose of television advertisements.

The investigative approach used by the authors was Jean Piaget's "clinical examination and critical method" (Piaget, 1965). In its simplest form, Piaget's method consists of asking children direct questions about their perceptions and explanations of the existence of things and feelings; of careful clinical "probing" to determine the precise basis of a child's reasoning; and then of categorization of these "reasonings."

Cognitive developmental theorists assume that all children progress through discrete stages of perception and cognition. Lower stages of reasoning are more concrete, literal, and undifferentiated; higher stages are more complex, involve greater degrees of "abstract thinking" in symbol recognition and analysis, and in general show more differentiation and integration of perception and cognition. For example, children universally mature through the following stages in their conception of life (responses to the question: "what is alive?"): stage one—"everything is alive;" stage two—"everything that moves is alive (e.g., bicycle);" stage three—"only things which move by themselves (are capable of spontaneous movement) are alive" (e.g., a car); stage four—"only plants and animals are alive (for various scientific reasons)." Similarly, children in every culture have been found to go through the following stages in their understanding of dreams: stage one—dreams are "real," come from outside the self, and remain external; stage two—dreams are caused by (arise within) the self, but remain external and "real"; stage three—dreams are of internal origin, take place internally, and are "not real." In each example, it can be seen that children progressively refine their conceptions of the reality, locus, purpose, and explanatory reasoning for the objective or subjective occurrences they perceive.

The investigators hypothesized that, in their perceptions and judgments about television commercials, children would demonstrate similar developmental trends to those Piaget and others have identified in their assessments of children's understanding of physical realities. These trends have þeen mentioned, but not explicitly developed, by several studies in the literature. Schramm, Lyle, and Parker (1961) have noted that television appears "real" to young children (e.g. there are "real little people" inside the box), and Thompson (1959) has shown that the ability to discriminate reality increases with age and viewing experience. Wells (1965, 1966) notes that young children have difficulty in discriminating and evaluating the advertisement as separate from the product being advertised. McNeal (1964) found that preteenage children make increasing and increasingly negative affective and credibility judgments about television commercials as they grow older.

Numerous researchers in human development have further recognized that children progress through various stages of affective concern and cognitive—judgmental reasoning. Ericson (1950, 1968) has described eight stages of development during the human life cycle: (1) basic trust (concern with basic oral needs), (2) autonomy (concern with control over one's own body), (3) initiative (concern with personal expression and sex role identity), (4) industry (concern with competence and peer cooperation), (5) identity (concern with stable and positive self image), (6) intimacy (concern with love and finding a mate), (7) generativity (concern with one's life's work), and (8) integrity (a final judgment on the work of one's life).

Loevinger and Wessler (1970) have described five stages of ego development: (1) impulsive/self-protective (concern with need satisfaction), (2) opportunistic (hedonistic concern with getting one's own way), (3) conformist (concern with social approval and role competency), (4) conscientious (concern with duty and purpose), and (5) integrated (concern with self-actualization).

Kohlberg (1968), expanding on early work of Piaget, has identified six universal stages of (cognitive-judgmental) reasoning in moral situations: (1) decisions made on the basis of deference to superior authority and avoidance of punishment (what is right is what a superior tells you to do, what is wrong what you get punished for); (2) decisions made on the basis of hedonistic self-interest (what is right is what gets you what you want); (3) decisions made on the basis of conformity and social approval (what is right is what others are doing, what society considers "nice"); (4) decisions made on the basis of enduring rules of law (what is right is what is decreed by the established order of society); (5) decisions made on the basis of social utility (what is right is what is best for all men, the democratic majority), and (6) decisions made on higher moral principles (e.g., the sanctity of life).

Elements of these affective and judgmental stage conceptions would be expected to have relevance for the responses of children to television advertising. Small children might be expected to respond more to concrete, "basic need," "hedonistic," and "authoritarian" themes ("buy this toy because it's fun for you"; an "authoritarian" announcer "ordering" a child to "tell your mother to buy this every time you see it in the store").

Older children might be expected to respond more to symbolic, competency, mastery, sex-role identificatory and conformist themes ("don't be left out, get this toy—all the boys are getting them" or "this cosmetic will make you beautiful and popular"). More mature children would be expected to respond to more rational, "conscientious" themes, those that deal with the factual characteristics of products or with their social utility.

METHODOLOGY

Blatt interviewed four groups of five children each from kindergarten, second, fourth, and sixth grade classes at the Lawrence Public School in Brookline, Massachusetts. While an attempt was made to choose groups of children with different racial, socioeconomic, and intellectual characteristics, the subjects were primarily white, middle-class, and slightly above average in intelligence and verbal ability.

The day before the interview, each group of children was shown an hour-long videotape of typical "Satuday morning" children's television programming. This tape included a cartoon show, *Sabrina and the Groovy Goolies* (a "fantasy" offering), *Joesie in the Know* (a factual "news" or "reality" offering describing a fishing operation for king crabs off Alaska), and approximately fifteen commercials. Most of the commercials presented were for food and toy products; one was a "public service" message for the Boy Scouts.

On the day of the interview, the groups of children were taken from their classes and questioned for one hour. The interview was conducted in the "open-ended, group discussion" format: children were asked specific questions, allowed to discuss one another's responses, encouraged to "make up and act out" a television advertisement of their own, and presented with and then questioned about a moral dilemma. The questions used were designed to elicit responses that would indicate the perceived reality, purpose, content discrimination, affective reaction, credibility, and level of judgmental reasoning (or ego functioning) characteristic of each grade level.

Due to the "exploratory" format of the interviews, the order and working of the questions varied, but each group was presented with the following questions:

1. "What did you see yesterday?" The purpose of this question was to determine which (if any) commercials children would spontaneously recall, and the degree to which they were able to differentiate commercials from cartoons (fantasy) and news or factual programs (reality).

2. "What is a TV commercial you like? Dislike? Describe it in detail. What does it say? Why do you like/dislike it?" This question attempted to elicit the detail with which children remembered commercials, whether they could distinguish products from commercials and the basis on which this discrimination was made, their affective reactions to commercials and the reasons for this reaction.

3. "What is something you want that you saw in a commercial? Don't want? Describe in detail. Why do (or don't) you want it?" This question attempted to elicit responses which would indicate the effectiveness of commercials and the "reasons" for this effectiveness or lack of it; analysis of these "reasons" provided data for determining level of ego and developmental judgment. Responses to this question also provided data about the degree to which advertisements were differentiated from products advertised.

4. "Do you know what a television commercial is? What are they for? What are television programs for? Who makes TV commercials? TV programs? Why?" This question probed children's understanding of the purpose and source (hence reality and credibility) of commercials and programs, and the degree to which these are differentiated.

5. "Do TV commercials (programs) always tell the truth? Why or why not? How do you know?" This question further probed the children's judgment about the purpose and credibility of commercials.

6. "If you had to sell (another child in the group) a product how would you do it? Make up a commercial." (Ask response of the viewer. Did he/she like it or dislike it? Why?) How could it have been better? (Ask actor for reasons for choice, format, content, etc. of "commercial"?) This question was designed to provide children with an alternative active, "role playing" method of communicating their responses in each of the issue areas probed by the preceding questions: origin, reality, purpose, affective response, level of discrimination and judgment.

Group interviews were taped and transcribed. Transcript data were organized by a "content analysis" procedure which attempted to identify the model or "stage" response for each age group in nine categories: (1) the perceived reality of television commercials; (2) their perceived purpose; (3) the degree of discrimination between the advertisement and the product advertised; (4) classes of products and/or advertisements recalled; (5) complexity of recall; (6) significant others responded to in the commercial; (7) perceived validity and credibility of advertisements; (8) affective response to commercials; and (9) cognitive-affective (ego level) basis of response to commercials. These conceptual categories were derived empirically from inspection of the data; while not exhaustive, they appear to capture most of the meaningful information in the transcripts, constitute dimensions on which clear cognitive developmental trend progressions take place, and provide a framework for preliminary theory construction.

FINDINGS

Findings in each conceptual category consist of summary or "stage" descriptions which appear to be applicable to children in a given grade level group ("K" stands for the kindergarten group, "2G" for the second graders, "4G" for the fourth graders, and "6G" for the sixth graders). All examples for graded summary descriptions are taken from the transcript of the interview of that grade level group.

Reality

The "reality" category refers to children's judgments about "what a commercial is" and "how real they are" compared with cartoon (fantasy) and news or documentary (reality) programs. A child's basis of cognitive reasoning can be "parataxic" (coincidental or associative) or "syntaxic" (logical, causal or purposive); both the discrimination and the basis of discrimination are important in judgments about reality. For example, kindergarten children reason that news programs are "more real" than advertisements or cartoons, but they explain this perception by saying news is more real because "it tells about the weather" or "it always comes at the same time." Older children are better able to make this distinction on the basis of specific differences in information presented or in purpose. In the examples below, the perceived "reality" of commercials is compared directly with that for cartoons and news/documentary programs.

K: *reality confused, judgment based on coincidental reasoning or affect*

> *Example:* (Q: What is difference between news and commercials?) "I like TV commercials much better" (affect). "The news tells weather and the news is at 7:00 (coincidental).(Q: How do you know one (crab) is real and one (cartoon) isn't?) "It looks not real." "It had too many legs" (confusion). "Commercials are more funny." (affect).

2G: *reality confused; judgment based on reality of object or person portrayed (similarity to objects, persons, or events in the real world); perceived "importance", factualness, or confirmation by outside evidence*

> *Examples:* (Q: Does the news have real people on it?) "Yes: They say real things. The news tells us what is happening in different places and what the temperature is and stuff and commercials they just tell us one thing like the doll or racing cars." (Q: Is Joesie [cartoon character drawn to look like real person who introduces a "news" documentary film with real people in it] real?) "I think she is because I saw... the program showed

her with other (real) people." "At first I didn't know and I thought she was just pretend, but then I read the paperback book." (Q: Is Sabrina (a cartoon witch) real? "No—I don't think there are such things as witches."

4G and 6G: *reality understood; no questions*

Purpose

The "purpose" category refers to the perceived intent or "message" of commercials, and the reasoning children use in making this judgment.

K: *confused (some thought "information," others "didn't know"), semirecognition that ads were intended to sell*

Example: (Q: What are commercials for?) "If you want something, so you'll know about it. So people know how to buy things. So if somebody washes their clothes, they'll know what to use. They can watch what to use and buy it."

2G: *clear recognition that advertisements were intended to sell; semirecognition of advertisers' motives*

Example: (Q: What are ads for?) "To make you buy (product)." (Q: Why do they want you to buy it?) "So they can get more money and support the factories they have."

4G and 6G: *clear recognition of purpose of commercials, motives of advertisers, and emerging understanding of the techniques advertisers use in constructing commercials*

Example: 4G: "They put the free things inside so you'll buy it (cereal box)." (Q, referring to discussion of the staging, tricks" etc., advertisers use: Why do they do that?) "Because they want you to buy it," 6G; "To advertise the product, to make people buy it, to benefit them because then they get more money."

Discrimination between advertisement and product

This category refers to children's ability to differentiate the product being advertised from the advertising message itself. Small children tend not to be able to make this distinction; they may, for example, dislike an advertisement because they dislike or fear the product (e.g., razor blades). Older children tend to be able to make the distinction; they may clearly like a product while disliking the advertisement for it, or vice versa.

K: *no discrimination between advertisement and product advertised*
Example: (Q: What's an ad that you liked?) "I like the one about the space men." (Q: Why?) "It was Hostess Twinkies."

2G: *confusion (can like product but not like commercial, but confuse product advertised with advertisement)*

Example: (Q: Which commercials did you like?) "Well, I like the advertisements about model electric shavers...I don't like those about blades, that are called shavers, because they cut and I don't think its good to use those kinds of shavers."

4G and 6G: *clear differentiation between advertisement and product adver-*
              tised

              Examples: (4G) "I like that ad (for coffee), its so funny I just love
              it!" (Q: If you had to buy coffee, would you buy that brand?) "I
              don't know. . .I don't even drink coffee."

6G: "It (an Alka Selzer advertisement) was really funny. It was the best com-
       mercial." (Q: Would you buy it?) "I've tried it and it made me even sick-
       er."

Classes of products recalled

Transcript data revealed marked differences in the kinds of products
and/or advertisements spontaneously mentioned or recalled by each age
group. These differences appear to be relevant to the cognitive-affective
or "level of ego development" dimension (see below).

K: *food (oral) products:* Hostess Twinkies, Yodels, cereal (Dune Buggies),
      waffles

      Example: (Q: What do you buy with your allowance?) "Candy, gum (sev-
      eral responses)."

2G: *identificatory competence products* (sex-specific)
       Example:
       2G Boys: crazy car, miniature hockey, electric car set
       2G girls: Suntan Barbie, fashion doll, dancing doll

4G: *household (cleaning) products:* dishwashing liquid, SOS, Lemon Pledge,
       Windex Cleaner, nonpolluting soap, rug cleaner, Lysol spray

6G: *no consistent pattern; emphasis on "message," not products*

Complexity of recall

Children in different age groups differ in their ability to perceive and
recall details of commercials. Younger children may be able to absorb
and parrot back repetitious material like commercial jingles, but they are
unable to understand it on more than one or very few dimensions. (Piaget calls this phenomena "unidimensionality" and gives as an example
the little girl who, when told her friend was a Catholic, said, "Oh, I
thought she was French"; the child could only reason on one dimension
—religion or nationality—at one time). Factual details or "pieces" may
be perceived and remembered, but only "at random"; young children
are not capable of organizing their perceptions into a coherent understanding of the "message" of the commercial. Older children selectively
perceive and remember relevant details and organize these perceptions
into focused *gestalts* which convey an image or message.

K: *recall is unidimensional, concrete and descriptive—only one aspect or
      image from a commercial is remembered, not the commercial's "mes-
      sage"*

      Example: (Q: Describe the Hostess Twinkies commercial): "They all had
      space hats on." (Q: Describe the cigarette commercial) "There was a
      cowboy on a horse."

2G: *recall is multidimensional, concrete, and descriptive, but recaptured only
       with probing; memory of details is "random," without order or under-
       standing of their relevance to the advertising message.*

Example: (Q: What were those commercials like?) "...she moves her arms and legs and hands and hips." (Q: probe) "She looks like a fashion model..." (Q: probe) "There's a thing in back and you turn it and there are a whole bunch of buttons and then you pull a little thing and a little stock of hair (grows out)..." (Q: probe) "She has eyes that open and close, a nose of course..." (Q: probe) "and she has red hair and an orange dress and shoes."

4G: *recall is multidimensional concrete, descriptive, spontaneous and coherent, with understanding of relevance of details to ad message*

Example: "well, the commercial about SOS pads, they have all different kinds of cleaners in the frying pan, and SOS skates around and the whole frying pan gets clean and all the other cleaners are so embarrassed they just jump out..."

6G: *recall is a "gestalt," ad elements are remembered precisely and repeated in a way that conveys the advertising message; message is the focus of recall, not the elements*

Example: "Well there is this guy who is at a bar and Mr. Eddie Fitz of the concerned drinkers of Gansett in New England stands up and he talks about Gansett and says that there are rumors that they were probably going to make an imitation Gansett and call it something else trying to fool 'we the people' and he says 'if anyone asks you about Gansett tell them to buzz off. Sez who? Sez me, Eddie Fitz. And all of these guys are congratulating him at the end."

Significant others

This category refers to the human beings spontaneously recalled or cited by child viewers in their reactions to or evaluations of advertisements. The persons or category of individuals a child focuses on provides a cue to what he considers important to his own interests and self-image, and to whether his judgments tend to be "other-directed" (a less mature cognitive-development mode) or "inner-directed" (more mature).

K: *significant others are recalled concretely and are coincidental-associative, without real affective response*

Example: (recalling the cigarrette commercial): "There was a man on a horse."

2G: *significant others tend to be parents and family members, relations dealing with mastery, sex-role or identity, or authority themes*

Example: (discussing cigarette commercial): "My little sister would find my mother's cigarrettes...so we'd hide them and bring them to my mother and she couldn't find them so finally we made deals, and she got them back."

4G: *significant others tended to be celebrities or entertainers, social role models ("other-directed" basis for judgment)*

Examples: John Wayne, Bob Hope, Danny Thomas, Cary Grant

6G: *the significant others tended to be the viewer himself ("inner-directed basis for judgment)*

Example: (Q: What about other people?) "...I'd like my own opinion. That might be just their opinion." (Q: If they had A. J. Foyt or Mario Andretti advertise a race car, would you buy it?) "They probably pay him to say it...I'd try it out first."

Perceived validity and credibility of advertisements

This category refers to the degree to which children at each age level perceive television commercials as "true" and/or "trustworthy."

K: *confused—no real understanding of purpose, so no basis for judgment*

Examples: (Q: Do you think commercials always tell the truth?) "Noooooo!" However, with regard to commercials' information value: "So if someboy washes their clothes they'll know what to use" (implied belief).

2G: *distrust, but concrete, empirical distrust on the basis of things wrong with the product advertised, not the advertisement* (Commercials are only bad if the products they promote are bad, because a clear discrimination is not made between products and ads.)

Example: (Q: Why do you think that sometimes ads don't tell the truth?) "Sometimes you buy things and they all of a sudden fall apart or something happens to it." Reasons for mistrusting a commercial about a "Corgi Racing Car" that wins: "I think maybe they made the Corgi a little more powerful than it is or maybe the other car isn't as good."

4G: *specific mistrust and contempt for specific commercials (i.e. "this one, this one and this one are untrue"), recognition of specific "tricky" devices, but not generalized or global mistrust*

Example: (Q: Do commercials sometimes not tell the truth?) "YES!" (overwhelming consensus). "They always exaggerate it. . .You know, there's some special kind of clothes and so they pick this lady and get her all dressed up and they put all kinds of makeup and cover her with all kinds of stuff and they take her and she looks great and they put the dress on a regular housewife and she looks ugly. . .they just slop on a whole bunch of stuff and make her look good!"

6G: *global (generalized) mistrust: all commercials are bad (except, if probed, public service advertisements)*

Example: "They sort of brainwash kids and they go out and buy it and then they make a lot of money." "The things advertised aren't as good as the things that aren't. If they're really good, they don't need advertising." (Q: Are there any ads that are useful?) "Peace Corps, Vista, because their organizations help people."

Affective response to commercials

This category refers to the emotional reaction, likes or dislikes, expressed by children.

K: *positive response to entertainment value but no real affective discriminations*

Example: "I like it 'cause it's silly!"

2G: *slight negative association, but not strongly felt*

    Example: (bored) "Oh, that was just a commercial. . ."

4G: *distrust, but active enjoyment of (sadistic) humor*

    Example: "It's real funny. . .it was this new commercial for this cereal or something. . .it was really funny and this guy falls down and they make it hilarious. . .you know these three clowns like and they fool around and everything and its really hilarious." Example of a good "made up" advertisement: "Ri-Jong here at the Japanese Market. . .There is a stampede on. Everyone has a headache from the last atom bomb explosion and the stampede on Bayer Aspirin is now commencing. Better get some before they're all sold out!"

6G: *some enjoyment of humor, but general contemptuous rejection*

    Example: "It was really funny. It was the best commercial." "I don't like any commercials. It's a contest to see who can come up with the corniest and really dumbest commercial ever."

Cognitive-affective (ego level) basis of response

This category refers to the central theme or basis of response which appears to underlie the reactions of each age group to television commercials. The cognitive-affective and judgmental stage theories and categories of data findings discussed above suggests a summary "stage" framework for the present study.

K: *basic (oral) needs orientation:* children's memory, reasoning and responses at this level are primarily concerned with concrete products (especially food products) which relate to their immediate impulsive needs

2G: *competence (mastery) and sex-role identification orientation*

    children's spontaneous recall, reasoning and affective responses at this level are primarily concerned with competence in their sex roles: for girls, looks; for boys, power and strength, hence with products (for girls, dolls; for boys, racing cars, sports equipment, foods which make one "strong"), advertising themes and symbolism which appeal to these interests

    Examples: girl—"I want her (a doll) because she has long blond hair and is pretty;" boy—"It (a cereal) will make your muscles very strong. . .it will make you beat up a big beast."

4G: *conformity and social approval orientation:* children at this level appear to be most concerned with social relationships and the reactions of others to approved roles. (There is also a theme of "hedonistic/opportunistic" sadism and appreciation of exaggerated symbolic "fantasy material" on an affective level.) For example, in responding to a husband and wife coffee commercial, fourth grade children put emphasis on the importance of being a good wife.

6G: *conscientious and altruistic social utilitarian orientation:* children at this level tend to evaluate advertisements on rational, "conscientious" bases, examining them for factual truth and purpose, rejecting those which appeal to lower levels of reasoning or enjoyment (materialism, exaggerated claims, fantasy and symbolism), and responding (at least consciously) only to those with a "worthwhile" message

SUMMARY AND CONCLUSION

It should be emphasized that for a number of methodological reasons (a very small sample and "clinical" rather than quantitative content analysis, no interrater reliability standardizations, no frequency count in categories, and no statistical comparisons), the results of this study are highly tentative. However, the data do suggest "developmental" trends in the ways children perceive and react to television advertisements. These trends are summarized in Figure 1, in terms of four dimensions which appear to change with increasing maturity.

Cognitive-affective focus refers to the kind or qualify of physical, emotional, or intellectual stimuli which are most likely to appeal to (be perceived by, remembered by, or reacted to) members of advancing age groups. Young children tend to "focus" on concrete products which are relevant to their immediate physical impulses and needs, a cognitive-affective reaction which can be labeled "concrete/impulsive." More complex symbolic or explanatory presentations are probably irrelevant to young children, who are only interested in and capable of absorbing, remembering, and acting upon simple, specific messages for concrete products.

Older children tend to focus on affective and symbolic elements in advertisements—humor, emotional appeals, exaggeration, fantasy—a cognitive-affective response mode which can be labeled "affective/symbolic." (Most television commercials—e.g., such highly symbolic productions as the "knight on a white charger" advertisement for a detergent cleanser—seem to be constructed in this mode, and are apparently correctly targeted for the "ten-year-old mind" frequently claimed for the general television audience.) More mature viewers, as they develop powers of logical discrimination, appear to focus increasingly (at least consciously) on the thematic content of commercials, in an attempt to extract and test the validity of factual details of advertised products, and to judge both commercial and product in terms of objective utility and worth. This cognitive-affective focus is labeled "rational/thematic." Sixth graders—12-year-old children—already can be seen to tend toward this more "adult" mode of reasoning.

Mode of assimilation refers to the ways in which children recall and use the information they receive from television advertisements. These modes parallel the cognitive-affective focus dimensions. Small children tend to recall "imitatively" and "coincidentally"; they can "parrot" advertising messages and remember (usually one) element or image from an advertisement, but they do not really understand what the message means or how the elements recalled are related to the message or product. Older children remember advertisements on the basis of their "responses or associations" to the commercial stimulus—"it made me laugh" or "it had to do with growing up and being real strong." "Affec-

Category-Advertising Element	Concrete/impulsive → Affective/symbolic → Rational/thematic				Cognitive-Affective focus
	Imitative/coincidental → Responsive/associative → Content evaluative purposive				Mode of assimilation
	Undifferentiated → Specific → Abstracted-generalized				Differentiation
	Impulsive/submissive → Mastery → Hedonistic → Conformist → Conscientious Utilitarian				Level of judgment
	K	2G	4G	6G	Age group
Product	+	+	−	−	increasing age
Significant others	0	−	+	−	
Affect/symbolism (humor, etc.)	0	−	+	−	
Purpose	0	−	+	+	
Credibility/validity	0	−	+	+	
Thematic content/utility	0	0	−	+	

Increasing:
·complexity
·abstraction
·judgmental quality
of element

Cell symbols refer to "Importance" (frequency of mention) of category elements to each group in reacting to and evaluating advertising stimuli:

0 = no importance, or very low impt.
− = relatively low importance
+ = relatively high importance

Figure 1: Trends in cognitive-affective focus, mode of assimilation, differentiation, and judgment in children's reactions to television advertising

tive/symbolic" advertisements depend on such nonlogical "response/ associative" recall mechanisms for their impact (e.g., the frustrated housewife's intended association to the knight on the white charger clearly depends on nonrational associations to the advertisement). More mature viewers, better able to discriminate and understand the purpose of commercial elements, tend to remember on the basis of an advertisement's "content" and "purpose" ("it was about this. . .") and of their evaluative use of this information ("and I didn't believe it, because it exaggerated, and white knights don't have anything to do with cleaning floors").

Differentiation refers to the degree to which children can distinguish fantasy (cartoon characters perceived as "real") from fact, products advertised from advertisements themselves, and elements of commercials from an "undifferented" to an abstracted or "*gestalted*" integrated whole. Small children have difficulty distinguishing fantasy from reality and products from advertisements, and do not distinguish (or distinguish on only one dimension) elements of advertisements from their unified "whole," purpose, and meaning. Older children are capable of discriminating between reality "facts" and fantasy and exaggeration (although they tend to focus on fantastic emotional and symbolic elements), of judging products and their advertisement separately, and of breaking commercials up into their constituent elements. This differentiation lacks integrative accommodation (abstraction of purpose and judgment), however; children at this level remember "pieces" ("the ad had this, and this, and this in it"), but fail to grasp the "whole" ("the message was this"). More mature viewers are increasingly able to differentiate fully and reorganize their perceptions into fully formed *gestals* and abstracted generalizations about the nature and purpose of advertising stimuli.

Level of judgment refers to the stage of cognitive or ego development at which a child judges or is susceptible to appeal to a commercial message. These "levels" appear to parallel the stages of development suggested by developmental and psychosexual theorists. [See Erikson (1950, 1968), Loevinger (1970) and Kohlberg (1964).] Small children judge on the basis of their personal "impulsive" needs ("I want gum when I'm hungry") or "submissively" in deference to commands from real or cartoon announcer "authorities" ("*YOU* TELL *YOUR* MOTHER TO BUY YOU *THIS*"). Older children appear to respond to appeals resonant with their psychosocial stage of development—mastery (sex role identity and "hero worship"), to conformist (peer group popularity) themes, and to more sophisticated affective/symbolic appeals to hedonistic self-interest and slapstick, sadistic humor. More mature viewers tend to evaluate advertisements (and products) more on the basis of factual attributes, utility, and "conscientious" (duty, realistic functional and role requirement) concerns.

Figure A-1 illustrates these trends by weighing various advertising elements on the basis of their importance (frequency of mention, emphasis, or focus) to the age groups interviewed. As elements increase in complexity, abstraction, and judgmental relevance, their importance can be seen to decrease for younger children and increase for older children.

These developmental trends are not rigidly age-sequenced. Any less abstract element or mode of reasoning can occur at any later age, but it is likely to occur less frequently and be less important as a focus or basis for perception and judgment as individuals increase in maturity. (For example, adults may still experience "ad jingles running through their heads"—an imitative basis of recall, and a majority of the adult television audience may remain "hooked" by affective/symbolic themes approriate to the reasoning processes of ten-year-olds. If probed about the meaning of an advertisement or asked to make an actual purchase decision, however, these same adults are much more likely than are ten-year-olds to weigh the factual merits of a product.

The present study suggests numerous avenues for further research. It should be possible, for example, to develop a rating system for commercial messages (and their constituent elements) on the basis of the cogni- .

tive developmental level of judgment they appeal to and to develop norms for the differential affects of these appeals on various age groups.

A preliminary stage conception, suggested by data from the present study and a synthesis of the developmental ideas of Erikson, Loevinger and Kohlberg, might be:

Level 1: Impulsive, self-protective, and submissive. At this level, viewers respond principally to basic needs and fears, and tend to be most receptive to commercials which demand, threaten, or use "hard sell" commands to stimulate impulsive reactions or beliefs and behaviors adopted in deference to a "superior authority." Advertisements aimed at this level tend to be blunt, direct and concrete.

Level 2: Intentional self-interest. Viewers at this level are most susceptible to appeals to "hedonistic" personal desires, "mastery" and "power" themes which appeal to self-image, ideal role models, and sexual identity. Level 2 is differentiated from and "higher" than Level 1 in terms of cognitive growth because appeals assume individual autonomy and intentionality and an active, preference-seeking sense of self; at Level 1, individual reactions are pursued on a "stimulus-response" or "knee jerk" reflex basis. Advertisements at this level tend to be rich in "selfish" fantasy and symbolism.

Level 3: Conformity. Viewers at this level are most susceptible to "other directed" appeals—comparisons with others, themes based on individual needs for social approval, popularity, and status ("not being left out"). Level 3 is differentiated from and more developmentally advanced than Level 2 because thinking at this level recognizes the existence and influence of others in addition to the self. Level 3 advertisements employ symbolism, are more realistic and "social" in format and theme than those targeted to Level 2 thinking, but depend on emotional reactions rather than rational evaluation for their effects.

Level 4: Conscientiousness. At this level, viewers preferentially respond to appeals to duty, functional utility, and rational role requirements. Level 4 advertisements tend to be objective and factual (e.g., straight-forward industrial marketing: "Our company's new microwave tube delivers higher power at lower cost because it is designed to the following technical specifications.") This stage is "higher" in a cognitive-developmental sense than those which precede it because it requires greater differentiation of facts and rational evaluation.

Level 5: Social utilitarian, integrative, and self-actualizing. Viewers at this level respond preferentially to aesthetic, altruistic, moral social concern appeals and self-actualization: "Buy this and you will improve society while attaining your own highest potential" (e.g., advertisements based on ecological themes). Advertisements targeted at this level attempt to edify and appear as "art."

It is the authors' hypothesis that viewers are differentially sensitive and receptive to advertising appeals, and that this differential susceptibility parallels recognized stages in the maturation of cognitive affective, moral, and ego reasoning abilities. Small children are most likely to be susceptible to manipulation by "low level" appeals.

REFERENCES

Erikson, E. *Childhood and society*. New York: Norton, 1959.

Erikson, E. *Identity, youth, and crisis*. New York: Norton, 1968.

Flavell, J.H. *The developmental psychology of Jean Piaget*. Princeton, N.J.: D. Van Nostrand Co., 1963.

Kohlberg, L. The development of moral character and moral ideology. *Child Development*, 1964, 1, 415-24.

Kohlberg, L. Moral development. *International Encyclopedia of Social Sciences*, Vol. 10. Crowell Collier and Macmillan, 1968.

Loevinger, J. and Wessler, R. *Measuring ego development*. San Francisco: Jossey Bass, 1970.

McNeal, J.U. Children as consumers. No. 9, Marketing Study Series. Austin: University of Texas Bureau of Business Research, 1964.

Piaget, J. *The child's conception of the world*. Totowa, N.J.: Littlefield, Adams & Co., 1965.

Schramm, W., Lyle, J., and Parker, E. *Television in the lives of our children*. Stanford: Stanford University Press, 1961.

Wells, W. Communicating with children. *Journal of Advertising Research*, 1965, 5, 2-14.

Wells, W. Children as consumers. In Newman, J. (Ed.) *On knowing the consumer*. New York: Wiley & Sons, 1966.

Children's Perceptions, Explanations, and Judgments of Television Advertising: A Further Exploration

Scott Ward
Greg Reale
David Levinson

The purpose of the study reported here was to extend the data gathered in an initial, exploratory study of young children's perceptions, judgments and explanations of television advertising.[1] The initial study (Blatt, Spencer, and Ward, 1971) involved focused group interviews with children from kindergarten and second, fourth, and sixth grades. Five children from each grade level were shown a videotape of typical "Saturday morning" children's television programming, including commercials. The following day, the children were interviewed, in groups, for about one hour. Tape recordings of the interviews, and subsequent content analysis, revealed the following "conceptual categories" of responses to television advertising:

1. Reality—referring to children's judgments about "what a commercial is" and "how real they are" as compared to cartoon (fantasy) and news or documentary (reality) programs.
2. Purpose—referring to children's ability to perceive the intent or "message" of commercials, and the reasoning they use in making this judgment.
3. Degree of discrimination between advertisement and product advertised—referring to children's ability to differentiate the product being advertised from the advertising message itself.

4. Classes of products recalled—referring to the kinds of products and/or advertisements spontaneously mentioned or recalled by children.

5. Complexity of recall—referring to differences in children's ability to perceive and recall details of commercials.

6. Significant other—referring to the human beings spontaneously recalled, cited or associated by children in the reactions to or evaluations of advertisements.

7. Perceived validity and credibility of advertisements—referring to the degree to which children at each age level perceive television commercials as "true" and/or "trustworthy."

8. Affective responses to commercials—referring to the emotional reactions, likes and dislikes, expressed by children about commercials.

9. Cognitive-affective (ego level) basis of response—referring to the central theme or basis of response which appears to underlie the reactions of children to commercials. These responses ranged from 1) basic needs orientation; 2) competence (mastery) and sex role identification orientation; 3) conformity and social approval and 4) conscientious and altruistic social utilitarian orientation.

The central findings of the Blatt et al. study may be summarized as follows:

1. Reality—children in all age groups could identify the term "commercials", but kindergarten children exhibited confusion, and judged the relationship between commercials and reality based on coincidental reasoning or affect;

2. Purpose—kindergarteners showed no understanding of the purpose of commercials, 2nd graders understood their purpose was to sell goods; 4th and 6th graders could comment on techniques employed in constructing them;

3. Discrimination between product and advertising—kindergarteners do not discriminate between commercials and products, and with increasing age clearer discriminations are made between commercials and actual products;

4. Classes of products recalled—kindergarteners spontaneously recall food product advertising, second graders recall products with which they can identify (toys), fourth graders mention household cleaning products, sixth graders show no consistent pattern of recall;

5. Complexity of recall—recall becomes more multidimensional and complex with age;

6. Significant other children associated parents and celebrities as significant references, and sixth graders view themselves as significant references;
7. Perceived validity and credibility of advertisements—as children get older they exhibit increasing distrust of commercials;
8. Affective responses to commercials—young children enjoy commercials; with increasing age children are increasingly contemptuous of commercials but continue to enjoy humor in some.

While some earlier research employing similar groups of children generally supports the Blatt et al. findings (McNeal, 1964), small sample size and the qualitative nature of the research force one to regard the data as highly tentative. However, the data were useful in suggesting dimensions for analysis in the present study. Our purpose was to gather additional data using personal interviews, relevant to several of the categories of responses to commercials suggested in the exploratory research.

METHODOLOGY

Sixty-seven children, ranging in age from five to twelve years, were interviewed by trained research assistants during the summer of 1971. The children were selected from a sample of Boston-area families which had been used in other research. While the families varied in socioeconomic status, the tendency was toward the middle- to upper-middle class.

Mothers of the children were contacted first by letter, explaining the purpose of the research. Arrangements were made for an in-home interview in a followup phone call. All but two of the mothers cooperated in making their children available to be interviewed. Children (or their families) were paid $5 for their participation.

Once in the home, one interviewer conducted the interview, while the other transcribed the child's responses. Tape recorders were found to inhibit responses, so written transcriptions were taken. Efforts were made to be alone with the child, or at least to minimize interruptions and obtrusions by other family members.

The interviews lasted an average of one hour. While questions were asked relevant to other purposes of the study during this time, the questions pertaining to the present purposes are in the Appendix. The interview forms were coded independently by two research assistants, and discrepancies were reconciled.

Data were gathered concerning several of the dimensions or categories of responses suggested by the Blatt et al. data. Data were not gathered for two categories—significant other and cognitive-affective basis of response. These dimensions were revealed through considerable analysis of qualitative data generated in the group interviews. Such extensive probing and analysis are not possible given the limitations of open-ended personal interviews employing questionnaires.

FINDINGS

Data in Table 1 concern children's responses to a direct question about their perceptions and explanations of "what a commercial is".

Table 1: Awareness of "what a commercial is" by age group[a]

		Age			
		5 – 7	8 – 10	11 – 12	
	Low	15	2	3	20
	Med	6	14	15	35
	High	1	1	2	4
Level of Awareness	d.k.	4	1	0	5
	n.a.	2	1	0	3
	n.	(28)	(19)	(20)	(64)

$$X = 22.7, \ df = 4, \ p < .001$$

[a]Low awareness=confused perceptions; low discrimination between commercial and program; definition in terms of product category. Perceptions based on coincidental reasoning or affect.

Medium awareness=identification of "advertising" concept; notion of information about products; judgment based on reality of object or person portrayed.

High awareness=notion of "sponsorship" concept; awareness of selling motives.

The earlier study suggested three levels of awareness: (1) low awareness—confused perceptions, based on coincidental reasoning or affect; (2) medium awareness—judgment based on reality of object or person portrayed (i.e., similarity to objects, persons or events in the real world); (3) high awareness—judgment based on understanding nature of sponsorship, basic purposes of advertising.

Few children were classified in the "high awareness" category, but the data show a clear trend from low to medium awareness with increasing age. "Medium" awareness appears to be reached by age eight, but few children exhibit high awareness by age 12.

Typical "low awareness" responses (Table 2) include children's naming specific categories of commercials or products in attempting to explain what a commercial is (e.g., "A commercial is when they show toys"). "Medium level" responses exhibit some minimal understanding of the notion of advertising, and some explaining of commercials with reference to the fact that they are "advertising." Responses were coded as high awareness only if the child exhibited clear understanding of commercial's intent (" to get people to buy the product").

Table 2: Types of responses: "What is a TV commercial?"

Responses	Frequency
Low awareness responses (Total=20)	
—— name specific product category of ads or products	8
—— "part of show"	3
—— interrupts show	3
Medium awareness responses (Total=35)	
—— "advertises things"	18
—— "informs people about products, shows, things to buy"	16
High awareness responses (Total=4)	
—— "tries to get people to buy products"	3
—— "sponsor show"	1

Purpose

The Blatt et al. study suggested three levels of understanding of the purpose of commercials. While one could evaluate advertising's purpose in the context of the general economy, our essential concern was whether children could understand that commercials intend to sell goods

and services. The levels of understanding range from no or little understanding of selling motives to indications that the child understands this
purpose of commercials—that advertisers seek profit and/or that advertising "pays for" programming.

Table 3: Level of understanding of the purpose of commercials, by age group

Level of understanding purpose[a]		5 – 7	8 – 10	11 – 12	
I		11	6	3	20
II		7	8	12	27
III		2	2	5	9
d.k.		7	1	0	8
n.a.		1	2	0	3
n.		(28)	(19)	(20)	(67)

$$x^2 = 8.0, \ df = 4, \ p < .05$$

[a] I = Low: confused, unaware of selling motive, profit-seeking
II = Medium: recognition of selling motive, some awareness of profit-seeking
III= High: clear recognition of selling and profit-seeking motives

Data in Table 3 indicate that understanding of the purpose of advertising increases with age, although few children exhibit relatively complete understanding of selling and profit motives and/or that commercials sponsor programming. Most Level I responses (low awareness of

purposes) are quite general—e.g., "to help and inform you about things they show" (Table 4). The typical Level II response (medium awareness of purpose) is "to make people buy things," but only five of the 20 eleven- and twelve-year-olds exhibited understanding of selling motives and of the purposes of sponsoring programming.

Table 4: Types of responses: "Why are commercials shown on TV?"

Responses	Frequency
Level I responses (Total=20)	
—— "to help and inform you"	14
—— "for entertainment"	2
Level II responses (Total=27)	
—— "to make people buy things"	22
—— "to sell products"	5
Level III responses (Total=9)	
—— "get people to buy and they pay for the show"	8

Degree of discrimination between program and commercial

While the Blatt et al. study did not deal with this discrimination direct-ly, children were asked to describe the differences between programs and commercials. Level I responses indicated a low level of ability to discriminate, based on coincidental reasoning or affect (e.g., "commer-cials are shorter than programs," "programs are better"). Level II re-sponses indicated more complex discrimination, based on accurate de-scriptions of programs or commercials (e.g., "programs have a story, theme or moral," "commercials are supposed to sell, programs to enter-tain").

Data in Table 5 indicate clear differences between younger and older children in degree of discrimination between programs and commercials. About two-thirds of the younger children exhibit a low level of differen-tiation, while over two-thirds of the older children exhibit a high degree of differentiation. Younger children, in particular, were likely to distin-guish between commercials and programs on the basis of their length: "commercials are shorter than programs" (Table 6).

Table 5: Program-commercial differentiation by age group

		Age		
		5 – 8	9 – 12	
	I	22	6	28
Level of Differentiation[a]	II	7	24	31
	other	5	3	8
	n.	(34)	(33)	(67)

$$x^2 = 19.5, 4 \text{ df}, p < .01$$

[a] I = difference based on affect or coincidental reasoning
II = difference based on reality

Table 6: Types of responses: "What is the difference between a TV program and a TV commercial?"

Responses	Frequency
Level I responses (Total=28)	
— "commercial short, program long"	20
— "before or after show"	2
Level II responses (Total=31)	
— "program has story, theme, moral"	10
— "program supposed to entertain"	7
— "commercials sell, make money"	3

Classes of products/advertisements recalled

Children were asked to recall their favorite television commercial and the commercial they disliked most. For both liked and disliked advertising, almost all children mentioned at least one commercial, and over half mentioned two; only a few children mentioned three commercials.

Data in Table 7 indicate commercials cited as "favorites" by children. Almost one-third of the mentions refer to food advertising, while about one-tenth of the mentions refer to toys and one-tenth to program announcements. Eight of the children said they did not have a favorite commercial, while 12 said they considered one a favorite but couldn't remember it.

Table 7: Classes of products/advertised recalled: Favorite commerial[a]
(Total mentions, n=103)

	Age			
	5–7	8–10	11–12	
Food	12	13	8	33
Toys	6	2	2	10
Program Announcements	6	2	1	9
Soft drinks	2	0	4	6
Autos, gas	1	1	3	5
Public Service Local Adv.	0	0	3	3
Other[b]	8	4	5	17
Can't remember	8	2	2	12
None	3	2	3	8
Total mentions:	46	26	31	103
n.	(28)	(18)	(20)	(66)

[a] 1 mention = 64
2 mentions = 36
3 mentions = 4

[b] "Other" includes personal products (Total=5); drugs and patent medicines (Total=4) cleansers (Total=2) and misc. (Total=6)

Data in Table 8 indicate commercials cited as disliked. Food advertising is the most disliked product category, but only 15 of the 101 mentions refer to food advertising. Advertisements for household cleansers and for personal products are referred to in under one-tenth of the mentions. Interestingly, almost one-third of the mentions are categorized as "can't remember"—i.e., children said they did consider an advertisement as "disliked," but they couldn't remember it. This is in contrast with only 12 of the mentions for favorite advertising which could not be recalled. This finding may be due to the fact that the question about disliked advertising always followed the question about favorite advertising in the questionnaire, however.

Table 8: Classes of products/advertising recalled: disliked commercial[a]
(Total mentions, n=101)

	Age			
	5–7	8–10	11–12	
Food	7	2	6	15
Cleansers	0	2	6	8
Personal products	2	1	4	7
Soft drinks	1	2	2	5
Toys	0	2	2	4
Public service Local adv.	1	1	1	3
Other[b]	8	7	7	22
Can't remember	14	8	5	27
None	4	5	1	10
Total mentions:	37	30	34	101
n.	(28)	(19)	(20)	(67)

[a] 1 mention = 63
2 mentions = 35
3 mentions = 4

[b] "Other" includes: autos (Total=2); drugs and patent medicines (Total=4); program announcements (Total=4) and misc. (Total=12)

Table 9 compares liked and disliked advertising, based on total mentions (n=204) for the total sample (n=67). About one-quarter of all mentions concerned food advertising, reflecting that product category's predominance during children's viewing times. In other research, the incidence of commercials for different product types was recorded during six to ten hours of normal viewing for 5-12-year-old children (Ward, Wackman, and Levinson, 1971). The data in Table 10 indicate that between 29 and 37 percent of the commercials to which 5-12-year-olds are exposed are for food products (including gum and candy). Exposure to commercials for personal products and for drug and patent medicines increases with age, reflecting the changing program tastes and viewing times of

Table 9: Summary: Classes of products/advertisements recalled as favorite, worst commercials

(Total mentions, n=204)

	Liked	Disliked	Total mentions
Food	33	15	48
Toys	10	4	14
Program announcements	9	4	13
Personal products	5	7	12
Soft drinks	6	5	11
Cleansers	2	8	10
Drugs, patent medicines	4	4	8
Autos, gas	5	2	7
Public service Local adv.	3	3	6
Other	6	12	18
Can't remember	12	27	39
None	8	10	18
Total mentions:	103	101	204
n.	(66)	(67)	

older children. The data on liked and disliked commercials reflect the different types of product advertising which children in different age groups are likely to see. Interestingly, however, children rarely cite local advertising and public service advertising as "liked" or "disliked" advertising despite the fact that advertising in these categories comprises between six and nine percent of the commercials to which they are exposed. A possible explanation is that (for local advertising at least) the commercials stimulate little affective response because they are frequently quite straightforward—showing only static pictures of products and slides illustrating a store's address, hours of business, etc. Advertising for products like food and toys, however, usually contains stories

Table 10: Incidence of exposure to commercials in various product and content categories by age group[a]

	Age		
	5–7	8–10	11–12
Food, gum	37%	30%	29%
Personal products	6	12	10
Drugs, patent medicines	4	5	7
Public service	7	8	9
Local	8	7	6
Toys, games	14	8	5
Program announcements	6	3	4
All others	18	27	30
	100%	100%	100%
n.	(532)	(336)	(320)

[a]Data based on a sample of 6,465 commercials to which children were exposed during six–ten hours of normal viewing. Recording of type of commercial and other information was done by mothers of 5-12-year-old children. See Ward, Wackman, and Levinson, 1971.

and more complex visual and verbal stimuli. Additionally, of course, children simply may not be as interested in local advertising as they are in advertising for products, like food and toys, which reflect their immediate interests.

The heterogeneity of liked and disliked commercials parallels the finding among adolescents (Ward and Robertson, 1971). Reflecting the changing tastes and viewing times of adolescents, food advertising is infrequently mentioned as either liked or disliked advertising. Food and drug advertising is cited as both liked and disliked by adolescents: most commercials in the product category are disliked, although one series of commercials was liked because of humorous aspects. Automobile and soft drink advertising was also liked by the adolescents. Aside from the predominance of affective responses to food advertising among preteenage children, both preteenage and teenage groups reflected quite heterogeneous patterns of liked and disliked television advertising.

Reasons for liking and disliking commercials

Children were asked why they liked or disliked specific commercials they mentioned.

Data in Table 11 indicate that over half the reasons given for liking a particular commercial concern the entertainment value of commercials; however, a substantial number of mentions by younger children indicate that their liking for the commercial is based on their liking for (and/or possession of) the product.

Data in Table 12 indicate the children also *dislike* commercials primarily for "entertainment" reasons: they dislike commercials which are seen as "boring," "dull," etc. Almost one-third of the responses do not fit into the major categories of reasons, indicating a high degree of heterogeneity of reasons children dislike commercials.

Comparing the reasons for liking and disliking for all age groups, data in Table 13 indicate that entertainment reasons predominate for both liked and disliked commercials. Affective attitudes toward the product itself only are given as a reason for liking commercials; no children mentioned attitudes toward the product as a reason for disliking commercials.

Complexity of recall

In addition to being asked why they liked or disliked spontaneously recalled commercials, the children were asked to "tell what happens" in the recalled commercials. The Blatt et al. study suggested four levels of complexity of recall, ranging from recollections of a single, random image in a commercial to multidimensional recall and recall focusing on

Table 11: Reasons for liking commercials by age[a]
(Total mentions, n=81)

	Age			
	5–7	8–10	11–12	
Entertainment	14	12	18	44
Aesthetics	2	2	2	6
Product	15	4	2	21
Other	4	2	4	10
Total mentions:	35	20	26	81 (5 na)
n.	(28)	(19)	(20)	(67)

[a]Reasons include:

Entertainment:	likes humor, music, cartoons
Aesthetics:	commercial is "fun", "happy", acting good, nice people, etc.
Product:	likes product, has product
Other:	"effective", "has free offer", "just like it", etc.

Table 12: Reasons for disliking commercials recalled by age[a]
(Total mentions, n=67)

	Age			
	5–7	8–10	11–12	
Entertainment	3	11	11	25
Aesthetics	7	1	5	13
Effect	1	1	5	7
Other	11	5	6	22
Total mentions:	22	18	27	67 (18 na)
n.	(28)	(19)	(20)	(67)

[a]Reasons include:

Entertainment:	"dull"; "boring"
Aesthetics:	"scary"; "people are rude to each other"; "brags"
Effects:	repetition irritating; aimed at opposite sex
Other:	"just don't like it"; "product no good"; etc.

the message themes and techniques, rather than simply on elements of commercials.

Complexity of recall did not vary markedly for liked and disliked commercials. Therefore, data in Table 14 reflect complexity of recall levels for both liked and disliked commercials recalled. The data show increasing complexity of recall with age, although few children were categorized in level IV—recall focusing on the commercial message theme, and/or techniques, rather than on elements of commercials.

Table 13: Summary: Reasons for liking and disliking commercials recalled[a]
(Total mentions, n=148)

Advertising Cited As . . .

	Liked	Disliked	Total
Entertainment	44	25	69
Aesthetics	6	13	19
Product	21	——	21
Effect	——	7	7
Other	10	22	32
Total mentions:	81	67	148
n.a.	(5)	(18)	(23)

[a]Based on total sample, n=67

Perceived credibility and validity of commercials

Children were asked if they felt commercials always tell the truth; how they judge whether commercials tell the truth or not, and why they do or do not tell the truth. Blatt et al. (1971) suggested that by second grade, some children indicated distrust of specific commercials, often based on negative experiences with the product. Older children were found to feel that commercials often do not tell the truth; this feeling is apparently based on reactions to specific commercials, to exaggeration, and to "tricky" techniques in specific commercials.

Almost half the children interviewed in the present study felt that commercials do not always tell the truth (Table 15). Only about one-fifth

Table 14: Complexity of recall for liked and disliked commercials by age group

		—————— Age ——————		
		5–7	8–10	11–12
	I	11	2	2
	II	18	11	13
Complexity of recall[a]	III	6	9	14
	IV	4	1	4
	d.k. n.a.	17	15	7
		(28)	(19)	(20)

[a]I = Unidimensional recall — child remembers single picture or image, e.g., "there was a man on a horse"

II = Multidimensional recall — child remembers several images, but no unified recall, sequence of ad not remembered

III = Multidimensional recall — child remembers several images, in coherent, unified sequence

IV = Recall centers on commercial message, not on descriptive elements of commercials

felt that commercials always tell the truth, and the majority of these children were in the youngest age group. The youngest children were also most likely to respond to the question by saying that commercials do "not always" tell the truth.

Data in Table 16 suggest how children judge whether commercials tell the truth or not. Younger children indicating that commercials are "true" may base this evaluation on their observation that the product exists. Children feeling that commercials are "untrue" seem to base this evaluation on three kinds of "reality tests." They may evaluate truthfulness of commercials in terms of their experiences with products, and 12 of the 33 older children (ages 9-12) indicate that commercials are not true because products "are not like ads say they are." A second "reality test" involves evaluation of truthfulness on the basis of the messages themselves. Children feel commercials are not true if they exaggerate, contain unreal people, objects or actions, or just "don't look right." Finally, a few children said they felt commercials were not true because they had heard this from others.

Table 15: Perceived credibility and validity of commercials, by age group

"Do commercials always tell the truth?"		Age			
		5–7	8–10	11–12	
	Yes	8	3	1	12
	No	6	12	14	32
	Not always	10	3	4	17
	d.k.	0	0	1	1
	n.a.	3	0	0	3
	n.	(27)	(18)	(20)	(65)

$$x^2 = 9.7, 4 \text{ df}, p < .05$$

Table 16: Perceived credibility and validity of commercials

"How do you know commercials (don't) tell the truth?"

	Age	
	5–8	9–12
Untrue		
Reality test: messages		
....unreal people, objects, actions	3	2
...."don't look right"	2	1
....ads don't show everything	0	2
....general "exaggeration"	0	2
Reality test: interpersonal		
....heard from others ad(s) not true	0	3
Reality test: consumer experience		
....don't see things advertised in store	2	0
....products "not like ads say they are"	6	12
....must buy product to be sure	0	2
True		
....true because products and objects portrayed exist	4	1
....true because see product in store	1	0
....don't know	4	0
....other	9	7
....na	3	1
	34	33

When asked why commercials tell the truth or do not tell the truth, 24 of the 33 older children (ages 9-12) said they feel that commercials are untrue because the motives of commercials are suspect—e.g., "they just want to make money"; "they want you to buy their product" (Table 17). Some of the younger children, on the other hand, feel that commercials are untrue because of a "mistake"; they may feel commercials are "true" because they see advertised products in the store, and feel commercials help people and minimize confusion.

It should be noted that children's perceptions of the validity and credibility of commercials are frequently based on the perceived intent of commercials (i.e., if commercials are trying to sell, they are not entirely true) and, particularly among younger children, are based on evaluating what is seen in commercials in terms of their literal perceptions of reality. (If commercials contain unreal episodes or scenes, such as a man flying through the air, commercials are not true because men do not really fly through the air).

Table 17: Perceived credibility and validity of commercials

"Why do (don't) commercials tell the truth?"

	Age	
	5–8	9–12
Untrue		
Suspect motives		
...."they just want you to buy their product	1	9
...."they want you to buy one brand and not others"	0	2
...."they just want to make money"	5	13
Other		
...."it's a mistake"	2	0
...."they don't know if product works"	1	0
....other	4	2
True		
Aid consumers		
...."help people, don't want people to get confused"	2	0
Reality test: consumer experience		
...."you see products in the store"	2	1
....don't know	4	0
....other	9	3
....na	4	3
	34	33

Our data are not sufficient to indicate the extent to which children generalized their feelings about commercials' credibility from one commercial, or group of commercials, to all commercials. It does appear that older children reason that commercials are not always true because of their selling motives. However, examination of attitudes toward commercials—as indicated by reasons for liking or disliking—reveals that children do not mention truthfulness as a reason for liking or disliking. Similarly, the "unreality" of commercials is not explicitly mentioned as a reason for disliking commercials. In fact, children may also perceive that programs are "not real," but like them nevertheless. "Unreality" fantasy can be entertaining or not entertaining, as the data concerning reasons for liking and disliking commercials suggests.

Future research might examine the specific elements of entertainment to which children respond positively or negatively. Similarly, future work might be devoted to understanding the generality of children's perceptions that commercials are not true because of their selling motives, and to understanding how these perceptions and attitudes relate to children's evaluation of products.

SUMMARY

This study sought to extend the data gathered in an exploratory investigation in which children's responses to television advertising were analyzed in a series of group interviews with kindergarteners and second, fourth, and sixth graders (Blatt et al., 1971). This preliminary study suggested several categories of perceptions, explanations, and judgments of young children concerning television advertising. The findings suggested that children's responses to commercials may be related to stages in cognitive development (Kohlberg, 1964; Loevinger and Wessler, 1970; Piaget, 1965).

The present study involved personal interviews with 67 children, ranging in age from five to 12 years. The children were selected from a sample of families in the greater Boston area used in previous research. The sample is slightly skewed toward the upper-middle class.

The data generally confirm the findings of the exploratory research. Younger children exhibit low awareness of the concept of commercials, frequently explaining them as "part of the show" or simply naming a category of products. Older children exhibit greater awareness, explaining commercials in terms of their purpose (to sell) and occasionally in terms of the concept of sponsorship. Similarly, older children show greater understanding of the purpose of commercials, and more readily discriminate between programs and commercials, than younger children do.

When asked to recall both their favorite commercial and the one they "really don't like," most children spontaneously recalled food advertising, regardless of age. Younger children were slightly more likely to name advertising in this category as liked or disliked, reflecting food advertising's predominance during children's prime viewing times. Other than food advertising, children's "liked" and "disliked" advertising choices are quite varied.

Children cite "entertainment" reasons as explanations for liking or disliking specific commercials. They liked commercials seen as humorous, containing good music or cartoons, and disliked commercials seen as "boring" or "dull." Younger children, however, often said that they liked specific commercials because they liked (and/or possessed) the product.

Complexity of recall increases with age: older children are more likely to recall several images from advertising in a coherent, unified sequence.

Most children do not feel advertising always tells the truth. Younger children, in particular, feel many commercials do not tell the truth because they contain elements which do not match the child's literal perception of reality. Older children often suspect the motives of commercials and appear to reason that since commercials are "trying to sell," they do not tell the truth. The extent of generality of this feeling is not made explicit by the data, however.

While the study has extended the earlier data generated in an exploratory study, the sample size does not permit broad generalizations. In particular, important questions remain concerning responses to commercials among children from different socioeconomic backgrounds. Moreover, future research should focus on the relationship of other variables to the various responses to television advertising examined here. For example, future research might focus on intrafamily communication, and on variables concerned with aspects of learning consumer skills as they relate to responses to television advertising. Such research can more accurately assess the various predictors of various responses to commercials which are indexed by age, and can suggest some consequences of responses to commercials, reflected in levels of knowledge about such consumer skills as brand awareness and accuracy of price perception.

FOOTNOTES

1 The authors wish to thank Rod Uphoff, Cathy McCarthy, and Wing-Hing Tsang for their contribution to this research.

REFERENCES

Blatt, J., Spencer, L., and Ward, S. A cognitive development study of children's reactions to television advertising. In *Television and social behavior*, Vol. 4 (this volume). Washington, D.C.: U.S. Government Printing Office, 1971.

Kohlberg, L. The development of moral character and moral ideology. *Child Development*, 1964, **1**, 415-24.

Loevinger, J.,and Wessler, R. *Measuring ego development*. San Francisco: Jossey-Bass, 1970.

McNeal, J.U. Children as consumers. Marketing Study Series, No. 9. Austin, Tex.: University of Texas of Texas Bureau of Business Research, 1964.

Piaget, J. *The child's conception of the world*. Totowa, N.J.: Littlefield, Adams & Co., 1965.

Ward, S., Levinson, D., and Wackman, D. Children's attention to television advertising. In *Television and social behavior*, Vol. 4 (this volume). Washington, D.C.: U.S. Government Printing Office, 1971.

Ward, S., and Robertson, T.S. Adolescent attitudes toward television advertising: preliminary findings. In *Television and social behavior*, Vol. 4 (this volume). Washington, D.C.: U.S. Government Printing Office, 1971.

Appendix: Questions

Questions used in personal interviews with 67 5-12-year-old children regarding perceptions, explanations, and judgments of television advertising; based on Blatt et al., 1971.

1. What is a TV commercial?
2. Why are commercials shown on television?
2a. What do commercials try to do?
3. What is the difference between a TV program and a TV commercial?
4. What is your favorite TV commercial—the one you like the most?
4a. Tell me what happens in this commercial.
4b. Why do you like it?
4c. Why do you like them?
5. Now tell me about the commercial that you really don't like — the one you don't like the most.
5a. Tell me what happens in this commercial.
5b. Why don't you like it?
5c. Are there other commercials that you really don't like? Which ones?
5d. Why don't you like them?
6. Do TV commercials always tell the truth?
6a. How do you know they (don't) tell the truth?
6b. Why do (don't) they tell the truth?

Children's Attention to Television Advertising

Scott Ward
David Levinson
Daniel Wackman

Watching television commercials would seem to be a necessary condition for learning from them, although the low-involvement nature of commercial viewing may mean that this learning is relatively gradual, subtle, covert, or "unconscious" (Krugman, 1965, 1968, 1971). Nevertheless, young children may form attitudes and impressions of products, of services, and even of people, as a function of viewing television advertising. Further, they may begin to acquire cognitive orientations and consumer skills. Such learning becomes increasingly important during adolescence and early adulthood, when young people assume roles which require consumer behavior (Cateora, 1963). Thus, early learning may have important effects on later learning.

This paper presents an empirical investigation of the nature of children's commercial watching behavior.[1] It focuses on understanding the extent and nature of watching behavior, determinants of watching behavior, and some short-term consequences of commercial watching.

Watching behavior has several dimensions and characteristics. One dimension is the extent or amount of viewing of commercials. A second is the degree of attention to the commercials. A third is the alternative and/or coterminus activities a person engages in while viewing commercials, such as walking around the room, talking, and so on. (Talking about the commercial and/or product can be viewed as a short-term consequence of watching, or it can be discussion of other matters, an alternative to commercial watching.) This paper focuses primarily on the second and third dimensions of commercial watching behavior.

With respect to these two dimensions of watching behavior, we are interested in: (a) the frequency of occurrence of different kinds of watching behavior while commercials are being shown; (b) changes in behavior when a commercial is broadcast; (c) elements in the stimulus sequence influencing these behaviors (e.g., place of the commercial in the program, characteristics of the commercial itself like length, position in a sequence of commercials, type of product advertised); (d) characteristics of the child affecting these behaviors (e.g., age and sex); and (e) elements in the viewing situation influencing level of attention (e.g., time and day of watching, who the child is viewing with).

Since our primary interest is watching *behavior*, we have adopted an observational methodology based on Steiner's (1966) study of watching behavior of adults. In that study, Steiner used college students to unobtrusively observe the watching behavior of one of their family members. In this study, we used mothers to observe commercial watching behavior of one of their children.

In the present study, data were gathered on the following aspects of commercial watching behavior:

Determinants of watching

1. Personal characteristics
   a. sex and age of child
2. Viewing situation
   a. time and day of viewing
   b. who child is viewing with
3. Characteristics of television stimuli
   a. duration of commercial (seconds)
   b. position of commercial within a "block" of commercials
   c. position of commercial within programming schedule
   d. object of commercial (product and brand)
4. Prior watching behavior
   a. attention to program before commercial appears

Watching behavior

1. Attention and behavior at commercial onset
2. Attention and behavior during commercial

Short-term consequences of watching behavior

1. Affective verbal comments on commercial or product

The variables listed above include only some of the range of determinants and consequences of watching behavior. Figure 1 illustrates these and other variables associated with watching behavior.

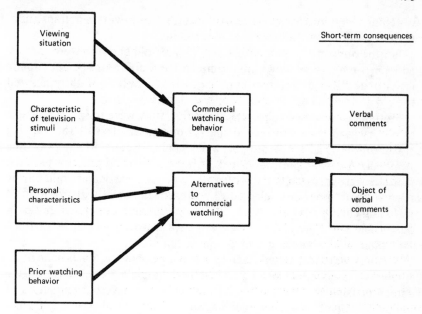

Figure 1: Major variables for study of children's commercial watching behavior

METHODOLOGY

Observation of behavior is often undertaken because of lack of confidence in the reliability of verbal reports of behavior. Since techniques for observation studies are normally quite expensive, they have traditionally been used by social psychologists dealing with small samples of individuals. Even with observation techniques, however, some coding by judges is usually necessary (Bandura and Walters, 1963). Interjudge reliability estimates can be computed, however, while possible sources of unreliability and invalidity in self-report surveys are difficult to estimate.

Observation techniques have been used in advertising research (Allen, 1965) and in marketing research (Wells, 1966). Another study in this volume (Bechtel, Achelpohl, and Akers, 1971) assessed correlates of television viewing behavior and compared the information gathered by in-home cameras for observation with self-report (diary) measures.

The present study applies unobtrusive observation techniques to the commercial watching behavior of children. Our procedures follow closely those of Steiner (1966). He used college students to unobtrusively observe the watching behavior of one of their family members over a nine-day period; his data show variations in attention to commercials depending on such characteristics as type and length of commercial, program context, time of day, and sex and age of subject. In addition to watching behavior, Steiner was also interested in overt reactions, non-verbal reactions, and alternatives to watching.

For the present study, mothers of 5-12-year-old children were recruited from women's service clubs sampled from different socioeconomic areas of the Boston metropolitan area. The sample is slightly skewed toward middle and upper socioeconomic levels (see Table 1).

Mothers who agreed to participate in the study were trained in the use of observation sheets to record the various parameters of the viewing situation, the child's watching behavior, and subsequent behavior. (See Appendix A for sample code sheet.) After training and practice periods, mothers were instructed to unobtrusively watch a particular child during normal viewing periods selected to represent the child's distribution of watching during a typical week. Data were gathered over ten-day periods in April and May 1971. Mothers were instructed to observe for a minimum of six hours and a maximum of ten hours.

Mothers were instructed to code watching behavior. Variations in attention were coded according to whether the child's eyes were on the screen consistently. Overt behavior included such verbal responses as annoyance or pleasure, and such actions as leaving the room. If comments were made about a commercial or a product, the nature and the object of the comment were also noted (see Appendix B).

Table 1: Comparison of socioeconomic levels; survey sample and Boston SMSA

	Survey sample	Boston SMSA[a]
Professional	12%	26%
Managers, proprietors	39	15
Clerical	7	6
Sales	14	5
Skilled labor	17	21
Operatives	6	12
Service	3	12
Laborers	2	3
	100%	100%
N	(109)	

[a]Boston Area Survey: Joint Center for Urban Studies, Cambridge, Mass. 1969

Of the 180 mothers initially recruited, 135 returned usable observation sheets. For the analyses reported here, data from 65 children were coded in three age groups: 5-7 years (N=29); 8-10 years (N=18) and 11-12 years (N=18). Data are based on a sample of one-fifth of the 6,465 commercials watched by these 65 children during the ten-day period.

FINDINGS

Analysis of marginal data indicates that observations of commercial watching behavior occurred most often during children's programs and movies. Reflecting the changing program tastes of the three age groups, the number of observations made during adventure programs and during educational and sports programs increase with age (see Table 2). Additionally, younger viewers are more likely to watch television on Saturday mornings, while older children watch more on weekday evenings (See Table 3).

Table 2: Percent of observations during program types by age groups

Programs watched	Age group 5—7	8—10	11—12
Children's programs and movies	50%	32%	41%
Adventure	6	20	15
Dramatic	6	7	7
Family	28	31	18
Variety	3	4	5
Education and sports	7	5	14
N	100% (578)	100% (356)	100% (359)

Observations of watching behavior for commercials in different product categories reflect the different programs watched by children of different ages (see Table 4). Younger children are more likely to be exposed to advertising for foods, gum, and toys and games, while older children are more likely to be exposed to advertising for personal products.

Most watching was done in the company of one or more siblings; watching with the mother only (necessary *de facto* due to study design) or with father and siblings occurs about equally, while watching with father only (not counting mother who was observing) occurs quite infrequently among all three age groups (see Table 5).

Determinants of watching: age and sex differences in watching behavior

Data in Table 6 are marginal percentages of observations of attention to programming just before commercial onset, reaction at commercial

Table 3: Percent of observations made at different times, by age group

Time of viewing	Age group 5–7	8–10	11–12
6–10 a.m. weekday	10%	4%	6%
10 a.m. – 1 p.m. weekday	8	1	0
1–6 p.m. weekday	11	10	14
6–9 p.m. weekday	27	43	33
9 p.m. – 1 a.m. weekday	1	1	2
6 a.m. – 1 p.m. Sat.	14	7	9
1–6 p.m. Sat.	3	1	3
6 a.m. – 1 p.m. Sun.	5	3	5
1– 6 p.m. Sun.	1	3	0
6 p.m. – 1 a.m. Fri. night	8	15	7
6 p.m. – 1 a.m. Sat. night	3	6	12
6 p.m. – 1 a.m. Sun. night	9	6	9
N	100% (564)	100% (356)	100% (351)

Table 4: Percent of observations of watching commercials
for different product types, by age group

	Age group 5–7	8–10	11–12
Food, gum	37%	30%	29%
Personal products	6	12	10
Drugs, patent medicines	4	5	7
Public service	7	8	9
Local	8	7	6
Toys, games	14	8	5
Program comments	6	3	4
All others	18	27	30
N	100% (532)	100% (336)	100% (320)

onset, behavior during commercial, and the incidence and object of verbal comments. The data indicate that children in the two youngest age groups (5-7, 8-10) pay greater attention to programming than do children in the older group (11-12 years old). Conversely, the incidence of paying "no attention" to prior programming increases with age.[2]

Table 5: Percent of observations made during viewing with others, by age group

		Age group	
	5–7	8–10	11–12
Others			
Mother only	26%	15%	19%
Sibling(s)	60	60	54
Father	3	8	6
Father and siblings	11	17	21
N	100% (574)	100% (352)	100% (357)

At commercial onset, the most common observation was that the children did nothing, although older children were slightly more likely to express a "dislike" reaction ("oh no, not another one") while younger children (under ten years old) were somewhat more likely to express a liking reaction ("now watch this"; "this is a good one").[3]

During the commercial, "full" attention seemed to decrease with age, although "partial" attention increased slightly. Talking with others during commercial broadcast occurred most often among the oldest children.[4]

The data in Table 6 indicate that younger children were somewhat more likely than the oldest children to make some comment about the advertisement or the product.[5] This was the case even though older children talked more during television viewing than younger children. This result provides a further indication that young children paid more attention to the commercial, since when they did talk, their conversation focused on the commercial or product more often than did that of older children.

Younger children's comments were more likely to be positive comments, and they were more likely to be about the product than about the commercial. Comments about the commercial itself increased with age.

No significant differences were observed between males and females in watching behavior. One finding, however, was that boys in the youngest category talked during commercials slightly more than girls. However, the pattern was reversed among the oldest age group: girls talked during 28 percent of the commercials, the boys during 20 percent.

Table 6: Watching behavior and verbal comments, by age group

| | | Age group | | |
		5—7	8—10	11—12
Attention	Full	58%	58%	50%
before	Partial	23	21	25
commercial	None	19	21	25
		100%	100%	100%
Commercial	Dislike	2%	3%	8%
onset	Break	5	7	6
	Like	14	16	9
	Nothing	78	75	77
		100%	100%	100%
Attention	Full	50%	46%	33%
during	Partial	16	22	25
commercial	Up, in room	9	6	6
	Talks	18	15	25
	Up, leaves	4	4	5
	Not in room	4	7	6
		100%	100%	100%
Verbal comment	Positive	12%	13%	8%
about product	Negative	2	4	6
or commercial	Neutral	7	7	4
	None	79	76	83
		100%	100%	100%
	N	(570)	(350)	(348)
		60%	56%	51%
		40	44	49
		100%	100%	100%
	N	(63)	(41)	(41)

Determinants of watching: the viewing situation

One aspect of the viewing situation is the time during the week when children watch television. Two peak viewing periods were Saturday mornings and early weekday evenings (see Table 3). Because of cell entries when data are analyzed by three age groups, data in Table 7 are based on two age groups: 5-8 years old and 9-12 years old, instead of the 5-7, 8-10, and 11-12 age categories which are used in every other table in this paper.

Observations of watching behavior before commercial onset suggest that older children, when they do watch on Saturday mornings, do not pay as much attention to the television as younger children do, although both groups seem to pay relatively high attention during weekday evening viewing.

Table 7: Time of viewing, watching behavior, and verbal comments[a]

		Saturday morning (6 am – 1 pm)		Weekday evening (6 pm – 1 am)	
		Age		Age	
		5–8	9–12	5–8	9–12
Attention	Full	67%	38%	57%	61%
before	Partial	20	31	22	18
commercial	None	13	31	21	22
		100%	100%	100%	100%
Commercial	Dislike	2	20	2	6
onset	Break	7	13	6	5
	Like	17	16	12	14
	Nothing	75	51	80	75
		100%	100%	100%	100%
Attention	Full	50	33	46	45
during	Partial	15	20	21	24
commercial	Up, in room	3	13	11	4
	Talks	18	16	16	18
	Up, leaves	9	9	2	3
	Not in room	6	9	4	6
		100%	100%	100%	100%
Verbal	Positive	18	21	15	7
comment	Negative	2	14	3	7
	Neutral	12	7	5	3
	None	68	58	77	83
		100%	100%	100%	100%
	N	(91)	(45)	(195)	(323)

[a]Data are percentages of commercial exposures, based on a sample of 6, 465 commercials observed by 35 children, 5–8 years of age, and 30 children, 9–12 years of age. 5–8 age group sample = 694 commercial exposures; 9–12 age group sample = 591 exposures.

Interestingly, 20 percent of the observations made at commercial onset by older viewers on Saturday mornings were "dislike" reactions ("Not another one"; "Here we go again"). This reaction was not nearly as frequent during commercial exposures on weekday evenings. The groups differed again in attention level during the commercials, with older children paying full attention during only 33 percent of the commercials on Saturday mornings, while younger children paid full attention during 50 percent. The groups did not greatly differ in "full" attention paid during weekday evening commercial exposures. The older children seemed to pay attention to considerably more commercials during weekday evening viewing than on Saturdays.

This pattern among older children may reflect their lessening interest in "kid's products" and their developing interest in the more general kinds of products advertised during early weekday evening programs. Such an interpretation may not be entirely accurate, however, since older children made *positive* verbal comments about 21 percent of the Saturday morning commercials but only 7 percent of the weekday evening commercials. However, the older children also made *negative* comments about 14 percent of the Saturday commercials but only 7 percent of the weekday commercials.

Another aspect of the viewing situation which should affect watching behavior is the number and types of people who are watching television with children. A limitation of this study is that the child's mother became a *de facto* viewing companion since she had to be present to unobtrusively observe the child. Thus no data are available on the child's viewing behavior when he or she watched alone.

Roughly equal proportions of children from each group watched with siblings and/or friends, and with fathers alone (see Table 5). Viewing with siblings and father—"family" viewing—increased with age. However, the data in Table 8 suggest that, while the incidence of family viewing increased somewhat with age, paying full attention to commercials during family viewing (father and mother present) decreased with age. One possible interpretation of this finding is that older children use the occurrence of "family" viewing for interpersonal communication, either as an alternative to watching commercials or possibly as a consequence of commercial watching (in the sense that children and others may talk about the commercial).

Determinants of watching: characteristics of television stimuli

Various characteristics of television commercials were related to watching behavior. One was the length of commercials. Four commercial lengths were coded: ten, 20, 30, and 60 seconds. Data presented in Figure 2 indicate that the oldest children pay full attention to commercials less often than the younger children, regardless of commercial length. Within all three age groups, least attention was paid to ten-second commercials. With the exception of the youngest age group, most attention was paid to 60-second commercials.

A second characteristic of television stimuli is the position of a given commercial within a "block" of commercials. Only one commercial may be broadcast between programs or during breaks in a program, but more often two to four commercials are aired in a block.

Table 8: Watching behavior (full attention, talking, and other) while watching with other viewers, by age group

	Mother only			Other Viewers — Siblings			Father only			Father and siblings		
Age group:	5–7	8–10	11–12	5–7	8–10	11–12	5–7	8–10	11–12	5–7	8–10	11–12
Behavior during commercial Full attention	47%	39%	36%	49%	46%	35%	47%	43%	22%	59%	51%	28%
Talking	16	16	19	19	14	24	27	25	22	16	14	34
Other (partial attention, up, in room, leaves room, not in room)	37	45	45	32	40	41	26	32	56	25	35	38
N	(148)	(51)	(69)	(350)	(213)	(190)	(151)	(28)	(23)	(63)	(59)	(76)

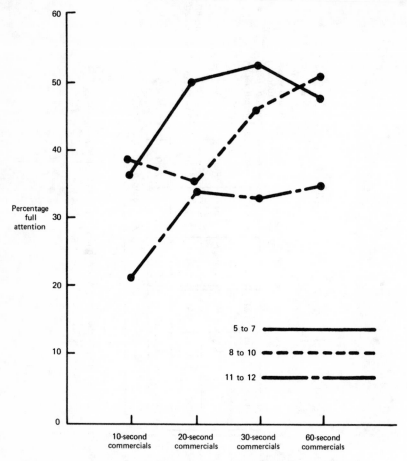

Figure 2: Full attention to commercials by commercial length and by age group

Data in Figure 3 indicate that children of all ages have similar (and high) attention to the program, but the attention level decreases much more rapidly during the sequence of commercials for the oldest children. For them, full attention fell from 50 percent for the program to 43 percent for the first commercial, to only 24 percent for later commercials. On the other hand, the youngest children were paying full attention to prior programming for nearly 60 percent of the observations; this percentage decreased slightly for later commercials.

Analyzing the data by the position of a commercial in the program context (beginning, middle, end of program), Figure 4 indicates that, while older children generally paid less attention, the incidence of full attention for all three groups was greatest to commercials at the beginning of programs. Further, full attention among older children decreased as the program progressed, while the younger children showed little difference in full attention regardless of the commercial's position in program context. For both 8-10 and 11-12 age groups, attention was particularly low to commercials at the end of the show. This may indicate that the youngest children did not know the show was ending, and it may be further evidence of young children's difficulty in discriminating be-

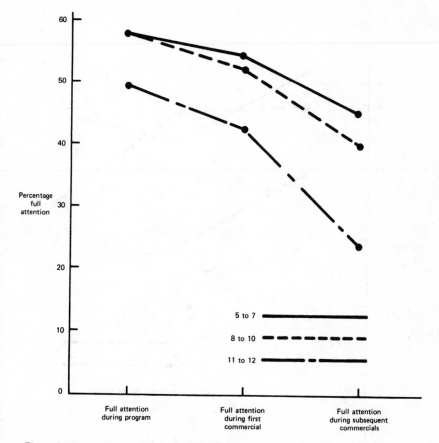

Figure 3: Full prior attention to program and full subsequent attention to commercials by age group

tween commercials and the program. Evidence that young children may be less aware that the program is ending is that only 26 percent of the youngest children had left the room or were talking during commercials at the end of the program, compared to 36 percent of the 8-10-year-olds and 47 percent of the 11-12-year-olds.

Data presented earlier (see Table 4) indicated the product categories of commercials to which children were exposed during the ten-day observation period. Because of the wide variety of products and the different times of viewing across the three age groups, cell sizes do not permit extensive analysis of watching behavior by product category of commercial. However, by combining several product categories, we can perform some analyses. Data in Table 9 indicate attention to programming before commercial exposure and watching behavior during com-

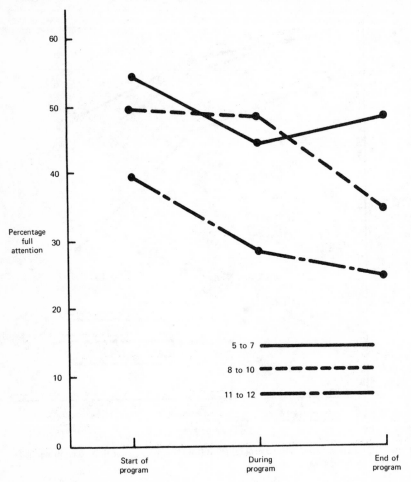

Figure 4: Full attention to commercials by position of commercial in program context and by age group

mercial broadcast for three product categories: food products, personal items (cosmetics or patent medicine), and household cleaners. Food products are generally more relevant to children than are products in the other categories (Ward and Wackman, 1971), while household cleaners and personal items should be less relevant.

Table 9: Relevance of product category, attention to prior programming, and subsequent attention during commercials, by age group

		Relevance of commercial product category					
		More relevant food			Less relevant hshld. cleaners, cosms. etc.		
	Age:	5–7	8–10	11–12	5–7	8–10	11–12
Attention before commercial	Full	61%	61%	46%	44%	55%	61%
	Partial	22	18	27	27	20	15
	None	17	20	27	29	26	24
	N	100% (193)	100% (98)	100% (95)	100% (63)	100% (82)	100% (62)
Attention during commercial	Full	52%	47%	35%	46%	40%	33%
	Partial	19	24	26	21	24	22
	Talks	12	14	23	16	23	19
	Other	17	15	16	17	13	26
	N	100% (193)	100% (98)	100% (95)	100% (63)	100% (82)	100% (63)

Children in the younger two age groups were observed paying more attention than 11-12 year olds just before commercials for food products. The pattern was just the reverse prior to commercials for less relevant products, probably reflecting the different program contexts for the types of commercials. The less relevant products are perhaps advertised during more adult programming, which are more engaging to older children.

The drop in full attention during the commercial was roughly equivalent for all three age groups for food commercials. However, as Figure 5 indicates, children in the 5-7 age group actually *increased* their attention during less relevant commercials over their attention to prior programming. As age increases, attention to the "less relevant" commercials decreases.

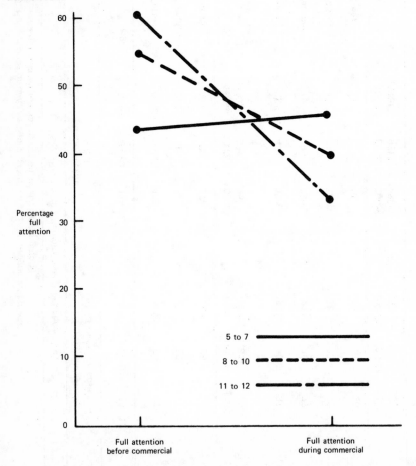

Figure 5: Full attention to the program and "less relevant" commercials by age group

This finding illustrates the danger of attempting to assess the "relevance" of types of advertising for children. If one defines relevance of products in terms of a child's direct consumption of them and/or his ability to directly buy them (low-price items), then clearly food products are more relevant than commercials for cosmetics and household cleaners. However, it may be that children are so familiar with food products —through advertising exposure, direct consumption, and intrafamily influence attempts—that advertising for food products is actually less relevant than advertising for products associated with adult roles. If one defines "relevance" in these terms, as products which illustrate adult roles, then our "less relevant" product category of cosmetics, patent medicines, and household cleaners is actually the *most* relevant product category.

Determinants of commercial watching: prior watching behavior

A final determinant of commercial watching behavior is the behavior of the child just before the commercial. Data in Table 10 indicate that, among children paying full attention to prior programming, attention falls off during commercial exposure for all age groups. The smallest drop in attention is among the 5-7-year-olds; the greatest is among the 11-12-year-olds. Conversely, older children are more likely to engage in other behavior—partial watching, getting up and moving around the room or leaving the room, talking—than younger children.

Table 10: Attention stimulation by commercials: behavior during commercials among children paying full prior attention to programming, by age group

		Age group		
		5–7	8–10	11–12
Subsequent attention to commercial	Full attention	78%*	70%	57%
	All other (partial attention, talking, up in room, leaves room)	22	30	43
	N	100% (329)	100% (201)	100% (180)

* Should be read: Of all observations of 5–7-year-old children paying full prior attention to programming, 78% of the subsequent observations indicated that these children continued to pay full attention to commercials.

An observation commonly made in the popular media and among commercial television's detractors is that young children actually pay attention to commercials when they do not pay attention to prior programming. Data in Table 11 do not support this generalization. Of the children who were observed paying no or partial prior attention to the program, only 12 percent showed an increase to full attention during the commercial; there were no differences among children of different ages.

Table 11: Attention stimulation by commercials: behavior during commercials among children paying no or partial prior attention to program, by age group

| | | Age group | | |
		5-7	8-10	11-12
Behavior	Full	12%*	13%	12%
during	Partial	29	30	37
commercial	Other	59	57	52
		100%	100%	100%
	N	(244)	(148)	(127)

* Should be read: Of all observations of 5–7-year-old children paying no, or partial prior attention to programming, 12% of the subsequent observations indicated that these children increased their watching behavior to full attention during commercial exposure.

Short-term consequences of watching: affective comments

Data in Table 6 indicate that verbal comments after commercials (and about the commercial or the product advertised) occurred after about 20 percent of commercial exposures. Younger children were more likely to comment about the product advertised, while older children are more likely to comment about the commercial itself.

Data in Figure 6 indicate the nature of these comments. Overall, when comments are made, they are likely to be positive comments. However, positive and neutral comments decrease after ten years of age, while negative comments increase steadily from 5-12 years of age.

CONCLUSIONS

The focus of this paper has been two aspects of the commercial watching behavior of young children: attention to commercials and co-terminus or alternative activities during commercials. A number of general tendencies in viewing behavior emerged.

Certain behaviors during commercial viewing are exhibited by all children. All children exhibit a drop in attention when a commercial is shown, compared with attention to prior programming, and attention continues to decrease during later commercials in a series. For all children, full attention to commercials is highest at the beginning of programs, lowest for those shown during the program or at the end of the

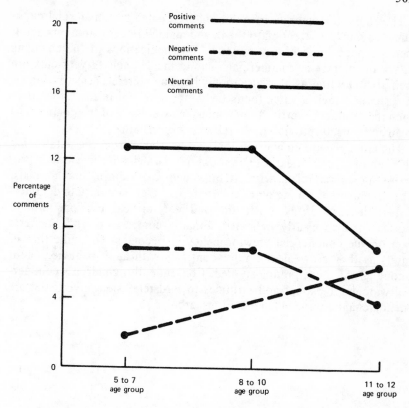

Figure 6: Percent of positive, negative, and neutral comments by age

program. Verbal comments about the product advertised or about the commercial itself are infrequent, but positive comments are more frequent than neutral or negative ones. Comments more often concern the product advertised than the commercial itself.

Despite these general tendencies, some important differences occur by age. For older children, the trend is toward less attention to commercials and more negative, critical, and sophisticated reactions to television advertising. The greatest changes in behavior, and presumably in attitudes, occur among 11- and 12-year-olds. For them, we see less attention to commercials in every viewing context. Further, decreases in attention from programming to initial commercials to later commercials are substantially greater for this age group than for younger children. The oldest children talk more during commercials but make fewer comments about the product advertised or the commercial itself. Also, although positive comments are still most frequent for older children, negative comments are nearly as frequent. Comments are increasingly likely to concern the commercial itself rather than the advertised product.

Thus a picture emerges of older children jaded to commercial exposures, paying less attention to them, and making fewer comments about them—especially positive comments. Two indications of the changing nature of interest in commercials among the 11- and 12-year-olds are their greater withdrawal of attention when commercials occur during the program and their greater focus on the commercial itself, rather than upon the product advertised, indicating an awareness of the commercial as an entity itself, providing entertainment or irritation.

The most general conclusion that can be drawn from the data is that children of all ages clearly exhibit differential behavior in viewing programs and commercials, with attention decreasing during commercials. The development among older children of greater immunity to commercials in the form of lower attention and more critical reactions to commercials is also clearly indicated. Finally, comparison with Steiner's data on the commercial viewing behavior becomes more like that of adults as they grow older, major contrasts with adult behavior occur among all three age groups studied. Consequently, children's commercial watching behavior and attitudes toward television advertising are phenomena requiring independent research.

FOOTNOTES

1. This research was supported by the National Institute of Mental Health (Contract No. HSM 42-70-74). Scott Ward is assistant professor, Harvard Business School, and research associate, Marketing Science Institute. David Levinson is a research assistant at the Marketing Science Institute. Daniel Wackman is director of the research division at the University of Minnesota School of Journalism and Mass Communication. The authors wish to express appreciation to Dr. Herbert Klugman, General Electric Company, for his suggestions and encouragement on this project.
2. The data indicate that children in the two youngest age groups were paying "full" attention during 58 percent of the observations made just before commercials. Children 11 and 12 years old paid full attention during 50 percent of these observations. Steiner (1966) found that adults paid full attention during 70 percent of observations made just before network commercials and during 68 percent of observations made before nonnetwork commercials.
3. The data indicate that the children engage in some behavior—liking, disliking, or taking a break—about 25 percent of the time. Steiner's (1966) data indicate that adults engage in similar behavior at commercial onset only about ten percent of the time.
4. Compared with Steiner's (1966) data, adults and the two younger age groups exhibit comparable incidence of "full" attention during commercials. The 11- and 12-year-olds exhibited far less "full" attention (33 percent) during commercials than either the younger children or Steiner's adults.
5. The incidence of verbal comments (after about 12 percent of commercials) is slightly greater than that observed among adults by Steiner (1966).

REFERENCES

Allen, C.L. Photographing the TV audience. *Journal of Advertising Research*, March 1965, 2-8.

Bandura, A., and Walters, R. H. *Social learning and personality development*. New York: Holt, Rinehart & Winston, 1963.

Bechtel, R.B., Achelpohl, C., and Akers, R. Correlates between observed behavior and questionnaire responses on television viewing. *Television and social behavior*, Vol. 2 (this volume). Washington, D.C.: U. S. Government Printing Office, 1971.

Cateora, P.R. An analysis of the teenage market. Austin: University of Texas Bureau of Business Research, 1963.

Krugman, H. Processes underlying exposure to advertising. *American Psychologist*, 1968, 23(4), 245-53.

Krugman, H. The impact of television advertising: learning without involvement. *Public Opinion Quarterly*, 1965, 29, 349-56.

Krugman, H. The television generation and the new research needs. Paper presented at a meeting of the American Association for Public Opinion Research, Pasadena, Calif., May 21, 1971.

Steiner, G. The people look at commercials: a study of audience behavior. *Journal of Business*, April 1966, 272-304.

Ward, S., and Wackman, D. Television advertising and intrafamily influence: children's purchase influence attempts and parental yielding. *Television and social behavior*, Vol. 4 (this volume).

Wells, W.D., and LoSciuto, L.A. Direct observation of purchasing behavior. *Journal of Marketing Research*, August 1966, 227-35.

Appendix A: Sample code sheet

Observation Sheets

Observer: _____

child: _____ age: _____ sex: _____

Date	with	time	channel	program	COMMERCIAL			BEHAVIOR				COMMENT	
					BRAND	SECS.	POSITION	BEFORE	AT ONSET	DURING	GENERAL		if p/c applic

BEHAVIOR codes:

BEFORE:
1. full att.
2. part att.
3. no att.

AT ONSET:
1. dislike
2. break
3. like
4. nothing

DURING:
1. full att.
2. part att.
3. up, in rm.
4. talks
5. up, lvs. rm.
6. not in rm.

COMMENT:
1. +
2. -
3. neutral
4. no comm.

Appendix B: Coding of commercial watching behavior

(excerpts from mother's training manual, adapted from Steiner, 1966)

I. BEHAVIOR BEFORE COMMERCIAL ONSET

This rating concerns your child's level of attention to television immediately before the onset of the commercial being rated, on the following 3-point scale:

1. Watching - full attention; eyes on set;
2. Watching - partial attention; eyes on and off set;
3. Not watching TV.

II. BEHAVIOR AT ONSET

This scale concerns reactions, if any, to the very beginning of the message. For instance, it is possible to have a very favorable (or unfavorable) reaction at the onset of a commercial and later change judgments on the commercial. The four possible "at onset" ratings are:

1. Annoyance, dislike ("not another one;" "here we go again," etc.)
2. Relief at break ("oh, good, here's my chance to get. . ." etc.)
3. Pleasure, liking ("now, watch this;" "this is a good one," etc.)
4. No overt reaction

III. BEHAVIOR DURING COMMERCIAL

This column relates to the degree of attention to the message itself, according to the following five-point scale:

1. Full attention - stays in chair and watches all or almost all; attention to visual and audio, eyes on set;
2. Partial attention - stays in chair but does not pay full attention (turns around talks, etc.) Exposure to visual and audio, but eyes on and off set.
3. Gets up but stays in room (gets something, makes phone call in room, etc.)

4. Leaves the room;
5. Not in room at onset.

IV. COMMENTS ON CONTENT

Here emphasis is on reactions to material within the commercial itself, whether form ("cute cartoon") or content ("think I'll try that"). Comments are to be classified according to these four categories:

1. Positive - (cute, interesting, clever, looks like a good idea);
2. Negative (stupid, boring, ridiculous, that looks useless, etc.)
3. Both, or neutral;
4. No comments about commercial content.

This refers strictly to verbal comments. If your child does not speak about the commercial, record "no comment." The last column refers to the child's comments on the content as recorded in the preceeding column. If the child responds either positively, or negatively, listen to the youngster's comment carefully. If it is clear whether the negative or positive reaction is for either the specific product (P) or the format of the commercial (C) mark this accordingly. If you are not able to readily determine the subject of the youngster's comments, put a dash in this column.

Television Advertising and Intrafamily Influence: Children's Purchase Influence Attempts and Parental Yielding

Scott Ward and Daniel Wackman

Traditionally mass communication research has been concerned with relatively immediate consequences of mass media use, such as attitude change. Considerably less attention is devoted to understanding second-order consequences of communication such as interpersonal communication and subsequent effects following the occurrence of more immediate and direct effects of mass media use.

The present study examines such second-order consequences of television use. The focus is on the influence of television advertising on aspects of mother-child interaction: children's attempts to influence mothers' purchases, and mothers' yielding to these attempts. We also examine mothers' perceptions of the frequency with which commercials influence their children.

Some previous research has examined relationships between mass media use, parent-child interaction, and subsequent effects. For example, McLeod and Chaffee and their associates have related adolescents' mass media use to parent-child interaction, and political socialization processes (Chaffee, Ward, and Tipton, 1970; McLeod, O'Keefe, and Wackman, 1969). Halloran et al. (1970) examined exposure to television and intrafamily communication among samples of delinquent and non-delinquent British adolescents.

Little empirical evidence has been brought to bear on the question of the extent of television advertising's influence on intrafamily interaction and subsequent behavior. For example, while much commercial research attempts to relate mass media exposure to aspects of consumer behavior, effort is rarely devoted to explicit examination of the intrafamily processes which intervene between media exposure and behavior. Studies of intrafamily consumer decision-making usually focus on husband-wife interaction and are not concerned with the influence of children (Granbois, 1967).

Some qualitative data indicate that mothers feel television commercials influence their children (Yankelovich, 1970). Most mothers cite commercials as influential in the formation of children's desires for various products; their influence is resented when these desires turn to overt attempts to influence parental purchase behavior. However, many mothers accept television advertising as a "necessary evil."

Such qualitative research, of course, does not explicitly link media exposure with specific intrafamily processes. Berey and Pollay (1968) examined intrafamily processes involved in mothers' purchases of children's breakfast cereals. While not concerned with mass media influences, the investigators found that highly child-centered mothers purchased their children's favorite cereals less frequently than less child-centered mothers. The child's assertiveness was not correlated with purchase.

The present study examines the influence of three kinds of variables on children's purchase influence attempts and parental yielding: demographics, variables relating to parent-child interaction, and variables related to mothers' mass communication behavior.

METHODOLOGY

Self-administered questionnaires were sent to 132 mothers of 5-12-year-old children in the Boston metropolitan area. The mothers had been recruited from service clubs in the Boston area previously for participation in another study. While attempts were made to sample service clubs from different socioeconomic areas of Boston, the sample was skewed toward the upper and upper-middle classes (see Table 1).

Table 1: Comparison of socioeconomic levels: survey sample and Boston SMSA*

	Survey sample	SMSA
Professional	12%	26%
Managers, proprietors	39	15
Clerical	7	6
Sales	14	5
Skilled labor	17	21
Operatives	6	12
Service	3	12
Laborers	2	3
	100%	100%

* Source: Boston Area Survey: 1969. Cambridge, Mass., Joint Center for Urban Studies.

The questionnaire took about one hour to complete, and women were paid for their participation. Each was instructed to answer items about the specific activities of one particular child in the household. Completed questionnaires were received from 109 of the mothers (83 percent response rate).

Various scales were recoded by summing responses to particular items, obtaining frequency distributions, and recoding the data for correlational analysis.

FINDINGS

Purchase influence attempts

Each mother was asked to indicate the frequency of her child's purchase influence attempts for 22 products. The products were all heavily advertised, but they varied in price, frequency of purchase, and relevance to the child (direct consumption or use by the child rather than by other family members).

Analysis of marginal data indicates that food products—particularly food products which are relevant to children—were frequently requested and that purchase influence attempts decreased with age. (See Table 2 for data on product requests.)

Durables which the child might use directly (record albums, bicycles, etc.) were the second most requested product category. As one would expect, games and toys were requested most often by younger children (5-7 years old), while clothing and record albums were most often requested by older children (11-12 years old). Across four product categories, it appears that purchase influence attempts decreased with age: younger children, more than older children, were likely to attempt to influence parental purchases of most products.

Parental yielding to children's purchase influence attempts

Data in Table 3 indicate that, unlike children's purchase influence attempts, which decrease with age, parental yielding to such influence attempts increases with age. Across most product categories, it appears that the older the child, the more likely mothers are to yield to influence attempts. This may be because older children ask for less. Mothers may also attribute to older children greater competence in making judgments about products.

Mothers are most likely to yield to purchase influence attempts for food products—the same products children most often ask for.

Estimated frequency of influence of commercials on children

Mothers were asked to indicate the frequency with which television advertising for the various products influenced their children to want the products. Data in Table 4 suggest that mothers of younger children feel

Table 2: Mother's reports of child's attempts to influence product purchases

	5-7 (n=43)	Age 8-10 (n=32)	11-12 (n=34)	Total (n=109)
Food products				
Relevant				
Breakfast cereal	1.26	1.59	1.97	1.59
Snack foods	1.71	2.00	1.71	1.80
Candy	1.60	2.09	2.17	1.93
Soft drinks	2.00	2.03	2.00	2.01
Jello	2.54	2.94	2.97	2.80
Overall mean	1.82	2.13	2.16	2.03
Less relevant				
Bread	3.12	2.91	3.43	3.16
Coffee	3.93	3.91	3.97	3.94
Pet food	3.29	3.59	3.24	3.36
Overall mean	3.45	3.47	3.49	3.49
Durables, for child's use				
Game, toy	1.24	1.63	2.17	1.65
Clothing	2.76	2.47	2.29	2.52
Bicycle	2.48	2.59	2.77	2.61
Hot wheels	2.43	2.41	3.20	2.67
Record album	3.36	2.63	2.23	2.78
Camera	3.91	3.75	3.71	3.80
Overall mean	2.70	2.58	2.73	2.67
Notions, toiletries				
Toothpaste	2.29	2.31	2.60	2.39
Bath soap	3.10	2.97	3.46	3.17
Shampoo	3.48	3.31	3.03	3.28
Aspirin	3.64	3.78	3.97	3.79
Overall mean	3.13	3.09	3.26	3.16
Other products				
Automobile	3.55	3.66	3.51	3.57
Gasoline Brand	3.64	3.63	3.83	3.70
Laundry soap	3.69	3.75	3.71	3.72
Household cleaner	3.71	3.84	3.74	3.76
Overall mean	3.65	3.72	3.70	3.69

Scale: 1 = often; 4 = never

commercials influence the desires of their children more than do mothers of older children.

Mothers report that commercials for food products which are relevant to children—Jello, soft drinks, breakfast cereal—seem to exert the most influence on children.

Correlates of influence attempts, yielding and perceived influence of commercials

Intercorrelations among the three dependent variables for the entire sample (see Table 5) indicate positive, significant relationships between

Table 3: Percent of mother's "usually" yielding to child's
purchase influence attempts, by product category

	5-7 (n=43)	Age 8-10 (n=32)	11-12 (n=34)	Total (n=109)
Food products				
Relevant				
Breakfast cereal	88%	91%	83%	87%
Snack food	52%	62%	77%	63%
Soft drinks	38%	47%	54%	46%
Candy	40%	28%	57%	42%
Jello	40%	41%	26%	36%
Overall %:	51.6%	53.8%	59.4%	54.8%
Less relevant				
Bread	14%	28%	17%	19%
Pet foods	7%	3%	11%	7%
Coffee	2%	0%	0%	1%
Overall %:	7.667%	10.33%	9.33%	9.00%
Durables, for child's use				
Game, toy	57%	59%	46%	54%
Clothing	21%	34%	57%	37%
Record albums	12%	16%	46%	24%
Hot wheels	29%	19%	17%	22%
Bicycle	7%	9%	9%	8%
Camera	2%	3%	0%	2%
Overall %:	25.6%	28.0%	35.0%	29.4%
Notions, toiletries				
Toothbrushes	36%	44%	40%	39%
Shampoo	17%	6%	23%	16%
Bath soap	9%	9%	9%	9%
Aspirin	5%	6%	0%	4%
Overall %:	16.8%	16.3%	18.0%	17.0%
Other products				
Laundry soap	2%	0%	3%	2%
Household cleaners	2%	3%	0%	2%
Gasoline	2%	0%	3%	2%
Automobiles	2%	0%	0%	12%
Overall %:	22.0%	.75%	1.50%	1.75%

children's purchase influence attempts and yielding (r=.35) and perceived influence of commercials (r=.71). The latter finding suggests that mothers may estimate the influence of commercials according to the frequency with which children attempt to influence purchases for advertised products. The magnitude of the relationship suggests that the measures are almost redundant.

While perceived influence of commercials and yielding are significantly correlated (r=.22), the relationship does not hold when purchase influence attempts are controlled. Thus, perceived commercial influence appears to be a function of the frequency of purchase influence attempts. Influence attempts may also lead to yielding, but the correlation between perceived influence and yielding seems a spurious one.

Table 4: Mother's estimated frequency of influence
of TV commercials on child's desires

	5-7 (n=43)	Age 8-10 (n=32)	11-12 (n=34)	Total (n=109)
Food products				
Relevant				
Breakfast cereal	1.43	1.50	1.94	1.62
Snack foods	2.10	1.66	1.86	1.89
Candy	1.91	1.94	2.29	2.04
Soft drinks	2.21	2.09	2.38	2.23
Jello	2.71	2.94	3.11	2.91
Overall mean	2.07	2.03	2.32	2.14
Less relevant				
Pet food	3.27	3.55	3.18	2.32
Bread	2.83	3.00	3.29	3.03
Coffee	3.91	4.00	3.91	3.94
Overall mean	3.34	3.52	3.46	3.10
Durables, for child's use				
Game, toy	1.29	1.45	1.83	1.51
Hot wheels	2.24	2.42	3.11	2.57
Bicycle	2.55	2.88	3.11	2.83
Clothing	2.95	2.81	2.82	2.87
Record album	3.26	2.71	2.74	2.94
Camera	3.88	3.88	3.77	3.84
Overall mean	2.69	2.69	2.90	2.76
Notions, toiletries				
Toothpaste	2.07	2.41	2.43	2.28
Shampoo	3.10	3.31	3.00	3.13
Bath soap	2.76	2.94	3.43	3.03
Aspirin	3.64	3.72	3.91	3.75
Overall mean	2.89	3.09	3.19	3.05
Other products				
Laundry soap	3.38	3.63	3.66	3.54
Automobile	3.59	3.81	3.57	3.65
Household cleaner	3.55	3.75	3.83	3.70
Gasoline brand	3.81	3.81	3.80	3.81
Overall mean	3.58	3.75	3.71	3.67

Scale: 1 = often; 4 = never

Table 5: Intercorrelations between dependent variables: child's
purchase influence attempts, parental yielding, and
perceived influence of commercials

	Child's purchase influence attempts	Parental yielding	Perceived influence of commercials
Influence attempts	--	--	--
Parental yielding	.35***	--	--
Perceived influence	.71***	.22**	--

** $p < .01$
*** $p < .001$

Data in Table 6 show relationships between the three kinds of independent variables and the three dependent variables. Visual inspection of the data revealed little intercorrelation among the independent variables.

Table 6: Correlations between child's purchase influence attempts, parental yielding, perceived influence of commercials, and the independent variables

	Child's purchase influence attempts	Parental yielding	Perceived influence of commercials
Demographics			
Child's age	−.13	.20**	−.14
No. of children	−.00	−.00	.01
Social class	−.01	.00	.03
Interpersonal variables			
Parent-child conflict	.18*	−.00	.12
Restrictions on viewing	−.01	−.24**	.06
Communication variables			
Mother's time spent with TV	.18*	.23**	.21**
Recall of commercials	.26**	.04	.27**
Attitudes toward adv.	−.00	.16*	.04

* $p < .05$
** $p < .01$

Essentially no relationships were found between the dependent variables and number of children in the family and social class. However, the relationship between age and influence attempts approaches significance ($p = -.13$). Thus, as seen in Table 2 influence attempts seem to decrease with age. A near-significant negative relationship also obtains between age and perceived influence of commercials. However, a positive correlation obtains between age and parental yielding to purchase influence attempts. Thus, while parents may receive many purchase requests from young children, they are more likely to act on them as the child grows older.

Two variables regarding parent-child behavior were examined: parent-child conflict and restrictions on television viewing. While many other variables may be important predictors of the dependent variables, conflict and restrictions are presumably related to types of control parents may attempt to exert over children. The data indicate a significant positive relationship between conflict and influence attempts ($r = .18$), suggesting that purchase influence attempts may be part of general patterns of disagreement and conflict between parents and children—perhaps a cause of them. However, no relationship is observed between conflict and yielding. Thus, it seems that failure to yield to a child's purchase influence attempts is not usually a mode of "punishment" employed by parents.

A negative relationship obtains between restrictions on viewing and yielding. Thus, the more restrictions parents place on a child's television viewing, the less they yield to purchase influence attempts. Interestingly, however, no relationship obtains between restrictions and influence attempts. It seems this form of parental control is not effective in reducing a child's purchase influence attempts.

The final set of independent variables concern aspects of mothers' mass communication behavior and their effect on the dependent variables. The data indicate positive relationships between mothers' time spent watching television and influence attempts, yielding, and perceived influence. This may simply reflect the greater availability to children of mothers who watch much television. Moreover, perhaps influence attempts, and promises of yielding, occur when mothers and children watch television together.

Mothers' recall of commercial content, measured by a series of fill-in-the-blank advertising identification items, is related to purchase influence attempts and perceived influence of commercials on children. This may suggest a general sensitivity of mothers to commercials which seem to affect their children. However, some evidence suggests that recall of commercial content is a function of intelligence (Ward and Wackman, 1971). Thus the lack of relationship between recall and parental yielding may suggest that more intelligent mothers are less likely to respond to influence attempts by yielding. Finally, a mild positive relationship obtains between attitudes toward advertising and yielding: mothers with more positive attitudes toward advertising are more likely to yield to purchase influence attempts than mothers with less favorable attitudes.

Examination of partial correlation coefficients (controlling for age) reveals only slight changes in the patterns of relationships analyzed above.

SUMMARY

Mothers feel that commercials influence younger children more than older children, and they appear to guage this influence by the frequency of purchase influence attempts for particular products. While influence attempts may decrease with age, yielding to requests increases with age, probably reflecting the perceived increased competence of older children to make purchase decisions.

Aspects of parent-child conflict are related to influence attempts and yielding. The data suggest that influence attempts may be part of more general parent-child conflict; furthermore, mothers who restrict viewing are likely not to yield to purchase influence attempts. Finally, mothers' time spent watching television is positively related to influence attempts, yielding, and perceived influence, while recall of commercials is related to influence attempts and perceived influence. Mothers with positive attitudes toward advertising are more likely than mothers with negative attitudes to yield to influence attempts.

In future research, other aspects of parent-child interaction and their influence on the dependent variables will be examined. Characteristics of the children should be related to influence attempts and yielding. Characteristics of the viewing situation should be considered. It may be that joint parent-child or family viewing increases the incidence of purchase influence attempts.

REFERENCES

Berey, L.A., and Pollay, R.W. The influencing role of the child in family decision-making. *Journal of Marketing Research*, February 1968.

Chaffee, S., Ward, S., and Tipton, L. Mass communication and political socialization. *Journalism Quarterly*, 1970, **47**(4), 647-59.

Granbois, D.H. The role of communication in the family decision-making process. Unpublished paper, 1967.

Halloran, J.D., Brown, R.L., and Chaney, D.C. *Television and delinquency*. Leicester, U.K.: Leicester University Press, 1970.

McLeod, J., O'Keefe, G., and Wackman, D. Communication and political socialization during the adolescent years. Paper presented to Theory and Methodology division, Association for Education in Journalism, Berkeley, Calif., 1969.

Ward, S., and Wackman, D. Family and media influences on adolescent consumer behavior. *Television and social behavior*, Vol. 4 (this volume).

Yankelovich, D. (Inc.) Mothers' attitudes toward children's programs and commercials. Newton Centre, Mass.: Action for Children's Television, 1970.

Adolescent Attitudes Toward Television Advertising: Preliminary Findings

Scott Ward and Thomas S. Robertson

Social scientists have long been concerned with the role of childhood and adolescent experiences in shaping a variety of later adult behaviors, but little attention has been paid to understanding the *development of consumer behavior*. Some recent attention is manifest in Herrmann's (1969) bibliography on the consumer behavior of children and adolescents.

The family, peer groups, and the mass media play major roles in shaping adolescent consumer behavior as they do in other aspects of socialization. This study concerns the effects of advertising on children and teenagers; we are particularly interested in television advertising, since television is the dominant advertising medium to which adolescents are exposed.

There is a gap in the research literature here. Most published studies of advertising's effects are not concerned with responses of young people, since adults are most often the target audience (Bauer and Greyser, 1968). On the other hand, most studies of effects of television on children ignore advertising; Schramm, Lyle, and Parker's (1961) classic study is a case in point.

In this paper,[1] we have two objectives. First, we want to provide some baseline data about attitudes of adolescents toward television advertising. These descriptive data are contained in Tables 1-3. Second, we test nine hypotheses; seven of these concern predictors of adolescent attitudes toward television advertising, and two concern effects of these attitudes on recall of commercials and on self-reported effects of purchase behavior.

METHODOLOGY

The data reported here were gathered last April in 12 schools in Prince Georges County, Maryland, through self-administered questionnaires.

The sample consisted of 1,094 students in grades eight through 12, providing reasonably good representativeness. However, black adolescents were underrepresented, because we were not permitted to interview in the predominantly black schools. The sample was slightly skewed toward the middle and upper classes; the lower class extends to the thirty-ninth decile (indexed by the Duncan Socioeconomic Status index) rather than the thirty-third.

Various indices employed in this research are described in Appendix A. The indices were derived by examining factor loadings for questionnaire items in various areas of a *priori* interest. Indices were constructed by recoding and summing items for each respondent. Groups were designated on the basis of frequency distributions for each index. Different cutting points resulted from the different distributions for the junior high, senior high, and total samples.

The main index, "Attitudes Toward TV Advertising," was constructed from five questionnaire items. The Spearman reliability coefficient estimate for the index is .55.

DESCRIPTIVE DATA

Tables D-1 through D-3 concern commercials mentioned as representing the "best" and the "worst" on television in response to open-ended questions. Tables report the data for the total sample, for the junior high and senior high respondents, and for each sex. The "percent of total mentions" column in Table D-1 represents an "overall salience measure" of commercials in various product categories for adolescents. Cigarette advertising, for example, is mentioned by 17 percent of the adolescents—making it a salient product category, but only 27 percent of these teenagers are favorable toward the cigarette ads. Drugs and patent medicine advertisements are in the second product category; the adolescents have mixed emotions about these ads.

Table 2 compares the junior with the senior high samples; there are no surprising patterns of differences. Table 3 compares responses of male and female adolescents.

Table 1 reports the advertising cited as "best," and Table 4 reports the reasons adolescents like the advertising they cite as best. Drugs and patent medicines, automobiles, and soft drinks are product categories most often cited as "best" television advertising, with predictable differences between junior and senior high students and between males and females. More older adolescents than younger adolescents, like automobile ads, and more boys than girls. The data in Table 1 indicate that the adolescents like ads that are "funny" and "straightforward."

The data in Table 5 indicate that cigarette advertising is the single most important product category accounting for negative attitudes. Table 7 shows that the major reason for the dislike is that adolescents feel the "worst" commercials are "stupid"—that they "insult intelligence."

Table 1: Major product categories cited as
"best" or
"worst" television advertising
(Total sample N = 1,094)

Product category	% of total mentions	% specifying product category as best, worst	
		Best	Worst
Cigarettes	17%	27%	73%
Drugs, patent medicines	15	58	42
Autos	9	79	21
Deodorants, cosmetics	9	43	57
Public service: antismoking	8	80	20
Soft drinks	7	96	4
Food, gum	6	53	47
Other*	29	20	80
	100%		
N	(1,535)		

* "Other" includes beer, wine, laundry soap, household cleaners, personal soap, gasoline, airlines, and public service.

Table 2: Comparison of junior and senior high samples:
percent of total mentions by product categories;
percent citing product category as
"best" or "worst" television advertising

Product category	Percent of total mentions		Percent citing product category as "best" TV adv.		Percent citing product category as "worst" TV adv.	
	Jr. high	Sr. high	Jr. high	Sr. high	Jr. high	Sr. high
Cigarettes	16%	18%	26%	28%	74%	72%
Drugs, pat. med.	16	13	55	60	45	40
Deodorants, cosmetics	9	9	40	46	60	54
Public service: antismoking	8	8	81	80	19	20
Autos	6	12	75	82	25	18
Soft drinks	8	6	96	96	4	4
Food, gum	7	6	58	48	42	52
Laundry, soap, household cleaners	7	5	13	19	87	81
Other*	23	23	47	42	53	50
N	(699)	(836)				

* Other responses include: beer and wine, personal soap, toothpaste, gas and oil, airlines, other personal, public service (other than antismoking).

Table 6 and 7 present the reasons adolescents give for liking and disliking television commercials, by the product categories, for the total sample and for the junior and senior high samples. Our sample sizes were quite small in these analyses, due to the fact that many adolescents failed to specify a commercial and/or a reason for liking or disliking it. In any case, some current advertising campaigns were reflected in the data: in Table 6 for example, of all the adolescents who gave "funny" as

Table 3: Comparison of males and females:
percent of total mentions by product categories;
percent citing product category as "best" or
"worst" television advertising

Product category	Percent of total mentions		Percent citing product category as "best" TV adv.		Percent citing product category as "worst" TV adv.	
	Male	Female	Male	Female	Male	Female
Cigarettes	17%	17%	21%	31%	79%	69%
Drugs, pat. med.	11	17	57	58	43	42
Deodorants, cosmetics	7	10	50	39	50	61
Public service: antismoking	8	8	78	82	22	18
Automobiles	16	4	86	59	14	41
Soft drinks	6	8	98	96	2	4
Food, gum	5	7	41	61	59	39
Laundry, soap, household cleaners	7	5	13	17	87	83
Other*	23	24	42	41	58	59
	100%	100%				
N	(673)	(853)				

* Other responses include: beer and wine, personal soap, toothpaste, gas and oil, airlines, other personal, public service (other than antismoking).

Table 4: Major reasons for liking "best" television
advertising by total sample, Jr. and Sr. high samples,
and male and female adolescents

Reasons for liking	Total (N=1,094)	Jr. high (N=537)	Sr. high (N=557)	Male (N=510)	Female (N=574)
Funny	15%	17%	14%	16%	15%
Straightforward	13	10	15	11	14
Different, unique	6	6	7	6	6
Interesting, clever	5	6	5	5	6
Beautiful	5	5	6	5	6
Other*	23	13	13	20	26
No response	33	34	32	37	27
	100%	100%	100%	100%	100%

* "Other" responses include: "contemporary style," "good music", "like product anyway", "real", "makes me think", and "fast moving."

Table 5: Product categories most cited as "worst" television
advertising, by total sample, jr. and sr. high samples,
and male and female adolescents

Product category	Total (N=1,094)	Jr. high (N=537)	Sr. high (N=557)	Male (N=510)	Female (N=574)
Cigarettes	17%	16%	19%	18%	17%
Drugs, patent medicines	9	9	8	6	11
Deodorants, cosmetics	7	7	7	5	9
Laundry soap, household cleaners	7	8	6	8	7
Other*	29	23	28	23	23
No response	31	37	27	36	27
	100%	100%	100%	100%	100%

* "Other" responses include: beer and wine, food and gum, toothpastes, automobiles, personal soap, antismoking, and other personal products.

a reason for liking the "best" television commercials, 26 percent cited drug or patent medicine advertising as the product category exemplifying this humor. This suggests that much reaction is directed at the current Alka Seltzer campaign.

Table 6: Major reasons for liking "best TV advertising"
by most often cited product categories: total sample (N=705)*

Major Reasons For Liking "Best TV Ads"

Product category	Funny	Straight-forward	Interesting, clever	Good music	Total
Drugs, pat. med.	26%[1] (75)	9% (7)	18% (14)	– –	19%[2] (127)
Autos	16% (41)	13% (10)	12% (9)	– –	14% (96)
Soft drinks	– –	– –	– –	60% (56)	14% (100)
Antismoking	– –	37% (28)	9% (12)	– –	11% (80)
Cigarettes	8% (19)	– –	– –	16% (15)	9% (63)
Deodorants	18% (44)	– –	– –	– –	7% (53)
Food, gum	– –	– –	22% (17)	– –	6% (44)
Other	– –	– –	– –	– –	20% (142)
% TOTAL REASONS:	33%[3] (245)	11% (75)	11% (77)	13% (93)	100% (705)

*   389 adolescents were eliminated from analysis due to missing data.

[1]   Should be read: Of the 245 adolescents who gave "funny" as a reason for liking the "best" TV advertising, 75, or 26%, cited drugs or patent medicines as the product category exemplifying this reason for liking.

[2]   Should be read: Of the 705 adolescents who specified both a product category as "best" TV advertising, and a reason for liking, 127, or 19%, specified some reason for liking drug or patent medicine advertising.

[3]   Should be read: Of the 705 adolescents who specified both a product category as "best" TV advertising, and a reason for liking, 245, or 33% cited product categories for "funny" commercials.

In table 7, cigarette advertising is disliked for a variety of reasons—primarily because adolescents see it as hypocritical.

HYPOTHESES

The first three hypotheses we formulated concern adolescents' characteristics which may affect their attitudes toward television advertising: social class, amount of television exposure, and intelligence.

Studies of effects of television programming on adolescents suggest that lower-class adolescents often use television as a learning device and that they have more favorable attitudes than higher-class adolescents (Greenberg and Dominick, 1968). Thus, we reasoned that lower-class adolescents would have more positive attitudes toward commercials than middle and upper class adolescents. The data in Table 8 support our hypothesis, although the main attitude difference is between lower- and upper-class adolescents. This finding holds only among the senior high adolescents, even when amount of television exposure is controlled.

Table 7: Major reasons for disliking "worst TV advertising"
by most often cited product categories: total sample (N=667)*

Product category	Major Reasons For Disliking "Worst" TV Ads					
	Stupid		Fake	Hypocritical	Bad taste	Total
Cigarettes	17%[1]	(41)	15% (11)	58% (40)	27% (16)	22%[2] (147)
Deodorants	13%	((30)	– –	– –	15% (9)	8% (56)
Food, gum	13%	(31)	8% (6)	– –	– –	9% (62)
Laundry soap, household cleaners	– –		33% (24)	10% (7)	12% (7)	19% (127)
Other	10%	(23)	12% (9)	– –	8% (5)	38% (275)
% TOTAL REASONS:	35%[3]	(236)	11% (73)	10% (69)	9% (60)	100% (667)

* 427 respondents were eliminated from analysis due to missing data.

[1] Should be read: Of the 236 adolescents who gave "stupid" as a reason for disliking the "worst" TV advertising, 41, or 17% cited cigarettes as the product category exemplifying this reason for disliking.

[2] Should be read: Of the 667 adolescents who specified both a product category as "worst" TV advertising, and a reason for disliking, 147, or 22% specified same reason for disliking cigarette advertising.

[3] Should be read: Of the 667 adolescents who specified both a product category as "worst" TV advertising, and a reason for disliking, 236, or 35% cited product categories for "stupid" commercials.

Hypothesis 1: The higher an adolescent's social class, the greater the negative attitudes toward television advertising.

Table 8: Family social class and attitudes
toward TV advertising (total sample)

		Social class		
		Lower	Middle	Upper
Attitude toward TV advertising	pos.	51% (150)	47% (150)	41% (134)
	neg.	49% (145)	53% (172)	59% (190)
		100% (259)	100% (322)	100% (324)

N=941

$X^2 = 5.64$, 2df, $p < .05$

Previous studies of effects of programs on children also led us to hypothesize that adolescents who watch a great deal of television will have more positive attitudes toward commercials than adolescents who watch less television and that less intelligent adolescents will have more positive attitudes than more intelligent adolescents (Schramm, Lyle, and Parker, 1961). The data in Table 9 support our hypotheses about exposure and attitudes, but the relationship holds only for middle- and upper-class

Hypothesis 2: Greater amounts of exposure to television will result in more positive attitudes toward television advertising.

Table 9: Amount of television exposure and attitudes toward TV advertising (total sample)

Amount of exposure

		Low	High
	pos.	40% (165)	49% (320)
Attitude toward TV advertising	neg.	60% (243)	51% (328)
		100% (408)	100% (148)

N=1056

$X^2 = 7.70$, 1df, p. $< .005$

adolescents when social class is held constant. The data in Table 11 support our hypotheses concerning intelligence and attitudes: the greater the intelligence, the greater the negative attitudes toward television advertising. Both these findings are consistent with previous research concerning effects of programs of young people.

Table 10: Amount of television exposure and attitudes toward television advertising, controlling for social class (total sample)

		Lower social class (n=292)		Middle social class (n=318)		Upper social class (n=321)	
Amt. Exp:		Low 55%	High 50%	Low 37%	High 51%	Low 35%	High 47%
	+	(55)	(95)	(43)	(103)	(52)	(82)
Attitude							
	–	45% (46)	50% (96)	63% (74)	49% (98)	65% (95)	53% (92)
		100% (101)	100% (191)	100% (117)	100% (201)	100% (147)	100% (174)

$X^2 = .41$, 1df, n.s. $X^2 = 5.68$, 1df, p$<.01$ $X^2 = 4.06$, 1df, p$<.04$

Hypotheses 4-7, reported in Tables 12-15, concern processes which presumably affect attitudes toward commercials. In other research (Ward and Robertson, 1971), we found that television advertising often complements interaction between parents and teenagers about the consumption of goods and services. Thus, we reasoned that adolescents from homes characterized by a great deal of communication about consumption should have more positive attitudes toward television advertising than adolescents from homes characterized by less communication about consumption. The data in Table 12 support this hypothesis.

Hypothesis 3: More intelligent adolescents will have more negative attitudes toward television advertising than will less intelligent adolescents.

Table 11: Intelligence and attitudes toward
TV advertising (Jr. High sample)

Intelligence

Attitude		Low	Med.	High
	+	59% (40)	47% (85)	43% (107)
	−	41% (28)	53% (95)	57% (141)
		100% (68)	100% (180)	100% (248)

N =496

$$X^2=5.29, 2df, p=0.7$$

While a slight majority of all adolescents express negative attitudes toward commercials, adolescents from high communication homes have more positive attitudes than adolescents from low communication homes.

Hypothesis 4: As communication increases within the family about consumption of goods and services, adolescents will hold more positive attitudes toward television advertising.

Table 12: Family communication about consumption
and adolescent attitudes toward
television advertising (total sample)

(total sample)

Family communication about consumption

Attitude		Low	High
	+	41% (202)	49% (219)
	−	59% (292)	51% (232)
		100% (494)	100% (451)

N = 945

$$X^2 = 5.56, 1df, p=.025$$

Hypotheses 5 and 6, reported in Tables 13 and 14, concern the aspirations of adolescents. We reasoned that for some adolescents television commercials portray attractive life styles and means of achieving them. Adolescents who aspire to these life styles should therefore have positive attitudes toward commercials. We used two measures of aspiration: the perceived parental expectation for the adolescent's occupation and social class level, and the adolescent's own aspiration. Both measures

Hypothesis 5:   Adolescents who perceive that their parents want them to achieve higher social-economic status, than the family's present social-economic status, will have more positive attitudes toward television advertising than adolescents who do not perceive this partial expectation, or who perceive it to a lesser degree.

Table 13: Perceived parental expectation
for adolescent's social class status
(total sample)

Perceived parental expectation

		No difference or slightly higher than present SES	Much higher than present SES	
	+	49% (79)	46% (82)	
Attitudes				
	−	52% (84)	54% (95)	
		100% (163)	100% (177)	N = 340

$X^2 = .082$, 1df, n.s.

are based on the Duncan Socioeconomic Index (see Robinson et al. 1969) which provides a sensitive measure of social class status based on an extensive occupational code.

The data in Tables 13 and 14 do not support our predictions, perhaps because adolescents are not firmly set on future occupations and class levels, perhaps because they do not clearly perceive their parents' expectation for them.

The seventh hypothesis concerns the effects of "materialism" on attitudes toward advertising. By "materialism," we mean valuing of physical possessions and money as important for personal happiness and for social progress. In this era when many young people seem to desire a less materialistic existence, we would expect less materialistic adolescents to have less favorable attitudes toward television advertising than highly materialistic adolescents. The data in Table 15 support this expectation. However, when social class is controlled, the relationship holds

Hypothesis 6: Adolescents who desire a higher SES level than their family's present SES level, will hold more positive attitudes toward television advertising than adolescents who have less desire for higher SES.

Table 14: Adolescent aspiration for SES, and
attitudes toward television advertising
(total sample)

Aspiration

		No difference or slightly higher than present SES	Much higher than persent SES	
	+	43% (131)	47% (165)	
Attitudes				
	−	56% (171)	53% (188)	
		100% (302)	100% (353)	N = 655

x^2 = .747, 1df, n.s.

Hypothesis 7: Adolescents who hold highly "materialistic" values will hold more positive attitudes toward television advertising than adolescents who hold less materialistic values.

Table 15: Materialism and attitudes toward
television advertising
(total sample)

Materialism

		Low	High	
	+	41% (227)	50% (245)	
Attitudes				
	−	59% (327)	50% (242)	
		100% (554)	100% (487)	N = 1041

x^2 = 8.74, 1df, p.=.003

only for middle-class adolescents—suggesting that materialism is a middle-class phenomenon, at least as measured by the items comprising our materialism index.

Hypothesis 8: The more positive an adolescent's attitude toward television advertising, the greater the recall of TV commercial slogans and descriptions

Table 16: Attitudes toward television advertising
and recall of commercials
(total sample)

Attitudes toward TV advertising

		+	−	
	Low	21% (102)	19% (111)	
Recall*	Medium	19% (91)	23% (134)	
	High	34% (168)	32% (183)	
	Very High	26% (126)	25% (145)	
		100% (487)	100% (573)	N = 1060

$$X^2 = 3.62, 3df, n.s.$$

*16-item scale:

Low	= 10 items or less	(22% of total sample)
Medium	= 11-12 items	(22% of total sample)
High	= 13-14 items	(32% of total sample)
Very high	= 15-16 items	(24% of total sample)

The final two hypotheses treat attitudes toward television advertising as the independent variable. We expected adolescents who have more positive attitudes toward commercials to recall more commercial content, and to report greater influence of commercials on buying, than adolescents with negative attitudes. However, the data in Tables 16 and 17 do not support our predictions. Attitudes toward television advertising were not related to recall or to self-reported effects on buying.

Hypothesis 9: Adolescents who hold more positive attitudes toward television advertising will report more effects in buying of TV commercials than adolescents who hold negative attitudes toward television advertising.

Table 17: Attitudes toward television advertising
and self-reported effects on buying of commercials
(total sample)

		Attitudes	
		+	−
	High	22% (105)	21% (123)
Self-reported effects on buying*	Meduim	28% (138)	27% (154)
	Low	50% (245)	52% (299)
		100% (488)	100% (576)

N = 1,064

$$X^2 = .382, 2 \text{ df, n.s.}$$

*Low effects = nothing purchased
*Medium effects = one item purchased
High effects = two or more items purchased

SUMMARY AND CONCLUSIONS

Adolescents do not have extensive, firm attitudes toward television advertising. Many adolescents we surveyed did not list a commercial as representative of the "best" or "worst" on television or did not give a reason for liking or disliking particular commercials. As much as marketers may wish advertising to be somewhat salient to adolescents, this does not seem to be the case. This "low salience" finding is consistent with other studies of adult samples (Bauer and Greyser, 1968).

However, the lack of clear, well-developed attitudes is not sufficient reason to ignore this aspect of the process of learning to be a consumer. At least some adolescents are quite responsive to some kinds of television advertising, and marketers should be interested in understanding their likes and dislikes.

Our findings suggest that other cognitive phenomena should be more extensively investigated. For example, although we did not find a relationship between attitudes and recall, the absolute level of recall was high. On the 16-item recall scale used to test Hypothesis 8, for example, over 50 percent of the sample correctly identified 13 or more of the 16 items. Learning may occur independent of attitudes, but further research should examine the prediction and consequences of differential learning of commercials.

We found social class, amount of television exposure, and intelligence to be related to attitudes toward commercials. Lower-class adolescents had somewhat more positive attitudes toward commercials than their higher-class counterparts. Middle- and upper-class adolescents who watched relatively high amounts of television were more positive than adolescents who watched less television. More intelligent adolescents were more negative in their attitudes toward commercials than less intelligent adolescents.

We found that adolescents from homes characterized by high communication about consumption, as well as adolescents who held relatively materialistic values, were relatively positive toward commercials. However, we did not find a relationship between the occupational and social class aspirations of adolescents and attitudes toward commercials. Finally, we did not find attitudes toward commercials to be a good predictor of recall or of effect on buying.

The failure to confirm some of our hypotheses may be due to difficulty with some of our measures, including the attitudes-toward-advertising index. In future research, we plan to focus on the dimensions of the concept which our data suggest are particularly salient for adolescents: stylistic or presentation characteristics, belief in claims, and humor. Such an improvement in the measure may lead us to a more complete picture of the role of television advertising in shaping the development of consumer behavior.

FOOTNOTES

1. This paper was presented to the meeting of the American Marketing
   Association, September 1970.

REFERENCES

Bauer, R.A., and Greyser, S.A. *Advertising in America: the consumer view*. Boston: Harvard Business School Division of Research, 1968.

Greenberg, B., and Dominick, J. Television usage, attitudes and functions for low-income and middle-class teenagers. Department of Communications, Michigan State University, unpublished paper, 1968.

Herrmann, R.O. *The consumer behavior of children and teenagers: an annotated bibliography*. Chicago: American Marketing Association, 1969.

Robinson, R., Athanasiou, R., and Head, K. *Measures of occupational attitudes and occupational characteristics*. Ann Arbor, Mich.: Survey Research Center, 1969.

Schramm, W., Lyle, J., and Parker, E. *Television in the lives of our children*. Stanford: Stanford University Press, 1961.

Ward, S., and Robertson, T. Family influences on adolescent consumer behavior. Cambridge, Mass.: Marketing Science Institute, 1970 (working paper).

Appendix A: Summary of indices

Index	Operational definition	Measure
Attitudes toward TV advertising	Cognitive and affective orientations concerning liking of and belief in TV advertising; advertising as indication of product quality; efficacy of advertising	4-point frequency and "agree-disagree" items, such as: "TV commercials tell the truth"; "TV advertising makes people buy things they don't really want."
Socioeconomic status; social class	Duncan Socioeconomic index	5-digit occupational code including 3-digit IRS code, 2 digit code indicating population decile of occupation
Family communication about consumption	Overt parent-adolescent interactions concerning consumption of goods and services	4-point "often-never" items, such as: "How often do you ask your parents for advice about buying things?"
Media use	Self-reported average time per day spent watching television, listening to radio; number of periodicals subscribed to or read, time spent reading newspaper	Closed-end time spent items; open-end items for periodical subscriptions or reading
Intelligence	School test scores (IQ, etc.)	Track in school
Materialism	Orientation emphasizing physical possessions and money for personal happiness and social progress	4-point frequency and "agree-disagree" items, such as: "It's really true that money can buy happiness."

Advertising recall	Aided recall of national TV advertising campaigns aired during 1969-70	16 incomplete slogans or descriptions of commercials, such as: "The Green Phantom..."
Effects on buying	Self-reported influence of commercials on purchase behavior; single effect of commercial, or effect of commercial for product already known about	Open-end question

Racial Differences in Responses to Advertising Among Adolescents

Daniel B. Wackman
Greg Reale
Scott Ward

The major purpose of this paper is to compare the responses of black and white adolescents to television advertising.[1] In particular, three dimensions of these responses are compared: choices of "best" and "worst" ads and the reasons given for these choices (including responses to specific aspects of ads); media behavior of black and white adolescents, with particular emphasis on the reasons adolescents have for watching commercials; and learning of several aspects of consumer roles.

Little research has compared blacks with whites on each of these dimensions, and almost no research has compared black with white adolescents. Barban has compared black and white adults' reactions to ads in several studies, generally finding that their reactions are very similar (Barban and Cunditt, 1964; Barban and Granbaum, 1965). Bauer and Cunningham (1970) also found a high degree of similarity between black and white adults' attitudes toward advertising and specific reactions to ads.

Only one study examined black and white adolescents' reactions to ads. In this study, Parente (1969) showed both all-white and integrated ads to black and white sixth graders. He found no differences in semantic differential responses to either the all-white or the integrated ads.

Somewhat more research has been done in the area of media behavior and reasons for media use. A number of studies have compared media use and program preferences of black and white adults—Carey (1966), CBS (1968), Greenberg and Irwin (1970), Larson (1968), but few studies have surveyed black and white adolescents. Dominick and Greenberg (1971) compared amounts of use of various electronic and print media among black, low-income white, and middle-income white tenth and eleventh graders. They that found the two groups of white youth were similar to each other and different from blacks in program preferences and in use of all mass media. This contrasts with findings from Greenberg and Dervin's (1970) study of adult media behavior, in which low-income blacks and whites were similar to each other and different from a general population sample of whites. In a study of reading interests, Olson and Rosen (1967) found several differences between groups of black and white ninth graders.

Gerson (1966) found that black adolescents were more likely to watch television shows and movies and read magazines and books to learn about dating than were white adolescents. Similarly, Dominick and Greenberg (1971) found that black adolescents were more likely than whites to watch television to learn "what life is really like," "how others solve the same problems I have," and so on. No research, however, has compared black and white adolescents' reasons for watching commercials.

Finally, no research has compared consumer learning among black and white adolescents.

In short, little research regarding racial differences in responses to advertising has been done, and almost none of this research has investigated racial differences among adolescents. The research presented in this paper will bring some empirical data to this area.

METHODOLOGY

The data reported here were gathered in April 1970 in 12 schools in Prince Georges County, Maryland, through self-administered questionnaires. The sample consisted of 1,149 students in eighth through twelfth grades—1,049 white and 100 blacks.[2] Open-ended questions were used to measure ad preferences, reasons for liking or disliking ads, and amount of television and magazine use. Close-ended questions were used to measure all the other responses discussed in the paper.

The black and white samples were nearly identical in distributions of age, sex, and grade in school. The white sample was higher than the black sample in social class as indexed by father's occupation.

Tables reported here show differences between black and white adolescents without control for social class. Data analyses run with control for social class are not different from the data reported here. Indeed, social class in both the black and white samples was not significantly related to the overwhelming majority of measures discussed in the paper.

FINDINGS

Reactions to television advertisements

Choices of "best" and "worst" ads, reasons for these choices, and responses to features of ads are presented in Tables 1 to 6. Table 1 indicates that white adolescents were more likely to choose a "best" ad or a "worst" ad than were black adolescents. This result is not due to a response bias; on other open-ended items, the same percentage of black and white adolescents failed to respond. A possible explanation of the lower choice rate among black adolescents is that television commercials are less relevant to them, since the commercials depict products which are less a part of black adolescents' lives and show people with whom they do not identify. However (as will be seen below), black adolescents were more likely than whites to say they watched television commercials for "social utility" reasons (to find out how others live, to find out how to make a good impression on others, etc.). This finding seems to conflict with the present interpretation.

Table 1: Percent of adolescents choosing a
"best" and a "worst" commercial

	Black	White
Percent choosing a "best" commercial	58%	72%
Percent choosing a "worst" commercial	58%	68%
N	(100)	(1049)

Tables 2 and 3 indicate that black and white adolescents choose highly similar types of commercials as "best" and give similar reasons for liking them. The only major difference in types of commercial chosen is that blacks were more likely to choose food and gum ads as "best." The reasons given for liking the ads were quite similar for blacks and whites, the major differences being that blacks were more likely to say the

Table 2: Types of commercials chosen as "best"

	Black	White
Drug, patent medicine	12%	17%
Automobiles	12	14
Soft drinks	14	14
Food, gum	19	7
Antismoking	10	12
Other	33	36
	100%	100%
N	58	767

"best" ad was "beautiful," while whites were more likely to say it was "different" or "interesting." These data support Barban's (1965) finding that black and white adults have essentially the same structure in their reactions to ads, and Parente's (1969) finding that black and white sixth graders have essentially the same (favorable) evaluation of all-white and integrated ads.

Table 3: Reasons cited for liking "best" commercial

	Black	White
Humor, funny	34%	32%
Straightforwardness	20	18
Beautiful	18	12
Stylistic, visual	11	11
Different, interesting	9	17
Other	8	10
	100%	100%
N	(56)	(726)

On the other hand, blacks and whites' choices of "worst" ads and their reasons for disliking these ads were somewhat different (Tables 4 and 5). Blacks were more likely to choose deodorant-cosmetic, automobile, and food-gum ads as "worst"; whites were more likely to choose cigarette and laundry soap ads as "worst." Further, blacks were more likely to say the ads were bad for stylistic reasons or because they were boring and too long. Whites were more likely to say the ads were stupid and insulted their intelligence or were in bad taste.

Table 4: Type of commercial chosen as "worst"

	Black	White
Cigarettes	14%	23%
Deodorant, cosmetics	22	15
Laundry soap	12	19
Automobiles	12	5
Food, gum	16	9
Other	24	29
	100%	100%
N	(58)	(712)

Table 6 indicates that black and white adolescents were similar in their negative evaluation of several specific aspects of television commercials, although whites are more negative on three of four items. Only on the general attitude item is the difference between the two groups statistically significant.

Table 5: Reasons cited for disliking "worst" commercial

	Black	White
Stupid, insults intelligence	30%	38%
False, hypocritical	21	21
Stylistic	25	14
Boring, too long	16	10
Bad taste	2	9
Other	6	8
	100%	100%
N	(51)	(670)

These data indicate that, in most ways, black and white adolescents have quite similar reactions to ads. Though whites were more likely to select an ad as "best" or "worst," the types of commercials chosen as "best" and the reasons for this choice were very similar for blacks and whites. Blacks and whites were also quite similar in their generally negative evaluation of TV commercials. Major differences between blacks and whites appear only in the choice of "worst" ads and the reasons given for this choice—though even here, in two of the three categories with the largest percent of responses (stupid, insults intelligence, and fake or hypocritical) blacks and whites show quite similar percentages.

Table 6: Attitudes toward television commercials[a]

	Black	White	Difference[b]
Most commercials are too long	72%	76%	n.s.
Most commercials are in poor taste and are very annoying	64	68	n.s.
TV commercials tell the truth	30	35	n.s.
I like TV commercials	43	30	B > W
N	(98)	(1032)	

[a]Table entries are percent of respondents agreeing with the item.

[b]B > W indicates a difference statistically significant at p < .05.

Media behavior and reasons for watching commercials

Differences between black and white adolescents in time spent using various media are reported in Table 7. Blacks watched substantially more television daily than whites, and they listened to the radio more. These results support Dominick and Greenberg's (1971) finding regarding television use but contradict their finding that whites listen to the radio more than blacks. In the present study, whites reported reading newspapers and magazines more frequently than did blacks; these results support Dominick and Greenberg's findings.

Thus, in our sample, blacks were relatively more oriented to "electronic" media than whites, and whites were relatively more "print" oriented than blacks. However, for both blacks and whites, the dominant medium was television.

A consistent pattern of difference between blacks' and whites' reasons for viewing commercials is found in the data (Table 8). Blacks were more likely than whites to say they watched commercials for social utility reasons (to learn how to solve problems, learn how to make a good impression on others, learn how to be successful), for communication utility reasons (to provide something to talk about with parents and friends), and vicarious consumption reasons (to see things I'd like to

Table 7: Amount of media use

	Black	White	Difference[a]
Electronic			
Hours spent watching TV yesterday	4.4	3.1	B > W
Hours spent listening to the radio yesterday	2.7	1.6	B > W
Print			
Percent reading a newspaper at least four times per week	51%	62%	W > B
Percent reading two or more magazines regularly	34%	46%	W > B
N	(99)	(1035)	

[a] B > W indicates a difference statistically significant at p < .05.

have, let me dream of the good life). These results support Gerson's (1966) finding that blacks use media more than whites for information about dating, and Dominick and Greenberg's (1971) finding that blacks are more likely than whites to watch television shows to learn such things as "what life is really like" and "how others solve the same problems I have." Of course, the difference in the present study is that blacks are more likely than whites to report watching *commercials* for these purposes.

Table 8: Reasons for viewing TV commercials

	Black	White	Difference[a]
Social utility reasons[b]	7.2	5.2	B > W
Communication utility reasons[c]	1.8	1.3	B > W
Vicarious consumption reasons[d]	2.8	2.4	B > W
N	(96)	(1015)	

[a] B > W indicates a difference statistically significant at p < .05

[b] The index of social utility reasons consisted of seven items:
  1. I find out what kinds of people buy the things advertised.
  2. Commercials show how other people solve the same problems I have.
  3. Some of the people they show are examples of what I wish I were.
  4. Commercials help me learn how to make a good impression on others.
  5. Commercials tell me the "in" things to buy.
  6. I watch them because they show what qualities people like in others.
  7. Commercials tell me how to be successful.

[c] The index of communication utility reasons consisted of two items:
  1. I watch commercials to give me something to talk about with my parents.
  2. I watch commercials to give me something to talk about with my friends.

[d] The index of vicarious consumption reasons consisted of two items:
  1. They show me things I'd like to have.
  2. They let me dream of the good life.

It should be noted that these findings refer to relative differences. Most black and white adolescents do *not* watch television commercials for these reasons. To measure these reasons, the respondents were asked whether a given reason for watching commercials was "a lot like me" "a little like me," "not much like me," or "not at all like me." In response to the social utility item ("Commercials show how other people solve the same problems I have"), only 34 percent of the blacks and 19 percent of the whites reported the statement was a lot or a little like them. For the social utility item ("I watch TV commercials because they show what qualities people like in others"), 37 percent of the blacks and 22 percent of the whites said this was either a lot or a little like them. For the communication utility item ("I watch commercials to give me something to talk about with my friends"), 30 percent of the blacks and 21 percent of the whites reported this was a lot or a little like them.

As noted previously, social class was not significantly related to media use or reasons for watching commercials. However, age was related to several of these variables. Junior high blacks and whites were more likely to watch commercials for social utility, communication utility, and vicarious consumption reasons than were their senior high counterparts. It would seem, then, that younger students, who are probably in an earlier stage of learning social norms and how to behave socially, are more likely than older students to try to find this kind of information in the media—in this case, in television commercials. Older students, with more social experience, probably have less need for this kind of information and/or have found the information presented in commercials not very useful for social purposes.

Clearly, then, television commercials do *not* have high "social utility" or "communication utility" for most adolescents. But they do seem to have somewhat more utility for black adolescents than for white adolescents and more for younger than for older adolescents. Apparently, not only do television shows and other media supply more socially useful information for black adolescents, as previous research indicated, but television commercials also do the same—at least, as the adolescents perceive it in terms of their reasons for watching commercials.

Consumer learning

Consumer learning—acquiring attitudes, values and skill relating to buying behavior—involves several different kinds of learning, which can be ordered according to levels of complexity. The simplest level of learning is recall of commercials, indexed here by a test of identification of product and company slogans used in television advertising ("_____has a better idea"). A somewhat more complex level of learning involves orientations toward marketing institutions (indexed here by a measure of attitudes toward advertising) and toward consumption (indexed here by a materialism scale). Finally, a higher level of learning complexity involves behavioral response to advertising, indexed here by an adolescent's report of buying products after seeing ads for the products.

Table 9 indicates no difference between black and white adolescents in recall of commercial slogans and attitudes toward advertising. Both black and white adolescents have a rather high recognition of commercial slogans, and both are somewhat negative toward advertising. Blacks are more materialistic than whites, and they report more purchases of products in response to ads than do whites. It may be that black adolescents, who are probably from a relatively more deprived material environment, feel a stronger need to have consumer goods than whites do; this may also account for their being more responsive to ads in subsequent purchase behavior.

Table 9: Consumer learning

	Black	White	Difference[a]
Recall[b]	11.9	12.4	n.s.
Attitudes toward advertising[c]	6.5	6.1	n.s.
Materialism[d]	12.2	11.5	B > W
Effects of ads on buying[e]	.9	.7	B > W
N	(98)	(1033)	

a B > W indicates a difference statistically significant at p < .05.

b The recall scale consisted of 16 fill-in the blank items requiring recall of commercial slogans, e.g., _____ has a better idea.

cAttitudes toward advertising was a three item agree-disagree scale
  1. Most commercials are too long.
  2. Most commercials are in poor taste and are very annoying.
  3. I like TV commercials.

d Materialism was a five item agree-disagree scale:
  1. A lot of social problems today could be solved if all people could just have more material possessions—like cars, televisions, etc.
  2. It's really true that money can buy happiness.
  3. All the things you can buy today really show how great America is.
  4. People judge others by the things they own.
  5. I buy some things that I secretly hope will impress other people.

e The effects of ads on behavior scale consisted of one open-ended question:
   Have you bought anything for yourself or others because of TV advertising?
   What? Respondents could write-in two products.

On none of these measures did junior high and senior high students within the black or white subgroups differ significantly from each other. Apparently, in terms of the measures of consumer learning used here, most learning had occurred by the time the students reached seventh and eighth grades.

SUMMARY

The overall impression of black and white adolescents' responses to advertising is that they simply are not very different. The two groups were very similar in their choices of types of commercials as "best" ads and in the reasons for these choices. They did differ somewhat in the types of commercials chosen as "worst" ads and in the reasons for these choices, although for two of the three largest categories of reasons for disliking the "worst" ads, blacks and whites had quite similar percentages.

Black adolescents were more likely than whites to say they watch commercials for social utility, communication utility, and vicarious consumption reasons, but relatively few adolescents in either group watched commercials for these reasons. Blacks and whites were no different in recall of commercial slogans and in attitudes toward advertising. Blacks were more materialistic and more likely to report purchasing products in response to ads, but differences between blacks and whites were not large.

Thus, black and white adolescents do not differ very much in most of their responses to advertising. This is the case even though blacks spend an hour and a quarter more per day watching television and an hour more per day listening to the radio than whites and therefore are subjected to many more commercials. Apparently this greater exposure does not have much impact on black adolescents which might differentiate them from their white counterparts.

FOOTNOTES

1. This research was supported by the National Institute of Mental Health (Contract No. HSM 42-70-74). Dr. Wackman is an assistant professor and director of the Research Division of the School of Journalism and Mass Communication, University of Minnesota. Mr. Reale is a research assistant at the Marketing Science Institute. Dr. Ward is an assistant professor at the Harvard Business School and senior research associate, Marketing Science Institute.

2. Because of racial problems in the Prince Georges County schools, we were unable to interview in predominantly black schools in the spring. Therefore, to increase the sample of black adolescents, we administered additional questionnaires in October 1970. Approximately half the black sample completed questionnaires in the spring, half in the fall.

REFERENCES

Barban, A.M., and Cundiff, E.W. Negro and white response to advertising stimuli. *Journal of Marketing Research*, 1964, **1**, 53-56.

Barban, A.M., and Grunbaum, W.F. A factor analytic study of Negro and white responses to advertising stimuli. *Journal of Applied Psychology*, 1965, **49**, 274-79.

Bauer, R.A., and Cunningham, S.M. *Studies in the Negro market.* Cambridge, Mass.: Marketing Science Institute, 1970.

Carey, J.W. Variations in Negro/white television preference. *Journal of Broadcasting*, 1966, **10**, 199-212.

Columbia Broadcasting System. *White and Negro attitudes towards race related issues and activities.* Princeton, N.J.: Public Opinion Research Corp., 1968.

Dominick, J.R., and Greenberg, B.S. Mass media functions among low-income adolescents. In Greenberg, B.S., and Dervin, B. *Use of the mass media by the urban poor.* New York: Praeger, 1970.

Gerson, W.M. Mass media socialization behavior: Negro-white differences. *Social Forces*, 1966, **45**, 40-50.

Greenberg, B.S., and Dervin, B. The role of the mass media for urban poor adults. In Greenberg and Dervin, *Use of mass media by the urban poor.* New York: Praeger, 1970.

Larson, C.M. Racial brand usage and media exposure differentials. In Cox, K., and Enis, B. (Eds.) *A new measure of responsibility for marketing.* Philadelphia, Pa.: American Marketing Association, June 1968.

Olson, A.V., and Rosen, C.L. A comparison of reading interests of two populations of ninth grade students. *Adolescence*, 1967, **1**, 321-26.

Parente, D.M. An investigation of the responses of Negro and white children to integrated advertising stimuli. Unpublished master's thesis, University of Illinois, 1969.

Family and Media Influences on Adolescent Consumer Learning

Scott Ward
and
Daniel Wackman

The focus of this paper is on "consumer learning" processes—processes by which adolescents acquire skills and attitudes relating to the consumption of goods and services.[1] We examine intrafamily and mass media communication as they affect consumer learning processes, and describe some demographic predictors of consumer learning.

While the area of consumer learning has received little attention in published research sources (Herrmann, 1969), it would seem to be an important area for research for several reasons. Young people comprise a large specialized market segment for many products and services. They influence purchases within family and peer groups. In addition, childhood and adolescent experiences relating to consumption presumably affect patterns of consumer behavior in adult life.

From the point of view of communication research, the area of consumer learning is important for two reasons. First, television advertising comprises a large amount of air time. On the average, between one and two of every ten minutes is devoted to advertising. Commercials are the number three content category, behind movies (32 percent) and comedy-variety (17 percent) but ahead of action (13 percent) and eight other categories (Steiner, 1963). Therefore, young people are likely to be exposed to a great deal of television advertising. In light of the high incidence of television advertising, it is particularly surprising that communication research has focused on effects of television programming on young people, to the virtual exclusion of examination of effects of television advertising.

Reprinted from AMERICAN BEHAVIORAL SCIENTIST
January/February 1971, Volume 14, Number 3
c 1971 by Sage Publications, Inc.

A second reason for the relevance of consumer learning to communication research is that the area offers the possibility of studying effects of communication on overt behavior, as reported by adolescents.

BACKGROUND

Research relevant to the study of adolescent consumer learning is typically of two types: research examining family consumer processes, and research examining consumption-related variables within static age groups of children. Research examining family processes, however, usually is limited to consideration of husband-wife dyads (Granbois, 1967; Kenkel, 1961; Komarovsky, 1961; Pollay, 1969; Wolgast, 1958). Little systematic evidence exists concerning the role of parent-child interaction in affecting consumer learning processes of offspring (see Ward and Robertson, 1971).

Research focusing on static age groups has examined such topics as attitudes toward saving vs spending and marginal propensities to consume (Cateora, 1963; Phelan and Schvaneveldt, 1969). Additionally, research has examined developing patterns of consumer behavior among young children to commercial messages (Wells, 1965, 1966).

Communication research, on the other hand, has generally ignored television advertising's effects on young people, while concentrating on programming effects. Published studies of advertising's effects have generally focused on adults rather than on young people (Steiner, 1963; Bauer and Greyser, 1968).

Nevertheless, several points of view developed in consumer and communication research are relevant to the present study of family and media communication influences on consumer learning. Communication research has examined the interactions of family and mass media as primary factors in socialization processes, especially political socialization (Chaffee et al., 1967; Jennings and Niemi, 1968; Hess and Torney, 1967). Communication research has also focused on reasons for watching television (Greenberg and Dominick, 1968) and simple measures of time spent watching, which characterized earlier media research.

With respect to the dependent variables, recent research has demonstrated that communication effects—particularly mass communication effects—do not operate in simple stimulus-response fashion (Klapper, 1960; Bauer, 1963). It would also be inaccurate, however, to consider communication as merely a reinforcer of existing cognitive states or behavioral patterns, as one prevalent view of mass media effects would have it (Klapper, 1960). Most of the evidence for this point of view is from studies of attitude change. However, socialization processes are characterized by attitude formation and learning processes. Thus, variables other than attitude change, such as attitude formation and learning, more accurately indicate mass communication effects and, perhaps, predict behavioral effects.

In the present research, our interest is in four criterion variables: recall of commercial content, attitudes toward television advertising, materialistic attitudes, and self-reported effects of commercials on buying behavior. We expect that various demographic indices will be related to these criterion variables. Our interest is in demographic characteristics of adolescents which, in effect, "locate" the adolescent in the social environment—socioeconomic status, intelligence, and available money.

Within demographically defined groups, however, we expect that adolescent consumer learning will vary depending on the relative presence or absence of intrafamily communication about consumption matters and on the adolescent's media use. Our concern is with two dimensions of media use: amount of print and television use, and motivations or reasons adolescents watch television commercials. Thus we are concerned with the *reasons* adolescents watch commercials, as well as with the amount of television and print use.

Previous writers suggest that people may attend to mass media communication for social reasons. For example, by watching commercials they may form impressions of what kinds of people buy certain products or brands, and they may develop associations of products with various life styles (Ogilvy, 1963). These "social utility" reasons for watching commercials may provide a means of conforming to the perceived expectations of others—that is, individuals may feel that if they buy a certain product or brand, they can manipulate the impression others have of them (Ward and Gibson, 1960).

Individuals may also attend to mass communication in order to provide a basis for later interpersonal communication (Chaffee and McLeod, 1967). Such "communication utility" motivations may also apply to watching television commercials.

Finally, people may attend to commercials as a means of vicarious participation in desired life styles or as a means of vicarious association with attractive others.

METHODS

Data for this study were obtained in a 1970 survey of 1,094 eighth through twelfth graders in the Prince Georges County, Maryland, school district. The adolescents received self-administered questionnaires in randomly selected classrooms in twelve schools. The questionnaires took about 45 minutes (one class period) to complete.

While Prince Georges County provides a good cross-section of American social classes, the sample distribution slightly overrepresents the middle class. This may result from the undersampling of classrooms from predominantly black schools. Because of racial tensions at the time of the survey, these schools refused to permit questionnaire distribution.

The sample is divided into junior high school students (eighth and ninth grades, n=537) and senior high school students (tenth, eleventh, and twelfth grades, n=557).

The variables in this research consist of scales formed by summing several items.[2] The procedure for developing the scales was to factor-analyze items relevant to areas of a *priori* interest where appropriate. Items which failed to load on the hypothesized factors were discarded and remaining items were summed to form the scale.

RESULTS

A primary concern is the extent to which different kinds of consumer learning change over time—or, to put it somewhat differently, what developmental changes occur during adolescence in different kinds of consumer learning. Comparisons between junior and senior high respondents indicate no differences on the several learning criteria—recall, attitudes, materialism, and effects on buying behavior. Thus it would appear that there are no gross developmental changes during the adolescent period, at least in terms of our criteria of four kinds of consumer learning shown in Table 1.

In contrast to the lack of differences on the criterion variables, however, we find differences between junior and senior high respondents on nearly every communication variable. In general, younger adolescents engage in more communication and are more likely to watch commercials for social utility reasons than older adolescents. The data in Table 1 also indicate that younger adolescents watch more television than older adolescents and talk more with their parents about consumption.

Table 1: Consumer learning and communication
variables by age group[a]

	Younger	Older	Differences
Recall of ads	12.4	12.3	n.s.
Attitudes toward TV ads	6.2	6.1	n.s.
Materialism	13.4	13.4	n.s.
Effects of ads on buying	0.7	0.7	n.s.
Exposure to TV	3.6	2.8	Y > O
Exposure to magazines	2.6	2.6	n.s.
Family communication about consumption	8.8	7.5	Y > O
Social utility reasons	6.0	4.7	Y > O
Communication utility reasons	1.6	1.1	Y > O
Vicarious consumption reasons	2.6	2.4	n.s.

[a] Table entries are the mean scores for the age gorup on particular scales. Unless n.s. indicated, differences between younger and older samples are significant at the .05 level or beyond.

Younger and older adolescents are equal in their use of magazines. Furthermore, while junior high respondents watch television commercials for social and communication utility reasons to a greater extent than senior high respondents, the two groups do not differ in watching television commercials for vicarious consumption reasons.

These results suggest that although younger and older adolescents may be at the same level in terms of consumer learning, the processes of learning may differ for the two age groups. Mean scores for the two groups differ on the independent and mediating variables. We defer a closer examination of this question until later.

A second consideration is to examine to what extent the different kinds of consumer learning occur together or occur independently of each other. Moreover, do the patterns of relationships among the criterion variables change over time? If the relationships among the criterion variables were stronger for older than for younger adolescents, this would indicate an increase in the integration of different aspects of consumer learning during adolescence. However, this kind of development does not seem to occur, as can be seen in Table 2. Correlations among the criterion variables for both younger and older adolescents are nearly all essentially zero. Thus, it would seem that the several criteria of consumer learning we have used in this study are quite independent of each other, including the general orientation measures of attitudes toward advertising and materialism.

Differences in consumer learning between younger and older adolescents

The remainder of the analysis concerns differences in consumer learning processes for younger and older adolescents. Our procedure is to examine the relationship between a set of independent variables and each criterion variable.

Table 2: Correlations among consumer learning variables for younger and older adolescents[a]

	Recall	Attitudes	Materialism	Effects on Buying
Recall of ads	– –	−.01	−.08	.08
Attitudes toward TV ads	.08	– –	.05	.04
Materialism	.01	.07	– –	.11
Effects of ads on buying	.05	.13	.06	– –

[a] Table entries are product-moment correlation coefficients. Entries in the upper right triangle of the matrix are correlations for younger adolescents; entries in the lower left triangle are correlations for older adolescents.

With each criterion variable, a step-up regression analysis was conducted with three sets of independent variables. Demographic variables included the adolescent's social class, available money, and intelligence. Communication variables included amount of time spent watching television yesterday, number of magazines subscribed to and read, and amount of family communication about consumption. Reasons for watching television commercials included social utility, communicatory utility, and vicarious consumption reasons. Analyses were carried out separately for younger and older adolescents.

Recall of television advertising

Recall of television advertising is a measure of the simplest kind of consumer learning, basically indicating an awareness of the themes and slogans of American companies and consumer products. For younger adolescents, the respondents' intelligence and their magazine reading were the two variables that met our criterion of accounting for at least one percent of the variance of the criterion variable. As can be seen Table 3, intelligence was a much better predictor of recall than exposure to magazines. For older adolescents, intelligence was again the strongest predictor, with television time the only other important predictor.

Intelligence, which in school tests mainly reflects verbal skills, is the primary predictor of commercial retention. Perhaps one should not be surprised that amount of media exposure is a less certain correlate. Considering the redundancy of commercial messages, it takes limited contact with the media to gain exposure to most prominent ads. However, storing and retrieving their content depend on the verbal skills that govern performance at a wide range of communicatory tasks in modern society.

Attitudes toward television advertising

Attitudes toward television advertising are a measure of a more complex kind of consumer learning. Table 3 indicates that, among younger adolescents, two variables accounted for much of the variance: social utility reasons for viewing commercials, and time spent watching television. By contrast, among older adolescents three different variables accounted for much of the variance: vicarious consumption reasons for viewing commercials, family communication about consumption, and socioeconomic status. Thus, it would appear that markedly different processes are involved for the two groups of adolescents in learning general attitudes toward advertising.

Materialism

Like attitudes toward advertising, materialism is a measure of more complex kinds of consumer learning, indicating an orientation which

Table 3: Relationships between recall of ads, attitudes toward TV advertising, materialism, effects of advertising on buying, and the independent variables for younger and older adolescents[a]

	Recall		Attitudes		Materialism		Effects	
	Young	Old	Young	Old	Young	Old	Young	Old
Socioeconomic status	.07	.08	.02	−.11	.06	−.02	−.01	.02
Intelligence	.34[b]	.29	.04	.07	.07	−.17	.06	.02
Available money	.00	.01	.07	.08	.11	.01	.07	.08
Family communication	.00	.06	.06	.13	.03	.07	.18	.26
TV exposure	.10	.16	.10	.03	−.01	−.07	−.09	−.09
Print exposure	.13	.07	.01	.04	.07	−.01	.12	−.03
Social utility	.06	.06	.14	.02	.17	.11	.21	.08
Communication utility	.01	.02	.03	.06	.09	.05	−.16	.08
Vicarious consumption	−.02	.02	.06	.16	.11	.17	.12	−.03
Multiple correlation coefficient (R)	.39	.31	.25	.29	.34	.38	.37	.31

[a]   Cell entries are beta-weights between the independent variables and the four dependent variables. These standardized partial regression coefficients represent the relationship between the independent and the dependent variable with all other independent variables controlled.

[b]   The boldface entries indicate those variables, when added in the step-up regression equation, increased the amount of variance accounted for by at least one percent.

views material goods and money as important for personal happiness and social progress. For younger adolescents, three factors accounted for much of the variance: social utility, vicarious consumption reasons for viewing television commercials, and the amount of money an adolescent usually has available. For older adolescents, social utility and vicarious consumption reasons for viewing commercials were also important predictor variables; however, the third variable for this age group was intelligence, which was negatively related to materialism.

These results suggest that among both age groups, the processes involved in learning a materialistic orientation are quite similar and quite strongly related to the adolescent's television viewing behavior, especially reasons for watching commercials.

Effects of television advertising on buying behavior

Our measure of effects of television advertising on buying behavior is a self-report item which asks whether the adolescent feels he has been directly influenced by television advertising in buying a specific product. This variable is essentially a measure of behavioral effects of advertising.

Table 3 indicates that three variables are important predictors of this kind of learning for both younger and older adolescents: communication in the family about consumption, social utility reasons for viewing television commercials, and the amount of exposure to magazines. In addition, for younger adolescents, a fourth variable is important: communicatory utility reasons for viewing commercials, which is negatively related to effects of advertisements on buying.

Consumption as a social process

These results suggest that simple exposure to advertising is not a sufficient condition for buying behavior. Rather, other variables involving the processing of information about consumption intervene between exposure to the commercial and purchase. Communication about consumption with parents seems to be a particularly important variable intervening between exposure to commercials and actual purchase, especially among older adolescents. This finding indicates clearly that consumption behavior is a *social* process, involving overt communication with others, not simply an individual psychological process triggered by exposure to advertising.

For younger adolescents, reasons for watching commercials are also important intervening variables between exposure and purchase. Social utility reasons for viewing are positively related to purchase behavior, further supporting the interpretation that consumption behavior is a social process.

The nature of this social process requires further study, however. Communicatory utility reasons for viewing commercials correlate negatively with purchasing behavior among younger children. Thus, purchasing seems to be a function of social comparison motivations, but not of interest in social communication. Among older respondents, both reasons for watching commercials emerge as modest but significant correlates.

SUMMARY AND DISCUSSION

We can conclude the following from the data presented in this study:

(1) Different aspects of consumer learning are not well integrated among either younger or older adolescents.

(2) Different clusters of variables have effects on the different kinds of consumer learning examined in this study.

(3) For any particular kind of consumer learning, essentially the same cluster of variables affects that kind of learning for both younger and older adolescents. Therefore, even though younger adolescents are exposed to more commercial content on the media, talk with parents

more about consumer goods, and watch commercials more for social utility and communicatory utility reasons, the predictive power of these variables is essentially the same in both groups of adolescents.

(4) Amount of exposure to television is not a very important variable in predicting different kinds of consumer learning. This finding adds to the growing body of literature which indicates that media exposure time is simply not a powerful explanatory variable of communication effects.

(5) *Three* major processes seem to be involved in the different kinds of consumer learning.

The learning of advertising slogans seems to be mainly a function of the intelligence of the adolescent.

The learning of more cognitive orientations, such as attitudes toward television advertising and a materialism orientation, seems to be mainly a function of the adolescent's reasons for viewing commercials. Thus, these cognitive orientations develop as a function of the adolescent's television behavior, but not simply of his exposure time. Rather, the orientations develop as function of the uses the adolescent makes of commercial content, several of which are basically social uses.

A third process, which seems to be involved in the learning of purchasing behaviors, is clearly an *overt social process*. In this process, communication with parents about advertising, consumer goods, and consumption processes seems to be an important variable intervening between exposure to advertising and the purchase of consumer goods.

This finding, indicating the occurrence of an overt social process between exposure to the media and decision-making, is similar to Chaffee and McLeod's (1967) finding regarding the occurrence of an overt social process between exposure to political content on the media and voting decision. Further, our finding that adolescents use commercials for social purposes parallels their finding that media political content is used for social purposes as well as for making political decisions.

Adolescents' consumer learning is not simply an individual stimulus-response phenomenon, but is a social learning process. It may be fruitful to think of media advertising as shaping the content and form of interpersonal perceptions and communication, rather than considering the media as dispensers of product information. Cross-sectional research with wider age samples than studied here would help reveal developmental changes in youngsters' consumer orientations.

FOOTNOTES

1. The research on which this paper is based was supported by the National Institute of Mental Health (Contract No. HSM 42-70-74) and by a grant from the Marketing Science Institute, Cambridge, Mass. The authors wish to acknowledge the help of Greg Reale (Northwestern University and MSI) for research assistance and that of Wing Hing Tsang (MSI) for computer assistance.

2. The following is a summary of the indices used in the present study:

INDEX	OPERATIONAL DEFINITION	MEASURE
Socioeconomic status: social class	Duncan socioeconomic index	5-digit occupational code, including 3-digit IRS code, 2-digit code indicating population decile of occupation
Intelligence	School test scores (IQ, and the like)	Track in school
Available money	Total money acquired in average week	Open-end item concerning allowance, jobs, "all other ways" money acquired
Family communication about consumption	Overt parent-adolescent interactions concerning consumption of goods and services	4-point "often-never" items, such as: "How often do you ask your parents for advice about buying things?"
Quantity of media use: A. television	Self-reported average time spent watching television, time spent watching yesterday	Open-end responses to questions about time spent with TV yesterday
B. print	Self-reported subscriptions and readership magazines	Open-end items for periodical subscriptions or readership
Reasons for watching commercials: A. social utiltiy	Motivation to watch commercials as a means of gathering information about life styles and behaviors associated with uses of specific consumer products.	4-point agree-disagree items. Scales such as: "I find out what kinds of people buy the things that are advertised."
B. communication utility	Motivation to watch commercials in order to provide a basis for later interpersonal communication	4-point agree-disagree items. Scales such as: "I watch commercials to give me something to talk about with my friends."
C. vicarious consumption	Motivation to watch commercials in order to identify with or vicariously participate in attractive life styles	4-point agree-disagree items. Scales such as: "Some of the people they show are examples of what I wish I were."
Attitudes toward TV advertising	Cognitive and effective orientations concerning liking of and belief in TV advertising; advertising as indication of product quality; efficacy of advertising	4-point frequency and "agree-disagree" items, such as: "TV commercials tell the truth"; "TV advertising makes people buy things they don't really want."

Materialism	Orientation emphasizing possessions and money for personal happiness and social progress	4-point frequency and "agree-disagree" items, such as "It's really true that money can buy happiness."
Advertising recall	Aided recall of national TV advertising campaigns aired during 1969-1970	16 incomplete slogans or descriptions of commercials, such as: "Fly the Friendly Skies of _____."
Effects on buying	Self-reported influence of commercials on purchase behavior; single effect of commercial, or effect of commercial for product already known about	Open-end response to "Did you ever buy a product after seeing it advertised on TV?"

REFERENCES

Bauer, R.A. The initiative of the audience. *Journal of Advertising Research*, 1963, **3**, 2-7.

Bauer, R.A., and Greyser, S. Advertising in America: the consumer view. Cambridge, Mass.: Harvard Business School, Division of Research, 1968.

Cateora, P.R. An analysis of the teenage market. Austin: University of Texas Bureau of Business Research, 1963.

Chaffee, S., and McLeod, J. Communication as coordination: two studies. Paper presented at a meeting of the Theory and Methodology division of the Association for Education in Journalism, Boulder, Colo., 1967.

Chaffee, S., Ward, S., and Tipton, L. Political socialization via mass communication in the 1968 campaign. Paper presented at a meeting of the Theory and Methodology division of the Association for Education in Journalism, Boulder, Colo., 1967.

Granbois, D.H. The role of communication in the family decision-making process. Unpublished paper, 1967.

Greenberg, B., and Dominick, J. Television usage, attitudes and functions for low-income and middle-class teenagers. Department of Communication, Michigan State University, 1968 (unpublished).

Herrmann, R.O. *The consumer behavior of children and teenagers: an annotated bibliography.* Chicago: American Marketing Association, 1969.

Hess, R., and Torney, J. *The development of political attitudes in children.* Chicago: Aldine, 1967.

Jennings, M.K., and Niemi, R.C. Patterns of political learning. *Harvard Educational Review*, 1968, **38**, 443-67.

Kenkel, W.F. Family interaction in decision-making on spending. In Foote, N. (Ed.) *Household decision-making*, Vol. 4. New York: New York University Press, 1961.

Klapper, J.T. *The effects of mass communication.* New York: Free Press, 1960.

Komarovsky, M. Class differences in family decision-making on expenditures. In Foote, *Household decision-making*, Vol. 4. New York: New York University Press, 1961.

McNeal, J.U. Children as consumers. No. 9, Marketing Studies Series. Austin: University of Texas Bureau of Business Research, 1964.

Ogilvy, D. *Confessions of an advertising man.* New York: Dell, 1963.

Phelan, G.K., and Schvaneveldt, J.D. Spending and saving patterns of adolescent siblings. *Journal of Home Economics*, 1969, **61**.

Pollay, R.W. A model of family decision-making. 1969 (unpublished).

Robinson, J., Athanasiou, R., and Head, K. *Measures of occupational attitudes and occupational characteristics*. Ann Arbor, Mich.: Survey Research Center, 1969.

Schramm, W., Lyle, J., and Parker, E. *Television in the lives of our children*. Stanford: Stanford University Press, 1961.

Steiner, G. *The people look at television*. New York: Alfred A. Knopf, 1963.

Ward, S., and Gibson, D. Social influences and consumer uses of information. Paper presented at a meeting of the Advertising division of the Association for Education in Journalism, Berkeley, Calif., 1969.

Wells, W. Children as consumers. In Newman, J. (Ed.) *On knowing the consumer*. New York: John Wiley, 1966.

Wells, W. Communicating with children. *Journal of Advertising Research*, 1965, **5**(2), 2-15.

Wolgast, E.H. Do husbands or wives make the purchasing decision? *Journal of Marketing*, 1958, **22**, 151-58.

Appendix A: Other papers

Ward, S. Effects of television advertising on adolescents: preliminary research results. Paper presented at first national Symposium on Children and Television, Boston, Mass., 1970. (New York: Avon Books, in press.)

Ward, S. Television advertising and youth: a behavioral scientist's perspective. Paper presented at Drake University, Des Moines, Iowa, 1971. (Reprinted in *The Congressional Record*, May 3, 1971.)

Ward, S. Television advertising and children: two studies. Paper presented at a meeting of the American Association for Public Opinion Research, Pasadena, Calif., 1971. (Preliminary version of Appendix B.)

Ward, S., and Robertson, T.S. Family influences on adolescent consumer behavior. Paper presented at annual meeting of the American Psychological Association, Miami, Florida, 1970.

Toward Defining the Functions of Television

John P. Robinson

National Institute of Mental Health

Researchers who have conducted empirical studies of the impact of the mass media often have come away feeling that by the time any promising principles of mass communication are developed, they have become so laden with qualifications and exceptions that they are all but inoperable. Such ambiguities have also characterized other subjects of applied social science; research in the closely related field of attitude change has also been characterized by inconsistent and ungeneralizable findings.

Daniel Katz (1960) has performed the laudable service of drawing together many of the disparate findings of attitude change research, using a "functional approach to the study of attitudes." Katz outlined three values of the functional approach:

1. It reduced all factors to the same level of analysis: "Dealing with nonfunctional variables makes. . .generalization difficult, if not impossible."

2. It avoided the great error of simplification—the error of attributing a given cause to a single phenomenon. Not only must a number of motivational forces be taken into account in explaining behavior, but the same behavior can have different motivational bases and consequences for different people.

3. In recognizing the complex motivational sources of behavior, it helped fill the gaps in several theories which lack specification of conditions under which given types of behavior will occur.

It is not the present author's ambition to set forth as exhaustive and helpful a set of functions for television viewing as Katz has done for attitudes.[1] The functions that will be proposed are far too tentative and disconnected for that. Nevertheless, even a modest attempt in this direction is required if the social psychological processes whereby television does or does not influence its audience are to be identified. Even if only partially complete, such a set of functions could be used to anticipate certain consequences of such changes in television programming as the removal of programs with violent content or the institution of new educational programming.

The data upon which this paper's analyses and conclusions are based come from five studies in which the present author was involved:

1. The National Inventory of Television Viewing Behavior (LoSciuto, 1971), in which a national sample of 512 viewers gave their attitudes toward television and recorded their television viewing during a one-week period.

2. A study of the viewing habits and news exposure of 949 high school students in a suburban Maryland county, conducted as part of the McIntyre and Teevan (1971) study. This survey has been supplemented by comparable data from college students and high school teachers in the Ann Arbor, Michigan, area.

3. A cross-national comparison of the differences in daily activities between set owners and nonowners (Robinson, 1971) from data collected by the Multination Time Budget Research Project.

4. A delineation of demographic characteristics of heavy viewers of violent dramatic programs and of news programs (Israel and Robinson, 1971) from data collected by the W. R. Simmons research organization.

5. In-home camera studies of 20 families' television viewing habits (Bechtel, Achelpohl, and Akers, 1971).

Figure 1 lists the areas of concern in this examination of data, and shows the relevance of each of these studies to the issues.

The samples, procedures, and results of these studies are detailed elsewhere in this volume.[2] The present paper will build upon and attempt to integrate the analyses they present.[3]

	National inventory	Maryland teenagers	Time study	Demographic characteristics	Camera study
Amount of viewing	xx	xx	xx	x	xx
Time trade-off	xx		xx		x
Learning	xx	xx			
Pleasure	xx				
Violence	xx	xx		xx	x

KEY: xx = highly relevant
      x = somewhat relevant
      blank = not relevant

Figure 1: Studies bearing on each of the issues in this report

Since a considerable portion of the following discussion is based on cross-tabulation from the national survey, the author wishes to make clear at the outset that sample sizes in this pilot project were too small to permit strong statistical confidence in these results. If it appears that firm conclusions are drawn, the author's intention of advancing these as hypotheses for further testing should be firmly kept in mind.[4]

TIME SPENT VIEWING

Considerable effort in these five studies was devoted to estimating how much of the 24-hour day Americans do in fact spend with television. This question of time spent viewing is almost completely independent of concerns about the functions of television, since both heavy and light viewers may view a program for the same reasons, and a person who views five hours a day can derive the same benefits from an episode of *Beverly Hillbillies* as the person who views only one hour a day.

Like other investigators (Schramm et al., 1961; Bogart, 1968), we found that estimates of viewing time varied widely according to the method of estimation used. In order to increase standardization, several surveys asked the same question used by the Roper organization in their surveys for the Television Information Office (Roper, 1971): "On an average day, about how many hours do you spend watching television?"

This question resulted in the highest viewing estimates for the population (over three hours on the average for the national sample), such estimates being about 50 percent higher than those obtained when the respondent was asked about his viewing "yesterday."[5] Such differences conceivably might have occurred because respondents interpreted the question to ask about an ". . .average day that you do watch television. . ." and forgot about nonviewing days in their estimates. However, even among those who did view on a particular day, the average viewing time was still well under three hours. Thus, as Bechtel et al. found in their in-home camera study, Americans persistently tend to generously overestimate the time they spend viewing.

This finding suggests that people feel little social pressure to conceal television viewing or to report it at lower than actual levels (as many social observers fear).[6] That few respondents (16 percent of the total) in the national sample felt they spent "too much time" watching television —even though they appeared to report more viewing than they actually engaged in—further reinforces this conclusion. Even among people who estimated that they watched more than eight hours on an average day, almost twice as many respondents felt they did not spend too much time watching television as did feel they watched too much.

The in-home camera study and the national survey suggest a further reason for these generous estimates: that many viewers count programs they view only sporadically or partially as viewed full time. We shall have more to say on this point later when considering the potential cognitive impact of such disjointed viewing patterns. For now, it is sufficient to comment that ascertaining actual viewing times seems a rather modest scientific goal, perhaps no more noteworthy than to remark that most estimates of viewing times and viewing audiences are highly exaggerated. The fact that Americans watch two hours rather than three hours of television per day may tell program sponsors and network executives that their audiences are not as large as projected, but it does little to alter the conclusion that viewing times are considerable, especially when aggregated across the span of a person's lifetime or during periods like childhood. It is because time is such a finely measurable entity and because social commentators use the more generous and inaccurate viewing estimates to comment on the poor use that Americans make of their leisure that we are led to devote as much discussion to it as we have already.

We feel confident enough of the *relative* validity of the question used to estimate viewing that we have used it as a predictor variable in several of the analyses which follow. There is a clear and strong relation in the aggregate between estimate times and "yesterday" viewing times, even though the estimated times are larger. (In other words, people who estimate they watch four hours per day on an average day do watch more television than those who claim to watch two or three hours on an average day.)

A far more interesting question is how viewing times vary by background factors like age and education. Almost all available data suggest a strong negative correlation between viewing and education. A curvilinear pattern of viewing exists with age, if one examines the whole life cycle. Steady viewing begins around age three and continues to stay at relatively high levels until age 12, when a gradual decline begins as shown in Figure 2. Figure 2 combines data from the W.R. Simmons national survey and data from the Maryland teenage sample. The data suggest that the decline "bottoms out" in one's early twenties and begins to rise again with the onset of marriage (especially for women). A noticeable jump in viewing (especially for men) also occurs around age 50, when children depart from home and leave more time for their parents to devote to television. Viewing times seem to increase further after retirement, when available leisure reaches a maximum.

The critical point in the life cycle during which viewing begins its decline in this generally U-shaped pattern comes during junior high school, as documented by the data from the Maryland teenage sample in Figure 2. It can be seen that the drop in viewing by age occurs differentially according to how well the student is doing in school. Even at the beginning of junior high school, students with A grades watch about one-half hour less television than C students. In the last four years of high school, this differential increases to over an hour, even as the viewing among C students drops dramatically lower as well.[7] By the time the students reach 19 years of age, data from the nationwide Youth-in-Transition study (reported by Robinson and Bachman, 1971) suggest, viewing continues to decline for both those who go on to college and those who do not, both groups estimating less than two hours viewing per day.[8]

While other background differences do exist, they are not as demonstrably great among the high school student sample, once the two factors of age and grades in school are controlled. Children of higher-status parents do tend to watch somewhat less, as do those with fewer sets and noncolor sets in the home. Teenagers with three or more sets in their homes reported more viewing (4.2 hours) than those with two sets (3.8 hours) or one set (3.6 hours). The five percent of fortunate teenagers with two or more color sets in their homes estimated they watched 4.6 hours per day, compared to 3.7 hours for those with one color set and 3.9 hours for those with no color set. Unlike other investigators, we found little relation between social isolation and increased viewing, except among that one percent of the sample who said they had "no" close friends. Among these, estimated viewing was reported at a remarkable 5.5 hours per day, but the small sample size renders this finding highly tentative.

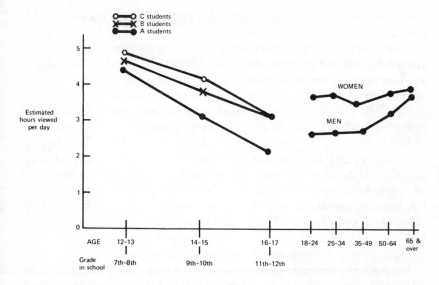

Figure 2: Hours of television viewed per day by teenagers, by grade in school and age (data from Maryland suburban county survey, spring 1970). Hours or television viewed per day by adults, by sex and age (data from W.R. Simmons national sample, described in Israel and Robinson, 1971).

Television's role in the lives of adults with infrequent social contacts or who have time on their hands comes across clearly in the national survey. Respondents who felt that they had "time on their hands with nothing to do, almost every day" estimated 4.9 hours of daily viewing, compared with 2.9 hours for respondents who had such time available less than once a week. Among respondents who reported spending none of their evenings away from home in an average week, estimated daily viewing time was 3.6 hours, compared with 2.8 hours for respondents claiming to be away from home more than three nights a week. Probably related to these findings is the higher viewing among persons scoring relatively low on a self-esteem scale (4.0 hours) or relatively high on an alienation scale (3.7-4.0 hours).

Each of these four variables is related to respondents' social class; the question naturally arises whether these variables provide extra explanatory power beyond social class or other background differences. One response to this question is provided by a Multiple Classification Analysis,[9] in which the effects of many other variables (including number and type of sets, channels received, use of other media, sex, race, education, age) were held constant to see whether any of these variables were responsible for explaining significant portions of variance in television viewing that the above variables appeared to explain. These results are presented in Table 1.

Table 1: Estimated average daily viewing time—national sample

TOTAL SAMPLE	3.3 Hours	Deviation Before*	Deviation After**
One set in household (N=203)	3.4	+.1	−.1
Two sets in household (N=123)	3.3	0	+.1
Three sets in household (N=27)	3.3	0	+.7
Color set (N=139)	3.4	+.1	+.2
Black and white (N=214)	3.3	0	−.1
1-3 channels received (N=76)	3.2	−.1	−.2
4-5 channels received (N=135)	3.4	+.1	+.1
6-7 channels received (N=76)	3.4	+.1	−.1
8 + channels received (N=66)	3.5	+.2	+.3
No magazines read (N=123)	3.5	+.2	−.2
One-two magazines read (N=135)	3.4	+.1	+.2
Three-eight magazines read (N=99)	3.0	−.3	−.1
No movies seen (N=214)	3.5	+.2	0
One-two movies/month (N=107)	3.1	−.2	0
Three or more movies/month (N=36)	3.2	−.1	0
No radio (N=96)	3.4	+.1	+.1
One hour/day (N=101)	3.3	0	−.1
Two-three hours/day (N=84)	3.4	+.1	+.2
Four or more hours/day (N=80)	3.3	−.1	−.2
Men (N=163)	2.9	−.4	−.3
Women (N=194)	3.8	+.5	+.3
Black (N=42)	4.5	+1.2	+.9
White (N=315)	3.2	−.1	−.1
Less than high school (N=96)	3.8	+.5	+.3
High school graduate (N=105)	3.3	0	+.5
Some college (N=36)	3.1	−.2	0
College graduate (N=36)	2.2	−1.1	−.9
No evenings away from home (N=65)	3.6	+.3	+.2
One-two (N=177)	3.6	+.3	+.2
Three-four (N=69)	3.0	−.3	+.1
Five-seven (N=46)	2.6	+.7	−.8
Time on hands every day (N=25)	4.9	+1.6	+1.3
Time on hands 2-3 times/wk (N=55)	4.2	+.9	+.8
Time on hands once/wk (N=72)	3.5	+.2	+.3
Time on hands less often (N=205)	2.9	−.4	−.5
Low alienation (N=100)	2.7	−.6	−.2
Low-medium alienation (N=101)	3.2	−.1	−.2
High-medium alienation (N=100)	4.0	+.7	+.4
High alienation (N=56)	3.7	+.4	+.1
Low self-esteem (N=23)	4.0	+.7	+.6
Middle self-esteem (N=143)	3.6	+.3	+.1
High self-esteem (N=191)	3.1	−.2	−.1

 * Deviation of average figure for that grouping of the sample from the whole sample
 ** Deviation of average figure corrected for effects of all other variables by Multiple
   Classification Analysis

The Multiple Classification Analysis indicates that the available time, time at home, and alienation differences were attenuated only slightly after adjustment for other background factors. Thus, persons who have a great deal of time on their hands estimate that they watch 1.3 hours more television on an average day than other citizens; those who are away from home five or more nights per week watch .8 hours less. Respondents who feel alienated or who have lower self-esteem estimate they watch about a half-hour more than other viewers, other factors being equal. Among other factors included in this analysis, only education and race produced anywhere near as much variation in estimates of amount of television viewed as did these four variables.

These analyses thus provide a preview of at least one function of television: supplying something to fill in time for many people who have nothing better to do. Moreover, the decreased viewing of older adolescents suggests that these youngsters are entering a more active period of the life cycle during which other media, like radio and movies, provide the more restricted content satisfying the demands peculiar to this age grouping. Television does not currently supply the more specialized and privatized content that adolescents' life styles require. Indeed, the high proportion of teenagers in the national sample who reported "time-killing" as a reason for television viewing or who could give no suggestions for changing television suggests that television would be hard put to cater more effectively to this segment of the audience.

SOME FUNCTIONS OF VIEWING

Social observers have identified several functions that television performs in everyday life. Television has been said to provide relaxation, to foster escapism and passivity, to affect family life, to define the broad outlines of the outside world, to set social norms and expectations, to homogenize language and customs, to destroy economic competition, to encourage consumption of trivial goods, to engender development of superficial personality traits (rather than "inner" personal qualities), to redesign the schedule of everyday living patterns, and to increase the feeling of national identity. There would appear to be no suitable way in which all of such functions could be subsumed into a single framework; some of these functions refer to processes within individuals, some to interpersonal relations among individuals, and some to the society as a whole.

Because of the limited scope and time of the current inquiry, the more complex and longer-range aspects of television's effects could not be properly investigated. Instead, we will examine three aspects or functions of television on which considerable information was collected: time trade-off, learning, and pleasure. They operate mainly at the social psychological level, rather than involving deeper personality dynamics or properties of the social system. These three functions are proposed as a selective rather than an exhaustive listing of the functions of television, and there is considerable overlap among them. It is possible that an individual's viewing of a particular program could be simultaneously fulfilling each of these functions.

Television as a time trade-off

Most individuals would probably be appalled at the thought that each activity they engage could be formally coded as performing some sort of behavioral function. While there are several conscious and unconscious motivations for each activity engaged in during the day, it would be most difficult for a social scientist to believe that individuals use rational accounting criteria to determine each and every activity in which to participate. Nevertheless, it is possible to draw a number of interesting inferences from the behavior choices that people do make; particularly interesting to us is the way television fits in with other activities during the day.

The data from the Multination Time Budget Research Project provide an instructive example in this regard. Almost from its inception, social scientists noted that people who acquired television sets began to spend less time with the other mass media. This was explained by television's subsuming and performing more efficiently the functions of these other media; television became a "functional equivalent" favored over radio, movies, and the reading of fiction (Schramm et al., 1962; Weiss, 1970).

The time budget data, however, suggest that several nonmass media activities in most Western societies may be replaced or filled by television as well. One of these—conversation—is also a communication or media activity; television set owners report 25 percent less conversation than nonowners. However, the three other activities that are lower for television owners—sleep, visiting, and hobbies—would take some redefinition to be visualized as functional equivalents to television. It is not difficult to construct *post hoc* rationalizations for such trade-offs for television. But we doubt that an investigator operating from a functional equivalence perspective would have been successful in predicting these three activities as the ones most affected by television. Several other activities—such as relaxing or eating—seem more likely candidates to be traded with television than sleep, visiting, or hobbies.

Research has shown that *sleep* does play an important role in allowing individuals to process and integrate the divergent information encountered during the day or previously. In this sense, sleep can be considered a functional equivalent of television, although it is hard to argue that this is the only "trade-off" between sleep and television. It is more provocative to describe sleep and television as sources of escape and fantasy or to describe television for many viewers as a stage of semisleep, inducing viewers into full sleep or into "daydreaming." Some recent physiological evidence does infact suggest parallelisms in brain wave reactions during sleep and while watching television.

The exact nature of the trade-off between *visiting* and television is also not entirely clear. How much of the replaced visiting was just low-involvement activity to break the monotony of some extra time? How much "company" does the television set provide? How does the viewer's interaction with actors on the screen different from his interaction with visitors? Is the interaction with the set more directed than the replaced conversation, more or less likely to focus on "realism" rather than "fantasy?"

At the same time that he has cut down on visiting, the television owner now does spend more time at home with members of his family. Television may thus be fulfilling a revolutionary role in altering mass patterns of informal communication, which are focused around more standardized media content than probably was true with regard to topics discussed with friends and neighbors.

The lower time owners spend on *hobbies* becomes both more and less understandable when we find that the major affected components of such activities are correspondence and handiwork (like knitting). Since correspondence is a medium of communication and handiwork is a low-involvement pastime, both are understandable as possible functional equivalents; on the other hand, the two activities themselves differ quite widely in the social functions they perform.

We might well conclude that one of the main effects of television's introduction (in addition to increasing time in communication activities) has been that individuals receive less communication inputs from informal sources (conversation and correspondence with friends and acquaintances) and more from structured, formal, and standardized sources (the mass medium of television). At the same time, it has brought the family into greater proximity (even though figures indicate that they may not communicate among themselves more as a result), perhaps at the expense of aimless visiting and low-involvement leisure activities like knitting.

That television watching itself may be characterized as an aimless or low-involvement activity is suggested by several facets of respondents' viewing activity in the national sample:

Somewhere between 30 and 40 percent of all programs viewed were seen either because the show simply came on a channel the person was already viewing or because some other member of the household wanted to watch it.

Of all programs seen, again between 30 and 40 percent were not watched from beginning to end.

Very nearly the same percentage reported engaging in second-ary or tertiary activities while viewing, with conversation being a particularly prevalent distracting activity while viewing (half of such conversations do not refer to the content on the screen).[10]

Another 30 to 40 percent by interviewers' (or coders') standards were unable to give an accurate recount of what the programs last seen were all about.

Such indices of low attention to or low involvement with television programs are not independent of one another. Otherwise we would be unable to locate any "true" viewing of television. Thus, respondents who see less than half of a program are more likely to have engaged in secondary activities, are likely not to have personally planned to watch the program, and are less likely to be able to recall what the program was about than are viewers who watched the show from start to finish. Less than half of all programs viewed, nonetheless, meet all four criteria of serious viewing: planned viewing, viewing of the entire program, absence of disrupting secondary activities, and recall of the major story line of the program.

Such findings on how television time is consumed are not without theoretical implications. It appears that the ways people watch television are at least as discontinuous and "mosaic" as McLuhan's (1964) description of the stimulus properties of the medium; many of the provocative effects of television that McLuhan describes as flowing from the mosaic image properties of the television picture could be due to the properties of the viewing environment.[11] Another factor detracting from attention was not even included in this study—daydreaming that is either provoked or begun independently at various points during the program.

Nor are these findings devoid of empirical ramifications, especially in the context of the debate over the relevance of laboratory studies relating filmed violence to aggressive behavior (Weiss, 1970). It seems virtually impossible to recreate in the laboratory the discontinuous setting in which most programs are viewed. The laboratory situation approximates movie viewing, with its lack of interruptions from either the environment or the viewing schedule, more closely than it does the usual television viewing experience. On the other hand, criticism of many laboratory experiments because they show segments of violent material outside the context of the scriptwriter's intended story line seems less applicable in light of the finding that so much television is normally seen out of context through the interrupted viewing patterns of the audience.

Considerable portions of viewing, however, are seen in context and are of a nature sustained enough to be suitably replicated in laboratory settings. The point is that laboratory experiments can replicate only certain facets of the television viewing environment or certain types of viewing. This point is especially relevant considering the effects of long-term habitual viewing patterns of most of the audience, which would seem impossible to recreate in controlled settings.

The bulk of the above findings should not be taken as evidence that television only "fills up" time that would be frivolously spent anyway. On an average day, almost 25 percent of respondents in the national survey were so attracted to available fare that they reported missing a program that they wanted to see. While the most frequent reason for missing the program was that another program was viewed instead (usually because another family member wanted to see the program, again pointing to television's role as a focus of family activity), the first column of Table 2 shows that about half the missed viewing time was taken up with obligatory (rather than "free-time) activities such as work, housework, shopping, school work, and organizational activity.

Table 2: Activities engaged in during periods when respondents either:
a) missed watching a program they wanted to see, or
b) did not watch television because no programs were worth watching
(national sample)

Alternate activity	Missed programs	Boycotted programs
Work	15	4
Housework-child care	12	27
Shopping-personal care (sleep, eat, etc.)	15	9
Study and homework	5	4
Organizational activity	7	3
Entertainment-visiting	15	6
Other leisure	25	28
Other	2	3
No answer, don't know	4	16
Total	100%	100%

Moreover, almost 20 percent of the sample reported feeling obliged to turn off their set sometime during the day because the choice of programs was so unpalatable, an indication that at least some viewers refuse to sit perfunctorily through a program of little consequence to them. Again, about half of the activities performed in place of television were more obligatory in nature (see the second column in Table 2); a good deal of extra housework apparently is inspired by the lack of acceptable television content. It is interesting to note in Table 2 that, while housework is highly likely to be a *post hoc* substitute for television, work, shopping, personal care, and entertainment-visiting are considerably more likely to prevent viewing than to be substitute activities once the television menu is rejected.

In any event, it is obvious that television's function in the daily round of activities goes well beyond a mere filling in of time when there is nothing better to do, even though a considerable portion of viewing time may have no more function than that.

Since the more positive terms "entertainment" and "relaxation" were three times as likely as "killing time" to be spontaneously mentioned by national survey respondents as reasons for viewing, it might be safely assumed that viewers do see their viewing fulfilling mainly positive and legitimate functions. The low porportion of viewers who describe programs they have recently seen as a "waste of time" substantiates the view that only a minority audience *perceives* television viewing as merely filling up time during which there is nothing better to do.

Learning

It is obvious, not only from our surveys but also from previous research and common observation, that few viewers consciously turn on their sets for educational purposes. The high mortality rate and small audiences for documentaries and news specials offer ample supplementary testimony. Only ten percent of the national sample spontaneously brought up information-seeking as a reason for watching television. This figure may, of course, represent an increase over ten or twenty years ago, since younger persons and persons with college and post-college training (a group whose size has increased significantly in the last two decades) are most likely to give these information-related reasons for viewing.

News. That less than 20 percent of the national sample listed a news or educational program as one of their four favorites may be taken as one indicator of the relatively low salience of this type of programming among viewers. On the other hand, one could hardly expect such programs to come to mind when a respondent is asked to name "favorite programs." Although the figure was closer to 40 percent among college graduates, it is not an unheard-of response. The figure is also noteworthy compared with the widely circulated poll finding (Roper, 1971) that most people claim to get most of their information about the world from television. In the Simmons survey, over a two-week period less than half the sample recorded watching a national news program.[12]

Both the study of Maryland teenagers and the national survey attempted to find out whether viewing of news programs was associated with greater awareness of news stories or of people in the news. As a standard of comparison, parallel information was also collected on news habits with regard to newspapers and magazines. Separate multidimensional analyses were performed on the Maryland and national survey data to gauge the impact of television news viewing on recognition of news material, to contrast it with use of other news media; the effects of other media usage and background factors such as education and age were controlled.

Recognition of people in the news was measured by how many out of seven persons in the news (Robert Finch, Bob Dylan, Calvin Hill, Ralph Nader, Joseph Tydings, Martha Mitchell, and Tom Hayden) the respondents could at least partially identify. These seven persons were not chosen by any systematic sampling from some universe of news personalities, but were thought to represent a reasonable cross-section of individuals in the news. The questions are obviously sex-biased, since in both samples males did significantly better on the quiz than did females.

The average number of correct identifications for various groupings in the Maryland student sample is given in Table 3; the effects of media exposure are shown separately according to two prime predictors of recognition about people in the news—year in school and average grades. Within practically all year-by-grade groupings, heavy viewers of television are less likely to recognize persons in the news than light viewers, and heavy news viewers show almost no more recognition than light news viewers. However, print media users are far more likely to be informed than are students who do not use these media, suggesting that print is a more powerful variable than television in explaining recognition.

Table 3: Average number of correct identifications of persons in the news by year in school, grades in school, and mass media usage (Maryland student study, total N=949)

Year in school	7 & 8th			9 & 10th			11 & 12th		
Average grades	A's	B's	C's	A's	B's	C's	A's	B's	C's
Hours of TV on average day									
Less than two hours	2.4	.8	.4	2.8	2.0	1.2	3.1	2.4	2.2
Two-four hours	1.6	.6	.7	2.3	1.6	1.0	3.2	2.0	1.6
More than four hrs.	1.1	.5	.3	1.5	1.3	.8	*	2.1	1.2
Frequency of news viewing									
At least twice a week	1.7	.5	.6	2.3	1.8	1.0	3.6	2.4	1.9
About once a week	*	.6	.3	2.2	*	.8	*	2.5	1.4
Never	*	.7	.5	2.5	1.2	1.4	*	2.7	2.5
Reads a news magazine (i.e., *Time, Newsweek, U.S. News*)									
Yes	1.8	.7	1.4	2.7	2.2	1.2	3.7	3.0	3.0
No	1.6	.6	.3	2.2	1.5	1.0	2.8	1.8	1.4
Reads newspaper									
Everyday	1.9	.9	.6	2.8	2.0	1.5	3.9	2.5	2.0
At least once a week	.3	.3	.5	1.7	1.4	.9	2.8	1.9	1.8
Less often	1.4	.6	.4	1.6	.5	.3	*	1.5	1.4

*Sample size less than 10

The question then arises whether enough control variables are included in the Table 3 analysis. For this reason, a multiple regression analysis based on a procedure outlined in Williams (1959) was performed on these data in order to test for the simultaneous effect of eleven other variables in addition to those examined in Table 3. Like the Multiple Classification Analysis described earlier, this procedure provides estimates of differences of each variable when controlled for the effects of all other variables, assuming no interaction effects. In this procedure, however, a simple Student t-test value is provided as the indicator of whether each independent variable shows significant associations with the dependent variable (here, recognition of persons in the news). The independent variables are ranked in Table 4 according to the strength of their association (in terms of t-test values) with recognition of people in the news.

Table 4 verifies the general findings of Table 3, but indicates that the students' preferences for psychedelic (or underground) music[13] and students' professed interest in the news are also prime predictor variables of recognition of people in the news—although weaker predictors than the student's age, grades in school, and print media readership respectively. The data also corroborate Table 3 in indicating total amount of television viewing to be significantly negatively associated with recognition of personalities. None of the other nine predictor variables is significantly associated with recognition (significance being attained by a t- value above 1.96).

Table 4: Values for t-test regarding the strength of linear association between each of 16 predictor variables and knowledge of people in the news and characteristics of foreign countries (Maryland teenage sample)

	Identification of people in news	Knowledge of foreign countries
Year in school	5.9 significant	3.5 significant
Grades in school	5.5 significant	4.1 significant
Read news magazines	5.2 significant	1.9 not significant
Frequency of newspaper reading	4.3 significant	2.7 significant
Preference for psychedelic records	3.7 significant	3.5 significant
Interest in news	3.3 significant	1.4 not significant
Father's occupational status	1.6 not significant	1.5 not significant
Mother's education	1.6 not significant	2.6 significant
Frequency network news	1.1 not significant	1.0 not significant
Frequency family conversation	.7 not significant	2.8 significant
Number of close friends	.7 not significant	.9 not significant
Number of TV specials seen	.2 not significant	2.3 significant
Read general interest magazines	− .3 not significant	.1 not significant
Amount of radio listening	− .5 not significant	−1.3 not significant
Amount of movie going	−1.2 not significant	.5 not significant
Amount of daily television viewing	−3.4 significant	−2.3 significant

The Maryland student sample was also asked to identify whether each of four countries (Poland, Spain, China, and India) had a communist government or not and whether each of four countries (Ecuador, Ghana,

Afghanistan, and Morocco) was or was not in Africa. A knowledge score, based on how many of these eight true-false items the students answered correctly, was constructed, and the same predictor variables were run against this score in a multiple regression analysis. The results are portrayed in the right column of Table 4.

Age and grades in school again emerge as prime predictor variables, but while newspaper reading and preference for psychedelic music strongly predict knowledge of foreign countries, news magazine reading and interest in the news do not. Three variables not significantly associated with the foreign country questions now appear as significant predictors of country recognition: extent of family conversation, mother's education, and (perhaps most interestingly) number of television specials of an educational nature seen over the preceding four months.[14] This last variable indicates that at least one aspect of television use has a beneficial effect on enlightment—since, once again, television *news* viewing does not explain significant amounts of variance in knowledge and since heavier television viewers have significantly lower knowledge levels.

Although there seems no way to read causal inferences into these data (since the data were collected at only one point in time), it seems doubtful that heavy television viewing yields much in the way of educational benefits in the topic areas examined here: it seems actually to be associated with considerably lower assimilation of this type of knowledge of the outside world.

Very much the same conclusion appears to emerge from an analysis of the national sample's replies to the same set of person recognition items.[15] We have set out, in the first column of Table 5, variations according to levels of media use in the recognition of these seven persons in the news. Heavier television viewers and nonusers of the printed news media again emerge as much less aware of people in the news than do light viewers or print media users. Paralleling the results from the high school sample is the lack of higher recognition levels among most frequent national news viewers—although the recognition level of respondents who claim never to watch either national or local news programs is strikingly low (less than one person recognized on the average).[16]

Again the question of how much such "effects" may be due to other related variables (such as sex, age, education, and other media use) arises. A Multiple Classification Analysis was undertaken to control for such possibly spurious influences; these results are portrayed in the final columns of Table 5 in terms of deviation above or below the average level of 1.5 persons recognized. Practically all the above differences become considerably attenuated once these other factors (particularly education) are taken into account. The original 1.3 point difference be-

Table 5: Average number of news personalities recognized according to media use
(national sample)

| | | Deviation from overall mean | |
		Before correction	After correction*
Total sample	1.5		
Hours of TV on an average day:			
Less than two hours (N=64)	1.9	+.4	+.1
Two-three hours (N=172)	1.8	+.3	+.1
Four-five hours (N=127)	1.3	−.2	−.1
Six or more hours (N=67)	.6	−.9	−.2
Frequency of national news viewing:			
At least twice a week (N=270)	1.6	+.1	+.1
About once a week (N=81)	1.8	+.3	+.1
Never (N=82)	.7	−.8	−.3
Frequency of local news viewing:			
At least twice a week (N=229)	1.7	+.2	+.1
About once a week (N=44)	1.3	−.2	+.1
Never (N=60)	.7	−.6	−.4
Reads a news magazine:			
Yes (N=60)	3.0	+1.5	+.6
No, but reads other magazines (N=214)	1.5	0	0
Does not read any magazines (N=159)	.8	−.7	−.2
Reads a newspaper:			
Everyday (N=293)	1.8	+.3	+.2
At least once a week (N=99)	1.1	−.4	−.3
Less often (N=41)	.3	−1.2	−.5
Hours of radio on an average day:			
Less than two hours (N=235)	1.5	0	0
Two-three hours (N=113)	1.6	+.1	0
Four-five hours (N=34)	1.2	−.3	−.3
Six or more hours (N=51)	1.5	0	+.1
Number of movies seen: (in previous three months)			
None (N=270)	1.2	−.3	−.1
One-two (N=116)	2.2	+.7	+.1
Three or more (N=47)	1.4	−.1	+.1

*After correction for usage of other media, sex, race, and education.

tween lightest and heaviest viewers (.6 vs. 1.9 persons recognized) becomes reduced to a .3 difference after suitable controls are introduced.

For the national sample data, Table 5 corroborates the results of Tables 3 and 4: differences in recognition levels by use of any of the broadcast media (television news, radio, movies) are not as significant as those by print media use. At the same time, with the exception of those few respondents who never watch television news programs, there is no evidence that television has any beneficial effect on recognition levels.

This conclusion is further supported by parallel analyses of self-reported awareness of several recent news stories (included in both the teenage and national surveys). On these items, print media differences again overshadow television use differentials in explaining professed awareness. There was a tendency in both samples, however, for heavier national television news viewers to show higher awareness levels, suggesting that watching television news may have demonstrable effects depending on the aspects of awareness asked and the format of the question (self-reported awareness as opposed to hard-and-fast information quiz items). The story recognition items, if not contaminated by respondent response set, may reflect assimilation of those "headlines" of information that television news is thought to convey most effectively. Such a suggestion—that television is able to effectively "teach" certain kinds of material but not others—will be further discussed in the following section.

Weather. Two information questions about weather were included in both the Maryland and the national surveys. Although weather programs are often scorned by viewers and mimicked by entertainers, one can well imagine that exposure to weather program map presentations night after night could inculcate in the minds of the public a good deal of "incidental learning" about the geography of this country. Since this effect would be hard to measure because of the many other factors that account for geographical map knowledge, the investigation focused on more direct questions about two principles implicit in television weather forecast presentations—that the prevailing weather flows from west to east and that low pressure systems are associated with cloudier weather conditions—in order to test the potential learning associated with viewing weather forecasts on television.

Few respondents (22 percent in the Maryland student survey and 24 percent in the national survey) were able to specify that the weather comes from the west,[17] while 48 percent in the student survey and 53 percent in the national survey knew the implications of a low pressure system. Our interest, however, is less in these levels of performance *per se* than in the way such levels relate to respondents' contacts with weather programs on television. This relation is examined in Table 6, along with differences by sex, age, and education in the national sample.

Respondents who claim to watch weather programs more often tend to answer both questions correctly, although differences are neither dramatic nor monotonic. Correct answers to both questions are found most often among respondents who feel that television weather programs have helped them understand weather maps or who feel that the weather forecasts are accurate predictors; both these variables, however, are themselves related to frequency of viewing, so they may not be pure indicators of what they purport to represent. Correct answers also tend to be given by men, by older persons, and by the better educated.

All of these variables, along with general mass media use questions, were thus subjected to a Multiple Classification Analysis, to ascertain how well each of them held up as predictors of weather knowledge once

Table 6: Percentage of the national sample knowing direction of weather
and implications of low pressure system by various factors
before and after correction for other variables

	Percent knowing weather comes from west			Percent knowing what low pressure means		
		Deviation from mean			Deviation from mean	
		Before	After*		Before	After*
Total sample	36%			54%		
Watches weather programs						
Every night (N=233)	40	+4	+2	60	+6	+5
Two-three per week (N=108)	36	0	−1	53	−1	−1
Once a week (N=43)	23	−13	−8	36	−18	−14
Less often (N=65)	31	−5	−1	44	−10	−5
Weather programs have helped understand weather maps						
Not at all (N=146)	28	−8	−4	37	−17	−13
A little (N=118)	33	−3	0	57	+3	+4
Somewhat (N=116)	47	+11	+9	65	+11	+7
A great deal (N=69)	37	+1	−5	66	+12	+8
Percent of time weatherman is correct						
0-30% (N=39)	20	−16	−13	37	−17	−9
31-50% (N=147)	39	+3	+6	51	−3	+10
51-70% (N=68)	30	−6	0	59	+5	+3
71-100% (N=195)	35	−1	−2	58	+4	+1
Sex						
Women (N=247)	31	−5	−4	50	−4	−4
Men (N=202)	43	+7	+5	59	+5	+4
TV viewing per day						
0-1 hours (N=80)	39	+3	+3	52	−2	−2
2-3 hours (N=176)	41	+5	+4	60	+6	+6
4-5 hours (N=124)	29	−7	−5	44	−10	−4
6-8 hours (N=67)	30	−6	+1	59	+5	+6
Age						
Under 20	30	−6		44	−10	
20-39	31	−5	Not	52	−2	Not
40-59	39	+3	calcu-	62	+8	calcu-
60-89	44	+8	lated	52	−2	lated
Education (adults only)						
None-11th grade (N=125)	31	−5	−2	52	−2	−2
High school graduate (N=125)	34	−2	−6	57	+3	+2
Some college (N=43)	42	+6	+5	61	+7	+1
College graduate or more (N=45)	53	+17	+9	54	0	−3

*Figures refer to deviations above and below the overall mean before and after corrections
for the effects of all other factors by Multiple Classification Analysis.

the other variables were taken into account. Results of this analysis indicate that of the variables in Table 6, only frequency of viewing weather
forecasts consistently and significantly relates to increased ability to

answer both weather knowledge questions correctly; even here the relation does not extend to people who profess to watch these programs less than once a week. One other group also gave more (but not significantly more) correct answers to both questions: respondents who reported watching six or more hours of television on an average day. In this one knowledge area, television use seems to predict greater awareness.

In the high school sample, differences in knowledge of these two items was again higher among more frequent viewers of weather programs, those who felt that such programs were instructive, those who thought forecasts more correct, males, older students, and students with better grades (who presumably as adults will have completed more education than their peers). However, such differences are not nearly so pronounced as they are in Table 6. Indeed, when the multivariate regression program using these and media usage variables to predict weather knowledge was conducted, not one variable predicted significantly to weather knowledge in the teenage sample.

Perhaps the most significant result in both samples, however, is that for this knowledge area—which is closer to "life knowledge" and has more day-to-day applicability than the more abstract "school knowledge" required to identify distant persons in the news or characteristics of foreign countries—heaviest television viewers emerge as well or slightly better informed than less frequent viewers. This is quite opposite to their performance on the more academic knowledge questions about news. Television, therefore, may well be an effective transmitter of information that it specifically and repetitively "teaches," reducing the "knowledge gap" between those of higher and lower educational achievement that the media are usually found to increase (Tichenor, 1970). The knowledge area (weather) upon which this suggestion is advanced is much too circumscribed to allow further generalization, and we have not been able to measure the degree to which weather viewers have picked up this information from other sources. However, the basic hypothesis does warrant attempts at replication in future research.

Other learning. Surprisingly little research has been devoted to estimating how much learning transpires as a result of viewing typical noninformational programs on television. McLuhan has claimed that in the presence of the electronic media, a child goes to school "to interrupt his education." Not many students seem to agree with McLuhan's pronouncement; when we directly asked Maryland high school students to estimate whether they had learned more about life from television or in school, they overwhelmingly chose school, as Table 7 shows. Not surprising, but still noteworthy, is the finding that less successful students are most likely to claim to have learned more from television.[18]

Such subjective estimates, while instructive, are, of course, of limited value in gauging possible learning from television. It seems implausible to imagine that if so few viewers feel that programs they watch are a

Table 7: Percentages of various youth samples estimating whether they have
learned more from television or in school

"All things considered, would you say you have
learned more about life . . . .

	From television	In school	Both		Total
Maryland students (N=949)	14%	59%	27%	=	100%
National sample of 19-yr. old boys (N=1534)	16%	80%	4%*	=	100%
University of Michigan advanced journalism students (N=73)	4%	79%	18%	=	100%

*This specific alternative was not read to respondents in this survey, although it was listed on
the questionnaire forms filled out by the other two groups.

waste of time, the gratifications they derive from viewing perform only
the "maintenance" functions of time consumption, escapism, or pleasure and do not provide viewers some partially realistic or instructive
experience.

This viewpoint is supported by the national sample's estimates of the
learning and the realism inherent in their favorite dramatic programs.
Majorities of viewers claimed their favorite dramatic programs to be
both realistic and instructive. Programs receiving particularly high mention in this regard were soap operas and the medical programs like *Marcus Welby, M.D.* and *Medical Center.* Respondents say they derive lessons and solutions to real-life problems from soap operas and acquire
medical knowledge from "doctor" programs. Several respondents also
mentioned learning about methods of tracking and catching criminals
from police-detective series; two of these programs, *Ironside* and *FBI*,
were described as "showing life as it really is" by over 85 percent of
viewers claiming these programs to be among their favorites.[19] Very few
respondents claimed that situation comedies were realistic or fostered
learning; *Eddie's Father* and *Family Affair* were seen as closest to reality.

With their more frequent mention of soap operas and medical programs, women are half again more likely than men to perceive favorite
dramatic programs as either realistic or instructive. Blacks and people
under 30 are also more likely than whites or people over 30 to feel that
they learn something from their favorite programs and to feel that these
programs show life as it really is. Persons with more formal education
are more likely to claim to learn something from their favorite dramatic
programs than the less educated, but at the same time they are less likely
to describe these programs as realistic.

Because of the wide variety of dramatic programs that people enjoy
watching and the diverse facets of these programs to which people at-

tend, it would seem impossible to design a study to adequately capture all the various "learning" that goes on from these programs over the course of a season—from the styles of dress and behavioral mannerisms expressed in the visual dynamics of the program to the moral precepts and philosophy of the world inherent in the scriptwriter's mind.[20] Yet it is precisely from such research that identification of the most telling impact on its audience is likely to emerge.

Pleasure

The replies in the national survey leave little doubt that television is a source of considerable daily pleasure in the lives of Americans. Few favorite programs mentioned are not predominantly entertainment-oriented. Viewers describe more than five times as many programs as "really worth watching" than as "a waste of time." While 82 percent of programs viewed evoke some pleasurable remark, only 17 percent had some element that was disliked. More viewers could name a program they wanted to watch but could not, than could cite some time period in which they had to turn off their sets because nothing was worth watching.[21] When asked specifically if there were anything on television they would like to see changed, 28 percent were unable to find any fault with television as it is; among those who did find fault, commercials rather than programs were the prime targets.

While these findings bear only indirectly on television's role in generating a purely pleasurable experience devoid of action consequences, as described by Stephenson (1967), they do suggest that much of television does perform this function. For many people, the set alone provides enough company to dispel feelings of loneliness. It can also transport them into situations they dare not enter or to places they know nothing about. Our surveys did not inquire specifically into such psychologically pleasurable experiences of viewers (if indeed the typical social survey is an appropriate setting for pinpointing such functions of television).

Nevertheless, several sources of displeasure were voiced. Most frequent, by a wide margin, were complaints about commercials on television—especially that there were too many of them.[22] A minority, but a substantial one, felt there was too much violence on television. Feelings that television overemphasized sex also received frequent endorsement, particularly among older people. A true generation gap emerged in responses to this question, more so than on any other question in the survey; two-thirds of the over-60 age group agreed that sex is overemphasized, compared with half of the 40-59 age group, one-quarter of those aged 20-39, and just over one-tenth of teenagers. Women and persons with less education were also more likely to agree with this assertion.

While substantial numbers of viewers reported encountering television content that had bothered or upset them, newscasts rather than entertainment programs were the predominant source of such unpleasant content.

The proportion of the audience claiming to boycott television because of poor program choice was twice as high as that reported in a national survey six years earlier (Robinson, 1969). This may well signal an increasingly critical audience for television programming, even though the bulk of this boycotting, as in the earlier study, occurred during nonprime time.

Indicators of the ways in various program content gives pleasure and performs other functions are summarized in Table 8. The data base for Table 8 consists of the reactions of diary keepers in the national survey to each of the 2,796 programs[23] they viewed as a group over a one-week period. The reactions registered in the diaries indicated notably greater attention to the set, greater viewer involvement, and more complete viewing than was found when respondents were asked in the interview portion of this survey, to give their reactions to the most recently viewed programs, so the Table 8 data may picture a more involved audience than actually exists.

Table 8 shows that newscasts and soap operas were the most-often viewed programs, although if all the adventure or situation comedy programs were grouped together, they would be heavily viewed categories as well.

With regard to types of programs that are pleasurably evaluated, fictionalized programs in general fall in the middle range of evaluation—with the exception of cartoons and movies, both of which are highly likely to be described as a "waste of time" or as having some element disliked by their viewers. These reactions seem to be a function of the accidental nature in which movies and cartoons are viewed; relatively few of them are chosen by the viewer, planned beforehand, or watched from beginning to end. (It is possible that such responses are due to the fact that these programs are not viewed in prime time hours, although it has not been possible to separately analyze movies by the time of day they were shown.) The Table 8 results also diverge from some results of Bechtel et al.'s in-home camera study, which found more attention devoted to the screen when movies were on than for any other program.

The most positively evaluated (and least negatively evaluated) programs were educational shows, newscasts, religious programs, local variety shows, and children's programs (children's programs—not surprisingly—being seldom chosen or viewed from start to finish by this largely adult sample).[24] This would suggest that while this set of programs does not attract relatively large portions of the television audience, they do give viewers the feeling that their viewing time has been well spent.

Table 8: Facets of viewing behavior for various types of programs

	Number of programs	Distractions			Involvement		Evaluation			
		Watched entire program	Talked during program	Doing anything else	Planned to watch	Had say in program choice	Really worth watching	Waste of time	Liked	Disliked
FICTION										
Dramatic programs										
Crime-detective (e.g. *Mod Squad, Mannix*)	166	81	40	29	79	87	46	7	81	14
Westerns (e.g. *Gunsmoke, Bonanza*)	59	81	48	25	75	81	25	5	80	12
Other adventure (e.g. *Mission Impossible*)	114	73	45	29	62	77	25	7	74	21
Other drama (e.g. *Marcus Welby, M.D.*)	118	85	37	26	71	84	46	3	81	16
Soap operas (e.g. *Edge of Night*)	304	90	22	40	96	97	30	4	88	18
Situation comedy										
Emphasis on young children (e.g. *Eddie's Father*)	129	83	30	26	83	80	29	1	88	9
Emphasis on adults (e.g. *Arnie, That Girl*)	178	84	32	32	62	80	31	4	86	6
Rural emphasis (e.g. *Mayberry RFD*)	112	80	44	21	60	76	32	4	83	14
All movies	226	56	53	35	57	77	31	12	73	36
All cartoons	48	62	40	29	30	42	25	19	65	23

Table 8: Continued

NONFICTION										
Variety programs										
Comedy (e.g. *Laugh-In, Flip Wilson*)	118	63	48	40	71	77	41	10	81	27
Singer (e.g. *Dean Martin*)	214	72	42	28	79	79	41	6	84	20
Talk shows (e.g.*Johnny Carson*)	94	51	36	58	82	94	52	5	81	20
Other										
News	397	80	31	50	89	83	52	1	77	10
Education	92	65	28	38	73	83	71	1	91	11
Sports	129	51	54	37	71	81	50	5	85	25
Game shows	190	86	32	34	83	87	38	4	88	13
Childrens shows	53	45	59	40	57	55	60	9	89	15
All programs	2843	75%	38%	32%	74%	82%	42%	5%	82%	17%

Several other interesting findings are continued in Table 8: the high degree of viewer involvement in and complete attention to soap operas (a finding supported by the Bechtel et al. data), and the great amount of conversation that accompanies children's programs, movies, sports, and comedy programs (suggesting these programs promote rather than retard social intereaction). Perhaps the most curious findings, however, center around differences between situation comedies and live comedy shows. The situation comedies seldom offend viewers, although their generally "wholesome" humor seldom seems to provide great pleasure either. Live comedy programs (with the exception of the *Flip Wilson* show, which pulls the favorability ratings for live comedy in Table 8 up considerably) often offend viewers and fairly often invite distracting activity.

In all, Table 8 suggests a variety of pleasurable functions that different programs provide: news and education programs keep viewers adequately in touch with the outside world; situation comedy offers a pleasurably bland entertainment; sports, comedy, and movies serve as a stimulus or an opportunity for social conversation; and game shows and soap operas provide diversions from household chores for housewives. Such results need to be replicated on much larger samples, however, to verify these impressions.

THE FUNCTIONS OF TELEVISION VIOLENCE

The data from the Simmons surveys clearly indicate that most television programs emphasizing violence draw disproportionate numbers of their audience from the less educated, black, and elderly segments of the population—even when the heavier overall use of television among these groups is taken into account. These population groups were also reported to describe their lives as "dull and routine" by a Gallup poll, which suggests that television violence may fulfill the function of providing vicarious excitement to these citizens.

On the other hand, higher viewing of violence may perform quite a different function for high school dropout youth. Although the data are not available in these studies, other research has found this group reporting higher participation in (and desire for participation in) certain forms of aggressive behavior than the rest of the population.[25] If true, this would comprise more concrete evidence for the common-sense proposition that television violence serves dramatically different functions for different segments of the audience. The need for wider and more complex measures of audience effects than are now usually considered becomes obvious.

The Simmons data also reveal that programs high in violence are viewed far more attentively than other television content, especially by male viewers. Parallel data from the national survey (see Table 8) and from the in-home camera study do not reveal this relation as strikingly, but they still show that violent programs attract more than average attention to the set. Perhaps if the data from these two studies were analyzed run separately for males, they would more closely approximate the Simmons results, which strongly suggest that violent content captures the attention of the male television audience far more than other fare.

Negative reactions to violent programs have also been examined. In the national survey, only 11 percent of respondents spontaneously mentioned excessive violence when asked about things they would like to see changed on television—although this was still the most frequent specific content complaint about television. When asked directly, some 43 percent agreed that there was too much violence on television. As with complaints about sex, substantial age differences emerged in views about violence; 25 percent of the under-20 segment of the sample agreed that there was too[26] much violence, compared with 65 percent among persons over age 60. More women than men agreed that there was excessive violence, but the overall difference was less than ten percent. A U-shaped relation held for education: college graduates and those with eighth-grade education or less (this group being disproportionately older) were more likely to endorse this complaint about violence than those with middle ranges of educational achievement—differences in some cases being as high as 20 percent between extreme and middle educational groups.

To a great extent, these results parallel viewing patterns for violent programs: young people and the less educated (who watch more than normal television violence) are least likely to complain about too much violence. Indeed, at the individual level in the national sample there is a mild negative relation between complaints about excessive violence and the amount of violent content in the respondents' favorite television programs. However, the relation is not strong enough to suggest that the two are intimately codetermined. Furthermore, there are interesting exceptions to this relation at the group level, especially among college graduates in the national sample, who complained disproportionately about excessive violence while describing favorite programs that were well above average in violent content. If their generally expressed attitudes about television violence were implemented, college graduates and older people might find many of their favorite programs taken off the air.[27]

It was obvious, from replies to several questions asked of the national sample about content that had upset them, that television news coverage underlay many of these complaints about excessive violence. One-third of the total sample (and 40 percent of news viewers) said too much attention was paid to violence on network news programs. The older and better-educated segments again tended to agree that news coverage of violence was excessive; there was no sex difference on this question, however, as there was for the question about television violence in general. There was a moderate correlation between the two attitudes; persons who felt there was too much violence on television were more likely to feel that network news paid too much attention to violence.

No relation was found between attitudes about news violence and preference for violent fare in favorite television programs. Nor was preference for violent television related in any notable way to either of the aggression measures (described near the end of the LoSciuto report) employed in the general national sample. However, among adult males (but not among male teens or women), some moderate differences do occur with one of the measures—the agree-disagree aggression items—but not with the other aggression measure, which was in forced-choice or open-end format. When male viewers were divided into three groups by the amount of violence in their four favorite television programs, progressive increases in agreement with aggressive responses were found. Respondents with low amounts of violence gave an average of 1.6 aggressive responses to these five items; those with medium television violence, 1.8 aggressive responses; those listing most violence, 2.0 aggressive responses. Such differences border on standard criteria of statistical significance and hence suggest that replication on larger representative samples is in order. The fact that such differences were not obtained with the other aggressive measure and that these differences are not overwhelming does indicate that the link between the two variables is not likely to be a strong one, however.

SUMMARY AND CONCLUSION

A number of functional aspects of television use have been identified and explored: television's functional relationships with other everyday activities; the way television functions vis-a-vis other media in informing the public; the sources of pleasure and displeasure that television provides; and some possible functions of television violence. Americans devote a considerable portion of their lives to television viewing, although not nearly as much nor with as much concentration as some estimates from previous research would lead us to believe. Nor are many viewers willing to agree with academic critics who contend that most viewing is merely a way of killing or filling extra time.

However, it has been far easier to demonstrate that television time results in a pleasurable diversion from the more serious concerns of everyday life than to demonstrate any benefits of an educational nature. Nevertheless, considerable numbers of viewers feel they are vicariously experiencing and learning about real-life situations from their favorite dramatic programs, and there is modest evidence of some learning transpiring in the process of watching television weather forecasts or in becoming aware of top news stories from television news. However, deeper understanding of more complex media content was decidedly lower among heavier viewers.

The category scheme employed here was meant as neither a comprehensive nor a thorough cataloguing of television's functions. Of those functions that have been discussed, "learning" is probably of greatest interest, since it seems to be the function that has important social *consequences* beyond the simple "social maintenance" function that time consumption or pleasure infer. Research is needed—perhaps from clinical psychological perspectives—on what goes through people's minds as they watch and on how such mental processes relate to the particular viewer's style of life and psychological goals. With such data, a comprehensive measurement scheme could be developed that could tell how viewers are affected by what they watch, what they "carry away" from their television experience.

Some attempt has been made here to see how well television use predicts to specific items of knowledge. The more laborious task of indexing how people's horizons are opened or restricted by the things they see on television now must be undertaken. Instead of asking, in essence, "What have you learned?" we need to ask, "Has anything you've seen changed your way of looking at the world?" Without such information, our knowledge of television's effects—with respect to violence, to political attitudes, or to information accrual—will continue to be excessively limited.

FOOTNOTES

1. With some modification, the four functions that Katz proposes that attitudes perform for individuals can be seen to have some parallels in television use:

Katz's function	Purpose for attitudes	Possible examples of function for television viewing
Utilitarian	Maximize rewards and minimize dissatisfactions	Television as a purely pleasurable or relaxing experience
Ego-defensive	Protection from harsh realities about oneself or the outside world	"Escapist" viewing; finding out everybody has problems; enjoying Don Rickles
Value expressive	Expression of appropriate personal values	Reinforcement and extension of viewers' values and life styles
Knowledge	Provides structure and meaning to one's environment	Educational or news viewing; keeping up with "what's going on"

Since there are enough problems identifying and separating Katz's functions in the study of attitudes (e.g., all functions are essentially utilitarian), we have decided on a more mundane and direct task of proposing three more limited functions of television, which certainly do not exhaust its potential functions as well as Katz's scheme does for attitudes.

2. The Maryland teenagers' data was collected in connection with the McIntyre and Teevan survey; it was not written up as a separate paper for this research program.

3. The author wishes to thank Nils Mattsson of the NIMH computer facility (for his skillful assistance and guidance in processing several difficult analyses), Deborah Cutler, and Eileen Marchak.

4. If perchance it may appear that firm conclusions are drawn, the author's intention to advance these as hypotheses for further testing should be kept in mind. Time limits have made it impossible to probe in detail any but a few of the many aspects of television view-

ing examined in the national survey; it is hoped that resources will become available so that we can more fully mine these data in the future.

5. In such comparisons, "yesterdays" are spread proportionately across all days of the week to offset the higher-than-average viewing which occurs on Sundays and the lower-than-average times for Saturday. It should be noted that several television rating services like Nielson and Simmons also estimate three hours of viewing per day per respondent.

6. There is a suggestion in the national survey data that the college-educated do underestimate their viewing on an average day compared with "yesterday viewing," so the critics receive partial justification on this score.

7. C students in eleventh and twelfth grades may be slightly better students than their counterparts in grades seven and eight, since some C students in grades seven and eight eventually drop out of school before reaching grades 11 and 12.

8. Among University of Michigan journalism students asked the same question, the estimate is just over one hour of viewing per day, which may represent one of the lowest group viewing figures.

9. The computer program is described in Andrews et al. (1967). It is based on a general linear regression model and hence does not extend to situations where there are strong interaction effects among the independent variables. Unfortunately there was no opportunity to check for interaction effects in this analysis.

10. The 40 percent reporting conversation during the program rises in significance when it is noted that 32 percent of all programs seen are reported viewed alone.

11. In a recent address to the American Association of Public Opinion Research, Herbert Krugman has suggested a further property of the television viewing experience that leads to the discontinuous perceptual style of "television man"—namely, the fact that almost all programs, serious or not, are constantly interrupted by frivolous and irrelevant commercials that draw viewers' attention away from the story line of the program.

12. Again respondents tend to overestimate their viewing with respect to news. Extrapolating from a general question on news viewing would place the proportion viewing national news on an average night at 43 percent and the proportion seeing any local news shows at 54 percent. In their week-long diaries, however, less than 30 percent reported any news program at all (20 percent seeing local news, 17 percent national news). In the Simmons data the average daily audience for all three network news shows combined was slightly larger, at 24 percent.

13. This finding suggests that the selection of news personalities in the information quiz may have been slanted toward personalities of more interest to followers of the "counterculture." Certainly a more systematic sampling plan to select news personalities may have been called for, but the fact that the same results were obtained with the information quiz about foreign countries indicates that conclusions reached from the news personalities' quiz do not suffer from serious deficiencies in this respect.

14. Even though students who watched most television were most likely to see such specials, and though students with lower grades watched most television, viewing of educational specials was slightly higher among students with better grades.

15. While the national sample averaged 2.4 persons recognized and the Maryland sample averaged 1.5, University of Michigan advanced journalism students averaged 4.5 persons recognized and a sample of Detroit area teachers recognized 4.3. Only Calvin Hill and Joseph Tydings were known to less than 50 percent of these higher education groups, while none of the news personalities were recognized by half of either the Maryland students or the national sample.

16. By and large, the more frequent news viewers are among heavier general users of television. However, almost one-third of the sample who estimated they watched over four hours of television a day claimed that they never watched national news programs, compared to less than 15 percent of the rest of the sample.

17. Another four percent in the student survey and 12 percent in the national survey did mention west and other directions (west and north, south and west), which are counted partially correct answers in Table 6 and other analyses. Among University of Michigan students and Detroit area teachers, clear majorities (73 and 64 percent respectively) knew the correct direction of the weather. The implications of a low pressure system were less well known, by 61 percent of the Michigan students and 70 percent of the Detroit teachers.

18. Among blacks in the national sample of 19-year-old boys, the proportion answering television was 30 percent, more than twice as high as the proportion of whites. This racial difference could not be accounted for by differences in educational attainment of either the boys or their parents.

19. More detailed personal interviews with some of the Maryland teenagers indicated that they predominantly felt crime-adventure programs to realistically portray the daily lives of police and government agents. The only vehement rejection of the reality of these programs came from the son of a police officer.

20. We did launch one half-hearted effort to locate a possible contribution of color cues in "learning" from television. In one subsample of Maryland teenagers, viewers of the program *Laugh-In* were

asked to describe the underlying joke of the Farkle family sketches. Since the brightly colored wigs worn by members of the family were such a tip-off to the neighbor's having fathered the Farkle children, we hypothesized that children who had color sets would be more aware of this implication than those who only had black and white receivers. In actuality, students without color sets were more likely to catch the joke, thus delivering a crippling blow to this line of research.

21. The two questions show a curious relation to education. The college-exposed, who watch least television, are far more likely to cite a program they wanted to watch but could not, and at the same time to note a time when they had to turn off the set because of poor program choice. The former finding suggests that, given fewer outside pressures, the better educated would watch more television; the latter finding suggests that, given more free time, they will boycott whatever is on anyway.

22. In the weekly diaries of viewing, excessive commercials received several mentions as something disliked about a program (especially movies), but almost no viewers noted infrequent commercials as something they liked about a program.

23. Several programs are counted more than once in this figure, since several respondents usually viewed a particular program. It is instructive to find the most popular programs on television—in this sample Marcus Welby, M.D. and Ironside—being recorded in only seven percent of respondent diaries. By our count across one week, several reruns (like Big Valley or Star Trek) come into the Top 10 programs viewed because they are shown many afternoons during the week by local stations.

24. Among the individual programs rated highest by viewers were Marcus Welby, M.D., Flip Wilson, Lawrence Welk, and Family Affair; over 60 percent reported these programs as really worth watching. The most unfavorable reactions were given to Laugh-In, Ed Sullivan, Johnny Carson, and Bonanza by respondents who saw these programs; less than 25 percent thought these were really worth watching.

25. The author has explored this relation in greater depth for a national sample of 19-year-old males in a separate report, co-authored with Jerald Bachman, which can be found in another volume of this report.

26. This percentage is almost exactly identical to that obtained in the Maryland teenage sample, where 23 percent agreed with the complaint of too much violence. An interesting interaction effect was noted between age and grades in school with this variable. Only among students with A grades did complaints about violence differ significantly from other students. The difference by grades did not

exist for the seventh and eighth graders, but it became evident among ninth and tenth graders and more evident among eleventh and twelfth graders—where about 44 percent complained about excessive violence. To some extent this interaction effect was concentrated among girls; however, it is of further interest to find this college-bound group resembling college students and teachers (at least at the University of Michigan, where close to 60 percent agree with this complaint) in their attitudes about television violence. This suggestion of "anticipatory socialization" for attitudes toward television violence among the academically successful teenagers most likely headed toward the university campus appears for other attitudes espoused by University of Michigan students as well: more negative views of big business, police, and the military; more positive views of college students, war protesters, and hippies; and greater appreciation of psychedelic music. The sample sizes are too small to speculate further, but it is interesting to find this group of older high school students with above-average grades to be the one group with such widely and consistently divergent attitudes from the rest of the teenage sample.

27. Few respondents probably made a conscious connection between the two questions; different results might be obtained if the two questions were explicitly linked. Moreover, the term "violence" has curious meanings to many Americans. A recent national survey conducted by the Survey Research Center found that more American males defined draft card burning as violence than defined police beating students as violence (Blumenthal et al., 1971).

REFERENCES

Andrews, F. Morgan J., and Sonquist, J. *Multiple classification analysis.* Ann Arbor, Mich.: Survey Research Center, 1967.

Bechtel, R.B., Achelpohl, C., and Akers, R. Correlates between observed behavior and questionnaire responses on television viewing. In *Television and social behavior,* Vol. 4 (this volume). Washington, D.C.: U.S. Government Printing Office, 1971.

Bogart, L. *Strategy in advertising.* New York: Harcourt Brace and World, 1969.

Blumenthal, M., Kahn, R., Andrews, F., and Head, K. *Justifying violence: attitudes of American men.* Ann Arbor, Mich.: Survey Research Center, 1971.

Israel, H., and Robinson, J. Demographic characteristics of television violence and news programs. In *Television and social behavior,* Vol. 4 (this volume). Washington, D.C.: U.S. Government Printing Office, 1971.

Katz, D. The functional approach to the study of attitudes. *Public Opinion Quarterly,* 1960, **24,** 163-76.

LoSciuto, L. A national inventory of television viewing behavior. In *Television and social behavior,* Vol. 4 (this volume). Washington, D.C.: U.S. Government Printing Office, 1971.

McIntyre, J., and Teevan, J. Television and deviant behavior. In *Television and social behavior,* Vol. 3 (this series). Washington, D.C.: U.S. Government Printing Office, 1971.

McLuhan, M. *Understanding media.* New York: McGraw-Hill, 1964.

Robinson, J. Television and leisure time. *Public Opinion Quarterly,* 1969, **33,** 210-22.

Robinson, J. Television's impact on everyday life: some cross-national evidence. In *Television and social behavior,* Vol. 4 (this volume). Washington, D.C.: U.S. Government Printing Office, 1971.

Roper Organization. An extended view of public attitudes toward television and other mass media 1959-1971. Press release from the Television Information Office, March 31, 1971.

Schramm, W., Lyle, J., and Parker, E.W. *Television in the lives of our children.* Stanford, Calif.: Stanford University Press, 1961.

Stephenson, W. *The play theory of mass communication.* Chicago, Ill.: University of Chicago Press, 1967.

Tichenor, P., Donohue, G., and Olien, C. Mass media flow and differential growth in knowledge. *Public Opinion Quarterly,* 1970, **34,** 159-70.

Weiss, W. Effects of the mass media of communication. In Lindzey, G., and Aronson, E. (Eds.) *Handbook of social psychology.* Reading, Mass.: Addison-Wesley, 1968.

Williams, E. *Regression analysis.* New York: Wiley, 1959.